DAN ALBONE – CYCLIST, INVENTOR, AND MANUFACTURER

RAY MILLER AND LEE IRVINE

The John Pinkerton Memorial Publishing Fund

Following the untimely death of John Pinkerton in 2002, a proposal was made to set up a fund in his memory.

The objective of the Fund is to continue the publishing activities initiated by John Pinkerton, that is to publish historical material on the development of the cycle of all types and related activities. This will include reprints of significant cycling journal articles, manufacturers' technical information including catalogues, parts lists, drawings and other technical information.

Cyril Hancock
JPMPF Chairman

PUBLICATION LIST:-

Lightweight Cycle Catalogue Volume 1: (2005)
An Encyclopaedia of Cycle Manufacturers - compiled by Ray Miller: (2006)
Frederick H Pratt and Sons - Complete Cycle Engineers - Alvin J E Smith: (2006)
The Electric-Powered Bicycle Lamp 1888-1948 - Peter W Card: (2006)
The Pedersen Hub Gear - Cyril J Hancock: (2007)
It wasn't that Easy. The Tommy Godwin Story - Tommy Godwin: (2007)
The End to End & 1000 Miles Records - Willie Welsh: (2007)
Lightweight Cycle Catalogue Vol II: (2007)
Origins of Bicycle Racing in England - Andrew Ritchie: (2007)
Here Are Wings - Maurice Leblanc (Translation by Scotford Lawrence): (2008)
The Origins of the Bicycle - Andrew Ritchie: (2009)
Lightweight Cycle Catalogue Vol III: (2009)
East Anglian Rides - Charles Staniland, Edited by Gerry Moore; (2009)
The Stanley Show, Review 1878 to 1889 & Catalogue 1890: (2009)
Flying Yankee - The International Career of Arthur Augustus Zimmerman - Andrew Ritchie: (2009)
An Encyclopaedia of Cycle Manufacturers - 2nd Edition- compiled by Ray Miller: (2009)
Cycle History 19- Proceedings of the 19th ICHC, Saint-Etienne, France, 2008: (2010)
Cycle History 20 - Proceedings of the 20th ICHC, Freehold, New Jersey, USA 2009: (2010)
Boneshaker Reprints Vol 5, Issues 41-50: (2010)
The Veteran-Cycle Club 1955-2005 compiled by Cyril Hancock: (2010)
Centaur Marque Album – compiled by Alvin Smith and Lionel Ferris (2011)
Cycling History No. 1 – The Malvern Cycling Club 1883 – 1912 – compiled by Roger Alma (2011)
Ivel Marque Album – compiled by Ray Miller and Lee Irvine (2011)

All publications are available through the Veteran-Cycle Club Sales Officer. www.v-cc.org.uk

Front cover – From the 1902 Ivel catalogue, the scene is the bank of the River Ivel, between Jordan's Mill and Mill Lane, Biggleswade.
Back cover – A montage of production by Dan Albone.

ACKNOWLEDGEMENTS

Ray Miller and Lee Irvine would like to thank a number of people and organisations without whom this work would not have been possible.

The Biggleswade History Society, and 'The Dan Albone Archive for Biggleswade'; in particular President Ken Page, past Secretary Mike Strange, and Editor, Jane Croot, who afforded every possible assistance.

Bedfordshire and Luton Archives and Records Service for access to various papers including the Hooper and Fletcher papers (Dan's solicitors).

The Science Museum Library, Wroughton (Mrs Eva Shell Dec'd, daughter of Dan's brother-in-law Richard Tingey, presented her research material to the Science Museum, including cuttings and family photographs).

Mike Benson of the Veteran-Cycle Club for his original research when Veteran-Cycle Club Marque Enthusiast.

Biggleswade Library for copy catalogues.

The Bodleian Library, University of Oxford, John Johnson Collection: Bicycles 1, for the reproduction of the 1890 catalogue.

The Cycles Curator of the Coventry Transport Museum, Lesley Robertson.

Tony Podmore of the Shuttleworth Collection.

The Library of the Vintage Sports Car Club.

Bonhams auctioneers

Also Mike Christy, David Higman, MBE, Rick Howard, Dorothy Pinkerton, James Peatling, Rodney Safe, Graham Thompson, and Frank Turner for their valuable contributions.

REFERENCES

The Ivel Story, by John Moffitt – ISBN 0-9540222-6-2. Recommended reading for those who wish to know more about the Ivel Agricultural Motor.

A Thorough Good Fellow, by Kathy Hindle and Lee Irvine - ISBN 1-85351-095-5.

Daniel Albone 1860 - 1906
Daniel Albone was the Inventor and Maker of the First Safety Bicycles, Motorcycles and Motorcars.
But is best known as the Inventor of the First Practical and Successful Farm Tractor the Ivel.
Father of the British Tractor Industry.

FOREWORD

When I joined the Southern Veteran-Cycle Club in 1979, I was curious about old cycles and cycling history but knew very little about the subject. It was not until a year or so later, when I was at a talk given by staff from the Bedfordshire Records Office at which Dan Albone was mentioned, that I became really interested. Here was cycling history on my doorstep, as it were. This led to my researching the history of Dan and the Ivel Company for an article in The Boneshaker.

Over the next few years I learned a great deal, not only about Dan, but about using the Bedfordshire Records Office, the Local Studies Centre at Bedford library, the Patents Office (quite near where I worked), the Science Museum library where a lot of documents about Dan were deposited, and the Public Records Office in Kew. I was very fortunate in that Dan's niece, Mrs. Eva Shell, had made a press cuttings book. This, together with Dan's obituary in the Biggleswade Chronicle (on microfilm in Bedford Library), and copies of many of the Ivel cycling catalogues in Biggleswade Library made writing my article easier.

At the same time, a few members of the Veteran Cycle Club who lived locally started the annual Ivel Ride, which was held for several years. I was also very fortunate to be able to acquire an Ivel bicycle. I worked very slowly on my article on Ivels and it was not until 1990 that it was finally published.

A year later, Lee Irvine published his little book A Thorough Good Fellow, with support from Bedfordshire County Council. The launch included television coverage on the BBC's "Look East" programme. I still have the video of that. In 2006, the Biggleswade History Society organised an event to commemorate the centenary of Dan's death. This included a cycle ride by members of the Veteran Cycle Club, a photographic exhibition and a church service in Biggleswade church which were very well supported locally. John Moffitt's book "The Ivel Story" was published in 2007. This is a very attractive book, but its main focus is on the tractor side of the business.

Dan Albone was an important figure in cycling during the 1880s and 1890s, not only as rider, inventor and cycle manufacturer but also as someone famous for providing hospitality for cyclists. He was not a major manufacturer but his influence was profound. He was also a great character and an important public figure in Bigglewade. The need for a biography that fully covers his early years was very clear. Dan's great nephew, Richard Shell, suggested that I should do this. It seemed to me, however, that Ray Miller would do a better job. Ray had recently published the very impressive Encyclopaedia of Cycle Manufacturers. I am delighted that he agreed to take up the challenge. He has produced an excellent and very well-researched and detailed book, that fills a much needed gap in the cycling history literature. I am glad that I have in some small way helped to make this possible and am very privileged to have been asked to write this foreword.

Mike Benson

INTRODUCTION

Today, Smiling Dan Albone is every bit as large as life as he was over a century ago. Many know him for his tractor, the Ivel Agricultural Motor, but he was a prolific inventor from the early days of the cycle with accomplishments for which he is still remembered, such as the 'hands-off' cross-frame safety bicycle, the first practical ladies bicycle, the tandem bicycle, the child carrier, and more.

Not only that, but he was a crack racing cyclist with many wins to his credit, publican of the Ongley Arms, and latterly the Ivel Hotel, proprietor of the Ivel Cycle Works, and a well-known public figure in Biggleswade.

We are fortunate that so much information has survived. Mrs Eva Shell (Dec'd), Lee Irvine, Mike Benson of the Veteran-Cycle Club, and Biggleswade History Society, have all helped ease the task of research. Indeed Mike Benson's article on Dan Albone and the 'Ivel' bicycle, published in The Bone-shaker, No. 124, Winter 1990, provided the basis for this book. Regretfully few of Dan's 'Ivel' cycles appear to have survived, with barely a dozen known to exist. Hopefully this work will enable more to be identified.

This book, 'Dan Albone – Cyclist, Inventor, and Manufacturer', is a semi-biographical work about one of Biggleswade's greatest personalities and his immediate family, but the real focus is on the famous Ivel Works and all that it produced. It is a collation of research from many sources and includes source material on Ivel Motor Bicycles, the Ivel Motor Car, and the Ivel Agricultural Motor, with reproduction of many cycle catalogues and patents.

As I was completing the manuscript, The Dan Albone Archive for Biggleswade was inaugurated by the Biggleswade History Society, following further donations of material by Lee Irvine. This creates a lasting memorial to Dan in the town of Biggleswade.

Ray Miller
Veteran-Cycle Club, 'Ivel' Marque Enthusiast

DEDICATION

This book is dedicated to the memory of Florence Maude Irvine, late wife of Lee Irvine. Maude was the great niece of Dan Albone and a charming, sweet-natured lady, who died in September 2010 at the age of 89.

Maude with Lady Shuttleworth's 'Ivel' bicycle

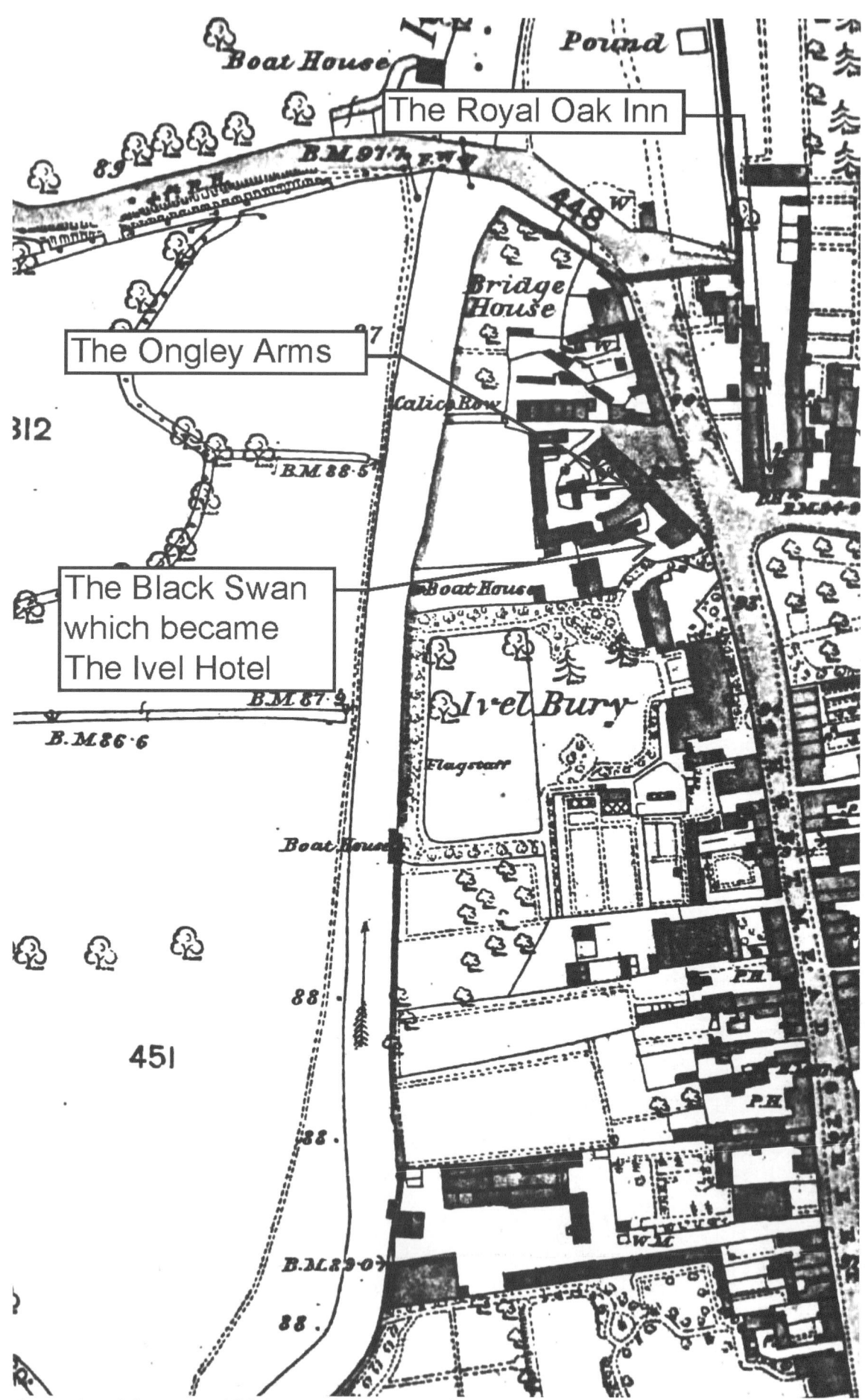

An extract from an 1884 map (courtesy of the Biggleswade History Society)

CONTENTS

Appendices

1860 – 1880 The Apprentice

Dan Albone was born on Wednesday, September 12th, 1860 into a large family in Biggleswade, Bedfordshire. His parents, Edward and Edith Albone, provided a living with several occupations. Originally a 'sawyer', Edward rented land for market gardening, employing a man. He also kept cows and sold their milk.

The name 'Albone' is not uncommon today in South Bedfordshire. In the Biggleswade Parish Registers it appears in the late 17th and early 18th Centuries as Aburn, Alborne, Aborn, or Albone, with minor variations. Thereafter fashion seems to have dictated the form. During the 18th Century we have Albone with one or two 'L's, with or without the 'E'. Dan's father, Edward, and his brothers and some of his sisters, seem to have received an education, but even then they changed their minds about the spelling of their name. In the 1830's they used the form Allbone. In 1847-48 it was written Alban, and finally in 1849 they seem to have settled for Albone and so it has remained in Biggleswade. However, and despite that, a number of the cycling journals continued to spell Dan's surname as 'Allbone' as late as 1885. Another local derivative is Hallybone.

The correct pronunciation would seem to be 'Al', as in Alfred, rather than 'All', as in altogether.[1] Confusion persisted though as one of the cycling papers thought otherwise, posing the question: *"Who is the thinnest cyclist in the world?" "Why, Dan All-bone of course!"* [2]

The family home was the Ongley Arms Inn, a Simpson's public house, in Shortmead Street, near the former stone bridge over the River Ivel. This is where Dan was born. There was a Quaker Meeting House on the site in 1715. Old deeds show that there was a blacksmith's shop in 1778. A newly erected public house built in 1785 followed the fire of 1783.

Lord Ongley owned land in this part of town near to the eastern end of his Old Warden estate. This accounts for the name. He was a local tradesman who became a director of the East India Company, and Sheriff of Bedfordshire. He was knighted in 1703 by Queen Anne.

Shortmead Street was then the Great North Road, along which all traffic passed. Although this part had a good surface it was then unmetalled and unlit, and would have been deserted at night. The Ongley Arms was not a major hostelry. When Dan's father had taken over the tenancy in 1853 its inventory shows it to have been a simple roadside hostelry, at a rent of £12 a year with a land-tax of 14s.4d. and in 1892 it was registered as a common lodging house for 15 lodgers. However, it backed onto the River Ivel, which lightermen used to take goods to and from King's Lynn although the river trade declined from the 1850s, when the railway came to Biggleswade. The Ongley Arms adjoined the Ivel Hotel and was fully licensed.

Ann, the Albone's eldest daughter, died in 1859, bringing the family's first taste of tragedy. Then, in 1864 Edward died, aged 43, leaving his wife Edith to look after their eight remaining children[3]. The eldest son, David, was fifteen. Edith Albone became the official publican, though there can be little

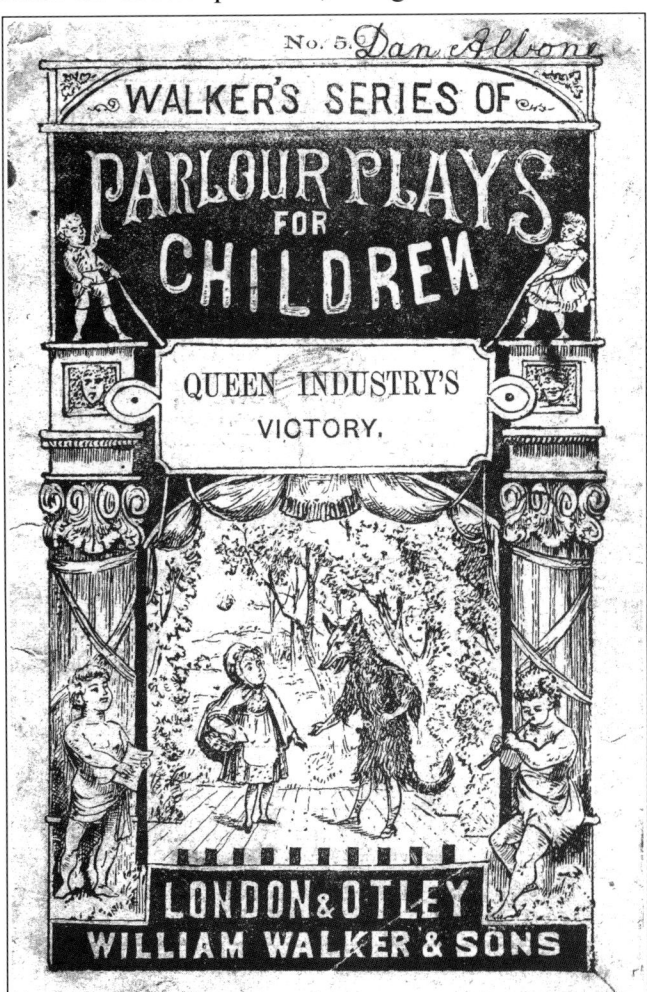

Fig.1: Dan's *Parlour Plays for Children*

---

1   Research by Mrs Jane Dale (née Albone) held in Biggleswade Library
2   *Wheeling*, February 27th 1889.

3   A number of the family died at an early age even for that time, male members in particular.

doubt that she had been running the pub for years while her husband was out at work. How did they manage? It cannot have been easy. Word-of-mouth, handed down within the family, had it that Edith Albone continued to send her children to school through these difficult times, at a cost of one penny a week. In addition, Edith had her mother, Mary Fielding, living with them until her death in 1871.

An interesting school booklet of Dan's has survived, '*Parlour Plays for Children*', which he had at age 9 (Fig.1). It tells of Queen Industry's Victory over King Laziness. It ends with a verse from Queen Industry:

"And yet I won't call Bertie rude,
But if he'll grow up kind and good,
If you'll each work, like a Busy-bee,
Both you and all around I see
Shall join me in that lovely place,
When you have run and won the race."

Fig.2: Dan with the Biggleswade & District C. C. badge on his cap

(courtesy Biggleswade History Society)

Maybe this had some influence on young Dan.

Another Edward Albone, Dan's cousin, lived with the family at the Ongley Arms. Bearing in mind the family carpentry background, he saw that the same tools which could be used to mend a coach wheel, or to shoe a traveller's horse, could be adapted to other purposes. So he obtained plans for the Boneshaker and made one, giving it to the nine-year-old Dan as a birthday present. Dan rode it round the streets causing a sensation amongst the children; everyone wanted to 'have a go' and there were even fights about it. Dan could hardly be parted from his Boneshaker, and travelled to and from school on it. [4]

Later, in 1873, Dan made a bicycle himself, aged just thirteen. This is how *Wheeling* magazine, interviewing Dan at the height of his fame and success in 1892, described his first effort:

"... there appeared in the streets of Biggleswade a spider[5] bicycle ... Dan at once determined to build a machine on the same lines and plan, and the youngster actually succeeded in producing an excellent bicycle with suspension wheels. He did all the work, his forge being the kitchen fire and his anvil a 100 pound weight. The machine did not of course have ball bearings, but on it he managed to scoop every race that he started in, and soon young Dan and his machine attained the reputation in Biggleswade and vicinity of being absolutely invincible."

Dan attended church and was a chorister. It is not known exactly when Dan left school to start work. Some apprenticeships began as early as twelve, and it's a fair guess that he started his working life at around thirteen. With his mother's agreement and encouragement he began an apprenticeship at Thomas Course and Son, engineers, of Hitchin Street, Biggleswade, a firm which covered every aspect of engineering a small country town might need, including the building and repair of mill machinery. Dan later worked for about a year as an improver at a millwrights in Bedford.[6]

---

4   *The Cycle Record Athletic Review and Diary* No. 35, April 27th 1889.
5   A general term used to describe the earliest form of Ordinary bicycle with direct wire-spoke wheels to distinguish from the wooden spokes of the Boneshaker, which came before, and the tangent wire-spoke wheels which came later.
6   The original Thomas Course in Hitchin Street was born in Bedford. Another Thomas Course was a millwright and publican at 17 Castle Street Bedford. His father William was a millwright at 2 Chandos Street, Bedford. In the 1871 census Thomas Course was a Millwright Master at 9 Thurlow Street employing two men and a boy.

By this time David Albone had become the publican of the New Inn on Market Square which he ran from 1872 to 1876. Then in 1877 he moved to Low Farm, Tempsford, and took up market gardening.

Emma Albone, housekeeper aged 27, was a visitor staying at the Ongley Arms in the 1881 census. She had married and moved to Felixstowe but it had been an unhappy marriage.

Although Dan had acquired a good deal of cycling experience he was not immune from accidents as this report indicates:

"On Sunday evening, an accident occurred to a youth named Daniel Albone, Shortmead Street. Riding around the corner near the church on a bicycle, to prevent a collision with another bicyclist, he turned too quickly which caused the tire to come off the wheel, throwing the youth violently to the ground. He sustained a cut on the head and sprained his ankle rather badly." [7]

The Biggleswade & District Cycling Club met for the first time on Tuesday May 11th, 1880. Its president was F. Whitbread, M.P., its captain was Arthur J. Hills[8] and its secretary Charles C. Whaley.

Other members of the club were Mr. White, who had an ironmongers in Shortmead Street; Mr. Marsh, the schoolmaster; Mr. Wheatley, the watchmaker, and Stamp Hutton, the postmaster.[9] Jim Cawse took time off from his jewellers in the Market Square to join, and C. B. Evans the printer did likewise. W. J. Robinson, another ironmonger, came and so did Mr. Taylor the blacksmith, an asset to any cycling club. Last among the list of members came Edward and Dan Albone. They wore a dark blue cyclists' uniform with polo cap. Dan was on the Club committee.

Fig.3: Dan's personal Biggleswade & District C.C. badge

(courtesy North Road C.C.)

Fig.4: Dan with Ordinary in Club uniform

(courtesy Biggleswade History Society)

The Club meetings were initially held at the Crown Hotel but from 1888 were held at the Ivel Hotel. The Club prospered for many years increasing membership to 232 by 1898. Edward Albone laid down a cycle race track for the use of Club members, whose main interests were road racing and road records.

The Ongley Arms, while not a grand establishment, had space for all the family. Dan even had room to work and keep his tools in the outhouses and yard that stretched down to the river, and here he started the construction of Ordinary bicycles. These outhouses were known as 'The Danneries', which became the telegraphic address for the Ivel Works (Fig.5).

In these modest surroundings the great Ivel Works, named after Biggleswade's river, were founded in 1880. The Ivel Works were to produce many world-famous machines and give pleasure to so many Victorians over the next few years. Dan had little money of his own at the time, yet he felt con-

---

7   Unnamed and undated newspaper report.
8   Worked as a solicitor with Thomas Hooper from 1878, later Hooper & Fletcher, Dan's solicitors.
9   Stamp was his real name. Born at Gainsborough, Lincs., in 1847, he married in June 1874 at Marylebone and was postmaster at Biggleswade from 1877 to 1892. Died March 1899 at Bedford.

fident that he would be successful, even though he was only twenty.

Dan never aimed at mass production. His aim was to produce reliable, light-weight machines, which required a minimum of effort to ride and which would be capable of considerable speed. 'Ivel' bicycles quickly became popular with racing cyclists, in spite of the undoubted attractions of the well-known factory-produced cycles. He believed in quality before quantity, but his charming personality and good nature probably also helped sales. In his first catalogue for 1880[10], Dan offered the 'Ivel' Roadster. Fitted with solid rims, ball bearings to both wheels, with hollow forks front and back, and plain pedals, there was a choice of handlebars. The price was £12.10s.[11]

Fig.5: The Danneries

10 According to the 1900-01 catalogue which stated it was now 20 years
    since his first, and the 1902 catalogue which stated that it was the 21st
    issue.
11 Science Museum Library, Wroughton

1881 – 1884 Open for Business

By 1881 the Ivel Works, proprietor Dan Albone, was advertising the 'Ivel Light Roadster' from £11 and the 'Ivel Racer' from £13.10s. Dan described himself in the advertisement as a *"Maker And Repairer of Bicycles And Tricycles"*. He was also the sole agent for the 'Facile' bicycle.

However, in the 1881 census he, or more likely his mother, didn't describe his occupation as cycle manufacturer; instead his occupation was given as 'Wheelwright and Engineer'.

His reputation had already spread to Stevenage as in May 1882 he was contacted by James Parker to build him a tricycle. Parker supplied plans requesting a 54 in. front wheel and 36 in. or 34 in. rear wheels, set 42 in. apart. Parker's letter indicates that he was contemplating taking out a patent. It seems that he later provided further plans for gearing and subsequent correspondence indicates the gear wheels were to be cast in brass (a somewhat unlikely material for this purpose). By February 1884, however, Dan's solicitors were pursuing Parker for payment of a claim to £20, having repeatedly requested a settlement. Dan offered to settle for £14 but did not hear further from Parker who had 'gone away'.[1]

Other early evidence of his being a manufacturer is the Copy of Indemniture of Apprenticeship between Daniel Albone and Richard Tingey and Tingey's father (of Caldecote Road, Northill), completed on July 14th 1882, as an apprentice engineer cycle maker for five years from August 2nd 1881.[2] The starting wage was one

Fig.6: Dan in race clothing c.1881
(courtesy Biggleswade History Society)

Fig.7: An 'Ivel' Ordinary of 1882

shilling a week, rising in one shilling increments each year to five shillings a week in the final year. Tingey's father undertook to provide board and lodging and generally ensure that Richard observed the agreement. Richard Tingey was bound not to compete with Dan within a 15 mile radius of Biggleswade.

Tingey had probably applied to an advertisement in the local press:

"Wanted, a Young Man, well up in making, repairing and riding."

Anyone taken on at the Ivel Works had to be able to turn his hand to anything. Tingey became Works Manager and married Ann Albone, Dan's sister.

The best way of selling cycles was to advertise and for a manufacturer who produced racing machines that was in the form of race reports. The best way to organise races was through a club. Locally that was the Biggleswade & District Cycling Club.

However, in 1882 there was a bit of a spat over handicapping. Arthur J. Hills, the captain of the Biggleswade & District C.C., wrote to The Cyclist complaining that Dan had been:

"... publicly rated at 40 yards from such a rider as Mr Cortis ..."[3]

1   Bedfordshire & Luton Archives Service, Hooper and Fletcher records, ref: HF 20/220/8.
2   Bedfordshire & Luton Archives Service, Hooper and Fletcher records, ref: HF 20/205/3.
3   *The Cyclist*, May 3rd 1882.

Fig.8: Dan being held on a racing Ordinary

This brought forth the response from Mr G. P. Coleman, Official Handicapper to the Bicycle Union:

"I concluded that Albone, having only ten yards in a mile and getting second prize, must be a very good rider indeed, and also having 35 yards ... from scratch in a five miles handicap, and again getting a second prize, I maintain I could not, on

the face of this, have done anything else than place him where I did."

A. J. Hills wrote in response that:

"it has been publically shown that that is not his proper mark" and *"The facts are not quite as stated by Mr Coleman."*

One cycling magazine, *The Cyclist*, took to referring to Dan, somewhat rudely, as *"the Biggleswade pet"*.

Soon Dan was adding to his advertisements the number of prizes his bicycles had won. Dan himself won quite a few of them. He became known as a racing cyclist, and found time, over and above his business interests, to attend track meetings and more formal occasions.

Experimentation was the name of the cycling game; there were no conventions as yet. In 1882 Dan introduced the 'Ivel' tricycle by displaying it at the first Biggleswade Fête held at the Fairfield meadow on August Bank Holiday. There was also a cycle race, the one mile bicycle handicap race, in which Dan was fourth.

Fig.10: 'Ivel' advertisement 1884

(courtesy Biggleswade History Society)

Tricycles became extremely popular so that in 1883 exhibits at the influential Stanley Show were to outnumber the bicycles displayed. The great advantage of the tricycle was that it was easier to ride and less perilous than the Ordinary bicycle. In some models the two wheels were at the front. There were also special racing tricycles, built as light as possible.

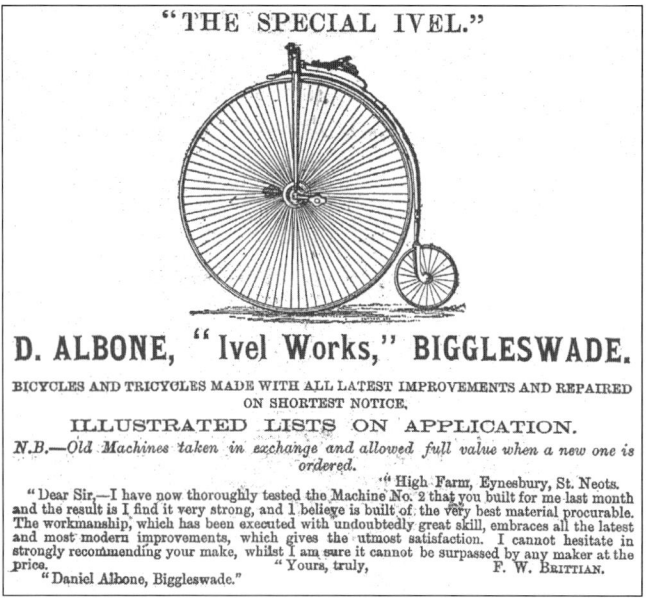

Fig.9: 'Ivel' advertisement c.1883

Fig.11: "Dan Albone's Place", 1884. Members of the North London Tricycle Club outside the Ongley Arms. Dan is standing to the right of the doorway

Fig.12: Dan, on right, with Biggleswade & District C. C. members, 1884

Around 1882 Dan drafted an agreement for the hire of cycles and accessories, based on a Singer agreement.[4] However it is not clear this was ever implemented.

Fig.13: 'Ivel' advertisement c.1884

(courtesy Biggleswade History Society)

Dan's brother, David, had given up market gardening and had become a fruiterer in Birmingham in 1881. There he met and married Emily. In 1882 they made a decision to emigrate and sailed to Sydney, Australia, on the three-masted sailing ship Hereford. They took with them their two children and also Alice Wells, daughter of Lucy, Dan's sister. Lucy had married William Armitage Wells, a basket maker. She died in 1881 in childbirth and asked Emily to look after the daughter.

D. ALBONE,

"IVEL" CYCLE WORKS, BIGGLESWADE

Prices of "Ivel" Bicycles and Tricycles on application.

DAN ALBONE being Proprietor of the Ongley Arms, Cyclists may depend upon being entertained at reasonable rates, and wheelmen may rely upon their machines receiving due and efficient attention on the premises.

Fig.14: 'Ivel' advertisement 1884, *The Cyclist*

At the Bedford Amateur C.C. annual dinner Dan proposed the toast to the Club and referred to the friendliness between the Biggleswade and Bedford clubs.[5]

Later in the year, Edith Albone died. Edith's belongings were put up for sale, as directed in her will, so that the money could be shared between her children. Dan was not mentioned in the will, and Edith directed that her son, Edward, should inherit the tenancy of the Ongley Arms. This was not because of bad feeling, but rather because Dan already had a thriving business of his own. Dan is on record as having bought some of his mother's belongings. Edward, Dan's brother, eventually went to farm livestock at Sibsey, and later Spridlington, in Lincolnshire.

Edith's death seems to have resulted in Dan's sister, Elizabeth, being placed in the Three Counties Hospital, Stotfold, with her affairs conducted by solicitors. She had lived with her mother, often being seen sitting outside making lace.

Dan took over the tenancy of the Ongley Arms from Edward and his sister Emma became housekeeper. William, another brother, became the landlord of the Royal Oak hostelry opposite in Sun Street. William was a bit of a character. He had dark hair and a tanned complexion. He ran the Royal Oak from 1883 to 1909.

Dan was now twenty four. He was accustomed to working all day at the workshops, running the inn, and also taking part in road races. At the same time, he was seeking better designs.

By 1884 cyclists knew of the Ongley Arms as a haven of rest. Dan understood the needs of the passing cyclist - he supplied liniment (or embrocation) as well as ale – and in addition was able to mend deficient machines. As an example, a tricyclist had broken the hollow handlebar of his tricycle. Reaching Dan at 3.15 a.m. he promptly turned out, lit his forge, and in three-quarters of an hour had effectively spliced the broken bar, so that the rider went on his way rejoicing.[6] Though the Ongley Arms was a simple country public house, few inns had as much to offer to the *"wheeling fraternity"*.

Dan now took on three men to help him produce the 'Ivel' machines so much in demand.

Fig.15: Biggleswade & District C. C. c.1884. Dan is eighth from the right.

(courtesy Biggleswade History Society)

---

4   Bedfordshire & Luton Archives Service, Hooper and Fletcher records, ref. HF 20/197/8.
5   *The Cyclist*, September 19th 1883, p.813.

6   *The Tricyclist*, October 24th 1884.

1885 The Kangaroo Hunt

The search for safety machines, especially for the less brave and hardy, resulted in developments which were fashionable at the time. Most important of these were the Beale & Straw 'Facile' and the Hillman, Herbert & Cooper 'Kangaroo' Dwarf Safety Bicycle.

Fig.16: The 'Facile'

The 'Facile', pronounced fah-seel, dated from 1878[1]. The driving levers pivoted on extensions of the forks below the front wheel hub and moved in an arc, which was unusual, but proved vastly more efficient than previous models. It was common practice just to tap the pedals at the top of each stroke, thus giving a sort of variable gear. With gearing the front wheel size could typically be 40-44 in. dia. The 'Facile' featured in record breaking rides; in 1883 'Facile' models broke the 24 hour re-cord five times, the most memorable of these being the ride of J. H. Adams, who pedalled 242 miles.

The 'Kangaroo' had arrived in 1884. It caused a sensation in the cycling world and its success was phenomenal. There was another factor; it prepared the popular mind for the rear-driver safety bicycle. The design, with sprockets fixed on extensions to the forks and a chain drive to the hub, was revolutionary. The facility to gear up using different-sized sprockets made the 'Kangaroo' one of the speediest machines around. The front wheel was only 36 in. dia., which substantially reduced its height by comparison with the Ordinary, whose 50 in. dia. or so wheel reached as high as the chest of an average man. Although the 'Kangaroo' was potentially more safe one contemporary commentator wrote:

"The upright forks and small back wheel rendered a cropper quite as easy of appearance as on an Ordinary."

The success of the 'Kangaroo' in races generated superb publicity. On Saturday September 27th, 1884, Hillman, Herbert & Cooper had promoted the first 'Kangaroo' race specifically to advertise their machine. All the official competitors rode 'Kangaroo's. It was a one hundred miles scratch road race, from Twyford to Norman Cross won by George Smith of the Merry Rovers club in 7 hr. 11 min. 10 secs.[2]

A little over a year later, in the second 'Kangaroo' race on Tuesday October 20th 1885, a new record of 6 hr. 39 min. 5 secs. was set by E. T. Hale. Dan, reported to be 5 foot 7 inches in height and weighing 10 stone 2 lbs, came in fifth with a time of 7 hr. 9 min. 58 secs., following a fall in which he hurt his leg.[3]

After the 1885 race, the 'Kangaroo Hunt Supper' (Fig.18) was held at the Ongley Arms. Dan, Hillman, Herbert, Cooper, Adams, Fraser, Duncan, other competitors, officials and, most importantly, members of the press, sat down to dine (Fig.18).[4]

An additional building, with galvanised iron roof, had been erected at the rear of the Ongley Arms to seat a large number of visitors.[5] This was

Fig.17: The 'Kangaroo'

1   Patent 1878/332 of 25 January.

2   *Bartleet's Bicycle Book*, p.81.
3   *The Cycle Record Athletic Review and Diary*, No. 35, April 27th 1889, p.147.
4   *Cycling Times*, October 1885.
5   *Cycling Times*, March 31st 1885 and *The Cyclist*, April 8th 1885.

often so well packed out that it was noted one bill was made out:

"Drinks, as far as counted, 5/3d". [6]

Fig.18: 'Kangaroo Hunt Supper' - Dan, Fraser, Duncan, Adams, Milthorpe and Buckingham

(courtesy Biggleswade History Society)

The Ivel Works was described as:

"although somewhat cramped for space, ... is a model of ingenious contrivance, and a regular multum in parvo (much in little) in the way of bicycle and tricycle works. A lathe or two are to be seen, whilst the forge and blowpipe arrangements were brought into work to secure the necessary adjustment of a spring on a new machine." [7]

It is apparent though that Dan must have been sending machines away to be completed as his catalogue states *"enamelled by Harrington"*. Harrington was at that time a bicycle manufacturer located in Coventry, Warwickshire.

Clearly Dan was on top of developments as he offered the 'Ivel Light Roadster Safety Bicycle'. This was similar in form to the 'Kangaroo' and used Kelsey's patent of 1884, No. 11,420, for the driving gear (Kelsey was also a manufacturer of this form of bicycle). Dan's machine had a 38 in. driving wheel, geared up to 55 in. Henry Sturmey described it as:

"Soundly and conscientiously built all through. The maker has himself proved that it can go". [8]

The 'Kangaroo' was offered at 17 guineas, whereas the Kelsey machine was £15.15s. Dan offered his 'Light Roadster' at £14. It was clearly a competitive market!

Dan also collaborated with Laurence Huber in order to produce the 'Ivel Automatic Steerer' tricycle, *"Suitable for either Lady or Gentleman"*, advertised at a price of £20 (Fig.19). *Wheeling* called it the 'Humber Ivel', no doubt due to its similarity to

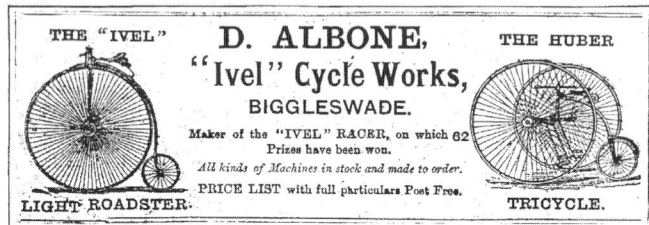

THE "IVEL"   **D. ALBONE,**   THE HUBER

"Ivel" Cycle Works,
BIGGLESWADE.

Maker of the "IVEL" RACER, on which 62 Prizes have been won.
All kinds of Machines in stock and made to order.
PRICE LIST with full particulars Post Free.

LIGHT ROADSTER.   TRICYCLE.

Fig.19: Huber tricycle advertisement

(courtesy Biggleswade History Society)

IVEL.

DAN ALBONE, Ivel Cycle Works, Biggleswade.

Description. ⅞in. and ¾in. moulded red tyres. Crescent rims. 42 and 20 No. 12 direct spokes. 2¾in. G.M. hubs, 7in. axle. Detachable cranks, 6in. throw. Rubber plain pedals. 38in. driving wheel, geared to 55in., 16in. back wheel.

Front wheel drives with chain gear. Edge's patent bearings to crank wheels. Morgan's chains. Edge's adjustment. Æolus ball bearings to both wheels. Steering like ordinary bicycle. Forks pass through bearings. 1½in. rake. Broad hollow front and semi-hollow back forks. Stanley head, 4in. centres. Thorn handles, 28in. cow-horn bars. 1¼in. 16 W.G. weldless steel backbone. Bolted scroll spring. Suspension saddle. Adjustable step. D.L.S. brake. Leg-guard. Valise, spanners, oilcan and bell. Weight 38lbs.

Specialities. Edge's bearings and adjustment (*page 23*).

IVEL.

PRICE.. .. .. .. £14 0s. 0d.

Sent out with bright handle-bar, head, hubs, cranks and spokes, rest enamelled black and green.

Extras. Hollow rims, 15/-; half-plated, 20/-; ball pedals, 15/-.

Remarks. Soundly and conscientiously built all through. The maker has himself proved that it can "go."

Fig.20: Extract from *Sturmey's Indispensable*, 1885

---

6   *The Tricyclist*, May 29th 1885.
7   *The Tricyclist*, May 15th 1885.

8   *Sturmey's Indispensable Handbook.*

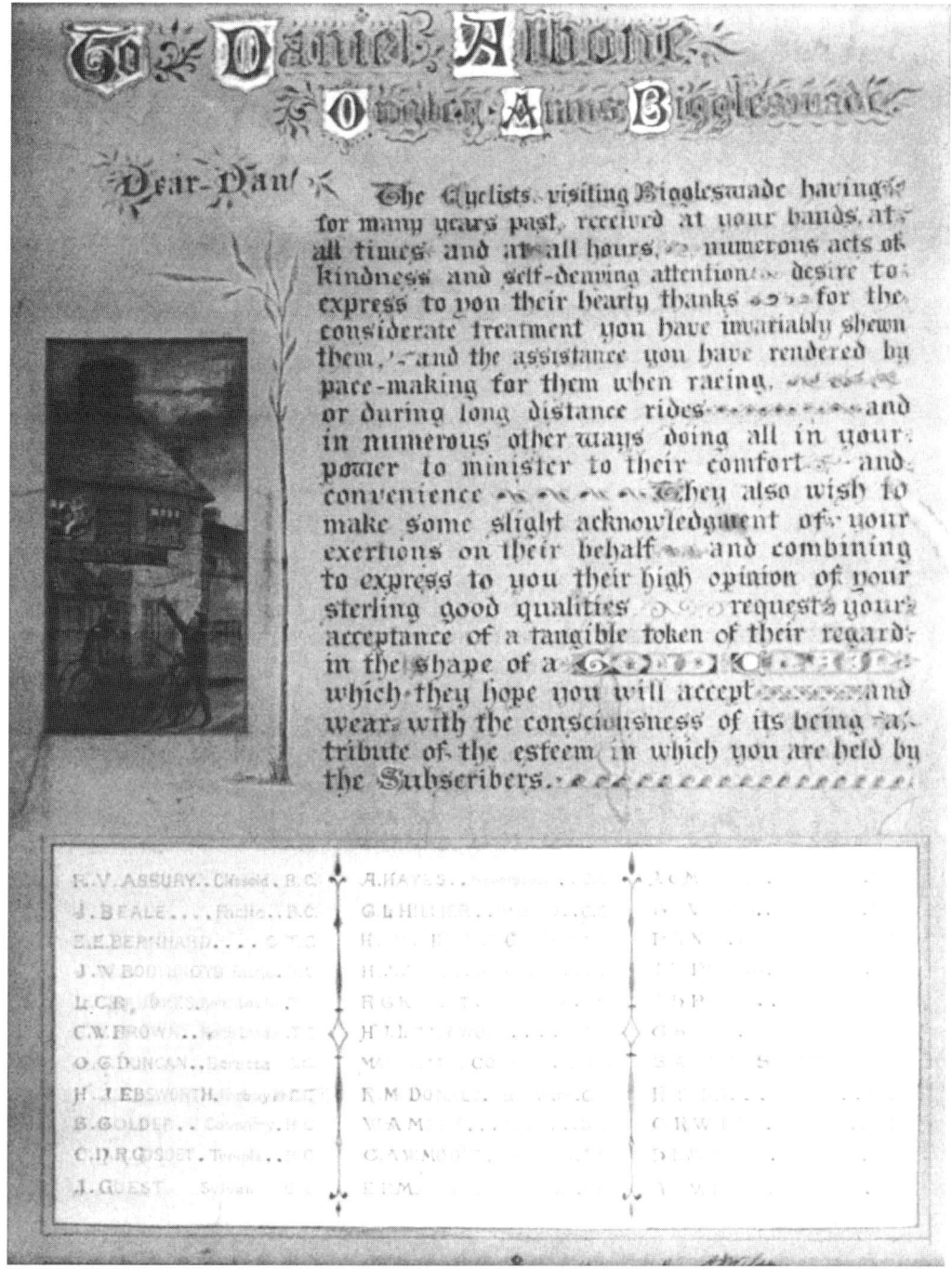

Fig.21: The Illuminated Testimonial

the Humber 'Cripper'.[9] The catalogue comment was that:

"This machine is at once the most comfortable form of tricycle extant, the steering is wonderfully easy and on a straight road, miles can be ridden almost without touching the handles."

Note that 'almost'. In fact, the tricyclist was still forced to steer the machine in a positive manner.

In addition Dan offered *"Any special pattern made to order, as Tandems, Sociables, Loop-frame Tricycles, etc."* We do not know if anyone placed an order and no survivor has been identified.

Also, as advertised in that catalogue, Dan was sole agent in the district for the 'Facile'.

On Sunday November 29th 1885 a special tribute of a framed illuminated testimonial was made to Dan, the illuminated part consisting of the Ongley Arms with Dan's head popping out of the window in the night to see what record breaker required his assistance, and a *"massive"* gold chain, spirited into the Ongley Arms in brown paper,[10]:

"subscribed for by 33 London and provincial cyclists, expressive of their gratitude for his painstaking efforts to aid in securing the comfort of

---

9   *Wheeling*, March 24th 1885

10 *Bicycling News*, December 4th 1885, p.179.

his guests, and in "pacemaking" for racing men and road-record breakers." [11] and

"... after the usual cyclists' dinner at the Ongley Arms" for *"... the painstaking zeal with which "Dan" of Biggleswade looks after the comforts of cyclists who are continually making rides on the Great North Road, (which) has become quite proverbial of late years: And a number of Metropolitan "habituees" of Biggleswade conspired to organise a "whip round" for the testimonial to Dan".*[12]

The illuminated testimonial read:

"Dear Dan, - The cyclists visiting Biggleswade having for many years past received at your hands, at all times and all hours, numerous acts of kindness and self denying attention, desire to express to you their hearty thanks for the considerate treatment you have invariably shown them, and the assistance you have rendered by pace making for them when racing, or during long distance rides, and in numerous other ways doing all in your power to minister to their comfort and convenience. They also wish to make some slight acknowledgement of your exertions on their behalf, and combining to express to you their high opinion of your sterling good qualities , request your acceptance of a tangible token of their regard in the shape of a gold chain, which they hope you will accept and wear with the consciousness of it being a tribute of the esteem in which you are held by the subscribers."

Dan Albone thanked all present for their kindness, which included a number who had ridden from London, and A. J. Hills, captain; W. J. Robinson, sub-captain; C. B. Evans; and Stamp Hutton of the Biggleswade & District C.C. He asked A. J. Wilson to convey to those absent subscribers his appreciation. The subscribers were:

R. V. Asbury, Clissold B.C.; J. Beale, Facile B.C.; E. E. Bernhard, C.T.C.; J. W. Boothroyd, Facile B.C.; L. C. Brookes and C. W. Brown, North London T.C.; O. G. Duncan, Berretta C.C.; H. J. Ebsworth, Finsbury Park C.C.; S. Golder, Coventry C.C.; C. H. R. Gosset, Temple B.C.; J. Guest, Sylvan B.C.; A. Hayes, Haverstock C.C.; G. Lacy Hillier, Stanley C.C.; Hillman, Herbert & Cooper; H. J. Jones, Haverstock C.C.; R. E. Knight, Southwark C.C.; Littlewood, C.T.C.; Marriott & Cooper;

R. McDonald, Southwark C.C.; W. A. Meek, York B.C.; G. A. W. Moore; E. P. Moorhouse, A. G. Morrison and T. A. Nelson, North London T. C.; P. A. Nix, Brixton Ramblers B.C.; J. H. Parish, North London T.C.; J. H. Price, Stanley C.C.; George Smith, Stoke Newington Harriers; Starley and Sutton; R. Todd, Stanley C.C.; G. R. White, Clissold B.C.; and H. T. Whorlow and A. J. Wilson, North London T.C.

Dan wrote to *Wheeling* to express his thanks:

"Dear Sir – Will you kindly allow me. through the medium of your paper to most sincerely thank those wheelmen who subscribed together to present me with a valuable testimonial of my services as they did on Sunday 29th. I am sure it affords me the greatest pleasure to find my efforts on their behalf and the sport generally, have been so generously acknowledged. The gold chain I am more proud of than any prize I have won while racing, and with the illuminated address will always be a lasting momento of the esteem in which I am held by the gentlemen named therein. My greatest efforts on behalf of record breakers and visitors generally will always be exerted to the utmost in future, as (I hope) I have done in the past. It is more especially for those riders who were unable to get down on Sunday, last, and therefore were not present at the time, that I write these few lines, thanking one and all most heartily and sincerely." [13]

It was proposed by 'Faed' Wilson[14], at a meeting of the subscribers to Dan's testimonial, that a club be formed for 'crack' riders. The North Road Cycling Club

Fig.22: North Road Cycling Club badge

was launched at a general meeting on Monday December 21st 1885 (essentially as a racing club open to cyclists who had ridden at least one hundred miles in a day, a circular having previously been issued on October 1st). 'Faed' Wilson, Dan Albone and G. P. Mills were founder members and the headquarters were at the Ongley Arms.

---

11 *The Cyclist Christmas Number,* 1885-86, p.98.
12 *Wheeling,* December 2nd 1885.
13 *Wheeling,* December 9th 1885.
14 Wilson was deaf, hence his nickname 'Faed'.

A full page article was subsequently published in *Bicycling News* setting out

"*... Its Origins, Its Aims, Its Men and Its Haunts*".[15]

In less than a year after *"fatherly Faed"* had proposed the idea, the Club had become an important feature in Metropolitan cycling circles and had members in many parts of the country.

"*Its policy is eminently of the anti-crawl type. Rightly or wrongly, it believes that club runs should be more correctly termed pub runs, and that pace and perfection are synonymous. This creed is carried out to the letter, and the eternal "man off" from the sub captain is not permitted by the N.R.C.C. men*".

'Faed' Wilson is quoted as saying:

"*I had frequently experienced the advantage of having fast riding companions to help make the pace hot on a return journey from Biggleswade ... how much more pleasantly the journey was made when a number of crack riders were with me than when I was grinding along alone... "*

Fig.23: Dan with North Road C. C. members, *The Wheeler*, October 4th 1893

(courtesy Biggleswade History Society)

The route up the Great North Road was already very popular, so it is hardly surprising that the Club took off so quickly. Of the *"Haunts"*, the report says that the Great North Road cannot come up to the celebrated Ripley view, though it says that Ickwell and Old Warden are the two prettiest villages in England. Of the road it says:

"*At Barnet ... the macadam ends and ... unusually stony road goes through Potters Bar to Bell Bar from whence to Hatfield it is stony. After Welwyn coaches turn right and go on the North Road*

proper to Biggleswade, but cyclists use the ... longer but flatter and better road via Hitchin and the beautifully flat road to Biggleswade and from then on a superb gravel surface."

Fig.24: Dan's Shanty – *Bicycling News*, June 25th, 1886

Dan had hung an Ordinary bicycle wheel from the inn sign of the Ongley Arms. It became a landmark on the Great North Road, and attracted comment in the press (Fig.24).[16] Production of machines was increasing, and the 'Ivel' name was well-known for quality. Dan himself was a salesman, prize-winning cyclist, design engineer and production manager, not to mention being the landlord of the Ongley Arms.

The Biggleswade & District C.C. continued to thrive. In the photograph (Fig.26) can be seen Capt. A. J. Hills (centre right, with hand on shoulder); Stamp Hutton, the postmaster (centre left with beard); Mr White, ironmonger, is at the end on the right; next to him is Mr Marsh, the schoolmaster; three to the left is Mr Wheatley, the watchmaker; sitting below Mr Hutton and slightly to the left is Jim Cawse, the jeweller; Mrs Tingey, Dan's sister Ann, is sitting, the second from the right; Dan is there too.

Dan was about to take some of the biggest steps so far in his career. The 'Kangaroo' as a form of safety bicycle was about to be eclipsed so how long the Ordinary wheel?

Fig.25: Ivel advertisement, *The Cyclist*

---

15 *Bicycling News*, June 18th 1886, p.546.

16 *Wheeling*, November 5th 1884

Fig.26: Biggleswade & District C. C.

(courtesy Biggleswade History Society)

Fig.27: Staged photograph at the Ivel Works.

(Letter addressed to Mrs Shell by A. J. Wilson, courtesy Science Museum. Dan, Ann Albone and Richard Tingey are in the background. The man at the anvil is Arthur Morrison, who wrote 'Duffersville' with 'Faed' Wilson, a thinly disguised name for Biggleswade. With the hammer is Major C. E. Liles, a champion cyclist.)

14

1886 The Golden Touch

This was an exceptional year for cycle development by Dan. He created the hands-off cross-frame safety, developed the tandem bicycle, and the first practical bicycle for ladies. These developments are covered in the chapters that immediately follow.

Much of this success can be attributed to his association with two individuals, 'Faed' Wilson and G. P. Mills, who assisted with the developments. Mills in particular gained valuable publicity for the 'Ivel' by his record breaking rides.

The Stanley Show of 1886 seems to be the first that Dan attended with a presentation of his bicycles. His 'Ivel Light Roadster Safety Bicycle' of 'Kangaroo' pattern, fitted with the 'Kelsey' bracket, was commented upon favourably.[1]

Dan's catalogue for 1886 offered six models.[2] The 'Ivel Racer' at £15.15s was in essence the machine that Dan was using to race. The catalogue claimed that during the previous season it had won no less than 110 prizes including the Championship of Bedfordshire for two years. The weight for a 54 in. was fairly light at 21 lb. and compared well with similar machines. Rucker, for example produced a Racer that he claimed weighed 23 lb.

The 'Ivel Roadster' was offered at £12 10s. (Griffin shows a different price) with hollow forks painted and lined but there was a cheaper version with solid forks at £10.

For those who didn't want an outright racing machine there was the 'Ivel Light Roadster'. This was an Ordinary *"specially suited for grass racing, or where the course is rather rough."* The weight was about 34 lb. and it was offered at £15.15s.

The 'Ivel Tricycle' was advertised as a *"fast machine"* and, although not claiming to be a racer, was very much styled as one of that time with two front driving and steering wheels, balance gear, backbone and trailing wheel. It cost £19.

In April Dan had applied for a Pony Trap patent (No. 1886-5909). It was granted in March 1887. The Pony Trap used tubular steel for the construction of the body. The wheels were 48 in. dia. wire-spoked with rubber tyres, and ran in ball-bearings,

No. 10. The Ivel Racer (Dan. Albone).—One commendable feature of this bicycle is the narrow tread (12½in.) between the pedal centres. To gain this, the hubs are only 4½in. apart. The latter are of a very neat and light pattern, and receive the 14-gauge direct spokes. Bown's (racing) ball bearings are bolted to the bottom of the broad (1⅛in.) hollow forks, which have rounded shoulders and a nicely-shaped Stanley head. A 27in. bent hollow bar has large cork knobs, forming a light and comfortable grip. To economise space, a spring is dispensed with, and the saddle fitted direct on the round backbone by an adjustable clamp. The wheels have Warwick's hollow rims and ⅝in. moulded tyres. Balls are fitted to all three parts (fixed cranks), and the machine is enamelled, with bright parts, and for quality is one of the cheapest mounts in the market. Price £15 15s.

No. 11. The Ivel Roadster.—This machine (see Fig. 6) has square-shouldered broad forks, which carry a straight Stanley head, with a long, hollow bar, dropped ends, and a good brake, with easily held lever.

A Humber pattern spring, with curled tail, supports a Long

FIG. 6.—THE IVEL ROADSTER.

Distance saddle. The spokes are of a heavier (13) gauge than in the Racer, larger hubs are put in, and the felloes are hollow. With balls to the three parts, detachable cranks, enamelled and plated, the price is—all sizes—£15 15s.

No. 12. The Ivel Dwarf Light Roadster.—There being no strikingly novel or original features in this machine, a lengthy description will be unnecessary. It is of the usual outline, as will be seen on reference to Fig. 7. A small 36in. or 38in. wheel is geared up to 54in. or more; the lower chain pulley, &c., are held by Kelsey's patent Duplex bearings, &c. In general details the machine is like that just described. save the difference in size. Abingdon chains are used, and the machine is a capital one of its kind. Fitted complete, balls all parts, enamelled and plated, the price is £15 15s.; or, with foot rests and mud guard, £16 7s. 6d.

FIG. 7.—THE IVEL DWARF LIGHT ROADSTER.

Fig.28: *Bicycles and Tricycles 1886, Griffin*

---

1   *Bicycling News* Supplement, February 19th 1886, page 5.
2   The catalogue might possibly be for 1885 – it is undated. The 'Ivel' Roadster is cheaper than Griffin indicates for 1886 which suggests the catalogue might be earlier. However, the two wins in the Championship of Bedfordshire point towards 1886 as the year for the catalogue.

both aspects being based on cycle materials and design. It weighed 112 lbs.[3] and sold for 35 guineas. The Pony Trap was first included in his 1887 catalogue. Later, wire-spoked carriage wheels with ball-bearings were shown in his 1891 catalogue, the wheels making an appearance with his cycles at a number of the Stanley Shows. The idea was not entirely new, apart from the use of ball-bearings, since Haynes & Jefferis advertised wire-spoked carriage wheels in their 1878 catalogue.

In 1886, cycling enthusiasm hit a new peak, and clubs flourished. When the weather prevented cycling, social activities, especially 'Cinderella' dances, as they were known, were organised, and well attended. Incidentally, many cycling clubs were off-shoots of 'Temperance' organisations.

With large parties of cyclists arriving at the Ongley Arms, the little country inn was crowded. Sometimes Dan sent customers across the road to his brother at the Royal Oak, but for cyclists, the Ongley Arms was the place to be. Dan was forced to plan the enlargement of his premises. Both the inn and the workshops had become inadequate.

Dan still took part in races. Indeed, it was essential that the 'Ivel' make should be associated with winners in the news. Dan took part in local races, such as those at the Biggleswade Fête at Fairfield Meadow, graciously lent by Colonel Lindsell, and now confidently expected to be an annual event. 'Ivel' racers featured strongly.

A typical race on public roads was reported as follows: Sheep's Bridge, Caldecote Road, through Upper Caldecote, Vinegar Hill, Poplar Corner, Beeston and Lower Caldecote, Upper Caldecote, Hill Lane and back to the start, a distance of roughly nine miles. Dan completed this race in thirty one minutes on his 'Ivel Racer' (an Ordinary) and so earned himself the title, 'Champion of the Biggleswade & District Cycling Club'. Only three out of the five competitors finished the race, probably due to the high winds and heavy condition of the unmetalled roads.

George Pilkington Mills (Fig.29) of the Anfield Bicycle Club, Liverpool, came to work for Dan in 1886. The Hooper and Fletcher records include a copy of an agreement (Fig.30), dated February 10th 1887, between Dan and G. P. Mills - to be partners.

£1 per week was to be paid to Mills. The term of the agreement was one year.

On November 5th Dan registered the 'Ivel' name as a trade mark, No. 58,621, for carriages, wheeled vehicles included in Class 22, bicycles and velocipedes.[4]

By the end of 1886 Dan was so well known in the cycling fraternity that the magazine *The Cyclist* published the following tribute:

"Daniel Albone, the most popular man in cycling and one of the best known, whether personally or by repute. Only twenty six years of age and looks even younger, comely, as all the Biggleswade fair know, and yet both an innkeeper and a cycle manufacturer. First rode at nine years of age and since then has won over sixty prizes on the wheel; is on the committee of his local club, the Biggleswade, and was its champion for five years. Dan Albone speedily built up for himself a steadily improving trade and is now known as the maker of some of the best cycles extant, employing a large staff of workmen."

This was compatible with comments elsewhere:

"whose cheery nature is proverbial, and who understands the Bohemian and unconventional habits of the record-breaker, and is never so happy as when laying himself out to plan routes and arrange for timekeeping, checking and pacemaking" [5]

Someone penned this little ditty:

DAN O'WRIGGLESWADE

In every record-ride, ye see,
In every record ride,
We're bound to go through Wriggleswade,
And call for Dan outside;
For every race he'll make the pace,
And have some jelly made;
And so a whip's been made for chips
For Dan o'Wriggleswade

A chain of gold he shall not lack
In honour of his care,
Nor words of thanks for all he's done,
Nor praises written fair;
Within the frame's a score of names
Of cycling men, who made
Their meaning plain, and gave a chainwheel
To Dan o' Wriggleswade

---

3 *Bicycling News*, February 11th 1888.

4 *The Cyclist Year Book* 1891, p.80.
5 *Wheel World*, October 1886, p.442 and 443

Fig.29: G. P. Mills

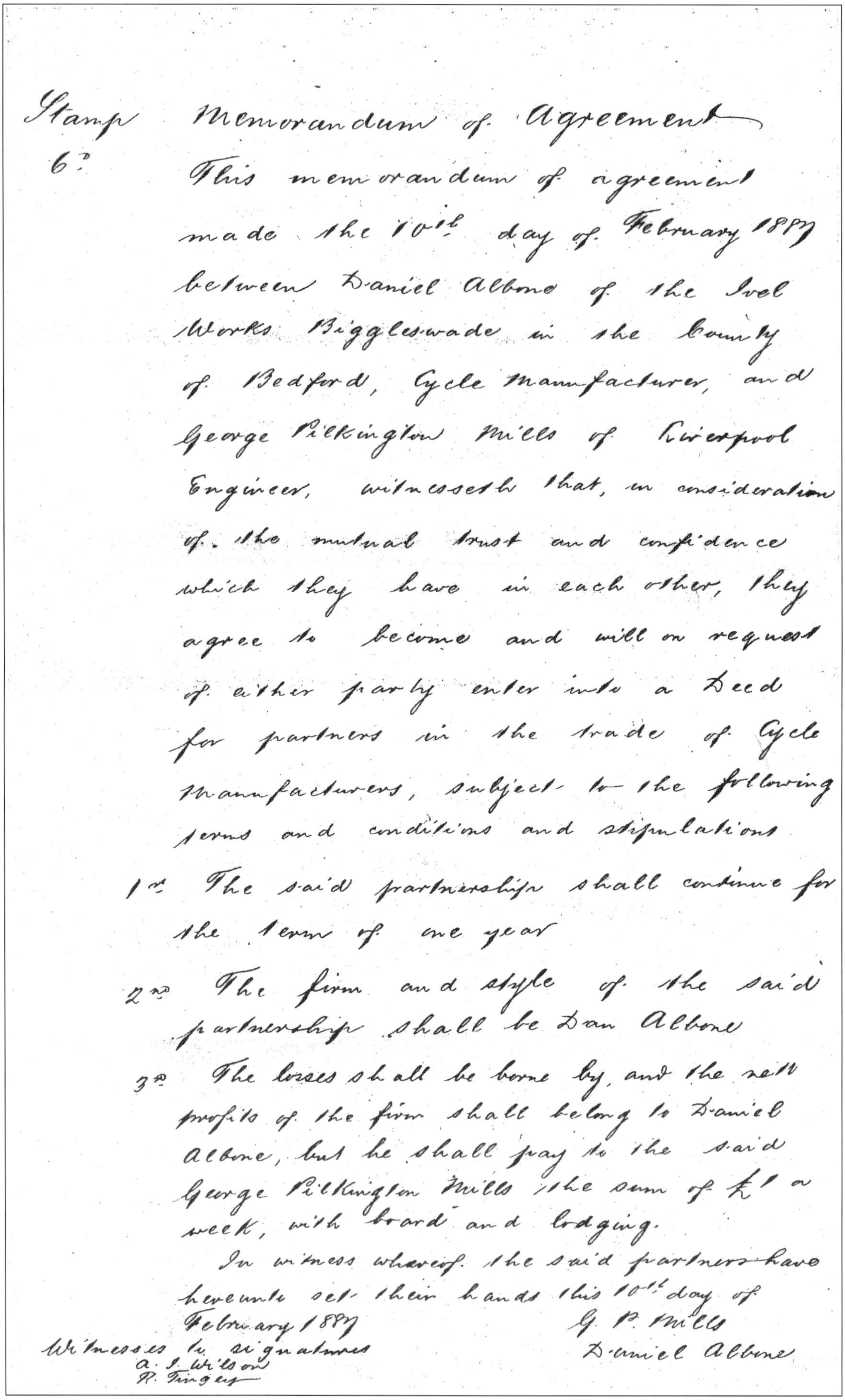

Stamp
6?

Memorandum of Agreement

This memorandum of agreement made the 10th day of February 1887 between Daniel Albone of the Ivel Works Biggleswade in the County of Bedford, Cycle Manufacturer, and George Pilkington Mills of Liverpool Engineer, witnesseth that, in consideration of the mutual trust and confidence which they have in each other, they agree to become and will on request of either party enter into a Deed for partners in the trade of Cycle Manufacturers, subject to the following terms and conditions and stipulations

1st The said partnership shall continue for the term of one year

2nd The firm and style of the said partnership shall be Dan Albone

3rd The losses shall be borne by, and the nett profits of the firm shall belong to Daniel Albone, but he shall pay to the said George Pilkington Mills the sum of £1 a week, with board and lodging.

In witness whereof the said partners have hereunto set their hands this 10th day of February 1887

G. P. Mills

Daniel Albone

Witnesses to signatures
a. I. Wilson
P. Finger

Fig.30: Dan's Agreement with G. P. Mills, concluded February 10th, 1887

(courtesy Bedfordshire & Luton Archives Service)

1886 The Hands-off Safety

Several attempts had been made over the years to invent a rear-driver bicycle where the rider sat between two moderate-sized wheels. Meyer is supposed to have made what might be classified as the first safety bicycle in 1869. About 1876 it is claimed George Shergold manufactured a bicycle with pedals and a chain drive to the rear wheel. Originally a shoemaker, he returned to his old trade and the 'Shergold' remained unique.

H. J. Lawson's first rear-driver was the lever-driven Safety Bicycle of 1876. Only a few were sold. He followed this up with the chain driven rear-driver 'Bicyclette' in 1879 but again only a few were sold before it was withdrawn in 1880. The public were not ready for it.

However, the development of a commercially-viable safety bicycle, that would become the model from which today's bicycle descended, did not take place until the mid 1880s. Sutton and J. K. Starley (nephew of James Starley of the Coventry Machinists' Company), brought their new 'Rover' model to the Stanley Show in February, 1885. With its clumsy indirect steering to the front wheel, the model had few customers and the public remained loyal to the 'Facile' and the 'Kangaroo'. Stephen Golder, a racing cyclist and clerk on *The Cyclist*, suggested that the indirect steering should be scrapped. It was. Like all good engineers, Starley and Sutton went back to the drawing board and re-designed the steering. In September 1885 the revised model emerged with direct steering.[1]

This revised 'Rover' bicycle, ridden by Golder, claimed the 50 mile record and then, ridden by George Smith, the 100 mile record, and suddenly the customers were interested. J. K. Starley continued to refine the design and The Cyclist penned the phrase: *"set the fashion to the world"*. This would turn out to be perfectly true. Cycle manufacturers suddenly saw the future of the bicycle going in a completely new direction, unthought of at the beginning of the decade.

The 'Rover' maintained its curved lines. Nevertheless the shape suggested a straight-lined frame to some. Cycle manufacturers aimed to bring their prototypes to the Stanley Show, and come away with a full order book. It was undoubtedly true that,

once a model was displayed, its novelties would soon be copied. Many disagreements and law suits came up at this time.

Hillman, Herbert & Cooper came up with their 'Premier' cross-frame safety idea in February 1886. They were granted a patent (No. 1775) for this incorporating a new method of chain adjustment, a new method of constructing a chainwheel, and the use of springs to keep the front wheel automatically in line, all of which were employed in their 'Premier'. Within two months, Dan had brought out a new version of the 'Ivel', a self-steering safety bicycle built on the cross-frame design. The vital difference was in the steering so that it could be ridden *"hands-off"* which was unusual (the 'Premier' design utilised springs to keep the front wheel in line). Although Dan was friendly with Hillman, Herbert & Cooper – witness their 'Kangaroo Hunt Supper' the previous year – it seems unlikely they would have allowed him to copy their design. There is a possibility that Dan was paying a royalty to them of £8.14s (per month?) based on some undated Albone papers.[2] If so, was this for the method of chain adjustment.

A claimed example of Dan's cross-frame in the Science Museum, is described as follows:

"The feature of this safety is the simplicity of the frame which consists essentially of a backbone, joining the rear hub to the steering head, crossed at right angles by a tube carrying the saddle and crank bracket. Later ... wire stays from steering head to saddle, and from rear hub to crank bracket

Fig.31: 'Ivel' Racer 1887, reputed to be Dan's, in Coventry Transport Museum

---

1   *A History of Rover Bicycles*, John Pinkerton and Derek Roberts, p.37.

2   Bedfordshire & Luton Archives Service, Hooper and Fletcher records, ref: HF 21.

Fig.32: Dan at Swiss Garden, Shuttleworth, 1886

(courtesy Biggleswade History Society)

were added. *The weight is taken by the backbone acting as a girder and hence the construction is heavy. The wheels have radial spokes and cushion tyres; the pedals are of rubber. Both wheels are 30 in. dia., the rear one is geared to 63.7 in. The radius of the pedals is adjustable between 5.75 in. and 6.25 in. The wheelbase is 43.7 in. and the weight is 45lb.*" [3]

Alfred H. Fletcher, an established rider, rode Dan's new safety bicycle in a 50 mile race on August 24th, setting a new record of 3 hrs. 9 min. 56 secs. This was not the 'Ivel' Racer but one that weighed 37 lbs., and was geared to 66 in. with 7 in. cranks. [4]

On September 1st Fletcher again rode Dan's new safety bicycle in a 24 hour race. Fletcher set a new record of 265½ miles, better than J. H. Adam's performance on a 'Facile'. A race report comments that:

"Dan Albone's 'Rover' pattern safety is a rare machine for pace". [5]

This makes it absolutely clear that Fletcher was not using the 'Kangaroo' type of safety but the modern cross-frame rear-driver.

In October the following review appeared:

A SELF-STEERING SAFETY CYCLE

"One of the great drawbacks to the dwarf bicycles of the 'Rover' type has hitherto been the impossibility of their being ridden without at least one hand on the steering bar, and even with 'automatic' or 'fly to centre' spring arrangements, it has not been found possible to balance and steer a rear-driving dwarf safety bicycle without the use of the hands. By some happy inspiration, Dan Albone has hit upon a means whereby this defect is overcome and without adding any extra parts to the steering appliances, he has constructed an 'Ivel' safety, on the plan of the 'Rover' or 'bicyclette', which can be ridden in a true and straight line, and even steered round easy corners without the use of the hands. This is accomplished entirely by the adjustment of the steering centres at a particular angle which, by its relative position as regards the wheelbase, the weight, and the driving power, automatically keeps the front wheel in a straight line when the rider sits upright and drives steadily forward and also deflects its course to the right or the left in obedience to the inclination of the rider's body. The result is of course that the steering is not only capable of being controlled with the hands-off, but also is vastly improved and rendered steadier when the hands are on the guiding-bar, the bicycle being indeed under the most perfect control and less subject to sudden swerves and lurches than it would be without this newly discovered self-steering angle." [6]

The reason why the 'Ivel' steered hands-off does not seem to have been satisfactorily explained.

Fig.33: Dan on hands-off safety, 1886

(courtesy Biggleswade History Society)

3   *H.M.S.O. Cycles*, Part 1, page 36 and Part 2, page 15. Inventory number 1924-74 and located in the Science Museum Wroughton store at the time of publication.
4   Ivel catalogue for 1887, p.12.
5   *Cycling Times*, September 1st 1886.
6   *Wheel World*, October 1886.

A REMARKABLE RECORD MACHINE!! 294½ MILES IN 24 HOURS.
ALTHOUGH ONLY ON THE MARKET FOR A FEW WEEKS,
THE "IVEL" SAFETY BICYCLE,
Which can be ridden and steered without using the handles, has achieved the unique reputation of being incontestably the fastest Bicycle ever made, as the undermentioned performances demonstrate.

The 50 Miles Road Record beaten by A, H. Fletcher, Esq. Time, 3h. 9m. 56⅔s. Aug. 24th, 1886.

The 50 Miles Road Record again beaten by G. P. Mills, Esq. Time, 2h. 47m. 35s. Oct. 2nd, 1886.

The 24 Hours Road Record beaten by A. H. Fletcher, Esq. Distance, 265¼ Miles. Sept. 1st, 1886.

The 24 Hours Road Record again beaten by G. P. Mills, Esq. Oct. 5th, the marvellous distance of 294¼ Miles, the ordinary Bicycle and every other record totally demolished by over 23 miles, in spite of fog and a collision.

Compare the actual figures with those of other makers claiming records for their machines.

PRICE £15 TO £17 10/-

"Mr. Mills spoke most highly of his mount, and gives it as his opinion that it is the best machine of its kind going."—*Cyclist*, Oct. 6th, 1886.

FOR FULL PARTICULARS, ADDRESS—

DAN ALBONE, "IVEL" CYCLE WORKS, BIGGLESWADE.

Agents:—Messrs. *Jennings & Co.*, Manchester; Thos. Redman & Co., Bradford; Herbert Smith & Co., London; A. Pallant, St. Albans; I. S. Earnshaw, Halifax; H. H. Halley, Edinburgh; Slade & Co., Liverpool; J. Elvidge, Duffield; Booth Bros, Dublin; D. E. Marvin, Ryde; Harrington, London; S. Moore, London; W. Olliffe, 13, Grainger Street West, Newcastle-on-Tyne, and Monsieur Louis Delaprax, 6, Rue de Saussure, Geneva.

Fig.34: 'Ivel' advertisement, *The Cyclist*, late 1886

Archibald Sharp[7] considered the generic question and concluded that:

"steering without hands should be easier the higher the speed, the larger the steering-wheel, and the heavier the rim of the steering-wheel."

He also contradicted M. Bourlet who had suggested that:

"the mass-centre of the front wheel and frame must lie in front of the steering axis; but this would mean that a bicycle with straight forks could not be ridden without hands; whereas some of the earliest 'Safety' bicycles, made with straight forks, were easily ridden without hands."

Sharp however did not comment specifically on the 'Ivel'.

The 'Ivel' safety was becoming well-known and Dan had as many orders as he could cope with. Bartleet notes that an outside 'liner' had been added under the main frame tube near the head to at least one machine after Mills had suffered a fracture at this point (he was commenting on what may have been Dan's own machine).[8] In addition, it seems

that after Mills had twisted the bracket riding up the hill to Old Warden church in 1886, extra stays from the bracket to the rear fork ends were offered for an additional £0.10s in 1887 at least on the No.2 and Semi-Racer.[9] By 1890 these stays were a standard fitting.

On October 2nd, Mills beat the 50 mile road record set by Fletcher on the Great North Road in a time of 2 hrs. 47 mins. 36 secs. He was riding an 'Ivel' rear-driver safety bicycle. This record was not beaten until 1889 and was the sort of publicity 'Ivel' cycles needed.

More was to come. Only a few days later on the 5-6th, Mills used the 'Ivel' rear-driver bicycle again to cover 295 miles in 24 hours[10], with Dan accompanying him for about 160 miles.[11] This record had previously been held by an American, Hollingsworth, who rode back and forward over a 13 mile stretch of road covering 281 miles. Mills started with the intention of beating his own record of 268½ miles on an Ordinary and did so by a substan-

7 *Bicycles and Tricycles*, 1896, p.232.
8 *Bartleet's Bicycle Book*, pages 78-79.
9 *The Cycle*, December 1894.
10 The initial measurement was 294½ miles but later ratified by the Records Committee of the N.C.U. at 295 miles.
11 *The Cyclist*, October 13th 1886.

Fig.35: 'Ivel's ready to race

tial margin. In the early stages Mills collided with a horse but was not hurt and continued although the 'Ivel' expired with 15 minutes to go.[12] Mills's famous ride is reported and this is an extract:

"Mills Puts in a Marvellous Performance

In our last issue, we stated that G.P. Mills was on Tuesday of last week riding in an attempt at the twenty-four hours' bicycle record, and were able to report that up to twelve o'clock he had accomplished 150 miles. We are now able to report one of the most wonderful pieces of riding on record. The route taken was from Biggleswade to Hitchin and back, then on by Peterborough to Wisbech, turning there back to Peterborough, Kate's Cabin[13] and back to Peterborough; south again to Eaton Socon; turning off sharp to St Neots, then to Godmanchester and back to St Neots; on to Cambridge and back via St Neots to Eaton Socon. From Eaton Socon to Bedford (etc.)... Mills finished half a mile outside Biggleswade exactly at 12 pm. on Tuesday having covered the wonderful distance of 294 miles in 24 hours. Several riders kindly gave their valuable assistance in pace-making; Mr D. Albone accompanied Mills for almost 160 miles; Mr C. B. Cooper of Sandy; Mr English of Peterborough; and Messrs. Huber, Marks and Hiatt of Biggleswade, all did good service; in fact Mills was unaccompanied only for a few miles. Mr H. F. Hardwick of the "Express" checked him at Hitchin on the Tuesday morning. Mr. Grant, of Cambridge, kindly got a bath, and had food and drinks ready for him. Mr

Mills rode all through the day at a marvellous pace, and running down nearly all his pace-makers, finished up as strong as when he started. The route taken is one of the very best that can be got, the roads were in good order and the weather most favourable. The rider was started and timed by Mr A. J. Hills, and as in his 50 miles record bestrode an "Ivel" rear-driving safety." [14]

He went on to break many more records on 'Ivel' bicycles and tricycles. One adversary was heard to say that Mills' great advantage was that he ate quickly and went on his way, but that cannot have been the total story of his success. Others said he had *"excessive brutal strength"*.[15]

Mills had this to say about preparation for road riding.

"there is nothing like plenty of long, hard road rides for giving you staying power. To ride such long journeys as 24 hours you need to train so thoroughly that you can eat and digest solid food at intervals during your ride. If you are not thoroughly in condition you cannot eat, and though many riders ride long distances on liquid food it is my opinion that a man can get himself in better condition than to be obliged to do that. When I was in my best form, no matter how long the journey, I never really felt knocked up, and could eat anything. In riding a 24 hours race I like to get my breakfast after riding about 100 miles. A good solid one. For stiffness I rub my muscles with whisky. To sum up, there is no way in which to get into thorough good "trim" for road riding but to do plenty of hard work." [16]

The 'Ivel' cross-frame safety had a brass head badge which stated:[17]

THE

IVEL

DAN ALBONE

BIGGLESWADE

BEDS

12 *Cycling*, August 21st 1919, p.140.
13 Kate's Cabin exists today as a transport cafe on the A1 at the northern end of the motorway section near Peterborough. There was originally a coaching inn at this location on the junction of the Oundle to Peterborough road and the Great North Road.

14 *The Cyclist*, October 13th 1886.
15 *The Boneshaker*, No.103, p.10.
16 *Cycle Racing and Road Riding*, 1890.
17 Based on a rubbing that was taken in the early 1980s.

A REMARKABLE RECORD MACHINE!

Although only on the market for a few weeks, the

"IVEL" SAFETY BICYCLE

Which can be Ridden and Steered without using the hands, has achieved the unique reputation of being uncontestably the

FASTEST BICYCLE EVER MADE,

As the undermentioned performances demonstrate :

The 50 Miles Road Record, beaten by A. H. Fletcher, Esq. Time, 3h. 9m. 56¾s.

The 50 Miles Road Record again beaten by G. P. Mills, Esq. Time, 2h. 47m. 3¾s.

The 24 Hours' Road Record beaten by A. H. Fletcher, Esq. Distance, 265½ Miles.

The 24 Hours' Road Record again beaten by G. P. Mills, Esq. Marvellous Distance, 294½ Miles. In this ride Mr. Mills accomplished 19 miles in the first hour.

The Record Machine on which Mills rode is now on view at Henry Hally's Stand, at the Edinboro' International Exhibition.

PRICE £15 to £17 10s.   For full particulars, apply

DAN ALBONE, "Ivel" Cycle Works, BIGGLESWADE.

Agents—Messrs. Jennings & Co., Manchester ; S. Readman & Co., Bradford ; Herbert Smith & Co., London ; A. Pallant, St. Alban's ; I. S. Earnshaw, Halifax ; H. H. Halley, Edinburgh ; Slade & Co., Liverpool ; J. Elvidge, Duffield : Booth Brothers, Dublin ; D. E. Marvin, Ryde ; Harrington, London ; and S. Moore, London.

Fig.36: 'Ivel' advertisement, 1886

Fig.37: Ready for the Off outside the Ivel Hotel c.1888

1886 Developing the Tandem

'Faed' Wilson had the idea of a tandem safety bicycle and collaborated with Dan in producing a new design.[1] Their first attempt in the Autumn of 1885 was to turn a 'Rover' type rear-driving bicycle into a tandem by the simple expedient of putting the front wheel of a 'Kangaroo' in place of the 'Rover' front wheel, and fitting a seat pillar and a pair of handle-bars from a Humber tricycle.[2] This machine was known as the 'Kangarover'. The trouble with this design was that the rear rider needed great strength to steer not only the front wheel but the weight of the front rider as well, because he was not supported on the frame as with a tradesman's bicycle. 'Faed' said that he broke several pairs of handlebars before deciding that the design was fated.

Fig.38: First attempt at a tandem, Autumn 1885. Dan on the front and 'Faed' on the rear

The second attempt in December 1885/January 1886 was by way of adaptation of an 'Ivel' cross-frame safety with a frame extending to the rear for another rider and drive gear. Unknowingly they had created the first 'donkey-back' tandem, later seen in use for track pacing in the late 1890's. The frame was just wide enough at the point of the rear axle to take a slotted fork-end in place of the usual washer. Not surprisingly, they found that the weight of the rear rider tended to lift the front wheel so making steering difficult if not impossible. Dur-

Fig.39: The second attempt

ing the trial runs they hung heavy weights to the head and Dan's men ran alongside to keep them upright if necessary.[3] However, note that the set-up is not dissimilar to the later-produced tandem tricycle.

'Faed' then sketched a tandem, while staying at the Ongley Arms in early 1886, with a frame long enough to accommodate two riders between the wheels but now the problem was fitting the (clumsy) chains of the time using the then (wide) bottom brackets. 'Faed' said:

"We thought that it would not do to make the rear rider's tread so wide as would be entailed by two broad chains alongside, whilst at the same time to put one chain on the left and the other on the right would hopelessly twist the bracket." [4]

The scheme was left in embryo for a while but another North Road Club rider, named Hall, did manage to make a suitable bracket using the narrowest chains, resulting in the 'Lightning' tandem. Hall took out two patents, assigned to J. H. L. Phillips, Patent Nos. 1887/13,191 and 1888/1,285.

Dan had finalised his 'Ivel' tandem during the Summer but it was not until early 1888 that it was available with both drive chains on one side.[5] The machine originally had connected steering. In January 1888 a second version with connected steering had lower connecting chains parallel with the cross-frame member. It was thought both riders must need to steer, until a connecting chain broke when Dan and Richard Tingey were on a 24 hour record attempt, and the rear rider could not steer, and they realised it was not necessary. Consequently from May 1888 there was no connected steering, al-

1 *Cycling*, December 1st 1933, p.543.
2 *Cycling*, July 19th 1940.
3 *Fellowship News*, 108/22 and Bartleet's notes. See also Cycling, December 1st 1933, p.543.
4 *Cycling*, December 1st 1933, p.543. 'Tread' is the distance between the pedal centres.
5 *Bartleet's Bicycle Book*, page 70.

though curiously the 1891 catalogue still refers to it. On this machine the saddle pillars were 31 in. apart. It was about the time that the connected steering was dispensed with that Dan invented a double clip for the rear handle-bars.

Fig.40: 'Ivel' tandem safety with the earlier connected steering

There followed in 1890 an action brought by Phillips for *"infringement"* of his patent, but he lost because he tried to claim too much. In part this was because Phillips conceded in court that the three elements required of steering, proper provision for carrying the weight of two riders, and proper provision for applying the force of both riders to effect proper propulsion, were not new as they had been anticipated by Howes and Rucker. Further, evidence was given that the Wilson-Albone tandem had been constructed and used in 1887 some weeks before the Phillips patent had been registered.[6] Accordingly, as 'Faed' Wilson later stated:

"The essence of a patent is the "Claim" at the end of the specification, and if the inventor claims parts already known, then his whole case fails. Such was the case with Hall" [7]

A short contemporary report congratulated Albone for fighting the case, rather than paying considerable royalties as several other companies had done.[8] It seems that Phillips subsequently attempted to claim costs from the Ivel Cycle Company but in another court decision had that turned down too.

'Faed' Wilson adds a delightful footnote to his account.

"What a small world it is! Forty five years later, I went to live in a village 150 miles away from Biggleswade, where, I found within a mile of my present little hut by the sea a parson named Hall, who told me how his brother had invented the tan-dem bicycle but had been done out of his rights by two bad wicked men named Wilson and Albone ...".

Later the respected cyclist and writer, H. W. Bartleet, had some interesting comments to make in an article titled 'Cycles That Made History – The Wilson-Albone tandem':

"I may be criticised for claiming that a machine which was never put on the market, and of which only a single experimental specimen was constructed, 'made cycling history', yet I feel quite justified in including the Wilson-Albone tandem bicycle in this series. It beat no records: it covered perhaps a total distance of 100 miles before its constituent parts were disassembled; but it was the means of preventing a later inventor obtaining a master patent which would have covered all tandem bicycles, so confining the type to one manufacturer. That such a monopoly would have restricted the development and sale of tandems will be appreciated when one realises how trade rivalry 'improves the breed' and prompts the various makers improvements in design and equipment, and – what is almost equally important to the public – to reduce prices.

On 29 September 1887 J. W. Hall applied for patent No. 13191 for a tandem safety bicycle with both riders within the wheelbase and alternatively a tandem bicycle converted to a single bicycle. The patent was accepted on 2 March 1888. He assigned his invention to H. L. Phillips. Not till February 1890 did the owner of the patent take steps to prove its validity, several ... practical tandems having appeared on the market in the meantime, Phillips took proceedings against the Ivel Cycle Co., Biggleswade 'for alleged infringement of plaintiff's patent for a tandem safety bicycle'.

The case was tried in the High Court, Chancery Division, before Mr Justice Kekewich, and the hearing took more than two days. Had Phillips won, and had Hall's patent been upheld, how very different would have been the history of tandem building and riding!

It was largely due to the evidence of our old friend A. J. ("Faed") Wilson, the man who has originated so many successful moments in and around the world of wheels, that the plaintiff's case failed.

Wilson's evidence was that in the year 1885 he possessed two bicycles of quite distinctive types, a front-driver 'Kangaroo' and a rear-driver 'Rover'. In the Autumn of that year it occurred to him to re-

6   *Bicycling News*, February 22nd 1890.
7   *Cycling*, December 1st 1933, p.544.
8   *Wheeling*, February 19th 1889.

move the backbone and rear wheel of the 'Kangaroo', and the front wheel and forks of the 'Rover', and combine the two machines, thus making a tandem, on which the rear rider shared and pedalled the 'Rover' portion, the front rider sitting astride the 'Kangaroo' part. The front man's handlebar was taken from the front of Wilson's Humber tandem tricycle.

Fig.41: 'Ivel' connected-steering tandem ridden by Sidney Faulkner (front) and Godfrey White

(courtesy *The Cyclist*)

In these experiments he was assisted by his friend Dan Albone, in whose cycle factory at Biggleswade the trials were carried out and the necessary mechanical alterations effected. Wilson and Albone jokingly dubbed the hybrid product their 'Kangarover'. Wilson tested it on the roads around Biggleswade before riding it to London with his young brother, aged 12, on the front saddle; he also rode it up Muswell Hill. The drawback of the 'Kangarover' was that the front rider's pedalling action caused his wheel to travel in a series of swerves, which had to be corrected by the steersman, thus putting a great strain on the handlebars. Faed recalls how he actually broke several bars before finally abandoning the hybrid and concentrating on a tandem with an extended wheel-base, with both riders between the wheels. This design he sketched early in 1886 and showed the drawing to several friends: unfortunately the sketch was destroyed but it was mentioned in the Phillips versus Ivel law case, and must have influenced the judge in arriving at his decision. The first commercially built Ivel tandem was made late in 1886 or early 1887 to this drawing.

Prior to making their 'Kangarover' Wilson and Albone had experimented with the former's 'Rover' single, putting a second rider behind the rear wheel (well outside the wheel-base) but the weight of the rear rider caused the front wheel to lift. So they procured a couple of 28lbs. weights and hung them on the front of the steering pillar to keep the front wheel on the ground, while six hefty 'Ivel' workmen ran alongside in an effort to help Wilson steer a straight course. It was the failure of this experiment which led to the 'Kangarover'.[9]

What fun these pioneers must have had, and what scope was provided for their experiments by the primitive mounts of their day. While signifying our appreciation of the mechanically perfect machines which we are privileged to ride today, we must pay a tribute to the experiments of 60, 50 and 40 years ago who risked their limbs and spent their money on 'trial and error' experiments, many of which were utter failures. Of these we hear nothing.

But, I repeat, how these old timers must have relished their rough and ready tests: how often – in the face of failure and perhaps a tumble in the gutter – must they have said to each other 'well turn it round and lets try it that way'! And then the joy when, at long last, success crowned their efforts."[10]

---

9   The accounts from Wilson and Bartleet differ: Wilson states that the 'Kangarover' came first.
10   From an undated manuscript draft article by H. W. Bartleet.

1886 First Practical Ladies Bicycle

Dan invented the first practical safety bicycle designed and marketed especially for ladies. It is a common misconception that Dan made the first lady's bicycle but that was not the case.

In France, Steiner patented a lever driven bicycle for ladies' use in 1869 and de Forville in 1870 claimed a provisional patent but it is not clear that any were made. In the United States in 1869 Pickering and Davis produced what they called a bicycle for ladies *"useable by velocipedestrienne"*.

In the UK, R. W. Thomas was granted a patent in 1870 for a two-track bicycle adapted for use by ladies. Then in 1874 James Starley was granted a patent for a two-track bicycle which could be ridden by a lady and could be converted into a sociable bicycle but no good one was made[1]. Thomas Sparrow followed with a patent in 1880 for his 'Amazon' roadster which was built, but there were drawbacks which inhibited its use by a lady. H. J. Lawson's bicycle stand patent of 1884 shows a single-tube open-framed bicycle which was chain driven. Two prototypes were produced by B.S.A. but crucially Lawson did not mention its suitability as a lady's bicycle, others did that much later and, although it might have been capable of use by a lady, there is no record of such use, and it was not considered a useable machine.[2] None of these attempts allowed for practical use by a lady.

The misconception crops up from time to time as this report from 1899 shows:

"A discussion has arisen as to the priority of invention of ladies bicycles, as THE CYCLIST says that Dan Albone's claim to have placed the first upon the market is untenable, because James Starley made such a machine fifteen years ago and H. J. Lawson built one twelve years ago. True enough, as far as it goes; and it might be added that Thomas Sparrow the evergreen veteran enthusiast not only made but exhibited a lady's bicycle which was ridden daily by a young lady at an exhibition in London some seven or eight years ago. But all these were mere experiments and never came to a practicable and marketable development; whereas Albone's "Lady's Safety" was a perfect machine in

exactly the same form as it was made and precisely the type which has been copied by all existing makers or bicycles for ladies' use so that the credit does belong to "Dan" after all. Palmam qui meruit ferit, Cyclist!" [3]

That it was the first practical ladies bicycle had been recognised rather earlier in 1887 by Violet Lorne, lady cycling journalist:

"Dan contemplates improving his lady's safety bicycle, but I do not believe that the fair sex will ever take seriously to the narrow gauger, but for those who do intend doing so, this is the first really practical lady's bicycle yet brought out." [4]

By 1906 it was generally accepted.

"The history of the lady's bicycle practically dates from 1886, and the names most intimately connected with its evolution are those of Dan Albone, who certainly made the first commercial

Ivel Safeties, Ivel Tricycles, Ivel Tandem-Safeties and Ivel Tandem-Tricycles have *all* beaten the road records.

Descriptive Price Lists Post Free on Application:
Ivel Cycle Co. Ltd., Biggleswade, Beds.

Fig.42: Lady's 'Ivel' safety advertisement

(courtesy Biggleswade History Society)

1 *Bartleet's Bicycle Book*, plate 16.
2 *Cycling History – Myths and Queries*, Derek Roberts, p.42-46. See *The Boneshaker*, 160/4.
3 *Irish Cyclist and Athlete*, January 16th, 1899.
4 *Bicycling News*, February 5th 1887.

drop-frame safety ..." [5]

What Dan did do, which is really much more of an achievement, is to design a lady's bicycle that worked, was copied by other makers, and has been essentially the design ever since. He replaced the straight front tube of the 'Ivel' safety with a curved or V-shaped tube from the head to the bracket. A leather dress-guard, laced onto a frame fashioned from a piece of flat iron and secured to the chain-stay, was also added. It had wheels of the same size.

Dan persuaded Miss Burrows, who lived nearly opposite, to sit on the machine while 'Faed' Wilson, who had assisted in producing the design, took a photograph. When Miss Burrows told her aunt what had happened, the aunt was horrified at the idea of her niece being depicted doing such a dis-graceful thing as riding a bicycle. Wilson was only able to pacify her by assuring her that the engraver would alter the face so as to be unrecognisable.[6] This picture was later used in the press. Much later Dan managed to persuade his wife, Elizabeth, to cycle down Biggleswade High Street but she did this very reluctantly.[7]

Although invented in August 1886[8] the bicycle did not appear in public until the Stanley Show of February 1887.[9] Dan was so ribbed by his racing friends that he went so far as to take the card off the show machine, as he almost felt he had done some-thing wrong in putting a bicycle on the market for the fair sex.[10] According to *Sturmey's Indispens-able*, the 'Ivel' was the only lady's machine on the market in 1887.

At the same time an advertisement appeared in *Bicycling News*.[11] It was not specifically included in the 1887 'Ivel' catalogue but as Dan states in the introduction to that catalogue:

"In the 'Anfield Ivel' Tricycle I have provided a machine unique in its simplicity, and which is more adaptable to the use of ladies than any other form of handle-bar steered tricycle. In its convertible form, too, this machine affords riders a means whereby they can ride either bicycle or tricycle ..."

The fact that the convertible form was in the catalogue and available in 1887 demonstrates that

the design of the solo form had been finalised by the Autumn of 1886. Sturmey included the solo machine in his *Indispensable*, remarking that it was *"convertible into a tricycle at will"*. [12]

ALBONE'S NEW TRICYCLE THE "ANFIELD" IVEL.

Fig.43: 'Anfield Ivel', *Bicycling News*, Feb. 5th, 1887

The 'Anfield Ivel' tricycle was made in several forms, according to one report by arrangement with Pausey using his patent No. 1884/12,084. The first was a non-convertible, gentleman's machine, the frame being similar to the safety but with a shorter rear fork, made to order with either two or four bearings to the axle.

This tricycle was, in the new direct-steerer form, a replacement for the Cripper-type (as it was ridden with great success by a noted amateur, Robert Cripps). Dan and Hillman, Herbert & Cooper were the first firms to adopt the new direct-steerer form.

For use by ladies the front of the frame was made in a V-shape. The conversion operation was simple. The tricycle back axle was removed, and one of the two wheels was set within the rear forks. This possibility, however, was not stressed, but to tempt husbands to buy the tricycle for their wives was the prospect that they could convert the ma-chine so as to have the use of a safety bicycle for themselves.

5   *Cycling*, April 25th, 1906.
6   *Bartleet's Bicycle Book*, pp.79-80 and 'Faed' Wilson writing in 1956.
7   Telephone conversation with Mr. Edward Albone on March 2nd 1990.
8   *Cycling*, April 25th 1906 and as claimed in the 'Ivel' catalogue for 1896.
9   *Cycling History – Myths and Queries*, Derek Roberts.
10 *Cycling*, April 25th 1906, p.349.
11 *Bicycling News*, February 5th 1887.

12 *Sturmey's Indispensable 1887*, p.312.

Fig.44: Ladies 'Anfield Ivel' convertible

(courtesy Biggleswade History Society)

Two other possibilities were the alternative conversion to an 'Ivel' tandem bicycle and an 'Ivel' tandem tricycle. There was nothing new about the conversion of a solo tricycle to a tandem tricycle as in November 1883 Thomas Humber had patented the idea of bolting an extra frame, fitted with saddle, chain wheel, cranks etc., to a solo tricycle. Others with similar concepts on the market were the Coventry Machinists' Company and Linley & Biggs. What Dan introduced was a much simpler design that permitted conversion to four types of machine which went far beyond the Humber design.

Further, for anyone who had purchased the 'Ivel' safety, the axle and wheels etc., could be purchased for £10 allowing full conversion to a tricycle, saving £12 on the cost of both machines.

Although convertible machines were very popular in the eighties, it was finally realized that most people found the conversion too much trouble to carry out and the type disappeared.

It could be speculated that Dan's particular interest in the lady cyclist, and his subsequent design of a drop-frame bicycle suitable for a skirted rider, could have arisen from his courtship of Elizabeth Moulden.

Women were not commonly seen on bicycles; tricycles were thought to be more suitable for females. Tricycles were more stable, yet equally they were heavier to ride. There was also much concern over the question of whether it was truly healthy for women to cycle, though this did not seem to be a great deterrent to women. Thanks to Dan's invention, the way was paved for women to take to the road in earnest.

1887 New Premises and Marriage

Dan started the year by extending his premises. He acquired a lease to the Ivel Hotel next door. This had previously been called the Black Swan having been built in 1760. It was situated next door to the house and wharf at Ivel Bury. The Black Swan appears to have survived the large fire in 1783 when Ivel Bury was burned down and rebuilt. Wells & Co. rebuilt the Black Swan in 1886, presumably in anticipation of Dan taking up occupation, and the name was changed to the Ivel Hotel.[1] The lease included meadows of 1½ acres to the west of the river. New workshops were built for the Ivel Works. The foreman of the Works was Mr Cottham. Dan moved into the new premises in February 1887.

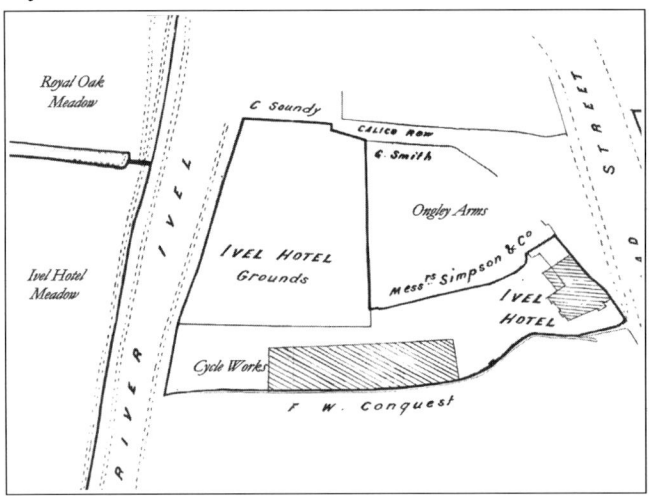

Fig.45: Site plan for the Ivel Hotel

(Biggleswade History Society)

The lease was not actually executed until August 24th 1888 between Frederick Archdale[2] and Charles Samuel Lindsell and Dan Albone. It provided for occupation of 21 years from September 29th 1887, terminable at seven or fourteen years, for a yearly rent of £22.[3] It seems that in order to proceed with the lease Dan had to make a statutory declaration that all his debts had been paid and that he was worth at least £2,000.

Despite all that work on the new premises, Dan still exhibited at the 1887 Stanley Show assisted by 'Faed' Wilson.[4] There was the 'Ivel Cycle Pony Trap', smooth running and fast, especially useful for showing the pace of a horse, a convertible tricycle, his new tricycles with steerer wheels larger than the drivers, the 'Anfield Ivel' lady's tricycle, the 'Ivel' safety, the 'Anfield Ivel' tricycle, the 'Ivel Roadster Safety', and the 'Irish Ivel' safety. Irish customers were clamouring for 'Ivel's, and Dan developed the 'Ivel' safety bicycle and tricycle specifically for the Irish market. In particular this machine had extra strong gauge tubing and larger tyres to cope with poor Irish roads. These came into production in January 1887. Also on the stand was a 54 in. 'Ivel Racer', a 48 in. 'Ivel Roadster', built for Mr Melano of the North Road C.C., and the 'Ivel Light Roadster Safety Bicycle'.

In the catalogue ten models were offered plus the Pony Trap although Dan made it clear that the cross-frame safety was now his speciality. Models were now numbered as had become fashionable with some manufacturers.

No.1 – The Cheap Ivel Safety. This machine primarily differed from the No.2 Best by having a fixed and painted, rather than plated, handlebar, and plain, rather than ball, pedals. It was offered at £16.

No.2 – The Best Ivel Safety differed from the No.1 as described above and was offered at £17.10s. It was the principal model in Dan's catalogue.

No.3 – The Irish Ivel Safety. This model was made with heavier gauge tubing (1¼ in., 14 W.G., rather than 1¼ in., 15 W.G.) for heavier riders and exceptionally rough roads. Also there were fore and aft stay rods. This model was offered at £18.

---

1 *Thirsty Old Town – The Story of Biggleswade Pubs*, Ken Page, p.85.
2 Frederick Archdale, 1827-1903, was a son of William Hogg of Ivel Bury. He changed his name to Archdale in 1866 by Royal Licence. William Hogge (added 'e') died in 1862 leaving his Biggleswade estate to Frederick, who then owned 50% of Wells & Co. Archdale moved to Baldock by 1871, travelling by horseback to Biggleswade daily. He would have known Dan quite well. It is possible that Wells & Co. built the workshops. In a preamble to the Wells & Co. sale particulars it was mentioned that the firm was managed on 'old fashioned lines'. When the brewery was sold, Frederick Archdale still owned 50% but Charles Samuel Lindsell owned 25% with other Lindsell's sharing the remaining 25%.
3 Bedfordshire & Luton Archives Service, Hooper and Fletcher records, ref: HF 20/376/1.

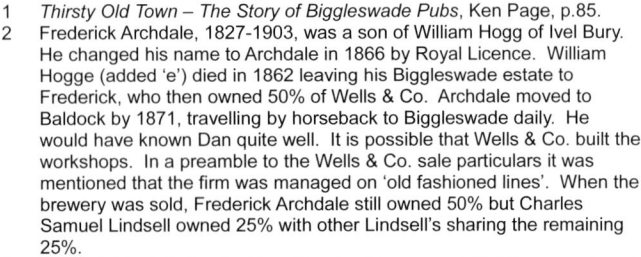
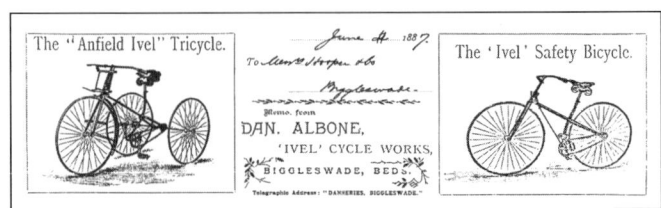

Fig.46: Ivel note paper

---

4 *Bicycling News*, January 29th 1887, pages 259 and 262.

IVEL ROADSTER.

D. ALBONE, Ivel Cycle Works, Biggleswade.

Description. ⅞in. and ¾in. moulded red tyres. Crescent rims. 60 and 20 No. 13 direct spokes. 16in. back wheel. 5in. G.M. hubs. 9in. axle. Detachable cranks, 6in. throw. Rubber plain pedals, 13in. tread. Æolus ball bearings to both wheels. Hollow front and semi-hollow back forks. Stanley head, 4¼in. centres. Pear-shaped horn handles, cowhorn bars, 28in. x 3in. 1⅜in. 16 W.G. weldless steel backbone. Humber scroll spring. Brooks's semi-racing saddle. Saw step. D.L.S. brake. Leg-guard. Spanners and oilcan. Weight 40lbs.

PRICE.

48in. to 54in. .. .. £13 10s.

Sent out enamelled in two colours.

Extras. Ball pedals, 15/- Half-plated, 20/-

Remarks. Sound and strong, built by a practical rider. (*See advertisement.*)

IVEL LIGHT ROADSTER.

D. ALBONE, Ivel Cycle Works, Biggleswade.

Description. ¾in. and ⅝in. moulded red tyres. Warwick's hollow rims. 50 and 20 No. 13 direct spokes. 16in. back wheel. 4½in. G.M. hubs. 8½in. axle. Detachable cranks, 6in. throw. Rat-trap ball pedals, 12½in. tread. Æolus ball bearings to both wheels. Hollow front and semi-hollow back forks. Stanley head, 4¼in. centres Pear-shaped horn handles, hollow cowhorn bars, 28in. x 2½in. 1⅜in. 17 W.G. weldless steel backbone. Humber scroll spring. Buffer saddle. Saw step. D.L.S. brake. Leg-guard. Valise, spanners and oilcan. Weight 34lbs.

PRICE.

48in. to 54in. .. .. .. £17 10s.

Sent out with plated handle-bar, head, hubs and cranks ; rest enamelled in two colours.

Remarks. A good and genuine article. Fit for use on good roads and grass courses. (*See advertisement.*)

IVEL RACER.

D. ALBONE, Ivel Cycle Works, Biggleswade, Beds.

Description. ½in. and ⅝in. moulded red tyres. Warwick's hollow rims. 50 No. 14 and 18 No. 15 tangent spokes. 16in. back wheel. 2½in. G.M. hubs. 7½in. axle. Detachable cranks, 6in. throw. Rat-trap ball pedals, 11¼in. tread. Æolus ball bearings to both wheels. Hollow front and semi-hollow back forks. Stanley head, 4¼in. centres. Elliptical cork handles, cowhorn bars, 28in x 1¼in. 1¾in. 19 W.G. weldless steel backbone. Gem racing saddle. Spanners and oilcan. Weight 21lbs.

PRICE.

48in. to 58in. .. .. £17 10s.

Sent out with plated handle-bar, head, hubs, cranks and pedals ; rest enamelled black.

Remarks. A really sound and well-made article at a moderate figure, and has figured very prominently for many years on Eastern Counties tracks. (*See advertisement.*)

Fig.47: *Sturmey's Indispensable 1887*

IVEL No. 1.—R.D.

DAN ALBONE, Ivel Cycle Works, Biggleswade.

Description. ¾in. red tyres. Crescent rims. 32 No. 13 and 32 No. 12 direct spokes. G.M. hubs. Detachable cranks, 5½in. to 7in. throw. Rubber plain pedals, 12in. tread. 30in. driving-wheel geared to 56in. 32in. steerer. Rear wheel drives with chain gear. Abingdon chain, slotted fork end adjustment. Æolus ball bearings to both wheels and cranks. Direct steering, sloping steering-post. Hollow front and back forks. American hinged head, 4½in. centres. Pear-shaped handle grips, 33in. bent back bars. Cross frame of 1⅛in. 15 W.G. weldless steel tube. Hollow straight seat pillar with split lug adjustment. Salter's No. 15 double scroll spring Long-distance suspension saddle. Saw step. Double lever spoon brake on front wheel. Mud-guards over both wheels. Valise, spanner, lamp-bracket and oilcan. Weight 40lbs.

Specialties. Convertible—with extra wheel—into " Anfield Ivel" tricycle.

Price .. .. £16.

Sent out with plated seat pillar, cranks and pedals; rest enamelled black.

Extras. Luggage-carrier, 10s. Extra wheel and axle for converting into tricycle, £10.

Remarks. The cheapest pattern made by this now celebrated maker. A sound, strong and reliable article. (*See advertisement.*)

IVEL No. 2.—R.D.

DAN ALBONE, Ivel Cycle Works, Biggleswade.

Description. ¾in. moulded red tyres. Crescent rims. 32 No. 13 and 32 No. 12 direct spokes. G.M. hubs. Detachable cranks, 5½in. to 7in. throw. Rubber ball pedals, 12in. tread. 30in. driving wheel geared to 56in. 32in. steerer. Rear wheel drives with chain gear. Abingdon chain, slotted fork end adjustment. Æolus ball bearings to both wheels and cranks. Direct steering, sloping steering-post. Hollow front and back forks. American hinged head, 4½in. centres. Elliptical handle grips, 33in. bent back hollow, detachable, adjustable bars. Cross frame of 1⅛in. 15 W.G. weldless steel tube. Hollow straight seat pillar

THE IVEL NO. 2.

with split lug adjustment. Salter's No. 15 double scroll spring. Brooks's semi-racing saddle. Saw step. Pull-up lever plunger spoon brake on front wheel. Mud-guards over both wheels and chain. Valise, spanner, lamp bracket and oilcan. Weight 46lbs.

Specialties. Convertible into " Anfield Ivel " tricycle with extra wheel.

Price .. .. £17 10s.

Send out with plated handle-bar, brake fittings, seat pillar, hubs, cranks, pedals and nuts; rest enamelled black.

Extras. Stay between crank shaft and back fork ends, 10/- Hollow rims, 10/-Victor square rubber pedals, 5/- Luggage-carrier, 10,- Ball bearing head, 20/-Wheel and axle for converting into tricycle, £10.

Remarks. Albone's chief pattern. A thorough roadster, and one of the easiest steerers in the market. Was the first machine of this type to be steered without hands. (*See advertisement.*)

Fig.48: *Sturmey's Indispensable 1887*

IRISH IVEL No. 3.—R.D.

DAN ALBONE, Ivel Cycle Works, Biggleswade.

Description. ¾in. and ⅞in. moulded red tyres. Crescent rims. 32 No. 12 and 32 No. 11 direct spokes. G.M. hubs. Detachable cranks, 5½in. to 7in. throw. Rubber ball pedals, 12in. tread. 30in. driving wheel geared to 52in. 32in. steerer. Rear wheel drives with chain gear. Abingdon chain, slotted fork end adjustment. Æolus ball bearings to both wheels and cranks. Direct steering. sloping steering-post. Hollow front and back forks. American hinged head, 4½in. centres. Elliptical handle-grips, 33in bent back hollow, detachable, bars. Cross frame of 1¼in. 14 W.G. weldless steel tube. Hollow straight seat pillar, with split lug adjustment. Double action Arab cradle spring. Brooks's semi-racing saddle. Saw step. Pull-up lever plunger spoon brake on front wheel. Mud-guards over both wheels and chain. Valise, spanner, lamp bracket and oilcan. Weight 52½lbs.

Price .. .. £18.

Sent out with plated handle-bar, brake fittings, seat pillar, hubs, cranks, pedals and nuts ; rest enamelled black.

Extras. Hollow rims, 10/- Victor square rubber pedals, 5/- Luggage-carrier 10/- Ball bearing head, 20/-

Remarks. A similar machine to the No. 2, but built extra strong throughout for use by heavy weights and on bad roads. The crank bracket and rear wheel are trussed by a compression stay. (*See advertisement.*)

IVEL SEMI-RACER No. 4.—R.D.

DAN ALBONE, Ivel Cycle Works, Biggleswade.

Description. ⅞in. moulded red tyres. Warwick's hollow rims. 32 No. 1 direct spokes. G.M. hubs. Detachable cranks, 5½in. to 7in. throw. Rat-trap ball pedals, 12in. tread. 30in. driving wheel geared to 60in. 32in. steerer. Rear wheel drives with chain gear. Abingdon chain, slotted fork end adjustment. Æolus ball bearings to both wheels and cranks. Direct steering, sloping steering post. Semi-hollow front and hollow back forks. American hinged head, 4½in. centres. Elliptical handle-grips. 33in. horn bent back hollow, detachable, adjustable bars. Cross frame of 1¼in. 17 W.G. weldless steel tube. Hollow straight seat pillar, with split-lug adjustment. Salter's No. 1 double scroll spring. Brooks's semi-racing saddle. Saw step. Valise, spanner, lamp-bracket and oilcan. Weight 35lbs.

Specialties. Convertible into tricycle with extra wheel.

Price £18

Sent out with plated handle-bar, brake fittings, seat pillar, hubs, cranks, pedals and nuts ; rest enamelled black.

Extras. Stay between crank bracket and back fork ends, 10/-. Victor rubber pedals, 5s. Ball head, 20s. Wheel and axle for converting into tricycle, £10

Remarks. A very fast and easy running mount. It was on one of these Mr G. P. Mills, Albone's partner, rode 295 miles in 24 hours, and also secured the fifty miles road record. It is specially built for fast work on good roads by good riders. (*See advertisement.*)

Fig.49: *Sturmey's Indispensable 1887*

33

Fig.50: 'Ivel' advertisement

(courtesy Biggleswade History Society)

No.4 – The Semi-racing Ivel Safety. This model had an extra light frame designed for road use (1¼ in., 17 W.G.) and wheels, detachable mudguards if desired, adjustable handlebar and adjustable saddle. It was the model, according to Henry Sturmey, that G. P. Mills rode to take the 24 hour record with 295 miles. It's price was £18.

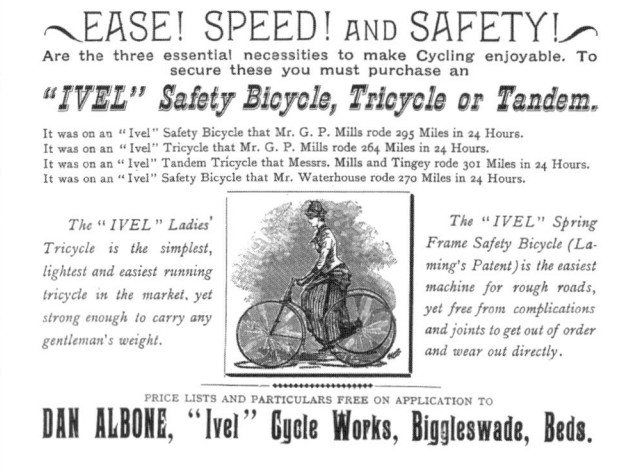

Fig.51: 'Ivel' advertisement, *The Cyclist* 1887

No.5 – The Racing Ivel Safety. This was made as light as possible for path (track) use with the handlebar and saddle fixed to suit the rider. Note too that the catalogue claimed the wheels were built with laced tangent spokes. Offered at £18.

No.6 – The Ivel Light Roadster. This Ordinary machine was unchanged from 1885 although the price had increased from £15.15s to £17.10s.

No.7 – The Ivel Strong Roadster. This Ordinary seems to be the Roadster of 1885 renamed. The price had increased from £12.10s to £13.10s.

No.8 – The Ivel Racer. This Ordinary machine was unchanged from 1885 although the price had increased from £15.15s to £17.10s.

No.9 – The Anfield Ivel Tricycle. Described below, this model was offered at £22.

No.10 - The Anfield Ivel Lady's Tricycle. The feature of this machine, as described in the catalogue, was *"tubing shaped so that a lady can ride it in ordinary costume, and can mount it and dismount it either in front or behind, the lowness of the*

Now it is on the Path!

—AT EASTER—

FIVE FIRST PRIZES ON TWO "IVELS."

At **STAPLETON** and **WESTON**, three first prizes were won o' an "Ivel" roadster by a novice.

At **OUNDLE**, two first prizes were won *from scratch* on an "Ivel" semi-racer.

At **HOUNSLOW**, a second prize was won *from scratch* on an "Ivel" roadster geared to 50in. only.

At **DUBLIN**, the first prize in the roadster tricycle race was won *from scratch* on an "Anfield Ivel" roadster.

RACERS can now be built to order weighing 20lbs. complete, wonderfully strong and rigid.

Look next week for RECENT Testimonials from independent riders.

Sole Inventor, Patentee and Maker:

DAN ALBONE,
Ivel Works, Biggleswade.

Fig.52: 'Ivel' advertisement

(courtesy Biggleswade History Society)

Fig.53: Dan with cross-frame safety c.1887

axle being a great point in favour of easy mounting and dismounting." As indicated in the last chapter, in convertible form this tricycle could become a bicycle. Dan wasn't explicitly saying so, indeed he was careful to avoid it, but here was the lady's bicycle in disguise. The price was £22.

The 'Ivel Cycle Pony Trap' was offered at £35.

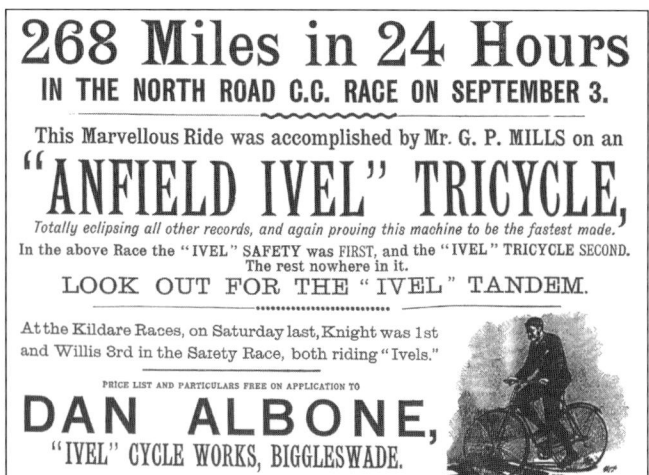

268 Miles in 24 Hours
IN THE NORTH ROAD C.C. RACE ON SEPTEMBER 3.

This Marvellous Ride was accomplished by Mr. G. P. MILLS on an

"ANFIELD IVEL" TRICYCLE,

Totally eclipsing all other records, and again proving this machine to be the fastest made.
In the above Race the "IVEL" SAFETY was FIRST, and the "IVEL" TRICYCLE SECOND. The rest nowhere in it.

LOOK OUT FOR THE "IVEL" TANDEM.

At the Kildare Races, on Saturday last, Knight was 1st and Willis 3rd in the Safety Race, both riding "Ivels."

PRICE LIST AND PARTICULARS FREE ON APPLICATION TO

DAN ALBONE,
"IVEL" CYCLE WORKS, BIGGLESWADE.

Fig.54: 'Ivel' advertisement, *Wheeling*, Sept. 21ˢᵗ 1887

No longer was the enamelling carried out by Harrington as Dan now had a suitable facility of his own. It is notable that the catalogue had a long list of agents where 'Ivel's could be seen or obtained, including several overseas. Dan had been busy!

It was reported:

"Dan contemplates improving the ladies 'Cripper' so that it can be also converted into a lady's safety bicycle. I do not believe that the fair sex will ever take seriously to the narrow gauger, but for those who do intend in doing so, this is the first really practicable lady's bicycle yet brought out." [5]

And even by this early stage that 'Ivel's were being faked:

"Even other machines are vamped up as Ivels in order to sell them, by unscrupulous dealers." [6]

Back from the Stanley Show[7], to celebrate the move to the Ivel Hotel, Dan gave out tokens worth three halfpence each to his workmen (Fig.55). The tokens could only be spent at the bar of the Ivel Hotel.

The Ivel Hotel 1ᴰ token, milled edge, brass, 23mm Countermarked "1" on reverse. 1½ᴰ also known.

Fig.55: The Ivel Hotel token

(courtesy *Token Corresponding Society Bulletin Vol. 5, No. 7, p.257*)

Bicycling News described the move to the Ivel Hotel as follows:

"Here, from small beginnings, Mr Daniel Albone, himself no mean performer upon the bicycle on the path and road, has built up a sound business and secured a reputation second to none in the cycling world. The Ivel cycles have a world wide reputation. The marvellous records which have been made upon all the various types (in each case the best performance of its sort accomplished by any rider the world over and thus dubbed par excellence world's records) bear the fullest testimony to the stability and excellence of these machines, whilst in Canada, the U.S.A.,Germany, China, Ja-

5   *Bicycling News*, February 5ᵗʰ 1887, page 278.
6   *Wheel World*, New York, January 14ᵗʰ 1887.
7   *Bicycling News*, February 11ᵗʰ 1888, page 308.

pan, Australia, Switzerland, Italy, Holland and all parts of the United Kingdom have secured agencies for these machines under notice.

Early in 1887, Albone removed from his old and far from commodious premises into a fine large shop erected next door, capable of accommodating nearly 100 men with offices, showrooms, engine house, enamelling and plating plant and a piece of ground about 1 acre in extent and there is plenty of room for further extension, whilst across the river a somewhat larger piece of ground is also rented by the Ivel maker. He leased the cycle factory, a garden and premises of the Ivel Hotel for 21 years.

As Albone moved into his new premises shortly after the Stanley Show of 1887 he commenced work there under great disadvantages, as Spring orders kept pouring in and the only thing for him to do was to keep on building machines as quickly as possible, no leisure time being available in which to reduce things to a system." [8]

The Ivel Works was in some disarray due to the move and Mills was quoted in the press as saying:

"Sometimes we'd have a couple of dozen machines made up and ready for packing when it would be found that there was not a mudguard in the place and the consignment would be delayed."

Dan restored order by working around the clock. Soon the Ivel Works was producing thirty cycles a week and these were sent all over the world. By October 1887, the output for the twelve months had risen to seven times that of the previous year.

On May 4th Dan issued a notice to the following effect:

"Owing to the extraordinary demand for 'Ivels', and the difficulties I have had to contend with in in-

Fig.56: 'Ivel' advertisement, 1887

(courtesy Biggleswade History Society)

8   *Bicycling News*, February 11th 1888, page 308.

Fig.57: Lady tandem tricyclists

(courtesy Biggleswade History Society)

creasing the output during the rebuilding and extension of my works, a number of Machines have been sent out lately, in reply to urgent demands for immediate delivery, without that perfection in finish which I could have desired. Notwithstanding, I am glad to find the general verdict of my customers is so eminently satisfactory, spontaneous testimony to the extremely easy-running qualities of the 'Ivel' being received daily.

I am now making many little improvements to obviate what I consider defects in the bicycles hitherto turned out, my arrangements for enamelling are much more perfect, and the finish of my Machines is consequently equal to the very best procurable.

Improvements in the detail and finish of the 'Anfield Ivel' Tricycle, convertible into an 'Ivel' Safety Bicycle, are also being made, and the demand for this remarkably light and easy-running Tricycle is steadily increasing as its good qualities become more known.

I am daily refusing applications for new agencies, the demand being so great that I can at present only supply on the usual retail terms of 5 per cent. off list prices."

The 'Ivel' safety bicycle was produced with 32 in. dia. front wheel and 30 in. dia. rear wheel. The 1887 Price List gives a rather curious reason for this, being:

ADVERTISEMENTS.

'IVEL.'

This is the name of the River upon whose banks the

"IVEL" CYCLE WORKS

are situated; and the word is registered as a Trade Mark, the property of DAN ALBONE.

It was on an **"IVEL"** Safety Bicycle that Mr. G. P. MILLS rode the marvellous distance of

295 MILES IN A DAY !

It was on an **"IVEL"** Safety Bicycle that Mr. G. P. MILLS rode **50 MILES ON THE ROAD in 2h. 47m. 36s.**

It was on an **"IVEL"** Safety Bicycle that Mr. G. P. MILLS rode **50 MILES OF VERY HILLY ROAD on an excessively windy day in 2h. 54m. 15s.;** beating every other Rider and every other Machine in the Catford C.C.'s open Road Race, for which 84 Entries were received.

Long-distance Road Records prove a Machine to be at once

FAST AND COMFORTABLE,

and the verdict of every owner of an "IVEL" endorses the evidence of the Records.

Every "IVEL" can be converted into an "ANFIELD IVEL" TRICYCLE.

Take notice that **THE ONLY GENUINE "IVELS"** are made by

DAN ALBONE, "IVEL" CYCLE WORKS, Biggleswade.

Fig.58: 'Ivel' advertisement, *Sturmey's Indispensable*

"so there is no tendency in the front wheel to deflect at each stroke of the pedals, as there is in all other forms of bicycles;"

While it is true that was the case for the Ordinary, where the pedals act directly on the wheel, it is not true of the rear-driver safety. A larger steerer wheel was generally considered desirable on account of the state of the roads.

Note also that, despite the contemporary illustrations of the 'Ivel' safety, the best version could be ordered with *"stay-rods"* between the crank bearings and the back wheel fork.

satisfactory to me, for, to use the vernacular, it is still "fresh as paint." [9]

Mills put up the fastest time of 2 hrs. 54 mins. 15 secs. in the Catford C. C. 50 mile race on June 1st riding an 'Ivel' safety against 76 competitors over a rough and hilly course. He then broke the 50 mile tricycle record on an 'Anfield Ivel' on June 10th, recording a time of 3 hrs. 7 min. 24 secs.

Mills was to break two other 24 hour records on 'Ivel' machines in September and October. First, on September 2nd -3rd, the tricycle record, when he covered 268 miles on an 'Anfield Ivel' in the North

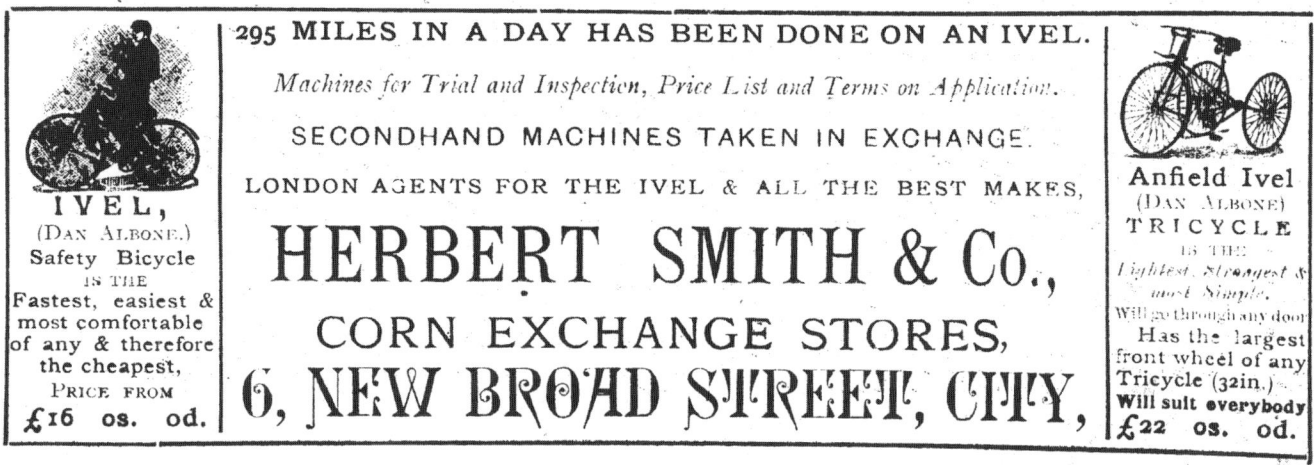

Fig.59: 'Ivel' advertisement, 1887

Some may think that Dan's 'Ivel' was only suitable for racing; that is not so as this account of a continental tour shows:

"A Tour on the Continent with an Ivel Safety

Having worked hard, I determined to see the world. Like most people of my ilk, being a free trader, I thought I would spend my money in places where I had not made it. Not knowing exactly what kind of roads I should have to travel in my journey I did not take my ordinary 'bike' and on viewing the stock of safeties in Mr Oliff's, Grainger Street, Newcastle, I selected one of Mr Dan Albone's Ivel safeties. Have I repented my choice! No! My machine proved sound and good in all parts, with the exception of the spring breaking, which is easily accounted for, and after doing about 800 miles, having run at times at a terrific rate down hills, forcing my way over continental cobble stones, and carrying baggage weighing 40 lbs., (besides your humble servant who makes the balance of the weighing machine tremble at the modest figures of 13st. 7 lb.). I consider the test severe enough for any machine and the Ivel has stood the test in a manner highly

Road Cycling Club 'All-Day Race' (Figs.54 and 56). The race was from Hatfield to Norwich and as far back as possible.[10] Dan advertised the race as *"again proving this machine to be the fastest made"*.[11] In that event Waterhouse had borrowed Dan's 'Ivel' Racer bicycle, geared to 63 in., to take first place with 270 miles, despite an accident which bent the front wheel, rectified shortly after.[12] Second was with Richard Tingey on October 4th, when they broke the tandem record by covering 301 miles on an 'Ivel' tandem. This was only the second 24 hour ride by Richard Tingey. The route for this record breaking attempt was the same as that used for the 'Kangaroo' race in 1885, though this time they started at Hitchin and went to Long Sutton and back.[13] Note that the distances are as confirmed rather than those initially reported.

On September 24th, Mills broke the 100 mile tricycle record on an 'Ivel' in a time of 7hr. 46min. 33secs.

9   *Northern Sports and Pastimes*, 1887.
10   *Bicycling News*, September 10th 1887.
11   *Wheeling*, September 21st 1887.
12   *Athletic News*, September 6th, 1887.
13   *Bedfordshire Express*, October 8th 1887.

SEPTEMBER 10th, 1887.

The North Road 24 Hours' Contest.

Fig.60: The North Road 24 Hours' Contest, *Bicycling News,* September 10th 1887

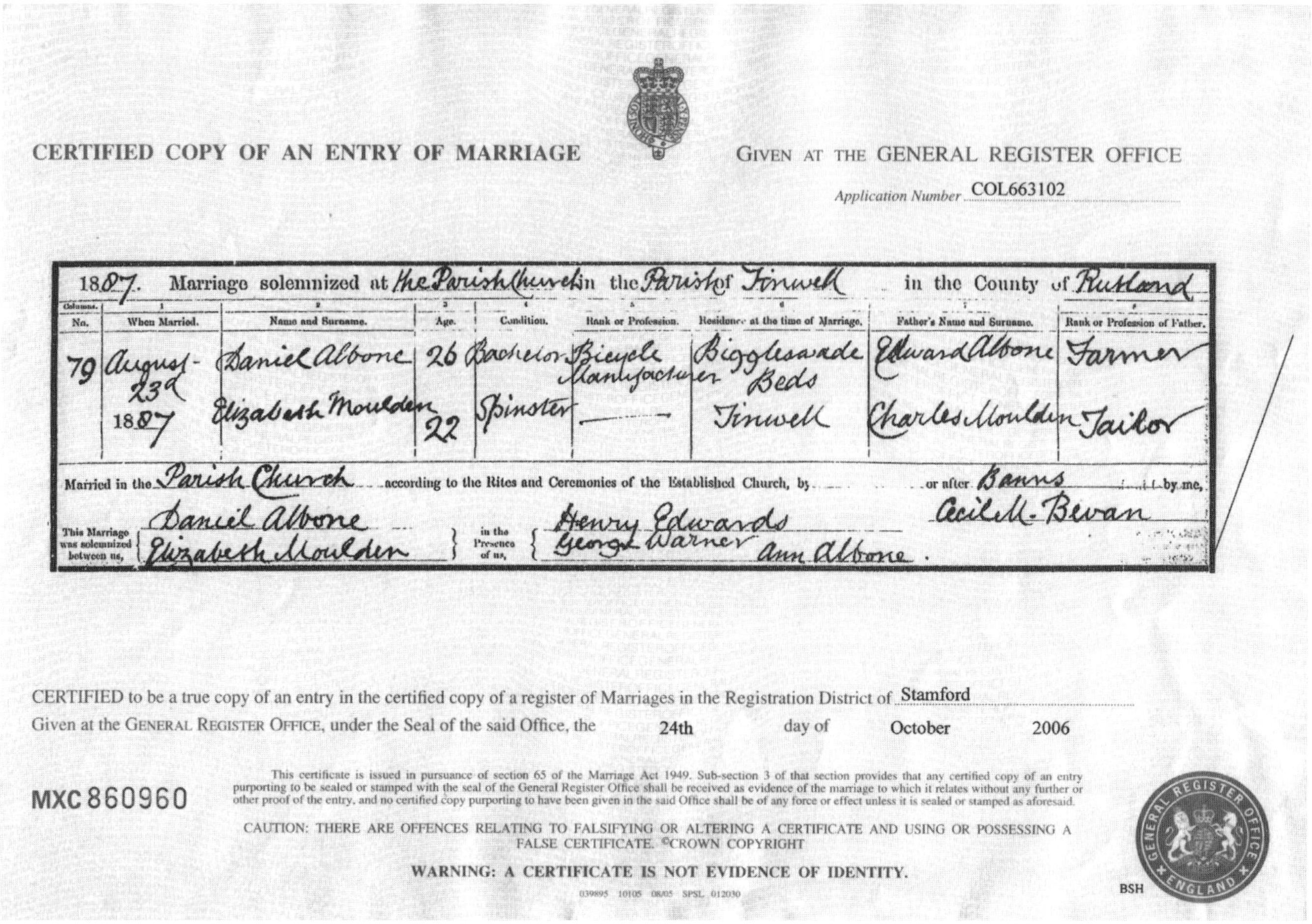

CERTIFIED COPY OF AN ENTRY OF MARRIAGE

GIVEN AT THE GENERAL REGISTER OFFICE

Application Number COL663102

1887. Marriage solemnized at the Parish Church in the Parish of Tinwell in the County of Rutland

No.	When Married.	Name and Surname.	Age.	Condition.	Rank or Profession.	Residence at the time of Marriage.	Father's Name and Surname.	Rank or Profession of Father.
79	August 23rd 1887	Daniel Albone	26	Bachelor	Bicycle Manufacturer	Biggleswade Beds	Edward Albone	Farmer
		Elizabeth Moulden	22	Spinster	—	Tinwell	Charles Moulden	Tailor

Married in the Parish Church according to the Rites and Ceremonies of the Established Church, by or after Banns by me, Cecil M. Bevan

This Marriage was solemnized between us, Daniel Albone, Elizabeth Moulden

in the Presence of us, Henry Edwards, George Warner, Ann Albone.

CERTIFIED to be a true copy of an entry in the certified copy of a register of Marriages in the Registration District of Stamford

Given at the GENERAL REGISTER OFFICE, under the Seal of the said Office, the 24th day of October 2006

MXC 860960

This certificate is issued in pursuance of section 65 of the Marriage Act 1949. Sub-section 3 of that section provides that any certified copy of an entry purporting to be sealed or stamped with the seal of the General Register Office shall be received as evidence of the marriage to which it relates without any further or other proof of the entry, and no certified copy purporting to have been given in the said Office shall be of any force or effect unless it is sealed or stamped as aforesaid.

CAUTION: THERE ARE OFFENCES RELATING TO FALSIFYING OR ALTERING A CERTIFICATE AND USING OR POSSESSING A FALSE CERTIFICATE. ©CROWN COPYRIGHT

WARNING: A CERTIFICATE IS NOT EVIDENCE OF IDENTITY.

039895 10105 08/05 SPSL 012030

GENERAL REGISTER OFFICE ENGLAND

BSH

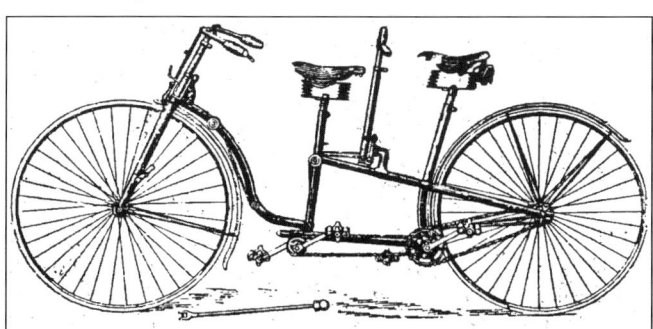

Fig.61: Copy marriage certificate

In 1887 Dan developed the 'Ladies Ivel Tandem' tricycle (Fig.57) which was adapted for two ladies or a lady on the front seat. The steering was connected to the rear handlebar, which gave control to both riders; the cost: £34.10s.

Fig.62: The Ladies 'Ivel' Tandem Safety

He also brought out the 'Ladies Ivel Tandem Safety' bicycle in the Autumn. The machine broadly resembled the 'Ivel' tandem for gentlemen except that connected steering was retained. The frame was dropped down much lower and the parts which carried the saddle and handlebars were given extra strength to avoid the kind of support which interfered with womens' dress. This machine cost £33. It was out of date by 1891 but was still exported to the U. S. A. An example survives: see Identification of Cycles.

At the end of August 1887, on the 23rd, Dan took some time away from his work to wed Elizabeth Martha Moulden of Hitchin.[14] His best man was George Henry Warner[15] of Hitchin. Elizabeth was married from her uncle's home at Tinwell in Lincolnshire, where she had been living since 1881. The ceremony was reported thus:

"The officiating clergyman was the Rev. Mr. Bevan, and the marriage was witnessed by a large party of relatives and friends of the bride and by many of the villagers, while, in addition, a good number of of well-known cyclists from all parts of the

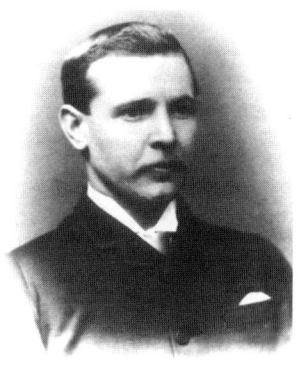

Fig.63: Dan

(courtesy Biggleswade History Society)

14 The Moulden family ran the Currier's Arms public house and lodgings in Back St., now Queen St.

15 George Warner married Elizabeth's elder sister, Mary Ann, on December 24th 1881.

Fig.64: Elizabeth

(courtesy Biggleswade History Society)

country were present. The bride was accompanied by two bridesmaids, and Mr. Albone was attended by Mr. G. Warner, of Hitchin, as best man. The bride was married from the house of her uncle, Mr. Edwards, of South View Farm, who also gave her away. After the ceremony the wedding party were entertained by Mr. Edwards to an elegantly served breakfast, the tables being ornamented by bouquets of flowers given by Lady Aveling, Normanton Hall. The remainder of the day was kept as a fête in the village, the bells ringing and the old people having a plentiful tea, whilst the choir, of which Miss Moulden was a member, were entertained at a substantial supper. Among the numerous presents given to the bride was a silver cake basket from the choir. During the afternoon the newly-married couple left, amid cordial good wishes and showers of rice, for Hunstanton for the honeymoon." [16]

On return Dan's very own lightweight trap was at the station. Instead of a pony, about 50 solo, tandem-riders, and tricyclists pulled them through the streets. The townsfolk cheered the entourage with wild enthusiasm.[17]

The *Bedfordshire Express* of August 27th carried the report of the wedding side by side with a report of Dan Albone's recent prize-winning races. In Au-

gust alone he had won ten prizes, in races as far apart as Ipswich and Oxford, on his new safety bicycle.

In September the *C.T.C. Gazette* apologised to Dan for some remarks about 'Ivel' cycles that were aimed at agents who had supplied them rather than Dan.[18]

On October 17th another marriage took place; this time it was Richard Tingey who married Dan's sister, Ann.

Prior to 1887 the finish of 'Ivels' had been found wanting but following the new works were found satisfactory by *Bicycling News* who viewed a safety weighing 23 lbs. and were told of another produced for the professional, Cattell, which weighed only 20½ lbs.[19] They also tried a new 'Ivel' tandem that weighed nearly 80 lbs.

Fig.66: 'Ivel Pony Trap' in Shortmead St.

(courtesy Biggleswade History Society)

Dan, however, needed capital to expand so his next step was to form a limited company. In November, Dan sent a note to G. Lacy Hillier, racing cyclist and stockbroker, 1 Crown Court, Threadneedle Street, London -

"Papers (Price lists etc.) sent as promised. Will see Major Shuttleworth as soon as possible. Have got a valuable secret for rubber sticking process. Hope will hurry on with making all preliminary arrangements as speedily as possible."

Lacy Hillier responded by requesting business information including a balance sheet, etc. Dan revealed he had been drawing over £400 a year from the business.[20] Matters proceeded quickly under Lacy Hillier's experienced guidance.

Fig.65: Some wedding guests

(courtesy Biggleswade History Society)

16 *Bedfordshire Mercury*, September 3rd 1887.
17 *Wheeling*

18 *C.T.C. Gazette*, September 1887, p.362.
19 *Bicycling News*, September 10th 1887
20 Bedfordshire & Luton Archives Service, Hooper and Fletcher records, ref: HF 21.

DAN ALBONE, Ivel Cycle Works, BIGGLESWADE.

Stand No. .

THE chief exhibit here will be specimens of the Ivel safety bicycle in different styles, including the **IRISH IVEL**, specially made with extra strong tubing and strutted frame, and the identical Ivel upon which Mr. G. P. Mills achieved

his celebrated best-on-record rides of 50 miles in 2 hours 47 minutes 36 seconds, and 295 miles in 24 hours, both on the road. As is well known, the Ivel safety can be ridden by any ordinarily expert rider, with the hands off the steering-bar, the balancing and guiding being accomplished entirely by the feet.

A striking novelty, and one possessing merit beyond mere novelty, is the "**ANFIELD IVEL**" tricycle, which follows closely the lines of the Ivel safety bicycle. It is made in several forms. The first is a tricycle, unconvertible, for the use of gentlemen only, the frame being like that of the Ivel safety, but with a shorter back-fork ; and this will be made to order with either two or four bearings to the axle. For ladies this type is peculiarly suitable, as the use of 30-inch driving-wheels makes the axle so low down as to render it very easy for a lady to step over in mounting and dismounting ; the front of the frame is made of a V shape, so as not to interfere with a lady's dress. But the most original feature of all is that the tricycle can, by a very simple addition, be made so as to convert into a perfect Ivel safety

THE IVEL SAFETY BICYCLE.

bicycle ; and in the case of the lady's tricycle, it can be made so as to convert into a bicycle which can be ridden by either a lady or a gentleman. Convertible cycles are usually inferior to non-convertibles, but in this case the conversion is so arranged that the rider gains benefit ; that is to say, instead of changing the position and action of the body when changing from bicycle to tricycle,—whereby power and comfort are usually lost,—the rider retains precisely the same position and action in every respect, the only difference being that the bicycle requires balancing, and the tricycle does not. This identical action will be appreciated by riders who have experienced the loss of power and comfort usually resulting from a change of machines ; and on the point of economy the invention is a very valuable one, as the price of all the parts requisite to convert the tricycle into the bicycle is only Six Pounds ; and any one who already possesses an Ivel safety bicycle can have the wheels, balance-geared axle, &c., to convert it into a tricycle at pleasure, for Ten Pounds, thus saving twelve pounds on the cost of the two separate machines.

THE "ANFIELD IVEL" TRICYCLE.
(PATENT APPLIED FOR)

The Ivel cycle (patent) ball-bearing pony-trap has given such complete satisfaction during 1886 that no alteration in its details has been considered necessary.

Detailed price lists will be sent post free upon application to

DAN ALBONE, Ivel Cycle Works, Biggleswade, Bedfordshire, England.

Fig.67: 'Ivel' Prospectus 1887

RECORD OF RECORDS!

The 24 HOURS' RECORDS for all classes of Machines are now held by the

"IVEL" CYCLES.

301 Miles on an "Ivel" Tandem.
295 „ „ „ Safety.
265 „ „ „ Tricycle.

Distances never approached by any other make.

Price Lists free on application to

DAN. ALBONE,

"IVEL" CYCLE WORKS,
BIGGLESWADE.

301

Miles in 24 Hours
ON AN

'IVEL'
TANDEM

On Tuesday, 4th October, 1887, by Messrs. Mills and Tingey.

The "IVEL" Cycles now hold the 24 hours' Records
for all three classes of Machines.

PRICE LIST AND PARTICULARS ON APPLICATION TO

DAN ALBONE, "IVEL" CYCLE WORKS, BIGGLESWADE.

DON'T BELIEVE IT

If you are told that there is a Machine as good or

BETTER THAN THE "IVEL"

The proof that it is not so lies in the fact that, striking an average for distance ridden on the Three classes of Cycles, Safety, Tricycle and Tandem, for 24 hours,

THE "IVELS" COME OUT WITH

22 MILES MORE THAN ANY OTHER MAKE.

THE "IVEL" SAFETY SPRING FRAME (LAMINGS' PATENT), THE SIMPLEST
AND EASIEST IN THE MARKET.

PRICE LIST AND PARTICULARS FREE FROM

DAN ALBONE,

"IVEL" CYCLE WORKS, BIGGLESWADE.

301

MILES IN 24 HOURS ON AN

"IVEL" TANDEM,

On Tuesday, 4th October, 1887, by Messrs. MILLS & TINGEY.

The "Ivel" Cycles now hold the 24 Hours for all three Classes of Machines.

Figure 68: A collection of 'Ivel' advertisments including one for the Spring Frame Safety sold by the Dublin agents and shown below

SAFETY, EASE, AND SPEED

Are only to be obtained by Purchasing an

"Ivel" Safety Tricycle or Tandem.

"IVEL" SPRING FRAME

The Ladies' "Ivel" Tricycle—Light, elegant, and easy to ride. Can be ridden by a gentleman, it being especially strong.

The Spring Frame "Ivel" Safety Bicycle — The simplest and most comfortable Machine of the class now in the Market.

(TAMIRE'S PATENT.)

Dublin Agents : BOOTH BROS., UPPER STEPHEN ST.

Manufactured by DAN ALBONE, "Ivel" Cycle Works, Biggleswade.

301 295 265

Are the respective distances that have been ridden on the

Ivel Tandem, Safety & Tricycle

In 24 hours, in each case the distance being

RECORD FOR THE WORLD.

PRICE LIST AND PARTICULARS FREE ON APPLICATION TO

DAN ALBONE, IVEL CYCLE WORKS, BIGGLESWADE.

1888 Incorporation

The Annual Dinner of the Biggleswade & District Cycling Club took place at the Ivel Hotel in January. Mrs Albone, described as a great social organiser, was evidently in charge of the kitchen and Dan toasted 'The Ladies' (Fig.69).[1]

DINNER OF THE BIGGLESWADE AND DISTRICT B.C.
PRESENTATION TO MR. A. C. HILLS.

By singular good fortune we were present on Monday last at the annual dinner of the above club at the Ivel Hotel, Biggleswade, the chair being filled by Mr. de Courcy Atkins, some thirty members and friends being present. Mrs. Albone sent in an excellent feed. The Chairman proposed "The Queen," and then Mr. A. H. Blake proposed "The Club," Mr. C. Whaley responding, and giving a very good account of the progress of the B. & D.B.C. Mr. Webster having given an excellent solo on the violin, the Chairman, in fitting and eulogistic phrase, presented to Mr. A. C. Hills a very handsome gold stop watch, value thirty guineas, as a testimonial from the club and its supporters. Mr. T. de Courcy Atkins bore very high testimony to Mr. Hills's merits as a lawyer and a citizen, and Mr. Hills responded at some length, though he had to conclude by admitting his inability to touch, at any length, upon the gift he had received, so much did he feel the compliment paid him. Mr. Blake having sung, Mr. Jno. Hern proposed "The Fire Brigade," Mr. D. M. Spong duly responding; and then, Mr. G. J. Webb proposed "Success to Cycling," Messrs. G. L. Hillier and D. Albone responding. Medals were then presented to Mr. Mills and several other members for their feats of road riding. Mr. C. G. Iliffe proposed "The Chairman," Mr. Atkins responding; and the toast list concluded with "The Ladies," proposed by Dan Albone, and "The Press," proposed by Mr. C. Whaley, and replied to by Messrs. Christie and Huber, after which the company broke up, a most pleasant evening having been spent.

Fig.69: Biggleswade & District C.C. Annual Dinner 1888

Also in January, Dan applied for a patent for his convertible safety bicycle idea. This allowed the machine to be converted into a tandem safety bicycle, a front-steering tricycle, or a rear-driving tandem tricycle. The patent was granted in December (No.1888-1098) and shows how the conversion was achieved using knuckle-joints.

Some fifty men were now employed as compared to just three, four years earlier.[2]

During 1887 one of the largest cycle dealers in London, West London Cycle Stores, of 79 Wells Street and 25 Castle Street, were appointed as his sole London agents. Their catalogue stated:

"These celebrated Machines can be had on hire for 1, 2, or 3 months, with option of purchase, or on the Easy Payment System." [3]

There were some interesting comments on Dan's 'Ivel's at the Stanley Show:

"On this stall we find several examples of the very popular "Ivel" cycles, amongst them the

identical machine upon which Messrs. Mills and Tingey performed their great feat of making the 24 hours' record for the road. This machine shows very few signs of the immense strain which has been put upon it, and looks like a sound and serviceable type of roadster. The exceedingly simple frame is fitted with very carefully placed stays, and the result is an exceedingly light machine. The rear wheels are of small diameter relatively to the front wheel, which is of larger size, and consequently makes the machine run considerably lighter; the plan of the machine throughout is very simple, and at the same time very effective, and it is certain to be during the coming season a most popular form of tandem. As Dan is a recently married man it is not astonishing that he should turn his attention to the production of a cycle suitable for the fair sex – in fact, we should imagine that Mrs Albone, resident as she is in such a hot-bed of cycling enthusiasm as Biggleswade, demanded that some such provision should be made for her, and the result is before us. The machine resembles as nearly as pos-

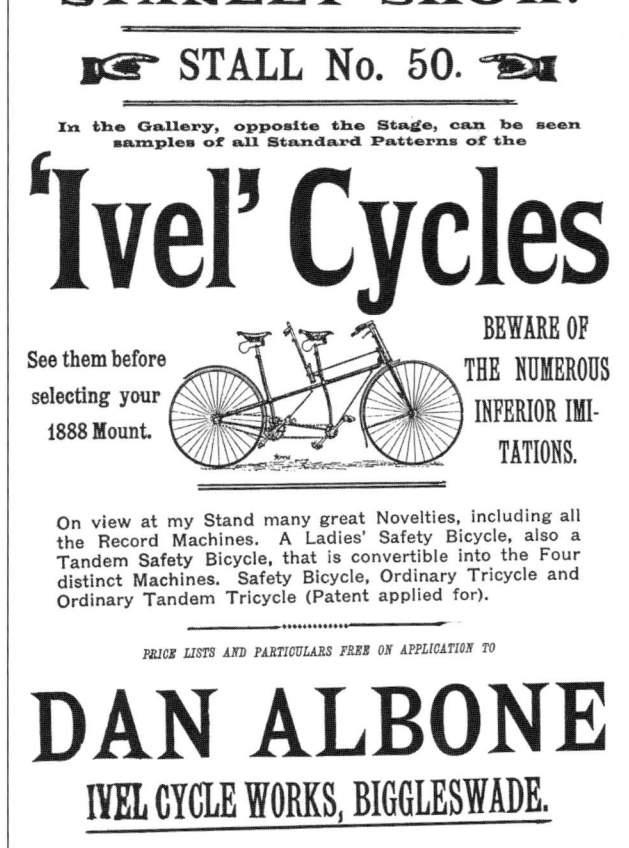

Fig.70: Ivel advertisement, *Bicycling News*, Feb. 4th

1   *Bicycling News*, January 28th 1888, page 271.
2   *The Bazaar*, February 1st 1888.
3   West London Cycle Stores catalogue 1888.

THE GREATEST NOVELTY AT THE SHOW
THE FASTEST CYCLE IN THE WORLD.
FOUR MACHINES IN ONE. £100 WORTH FOR £38 : 10 : 0
THE
NEW "IVEL" TANDEM SAFETY.
(PATENT APPLIED FOR.)

"Ivel" Safety.

"Ivel"

Safety Tandem.

"Ivel" Tricycle.

"Ivel" Tricycle

Tandem.

Having thoroughly tested this Machine on the road, we can now safely assert that it is perfect in every respect, and for speed it cannot be approached. It steers better than a single safety, and can be easily mounted and dismounted. Both riders steer, and it can be ridden by one rider alone in its double form. Enamelled black, parts plated.
PRICE (Not Convertible) £25.
It is also made convertible in a few minutes into an ordinary "IVEL" SAFETY—£2 extra charged for joints, &c.; and by the addition of our patent wheels and axle can be converted into an "IVEL" TRICYCLE, and also an "IVEL" TANDEM for £11 extra, making price in all £38 10s. for Four Machines, list prices of which amount to £100.
Can be seen and tried at London Agents, the West London Cycle Stores, 79, Wells Street, Oxford St., W. and 25, Castle Street East, Oxford St., W., both near Princess's Theatre.

Fig.71: 'Ivel' advertisement, *The Cyclist*, Feb. 8th

sible the outlines of the ordinary "Ivel" tandem; the frame is dropped down much lower, and the parts which carry the saddle and handles are stayed as little as possible so as not to interfere with the dresses of riders more than is absolutely necessary. There is no doubt that this tandem, simple as it is, will find much favour, the disposition of the stays between the brackets being very carefully calculated to withstand the strains; the brake power is fully adequate, a drum brake on the carrying wheels, and an ordinary brake on the front wheel, being specially fitted. We like the look of this machine very much, and it will no doubt find favour with the public." [4] and

"The 'Ivel' tandem is very different in appearance to the other machines of its class shown, the frame being that of an elongated single, with a sort of double cross frame. The rear rider drives by means of a chain on the left, and the front man by a chain on the right, running from the pedal axle to the rear rider's. The steering is made double by means of a connecting rod running almost parallel to the main tube. The machine is thoroughly well stayed in every part, and looks thoroughly practicable. It is convertible to a single by a simple arrangement." [5] and

"Mr Dan Albone, of Biggleswade, shows some very neat and simple tricycles capable of conversion into rear-driving safety bicycles. A special feature of the machines turned out by this maker is that all the component parts of his several machines are interchangeable, thus allowing any type of machine to be readily converted into any other type." [6]

A report on the Stanley Show states:

"So great and increasing is the demand for the Ivel machines that -although over fifty men are now employed against three four years ago - it is impossible to meet the demand...". [7]

4   *Bicycling News*, February 4th 1888, page 286.

5   *Bicycling News*, February 4th 1888, page 291.
6   *The Engineer*, February 17th 1888, page 131.
7   *The Bazaar*, February 1st 1888.

DAN ALBONE,

"Ivel" Cycle Works, Biggleswade,

MAKER OF THE CELEBRATED

'IVEL' CYCLES

Which, in spite of many inferior imitations, still prove themselves unbeaten. **Read the following** unsolicited testimonial as a clear proof:—

Mr. Dan Albone, Finchley, March 28th, 1888.

Dear Sir,

I think I ought to let you know how pleased I am with the "**Anfield Tricycle**" which you built for me last year. It was certainly the cause of my winning the two Finchley Tricycle Club handicaps. Having won them the previous year, and consequently being placed next to Scratchman (Mr. C. W. Brown), I should not have stood a chance, except for the fact that the "Anfield Tricycle" made a difference to me of at least 45 seconds in the two miles, and a proportionate amount in the five miles. I consider it the fastest and easiest machine made, and it turns corners splendidly. Since you altered the gearing to 60in. it has not given me a minute's trouble nor cost me a penny in repairs, although geared much higher than any previous machine I have had. I rode it up Muswell Hill on the first day I mounted it with far greater ease than any other machine I have ever tried.

You are at liberty to publish this letter if you wish.

Yours truly, (Signed) M. E. STEPHENS.

See you get the genuine article by sending for Illustrated Catalogue, with List of Agents, supplied free.

Fig.72: 'Ivel' advertisement, *The Cyclist*, April 18th

Such was the demand exceeding the capabilities of the works many of the parts had to be made elsewhere. The result was a number of breakages, particularly in the nuts and bolts.[8]

In response to cyclists' complaints about bumpy rides, the Ivel Works produced a spring-frame safety, under Laming's patent, called the 'Ivel Anti-vibration Safety'. This had a frame jointed in the middle with the two parts connected by a strong spiral spring. The Stanley Show report said:

"The "Ivel" safeties are shown on Dan Albone's stand in profusion, every sort, from a lady's machine to a light racer weighing 19½ lbs., finding a place. Laming's patent spring frame is fitted to one. The finish of these machines shows a marked improvement on that of former years, and the stronger stays, used without stint, should, if anything, increase the reputation of the record cycles par excellence." [9]

The Stanley Show report[10] of the Ladies Tricycle noted its moveable stay, between the top of the saddle pillar and the head, which could be fixed into position quite quickly, so

"The frame is brought very low, and a peculiarity of construction is that the front wheel is larger than the drivers. The steering can be managed without touching the handlebar."

On the 'Ladies Ivel Tandem Tricycle' the report stated that it:

"... is a very business-like machine, and simplicity in itself to make."

Probably the most remarkable cycle was the 'Ivel Convertible Safety'. For £38.10s the customer received a safety bicycle which could be converted into a tandem safety or a front-steering tricycle or a rear-driving tandem tricycle. This machine was held together with removable pins, allowing parts to be added or taken away as appropriate.

In tandem form, if it be desired to convert to a single, the pins holding the frame joints are removed, when, by undoing the stays and chain, the whole central portion lifts away, and the front portion is united by the joint just before the rear pillar,

8 *Irish Cyclist and Athlete*, c.1891.
9 *Bicycling News*, February 4th 1888, page 290.
10 *Bicycling News*, February 11th 1888, page 311.

and becomes a single safety. From this it can be changed into a single tricycle by removing the rear wheel and fixing the chain stays to the centre of the axle bridge, and putting the chain over the gear box.

Dan achieved a great deal of publicity with this novel machine. Reading between the lines for the assembly instructions for this design, it is apparent that Dan had streamlined his production methods so that key parts of the bicycles and tricycles were standardised and therefore interchangeable.

"The Ivel Ladies' Safety is certainly a very pretty little machine, and one on which there would be not the least difficulty for a lady to maintain her balance; though the excellent and ingenious inventors who have turned their attention to providing this class of machine seem not to have taken into their calculations the fact that the peculiar conditions of a woman's costume render mounting and dismounting a thing of infinitely more risk than either is with a man."

THE 'IVEL' CYCLES
STILL HOLD THE FOLLOWING
World's Records.
WHAT STRONGER EVIDENCE OF THEIR EXCELLENCE?

THE IVEL SAFETY.
Records passed by the N.C.U. 295 miles in 24 hours.
50 ,, 2hrs. 47mins.
THE IVEL TRICYCLE.
RECORD - - - - - 265 miles in 24 hours.
The IVEL TANDEM TRICYCLE.
RECORD - - - - - 298½ miles in 24 hours.
The IVEL TANDEM SAFETY.
RECORDS. - - - 50 miles in 2hrs. 52mins.
20 miles in 1 hour 2mins.

WORLD'S RECORDS FOR EACH TYPE OF MACHINE.

PARTICULARS AND PRICES OF ALL TYPES OF MACHINES ON APPLICATION TO
THE 'IVEL' CYCLE CO., LTD.
BIGGLESWADE, BEDS. MANAGER, DAN ALBONE.
OR THEIR AGENTS

Fig.73: 'Ivel' advertisement, *The Cyclist*

Some wry comment also appeared; the *Scottish Athletic Journal* of 1888 contained this paragraph:

"Dan Albone has a wonderful cycle which converts into almost anything. We cite a few of the uses at random, and no family should be without it. It converts into a Safety or Tandem for the road, into a lunch basket and foot warmer on the rail, a life-belt or lobster pot for those at sea, and a garden roller, hat rack or fire stove ornament for domestic use."

Dan took little notice of pundits such as the following from *Bicycling News* of 1888:

The writer of this piece, although he admitted that cycling for women was *"on the advance"*, concluded:

"Altogether, I don't think we shall live to see the Ladies' Safety drive the three-wheeler out of the field."

The writer probably lived to see just that. The safety bicycle was the very model which gave women cycling freedom. The Rational Dress Society had been formed in 1882[11]; some women began to cycle in plus-fours, bloomers (named after Mrs Bloomer) or leggings. Controversy raged for some

11 *King of the Road*, Andrew Ritchie, p.151.

RECORDS! RECORDS! RECORDS!

FOUR RECORDS in One Week on the "IVEL" CYCLES.

October 9th — 50 MILES in 2 hrs. 59 min. 38⅔ sec., on an "Ivel" Tandem Safety, ridden by Messrs. D. ALBONE and R. TINGEY.

October 13th — 50 MILES in 2 hrs. 52 min. 16 sec., on an "Ivel" Tandem Safety, ridden by Messrs. D. ALBONE and E. E. GLOVER.

October 15th — 20 MILES in 1hr. 2 min., on an "Ivel" Tandem Safety, ridden on the track by Messrs. D. ALBONE and E. E. GLOVER.

October 13th — 50 MILES in 3 hrs. 2 min. 44 sec. on an "Ivel" Tricycle, ridden by Mr. R. TINGEY, beating the previous Record by 6 min. 31 sec., which has stood untouched for 2 years.

The above Records are RECORDS FOR THE WORLD, thus showing that the 'IVEL' Cycles still maintain their position for road work.

"IVEL" CYCLE CO. LIMITED, BIGGLESWADE, BEDS.

Fig.74: 'Ivel' records advertisement

years, but women took to cycling in ever-increasing numbers. Keen female cyclists could be seen in the parks of London from the 1890s. Cycling for women came to be accepted as a healthy pastime, and this led to women being able to use cycles as a form of independent transport. Indeed, the cycle helped to liberate women from their homes, as accessories for carrying children were invented.

Following an agreement entered into on January 30th 1888, The Ivel Cycle Company Limited was formed on March 31st 1888 with capital of £15,000 divided into 3,000 shares of £5 each. Dan received £5,000 and shares equivalent to £3,500. The founders with one share each were: T. G. Welchman, Walter Morris, H. G. Welchman, Francis Ransom, George T. Langridge, Raymond C. Bennett, and Frederick W. Baker. Walter Morris was chairman of the board, H. G. Welchman the managing director, Dan the Works Manager with G. P. Mills as assistant manager and designer.

Notes on the draft company formation agreement contain some interesting comments such as:

"It would avoid misunderstanding if in a letter it were stated that the vendor does not include in the sale the machines which are personal and have been kept for own use. Nor the lathe which he won as a prize and which by the Rules of the N.C.U. he cannot sell." [12]

The Company acquired a 21 year lease from March 25th 1888 on May 16th 1888 to the *"Cycle Factory garden meadow land and premises"* at the rear of the Ivel Hotel, reaching to the bank of the River Ivel, which included offices, factory, engine house and repairing shed. Frederick Archdale and Charles Samuel Lindsell were the lessors and it is interesting to note that their signatures were witnessed by Arthur J. Hills, Captain of the Biggleswade & District Cycling Club. Dan signed on behalf of the Ivel Cycle Company. The lease was at a yearly rent of £28 for seven years and then at a yearly rent of £33. There was a provision for additional yearly rent of £5 should Dan cease to be the tenant of the Ivel Hotel. This lease was eventually surrendered on September 29th 1897. [13]

In July the American tandem 10 mile record fell to an 'Ivel'. Louis Hill and John Fuller of the Pennsylvania Club completed the distance in 30 min. 44.4 secs. It had been imported by B. B. Craycroft & Co. of Philadelphia, the sole agents for the 'Ivel' in the U. S. A.[14] William Read & Sons then claimed to have the sole agency[15] and, later in 1889, it seems that A. G. Spalding became an importer, and the lady-front tandem cost $200.[16]

About this time G. P. Mills parted company with Dan. Certainly Mills registered a trade mark for the 'Mills' on August 28th for *"bicycles, tricycles, and other velocipedes."* Mills was acting in partnership with Alfred Walcot Gamble, trading as Mills and

12 Bedfordshire & Luton Archives Service, Hooper and Fletcher records, ref: HF 21.

13 Bedfordshire & Luton Archives Service, Hooper and Fletcher records, ref: HF 20/376/1.
14 *American Athlete*, July 11th 1888.
15 *Bicycling News*, April 21st 1888
16 *Riding High*, 1956, p.105.

Gamble of 6 Hitchin Street, Biggleswade.[17] This partnership does not appear to have lasted very long as Mills was taken on by Humber not long after.

Dan travelled to Scheveningen, Holland, where on September 9th 1888, he won the prestigious international 5 kilometer tricycle race in 11 min. 10 secs. by half a wheel from the Dutch champion Scheltema Baldwin. His prize was a splendid silver wreath (Fig.75), value twenty guineas, property of the person who won it three times. For once, Mrs Albone went too, and the Dutch gave them a superb welcome. It was all good for business. The 'Ivel' machines won a prize each time they were ridden at this meeting; nine medals and three other prizes, including the silver wreath. The only problem was that Dan could not make himself understood enough to get his egg and bacon breakfast![18]

Away from his growing business, Dan still found time to win prizes and break records. On October 9th, with Richard Tingey, they broke the 50 mile tandem record with a time of 2 hrs. 59 min. 38.6 secs. On October 13th 1888, Dan rode with E. E. Glover on the 'Ivel Tandem Safety' and broke the 50 mile record, in 2 hrs. 52 min. 3 secs. They cycled from Peterborough to Hitchin, via Kate's Cabin, Norman Cross, Stilton, Buckden and Biggleswade, where it is reported, they had a cold collation. The riders also lost two minutes through waiting at Henlow Crossing for a luggage train to pass. A week later on Monday October 15th Dan and Glover lowered the 20 mile track record (and the times for the intermediate mile points).[19] In the same year, Dan competed at Harrogate (see below), Grimsby and Sheffield amongst other places. Richard Tingey also broke the 50 mile safety record that day on an 'Ivel' tricycle with a time of 3 hrs. 2 mins. 44 secs.

The North of England Cyclists' Meet Committee published a Souvenir in 1898[20] to mark the cycling camps which it had organised, principally at Harrogate. This Souvenir included a page setting out *"Some Cycling Celebrities who have attended past Harrogate Camps"*. Dan's name was included along with G. P. Mills. No further detail is provided about Dan's attendance. The Camps were held over the August Bank Holiday and included a race meeting. It is likely that the reference to Dan's attendance was for just the race meeting in 1888 but he may have attended more.

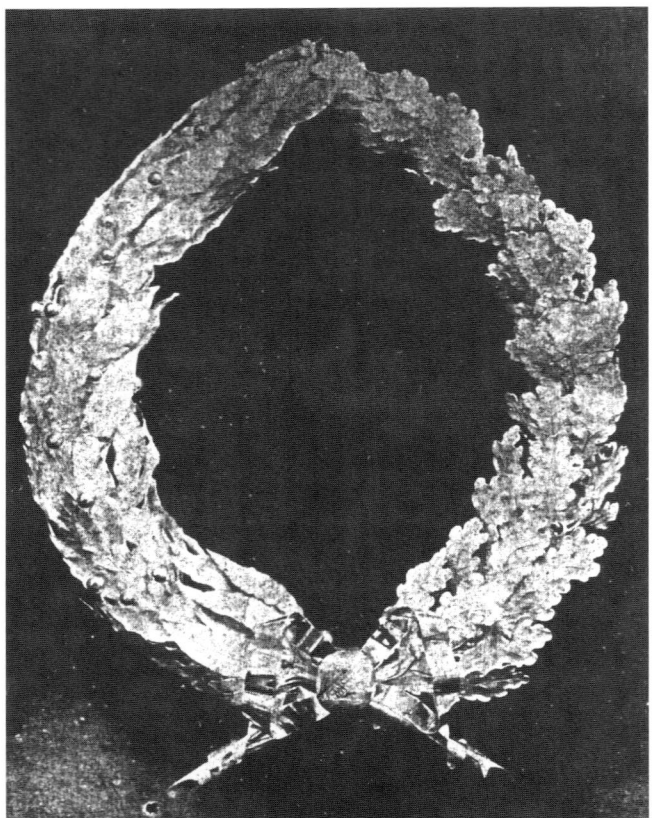

Fig.75: Scheveningen silver wreath

(courtesy Biggleswade History Society)

17 *The Cyclist Year Book*, 1891, p.82.
18 *The Cyclist*, September 19th 1888.
19 *The Cycle Record Athletic Review and Diary*, No. 35, April 27th 1889.
20 *North of England Cyclists' Meet and Camps at Harrogate, Scarborough and Bridlington, Stories and Reminiscences*, 1898

1889 Stanley Dan

The safety bicycle had now reached a new stage of refinement. Dan was a part of this trend particularly with his ladies' machines.

However Henry Sturmey wrote inaccurately in his Indispensable and was answered by Dan.[1]

"Mr Sturmey tried a little theorising last week, and among others the compiler of the Indispensable stated that safety bicycles, specially built with dress guard and dropped frames for the use of ladies, were introduced this spring. Practical Dan Albone, however, who, by the bye, had better in future be retained to compile the Indispensable, says straight from the shoulder; "The Ladies" safety bicycle is not quite so young, for I brought one out more than two years ago, and am pleased to say that it turned out a great success. I had blocks (which you still have) cut, with a lady riding the safety, for advertisements published in your valuable paper May 25th 1887, and in Bicycling News February 5th 1887".

The Stanley Show held early each year, was the major cycling exhibition for collecting orders. In 1889 the Ivel Cycle Company had fifteen models available to the public, plus four speciality models. An 'Ivel' military tricycle was shown (Fig.76). The

ammunition and valise were carried on the luggage carrier at the rear, and the bayonet and flag each side of the frame. The report about this concludes with a note that the design is not quite complete.[2]

Dan arranged for the Great Northern Railway to offer cheap excursions for the Stanley Show.[3]

No. 32. The Ivel Direct Steering Semi-Roadster (The Ivel Cycle Company, Limited, Biggleswade, Bedfordshire). —Like all other Ivel machines, the driving wheels are 30in., and the pilot wheel 32in. The details are very simple. Warwick's hollow rims and ⅞in. rubbers go to the wheels, which have light-gauge, direct spokes. To the axle there is the regulation four-bearing bridge, and the frame is of the single, or + pattern, with centres steering in front. A slight curve is given to the pillar, which carries the crank-bearing bracket in a ∩-shaped holder; the foot of the pillar is held by two stays from the axle bridge, and one from a lug held below the front end of the backbone by a strengthening rib brazed to the tube. Straight forks and pillar are put to the pilot wheel, and the saddle spring is held by a straight hollow plunger in the socket pillar; hollow handle-bars are bent into a convenient position, and have cork grips.

Every detail of the machine is highly finished, and made of the best material. It is a remarkably easy machine to guide. The usual weight is about 38lb. to 40lb., though one we scaled turned the balance at only 35lb. Neither brake nor mud-guards are used. The price, balls all parts, finished enamelled and part plated, is £24.

Fig.77: Extract from *Bicycles and Tricycles,* 1889, Griffin

While Dan was away at this show, Elizabeth had a baby boy, on January 31st and Dan left for Biggleswade as soon as he received the telegram. However, he did return to the show within twenty four hours!

In March the child was christened. His given names were Stanley Dan, because of his arrival during the Stanley Show. Within a short time Stanley would be the inspiration for one of Dan's practical cycle accessories.

During the Stanley Show, Dan wrote a letter to the cycling press about protection for cycle agents and that manufacturers should be more careful to whom they allowed agents terms. He indicated that he would not allow his appointed agents to offer more than a 5% discount to customers.[4] By 1895, following the voluntary liquidation of the Ivel Cycle Company, he was advertising prices net of the discount.[5]

The rigidity of the tricycle was improved by a re-designed bottom bracket. This was formed of a pair of V-arms swinging to adjust the chain, with the bearings contained in the lower extremity of the

Fig.76: 'Ivel' military tricycle

1   *Wheeling,* January 9th 1889.

2   *Bicycling News,* February 2nd 1889.
3   *The Cyclist,* January 9th 1889.
4   *Wheeling,* January 23rd 1889.
5   See for example 1897 catalogue, p.3

THE 'IVEL' CYCLES.

" *To* THE IVEL CYCLE CO.,   " ' Lyndale,' 90 Turnpike Lane, Hornsey, London, N.

       " BIGGLESWADE.   " *June 16th 1889.*

     " DEAR SIRS,—I like the 'IVEL' better than any other Machine because of the straight forks and easy steering. The following is a list of the prizes and places I have obtained this year :—

           " May 4th—Dunstable Road Cyclist League. Ten Miles Handicap Road Race. Sixth out of 13 starters.
           " May 9th—Southgate C.C. Five Miles Scratch Race. Second.
           " May 11th—Essex C.C. Sports at Leighton. One Mile Safety Handicap. Second.
           " May 25th—Southgate C.C. Ten Mile Road Handicap. First. Time 36 min. net.
           " June 6th—Southgate C.C. Five Miles Scratch. First.
           " June 15th—Dunstable Road Cyclist League. Fifteen Miles Road Handicap. First. Fastest time
                56 min. 33 sec. against W. G. JAMES, London, and MR. AYLOTT, Luton, and other men

                              " Yours faithfully, ROBT. L. EDE, *Southgate C.C. and D.R.C.L.*"

👉 AGENTS WOULD DO WELL TO WRITE FOR TERMS, &c., IN TOWNS NOT REPRESENTED.

Fig.78: 'Ivel' advertisement

"V", and an arm continuing downward, below the bearing, to a point below the bottom edge of the chainwheel, where a cross-piece connects the two arms under the chain, and the back stays are jointed to this. The result is an extremely stiff bracket.[6]

The ladies tandem safety had chains, rather than a bar, between the handlebars.

The 'Irish Ivel' embodied a number of suggestions from a well-known Irish rider, assumed to be R. J. Mecredy, a friend of 'Faed' Wilson, and was built stronger with stouter tyres.

There was a new pattern of semi-racing 'Ivel', which had direct spokes but on the tangent principle as the hub flange was cogged.

The 'Ivel' safety bicycle had its price reduced to £16.

All machines this year had a wide bearing to the rear hub with slots in the chain stays for adjustment.

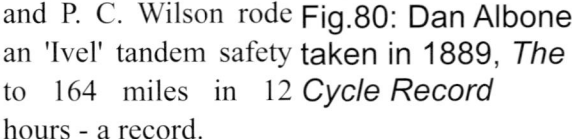

Fig.79: 'Ivel' Direct Steerer tricycle 1889

In June, the Ivel Cycle Company gave Power of Attorney to William Brockie of Walnut & Front Streets, Philadelphia, to settle a dispute with Strong & Green Cycle Co., 707 Arch Street, Philadelphia. It is not clear what the dispute was about.[7]

On August 16th, M. A. (Monty) Holbein and P. C. Wilson rode an 'Ivel' tandem safety to 164 miles in 12 hours - a record.

Fig.80: Dan Albone taken in 1889, *The Cycle Record*

The next day, on August 17th, Monty Holbein and J. Blair broke Dan's tandem 50 mile record with a time of 2 hrs. 51 mins. 51 secs. in heavy conditions on a standard 'Ivel' tandem weighing over 70 lbs.

Then in early September, Monty Holbein rode with P. C. Wilson on an 'Ivel' Tandem Safety Bicycle, breaking the records for 100 miles and 12 hours with 7 hr. 24 min. 10 secs. and 168 miles.

---

6   *Bicycling News*, April 13th 1889

7   Bedfordshire & Luton Archives Service, Hooper and Fletcher records, ref: HF 20/302/12.

1890 The Pneumatic Tyre

At the 1890 Stanley Show the following report was given:

"Better than ever are the Ivels, a year's experience having brought about great advances in the machines made at Biggleswade. The cross-framed Ivel safety, which did so much to popularize its type, is now stayed between the neck and the

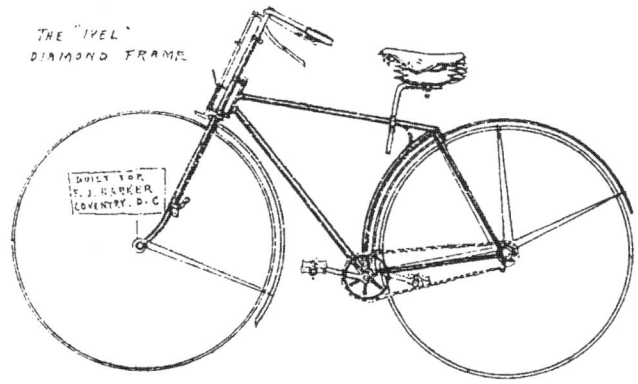

Fig.81: Diamond-frame, *Bicycling News*, Feb. 22nd

saddle-pillar, as well as below; and the diamond-framed Ivel has a curved down tube. Curved front-forks are used on some patterns, but the original straight fork is still recommended. A half-diamond framed safety is also stayed from neck to saddle-pillar, and the Lady's Ivel safety, which was the forerunner of modern ladies' safeties, is on view. The Ivel tricycles are mainly on the familiar cross-framed pattern, and the tandem tricycles, which still hold the 24 hours road record, have been found so satisfactory that the pattern is retained. A ladies' tricycle has drop frame and detachable stay; and all the tricycles have the powerful swing crank -bracket, peculiar to this firm. Ordinary bicycles, too, are again made, Dan Albone's first successes having been with the tall wheel; and the present patterns are fully up to the times. The general finish of all the Ivels is vastly improved, and bids fair to bring these excellent wheels into renewed favour in Ireland." [1]

Across the Atlantic the *New York Herald* thought Dan was worthy of mention:

"But let us push on, past Henlow Crossing and village, over level windswept surfaces to Biggleswade and dismount at the Ivel Hotel, known

in the early days of the (Great North) road's popularity as the Ongley Arms. Here we are welcomed by the genial host and thorough good fellow, Dan Albone ... He would turn out at all hours of the day or night to 'pace' and generally advise any rider. And should you chance to catch Dan (as everyone calls him) with an hour to spare, vastly interesting facts can he retail to you of the deeds of days gone by. His valuable help on record rides was acknowledged by the riders interested in the form of an address on vellum and presentation chronometer.

Biggleswade is a thoroughly cycle-loving town. Its postmaster is a cyclist, and will ride a couple of miles to a finishing point of a race, and back to the office wires with one's 'copy' of the result; and the town constable's awe-inspiring presence has been frequently found extremely useful in keeping a clear course for competitors at the end of a race."

Dan's catalogue offered eighteen models. There was a new 'Ivel Roadster Safety', which incorporated a top stay, at £18. Also, a diamond-frame had been introduced (Fig.81), late in the previous year, and was now listed as the 'Ivel Roadster Safety No.8' at £18.

He now had his own London office and showroom at 77 Fore Street and 14 Fore Street Avenue.

Fig.82: 'Ivel' advertisement, Stanley Show

---

1   *Irish Cyclist and Athlete*, Stanley Show Number 1890, p.67.

SEASON 1890.
Illustrated Catalogues
READY
1st JANUARY, 1890.

THE
Ivel Tandem Tricycle.
Mr. W. E. HAMMERTON (G.N.R., King's Cross) says: "Although the roads and weather have been most unfavourable for riding, I cannot speak too highly of the machine, either when ridden by myself and companion, or two of my sisters, and we are very pleased with its performance."—Oct., 1889.

Mr. J. W. HERRINGTON (Hon. Sec. Kemp Town Cycling Club, Brighton) writes: "Having ridden one of your light roadster safeties for nearly two years, I think you will be pleased to hear how well it has stood the test of the roads round about Brighton, which are never in the best condition. I am confident that the 'Ivel' machines are the best for workmanship and speed."—Sept, 1889.

"IVELS."

THE "IVEL" TANDEM SAFETY.
Messrs. LOUIS SHUTE and W. C. JONES (Polytechnic C.C.) write: "For ease of running, strength, design, workmanship, &c, we think it could not be surpassed. It was a pleasant revelation to us."—Oct., 1889.

THE
IVEL CYCLE CO.,
LIMITED,
BIGGLESWADE, BEDFORDSHIRE.

"I have now ridden the 'Ivel' Semi-racing Safety two years. I have found it to have no equal for easy running and steering."
R. L. EDE, Southgate C.C.
Oct, 1889.

Fig.83: 'Ivel' advertisement 1890, *The Cyclist Yearbook*

1890 was a year in which Dan was travelling round spreading the good news about 'Ivel' cycles. Not only did he go to cycle race meetings, but he also visited Dundee, Aberdeen, Cardiff, Dublin, Oxford and Manchester, persuading traders to take on agencies for 'Ivel' cycles. No doubt this was no easy task as it was a very competitive business.

Dan lent the Bedfordshire Constabulary two cycles, one stationed at Biggleswade and the other in Bedford, so that they could be assessed for police purposes. The police report stated:

"Although the winter is not the best time for trying them, I have found them of some use and although I cannot recommend that the County should be put to the expense of buying a bicycle for each Divisional Station I venture to express a hope that I may be allowed to purchase one to be kept at Head Quarters." [2]

The 'Ivel' tandem obtained a favourable mention:

"Other well-known representative machines are the Ivel (Dan Albone), [and the] Lightning (Lightning Cycle Co.). Both these are, however, confined

to gentlemen, owing to the shape of the framework; but the former, and one type (there are several) of the latter carry the steering connection parallel with the main tube, so that there is no high bar." [3]

'Faed' Wilson and Dan experimented with a 24 in. pneumatic-tyred steering wheel out of 'Faed's Humber racing tricycle. [4]

In early August 1890 Biggleswade folks who attended the fête were astonished to see Dan's 'Ivel' racer. In place of the solid rubber tyres the racer had *"cumbrous-looking"* pneumatic tyres. Dunlop had publicised his invention late in 1888, and Dan was among the first to use pneumatic tyres in cycle production. The *Bedford Express* reported that Dan was penalised fifty yards for using a cycle with pneumatic tyres in the half-mile Open Race: he came in a very close second.

Dan would have been very familiar with the early development of the pneumatic tyre as he knew Dunlop very well and his good friend Richard J. Mecredy was a director of the Pneumatic Tyre and

---

2 Bedfordshire & Luton Archives Service, Ref. QEV 1/2 .

3 *Cycles and Cycling*, Griffin 1890.
4 *Wheeling*, August 20th 1890.

Booth Cycle Agency set up in Dublin on November 18th 1889. On December 12th 1889 the company voted to allow the bicycle trade to have use of the pneumatic tyre.[5] The pneumatic tyre was released onto the market for 1890. From August 1890 pneumatic-tyred 'Ivel' racing cycles made a noticeable impact.

Meanwhile, cushion tyres tended to split but Dan had a special wheel rim manufactured that prevented the rim from cutting the tyre.[6]

On August 16th A. F. Ilsley won the 50 miles handicap of the North Road C. C. on an 'Ivel Safety' in a time of 2 hrs. 48 mins.

The Cyclist said of the Bath Road C. C. one hundred miles race run on August 23rd

Fig.84: 'Ivel' advertisement

"All riders of the pneumatic and cushion tyres left the other riders at the start."

Edmund Dangerfield won on an 'Ivel Safety' with pneumatic tyres in 6 hrs. 28 min., *"with roads in a vile condition and a heavy westerly wind"* and was *"highly pleased with his machine"*.

Then on August 30th T. A. Edge made 334 miles in the North Road C. C. 24 hours on an 'Ivel Semi-Racer Safety'. There was a terrific contest between T. A. Edge and Monty Holbein. Edge narrowly failed to beat Holbein who recorded 336½ miles riding a cushion-tyred 'Whippet'.

On September 15th the 100 miles tricycle record was taken by T. A. Edge of Manchester on an 'Ivel' in 6 hrs. 10 min.

Then on September 5th, the 50 miles tricycle record fell to P. C. Wilson on an 'Ivel' in 2 hrs. 44 mins. 20 secs.

Dangerfield was in action again on September 20th when he won the North Road C. C. 100 miles handicap on an 'Ivel Safety' in 6 hrs. 10 mins. 45 secs.

On September 22nd, T. A. Edge rode 100 miles in 6 hrs. 10 mins. on an 'Ivel' tricycle, breaking the existing record.

Then, on October 18th, T. A. Edge accomplished the fastest 50 and 100 miles ever. He was mounted on a new 'Ivel' diamond-frame light roadster weighing 30 lbs. His time was 2 hrs. 29 mins. 54 secs. for the '50' and 5 hrs. 27 min. 38 sec. for the '100'.

On October 23rd, Edge tackled the York to London record on an 'Ivel Safety', completing the distance in 14 hr. 33 min.

Record after record fell; the new tyres made all the difference. All these records were toasted in press advertisements.

A new private bar room was added to the Ivel Hotel for those who wished to retire into peace and quiet when the rest of the hotel was humming with cyclists in the season.[7]

The capital of the Ivel Cycle Company Limited was increased in December.

Fig.85: 'Ivel' advertisement

---

5   Information provided by David Higman, MBE. Booth Bros. were Dan's 'Ivel' agents in Dublin.
6   1891 Ivel catalogue, page 2. See also *The History of the Pneumatic Tyre*, page 37.

Nr.	Date.	Name.	Club.	REMARKS.
7	31.7.90	Chas S. Scarborow	Brighton Wanderers B.C.	Safety Tandem crew of B.W. B.C.
8	"	Harold Gaskill	Manchester Wheelers	
9	"	Chas Johnson	Unattached	
10	"	Fred. Bushby	Unattached	
August				
1	Aug 1	Harold Gaskill	Manchester Wheelers	
2	"	Frank Godwin	New Southgate	Rode my mare (none of your bloomin' cycles) from Lincoln here in a day and a half) came along Ermine Street now called High Dyke, stayed Station Hotel Peterboro and woke the town up at six o'clock. Wet through with rain yesterday and today with sweat, but not so dirty as these blanky 'wheelers'. Yorkshire ain't in it with Lincolnshire. (See preceding Page)
3	"	Arthur G.B. West	M.C.C.	
4	" 1st	Dan Albone	Biggleswade Tr. & D.C.C.	Pacing Holbein.
5	"	A.E. Bennett	Do.	Do
6	"	[illegible]	Catford & N.R.C.C.	Passed 3.50 P.M. E. Elliott
7	"	H. J. Howard	N.R.C.C.	Pacing Holbein.
8		P. Carlisle Wilson	Catford CC	

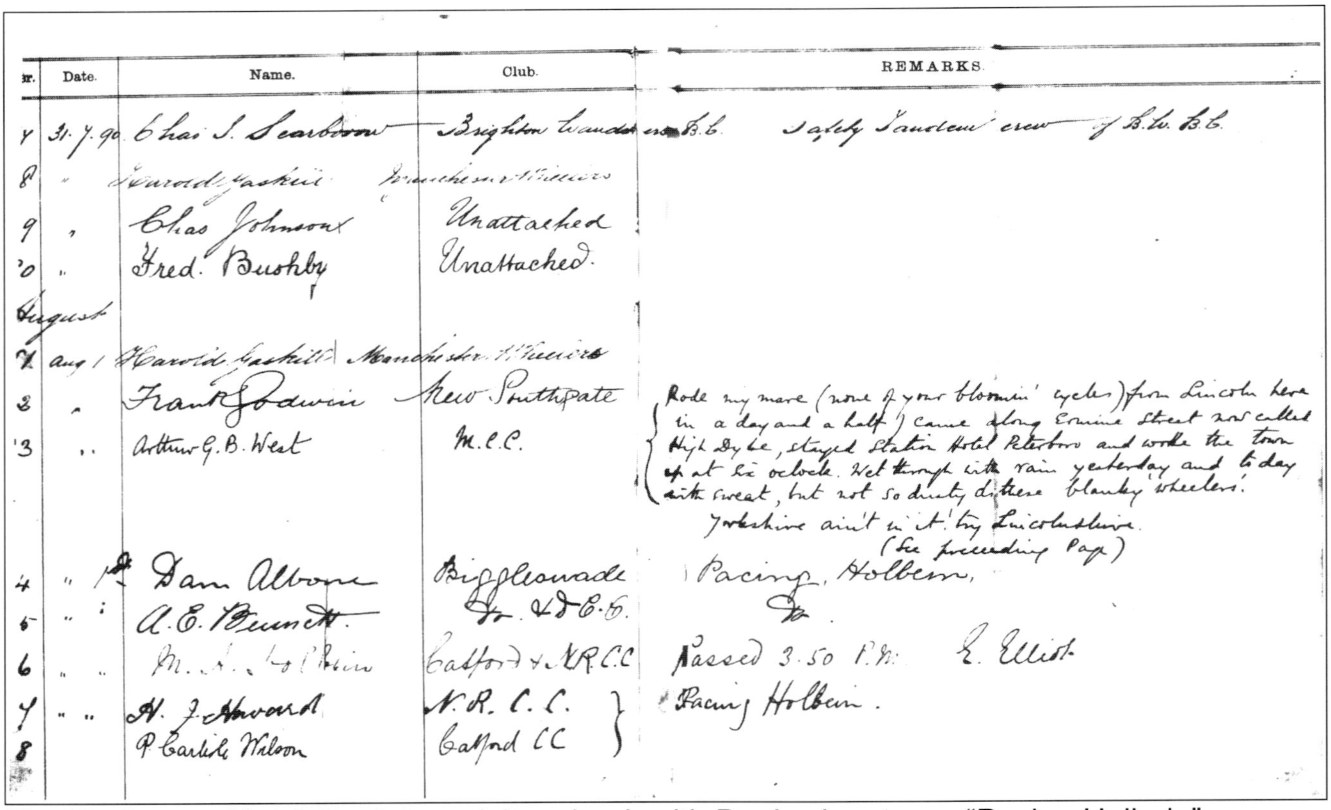

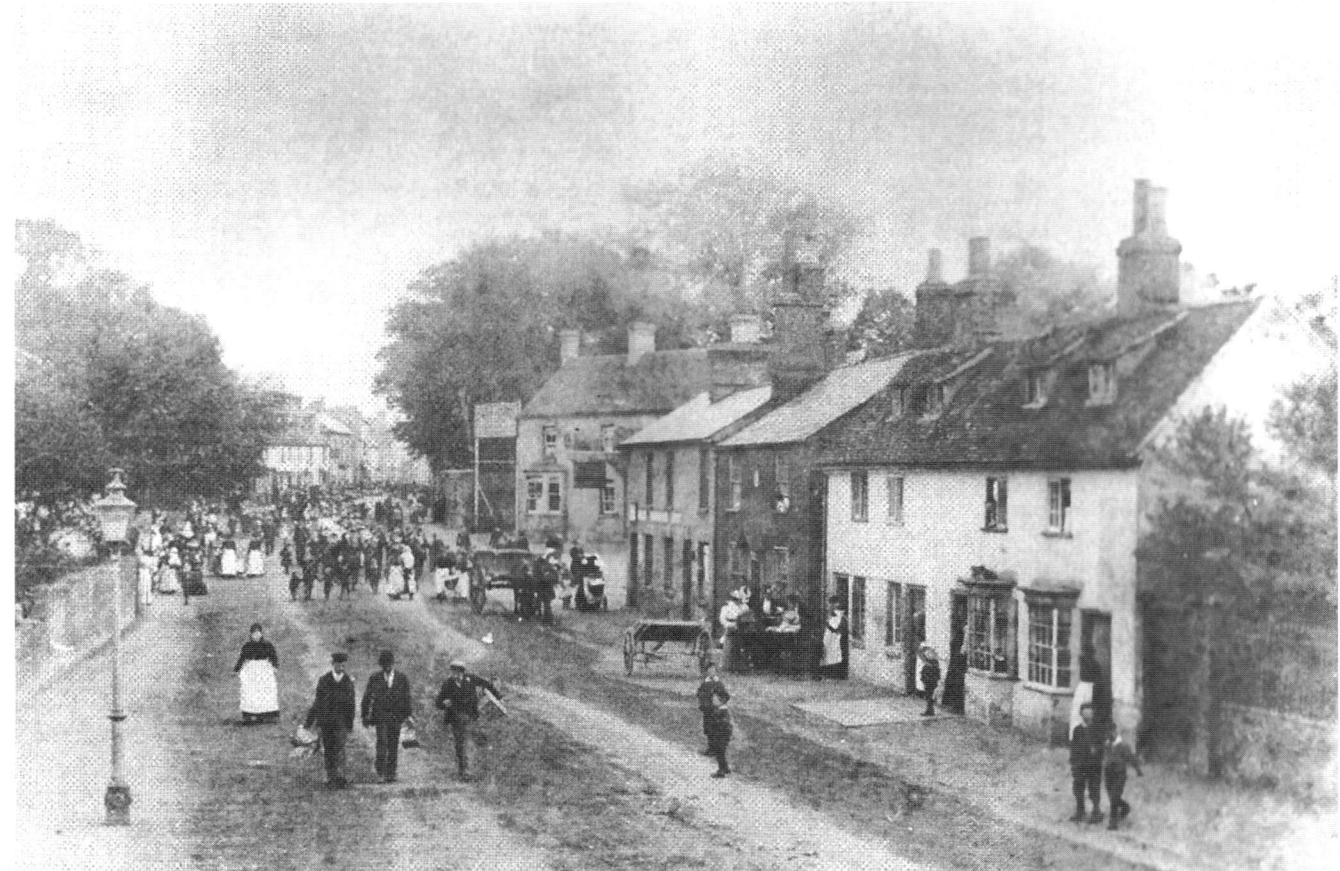

Fig.86: George Hotel, Buckden, visitors book with Dan's signature - “Pacing Holbein”

(courtesy North Road C. C.)

Fig.87: Shortmead St looking south towards the Ivel Hotel in the early 1890s. Crowds are walking to the Biggleswade Fête at Fairfield on the August Bank Holiday.

(courtesy Biggleswade History Society)

1891 The Child Carrier

Dan's catalogue for 1891 was his largest ever, displaying over twenty models. The cross-frame safety had evolved with top and bottom front bracing stays but there were also diamond-frames, several of which had a distinctive bracing strut to the seat pillar. The 'Ivel Lady's Safety' was offered with a stay rod for extra bracing if used by a gentleman. The 'Ivel Tandem Safety Bicycle' was there with the option of a lady-front model and a note that the right to offer them was no longer sub judice. Tricycles and tandem tricycles were there in various forms as well as two Ordinary models. There was no longer an 'Anfield Ivel' tricycle, following Mills' departure, although the 'Ivel Roadster Tricycle' was to all intents the same. The 'Ivel Anti-vibration Safety', introduced in 1888, was shown together with Laming's joint and spring.

Cushion and pneumatic tyres were now, of course, all the rage and Dan had models to accommodate them. The catalogue mentions the special rim manufactured for the Company, it is believed by Dunlop, which prevented the rim from cutting the tyre. Dan also offered inflated cushion tyres which were a hybrid form, allowing the machine to be ridden, even if punctured, as if on a cushion tyre.

Fig.88: The Child Carrier by George Moore, *Cycling*, May 9th 1891

Most machines appear to have larger front wheels (32 in./30 in.) but the Lady's Safety had 28 in. wheels front and rear.

Fig.89: Dan with Stanley in Child Carrier

A Child Carrier became one of Dan's most successful accessories, and caused a great deal of comment. A patent for this was applied for in April and granted the following January (No. 1891-7300).

"Some sensation was caused in Bedford High Street on Tuesday by Dan Albone of Biggleswade on a Pneumatic Safety with wicker chair in front, in which was seated his little boy. At two or three stopping places crowds assembled round the machine and took stock of the little voyager." [1]

The reaction of an 'old dame' from Southill was reported with the reporter's own comments added:

"Capital, capital! Good father, good father!" One felt she wished in her time husbands had all been cyclists and able to take the children out in the morning while the pudding was being made, what a blessing it would have been and how many years it would have added to her life ... Fathers, get a basket fitted to your machine and in future make a point of taking out your most troublesome child on your Saturday afternoon spin, instead of leaving them at home for the wife to look after." [2]

The Child Carrier was built of wickerwork over a light wire frame and was provided with a padded cover to the seat. The cost of the Child Carrier was just £2 and orders poured in in their hundreds.

"Dan Albone ... has four basket-makers at work making nothing else just now." [3]

---

1   *The Bedfordshire Times and Independent*, May 1891.
2   *Bedfordshire Standard*, May 9th 1891.
3   *The Cyclist*, August 1891.

Fig.90: Dan and Richard Tingey with child carrier outside corrugated Ivel Works

Indeed, he could not get them made fast enough to satisfy demand.

Orders from France exceeded supply for a time, and Irish riders placed their orders with alacrity. This design remained common in France until at least the Second World War.

A report of the Child Carrier reads:

"There were not many articles at the Stanley Show this year of interest to ladies, but we must make an exception to that statement when speaking of D. Albone's child-carrier. This ... is attached to the front of the cycle and is free from all jolting and vibration. There are many ladies who are using these carrier and the children never so pleased as when enjoying a trip in the 'Carrier'. The only difficulty is when they have to get out. Cycling is loud in its praises for this invention. "We understand that in Paris the sale is much more rapid than the supply". [4]

These instructions were issued for fitting:

"At the bottom of the basket you will find two bolts, to which the fork has to be fixed. Fasten the fork to axle of front wheel; if the axle should be short make the eyes on end of fork, or the eyes of the stay rod holding the mudguard, thinner. If the axle is still short it is best to send to the makers for a longer one (or the mudguard can be taken off). Then fasten the two gun-metal clips to handlebar in such a position as to allow the brake to work properly. To do this, in most cases, they have to be put near to the post of handlebar; the cranked pieces of

half-round steel should then be fixed to them. Spread them out wider at the bottom than the top; they will then be in a slanting position across the back of the chair. When this is done, put the bolts sent with it through the wickerwork wherever they come, and screw all nuts, etc., up tightly. If at any time an alteration of position of handlebar is required, the bolt must be altered to correspond in the wickerwork. The holes left in back of carrier are not for the bolts, but for the straps to hold the child securely in the chair. The basket is easily put on and taken off in two minutes by taking the bottom screws out of the clips, and leaving clips on handle-bar."

A brief article on Dan appeared in *Cycling* in May, under the heading *"Always Affable"*:

"Who has not heard of Dan Albone, the genial, ever-smiling Dan? With the big performances which have made the North Road famous, his name will ever be linked. There is not a man on record-breaking intent to whom he has not rendered some valuable assistance and though in the cycle trade himself, he never stops to enquire on what machine the record-breaker is mounted. He is a sportsman above all things. On the road Dan Albone is best known as an ever-willing pacemaker, but on the race path he has won a big sheaf of awards, which adorn the interior of the "Danneries" at Biggleswade." [5]

Also in May, Dan was one of a number of pacers who assisted Monty Holbein in setting a new tricycle 12-hour record at 174½ miles.

On June 5th, Dan entered into agreement with Viggo C. Eberth, Frederiksberggabe, 4 Copenhagen,

Fig.91: Ernie Chew with 'Ivel', 1891

(courtesy Biggleswade History Society)

4 *The Lady*, December 17th 1891.

5 *Cycling*, May 2nd 1891, page 233.

for patent rights in and sale of the Child Carrier in France, Germany, Denmark and Belgium. The Child Carriers were provided for the net price of £1 10s. each delivered to Biggleswade Railway station Dan agreed to pay Eberth's costs up to £25 and permitted him a commission of 4½d per Child Carrier per country. Dan also agreed to provide advertising blocks.[6]

On August 31st, 1891, Dan, and his brother-in-law Richard Tingey, applied for a patent (No. 1891-14705) for the invention of U-shaped clips to carry

Fig.92: "A Nice Baby to Carry", *Cycling*, June 25th

a cycle pump on a cycle. The clips were adjustable and were secured by a screw and nut. This patent was later subject to a dispute in 1892 with John Harrison of Porchester Foundry, Porchester Street, Birmingham whom Dan sued for infringement. It seems that Harrison claimed he had been assigned the patent. Harrison subsequently paid £28 10s to settle the matter but it dragged on into 1894 with the Birmingham Patent Office becoming involved.[7]

Dan also developed a parcel carrier, which he called the 'Postman's Friend'. Did Biggleswade's postmaster, Stamp Hutton, have an input we wonder?

On September 4th, the London to Brighton and back record was broken by F. Lowe on an 'Ivel' tricycle.

At the Stanley Show the parcel carrier was reported thus:

"Cheery Dan Albone will be showing his popular "Kid Konveyor", and it is sure to come in for a large share of the visitors' patronage. As well as the child carrier, Dan Albone has a new handlebar parcel carrier, which should sell with lightning rapidity. Dan and his smile should by no means be missed." [8] and

"The ever-smiling Dan Albone was at this stand with a couple of 'Ivels' fitted with his patent child-carrier. In one of the carriers was a handsome life-size wax doll. Its face was illuminated with a smile, which it seemed to have caught from its owner." [9]

There was no display of 'Ivel' cycles at the Stanley Show this year which was explained as follows:

"During the Stanley Show the Ivel Cycle Co. is going to run an opposition exhibition in Fore Street, City, in which, as is only natural, the Ivel of historic renown takes a very prominent part. Mr Albone informs us that the Ivel Cycle Company is not discontinuing any of its last year's patterns, as they appear to have given such general satisfaction, but that two or three new patterns are to be introduced, the chief of which is a diamond-frame Ivel, either roadster or racer, which is to be in happy possession of an extended wheel-base and an elongated ball-socket head. Of course, all the many other Ivels will be there to be seen, and which are too well-known to our readers to require minute description at our hands." [10]

The Child Carrier had led to some humorous cartoons such as "A Ride in Hyde Park!" (Fig.94) [11], and "The Baby Carrier in the Rain" (Fig.95).[12]

Fig.93: The result of an evening at the Stanley Show, *Bicycling News*, December 3rd

---

6 Bedfordshire & Luton Archives Service, Hooper and Fletcher records, ref: HF 20/324/22.
7 Bedfordshire & Luton Archives Service, Hooper and Fletcher records, ref: HF 20/341/5.

8 *Cycling*, November 28th 1891, page 304.
9 *Cycling*, December 5th 1891, page 342.
10 *Cycling*, November 28th 1891, page 310.
11 *Bicycling News*, May 30th 1891
12 *Bicycling News*, December 3rd 1892.

Fig.94: A Ride in Hyde Park with apologies to Dan Albone, *Bicycling News*, May 30th

Fig.95: "The Baby Carrier in the Rain"

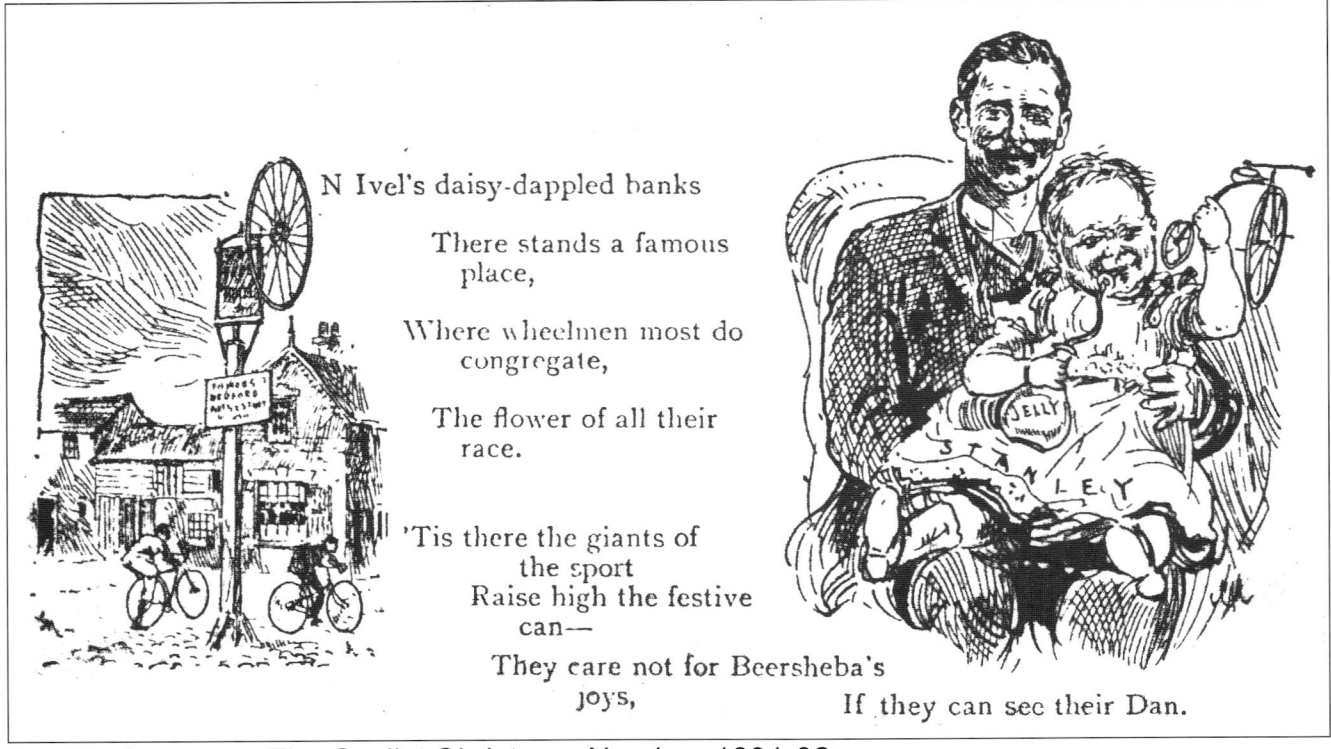

N Ivel's daisy-dappled banks

There stands a famous place,

Where wheelmen most do congregate,

The flower of all their race.

'Tis there the giants of the sport
Raise high the festive can—

They care not for Beersheba's joys,

If they can see their Dan.

Fig.96: Cartoons, *The Cyclist Christmas Number*, 1891-92

Fourteen were grouped around his
door,

Well known for form and pace,

When by them all dashed he
who rode

A couldn't-help-it race !

And there was mounting
in hot haste ;

Full soon a scorching
crew,

With curvèd backs, were
on his trail,

As down the road he
flew.

Each flier rode the best machine,
Each man was trained to stay,
And many shekels was it worth
To see them break away.

miles along the classic roads
The Biggleswaders spank,
Till mythic cramp and shameless nuts
Combine with perjured crank.

By ones and twos the crowd tailed off,
Till left were only three,
The very pick of England's best
All-day fraternity.

Fig.97: Cartoons, *The Cyclist Christmas Number*, 1891-92

1892 A Billiard Table Arrives

There were 16 models in the catalogue for 1892. The Ordinary models had been dropped. New models included a specially constructed diamond-frame 'Ivel Racer Safety'. This had an extended wheelbase, lengthened ball-socket head, raised bottom bracket and tangent-spoked wheels. With pneumatic tyres it weighed only 25 lb. The 'Ivel Semi-Racer Safety' is shown with a tangent-spoked rear wheel and direct or radial-spoked front. The 'Ivel Lady's Safety' now had ball socket head and improved dress and chain guards. It is notable that the 'Ivel Tandem Tricycle' was still, according to the catalogue, offered with connected steering when that had been discontinued on the Tandem for some time.

A new design of tricycle was also offered in convertible form with detachable top tube for use by either sex.

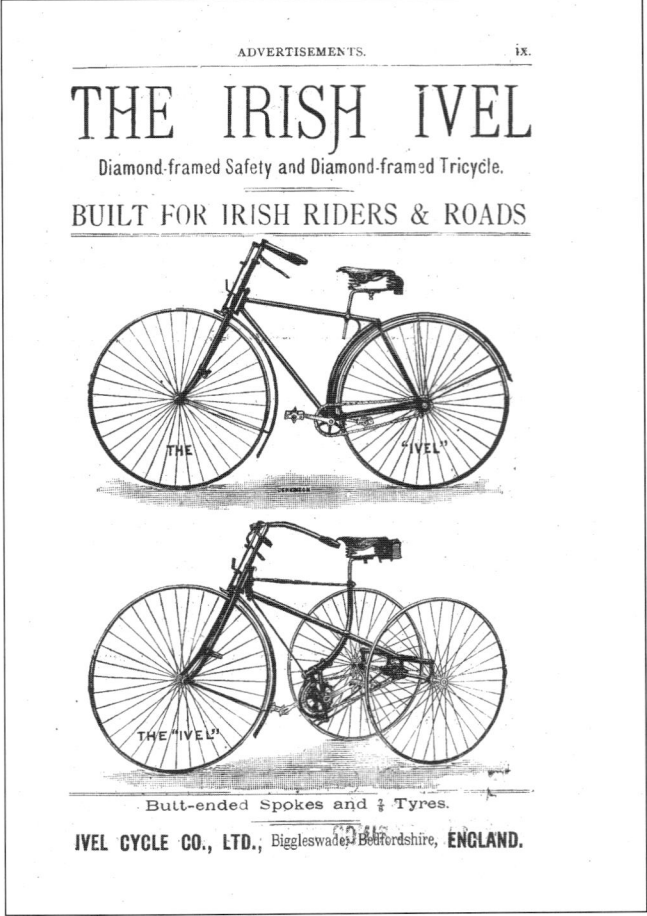

Fig.99: Irish Ivel advertisement

Cycling of March 1892 reported from the Copenhagen Show:

"A lady in a white dress, mounted on a white-enamelled Ivel Safety with a white baby carrier, carrying a white-dressed baby was one of the attractions .."

In 1892 Dan bought a full-sized billiard table, the only one in Biggleswade, for the Ivel Hotel.[1] The billiard table was a full size Thurston, the very best quality. Dan probably didn't know it when he bought his billiard table, but the Ivel Works was heading for a startling change in its fortunes.

At the Stanley Show, Dan again showed his child carrier.

"Of course a smile was reserved for all comers by cheery Dan Albone, who was always at hand to explain the virtues of his neat and comfortable child carrier. Two 'Ivel' safeties were shown with the carrier fitted to each, and no father could pass

Fig.98: Ivel Hotel advertisement

---

1 *The Cyclist*, November 2nd 1892.

this Stand without wishing at least for one of Dan's handy little child conveyances." [2]

In the Ivel Works photograph at the foot of this page a number of workers can be identified. At the front on the left is Ernest E. Smith, next to him with the bicycle is James Moulden[3], and standing to our right is 'Font' Gauge. Behind and to the left of Jim Moulden is Jim Handscombe, with 'Cuckoo' Page[4] on his left. David Tole is on the bicycle, then John Holmes and Frank Chivers behind 'Font' Gauge. Behind them is Tommy Cottam, and slightly further back and on the extreme right is George H. Smith.

Fig.100: 'Ivel' for 1892

Fig.101: The Ivel Works c.1892

(courtesy Biggleswade History Society)

---

2   *Cycling*, November 26th 1892, p.321.
3   James and George Moulden both worked at the Ivel Works. They were two of Elizabeth's four younger brothers and both were boarders at the Ivel Hotel in the 1891 Census.
4   'Cuckoo' Page was Henry Page who after the works closed, played football and became groundsman for the Town Cricket Club, Football and Hockey Clubs for 30 years.

1893 Voluntary Liquidation

This years' catalogue showed just seven models, all with pneumatic tyres although cushion or solid tyres were an option. The 'Ivel Anti-vibration Safety' had been dropped. No carriage wheels or tandems were shown and it was stated of tandem tricycles *"the demand is so limited that we have ceased to stock them."* However Dan was prepared to make to order. Also the catalogue stated there was *"a small surplus stock of machines of various patterns, of last and previous seasons' models, which we do not include in this list, having discontinued their manufacture. These we can offer at Very Attractive Prices ..."*

Despite this there were two new models, the 'Ivel Front Driving Safety' at £25.10s., and the 'Ivel Geared Ordinary' at £26. Although comparably priced to the Roadster Safety, not many could have been sold at these prices. The 'Ivel Front Driving Safety' (Fig.102) had 30 in. front, 24 in. back, direct-spoke wheels with Perry gearing to 60 in. or to order. The 'Ivel Geared Ordinary' had 36 in. to 40 in. front, 22 in. back, direct-spoke wheels with Crypto gearing. Both of these machines were ahead of the market since the Crypto 'Bantam' was only introduced in November 1893 with the name 'Bantam' appended in February 1894.

Fig.102: 'Ivel Front Driving Safety

The 'Ivel Roadster Safety' had been revised with 28 in. direct-spoke wheels front and rear and other detail changes. It was offered at £25.10s., the same price as in 1892.

The 'Ivel Light Roadster Safety' was similar but weighed 30 lb. as compared to 39 lb. for the 'Ivel Roadster Safety'. It was offered at £25.

The 'Ivel Racer Safety' weighed only 24 lb. and had 28 in. tangent-spoke wheels front and rear although a 26 in. rear wheel could be ordered. This model was offered at £26.

The 'Ivel Lady's Safety' had been completely revised, now with a double-tube drop-frame and a steering lock. The wheels were 28 in. direct-spoke wheels front and rear. It was offered at £26.

The 'Ivel Roadster Tricycle' was constructed as a convertible with the top tube being removable. There were 28 in. direct-spoke wheels front and back. It was offered at £35.

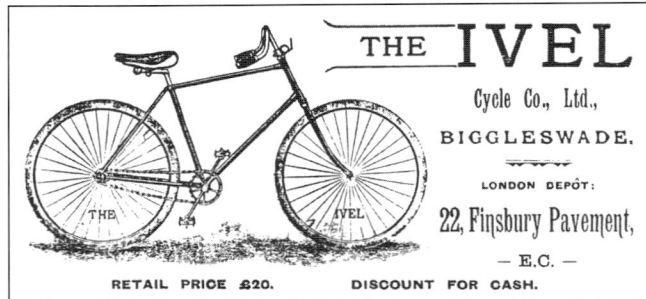

Fig.103: 'Ivel' advertisement

It is notable that all the bicycles are now shown with the chainwheel and drive on the conventional right-hand side whereas previously the left-hand side had been the case. There is no specific comment in the catalogue although there is a reference to the crank bracket being of greatly improved design and the narrowest tread that can be obtained.

The London Depot is now given as 22 Finsbury Pavement, London E.C. The change from the Fore Street premises was very likely a precursor to the liquidation that came later in the year.

In January the River Ivel froze and a skating match was organised for cyclists. There were sixteen entrants, and the race was run in eight heats, second round, and final. The course was three-quarters of a mile, and the fastest heat was timed at 2 min. 45.6 secs. The winner was H. Purser, who received a 40 yds start; second , F. Bennett, 100 yds start; and third, Dan who was the scratch man.[1]

Cycle manufacturers generally had expected endless growth in the market. In fact, the 1890s were a time of over-production, when too many manufacturers chased too few customers. Victorian cycles were sturdy, and for those indifferent to fash-

---

1   *The Wheeler*, January 11th 1893.

ion, a second-hand bicycle was adequate. Safety bicycles were now commonplace and it was the Ordinary bicycle which received the derogatory name of 'Penny-farthing'. There were also very few reports of cycle racing in 1893.

This malaise was reflected in all aspects of life in the 1890s. This decade saw even more bankruptcies than the 1880s, and even millers, bankers, solicitors and shopkeepers experienced hardship.

Workers at the Ivel Works, at the start of the decade, felt fortunate to be employed there, for the town of Biggleswade was suffering from a slump in farm produce prices, and people were moving out of the town in search of work.

So by 1893, and despite Dan's efforts to publicise the 'Ivel' bicycle, orders had dwindled. Over 700 machines were in stock and unsold at the Ivel Works.[2] The *Irish Cyclist* called it bad management[3] but the story was the same everywhere.

Fig.105: Charles Guy on his 'Ivel' tricycle outside the Union Workhouse in London Road where he was master.

(courtesy Biggleswade History Society)

Some manufacturers carried on longer than Dan, only to go bankrupt later.

Dan made a difficult decision; he put the business into voluntary liquidation. There was an Extraordinary General Meeting on October 13th., which passed a Special Resolution for the voluntary winding up, and a subsequent Extraordinary General Meeting on October 28th, which appointed the Liquidators.

Every shareholder received a full repayment of their investment. The employees who had been so proud to work for Dan, over a hundred of them when business was at a peak, were suddenly out of work. It was an immense blow to the town of Biggleswade.

At the Stanley Show, Dan just exhibited his Child and Parcel Carriers, of which the former could be fitted with springs when required at a small extra charge.[4]

The Child Carrier continued to attract humour in the cycling cartoons as the 'Triplet Safety' illustrates (Fig.106). All good for keeping the cycling public aware of Dan's carrier, though.

24 Hours' Jaunt. — Sept. 23rd, 1893.

Headquarters: THE IVEL HOTEL, BIGGLESWADE.

Telegraphic Address:
DANNERIES,
BIGGLESWADE.

REGULATIONS.

1.—The Start will take place Midnight (Friday) at the 46th milestone on the Main Road just north of Biggleswade. The timekeeper, Mr. M. A. Holbein, will be at Headquarters at 11.30 p.m. to sign riders' books, &c. All should report themselves by 11 p.m. to avoid confusion.

2.—Those taking part are requested not to ride with bare legs and knees, but should be completely clothed from the neck to the ankles, including sleeves to the wrists, and it is particularly hoped that the style and colour of costumes will be as inconspicuous as possible.

3.—Trains leave King's Cross (G.N.R) at 5.50, 7.0 and 9.35 p.m. The nearest Station on the Midland main line is Bedford, thence to Sandy (2 miles) or Southill (4 miles from Biggleswade).

4.—Riders cannot be too strongly warned against starting in too thin clothing, as the nights strike cold and many men give up long night rides in consequence.

5.—No detour should be omitted except with the consent of a Marshall, as checkers will only be at their posts for stated periods.

6.—Riders will be distinguished by a small white rosette on the left lapelle of the coat. Marshalls will wear red rosettes.

7.—Every assistance will be given to those unacquainted with the roads, but with reasonable care there can be no difficulty.

8.—The route will be from Biggleswade to Peterboro', Wisbech (57), Lynn (68½), Wisbech, Huntingdon (115), Wisbech (150), Downham Market, Wisbech (174), Long Sutton, Wisbech (190), Peterboro' (211¼), Bourne, Peterboro' (242½), Girtford Bridge (275½), Bedford, Girtford Bridge (290¾), thence Hitchin, &c., as per route card.

9.—Riders should provide themselves with checking books of stout paper and well sewn.

Further particulars can be obtained of

J. H. PRICE,
The Stanley Cyclists' Club,
261, Seven Sisters Road, London,

Or DAN ALBONE,
Ivel Hotel, Biggleswade.

Fig.104: Circular for a 24 Hours 'Jaunt' in 1893 based on the Ivel Hotel

2   *Biggleswade Chronicle*, May 26th 1894.
3   *Irish Cyclist*, November 7th 1906

4   *C.T.C. Gazette*, December 1893, p.320.

SHE: "And is that what you call a Triplet Safety?"

Fig.106: The 'Triplet Safety', *The Wheeler*, Mar. 29th

Note the new 'Ivel' Front Driving Safety

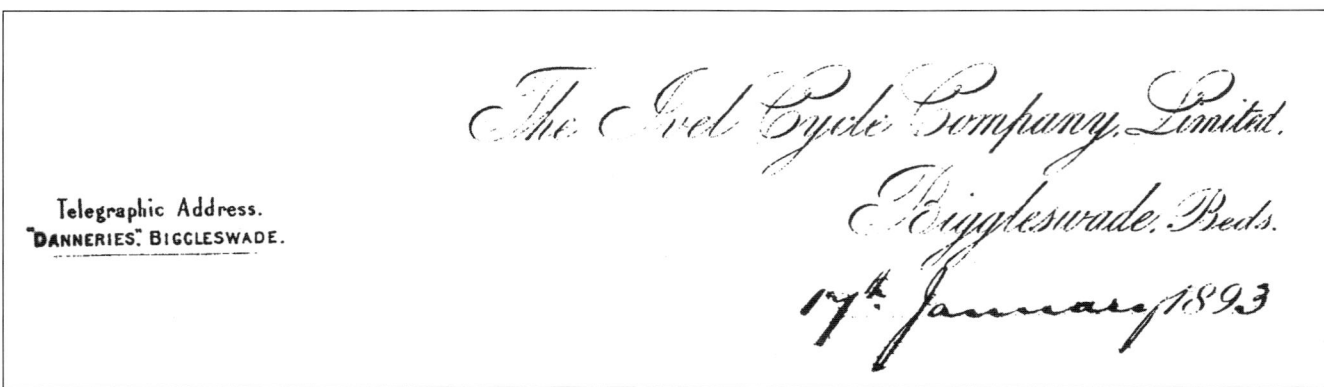

Telegraphic Address.
"DANNERIES". BIGGLESWADE.

The Ivel Cycle Company, Limited.
Biggleswade, Beds.
17th January 1893

Fig.107: Ivel Cycle Company letter head Jan. 1893

Fig. 108: A scene outside the Ongley Arms, *Cycling*, Jan. 9th 1907

1894 Back from the Brink

This was the year that Dan, along with some other manufacturers, introduced a larger chainwheel (Fig.109). His 11½ in. chainwheel, with five flat steel spokes, achieved a gear of 68 in. To onlookers the large chainwheel looked outlandish, but Dan considered that it lessened the load on the chain (making it travel at a higher rate to do the same work). To us today, it would look quite ordinary but it was then a subject of controversy and much discussion in the cycling press.

Fig.109: 'Ivel' with large chainwheel

Dan set to work to salvage what he could from the voluntary liquidation of the Ivel Cycle Company, assisted it seems by Elizabeth's uncle, Mr Edwards, who provided a guarantee to the bank which lent money until Dan recovered funds from the liquidation. The stock of cycles had been sold.

By an Indenture agreed with the Liquidators, Messrs Baker and Welchman, on June 8th 1894 Dan took over the lease from the Ivel Cycle Company for the sum of £5 for the residue of its unexpired term. This lease was later surrendered by Dan on September 29th 1897.[1] It is separately noted that the buildings at that time consist mainly of a large store with a boarded floor, length 80 feet and width 30 feet, and some smaller ones.

By a further Indenture agreed with the Liquidators on June 23rd 1894, he bought back the machinery, goodwill and trade mark of the Ivel Cycle Company and went into production with twenty men on the payroll, including George Course, previously London Manager of the Ivel Cycle Company.

A Circular was issued to announce that Ivel Cycles were back. From this point on, the Ivel

Works was producing a smaller number of bicycles, but many of them were custom-made for individuals. Lord Alwyne Compton, Unionist M.P. for North Bedfordshire, was one of the first to have such a bicycle. Lord Ampthill and Samuel Whitbread, M.P., followed. At the Stanley Show Dan took an order for a cycle for Countess Cowper.[2] The 'Ivel' name was still in favour with the nobility.

At the Biggleswade Fête, on August Bank Holiday, Dan again competed in the half mile open bicycle scratch race which included star riders such as A. A. Chase of the North Road C.C. An advertisement on the back page of the programme announced: Increased Velocity Effort Lessened.[3]

By September of 1894 Dan was once more showing his riding ability and this report taken from a local paper reveals something of Dan's character:

"A Mr Flanders of Bucklersbury in Hitchin had hired out a bicycle to a young man. Flanders had his suspicions that the man did not mean to return the cycle and thought it likely that the cyclist would head north. He got the local police to contact Dan Albone. Dan on his cycle met up with the cyclist, who related his plans to ride to Scotland. Dan kept

Fig.110: 'Ivel' advertisement, June 2nd

---

1   Bedfordshire & Luton Archives Service, Hooper and Fletcher records, ref: HF 20/376/1.

2   *The Wheeler*, December 5th 1894.
3   Bedfordshire & Luton Archives Service, Ref. SDBiggleswadeNAT9/1

level with the cyclist as far as Eaton Socon when Dan decided to speed ahead to alert the St Neots police. The culprit was arrested, but not without a scuffle. Eventually, the criminal was returned to Hitchin to stand trial for theft. An Ivel cycle was a considerable advance on police communications of the time!"

In November Dan issued a further Circular to announce that the Ivel Works were now in full and thorough working order and he was prepared to take orders (see appendix). He offered a machine at £15.15s net.

Dan was at the Stanley Show which was reported thus:

"Dan Albone, Biggleswade, Beds., will show nine safeties, a lady's safety, a tricycle, a parcel carrier, and a child carrier; also a pair of ball bearing carriage wheels and axle, fitted with pneumatic tyres. The hub of the carriage wheels is a novelty of which great things are expected. The large gear wheel and the Stop Thief lock will no doubt attract attention." [4] and

"A prominent feature on this stand is a pair of 48 in. carriage wheels, fitted with detachable axle,

ball bearings, wire spokes, and Dunlop pneumatics – a prototype of what will be common in our streets in a few years – and in this connection it is well to remember that Albone showed a vehicle with this axle (all save pneumatics) at the 1888 Show. He ought therefore to be remembered when the coming boom for reformed vehicles arrives. His cycles number 10, including an up-to-date Ivel road racing tricycle, about 36 lb., all on – a beautifully light mount. The other nine are single safeties. One of these, a road racer built for C. N. Bamyard, N.R.C.C., has a striking enlargement of the crank chain pulley to 11½ in. (17 teeth, every other removed). This necessitates a larger pulley on the driving wheel axle in (14 teeth) gearing the 28 in. wheel to 68 in., and scales 26 lb. A path racer on similar lines comes out 5 lb. lighter. The remainder are road machines, including a lady's." [5]

New features this year were the combined head adjustment and lamp bracket, the bolts of which also serve to lock the handle-bar in position, and the 'Stop Thief' steering lock, attached to the top tube and catching into a notch in the ball head cup.

The Start for the above Race will be made from the third milestone on the Bedford Road at 5.45 p.m. sharp. The route will be *via* Henlow, Clifton, and Caldecote to Girtford Bridge, turn *right* along the Biggleswade Road to Tingey's Corner, turn *right* to Caldecote, *right* again at Elm Tree to Girtford Bridge, round this course again to Girtford Bridge, on to Tingey's Corner and Caldecote, turn *left* at Elm Tree and finish at the fifth milestone from Hitchin.

Check at Elm Tree each time round. Checks *must* be given up each time. Competitor's Entry Fee and Subscription must be paid before the race or they will not be allowed to compete.

Competitors are requested to ride in as inconspicuous garments as possible, not to make undue noise going through villages or in passing anything on the road, as it is the wish of the Committee that the Race be carried out in a quiet and inoffensive manner.

Fig.111: Extract from 30-mile race programme 1894

Note the references to Tingey's Corner and race conduct

---

4   Supplement to *Wheeling*, November 21st 1894, page 3.

5   Supplement to *Wheeling*, November 28th 1894, page 16.

1895 Ball-bearing Axle Boxes

At the Stanley Show it was reported:

"Nine Ivel safeties neatly arranged in rows. The ladies' machines have duplex curved backbones, celluloid gear cases, and cord guards. Some of the men's safeties have direct spokes, and all have a very neat vertically-split-lug bracket adjustment. Dan's well-known pneumatic-tyred, wire-spoked, ball-bearing vehicle wheels are shown of course; and a novelty in this direction consists in applying the ball bearings to wooden wheels having the usual forms of naves. These have been supplied to the London Improved Cab Company. A good stand as usual." [1]

Dan also attended the National Show where his carriage wheels were on display.[2] He took the idea a stage further with a patent application in March for ball-bearing axle boxes for vehicles (No. 1895-4427).

He continued to be favoured by sales to nobility with orders by the Earl and Countess Grey[3]; the Earl of Jersey[4]; the Countess of Listowell; and Viscount Peel.[5]

In March there was correspondence with F. R. Beckett, a Maidstone cycle agent, regarding a cycle returned after 2 months in poor condition on the pretext of poor workmanship. Dan sought compensation of £1 and said he would probably have to re-enamel it. It is unclear how the dispute was settled.[6]

Dan ceased to be a member of the North Road Cycling Club in July. This is perhaps not surprising as there is no record of him having raced for nearly five years, and it was a racing man's club. He had obviously moved on to focus on restoring his business which, according to his 1896 catalogue, had a phenomenal year (in 1895). Also changes had taken place in the Club: *"Momentous events and decisions marked the beginning of the year"*, which included his friend 'Faed' Wilson stepping down from the position of Club President, and this may have had something to do with it.[7]

At about this time Richard Tingey left the Ivel Cycle Company and started his own business making 'Rowe' cycles in Peterborough. J. W. Rowe and M. F. Rowe were vice-presidents of the Peterborough B. C., so it appears there may have been a partnership. Tingey's Indemniture of Apprenticeship contained a restrictive covenant not to engage in a similar trade to Dan's within a radius of 15 miles and this undertaking was not limited to the term of the apprenticeship but Peterborough is greater than 15 miles from Biggleswade. Subsequently he went to work for Milner's in Liverpool as Works Manager. Perhaps on a recommendation

73. ALBONE, DAN, Ivel Cycle Works, Biggleswade, Beds.

28 and 30 in. No. 1 Roadster Safety, Clincher tyres	£16	10	0
28 and 30 in. No. 2 Light Roadster Safety, Clincher tyres, Grose gear case	16	15	0
28 and 30 in. No. 2 Light Roadster Safety, detachable pneumatic tyres	15	0	0
28 and 30 in. No. 2 Light Roadster Safety, Clincher tyres, Carter detachable gear case	17	10	0
28 and 30 in. No. 2A Road Racer Safety, Clincher tyres, hollow rims, Grose gear case	17	15	0
28 and 30 in. No. 2A Road Racer Safety, Dunlop tyres, hollow rims, Grose gear case	17	15	0

Fig.112: From the Stanley Show list

1   Supplement to *Wheeling*, November 27th 1895, page 11.
2   *The Road*, January 1st 1895.
3   *Bedfordshire Standard*, March 22nd 1895.
4   *Bedfordshire Mercury*, July 27th 1895.
5   *Bicycling News*, November 26th 1895.
6   Bedfordshire & Luton Archives Service, Hooper and Fletcher records, ref: HF 20/344/5.
7   *Fifty Years of Road Riding – The History of the North Road Cycling Club.*

by Mills who hailed from Liverpool. While there he invented a combined cycle brake and free wheel (Patent No. 1899/5213). Later it seems he became works manager at Components (Ariel).

The eighth meeting of the Institute of British Carriage Manufacturers was held in August at Tunbridge Wells. Dan was invited to attend and he was elected an associate member of the Institute. Papers were read on the various improvements to carriages, including ball bearings, the latter being discussed at length. Dan was called upon to explain the working of the 'Ivel' carriage ball bearings, and among the exhibits was the 'Ivel' ball bearing axle box for wooden wheels. The President, in his address, said:

"The great aim in life is to reduce friction to a minimum, and the pneumatic tyre affords great assistance in this direction, but it seems to me that in the efforts to reduce friction we have not devoted to ball bearings or roller axles the attention they deserve." [8]

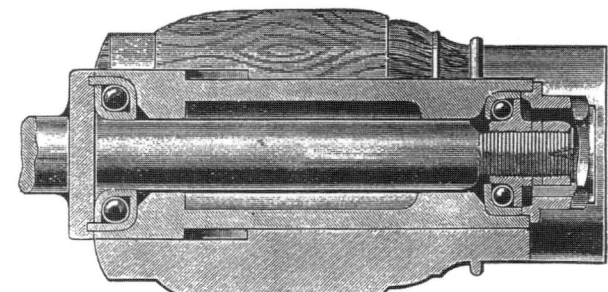

Fig.113: Ball-bearing Axle Box for Wooden Wheels

As well as being used by the London Improved Cab Company, the axle boxes were also fitted by a number of the landed gentry, including the Duke of Bedford, and the principle was utilised by the G.N. and L. & N.W. Railway.

8   *Bedfordshire Standard*, August 30th 1895.

1896 Made Specially to Order

Dan's 1896 catalogue revealed machines of similar pattern to the previous year. That they were individually made is revealed by this note in the catalogue:

"Most of my Machines are made specially to order, thus giving more satisfaction to the Purchaser and myself. All I require is the inside measurement of leg and the weight of the rider."

There is also an interesting comment with regard to his plating facilities:

Fig.114: 1896 Trade Mark

"All kinds of nickel plating done on the premises. I also have a special plant for silvering such articles as forks, spoons, cruets, trays, etc."

There was no longer a London depot but either Dan or his representative, George Course, would visit London once or twice each week. Further, the train service was such that a machine could be despatched from London to be in Biggleswade to be attended to in little more than an hour.

The No. 1 'Ivel Roadster' *"for Touring and General Purposes"* continued to be offered with 28 in. driving wheel and 30 in. steerer. It was priced at £16 10s.

The No. 2 'Ivel Light Roadster' was ten pounds lighter at 29 lb. It cost £15.15s.

The No. 3 'Ivel Road Racer' and No. 4 'Ivel Path Racer' were lighter still at 25 lb. and 20½ lb. respectively.

The No. 5 'Ivel Lady's Safety' was again offered with 28 in. wheels front and rear. It was priced at £17.

The No. 6 'Ivel Tricycle' was offered as a convertible with *"detachable stay for gent's use"*. It was priced at £26.

The No. 7 'Ivel Roadster' was effectively an 1895 model and priced at £14 *"on account of having in stock a large quantity of machined parts which I have decided to make up throughout this season."*

At the Stanley Show, Dan exhibited 12 machines:

"Dan Albone, Biggleswade, will have an exhibit consisting of six ladies' and six gentlemen's Ivel safeties, in praise of which it is unnecessary to say anything at this period of the cycling history of the world. He will also show a pair of Ivel patent ball-bearing boxes for wood wheels of any vehicle, and a pair of carriage wheels with cycle spokes and ball bearings." [1] and

"The ever smiling Dan Albone makes a very fair display indeed, with almost a dozen Ivels. He is one of the few exhibitors in the Hall who venture to retain a 30 in. steering wheel; but he does not pin his faith exclusively to it, as in some ladies machines he gives equal 28's. The Ivel is little altered from last year. The chief attractions about the stand are the Ivel ball bearing box for ordinary carriages. This is a massive affair in itself, and the pair of carriage wheels, which are shown fitted, are seldom still, the public taking quite a childish delight in keeping them moving. Of course, Dan has got his child carrier, or, as it is popularly called, kid carrier, which, however, we are glad to say, has never been a popular fitting to a cycle." [2]

There was a reference in another Show report that on the 'Ivel' stand there was displayed a beautiful little safety for Lord Napier of Magdala.[3] It was said this was a duplicate of one that Dan had made for his son Stanley.

Fig.115: Dan holding riders on a quad

(courtesy Biggleswade History Society)

1   Supplement to *Wheeling*, November 18th 1896, page 4.
2   Supplement to *Wheeling*, November 25th 1896, page 21.
3   Cycling.

The 'Ivel's at the Show were noted as being almost identical with the previous years' pattern.[4] However all machines on the Show stand had been sold to persons of title or distinction and labelled for all to see.

Dan collaborated with William Crawley of Brampton, Huntingdonshire, to patent a lathe chuck particularly for use in cycle manufacture (Patent No. 1896/24388).

The photograph below (Fig.116) shows Dan riding in Biggleswade High Street with Drum Clock in background. The Drum Clock was made in 1884 by clockmakers Richard Cawse and John Robert Jefferies. It was fixed on the original Post Office at 53 High Street, but belonged to the town of Biggleswade. A new postmaster, Richard E. Thomas was appointed in 1897 and asked the Urban District Council to move the clock as it was close to his principal bedroom and could only be reached for winding and maintenance with his permission. The clock was moved to the Town Hall in March 1898 and has been there ever since; much appreciated by the townspeople. In 1993 it was badly damaged by vandals and subsequently repaired by clockmaker Peter Fletcher at a cost of £2,500 borne by the Town Council.

Dan obtained an order to supply Bedfordshire Constabulary with six cycles as the following from the Chief Constable illustrates:

"I beg to inform you that your tender for six Bicycles for the Bedfordshire Constabulary, the back wheel to be fitted with thickened tubes for the tyres and including lamps and all other requisites, for £11 each, has been accepted. I will write at a future date concerning loan machines for men to learn to ride on. I do not wish the machines sent to the various Stations before the beginning of next month." [5]

Fig.117: The Ivel Works 1896. An Ordinary wheel is mounted above the sign.

One May morning at 4 am, Elizabeth was astonished to see Dan up and dressing and was told that he must go down to the Office and put a design down on paper for an agricultural motor which would be a great improvement on horses or traction engines. More was to come in 1902.

Fig.116: Dan riding in Biggleswade High Street, c.1896 with Drum Clock in background.

4   *The Irish Wheelman*, November 24th 1896.

5   Bedfordshire & Luton Archives Service, Ref. QEV 1/2, February 15th 1896.

1897 Riding the Cycling Boom

At the Stanley Show Dan exhibited 12 rear driving safeties and no tandems or tricycles.[1] It was noted that Dan had decided to fit some of his mounts with disc-adjusting hubs.[2] Also the tread had been reduced slightly on all machines.[3] Bicycling News commented:

Fig.118: New Trade Mark

"The fact that he does such a big recommendation business is a sufficient guarantee of the reliability of the wares of this maker." [4]

Business was obviously good as, although general prices had not increased, Dan had increased his prices by an average of 6.6% as compared to the previous year with the Lady's Safety up 8.8%. He introduced a new trade mark which remained in use through to 1906 (Fig. 118). Dan was riding the cycling boom.

The No. 1 'Ivel Roadster' continued to be offered with 28 in. driving wheel and 30 in. steerer, plus the option still of tangent or direct spokes. The weight had been trimmed by three pounds to 36 lb. It was now priced at £17.10s.

The No. 2 'Ivel Light Roadster' had also lost a pound at 28 lb and was now only offered with tangent spokes. It was though now claimed to be *"entirely suitable for touring purposes"*. It cost £16.16s.

The No. 3 'Ivel Road Racer' and No. 4 'Ivel Path Racer' appear to have been unchanged but, as with other models, the price had increased to £17.17s. and £18.18s. respectively.

The No. 5 'Ivel Lady's Safety' was changed slightly for 1897. Dan's catalogue states: *"I have decided to alter the pattern very little"*. However it

is clear that the frame design was changed, with the two down tubes being joined at a higher point. It was priced at £18.10s.

The No. 6 'Ivel Tricycle' was re-designed for 1897. No longer a convertible it had *"a light truss frame"* for use by either a lady or a gentleman at £28.

The No. 7 'Ivel Roadster' was again offered and built of *"last year's machined parts in stock"* It was priced at £14.14s.

Again Dan illustrated in his catalogue the Ball Bearing Carriage Wheels but this time had appended *"& Motor Car Wheels"* and added: *"During the past year I have also made a number of Motor Car Wheels on the same principle, sometimes leaving each hind hub longer to allow for the fixing of a sprocket wheel for driving purposes"*. His experiments towards making a motor car of his own had begun.

On September 29th 1897, Dan surrendered the leases to the Ivel Hotel and the Ivel Works to the lessors, Frederick Archdale and Charles Samuel Lindsell without apparently any payments being required (as it was not a terminable date as specified in the lease).[5] Dan continued in occupation paying a yearly rent of £55 for both properties. This arrangement may have been to facilitate a sale by the landlords in the next year.

Apart from making motor car wheels, Dan had earlier in the year acquired an Arnold sociable motor car, which he was using to the fullest extent. He decided to keep a stock of petrol for his own use and that of other motorists.

A report in the *Autocar* indicates that at this time his thoughts were turning to producing his own car. This was indeed the case as late in the year his prototype 'Ivel' was on the roads as this report demonstrates.

"Mr Dan Albone of Biggleswade, who has won 180 prizes as a Bicycle Rider and is well-known also as a Cycle Manufacturer, last week paid a visit to his uncle, Mr Henry Edwards, of Stamford. In company with his Electrical Engineer he performed the journey along the North Road on a Motor Car which he has perfected, and its performances

1   *The Cyclist Year Book*, 1898, p.108.
2   *Cycling*, November 27th 1897.
3   *The Scottish Wheel and Motor News*, November 24th 1897.
4   *Bicycling News*, November 26th 1896.

5   Bedfordshire & Luton Archives Service, Hooper and Fletcher records, ref: HF 20/376/3.

through the streets of Stamford caused a good deal of curiosity. Several gentlemen were favoured with short trips, and all bear testimony to the great comfort they experienced when riding.

It is a neat little phaeton to carry two persons, and is driven by a 1½ horse power motor, the force being obtained by little explosions of petroleum brought about by electric sparks, the effect being similar to a gas engine. The Power is transmitted by belts to a counter-shaft which is fitted with a balance geared at two different speeds and chains to drive the hind or driving wheels. The wheels are cycle spoked or tension, fitted with 1¾in. solid rubber, three feet to back or driving, and two feet to front or steering wheels, all on ball bearings.

The driver has full control of the carriage by various levers at hand, one for each speed a foot lever which actuates band brakes on each driving wheel. A powerful spoon applied to both wheels worked by a lever at the left hand, and a small lever which operates a throttle valve in the supply pipe of the Motor.

The carriage travels at from 10 to 16 miles an hour according to the state of the Roads. The electricity is stored in four accumulators. Mr Albone reached home without a single hitch through the heavy Roads after a journey in all of about 160 miles. On his way he called at the Fitzwilliam Meet at Abbotts Ripton Hall, the Motor causing considerable excitement among those assembled!" [6]

The fact that the prototype 'Ivel' Motor Car was on the roads by the end of the year is confirmed by Dan in his 1900-01 catalogue which states:

"Having now had some three or four years experience in the Motor Car industry .."

Another new invention was about to arrive.

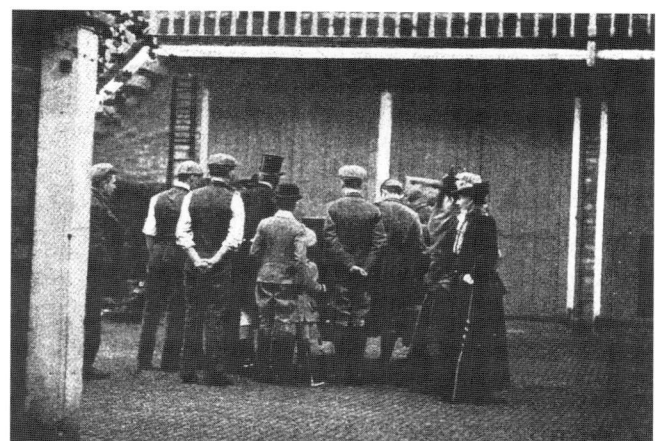

Fig.119: Great interest in the 'Ivel' Motor Car

(courtesy *Rutland and Stamford Mercury*, Jan. 7th 1898)

---

6   *Rutland and Stamford Mercury*, January 7th 1898.

1898 Enter the Motor Car

At the Stanley Show Dan exhibited 12 rear driving safeties and no tandems or tricycles.[1] These included two road racers and a racer. There were also ladies machines of a new pattern.[2]

His Motor Car had many new improvements, for example independent spring suspension, axle boxes, electric ignition so that the driver did not have to get out of the car to start the engine (there were four accumulators), and a great feature was that all control levers were within easy reach of the driver, while the steering was remarkably steady as the wheels could not be deflected by obstacles on the road. The wheels were cycle-spoked, fitted with 1¾ in. solid rubber, the front 24 in. dia. and the rear 36 in. dia.

The 'Ivel' Motor Car had a 1½ horse power engine. The power was transmitted by belts to a coun-ter-shaft which is fitted with a balance geared at two different speeds and chains to drive the rear wheels. Reverse gearing was also provided. With these advantages, and Dan's patent ball bearings, it was found that the 'Ivel' Motor Car was equal to other more powerful cars at very much less cost. The convenience of the driver was carefully studied, and noted that every part of the machinery could easily be reached so that all adjustments could be made with great ease.

Perhaps these developments led Dan to change his telegraphic address from "The Danneries" to "Dan Albone, Biggleswade".

It was reported:

"Dan Albone's motor car is becoming well known in many parts of the country other than Biggleswade ... Recently Dan took a trip to Stam-

---

131 ALBONE, DAN, Ivel Cycle Works, Biggleswade.

Description	£	s	d
28 and 28 in. No. 5 Ladies' Safety, geared 59 in., Dunlop tyres, Westwood hollow rims, Ivel gear case	£19	0	0
28 and 28 in. No. 5 Ladies' Safety, geared 56 in., Clincher tyres, Ivel gear case	18	10	0
28 and 28 in. No. 5 Ladies' Safety, geared 56 in., Clincher tyres, hollow jointless rims, Carter gear case	20	0	0
28 and 28 in. No. 5 Ladies' Safety, geared 56 in., Dunlop tyres, Westwood hollow rims, Bluemel gear case	19	10	0
28 and 28 in. No. 5 Ladies' Safety, geared 59 in., Fleuss tyres, jointless hollow rims, Ivel gear case	19	0	0
28 and 26 in. No. 5 Ladies' Safety, geared 58½ in., Clincher tyres, jointless hollow rims, Ivel gear case	19	0	0
30 and 28 in. No. 3 Gent.'s Road Racer Safety, geared 62 in., Clincher tyres, jointless hollow rims	17	17	0
30 and 28 in. No. 3 Gent.'s Road Racer Safety, geared 70 in., Palmer tyres, jointless hollow rims	17	17	0
30 and 28 in. No. 3 Gent.'s Road Racer Safety, geared 66½ in., Dunlop plain tyres, Westwood hollow rims, Carter gear case	19	15	0
30 and 28 in. No. 1 Gent.'s Roadster Safety, geared 59 in., Dunlop tyres, Westwood hollow rims, Ivel gear case	19	12	6
30 and 28 in. No. 2 Gent.'s Light Roadster Safety, geared 62 in., Fleuss tyres, jointless hollow rims, Carter gear case	20	0	0
30 and 28 in. No. 2 Gent.'s Light Roadster Safety, geared 62 in., Clincher tyres, jointless hollow rims, Carter gear case	20	10	0

Ivel Cycle Spoked Ball Bearing Carriage Wheels.
Ivel Patent Ball Bearing Box for ordinary vehicles with wood wheels.
Child Carrier.

Fig.120: Extract from Stanley Show catalogue

1   *The Cyclist's Indispensable*, 1899, p.191.
2   *The Irish Cyclist*, November 30th 1898.

ford and back, a distance of 160 miles [including demonstration trips, etc.], and though the roads were muddy and rough over a great portion of the way, the journey was most successfully carried through. The other afternoon at the invitation of Mr Albone, a representative of the Express had a most enjoyable run on it. The route taken was through Sutton - here Dan did a good piece of steering over the narrow footbridge, the water being too deep and the condition of the bed of the stream being too doubtful to allow the car to go through it - on to Potton, Gamlingay, through Waresley and home by another route. Over stones, mud and ruts the car seemed to travel alike, and the pace kept up through this ride fell little short of 10 to 15 miles an hour. There was no hitch from start to finish, and the enjoyment of the run was completed by the kind loan at Potton of an overcoat - we foolishly started without one - by Mr Fowler of the Rose and Crown hotel. The run we have mentioned strengthens the opinion we have always had that we are within measurable distance of the time when motor cars will be as common as horse and trap." [3]

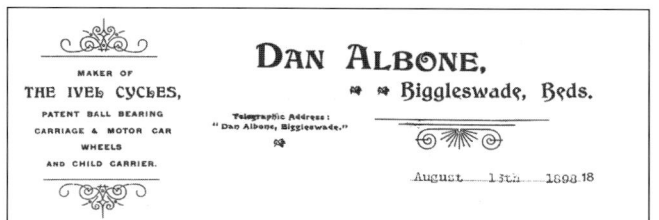

Fig.121: Dan Albone letter head 1898

(courtesy Biggleswade History Society)

Not all Dan's motoring excursions were as successful. On one occasion the motor car broke down and had to be towed home by a horse hired from a farmer. As the vehicle had no lights, there were many difficulties, and the horse seemed hard to manage. When Dan at long last reached home he found that the farmer had not bridled the horse properly.

In 1898 on February 21st the Ivel Hotel, the Royal Oak Inn, and other properties then owned by Wells & Co. were put up for sale. This is the text of the notice of sale:

"The IVEL HOTEL, Public-House, Bridge Street, Biggleswade. A substantial brick and tiled House, well-placed and of attractive appearance, containing good Entrance Passage and Enclosed Bar; Billiard Room, Private Sitting Room and Coffee Room; Tap Room, Larder, Bar Parlour, Kitchen and Scullery; Cellar in Basement; Six Bed Rooms, Box Room and w.c. above. Roadway at side of House, and Gates admitting to large Yard; also an Inner Yard, with Offices, Factory, Engine-house, Sheds and Buildings, and two large Gardens.

On the other side of the river is a meadow of about 1 acre 3 rods 1 pole. The whole let to Mr D. Albone on leases at rents amounting to £55 per annum.

NB. A Common Right attached to this property (i.e. a right to graze livestock on the common)."

The Royal Oak, a much larger establishment let to William Albone, was described as an *"old Coaching House"*, and let for some reason at a nominal rent of £20 per year. It was an ancient coaching inn first mentioned in 1669 and closed in 1970.

It is interesting to note that the Albone's did not buy either property as the whole brewery estate was sold to George Winch of Chatham in 1899 and he set up Wells and Winch Ltd. It was never the intention to sell the estate in lots, so there was no opportunity for tenants to buy.

Dan's Motor Car was in frequent use, appearing at the seat of the Earl and Countess Cowper in Wrest Park, near Silsoe, where he treated notable persons to a drive. It was also noted that on another occasion he drove from Biggleswade to Stamford, a distance of 46 miles in 3 hr. 5 min., his son and a small quantity of luggage being carried. [4]

Fig.122: Dan with Lord Compton at Biggleswade Fête 1898

(courtesy Biggleswade History Society)

---

3   *Bedfordshire Express*, January 1898

4   *The Autocar*, December 3rd 1898.

1899 First Motor Car Sold!

At the Stanley Show, Dan exhibited a varied form of Lady's Safety bicycle having a curved upper down tube and a straight lower down tube.[1] However the double curved tube model was also available.

Fig.123: Dan and Elizabeth in Victoria Combination

(courtesy Biggleswade History Society)

Fig.124: 'Ivel' motor car and Albone family

(courtesy Biggleswade History Society)

Dan was now motoring around in a Victoria Combination car (Fig.123), having presumably disposed of the Arnold. It seems that the development of his own car had taken some time as it was not complete by October 1899.[2] However, it seems that it was completed by early November as Dan applied for a Motor Stand at the Stanley Show but was too late.[3] The car was immediately purchased by the Duke of Bedford, who was a good friend of Dan's and regularly invited him to dinner.

Fig.125: Elizabeth in Benz car with cyclists

(courtesy Biggleswade History Society)

Fig.126: A motor rally outside the Ivel Hotel, *Bedfordshire Times*, April 28th 1899

(courtesy Biggleswade History Society)

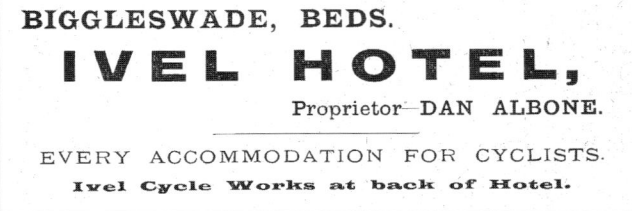

BIGGLESWADE, BEDS.
IVEL HOTEL,
Proprietor—DAN ALBONE.

EVERY ACCOMMODATION FOR CYCLISTS.
Ivel Cycle Works at back of Hotel.

Fig.127: Ivel Hotel advertisement

(courtesy Biggleswade History Society)

1   *C.T.C. Gazette*, January 1899, p.38.
2   *The Motor Car Journal*, October 20th 1899.
3   *The Autocar*, November, 25th 1899.

Dan Albone – Cyclist, Inventor, and Manufacturer

Fig.128: Stanley riding his bicycle on the Great North Road, 1899

Fig.129: 'Ivel' advertisement 1899

Fig.130: Biggleswade & District C. C. at Castle Ashby, July 1899 (Dan is sitting to the right of the triplet)

(courtesy Biggleswade History Society)

1900 Alwyne Patricia Edwards

Dan's first catalogue of the new century covered two years, 1900 and 1901. Presumably this was because it was issued late. Possibly it was because he had been much more involved in developing his 'Ivel' Motor Car, so much so that he was now able to announce:

"Having now had some three or four years experience in the Motor Car industry, I am pleased to state that I am now in a position to make and supply complete IVEL Motor Cars."

Fig.131: Dan, Elizabeth, Stanley and friend (courtesy Biggleswade History Society)

And so the 'Ivel Motor Car' figured prominently in his catalogue. In addition Dan offered the Ideal Car, fitted with a 3 h.p. Benz engine, and the Victoria Combination, fitted with 2¼ h.p. De Dion Bouton engine. This was fortunate as the cycle boom was over and prices had dropped.

Reviewing the machines now available, a Bowden cable operated rear brake, newly introduced to the market in 1899, was now an option.

The No. 1 'Ivel Roadster' continued to be offered with 28 in. driving wheel and 30 in. steerer but no longer the option of direct spokes. It was now priced at £16.

The No. 2 'Ivel Light Roadster' appeared to be unchanged and cost £16.

The No. 3 'Ivel Road Racer' and No. 4 'Ivel Path Racer' also appear to have been unchanged. They were priced at £15.10s. and £16 respectively.

The No. 5 'Ivel Lady's Safety' was unchanged. It was priced at £16.

There was the new No. 6 'Ivel Lady's Safety'. This had a curved upper down tube and was offered to meet customer demand. It too was priced at £16.

Whereas on previous occasions Dan had offered machines built of last years' stock, with the price reduced accordingly, he now offered a No. 5C Lady's Safety and a No.7 Roadster Safety. These he described as:

"Owing to the demand for Machines at a somewhat less price than that of the highest grade" and *"They are practically last season's patterns fitted with "B" Clincher tyres, and a little cheaper saddle, gear case, etc., than usually fitted"*.

The Tricycle was now the No.8 and priced at £28 but otherwise unchanged.

On March 17th, 1900 a daughter was born to Dan and Elizabeth. She was christened Alwyne Patricia Edwards, after Lord Alwyne Compton, a close friend of the family.

On May 17th, Richard E. Thomas the postmaster, telephoned the news that the siege of Mafeking had been lifted. Dan had organised dinners and

Fig.132: A lady riding her 'Ivel'

(courtesy Biggleswade History Society)

'send-offs' to volunteers during the South African war. He let the town know by sounding the klaxon at his works and went out in his motor car to spread the news to the townsfolk.

Everybody in town knew Dan Albone, a striking figure who was never without his buttonhole; a fresh carnation picked from his greenhouse each

Fig.133: The 'Ivel' Motor Car

(courtesy *The Gentleman*)

morning by the gardener. He was a great local character. He was a staunch conservative, and an ardent supporter of Lord Alwyne Compton, a former M.P. He was Secretary (since 1896) and later Chairman of the Licensed Victuallers' Association (in Biggleswade) and a great enthusiast. It is recorded that many local events would have fallen flat but for his support, spirit and organising power.

Dan was now working mainly on motor car design and, as with his cycles, it is likely that each vehicle he produced was different in detail, being built to order. He exhibited an 'Ivel Motor Car' in London; the motor was a single cylinder Benz-type (8 h.p.) with electric ignition. The vehicle had pneumatic tyres and independent suspension. The steering was by means of a lever on the right hand side (subsequent models had steering wheels). The car weighed about 9 cwt and could achieve seventeen miles an hour.

Mr R. C. Vyner of Newby Hall, Ripon, was one of Dan's satisfied customers. Another was Captain Fane. He bought an 'Ivel Landaulette' (Fig.134), a five-seater (including a seat for a servant at the back). This model was very much a carriage with a motor, but at 8 h.p. the double cylinder petrol en-

gine could cope with the extra load. It is reported the motor car cost £490.[1]

Another customer for the motor car, Mr Bateman Brown of Huntingdon, was so pleased with his car that he gave a dinner at the Ivel Hotel on August 11th for all the men at the Ivel Works.[2]

At the Stanley Show, eleven cycles were displayed nearly all of which had sold labels on them bearing names of distinguished clients. A lady's cycle, finished in black with gold lining and plated rims, was fitted with Bowden brakes, front and rear, and a Manchester two-speed gear. There was a truss-frame tricycle too, suitable for either sex. The Chater-Lea was the selected make of free-wheel. Also, it seems, at the Show was the 'Ivel' Motor Car:

"The latest and most interesting production from Biggleswade is the Ivel motor with "landaulette" body, which departs somewhat from the usual type, inasmuch as the frame is constructed of steel tubing, and the arrangement of the tubes is such that all the various strains to which the frame is exposed, both from road vibration and the motor itself, are scientifically taken up, a cantilever principle being adopted. A double cylinder petrol motor of eight horse-power is employed, of English make and with electric ignition. Every detail is studied so that the occupants of the car are entirely insulated from motor vibration and that caused by road inequalities. Moreover, a different body can at any time be attached to the frame in a short time, so

Fig.134: The 'Ivel Landaulette' (Reg. design 355912) (courtesy Biggleswade History Society)

1   *The Motor News*, January 1901.
2   *Bedfordshire Standard*, August 17th 1900.

that the purchaser may practically have two or three cars to one frame and motor. Three-speed gear and a reverse are embodied. Altogether the Ivel motor is fitted up in a style worthy of the name." [3]

Another review stated:

"Some time ago it was duly chronicled in these columns that a new motor-car was in course of construction at the works of Mr. Dan Albone, Biggleswade, Beds. We were afforded an opportunity of inspecting the new car ere it was completed, but in view of the many special features it comprises we postponed a description of the vehicle until it had been finished and put through its paces on the road. As will be seen ... the car is arranged to carry four persons. One of the special features is the under-frame, which is constructed of steel tubing after the same style of that of the ordinary cycle, the arrangement of the tubes being such that the various strains to which the frame is exposed, both from the road vibration and that caused by the motor itself, are scientifically taken up, a double cantilever system being adopted. The frame is car-

Fig.136: 'Ivel' ball bearing cap (courtesy David Bray)

ried upon four spiral springs, those from the rear axle being contained in steel cylinders, which are raked slightly rear-wards, so that the action of the springs may co-incide with the lines of vibration from the wheels.

These cylinders serve another very important purpose. The sliding pistons upon which the springs act are sufficiently long to obtain an ample bearing surface in the cylinders, and thus prevent any movement of one spring taking place without a corresponding motion on the part of the other. The object of this arrangement is to secure that the chainwheels are always in positive alignment, so that the wear upon the chains and the friction set up are greatly reduced. The front axle springs are vertical, and are designed to allow the wheels to rise or fall to accommodate themselves to the inequalities of the roads traversed.

The motor, which is of the Benz horizontal type of 3 h.p., with water jacket and electric ignition, is located about the centre of the frame; its position is exactly reverse to that adopted in the Benz cars, that is to say, the combustion chamber, not the flywheel, is located at the rear of the frame, the motor thus running in the same direction as the car. Two speeds forward and one reverse motion are provided, the power being transmitted by straight belts from the motor shaft to an intermediary shaft behind the rear axle, and from the intermediary to the hind road wheels by duplicate Renold "silent" chains.

The 'body' of the car, is mounted upon four C springs, and is entirely separate from the frame and working parts. The occupants are thus completely insulated from the vibration, not only of the road, but from that due to the motor. Through the floor of the car, in the centre, rises a tripod of three tubes, which carry a round fibre flat plate, upon the face of which appearing the variable speed gear. The plate is slotted, and through it pass two long levers,

Fig.135: A lady with her 'Ivel'

(courtesy Biggleswade History Society)

3   *Bicycling News*, November 28th 1900.

Fig.137: The Ivel Works from across the river

one being that of the reversing gear, and the other for applying the tyre brakes. This lever, when pushed forward, automatically opens a switch, thus breaking the electric circuit and so stopping the motor. The steering is controlled by means of a handle and a disc, after the manner adopted in the Benz cars, but the standard is located well on the right-hand side, the connection to the front wheel steering lever being made underneath the frame by means of a chain.

Provision is made that the motor-car can be started from the driver's seat, it being possible to stop the car and start again at any time without having to get out of the car. Both water and petrol gauges are fixed in front of the driver, and everything is so placed that all the working parts can be easily got at without undue trouble, and any adjustments which may have to be made can be done in a few minutes. The bearings of the wheels are very large ball bearings being employed wherever possible.

The main brakes are applied by the foot of the driver, and expand inside the drums formed by the chainwheels. These brakes, which take the form of double friction blocks, act both ways, so that, when on, the car cannot run backwards downhill. Both these brakes and those acting upon the tyres are provided with a compensating device, so that one side cannot be applied harder than the other. The petrol tank is carried under the front seat, and contains about nine gallons, while the water tank is also large, enabling the car to run a hundred miles without a fresh supply of water being required. Four cooling tubes with large mouths pass through

the tank, and as the tank is well above the motor, no pumps are required to maintain the circulation. The chains and the motor are entirely enclosed ... so that the amount of cleaning required is reduced to a minimum.

The accumulators and induction coil are carried on the car in a box placed at the rear, and all the necessary tools are also provided for in this arrangement. The car is fitted with cycle-type wheels and pneumatic tyres: it weighs complete about 9 cwt. and is speeded up to a maximum of from 16 to 17 miles per hour. Mr. Albone's object having been the production, not of a racing car, but of a comfortable, easy-running vehicle, capable of maintaining a fair speed. In the course of a conversation with Mr. Albone at the Stanley Show last week, he informed us that the car had been subjected to a number of trials, the results of which have exceeded his expectations, both as to the hill-climbing capabilities and to the absence of vibration." [4]

The reports of the 'Ivel' Motor Car vary in certain respects as regards specification. For example, in 1898 the engine was stated to be of 1½ h.p., later a 3 h.p. Benz engine. The 1900-01 catalogue refers to a 5 h.p. engine of English manufacture, and another report refers to an 8 h.p. engine of English manufacture. Likewise there is reference in the 1900-01 catalogue to the provision of two-speed or three-speed gearing. It is possible that all are correct either as evolutionary steps in development or according to customer specification. We shall never know for sure as detailed records have not survived and no 'Ivel' Motor Car is known to exist.

Fig.138: The Blacksmith's Shop in the Ivel Works

4   *The Gentleman*, December 8th 1900.

Fig.139: Dan with Elizabeth cycling across Biggleswade Square for the camera c.1900.

(courtesy Biggleswade History Society)

1901 The Motor Bicycle

In 1901 Dan now offered the 'Ivel Motor Bicycle'. This machine followed the lines of the Minerva and Excelsior motor bicycles. Based on a strengthened bicycle, the 1.5 h.p. Minerva engine used a twisted raw hide belt to drive the rear wheel. This machine had electric ignition, although it could be pedalled to start, and weighed about 70 lbs. The motor was fitted with a float-feed carburettor and automatic oiling. Two powerful brakes were fitted. The speed could be anything from a walking pace up to twenty five miles per hour. Examples were supplied to Lord Alwyne Compton, M.P., the Rt. Hon. George Kempe, M.P., and the Rt. Hon. Andrew Graham Murray, Lord Advocate for Scotland.

Fig.140: The 'Ivel' Motor Bicycle

Commenting on its use, not all the reports were glowing as *The Cyclist* had this to say:

"It is rather a task to mount or dismount a motor bicycle ... with a diamond frame. The rider has to lift one leg a considerable height to clear the connecting rod, and in a 'tight corner', in which we all get sometimes, trouble may result." [1]

Dan then came up with a lady's version (Fig.141); again the dropped frame suitable for a skirted rider, and many safety features were added,

Fig.141: The Lady's 'Ivel' Motor Bicycle

such as shielding the motor and belt, and guarding any parts likely to become heated. In practice, the refinements made the lady's motor cycle a better machine. Mrs Mary Kennard, an author, of The Barn, Market Harborough, chose one and wrote a fascinating account:

"The bicycle, I may tell you, resembles an ordinary safety, only built on stronger lines, but it is so neat throughout that the rider escapes being stared at – a great point in my estimation. Mr. Albone had carefully thought out a variety of details and has effectually shielded both belt and motor, so that one's dress can neither catch nor get unduly heated. Also, by some very efficient nickel guards placed over the engine and exhaust pipe, one can ride without having one's clothes smothered in grease. This, I can assure you, is a great point for a lady. Dust, of course, is not to be avoided, but it is easily brushed off and does not inflict permanent damage on one's attire.

I stipulated for a spring seat-pillar, and find it the greatest comfort, as it absorbs nearly all vibra-

Fig.142: Richard Tingey on an 'Ivel' Motor Bicycle

tion and adds enormously to the comfort of the rider. I did not care to depend upon a single accumulator, and had a battery-box fitted capable of holding a couple. Then I ordered a stout luggage-carrier fixed over the rear wheel of the machine, and on this I strap a bag, containing a waterproof cape, and, if I go far afield, a spare can of petrol. I may mention that I have a spray carburettor, and can do about seventy-five miles on three-quarters of a gallon of petrol. Another source of joy is a sight-feed lubricator containing five

---

1   *The Cyclist*, June 4th 1902.

Fig.143: The Ladies 'Ivel' Motor Bicycle

charges of oil. I have the satisfaction of seeing, when I pump the oil to the crank-chamber that it goes to the desired direction. The Clincher tyres are excellent, I could not wish for better, but in order to avoid the bother of puncture I ordered self-sealing air tubes. I rejoiced greatly at this when the other day I picked a sharp pin out of my back tyre. My coil is placed under the saddle, well tucked away, and I further protect it with an india-rubber covering. Every terminal is made secure with wax, and the wires are all well insulated. Now about the levers. I daresay you would think there are a good many when you begin, but it is astonishing how soon the moving of them to and fro becomes automatic. At the same time, I strongly advocate that they should all be placed on the handlebar within easy reach of the hands. In my machine I have the compression lever on the left and the regulating one on the right, but both are fitted some little distance beneath the head. Although the levers are made extra long, when going at high speed it is tiresome

Fig.144: 'Ivel' Motor Tricycle with trailer and Motor Car with Dan and Stanley

(courtesy Biggleswade History Society)

having to manipulate them. Mr. Albone has therefore promised me to mount the regulator lever on the handlebar, close to the right hand, which actuates the front brake, the advance ignition, and exhaust valve lifter.

To the left are assigned the switch, the rear brake, and the bell, and I can assure you that, just at first, one wishes one possessed an extra hand. To start the bicycle you mount as on an ordinary safety, but I may tell you that, owing to the difference in weight, this feat requires a little practice. It is not wise to attempt to start up a steep hill, but on the level or down hill the knack is quickly acquired. Once off, the sensation of sailing away, free-wheel-

Fig.145: The 'Ivel' Motor Tricycle

ing all the time, is most enjoyable, especially on a hot summer's day, when people feel indisposed to take much active exercise. Mr. Albone is an adept in the art of teaching, and inspired me with such confidence that I rode from his residence at Biggleswade, some fifty miles, entirely alone. I do not mind confessing that I felt exceedingly adventurous, and inwardly wondered what on earth I should do were anything untoward to happen. But I consoled myself with the reflection that nothing ever does happen to a brand new machine, with batteries fully charged and all in spick-and-span order.

They came later on. My belief was justified, for I had the most enjoyable ride home. I found that my little motor got up every hill I came across. If the hill were extra steep I pedalled a little to prevent the engine from slowing down too much, and experienced no difficulty in negotiating every ascent I encountered. Of course, one cannot get everything united. If you go in for a high-powered bicycle, it requires much more expert handling, adds extra weight to the machine, uses more petrol, and the vibration is materially increased. Now, I dislike the vibration excessively, and prefer occasionally pedalling a few strokes to being bumped and jolted about. I had enough of that with my De Dion tricycle. I do not think a lady wants a bigger horse-power than one and a half, unless she lives in an abnormally hilly country.

I greatly prefer the motor bicycle to the three-

Fig.146: 'Ivel' Motor Tricycle

(courtesy Biggleswade History Society)

wheeler. Certainly something is sacrificed to safety and stability, but the gain in handiness, in weight, and having only a single track is enormous. It is possible to wheel the bicycle about and even to push it up a steep incline, if necessary, by opening the compression and exhaust valve lifter; but I defy any woman to propel, by her sheer unaided strength, a tricycle weighing over 2 cwt. Having tried it, I can speak with authority on this point. In case of a real breakdown, too, it is a great consolation to know that, by taking off the belt one can pedal a few miles to the nearest station and not be stranded hopelessly. I quite think that in time a certain number of ladies will be seen riding motor bicycles.

I do not suppose they will ever become universal, because only a limited number of women will take the trouble to learn how to manage their engine and master the numerous points requiring attention. A great many ladies ride bicycles who have not an idea how to mend a puncture, or even to blow up their own tyres. I have seen them arrive at our local cycle agent's and request to have this simple office performed for them. Such fair cyclists as these had better not turn their thoughts towards the machine with a motor. But girls ... with plenty of "go" and nerve, accustomed to the hunting field

and with sufficient intelligence to take an interest in mechanical matters, will very soon overcome the initial difficulties." [2]

At the annual dinner of the Biggleswade and District Licensed Victuallers Association, Dan was presented with an illuminated address and gold watch having resigned after five years as its secretary. The address read:

"Dear Sir – We, the members of the above named Association, have learnt with much regret that owing to pressure of business and other important duties devolving upon you it has been necessary for you to resign the position of Honorary Secretary, which you have occupied since its formation to the great satisfaction of us all. We cannot allow you to vacate this office without an expression of our appreciation of your valuable services, in token of which we have much pleasure in asking your acceptance of this address, together with the accompanying gold watch. We trust, however, that although prevented from continuing as our Honorary Secretary, you may long continue to render us your valuable services in other directions. Signed on behalf of the Association, Samuel Wheatley, Chairman; Charles Marsom, Treasurer."

On Peace Day, Dan had the misfortune to lose one of his prized gold medals. He offered a considerable reward for its recovery. Nothing was heard for some time until it was found in the window slot of a brougham being repaired at Messrs Saunders Bros., coach builders of the Market Square.

At the Stanley Show, nine bicycles were shown of which three were Motor Bicycles. One of those three was a lady's Motor Bicycle.

Fig.147: Dan, with Stanley in the background. (courtesy Biggleswade History Society)

---

2   *The Car*, August 27th 1902. Later in that year Mrs Kennard advertised the Ivel for sale for £38 "as new, reliable, genuine machine."

Fig.148: Monty Holbein on an 'Ivel' Motor Bicycle

(courtesy Biggleswade History Society)

Fig.149: Monty Holbein at speed pacing a tandem

(courtesy Biggleswade History Society)

"IVEL" THE MOTOR BICYCLE.

THE most simple and practical Motor Cycle on the market. It has stood severe tests and can be thoroughly relied upon. The weight is equally distributed between the two wheels, the steering is not at all affected, and there is no unpleasant shaking to the rider, or any vibration to the machine. Compare the "IVEL" MOTOR BICYCLE with others and you will find it stands out far ahead as regards appearance, for most others are ungraceful, heavy, badly balanced, and altogether unsightly machines. Any ordinary intelligent person can ride and control an "IVEL" MOTOR BICYCLE in three lessons. Purchasers are given lessons free of cost by a competent instructor, on machines kept in stock for the purpose, and no pains are spared to give the purchaser every satisfaction, both as regards the lessons and the new machine specially made for him.

PRICE - - - £45.

High Grade 'Ivel' Safety Bicycles complete with Pneumatic Tyres from £12 upwards.

A number of shop-soiled and second-hand good Machines to be disposed of at very low prices.

All kinds of repairs to any make machine done on the premises, including plating and enamelling. Re-plating with pure silver also done on the premises.

INSPECTION INVITED.

Price Lists, with full particulars, sent post free on application.

DAN ALBONE,

Ivel Cycle and Motor Car Works, BIGGLESWADE.

Fig.150: November 1901 advertisement

1902 The Ivel Agricultural Motor

At the Crystal Palace Motor Show, Dan exhibited his Motor Bicycle but it seems not his Motor Car.[1]

Fig.151: Inside the Ivel Works c.1902

(courtesy Biggleswade History Society)

The No. 1 'Ivel Roadster' still continued to be offered with 28 in. driving wheel and 30 in. steerer which was now becoming a less than modern offering as the roads improved. Although the catalogue illustration had not been changed, the specification now offered two rim brakes and free or fixed wheel. Foot rests appear to have been discontinued commensurate with the brake upgrade. This model was

Fig.152: Dan on prototype 'Ivel' Agricultural Motor

Fig.153: The prototype Agricultural Motor

now offered with an extra top tube for exceptionally tall and heavy riders. It was still priced at £16.

The No. 2 'Ivel Light Roadster' also had two rim brakes and, as with the Roadster, standard gearing had been increased. It too cost £16.

The No. 3 'Ivel Road Racer' and No. 4 'Ivel Path Racer' appear to have been unchanged apart from the former being offered with a higher gear as standard. They were priced at £13.10s. and £14 respectively, both prices being reductions.

The No. 5 'Ivel Lady's Safety' appears to be un-

Fig.154: An early test

changed apart from being offered with two rim brakes and free or fixed wheel. It was priced at £16. Likewise the No. 6 'Ivel Lady's Safety' with curved top tube. It too was priced at £16.

Both the No. 5C Lady's Safety and the No.7 Roadster Safety were much the same as before, being offered with plunger front brake, but at reduced prices of £11.17s.6d. and £11.10s. respectively. A Bowden rear brake and a freewheel cost extra.

The No. 8 Tricycle was now priced at a reduced £25 and unchanged.

---

1   *Bedfordshire Express*, February 22nd 1902.

Star attraction in the catalogue was the Gent's and Lady's Motor Bicycle. These were priced at £45 and £47 respectively. The 1902 models had a more powerful engine with larger valves and other improvements to compression, sparking plug, trembler coil, etc. A rear attachment was available to carry a companion and a trailer could also be attached to carry a person.

We might conclude that sales had been weak and with much competition in the market it was not a viable proposition unless he obtained a specific order. Perhaps the motor car had been overtaken by events as other manufacturers brought out their own models and Dan had probably turned his attention to working on developing his tractor.

Fig.157: Name plate No.131, probably the 31st made.

In June, Dan was presented with a silver flask, as recognition of his services to the Bedfordshire Imperial Yeomanry. The flask was engraved "Presented to Dan Albone by the Officers, Beds. I.Y., 1902." The presentation was made by Captain and

Fig.155: The 'Ivel' Agricultural Motor, cover removed, engine side

So far as the 'Ivel' Motor Car was concerned, all the catalogue stated was *"I shall still be prepared to supply Motor Cars ...."*

Fig.156: Driving a Samuelson mower

Fig.158: The 'Ivel' Agricultural Motor, cover removed, transmission side

Fig.159: Pulling two reaping machines

Adjutant C. L. Graham. It is notable that Dan made many sales to former Army officers.

By November 1901, he had perfected his design of the tractor. Early in 1902 he had Phillips, his patent agent, apply for a patent at Chancery Lane in the City of London (No. 1902-3920).

The Ivel Agricultural Motor initially had an 8 h.p. twin-cylinder petrol-driven engine and weighed 17 cwt 71 lbs, even with its tank of water for cylinder cooling. Capable of hauling 2½ tons, it was light, powerful, very compact when compared with traction engines, and beautifully engineered. It could drive stationary machinery or work other implements. The make of engine was never officially revealed but is understood to have been supplied by Payne-Bates of Coventry or Aster.[2]

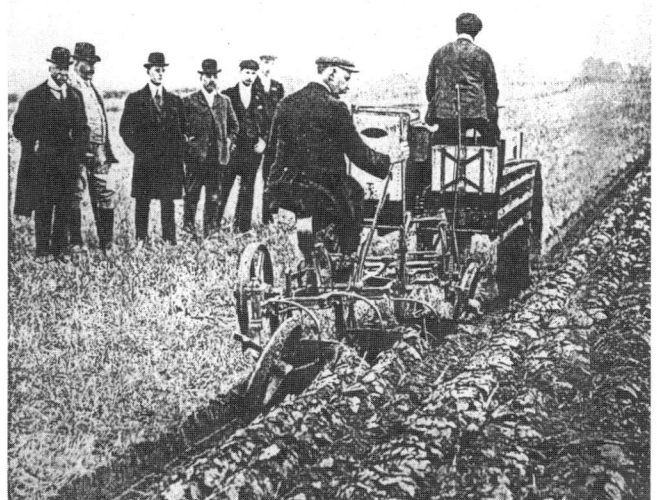

Fig.160: Pulling a three-furrow plough

George Farr, of Luton, answered an advertisement and was taken on as foreman for the tractor project. He was offered 6d per hour, but as a mechanics rate was then 4d per hour, he held out for and got 8d per hour.[3]

One of the early tractor trials was held in July 1902 by the invitation of Dan Albone and the kindness of Mr. C. Capon of Hill Farm, which lies between Biggleswade and Old Warden, who had placed a field of grass to be cut for hay at the dis-

Fig.161: Dan and Stanley with a two-furrow plough on demonstration

posal of Dan. A large company assembled to witness the trial of the new invention in taking round a mower. Amongst those present were Lord Alwyne Compton, MP, Mr. Edwards of Stamford, Mr. Capon and numerous farmers.

Fig.162: Returning from London with supplies of petrol

(courtesy *The Autocar*)

2   *Veteran and Vintage Magazine*
3   *Bedfordshire Times*, November 2nd 1956.

Fig.163: The 'Ivel' Agricultural Motor and implements on trial (Ivel Works in background)

The time announced for the trial was 12.30 and shortly after the motor was travelling round and around at the rate of 8 miles an hour, drawing a mower, and the grass was falling clean cut to the general satisfaction of everyone. For over an hour and a half the proceedings were watched with keen interest and not only was there no hitch in the working of the new machine, but no one had a word to say in disparagement of either its performance or its manifest capabilities.

Everyone appeared to be more than satisfied and the general opinion expressed was that this invention met exactly the want which had been felt for so long in agricultural circles. When finally the tractor was brought to a standstill amid the company, Dan

Fig.165: Mrs Loder with ladies 'Ivel' Motor Bicycle near Biggleswade

(courtesy Biggleswade History Society)

briefly introduced Lord Alwyne Compton who was heartily received. It was reported: *"He said he thought all would agree on one thing, and that was that they ought to pay a tribute to Dan Albone for his enterprise in working out that agricultural motor, because he had not the slightest doubt it had given him a great deal of thought and trouble and put him to much expense. He thought all in Bedfordshire and outside it owed him this debt.*

The machine was perfectly simple in its construction and therefore not likely to get out of order. It was well within its power and had not been strained anywhere by the work it had done, and as to whether it would be applicable to the farming industry, they could all form their own opinion, but he thought it would. Some of them remembered the tremendous fight against machinery because it was said it would take the bread out of poor people's mouths, but that objection did not exist any more

Fig.164: Dan in thought

because they had a difficulty in getting men to do the work. As far as agriculture was concerned, they had enough of competition to keep them awake, and if they were not to lag behind and machinery would help them, it seemed to him they ought to use it.

Of course, the only question that remained for them was what would the cost be. If it came within

Fig.166: Stanley with friend

their means, he did think it would be a vast gain for it would do the work of the horses on the farm and then go into the barn and do other work as well. It was a great stride in advance and if it came within their means - he spoke honestly - it would be a great boon.

He thought Dan recognised that as much as anyone and if he could only turn it out cheap enough, they would be very foolish if they did not take advantage of it. There was no doubt it was a very practical thing, in conclusion, he thought and spoke for all when he said they owed Dan their hearty thanks whatever the future of the machine might be. Mr. L Briggs of Stamford spoke very highly of what he had seen and believed it would fill a long-felt want. He was so much taken with it that he was willing to purchase it at once if Dan would sell it, for it was a splendid thing and he always believed in having such things at once it they were good."

Dan had built a drawbridge to the meadow on the other side of the river so that he could drive his tractor straight to the demonstration meadow (which was an area also used for trials – Fig.163). This caused some strife between Dan and his brother William, landlord of the Royal Oak, who let out boats for hire on the river.

For road use rubber sections could be fitted to the wheels and secured with nuts and bolts.

Charles Lindsell of Home Green Farm, near Biggleswade, permitted Dan to cut a field of wheat and then place an advertising board next to the Great Northern Railway line. Every passenger must have been aware of the 'Ivel' Agricultural Motor.[4]

Landowners were quick to see that one engine and a driver could do the work of several ploughmen and their horse teams. A 1905 letter stated that the 'Ivel' was cheaper than teams of horses or steam traction for ploughing.[5] By 1903, orders were rolling in from all over the world. The 'Ivel' performed well in trials and proved to be extremely rugged and reliable.

It's dimensions were: length 9 ft. 3 in., and width overall 5 ft. 4 in. Weight was 30 cwt when packed for shipping. The price was £300.

On December 12th 1902, Dan formed a limited company called Ivel Agricultural Motors Ltd with offices at 45 Great Marlborough Street, London (where Charles Jarrott had motoring offices and showrooms for Napier and De Dietrich). There were 10,000 shares of £1 each. The company pur-

Fig.167: Alwyne takes a few steps

4   *Implement and Machinery Review*, September 1st 1902.
5   *Implement and Machinery Review*, June 2nd 1905, p.209.

Fig.168: Alwyne marches outside the Royal Oak

chased Dan's motor business, including patents, for £4,500. Among the shareholders were the Marquis Granby, Lord Willoughby de Eresby, Lord John Scott Montagu and many other landowners who could see the tremendous potential of the 'Ivel' tractor. The directors of the Company were Charles Jarrott[6], John W. Hewitt, Selwyn Francis Edge[7], Lord Willoughby de Eresby (chairman), Adolph

Fig.169: Dan and family in the 'Ivel' Motor Car

(courtesy Biggleswade History Society)

6   Jarrott was a sportsman and racing cyclist who abandoned a legal career in 1896 for the automobile business. In 1905 he trialed cyclist scouts to provide advance warning to motorists of speed traps leading to the formation of the Automobile Association. His autobiography was called 'Ten Years of Motor Racing 1896-1906".

7   Edge had been a well-known racing cyclist and manager of the Dunlop offices in London and then became a prominent racing car driver. By the end of 1900 he was the up-and-coming man in the motor world.

Hoffman and Dan. It seems that Dan had close ties with some of the leading pioneers of motoring.

There are some who think that the tractor industry started in 1902 in the United States but they are mistaken as the American machine was more of a heavy traction engine powered by an internal combustion engine. It took quite some years for a light American tractor to come on the market.

It seems that the inception of Ivel Agricultural Motors Ltd signalled the end for the 'Ivel' Motor Bicycle and 'Ivel' Motor Car. Clearly the focus was now on the 'Ivel' tractor as there were many other competitors in the market offering motor bicycles and cars.

There was no attendance at the Stanley Show this year.

Fig.170: Great Marlborough Street premises prior to redevelopment in 2002. The building was built in 1901-2.

1903 The Armoured Car

Early in 1903, Dan and his works foreman, George Farr, were looking at an 'Ivel' tractor which had been cased in light metal to resolve the problem of dust when Dan suddenly exclaimed:

"You know, with a thicker cover, that could be used by the Army; it would resist guns."

Fig.171: The Armoured Car

(courtesy Biggleswade History Society)

Dan wrote to Cammell Laird for quarter inch bullet-proof steel shields and began to experiment. He put a cover on one of his tractors with a door at the rear, and called the new vehicle the 'Ivel Armoured Car'. Dan wrote to the War Office and arranged a demonstration in the meadow on the other side of the River Ivel.

The military visitors were impressed, and another demonstration was planned. High-ranking officers watched Dan drive the armoured car round the meadow while three expert riflemen shot at the vehicle with a variety of weapons. The armoured car did not falter, and neither was the armour

Fig.172: The Armoured Car demonstration

pierced. Dan stepped out of the car at the end of the demonstration, and said smiling: *"There you are gentlemen there's an idea for you for an armour-covered vehicle that could pierce enemy lines".* [1] Among the invited guests was Prince Christian of Denmark, who congratulated Dan on his invention.

Also present was Dan's friend, William Tritton. Five years later, Tritton invented caterpillar tracks for the armoured car, and received a knighthood for his invention.

Dan went on to adapt his design to an armoured ambulance with bulletproof screens to protect the wounded.

In 1903 the Ivel Agricultural Motor won the silver medal for the Royal Agricultural Society, and collected the same award again the following year. At agricultural fairs around the countryside, the 'Ivel' tractor won many medals after demonstrating its astonishing speed and efficiency.

Fig.173: Dan in the Armoured Car

Orders for the Ivel Agricultural Motor poured into the Biggleswade works from all over the world: Argentina, Australia, Austria, Brazil, France, Hungary, New Zealand, Romania, Russia and South Africa. Adolph Hoffman was in charge of exports and agencies were distributed world-wide.

On December 29th Dan had a four-seater 'Ivel' Motor Car registered to him with the registration plate BM 46 (cancelled May 13th 1914). A few days later he had an 'Ivel' Motor Bicycle with Minerva engine registered to him with the registration BM 67.

---

1   'Faed' Wilson, who was present, writing in 1956.

Fig.174: The Ivel Hotel c.1903 (note the C.T.C. sign)

(courtesy Biggleswade History Society)

Fig.175: Dan, holding Alwyne, and his workforce. Stanley is on the left.

(courtesy Biggleswade History Society)

1904 More Inventions

Dan continued to work on developing the motor tractor by extending its use with attachments and also experimented with other fuels, notably alcohol. By 1906 the tractor was capable of running on petrol, paraffin, kerosene or alcohol as a fuel.

Fig.176: 'Ivel' Agricultural Motor on test of multiple coupling

He applied on May 2nd 1904 for a patent for improvements in Automatic-Feed Oil Lubricators, (No. 1904-10064) and on June 16th a patent for Attachment of Mowers, Reapers, Binders and like Implements and Machines to Motor-tractors (No. 1904-13663).

Fig.177: 'Ivel' Agricultural Motor ploughing

Yet another of Dan Albone's inventions was Improvement in the Means for Vaporising Heavy Hydrocarbons for use in Internal Combustion Engines (No. 1904-24489).

Fig.178: Inside the Ivel Works

(courtesy Biggleswade History Society)

Dan's last invention was an Auto Potato Planter with two operations in one, which was not patented.

It was reported that a Lincolnshire company was being formed, with £3,000 of capital at £5 per share, to hire out the Ivel Agricultural Motor.[1]

Fig.179: Inside the Ivel Works

(courtesy Biggleswade History Society)

Records show that 24 Motor Bicycles were registered in Bedfordshire in the year so production continued albeit probably at a low level.

---

1   *The Autocar*, September 3rd 1904, p.311.

HIGHEST GRADE

"IVEL" CYCLES

Each complete with Free-wheel, Two Rim Brakes, Plated Rims, Mudguards and "Ivel" Gear Case, £12 12s.

THE VERY LATEST

2 h.p. "IVEL" MOTOR CYCLE £36.

A number of Second-hand Bicycles to be disposed of at very Low Prices.

One Second-hand "Ivel" Motor Bicycle, complete with 2 h.p. Engine, £23.

Also one ditto, complete with 2½ h.p. Engine, £28.

Both in Excellent Order.

CALL AND INSPECT MY STOCK.

Any kind of REPAIR to any make machine done on the premises, including plating and Enamelling.

If you do not want the whole of your machine renovated bring some of the rusty parts to be

Polished and Nickelled.

The prices for this work are very low ; Handle Bars costing only 2/6 ; Seat Pillars 1/4 ; Cranks, per pair, 2s. ; Bell Domes 7d. ; and other parts accordingly.

Lamps, Bells, etc., sold at the very lowest fixed retail prices.

DAN ALBONE,

'Ivel' Cycle and Motor Works,

BIGGLESWADE.

Fig.180: 'Ivel' Motor Bicycle advertisement, 1904

(courtesy Biggleswade History Society)

1905 – 1906 The End of a Legend

The 'Ivel' tractor collected gold medal after medal during 1905 and 1906. Added to this was the machine's growing reputation for reliability. Dan must have felt that he had found the key to lasting success; he had the ideal product at the right time. Yet he had not forgotten the bicycle.

His catalogue was smaller yet it still displayed his main models. In 1906 he introduced a new model, the 'Runwell' which provided a reliable but lower priced machine than the 'Ivel'.

Fig.181: 'Ivel' advertisement, 1905

Fig.182: Dan and family

(courtesy Biggleswade History Society)

The *Bedfordshire Express* reported on the new cycle shop which Dan had opened in Biggleswade's Hitchin Street in April 1906, under the management of Mr G. Lincoln.[1] The shop also sold 'Ivel' Motor Bicycles and gramophones!

The No. 1 'Ivel Roadster' now had 28 in. wheels front and rear and was geared higher at 68 in. no doubt reflecting an improvement in the state of the roads. There were Bowden brakes front and rear and the weight had been reduced by four pounds to 32 lb. The price had been reduced significantly to £11 although there was an optional extra of a two-speed or three-speed gear.

The No. 2 'Ivel Light Roadster' appeared to be much as before but its price had been reduced to £11.10s.

The No. 3 'Ivel Road Racer' had been discontinued and in its place was the No. 3 'Ivel Path Racer'

---

1   *Bedfordshire Express*, March 24th 1906.

which again appeared much as before but priced at £10.

Fig.183: Driving a threshing machine

The No. 4 'Ivel Lady's Safety' also had Bowden rim brakes front and rear and came with the extra cost option of a two-speed or three-speed gear. It was priced at £11. The curved top tube version had been quietly discontinued from the range.

Fig.184: Harvesting with two Wood binders

The No. 5 Lady's Tricycle was offered at £20 with the option of a back pedalling brake for £3, in addition to the front rim brake. A Gent's model was also offered with straight top tube.

Fig.185: The 'Ivel' demonstrated in Cumbria (courtesy Biggleswade History Society)

The 'Runwell No. 6 Roadster' was effectively a development of Dan's previous policy of offering a cheaper machine. The Runwell was offered with much higher standard gearing than the No. 1 at 75 in. It was priced at only £7.

There was a 'Runwell No. 7 Lady's Roadster' too with curved top tube. This was priced at £7.10s.

In addition, Dan now offered the 'Ivel' Juvenile Cycle for boys and girls at £5.5s.

Fig.186: Harvesting at night with lightning!

(courtesy Biggleswade History Society)

The Gent's and Lady's Motor Bicycle now had a more powerful engine of 2 or 2¾ h.p., priced at £29 and £32, respectively. The back attachment and trailer were no longer offered.

Fig.187: 'Ivel' with pump outside the Royal Oak (courtesy Biggleswade History Society)

The catalogue stated that a Motor Car was no longer manufactured and that Dan had sold *"a good number"* (we think no more than a dozen).

It was reported in March that the 'Ivel Agricultural Motor' had won two more gold medals in ploughing matches conducted in heavy conditions.[2]

---

2 *The Cycle and Motor Trades Review*, March 1st 1906.

In May 1906 Dan finalised his last invention, the 'Ivel Potato Planter', which together with his Agricultural Motor were again a great attraction at the Biggleswade Fête.

Fig.188: Dan demonstrating at the Royal Agricultural Society of England show

On June 1st, Stanley applied to join the Biggleswade & District Constitutional Club (Fig.191). His proposer was Dan. Stanley had been educated at Bedford Grammar School and went on to study with a Manchester engineering firm. His age on the application was claimed to be 18 but it wasn't! Stanley was born on January 31st 1889 so on the date of application he was aged 17 years, four months and one day. Stanley was accepted and this is perhaps a reflection of Dan's standing in the local community.

Fig.189: Ivel tractor and Albion binder being driven by one man in 1910

On August 2nd, Dan introduced the idea of harvesting at night with his 'Ivel' tractor, working a Walter A. Wood 5 ft. binder, cutting wheat. The light was provided by Costle acetylene motor lamps which were fitted to the motor as well as to each of the binders. This demonstration took place during a thunderstorm (Fig.186) and it will be observed that the lightning flash passed between the tractor and

the camera during the exposure of the photographic plate.

Also Dan used his tractor to power a fire fighting machine which was made by Merryweather & Sons for fire and irrigation purposes.

Fig.190: The 'Ivel' Agricultural Motor in 1912

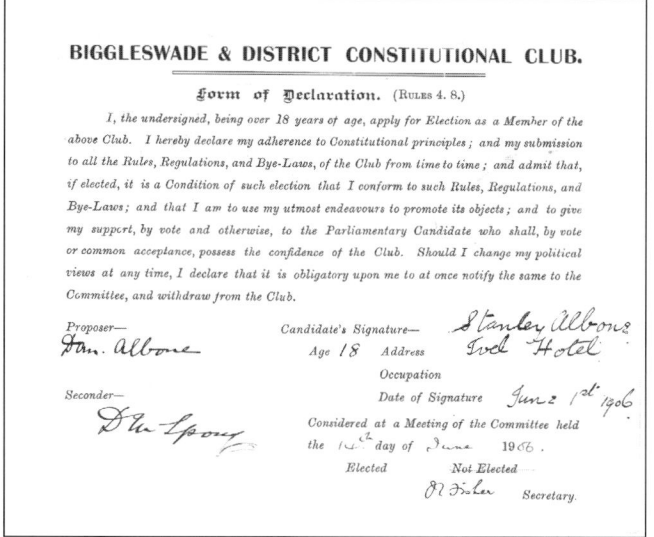

Fig.191: Stanley's application for the Biggleswade & District Constitutional Club.

(courtesy Biggleswade History Society)

On the morning of October 30th, 1906, Dan Albone rose early and went to his office. During a telephone conversation with Adolph Hoffman at the London office, in which he was advised he had won a patent law case against an American company[3], Dan collapsed from a major stroke. The foreman of the Ivel Works, Frederick Boswell, and an assistant, Mr. Horton, were in attendance. Within ten minutes

---

3 Telephone conversation with Mr. Edward Albone on March 2nd 1990.

he was dead. He was just forty-six years old. His death was reported in the cycling press.[4] At the inquest Mrs Albone described Dan as an excitable man and said she had been concerned that he would die of a stroke, as had his mother.[5]

It is understood that Dan had been recommended for a knighthood but did not live to receive it.

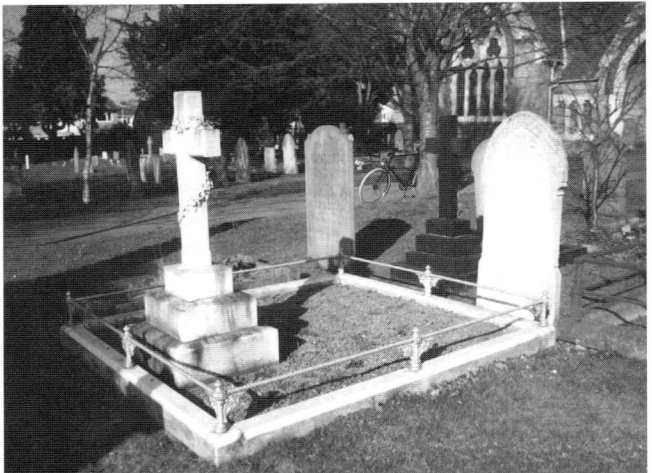

Fig.192: The Albone family grave

He was buried in Biggleswade Cemetery on November 2nd.[6] The procession of mourners was half a mile long and the town practically closed, according to newspaper reports. Thousands of people from the town and surrounding area came to pay their last respects. Colonel and Mrs Shuttleworth, Lord Alwyne Compton, and Montagu Holbein were among those who attended. There were about eighty carriages, and extra wagons had to be brought to carry the floral tributes. All the men from the Ivel Works were mourners, and there were representatives from the St Andrew's Lodge of Freemasons, the Licensed Victuallers' Association and Biggleswade and District Unionist Association, led by C. T. Lindsell.

The parish church was packed. This was the Reverend R. W. Barber's tribute to Dan:

"The hymn I shall shortly ask you to sing was Dan Albone's favourite hymn and it was characteristic of the man - 'Fight the good fight with all thy

The late Dan Albone.

Fig.193: The Late Dan Albone

(courtesy *Cycling*)

might. ' With all thy might! Surely that gives us the keynote of Dan Albone's life. Whatever thy hand findeth to do, do it with all thy might. He loved his work and was strenuous in it, endowed with undaunted and unbounded energy. He made himself famous throughout England and many parts of the world, but he is called away thus in the very prime of life. If anyone was in difficulty or wanted a helping hand, he went to Dan Albone, and did not go in vain, for he was warm-hearted and open-handed ... whether we knew him as an athlete, or as secretary of the Licensed Victuallers' Association, or as connected with the benefit society, or as a politician, or as an employer of labour and a business man, he ran a straight race."

---

4   *Cycling*, November 7th 1906, p.388.
5   *Bedfordshire Mercury*, November 3rd 1906
6   *Biggleswade Chronicle*, Obituary, November 2nd and 9th 1906.

'Ivel Dan' was written by the late Lucien Savournin, M.R.C.V.S., originally a member of the Finsbury Park Cycling Club, and later of the Stanley Cycling Club, when staying at the Ivel Hotel in June 1904. The author added this dedication in 1906:

To the memory of
One, who
In his capacity of
Inn-holder
and
Cycle-maker
Won the esteem of all
Frequenters of the Great North Road
These trivial lines
are reverently inscribed
by The Author, 1906

Fig.194: In Memoriam

IVEL DAN

You've heard of Ivel Dan,
The famous North Road man,
  That jovial and genial,
  Very convivial,
Biggleswade young man.

He runs the hotel here,
Dispensing out good cheer,
  To all and to sundry,
  The thirsty and hungry,
That come from far and near.

And build a bike he can,
As good as ever ran:
  With extra-or-dinnery
  Genius culinary
Braze up a dinner he can.

Imagine if you can,
This versatile young man -
  For a moderate figure
  He'll build you a jigger
And line your inner man.

He'll build you a motor car,
To carry you afar,
  A snuffing and snorting -
  A merry cavorting
Classy Ivel car.

Conceive him if you can,
With spanner and oiling can,
  This specially practical,
  Clever mechanical
Up to date young man.

He'll do the best he can
With the "crocks" of another man,
  For motors asthmatic
  And jiggers rheumatic,
Are sent to Doctor Dan.

So doff your cap to Dan,
The friend of cycling man,
  Be you an old sinner,
  or just a beginner,
Just thank your stars for Dan.

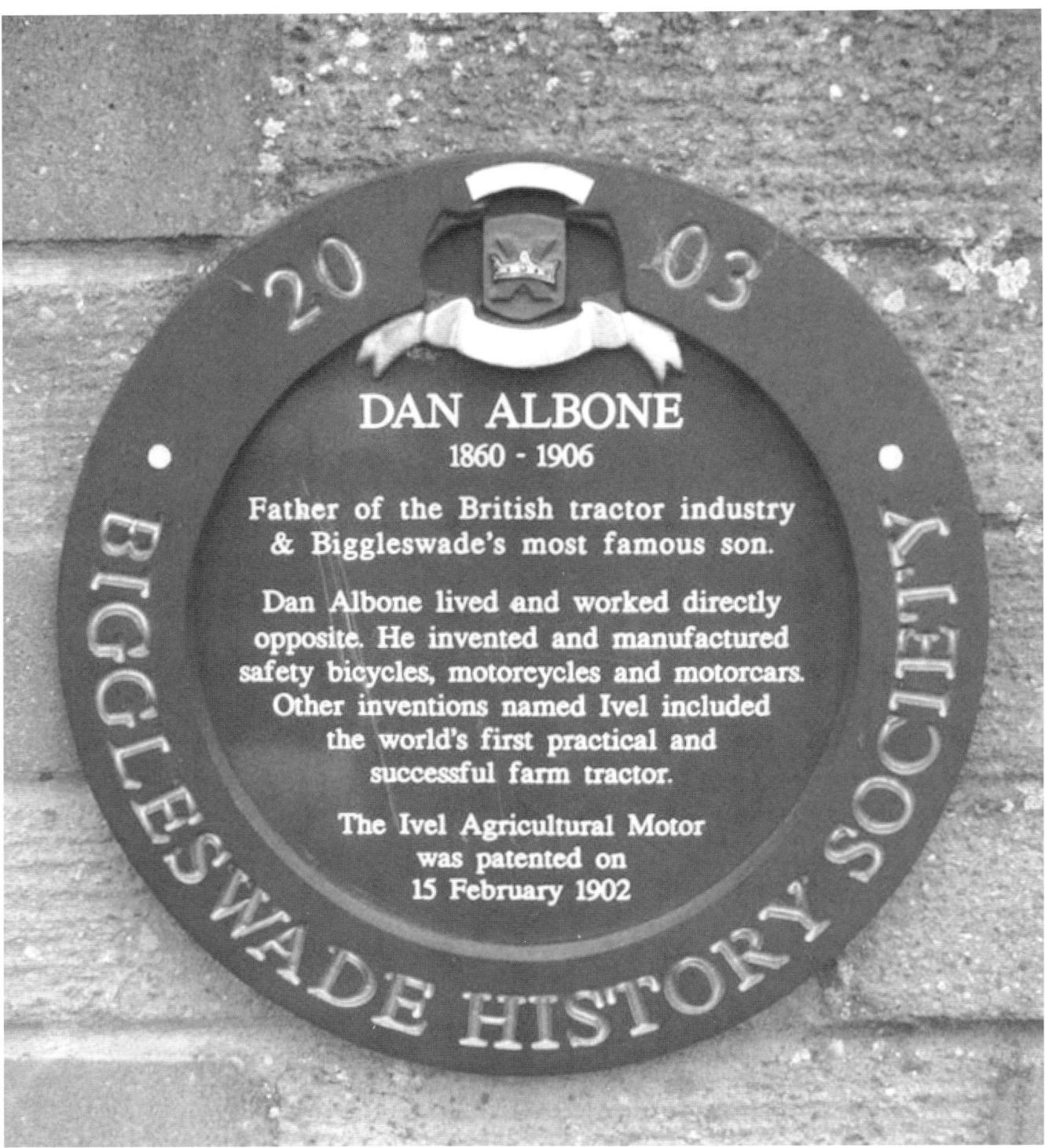

Figure 195: Memorial Plaque to Dan Albone erected in 2003 by the Biggleswade History Society

Addendum

When probate was granted on January 3rd 1907 Dan's estate was proven at £4,788 14s 4d. His Will left his estate on trust for Elizabeth, to pay her the income for her life, and then to his children. There was only one specific request: to Arthur J. Hills to select any three of Dan's prizes.[1]

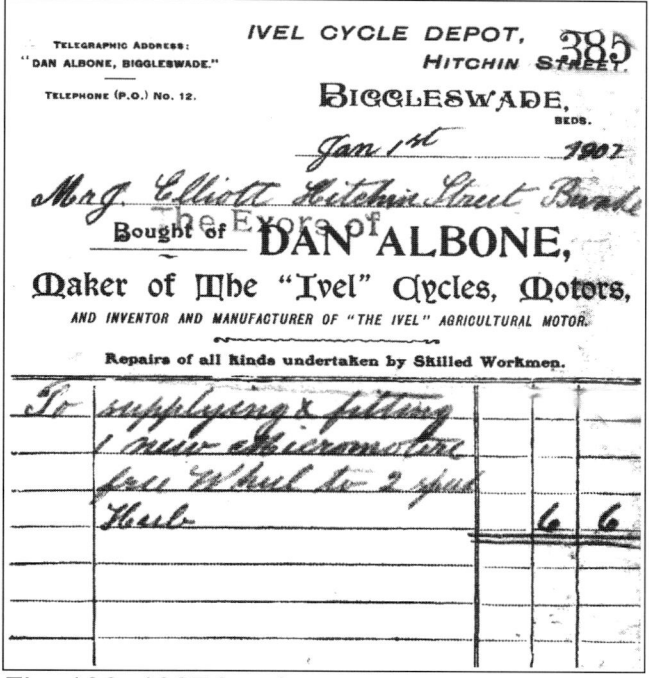

Fig. 196: 1907 Invoice

(courtesy Biggleswade History Society)

Cycle manufacture did not continue for more than a year or two after Dan died. Repairs to cycles continued for a while longer as the 1909 invoice for work done to a cycle illustrates (Fig.197). Note also that old letter head was still being used. Many records and documents were burnt by Elizabeth. She carried on as licensee of the Ivel Hotel and also went into partnership with George Course, former manager of the Ivel Works, trading as Dan Albone & Co.[2] George lived at 17 Fairfield Road where he died in 1946 and the Albone family were next door at No. 15. The partnership rented part of 3 Market Square from Saunders Bros., coachbuilders, from 1906 until 1927, when Biggleswade Gas Company opened their new showroom. In 1921 the partnership was advertising for sale from stock the Gents' Popular Ivel at £12 with ladies machines 10s. extra.

The 'Ivel Agricultural Motor' became known all over the world, whether manufactured in Biggleswade or made elsewhere under licence, as for example in the United States. The 'Ivel' was undoubtedly the inspiration for the British tractor industry. The tractor was produced for a number of years after Dan's death.

In 1908, Adolph Hoffman made it known that a number of the 'Ivel tractors would be made available to be let out on hire for an inclusive charge.[3]

In 1909 the London offices moved to 45/46 Poland Street.

In 1912 the magneto, which was formerly fitted in front of the engine and driven by gears from the crankshaft, was placed at the side, and driven direct from the camshaft. In addition, accumulator ignition was fitted. Also a new fixed cover was introduced for the engine.[4]

Despite continued interest and exports, Ivel Agricultural Motors Ltd began to lose money and production ceased in 1916.

In 1917 magistrates referred for enforced closure both the Ivel Hotel and the Ongley Arms, still a common lodging house. The usual reason was lack of facilities or low trade. Both closed in 1918. Elizabeth sold off various effects in the yard adjoining and the Ivel Works business moved to the Market Square in 1920. Sale of the Ivel Hotel to R. W.

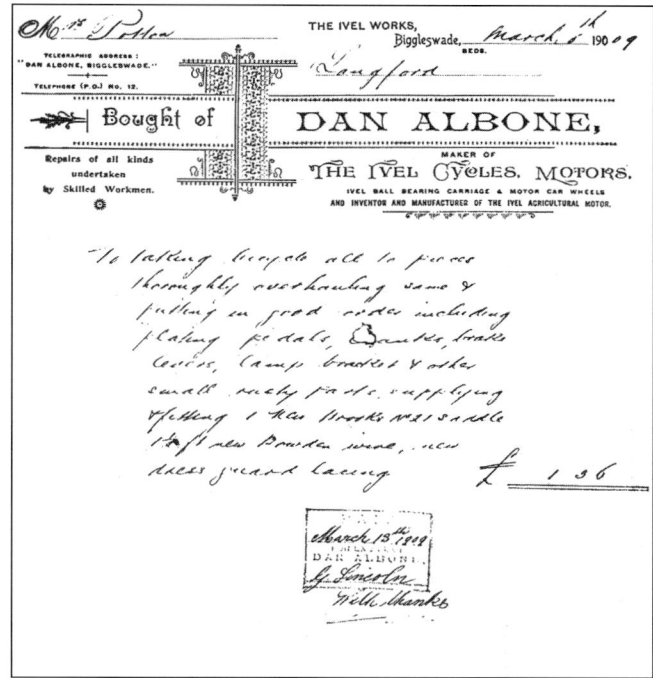

Fig.197: 1909 Invoice for bicycle service

(courtesy Biggleswade History Society)

1   Bedfordshire & Luton Archives Service, Ref. HF 4/32/5.
2   *Biggleswade Chronicle,* June 3rd 1927 'Partnership of Elizabeth Albone and George Course dissolved'.

3   *Implement and Machinery Review*, December 1st 1908.
4   *Implement and Machinery Review*, April 1st 1912.

Fig. 198: Medals won by the Ivel Agricultural Motor

Fig.199: Some images of Alwyne with her 'Ivel' and pet dog

(courtesy Biggleswade History Society)

Jordan and A. R. W. Jordan for use as a coachbuilding works was completed in 1921, but they were trading from the former Ivel Works buildings in 1920. R A Jordan Ltd was registered there in 1923. They closed about 1970. The original buildings were demolished in 1972 when Owen Godfrey Ltd opened their showroom and petrol station. That showroom in 2011 is occupied by Harvest Furnishing. Lea Valley Dairies occupied some of the factory buildings from about 1977 to 2000. The last owners were Rosper Safes before demolition in 2008. McCarthy & Stone opened Northgate Court in 2009 occupying most of the site with retirement flats.

Fig. 200: 1921 'Ivel' advertisement

(courtesy Biggleswade History Society)

Stanley, Dan's son, died of tuberculosis on December 7th 1913 aged 24 years. He did not marry. Elizabeth Albone died aged 70 years in 1935. Dan's daughter Alwyne (Winnie) also did not marry and lived in Fairfield Road, Biggleswade, until her death on April 4th 1954. She has been described as tall, slim, delicate, and reserved. The family is buried in Drove Road Cemetery, Biggleswade.

The Ivel Agricultural Motor Co. Ltd was put into receivership in 1920, concluded on December 31st 1921, and the company finally dissolved on July 6th 1923, all the assets having been purchased by the United Motor Industries Ltd of Hanover Square, London.

In 1920 the first 'Ivel' tractor was presented to the Science Museum by the Ivel Works. It was dis-

mantled and put into store and remained there until 1950. It was then cleaned and assembled and started on the first turn of the handle.[5] It headed a procession of farming machinery at the Royal Show, Cambridge, July 5th 1951.

Curiously, the *Bedfordshire Directory, 1924*, still carried an entry for Dan Albone & Co., manufacturers of 'Ivel' cycles, Market Square.

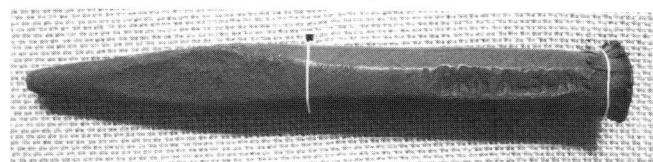

Fig. 201: Dan Albone punch in Ashwell Museum

A Dan Albone punch, marked with his name, and vice survive in Ashwell Museum.[6] These were recovered when Dan's workshop was cleared. It is understood that other tools were passed to Neville Smith, who had been apprenticed to Dan, and had a cycle shop in Biggleswade.

In the early 1950s, Mrs Eva Shell, the niece of Dan Albone and daughter of Dan's younger sister,

Fig. 202: Dan Albone vice in Ashwell Museum

---

5   *Evening News*, May 18th 1951.
6   A 'Kangaroo' is also on display in Ashwell Museum.

Ann, and Richard Tingey, collected together material for a scrap book and added a commentary. This was to result in her gathering sufficient enthusiasm locally for a plaque to be placed on Jordans coach-building works (the former Ivel Hotel) to commemorate the 50th Anniversary of Dan Albone's death in 1906.[7]

The plaque reads:

DAN ALBONE
1860-1906
PIONEER IN CYCLE, MOTOR CYCLE,
CAR AND TRACTOR MANUFACTURE
LIVED AND WORKED
IN THESE PREMISES

Fig. 203 G. H. Stancer, O.B.E., unveils the Dan Albone plaque.

(courtesy Biggleswade History Society)

The plaque was unveiled on October 30th 1956 by G. H. Stancer, O.B.E., then President of the Cyclist Touring Club, Road Racers Association, Road Records Association and Century Road Club, together with W. H. Cashmore, Director of the National Institute of Agricultural Engineering, Wrest

Fig. 204: Group photograph after the unveiling (courtesy Biggleswade History Society)

---

7 *Biggleswade Chronicle,* report of November 26th 1956.

Fig. 205: Guests at the ceremony

(courtesy Biggleswade History Society)

Park, Silsoe, and Alderman Leslie Chambers of Biggleswade Urban Council. The plaque was mislaid when the original buildings were demolished in 1972 but was recovered and is now displayed on the showroom occupied by Harvest Furnishing.

The original scrap book is in the care of the Biggleswade Town Council and contains many ori-

Fig. 206: The former Ivel Hotel in the 1960's. The former Ongley Arms is the white showroom. (courtesy Biggleswade History Society)

ginal cuttings from cycling and other papers of the second half of the 1880's and 1890's. Much material about Dan Albone has survived, a very large amount of which, many press cuttings, photograph albums which include family snaps, and some letters, together with Mrs Shell's own correspondence while she was doing her researches, is now in the Science Museum Library.

In 1964 the U.K. Antarctic Place-Names Committee named a deeply entrenched narrow glacier in

Western Antarctica, the Albone Glacier in recognition of his invention of the 'Ivel' tractor.

To mark the centenary of Dan's cycle inventions, a ride was held on April 9th 1977 starting from the Royal Oak Hotel, Biggleswade, to Bedford and back.

An exhibition at Biggleswade Library was held from February 7th to March 7th 1978, titled "Dan Albone – Biggleswade's Inventor Extraordinary".

Fig. 207: Memorial Leisure Area complete with c.1902 'Ivel'

In 1980 Biggleswade Town Council established a Memorial Leisure Area on the banks of the River Ivel as a tribute to Dan Albone. Not only is the site near Dan's home and place of work; it is very close to the original race track where the young Dan won races and tested so many 'Ivel' machines.

The Veteran-Cycle Club commenced an 'Old Warden Run' in 1981, taking in the old Ivel Works. The next year it was re-named as the 'Ivel Run'.

The book 'A Thorough Good Fellow' by Kathy Hindle and Lee Irvine was published on September 13th 1990.

Fig. 208: The modern 'Ivel' racing bicycle

Biggleswade Chamber of Trade held an Edwardian Day on October 6th 1990 which included a parade of cars and cycles with the Veteran-Cycle Club participating.

The Dan Albone Memorial Cycle Rally was proposed by Lee Irvine in 1991 along with the proposed formation of the Ivel Cycle Pioneers Club, relating to new cycle inventions.

Also in the 1990's, Lee Irvine created a modern interpretation of an 'Ivel' racing bicycle. This high quality machine has a frame made of Reynolds 753 tubing and is fitted with Shimano Dura-Ace equipment. The 'Ivel' name has been engraved on the frame.

Fig. 209: The modern 'Ivel' head badge

It now resides in Coventry Transport Museum.

Fig. 210: The modern 'Ivel' seat stay detail

Royal Mail held an exhibition in 1999 titled "Post Impressions – The Art of the Stamp & 1000 Years of Inspiration" which featured the Lady's 'Ivel' on a stamp titled "Liberation by bike" designed by Sara Fanelli and issued on February 2nd 1999.

Fig. 211: Royal Mail post impressions 1999-2000

In the year 2000 Les Williams of Pedals Cycles, Biggleswade, donated a number of unique cycle stands in the form of an 'Ivel' bicycle around the Market Square to commemorate Dan.

'The Ivel Story' by John Moffitt was published in 2003 and marked the centenary of the 'Ivel Agricultural Motor'. On Saturday June 21st 2003 the 'Ivel' tractor returned to Biggleswade, visiting the historic Market Square, Sainsbury's Store and the Shuttleworth Museum, Old Warden. In the evening there was a reception in the Russell Hall at Shuttleworth College followed by a charity celebration dinner.

Fig. 212: Ivel cycle stand at west end of Market Square

On Sunday June 22nd 2003 at Biggleswade, a Heritage Plaque was unveiled opposite the site of the Ivel Works by Alex Albone, Dan's great-great nephew, and Ken Page of the Biggleswade History Society while Maude Irvine laid a wreath on Dan Albone's grave at Drove Road Cemetery. Celebrations on the Market Square included a Farmers Market and various Youth Events.[8]

8 *Biggleswade Chronicle*, June 27th 2003.

Fig. 213: Ken Page unveiling the commemorative plaque in 2003 for the 'Ivel' Agricultural Motor

(courtesy Biggleswade History Society)

Three 'Ivel' bicycles were displayed at the 'Made in Bedfordshire' exhibition at the Shuttleworth Steam Fair on September 16th 2006.

A commemorative church service was held on October 29th 2006 at St Andrew's Parish Church. This service included the reading of a poem dedicated to Dan in 1904, a short history of his life, and accolades that appeared in his obituary and were read out at his funeral. It was well attended by people from Biggleswade, those with a cycling connection, and relatives.

A Lady's 'Ivel' featured in the 'Clocking In' exhibition at Bedford Museum from February 27th 2010 to May 23rd 2010. The exhibition explored the past, present and future working lives of the people of Bedfordshire.

Fig. 214: Three 'Ivel' bicycles at the 'Made in Bedfordshire' exhibition

In 2011 Biggleswade History Society instituted the 'The Dan Albone Archive for Biggleswade' and expects to formally open it in 2012.

Index

The Value of Money

The table below will help you find an approximate current value for Dan's prices. It shows a multiple for UK retail price inflation for a given year to enable an estimate of cost in today's money.[1]

Example 1:

The 'Best Ivel Safety', produced in 1887, was offered at £17.10s (£17.50). What is the value in today's money?

Look up the year column on the table and select the 1880s decade. To the right of the year 1887 is found the multiple 107.0. This means that prices have increased 107.0 times since 1887.

So, in today's money the 'Best Ivel Safety' would cost:

$$£17.50 \times 107.0 = £1,872.50.$$

Example 2:

The 'No.5 Lady's Safety', of 1902, was offered at £16. What is the value in today's money?

Look up the year column on the table and select the 1900s decade. To the right of the year 1902 is found the multiple 100.0. This means that prices have increased 100.0 times since 1902.

So, in today's money the 'No.5 Lady's Safety' would cost:

$$£16 \times 100.0 = £1,600.00.$$

Table

1880	97.9	1890	104.6	1900	100.0
1881	98.9	1891	103.4	1901	100.0
1882	97.9	1892	103.4	1902	100.0
1883	98.9	1893	104.6	1903	98.9
1884	101.1	1894	105.8	1904	98.9
1885	104.6	1895	107.0	1905	98.9
1886	105.8	1896	108.3	1906	98.9
1887	107.0	1897	105.8	1907	97.9
1888	105.8	1898	105.8	1908	97.9
1889	104.6	1899	104.6	1909	96.9

---

1   *Consumer Price Inflation Since 1750*, Jim O'Donoghue and Louise Goulding, Office for National Statistics. Based on RPI to July 2011.

Edward ALBONE – Edith GILBERT
b.1819, d.1864 – m.10.11.1845 - b.1819, d.1883
    Ann ALBONE
    b.1847, d.1859

    David ALBONE – Emily
    b.1849
        David William ALBONE
        b.1874
        Edith Emily ALBONE
        b.06.02.1875

    Lucy (May) ALBONE – William Armitage WELLS
    b.02.08.1850, d.1881 – m.08.03.1875

    William ALBONE – Mary Ann COMPTON
    b.1851, d.30.09.1914 – m.24.03.1884 – d.23.07.1937
        Edith Emma ALBONE
        Florence Annie ALBONE
        William Compton ALBONE
        Beatrice Louise ALBONE

    Emma ALBONE – William Henry BALL
    b.1853, d.04.1931 – m.22.05.1882
        Edward John BALL d.1956

    Elizabeth ALBONE
    b.1855, d.21.10.1908

    Edward ALBONE – Emma Ann
    b.1857, d.04.1931
        George ALBONE
        Edith Alice ALBONE – Joseph W. TEAR
            Dorothy Emma TEAR – Arthur MEW
                Pauline TEAR
            Florence Maude TEAR – Lee IRVINE
        Fred ALBONE
        Dan ALBONE
        Maudie ALBONE
        Walter ALBONE
        Horace (Dick) ALBONE

    Daniel ALBONE - Elizabeth MOULDEN
    b.12.09.1860, d.30.10.1906 – m.23.08.1887 – b.July-Sept. 1865, d.30.12.1935
        Stanley Dan ALBONE
        b.31.01.1889, d.07.12.1913
        Alwyne Patricia Edwards ALBONE
        b.17.03.1900, d.04.04.1954

    Ann ALBONE – Richard TINGEY
    b.1862 – m.17.10.1887 – b.1866,
        Eva TINGEY (SHELL)

Dan's Race Results

1880

At the first race meeting of the Biggleswade & District Cycling Club, held along the Bedford Road, on September 16th, Dan was third in the one mile club handicap and second in the five mile handicap.

1881

At another Biggleswade & District Bicycle Club meeting on August 18th, he was first in the one mile club handicap and second in the five mile club handicap.

1882

On Easter Monday, April 10th, Dan with ten yards start over scratch in the one mile, was placed second to F. Metcalf.

At the first Fête and Gala held in Biggleswade on August Bank Holiday on the Fairfield Meadow, Dan was fourth in the one mile bicycle handicap race.

1883

In a one mile handicap in June, Dan won his heat in a time of 2 min. 52.4 sec. but was beaten in the next round.[1]

At the Wisbech B.C. meeting on July 4th, Dan riding his special 'Ivel Racer' weighing 25 lb., was second in the one mile open handicap to A. Hood, Speedwell B.C., the prize for second being a handsome silver-plated cruet. In the three miles open handicap Dan was again second to Hood by a wheel. Time 12 min. 5.6 sec. The prize was a case of silver-plated knives and forks with pearl handles.[2]

At the second annual Fête Meeting held in the Fairfield Meadow on August 6th, Dan was first in the one mile open handicap; his brother Edward came second, thirty five yards behind. In the Club two mile open bicycle handicap, he also gained first prize and his brother second.

Dan was also very much to the fore in September, when J. H. Adams of the Facile B. C. was seeing how many miles he could do in 24 hours. Dan met him at Henlow Crossing before 3 am (Saturday morning) and paced him via Biggleswade, Bedford and St. Neots to Cambridge, whence he returned by train. Arthur J. Hills received a telegram in the evening asking for more help. Dan at once started for St. Neots and met Adams there and rode with him to the finish. Dan rode 116 miles altogether, besides doing a good day's work in between, which must be categorised as a very good performance. A race report lists Dan as a runner-up with Edward Albone.[3]

A few days after the above event, Dan won the ten mile Club Championship which took place along the Caldecote Road. Dan started a few yards behind the other competitors, as there was no room for everyone to start abreast. He soon went to the front, a place he maintained all the way.

1884

At Bedford on June 25th, he won second prize in the one mile club handicap from scratch, and in the County open mile handicap Dan obtained first prize (Richard Tingey was 4th).[4]

At the Biggleswade Fête meeting on August 13th he was first in the one mile tricycle open handicap. Dan was 2nd in the heat for the Mile Handicap and 3rd in the Final. He was also 3rd in the three mile handicap. The 'Facile' race was won by Dan.[5]

On September 11th Dan was narrowly beaten into 2nd in the four mile handicap at Cambridge, the winner G. N. Howes having a time of 12 min. 20 secs. Dan was one of the "Wheeling Celebrities" whose autographs appeared in "Wheeling" of the following week.[6]

---

1   *The Cyclist*, June 13th 1883, p. 537.
2   *Bicycling Times & Tricycling Record*, July 10th 1883, p.138.
3   *Bicycling News*, September 21st 1883.
4   *The Cyclist*, June 25th 1884.
5   *The Cyclist*, August 13th 1884.
6   *The Cyclist*, September 17th 1884 and *Wheeling*, September 24th 1884.

1885

Dan obtained his first win in April, at the two mile open in Oundle, Lincolnshire.[7]

At the Bedford Amateur C.C. event in the one mile handicap Dan came in first with a time of 3 min. 10.2 secs. to win a silver cup.

In May, riding at Alexandra Palace in the Keen Meeting, Dan was riding his 'Ivel Light Roadster' in the Safety Race against some of the best men of the day and was in third place but his foot slipped the pedal on the last lap.

Also in May, Dan was first in the one mile handicap, beating Baldwick and Middleton, with a time of 3 min. 47.6 secs., and second in the two mile at Peterborough Athletic Sports to M. Rowe, who had a time of 8 min. 16.4 secs.

At the Bedford Cycling and Athletic Club one mile handicap, Dan was riding his 'Ivel Light Roadster' and was second in the third heat at 3 min. 26 secs. to Ennals riding an ordinary, and fourth in the final.

At this year's Fête ten out of the eighteen prizes in the cycle races were won on 'Ivel' machines. In the mile tricycle race he was third, and first in the two mile club handicap.

In August at Cambridge in the one mile open handicap he came in first, and second in the two mile open handicap.

In September in Cambridge he was second in the four mile handicap and also won the Championship of the Biggleswade & District Cycling Club over a distance of about five miles.[8]

A few days later he obtained a first at the Peterborough B. C. event in an open handicap from scratch with a time of 2 min. 46.2 secs.

In October at the Alexandra Palace he obtained a first in the one mile open handicap, beating Adams.

In the 100 mile 'Kangaroo' race on October 20th a new record of 6 hr. 39 min. 5 secs. was set by E. T. Hale. Dan came in fifth with a time of 7 hr. 9 min. 58 secs., following a fall in which he hurt his leg. He was awarded a medal, which he lost on Peace Day 1901, but which was months afterwards found in a carriage window slot.

At Huntingdon Athletic Sports he obtained a first in the two mile handicap prize.

1886

At Oundle, on the Easter Monday, Dan came in last in the final. Bicycling News commented, somewhat cruelly, that *"Albone has the ingredients of a fine rider, which he will never improve upon until he takes regular practice and utilises the joints of his ankles."*[9]

At Wisbech in July he came second in the one mile handicap and second in the three mile handicap.

At the Fête in Biggleswade, he was second in the two mile open, second in the one mile open, and first in the half mile scratch.

1887

At Oundle Athletic Sports on April 11th, he was first in the bicycle one mile open, and first in the bicycle two mile open, both from scratch.

On April 19th he competed at Oxford and secured a first from 30 yds. in the bicycle mile open handicap with a time of 2 min. 46 secs. He was also placed first in the five miles bicycle race.

At Alexandra Palace on May 21st, Dan was placed second from 55 yds in the bicycle mile.

In Peterborough on May 30th, he placed second from scratch in the bicycle mile. He also placed third from scratch in the bicycle two miles.

At the sixth annual Biggleswade Fête on August 1st, with about 8,000 spectators present, he was second in the one mile bicycle open from scratch, beaten by H. A. Speechly by a length, time 3 min.

---

7   *Wheeling*, April 8th 1885
8   *Wheeling*, September 16th 1885
9   *Bicycling News*, May 7th 1886

7.4 secs., second by four yards in the two mile bicycle open from scratch, and first in the half mile bicycle open from scratch with a time of 1 min. 27.8 secs.

At Bradford Dan won second prize in the one mile and two mile bicycle races.

In Oxford on August 18th, Dan was second from scratch in the safety three miles to F. S. Buckingham by a length, and second from 75 yds., again to Buckingham by a foot, in the bicycle five miles, time 9 min. 20 secs.

On August 20th, Dan competed at Ipswich and was second from 20 yds. in the bicycle half mile.

Note that the above references to 'bicycle' and 'safety', taken from the same source, indicate that Dan was still competing on an Ordinary in 1887.

The Biggleswade and District C.C. championship race over five miles was won by Dan, from Richard Tingey, in a time of 14 min. 30 secs.[10]

1888

At Peterborough in May, he won a second and a third, and a second at the Alexandra Palace.

At Bedford on May 21st, Dan was first in the mile handicap from scratch with a time of 3 min. 42.8 secs. He was then placed second in the two mile handicap from scratch with a time of 7 min. 47.8 secs.

On July 4th he rode with J. W. Rowe in the mile tandem tricycle handicap at Wisbech coming third in 3 min. 40 secs. having been given 20 yds.

At Bradford on July 21st Dan rode the two mile safety handicap from scratch and came second with a time of 7 min. 34.4 secs.

At Harrogate on August 4th, Dan came first in the one mile tricycle handicap, having been given 40 yds., in 3 min. 50 secs. He also rode the two mile safety handicap and came second with a time of 9 min. 36 secs.

In Biggleswade on August 6th, Dan was third in the one mile handicap from scratch with a time of 3 min. 15.2 secs. He was also first in the one mile tricycle handicap from scratch with a time of 4 min. 9 secs.

Ten riders lined up for the N.C.U. National 25 mile Championship to be held on the new Grimsby Cycling Club track. H. Synyer, J. H. Adams of the Speedwell, F. B. Woods of Brixton B.C., D. Albone of Biggleswade & District C.C., B. Hinchcliffe of Derby B.C., W. J. Rowe of Peterborough B.C., G. W. Howard of Ilkeston B.C., R. M. Wright of Grimsby C.C., H. H. Sansom of Notts Castle B.C., and W. Price of Paddington B.C., with Adams being the eventual winner. Dan came in fifth with a time of 1 hr. 22 min.

At Bradford in August he came second in the one mile and two mile and at Ipswich in the half mile handicap.

On August 20th Dan rode at Sheffield coming second in the two mile open tricycle handicap to H. A. Sansom with a time of 6 min. 28 secs. He also rode the one mile safety bicycle handicap at this event coming first from 15 yds. with a time of 2 min. 59.8 secs.

The next day at Ketton Sports and Races, Dan was second to M. F. Rowe in the one and two mile bicycle handicaps.

At the seventh annual Fête, he was first in the half mile open scratch and third in the two mile.

On the Paddington track Dan rode with E. J. Willis on an improved 'Ivel' tandem over 20 miles which they completed in 1 hour, 5 minutes and 55.8 seconds.

At a cycle meeting held at Scheveningen, Holland on September 9th, Dan was first in the 5 kilometer International Tricycle Scratch Race, in a time of 11 min. 10 sec., for which the prize was a silver wreath, property of the person who won it three times. He was also second in a two and a half mile handicap safety race, first in the tricycle handicap of the same distance, and third in the half mile safety handicap. On his return to Biggleswade there was a welcome gathering in his honour.

On September 29th Dan won the Championship of Bedfordshire five mile race in Bedford Park on the grass. The race was rather tactical hence the time was only 21 min. 35 secs.

On October 9th, Dan rode with Richard Tingey on the 'Ivel Ordinary Tandem Safety' breaking the fifty miles record in 2 hr. 59 min. 39 secs.

Also on October 13th, Dan rode with E. E. Glover on the 'Ivel Ordinary Tandem Safety', weighing 49 lbs. and geared to 63 in., and broke the fifty miles record, in 2 hr. 52 min. 3 secs. They cycled from Peterborough to Hitchin, via Kate's Cabin, Norman Cross, Stilton, Buckden and Biggleswade, where it is reported, they had a cold collation. The riders also lost two minutes through waiting at Henlow Crossing for a luggage train to pass.

At the Paddington track on October 15th, Dan with Glover broke the 20 mile path record with a time of 1 hr. 2 min. 16.6 secs.[11]

1889

At the Biggleswade Fête Meeting, Dan was third in the one mile tricycle handicap and first in the half mile open scratch, which was immensely popular.

1890

August 4th, Dan was first in the 880 yards at the Biggleswade Fête, beating A. F. Ilsley.

On August 9th he was third in the mile safety handicap from 85 yards at Sheffield with a time of 2 min. 37.5 secs.

1891

From press comments in 1891 it seems that Dan had given up competitive racing although he still competed at the Biggleswade Fête.

---

11 *National Cyclists' Union Review and Official Record*, 1888, p.139

Identification of Cycles

Production

We do not know for sure what numbering system Dan Albone used. It is assumed the system was cumulative numeric, based on the known examples. The projection below is based on the reported facts and some assumptions. It must be stressed these are 'best guesses' since there are no records available to us now.

Year	Cumulative	Reported Facts
1880	10	Start of production by Dan working alone
1883	35	Mother died and became landlord of Ongley Arms
1884	75	Dan took on three men
1885	275	
1886	600	
1887	1000	Report that, following move to Ivel Hotel, production was 30 machines a week, seven times previous year
1888	1500	50 men now employed
1889	2100	
1890	2800	
1891	3600	
1892	4700	Over one hundred employees at peak
1893	5600	Over 700 machines in stock
1894	5800	Post liquidation started with just 20 men
1895	6000	
1896	6275	Idea for Agricultural Motor
1897	6600	Motor car development starts
1898	6900	
1899	7200	First motor car sold
1900	7500	
1901	7800	Motor bicycle production starts
1902	8100	Ivel Agricultural Motor announced
1903	8400	36 men in Works photograph, apart from Dan.
1904	8700	
1905	9000	
1906	9300	

Fig.215: c.1899 head badge

The known and probable 'Ivel' cycles are:

1. An Ordinary that was at one time in the Shuttleworth Collection but its whereabouts are currently unknown.

2. A claimed cross-frame solid-tyre safety in the Science Museum.[1] This machine has been attributed with a date of 1886 but it has top and bottom stays so probably dates to c.1889-90. Also, there are some detail differences from the machines in the 'Ivel' catalogues. Specifically, the actual position in which the top and bottom stays are located does not match any machine in the 1890 or 1891 catalogues; second, there are some detail differences with the seat pillar and the position of the mudguard stays which also differ from the catalogues; third, there is too much curvature to the front forks to match the machines in the catalogues and the general form of Ivel forks. It is understood that there are no markings, frame number, or badge, and no provenance that it is an 'Ivel'. It appears more likely the machine is an 'R&P'.

3. An 1888 tandem at one time in the Raleigh Collection, Nottingham, and then the National Cycle Museum, Lincoln, which was sold at auction in 1998 and is now believed to be in a private collection.[2]

4. A cross-frame solid-tyre safety in New Zealand. This appears to have the frame number 1487.

5. A cross-frame solid-tyre safety in Coventry Transport Museum. This may have been Dan's own racing machine used by G. P. Mills on grass tracks as there are several departures from standard.[3] On this machine a number of features have been noted:

- both hubs are stamped with patent No.1877/3531 (patentee J. N. Hughes, for 'Bown's' adjustable ball bearings);
- it has been re-painted a light olive green, understood to match the original colour;
- the front wheel has 36 spokes, is nominally of 30 in. dia. (29 in. actual), with 5/8 in. tyre;
- the rear wheel has 36 spokes, is nominally of 28 in. dia., with 3/8 in. tyre;
- the chainwheel has 16 teeth, and the rear sprocket has 7 teeth, for gearing of 64 in. (based on actual 28 in. dia.);

Fig.216: Lady's tandem sold at auction in 1998 (courtesy Bonhams auctioneers)

Fig.217: Cross-frame in New Zealand

Fig.218: Cross-frame, Coventry: detail below

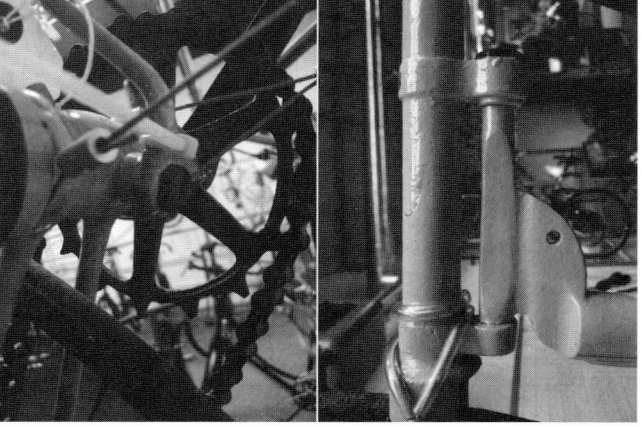

1   *Cycles – History and Development*, Part 1, Page 36, and Part 2, Page 15. Image opposite page 27 in Part 1. Inventory No.1924-74. Located in the Wroughton store at the time of publication.
2   Veteran-Cycle Club, *News & Views*, No. 114/3 and Phillips auction August 15th 1998, lot 364.
3   *Bartleet's Bicycle Book*, page 79.

Fig.219: Cross-frame rear drop-out detail

Fig.220: Cross-frame top stay tensioner

Fig.221: Frame No.8119 on top head lug

Fig.222: Rear drop-out 1902

- wheelbase is 40½ in. approximately;
- the stay is bolted to the under-side of the bottom bracket;
- the bottom bracket to chainstay lug distance is 14½ in.
- the cross-lug to end of dropout distance is 16½ in.
- the cross-lug to steering swivel distance is 17½ in.
- the distance from the top of the steering swivel to bottom is 4¾ in.
- the width of the handle-bars is 27 in.
- the distance from the bracket to the top of the seat tube is 23 in.
- the cranks are 7 in. max.
- the wheel axles and the crank axle are hol low.

6. An Anti-vibration Safety seen in 1979 at the Boston Veteran-Cycle Club Rally.[4]

7. A juvenile safety c.1896, believed to be either the one made for Lord Napier of Magdala or the one made by Dan for his son, was exhibited at Luton Museum in 1978. However its current whereabouts are unknown, but it is presumed to have survived.

8. A gent's safety with double top tube c.1899, frame 7032, size 24 in. This is just a frame and forks. Note that the top tubes are not parallel.

9. Lady Shuttleworth's No.5 Lady's Safety 1901, in the Shuttleworth Collection, frame 7736. This machine has lost its chaincase. It has 28 in. wheels. There is a three-speed hub gear in a wheel that appears to be a replacement as the rim does not match with the front.

10. A gents No.2 Light Roadster Safety c.1902, frame 7874, size 26 in., at one time owned by Mrs Munns of Biggleswade. This does not have the original wheels. It bears a nicely cast head badge modelled on the 1896 'Ivel' trade mark but this is not original. The cranks have pinch-bolts.

11. A No.5 Lady's Safety c.1902 in Evandale, Tasmania, Australia, frame 7934.

12. A No. 5 Lady's Safety c.1902 located in Bedfordshire, frame 8119, size 23 in. The cranks, which appear to be original, no longer have pinch-bolts to hold the pedal spindles.

4   Veteran-Cycle Club, *News & Views*, No. 151/8

Fig.223 Lady's No.5 front brake lever

Fig.224: Fork crown 1901

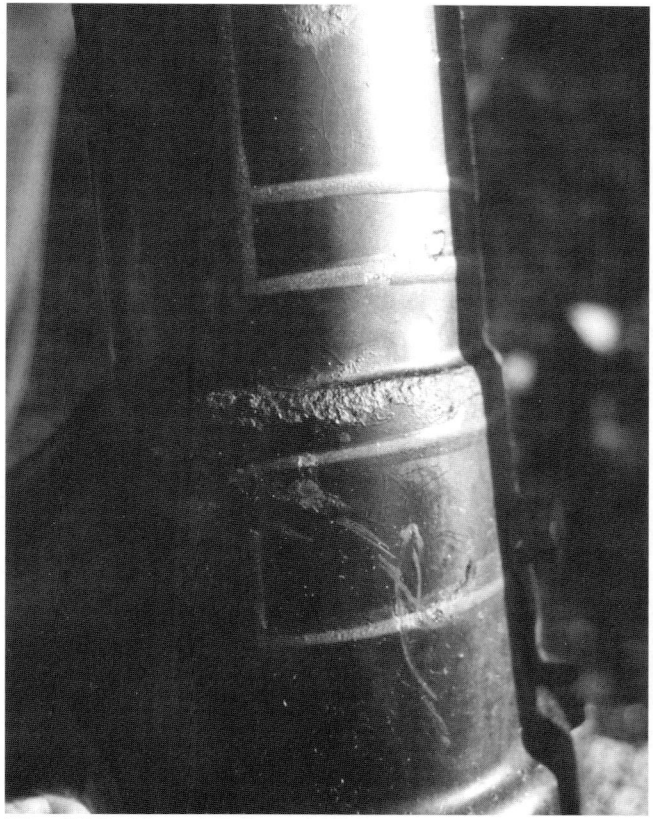

Fig.225: Head lining 1902

Fig. 226: Fork lining 1902

Fig.227: Front mudguard stay bracket

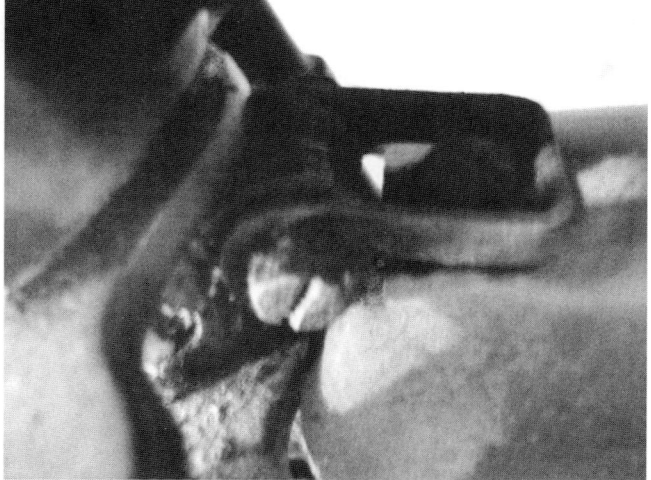

Fig.228: Front mudguard bracket 1901

Fig.229: Bottom bracket 1901

Fig.230: Seat stay 1901

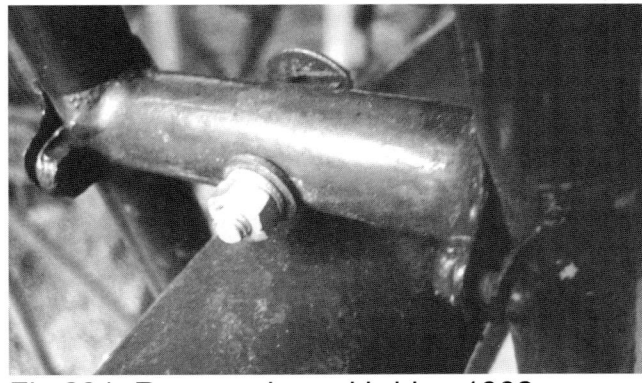

Fig.231: Rear mudguard bridge 1902

Cycle Features:

With the solid-tyre safeties there were some notable features, namely:

1.   A near-side or left-hand chainwheel. Until about 1893 'Ivel's had the chainwheel on the left or near-side. However this does not mean that every machine with a left-hand chainwheel is an 'Ivel'. For example, this was also a feature of the much larger concern of Hillman, Herbert & Cooper with their 'Premier' rear-drivers until about 1899. There were others too with a left-hand chainwheel such as the Howe Machine Co. 'Albemarle'; F. J. Rodgers 'Dreadnaught'; Robinson & Price 'R&P'; Tomes & Beard 'Reynard', the 'Onward' by Samuel Cotterill and the 'Wulfruna' by John Barratt; so this was not an unusual feature of its time. It is understood that the left-hand drive bracket assembly is 'handed' in that it could only be assembled that way.

2.   The No.5 Racing 'Ivel' Safety of 1887 had fixed seat pillars and handlebars, obviously made to measure for the customer. However note that the machine in Coventry Transport Museum does not have a welded seat pillar.

3.   The cross-frame safeties also had hollow bottom bracket and rear wheel axles.

4.   Straight forks were normal for early 'Ivel' cross-frames, but slightly curved forks were optional. Later models had curvature from c.1890.

5.   Larger front wheel than the rear. This was at least the case according to the catalogues up to 1896. From 1886 the front wheel of the rear-driver safety was of 32 in. dia. and the rear wheel 30 in. dia. Those dimensions continued to be the case into 1889. The 1891 catalogue does not spell out the sizes but the illustrations of cross-frame machines show a larger front wheel. Dan was still producing safety bicycles with a 30 in. dia. front wheel in 1902 according to the catalogue. However it should be noted that the surviving cross-frame machine in the Coventry Transport Museum has equal-size wheels which appears to be a bit of an anomaly.

6.   A double top tube frame was an option from c.1899 for the 'Ivel' No.1 Roadster Safety as can be seen in the 1901-02 catalogue.

7.   Threads. It appears that the 'Ivel' used a 30 t.p.i. thread on 5/16" front axle for the solid-tyre safety whereas Premier used 19 t.p.i. to prevent oth-

ers effecting repairs on their machines.

8. In general, 'Ivel' handlebars are notably wide and flat.

9. The frame number for machines from c.1899 is located on the front of the top head lug.

10. A double-plate fork crown was used up to c.1905.

11. The bottom bracket detail is distinctive for machines c.1900. In particular note the forward-facing clamp bolt for the near-side bracket cup. The off-side bracket cup is clamped by a screw beneath the bracket. In addition there is an oiler on the top of the bottom bracket on the near-side. The precise position of this might be variable according to the machinist as it is noted that the position of the oiler on Lady Shuttleworth's machine is inclined slightly forward whereas a slightly later machine has the oiler mounted in a vertical position.

12. The rear drop-out is particularly distinctive from c.1896 with its "kick-up" of the chain stay end combined with swinging seat stays. Interestingly it is quite similar to that of the Humber where G. P.

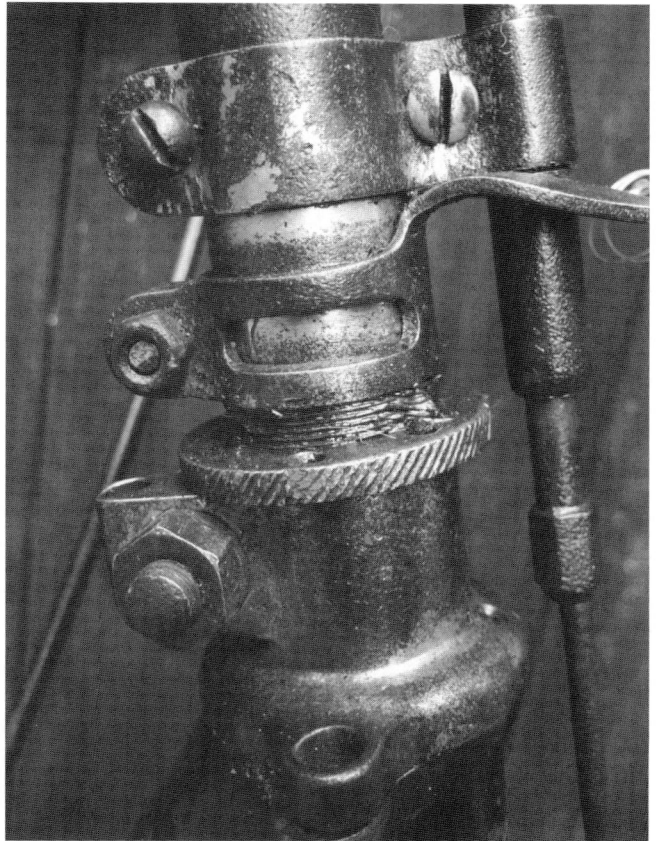

Fig.232: Head clamp and steering lock 1902

Mills worked as chief designer after leaving the Ivel Cycle Co.[5] It is presumed that G. P. Mills was happy for Dan to use it after he left Humber for Raleigh in 1894.

13. Often the seat stays differ between manufacturers. In the case of the 'Ivel' seat stay of c.1900 it has a simple crimped end to the tube.

14. The front mudguard stays c.1900 were joined before the spindle.

15. A rear brake operated by Bowden cable was available from c.1900 but could have been added after purchase.

16. The Lady's No.5 for 1901 has a single green line on black down the front fork blades, the frame tubes and the seat stays but not on the chain stays or mudguards.

17. From at least c.1899, if not before, there was a gold 'Ivel' seat tube transfer pierced by a double headed arrow. This transfer was positioned so that it could be read from the off-side.

The authors would be interested to hear from anyone with further information or a cycle for identification. Contact can be established via the Secretary of the Veteran-Cycle Club.

Fig.233: Rear brake (not Bowden) on 1901 'Ivel'

---

5   *Modern Cycles*, A. J. Wallis-Tayler, pp.173-175 and patent 1890-8890.

Fig.234: Double top tube frame No. 7032

Fig.235: Lady's No.5 frame No. 7934

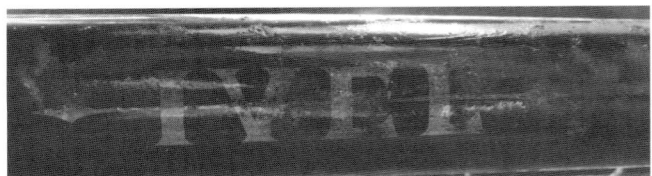

Fig.237: Seat tube transfer

Fig.236: Lady's No.5 frame No. 8119

Fig.238: 1902 Lady's No.5 and proud owner

Fig.239: Magnificent 1902 head badge

THE "IVEL" RACER.

A Machine that can be safely asserted to be second to none. It has, during the past season, been very successful, winning no less than 110 prizes, including the Championship of Bedfordshire for two years, and many other important events.

Weight for 54in., complete, 21lbs.

PRICE £15 15s.

This price includes ball bearings throughout, hollow rims, hollow handle-bar of most approved shape, plated hubs, handle bar, cranks, pedals, &c., rest enamelled by Harrington.

THE "IVEL" ROADSTER.

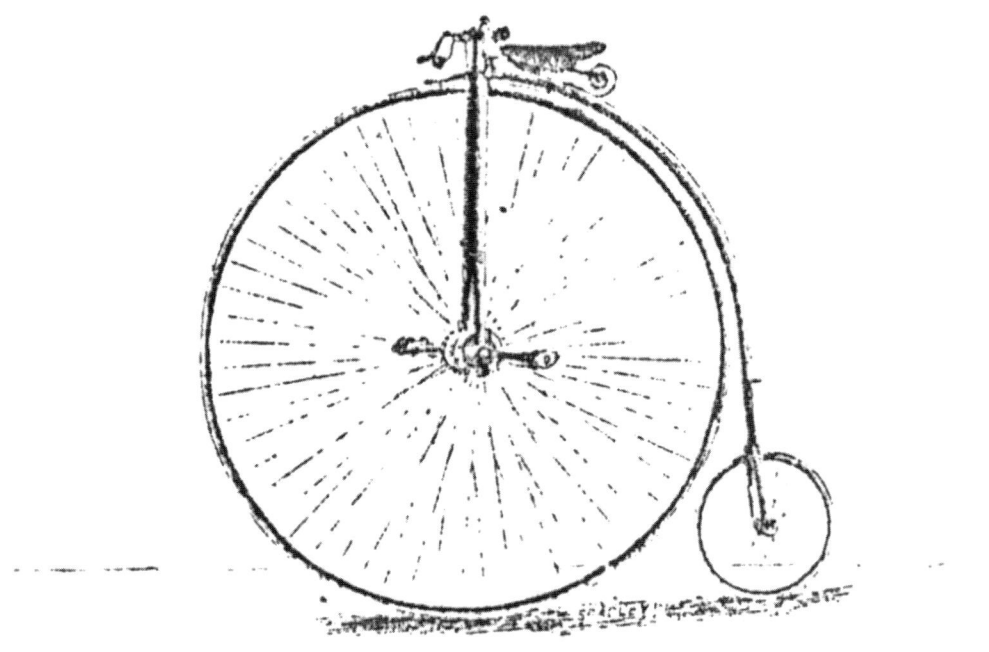

A Machine similar to the Light Roadster. Fitted with solid rims, ball bearings both wheels, hollow forks back and front, plain pedals, handle-bar (cowhorn or crank).

Painted and lined.

PRICE £12 10s.

EXTRAS.—Half-plated, £1. Enamelled, 10/-. Ball pedals, 15/-.

A still cheaper Machine than the above is fitted with solid forks, ball bearings front wheel, cones to back, &c.

PRICE £10.

A good, strong, sound, and reliable Machine.

The "Ivel" Light Roadster.

This Machine has been specially designed for those requiring a bicycle of stouter build than the Racer. but lighter than the Roadster. Is specially suited for grass racing, or where the course is rather rough.

Can be made with smaller hubs if desired.

Weight, complete, about 34 lbs.

PRICE £15 15s.

This price includes ball bearings throughout, hollow rims, hollow handle-bar (cowhorn or crank), plated head and handle-bar, brake-set, hubs, cranks, pedals. &c., rest enamelled by Harrington.

THE "IVEL" TRICYCLE.

Undoubtedly the favourite form of Tricycle for those requiring a fast machine. The action being similar to a bicycle, is easily learned by riders of the latter machine.

Ball bearings throughout, except pedals; balance-gear in the centre, fitted with powerful band-brake, thus giving full control over machine down steepest hill.

PRICE £19.

This price includes plated hubs, handle-bar, bearings, &c., rest enamelled by Harrington.

EXTRAS.—Hollow rims, 25/-. Ball pedals, 15/-.

THE "IVEL" LIGHT ROADSTER SAFETY BICYCLE.

This Machine is as fast as any luxury bicycle and as safe as a tricycle

Fitted with ball bearings throughout. Keisey's patent Duplex bearings to bottom chain-wheels (for particulars see page 9), hollow rims, hollow handle-bar (cowhorn or crank), Abingdon patent chain, &c.

Can be made geared to suit purchaser.

PRICE £15 15s.

This price includes plated hubs, head and handle-bar, brake set, bearings, &c., rest enamelled by Harrington.

EXTRAS.—Foot-rests, 7/6. Mud-guard, 5/-.

THE "IVEL" ROADSTER SAFETY BICYCLE.

A similar Machine to the above.

Ball bearings throughout, except pedals; Bown's patent adjustable crank and chain-wheel (for particulars see page 5), solid rims, hollow forks back and front, handle-bar (cowhorn or crank). Painted and lined.

PRICE £12 10s.

EXTRAS.—Half-plated, £1. Enamelled, 10/-. Ball pedals, 15/-. Foot-rests, 7/6. Mud-guard, 5/-.

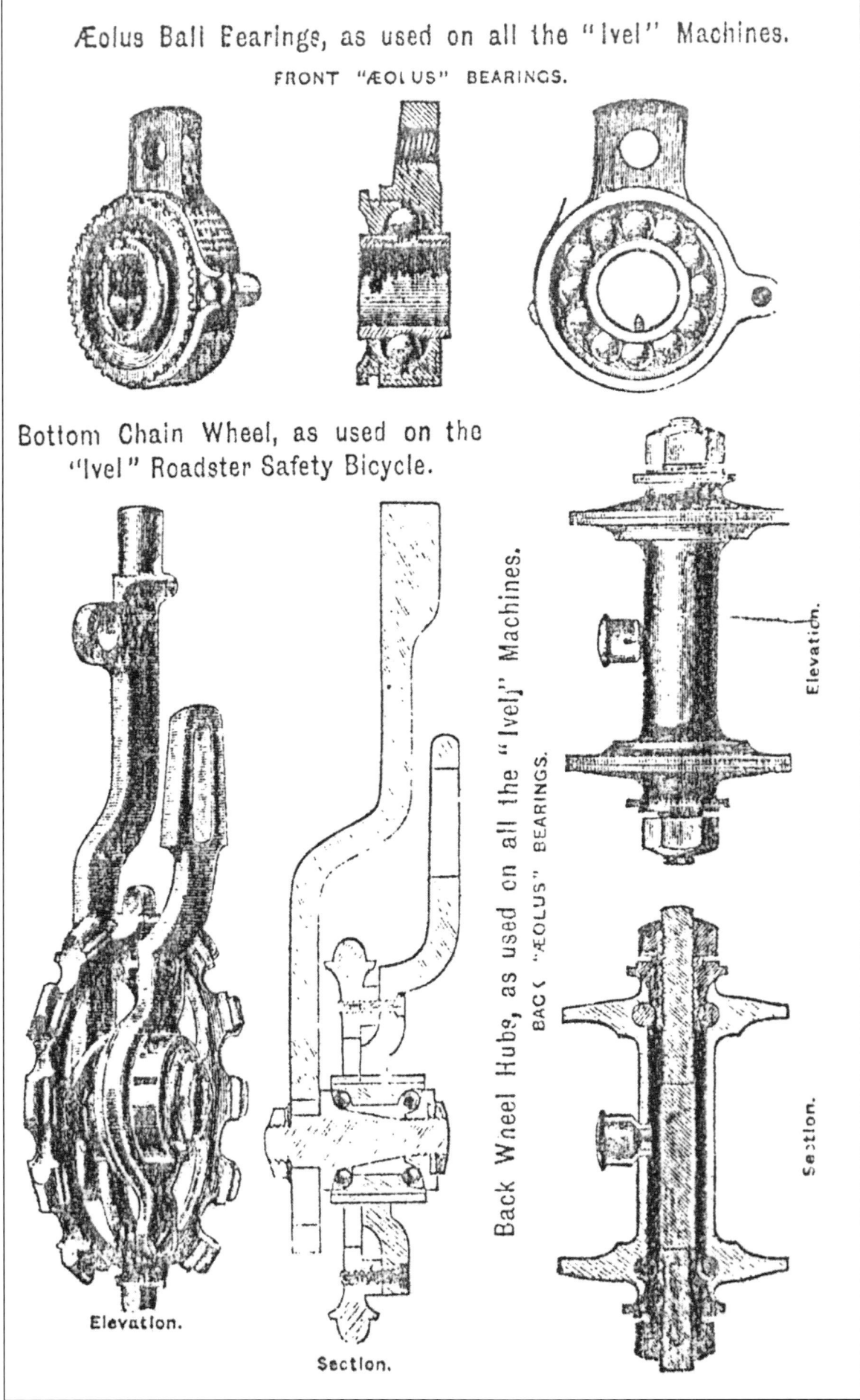

Æolus Ball Bearings, as used on all the "Ivel" Machines.

FRONT "ÆOLUS" BEARINGS.

Bottom Chain Wheel, as used on the
"Ivel" Roadster Safety Bicycle.

Back Wheel Hubs, as used on all the "Ivel" Machines.

BACK "ÆOLUS" BEARINGS.

Elevation.

Section.

Elevation.

Section.

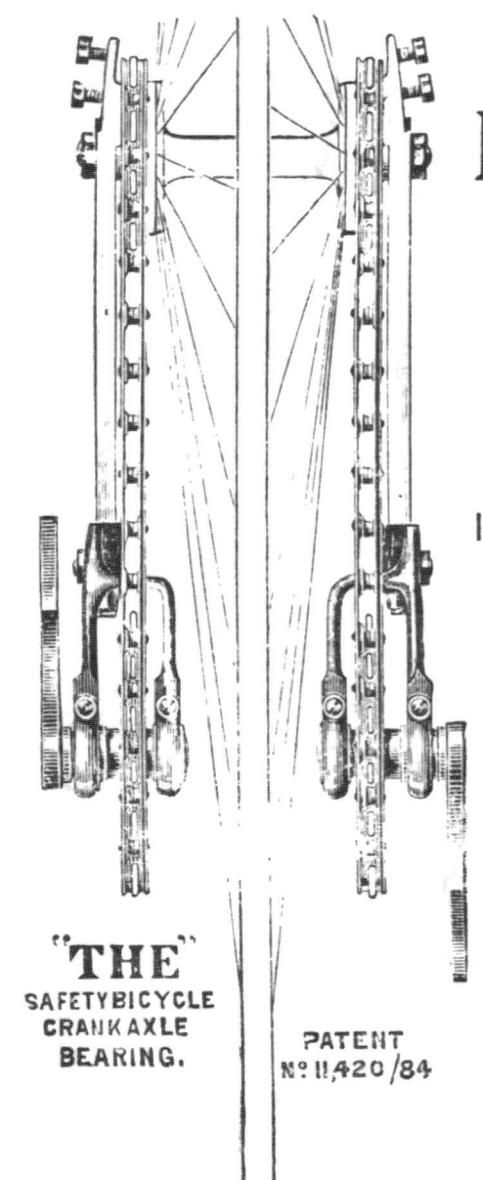
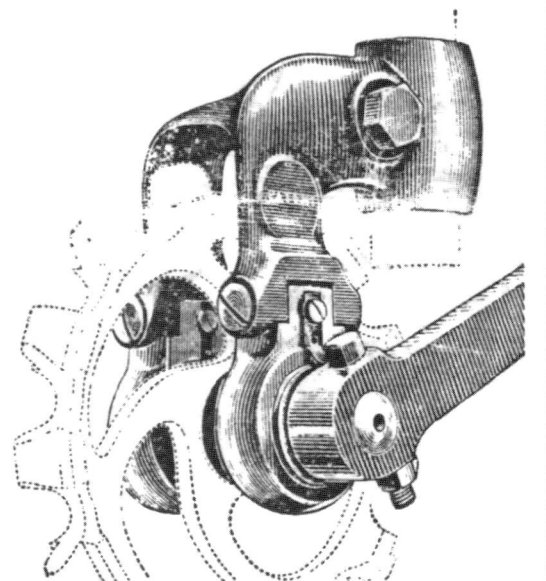

The 'Ivel' Automatic Steerer.

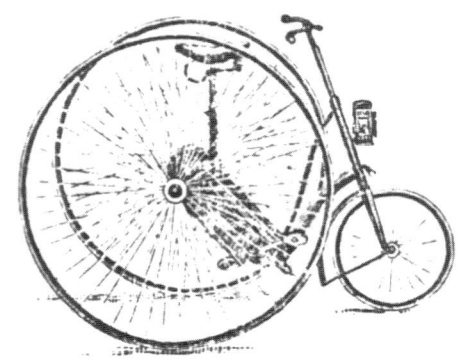

Suitable for either Lady or Gentleman.

This Machine is at one the most comfortable form of tricycle extant. The steering is wonderfully easy, and on a straight road miles can be ridden almost without touching the handles. Ball bearings throughout except pedals, balance gear, &c., fitted with powerful band brake.

PRICE £20.

This price includes plated hubs, handle-bar, bearings, &c.; rest enamelled by Harrington.

EXTRAS.—Hollow rims, 25/· Ball pedals, 15/-.

1887.

PRICE LIST OF

THE "IVEL"

(TRADE MARK REGISTERED),

BICYCLES & TRICYCLES,

MANUFACTURED BY

DAN ∴ ALBONE,

"IVEL" CYCLE WORKS

BIGGLESWADE,

BEDFORDSHIRE, ENGLAND.

AGENT :—

ALL PREVIOUS LISTS CANCELLED.

—AGENTS.—

Samples of the "IVEL Safety" can be seen at any of the following depôts :-

BRADFORD (and **KEIGHLEY**): Thos. Redman & Co., 172, Manningham Lane.

BIRMINGHAM: J. H. CLARKE.

DRIFFIELD: J. Elvidge, 58, Middle Street.

DUBLIN: Booth Brothers, Upper Stephen Street.

DUNDEE: Wm. Black, 94, Murraygate.

EDINBURGH: H. Hally, 22, Spittal Street.

GLOUCESTER: W. Stout, Westgate Street.

HALIFAX (and **MIDDLESBORO'**): J. S. Earnshaw, The Square.

HULL: Taffinder & Co., Spring Bank.

LIVERPOOL: Slade & Co.

LEICESTER: The West End Cycle Company.

LONDON (E.C. & E.): Herbert Smith & Co., 9, New Broad St.

LONDON (W.C.): R. Willis, 25, Castle Street East, near Oxford Circus, W.

MANCHESTER: Jennings & Co., 44, Deansgate.

NEWCASTLE-on-TYNE: W. Olliff, 13, Grainger St., West.

PAIGNTON (DEVON): W. Griffin, 2, Gerston Place.

RYDE (ISLE of WIGHT): D. E. Marvin, 75, Union Street.

St. ALBANS: A. Pellant.

The "Ivel" Cycles can also be obtained to order through any of the undermentioned Agents :—

Amsterdam, J. Holst ; Samuels and Co ; Boston (Lincs) A. W. Forinton ; Bristol, W. J. Herbert ; W. H. Grimwade ; J. S. Willway ; T. Morgan ; Bayern, Louis Schmetzer et Cie ; Bale, De Speyr and Co ; Brighton, Henry Moore ; Thompson and Gordon ; W. Halliwell ; Belper, W. J. Parker ; Carrington, J. Scott ; Derby, E. C. Clarke and Co ; Denmark, K. L. Momines ; Copenhagen ; Exeter, W. H. Casley ; Fulham (London) J. Harrington and Co ; Hereford, Naylor and Co ; Horgen, Hunerwadel and Co ; Holland, Em. Kiderlen ; Jersey, S. Dancaster ; London (W) Goy, Limited ; London (export) McLean Bros. and Rigg ; London (S.E.) G. Skudder and Co ; Lyons, P. Rousset and Ingold ; Leek, W. T. Cook ; Long Eaton, T. W. Youngman ; Munden, Carl Beuerman ; Oldham, J. Hoyel ; Preston, Baddeley and Co ; Prague, A. Rosenbaum ; Riga, Hugo Herman Meyer ; Rochdale, W. Greenwood ; St. Etienne, P. de Vivie ; Sheffield, Leadbeater and Scott ; Swindon, R. H. Nicholson ; Scarboro, J. H. Hackett ; Stroud, H. Nispel ; Tooting, F. T. Shaw ; Tralee, J. G. Hodgins ; Torquay, Edwards and Son ; Worcester Bowcott and Co. ; Wisbeach, J. Morris, Jr. ; Winsford, T. E. Leigh ; Widnes, W. Crabtree.

144

IVEL CYCLE WORKS, BIGGLESWADE.

————:o:————

The feature of Cycling in 1885 was the decisive advance in popularity of the rear driving form of safety bicycle ; and since I designed the " Ivel " Safety, its success has been so phenomenal that I have been inundated with orders, and have had to entirely re-construct my works, removing, in the present month, to much larger premises, which I have built especially for the purpose of Cycle construction, next door to my old factory. Here, with increased facilities for turning out the best class of work, I trust to always merit the favour which has been so freely bestowed upon me lately.

The " Ivel " Safety Bicycle is now my speciality, although I continue to make some of the patterns which attained so good a reputation previously to the Safety era ; and in the following pages I have set out details of the various modifications in design which I am prepared to supply to satisfy all requirements and tastes, from the " Racing Ivel," for path use, and the " Semi Racing " for good roads, to the " Irish Ivel " which I have especially constructed for exceptionally rough roads.

The speed of these machines is so conclusively proven by the records of fast performances detailed elsewhere, and their comfort is so exemplified by the remarkably long distances ridden upon them, that I need say no more on that point, except that these records of speed and endurance *on the road* are far more conclusive than any number of races won on smooth racing tracks.

In the " Anfield Ivel " Tricycle I have provided a machine unique in its simplicity, and which is more adaptable to the use of ladies than any other form of handle-bar steered tricycle. In its convertible form, too, this machine affords riders a means whereby they can ride either bicycle or tricycle, as circumstances suggest, at far less cost than would be incurred by the possession of two separate machines, and with the great advantage of not altering the position and action in the slightest,—a consideration which will appeal forcibly to all who have felt the discomfort inseparable from changing off one kind of cycle on to another.

Although I use the best materials, and the most skilled workmanship, in all my machines, it will be found that my prices all round are considerably less than those of other first-class makers.

January, 1887.   DAN ALBONE.

The " Ivel " Safety Bicycle.

The " IVEL " Roadster Safety Bicycle.

This bicycle, in addition to being faster, and easier to drive, than any other form of bicycle, is completely safe in every respect, a header being impossible, and a side-fall so difficult of accomplishment as to be almost an impossibility. The rear wheel (30 inches in diameter) drives, and the front one (32 inches) steers, so that there is no tendency in the front wheel to deflect at each stroke of the pedals, as there is in all other forms of bicycles ; and the steering is so arranged that any ordinarily expert rider can leave hold of the handles and ride along for many miles without touching the steering-bar driving in a straight line, or turning aside to dodge stones, ruts, &c., and turning corners, merely by an almost unconscious swaying of the body. The steering is not controlled by any spring or cam, but is entirely free ; and the correctness of the adjustment causes the guidance and balancing to be singularly easy, and free from the eccentricity so noticeable on other machines, including many bicycles which are apparently identical in construction with the " Ivel " It is much easier to learn than an ordinary bicycle, the steering and balancing not being affected by the alternate pressure on the pedals, while the proximity to the ground is a source of great confidence to the beginner

The simplicity of its construction, and freedom from complicated parts, renders it much less likely to get out of order than other safety bicycles; and it is made throughout of the best possible materials,—weldless steel tubing, direct spokes, accurately turned cogwheels, smooth-running patent hardened chain, and laterally adjustable ball-bearings, being used on all patterns; the only variety being in the details, not in the quality, of the parts.

SPECIFICATIONS AND PRICES.

No. 1.—THE CHEAP "IVEL" SAFETY.—Weldless steel tube frame; hollow back fork; shell front fork; hollow handle-bar; pear handles; double-lever spoon break; adjustable saddle; adjustable mud-guards; solid U rims; plain pedals; long cranks; stay-rod between crank bearings and steering centres; $\frac{3}{4}$ inch rubbers; lamp bracket for head lamp on extremity of front wheel spindle; enamelled black with plated hub, cranks and pedals.   £16 0s.

No. 2.—THE BEST "IVEL" SAFETY.—Adjustable handle-bar; pear or spade handles; plated handle-bar, cranks, seat-rod, hubs, and pedals; ball pedals; dirt-guard over chain if desired; $\frac{3}{4}$ or $\frac{7}{8}$ rubbers; all other details as No. 1.   £17 10s.

EXTRAS: Hollow rims, 10/-; stay-rods between crank bearings and back wheel fork, 10/-.

No. 3.—THE IRISH "IVEL" SAFETY.—Made with extra strong gauge steel tubing; hollow forks to both wheels; $\frac{3}{4}$ and $\frac{7}{8}$ in., or both $\frac{7}{8}$ in. rubbers; stay rods fore and aft; other details as No. 2.   £18 0s.

EXTRA: Hollow rims, 10/-.

No. 4.—THE SEMI-RACING "IVEL" SAFETY.— Extra light frame and wheels, suitable for road racing; detachable mudguards if desired; hollow rims; no break; ball pedals; adjustable pear or spade handles; adjustable saddle; half-plated.   £18 0s.

No. 5.—THE RACING "IVEL" SAFETY.—Made throughout as light as possible, with handle-bar & saddle fixed at height suitable to rider; laced tangent spoked wheels; rat-trap ball pedals.   £18 0s.

** *Gearing.*—Either of the above machines can be geared to within $1\frac{1}{2}$ in. of any height, to order, from 53 up to 66 inches. For ordinary roads and average riders the recommended gearing is 60 in.

No. 6., The " Ivel " Light Roadster.

This Machine has been specially designed for those requiring a bicycle of stouter build than a racer, but lighter than is usual with Roadsters. Is specially suited for grass racing, or where the course is rather rough.

Can be made with smaller hubs if desired.

Weight, complete, about 34lbs.

PRICE £17 10s.

This price includes ball bearings throughout, hollow rims, hollow handle-bar (cowhorn or crank); plated head and handle-bar, brake-set, hubs, cranks, pedals, &c., rest enamelled black.

No. 7., The " Ivel " Strong Roadster

A Machine similiar to the Light Roadster. Fitted with solid rims, ball bearings both wheels, hollow forks back and front, plain pedals, handle-bar cowhorn or cranked.

Enamelled black all over.

PRICE £13 10s.

No. 8., THE "IVEL" RACER.

A Machine that can be safely asserted to be second to none. It has during the past few seasons been very successful, winning an unprecedented proportion of prizes, including the Championship of Bedfordshire for four years, and many other important events.

Weight for 54in., complete, 21lbs.

PRICE £17 10s.

This price includes ball bearings throughout, hollow rims, hollow handle-bar of most approved shape; plated hubs, handle-bar, cranks, pedals, &c., rest enamelled black.

8   D. ALBONE, BIGGLESWADE.

No. 9., The " Anfield Ivel " Tricycle.

(Patent Applied for.)

This tricycle is made on the lines of the " Ivel " safety bicycle; and—like its two wheeled prototype——it can be steered in a straight line without the use of the hands, but without any spring or cam " controller " to tire the arms. It is made only in one quality—the very best; and in all details follows the " Ivel " safety lines as closely as possible. The wheels are respectively 32 in. (steerer) and 30 in. (drivers); and the axle is fitted with balance-gear to drive both the wheels. For very heavy riders, and bad roads, it is made with a long axle-bridge, and four bearings to the axle; and if desired it is made so that by loosening a couple of nuts the axle is removeable, and the machine can be converted into an " Ivel " Safety Bicycle, precisely the same position and action being maintained in both forms. The peculiar shape of the frame enables it to be kept very light, without sacrificing strength.

With solid rims; balls all over (including pedals) £22 0s.

EXTRAS:—Hollow rims, 15/-; four bearings to the axle 20/-; convertible into bicycle, £6.

No. 10.,
THE " ANFIELD IVEL " LADY'S TRICYCLE.

This machine is identical with No. 9; but has the tubing shaped so that a lady can ride it in ordinary costume, and can mount it and dismount it either in front or behind, the lowness of the axle being a great point in favour of easy mounting and dismounting. Prices, same as No. 9.

—SUNDRIES.—

£ s. d.

Spring-handled head-lamps, to suit brackets fitted to "Ivel" safety bicycles and tricycles, best make, post free 0 13 0

"The Gripper" non-vibrating spring-coil lamp-bracket, to fit on any ordinary bicycle or tricycle head, under a lock-nut, fits any sized lamp-socket and does not allow lamp to jump off; post free 0 2 3

"The Gripper" bracket, with annular clip to fasten on steering-post of "Ivel" safety or tricycle, clear of break-lever; post free 0 4 3

Luggage-carrier, as depicted on woodcut No. 9, fixes easily and rapidly on front of "Ivel" safety or tricycle, clear of break-lever; post free 0 10 0

Wheels, axle, &c., to convert any existing "Ivel" safety into an Anfield Ivel tricycle 10 0 0

Wallet, oilcan, fixed and adjustable spanners, sent out with every machine ... ... *Gratis.*

The " Ivel " Cycle Pony Trap.

(PATENT.)

The attention of gentlemen owning horses is directed to this vehicle. The wheels are built on the unequalled direct-suspension principle, and are fitted with rubber tyres of very best quality. The axle is hollow, and runs on patent double-row ball bearings, giving an ease in running, and freedom from friction, such as has never before been experienced on any vehicle whatever.

Carriages made on this principle run smoothly, and perfectly noiseless, and the saving in horse labour is incalculable; indeed, a horse will run as easy between the shaftes as if trotting alone; and the substitution of such a carriage for one of the ordinary type will add full ten years to a horse's working life, and keep him in a stronger and smarter condition. The light and elegant appearance of these vehicles is at once noticeable, no other carriages in any degree approaching them in this respect.

It may be imagined that the rubber tyres will soon become worn out. This, however, is not the case, the material being especially prepared for the purpose and equal to a surprising amount of wear. After long use the tyres can be turned at a merely nominal expense, when they will be equal to new again. Should new tyres be at any time desired, they can be supplied at a moderate charge ; the size of tyre recommended for an ordinary double-seated trap is 1⅜ in., but larger or smaller tyres can be fitted to order. Other pattern bodies can be fitted if required.

SPECIALLY RECOMMENDED FOR USE IN INDIA

and in other situations where it is desirable to reduce the labour of horses, and entirely abolish the irritating rattle and vibration inseparable from all other carriages.

Price for Trap, as shown, in best finish, 35 Guineas.

| EXTRAS | Hoods | - | - | - | 12 | ,, |
| | Lamps | - | - | - | 2½ | ,, |

These vehicles can, at a very small additional cost, be built specially light and stiff in the body, by the provision of a hollow steel frame. The panels can then be entirely removed in a few minutes, at once converting the trap into the strongest and fastest trotting machine made. The entire weight of the vehicle made thus, including all panels, splashboards, etc., is about 112lbs., and owing to its light draught and free running, it is the best possible vehicle for showing off a smart animal at a show or sale.

The spider wheels, rubber tyres, hollow axle, and patent double-row ball bearings can be fitted to any vehicle now in use without the slightest trouble, and without any alteration whatever, the bearings being merely bolted or clamped to the old springs. The price for these parts, viz., two 48 in. wheels, hollow axle, and patent double ball bearings, complete, is **15 Guineas,** advancing half-a-guinea for each additional two inches in height of wheels.

The ball bearings and axle only can be fitted to any vehicle now in use, the ordinary wooden wheels being still retained.

The maker will be pleased to answer any enquiries, or make arrangements for a practical trial.

TESTIMONIALS & OPINIONS OF THE PRESS.

(From an immense number of favourable letters and press notices, the following are selected almost at random.)

"I have carefully inspected Dan's compact little workshop, and examined the pieces and parts used in the construction of the 'Ivel' Cycles, together with samples of machines themselves, and can confidently recommend any one requiring a sound, neat, and excellent machine of any kind, at a reasonable figure, to give Albone a turn."—*Wheel Life.*

The " Ivel " rear-driving Safety appears to be in great request, and is Dan's principal " line " just now. He is turning these machines out in large numbers, and not only for England, but also for abroad. I was shown one for Germany that was on the stocks. Dan, as is very natural when a man has hit upon a very good thing, is mighty proud of his creation, and although I had never ridden one of these type of Bicycles before in my life—about the only pattern of safety, by the way, that I have not crossed—he must needs insist on trotting out his fancy and impress me into riding it. Having heard alarming tales of the difficulty in balancing and steering this class of machine, I was somewhat timid on making a commencement, but Dan was not to be denied, and after describing some very peculiar curves and angles, I got into the knack of the thing before I had ridden 20 yards, and pegged away for 20 miles. The result was to firmly establish my opinion that these machines are faster than the ordinary on the level, and far more comfortable than any other form of safety. Having only tried the " Ivel " of this type, it would be very unfair to attempt comparisons, but I may say at once that the " Ivel " is the fastest Safety I have ridden, it is very cleverly designed, built as lightly as strength and stability will admit, and is a good-looking, well finished machine.—*Cyclist*, Sept, 22nd, 1886.

"Fletcher's machine, on which he broke the 50 miles record, is a rear-driving Safety, framework of the Premier pattern, possessing the good points of the Rover and the former machine combined ; geared to 66 inches, with 7 inch cranks, it can move when a man like Fletcher gets aboard it. It weighs 37lbs, and is not a racer, and as it is built for use on the rough Lancashire roads, Dan tells us that he could make a racer to weigh 25lbs. If it moves in proportion to the manner of this, it would be a grand machine.—*Wheeling*, August 25th, 1885.

Dan Albone is jubilant. The " Ivel " Safety has got the best of the old scythe-bearer again, and holds two records which will stand for some time, fifty miles in 2hrs. 47mins. 36sec., and 295 miles in 24 hours. The marvellous performances speak for themselves as to the merit of the machine.—*Irish Cyclist*, October 13th, 1886.

One of the great drawbacks to the popularity of dwarf bicycles of the " Rover type has hitherto been the impossibility of their being ridden without at least one hand on the steering-bar ; and even with "automatic" or "fly to centre" spring arrangements, it has not been found possible to balance and steer a rear driving dwarf safety bicycle without the use of the hands. By some happy inspiration, Dan Albone has hit upon a means whereby this defect is overcome, and without adding any extra parts to the steering appliances, he has constructed an " Ivel " Safety, on the plan of the " Rover " or " Bicyclette," which can be ridden in a true and straight line, and even steered round easy corners without the use of hands. This is accomplished entirely by the adjustment of the steering centres at a particular angle, which, by its relative position as regards the wheel-base,

154

the weight, and the driving power, automatically keeps the front wheel in a straight line when the rider sits upright and drives steadily forward, and also deflects its course to the right or the left, in obedience to the inclination of the rider's body. The result is, of course, that the steering is not only capable of being controlled with the hands off, but also is vastly improved and rendered steadier when the hands are on the guiding bar, the bicycle being, indeed, under the most perfect control and less subject to sudden swerves and lurches than it would be without this newly-discovered self-steering angle.— *Wheel World*, October, 1886.

———

" It is worthy of remark that out of 18 prizes given in cycling events, 10 were won by " Ivel " machines of Dan Albone's manufacture. This speaks volumes in favour of our townsman's machines. Ten prizes in one day is something to be proud of."—*Beds. Mercury*.

———

6, Park Hall Place, East Finchley.

Dear Sir,—The 54in. " Ivel " roadster you built for me, has given entire satisfaction, and I find it to be one of the easiest running machines in the market. I am two miles an hour faster on your machine than my former one, although they each weigh the same.

Yours faithfully, G. R. WHITE, Vice-capt. Clissold B.C.
Mr. D. Albone, " Ivel " Works, Biggleswade.

———

Bancroft, Hitchin.

My dear Sir,—In answer to your letter I am glad to say that I still continue to like my tricycle you made for me last summer, and prefer it infinitely to my old one. It has stood a goodish deal of hard work on rough roads, and has shown remarkably little evidence of wear and tear for such a light machine.

I remain, yours faithfully,
RICHARD SHILLITOE.
Mr. D. Albone.

———

Perhaps the busiest maker at the present moment is Dan Albone, whose premises at Biggleswade are probably the smallest in the world devoted to the manufacture of high-class machines. He has been so successful as to construct a Safety Bicycle which has been demonstrated to possess unexampled good qualities. The fifty miles record and the 24hrs. record on the road have been handsomely beaten on this machine, called the " Ivel." and the reports of good material and workmanship put into his machines have resulted in his receiving a large influx of orders. It differs from the " Rover " in respect to its frame, which has none of the curves and flourishes of its antetype, but consists of a straight back fork, and three straight tubes, forming a **X**, and a front fork at right angles to the back fork. By some cunning arrangement of the steering-head, it can be driven straight, and even round easy corners, without the use of the hands. An especially strong pattern is being made for Irish roads, which would, I imagine, be just the thing for such districts of America as have roads too rough for the ordinary light type of bicycles.—*American Bicycling World*, 17 December, 1886.

We have at different times pointed out that when a horse is got into good hard condition, which is a work of time, strong exercise, and sound corn, it is a great pity to lose it, by turning the animal up for the summer in a loose box, or otherwise; and we have also advocated that condition might be kept up by a little regular exercise in harness. If anything can tend to strengthen our view, that this may be accomplished with ease and comfort to the horse, and pleasure to his owner, it is the introduction of the vehicle as shewn in our engraving, by Mr. D. Albone, of Biggleswade. Although brought out for a pony trap, we have no doubt it could be made suitable for any sized horse; the wheels, which are fitted with indiarubber tyres, of material specially prepared for the purpose, and equal to a large amount of wear, are built on the direct suspension principle. The axle is hollow, and runs on patent double row ball-bearings, which gives smooth, easy running, free from any motion, friction, or noise, which combination of freedom from disagreeables has, we believe, never before been attained in any kind of vehicle. It is almost needless to say that the carriage is light to a degree, and most elegant in appearance.—*Land and Water*, June 12, 1886.

" A stand whose contents attracted a great deal of attention was that of D. Albone, of Biggleswade, situated at No. 12. This pushing maker has a Pony Trap on view, with wheels as fitted to an ordinary bicycle. The frame is made of steel tube, and the axle runs in ball bearings. The whole is very light and fast, and should, we think, sell well......"—*Sportsman*, Feb. 15th, 1886.

Emmanuel College,
Cambridge, June 18th, 1886.

SIR,
    I have now given the PONY TRAP I purchased of you a good trial, and I am more than satisfied with it. It is without exemption, the most comfortable vehicle of any kind which I have ever used, and runs delightfully freely and noiselessly. It is a great saving of labour to the Horse, and answers my expectations and your own recommendations in every respect. The Tyres wear surprisingly well, and altogether I can conscientiously recommend your vehicle without the slightest reserve in any particular.

        Yours faithfully,
MR. DAN. ALBONE.   ....   HERBERT WILSON.

Cheriton, Alresford, Hants,
Sep. 5th, 1886.

DEAR SIR,
    The wheels arrived safely the day before yesterday, and I have had them put on the Cart and have driven it; they are perfect to travel with, and if the Tyres will stand the wear and tear of our roads, I could wish for nothing better. I drove the cart to a Lawn Tennis Party yesterday over a very stony road, several people looked at the wheels, and all agreed that the thing is just what is wanted.

        Yours truly,
        W. HIGGENS,
MR. DAN ALBONE.   ....   Late of the 90th Infantry.

THE "IVEL" HOTEL,

—BIGGLESWADE.—

DAN ALBONE, proprietor of the Ivel Cycle Works and the "Ongley Arms" inn, will shortly remove to the "Ivel Hotel," which is being built for him next door to the "Ongley Arms," where he will have greatly improved facilities for accommodating his patrons as economically as, and far more comfortably than was possible, at the old place so favourably known to cyclists as "Dan's Shanty." The new hotel is thus humourously described in *The Tricycling Journal* :—

"It is a fact which will doubtless be noticed with very general astonishment that I have lately been to Biggleswade,. And I have brought back a piece of news for North Road men. Dan (there is only one Dan, and the "Ivel" is his profit) is having an entirely new place built—hotel (a real one), workshops, and all. I have been over the site, and it was only because of the physical difficulties of the feat that I didn't surreptitiously bag and transplant that site to London, where I am informed such commodities are monetarily valuable. There is to be a small orchard (with a large man to mind it, please take notice); a foreshore, or bank, or wharf, or seaboard, or or coast, or quay, or something, abutting on the river or stream, with facilities for boating, swimming, and soaking string and worms in water (*vulgo* angling) ; and there is to be a lawn-tennis ground, an arbour, a pony, two cows, and a donkey, with other fittings ; and there is to be a revolver-butts for Mills, Faed, Adams, & Co., with a special target for the heavy artillery of my own Bull Dog ; and there is already a triangular meadow on the other side of the stream which is racking Dan's mind with mathematical chaos as how it can be made square or circular to hold a track ; and many messuages, tenements, holdings, estates, appurtenances, and dodgements. In the hotel are to be some ten or so large, airy, double-bedded bedrooms, beside a large club room, and dressing and rubbing-down room for scorchers, and a bath-room. Being a full and complete edition of all the fun of the fair. About the workshops, the dimensions of which Dan continually repeated to me, I shall say nothing, except that I don't recollect any of Dan's measurements, but I have an idea that one shop is to be seven or eight miles long, and proportionately wide, with several dozen stories—but I'm not quite certain about the stories, although one man to whom I mentioned these figures said he *was* quite sure about the stories. I wonder what he meant."

Telegraphic address :—"DANNERIES, BIGGLESWADE."

295 MILES in A DAY.

Although only on the Market for a few weeks, the

"Ivel" Safety Bicycle,

which can be ridden and steered without using the handles, has achieved the unique reputation of being incontestably the fastest Bicycle ever made, as the undermentioned performances demonstrate.

The 50 Miles Road Record beaten by A. H. Fletcher, Esq. Time, 3hrs. 9mins. 56¾secs., August 24, 1886.

The 50 Miles Road Record again beaten, by G. P. Mills, Esq. Time, 2hrs. 47mins. 36secs., October 2, 1886.

The 24 Hours Road Record beaten by A. H. Fletcher, Esq. Distance 265½ miles. September 1, 1886.

The 24 Hours Road Record again beaten, by G. P. Mills, Esq., October 5; the marvellous distance of 295 miles. The ordinary Bicycle and every other record totally demolished by over 23 miles, in spite of fog and a collision. Compare the actual figures with those of other makers claiming records for their Machines.

These Records are certified as correct by the National Cyclists' Union.

" Mr. MILLS spoke most highly of his mount, and gives it as his opinion that it is the best machine of its kind going."—CYCLIST, October 6th, 1886.

DAN ALBONE,

"IVEL" CYCLE WORKS, BIGGLESWADE.

J. C. SAWTELL, PRINTER, SHERBORNE, DORSET.

All Previous Lists Cancelled, January 1st, 1890.

1890

IVEL
CYCLES

MANUFACTURED BY THE

Ivel Cycle Company,
LIMITED.

Manufactories and Registered Offices:

BIGGLESWADE, BEDFORDSHIRE, ENGLAND.

London Agency and Showrooms:

77, FORE STREET,

AND

14, Fore St. Avenue,

London, E.C.

Telegraphic Address:
"DANNERIES,
BIGGLESWADE."

THE TEMPLE PRESS. (DANGERFIELD'S), 17½ BOUVERIE ST., FLEET ST., E.C.

All Previous Lists Cancelled, January 1st, 1890.

ILLUSTRATED PRICE LIST

OF

"IVEL"

BICYCLES AND TRICYCLES,

MANUFACTURED BY THE

"Ivel" Cycle Company,

LIMITED.

MANUFACTORIES AND REGISTERED OFFICES;

BIGGLESWADE, BEDFORDSHIRE, ENGLAND.

TELEGRAPHIC ADDRESS: "DANNERIES, BIGGLESWADE."

LONDON AGENCY AND SHOWROOMS:

77, Fore Street and 14, Fore Street Avenue,
London, E.C.

One Minute from Moorgate St. Station.

The Ivel Cycle Company, Limited,

THE IVEL CYCLE COMPANY, LIMITED, have pleasure in presenting their New Illustrated Price List for 1890, in which they trust may be found a sufficient variety of first-class machines to satisfy the diverse tastes and requirements of their numerous past and future customers.

They are happy to be able to inform their customers in the Metropolis, that from this date all their standard pattern machines will be stocked at the spacious show-rooms of their Agents. Messrs. BIGGS, WALL & COMPANY, No. 77, Fore Street, and 14, Fore Street Avenue, City, E.C. (one minute from Moorgate Street Railway Station).

Several new designs of Ivel Safeties, combined with many important improvements, will be found in the following pages, which we commend to careful perusal by all buyers of Cycles.

The Ivel Cycle Company, Limited.

January 1st, 1890.

Biggleswade, Bedfordshire.

The Ivel Cycle Company, Limited,

⇥ ❦ TERMS ❦ ⇤

PAYMENT.—Customers having no Ledger Accounts with the Company will be furnished with an Invoice of the goods ordered, against which remittance is to be made before the goods leave the Works, or approved References must be given.

REPAIRS are charged at NET CASH prices in all cases. CARRIAGE on Machines or parts must be PREPAID, and sender's name and address securely attached to prevent their refusal by the Company. PAYMENT for Repairs must be made BEFORE THE GOODS LEAVE the Works.

DELIVERY of all goods is made by the Company Free on Rail, and are signed for by the railway company as received in good condition. Thence they are FORWARDED AT THE RISK OF THE PURCHASER, by whom all charges are payable. Purchasers should therefore protect themselves by notifying any damage to the Carriers, against whom claim should immediately be made.

CRATES are charged at absolutely net cost, and are not returnable.

Biggleswade, Bedfordshire.

The Ivel Cycle Company, Limited,

4

Ivel No. 1 Roadster Safety.

The established popularity of this machine enables us to place it again before our patrons with every confidence. Owing to improved manufacture we were enabled to reduce the price from £18 to £16 in June last year, and now IMPROVED IN MANY IMPORTANT DETAILS, we continue to offer it at the same price, notwithstanding increased cost of materials.

SPECIFICATION.

Frame Work of best weldless cold drawn steel tubes, and steel stampings, strongly braced by front and back stay rods, hollow elliptical steel forks, adjustable handle bar, and saddle pin, improved crank axle bracket, and detachable Roadster cranks, with throw adjustable, from $5\frac{1}{2}$ to $6\frac{1}{2}$ inches, improved plunger brake lamp bracket, rubber foot rests, dirt guards.

Wheels.—Driving wheel 30 in. diameter, steerer 32 in., best gun metal hubs, of latest improved design, best high tension steel wire spokes, $\frac{3}{4}$ in. solid U rims, and best grey rubber tyres.

Bearings.—Æolus patent ball bearings throughout.

Fittings.—Abingdon Humber chain, improved patent combination tension saddle and spring, best Æolus ball rubber pedals, Ivel pattern black horn handles, Ivel pouch, adjustable wrench, oil can and spanners.

Gearing.—54 in., 57 in., or 60 in.

Finish.—Finest stoved black enamel, with nickel plated handle bar, brake set, saddle pillar, hubs, stay rods, cranks and pedals.

Price £16.

Extras.—Patent hollow rims, per wheel, 10s., $\frac{7}{8}$ in. tyres, per wheel, 5s., lining 7s. 6d., chain guard 3s. 6d., luggage carriers from 12s. 6d.

Ivel Roadster Safety No. 2.

SPECIFICATION.

As above, but built extra strong, with special stout frame and forks, and $\frac{7}{8}$ in. tyres. Suitable for bad roads and heavy riders.

Price £17.

EXTRAS AS TO No. 1.

Curved front forks and ⌐ saddle pins are also fitted to the above machines.

Biggleswade, Bedfordshire.

The Ivel Cycle Company, Limited,

Ivel Semi-Racer Safety, No. 3.

This machine is constructed to meet the requirements of those riders who desire a light yet strong machine for fast road riding and grass track racing. Upon it have been accomplished so many of those performances which have rendered the reputation of Ivel machines second to none.

SPECIFICATION.

FRAME WORK of best weldless cold drawn steel tubes and steel stampings, strongly braced by front and back stay rods ; hollow elliptical steel forks, adjustable handle bar and saddle pin : improved crank axle bracket, and detachable Racer cranks, with throw adjustable from 5¼ to 6½ inches, lamp bracket, rubber foot rests.

WHEELS.—Driving wheel 30 in. diameter, steerer, 32 in., best gun metal hubs of latest improved design, best high tension steel wire spokes, 5/8 in. patent hollow rims, and best grey rubber tyres.

BEARINGS.—Æolus patent ball bearings throughout.

FITTINGS.—Abingdon Humber Racer chain. Improved patent semi-racer combination tension saddle and spring. Best Æolus rat-trap ball pedals. Ivel pattern black horn handles. Ivel pouch. Adjustable wrench, oil can, and spanners.

GEARING.—57 in., 60 in., and 63 in.

FINISH.—Finest stoved black enamel and nickel-plated handle bar, saddle pin, hubs, stay rods, cranks and pedals.

Price £16 16 0.

EXTRAS.—Brake set 10/-, mud guards 10/-, cork handles 3/6, chain guard, 3/6, lining 7/6.

Ivel Racer Safety, No. 4.

SPECIFICATION.

FRAME WORK of best weldless cold drawn steel tubes, and steel stampings, strongly braced by front and back stay rods, hollow elliptical steel forks, fixed handle bar and saddle pin, to suit height of rider, improved crank axle bracket, and detachable racer cranks, with throw adjustable from 5½ to 6½ inches. The whole reduced in weight throughout as much as is consistent with strength.

WHEELS.—Driving wheel 28in. diam. ; steerer 30in., specially light gun metal hubs of the latest improved design. Best high tension steel wire spokes. ⅝in. patent hollow rims, and best grey rubber tyres.

BEARINGS.—Æolus patent ball bearings throughout.

FITTINGS.—Abingdon Humber Racer Chain. Best racing saddle. Cork handles. Best Æolus rat-trap ball pedals.

GEARING.—60in. and 63in.

FINISH.—Finest stoved black enamel and nickel-plated handle bar, saddle pin, hubs, stay rods, cranks and pedals.

WEIGHT —About 20lbs.

Price £18.

This machine is usually built to order. Delivery can be made in about 14 days from receipt of instructions. Straight front forks are also fitted to the above machines.

Biggleswade, Bedfordshire.

The Ivel Cycle Company, Limited,

6

Ivel Anti-Vibration Safety, No. 5.

The simplest and neatest spring frame made attaining the desired effect, whilst avoiding any series of complicated springs and joints so noticeable in many similar machines designed to reduce vibration to a minimum. Admirably suited to use on rough roads.

SPECIFICATION.

In every respect similar to that of No. 1, but fitted with Laming's improved patent joint and spring.

Price £18.

EXTRAS as No. 1.

The above patent is equally applicable to the design No. 6, the price of which is £20.

Biggleswade, Bedfordshire.

The Ivel Cycle Company, Limited,

Ivel Roadster Safety, No. 6.

This design is offered to our patrons as our specialty for the new season. It has been thoroughly tested during the winter months by many experienced practical Cyclists, whose high eulogiums commending its comfort, easy propulsion, and sound construction predict its speedy establishment as a popular favorite.

SPECIFICATION.

FRAME WORK.—Best weldless cold drawn steel tubes, and steel stampings, forged stay rods; elliptical hollow steel forks; adjustable handle bar and saddle pin; specially designed crank axle bracket, and detachable Roadster cranks with adjustable throw from 5½ to 6½ inches; improved plunger brake; lamp bracket, rubber foot rests, and mud guards.

WHEELS.—Driving wheel 30 inches diam.; steerer, 32in.; best gun metal hubs of latest improved design; best high tension steel wire spokes; ⅞in. solid U rims, and best grey rubber tyres.

BEARINGS.—Æolus patent ball bearings throughout.

FITTINGS.—Abingdon Humber chain. Improved patent combination tension saddle and spring. Best Æolus ball rubber pedals. Ivel pattern black horn handles. Ivel pouch, adjustable wrench, oil can, and spanners.

GEARING.—54 in., 57in., or 60in.

FINISH.—Finest stoved black enamel, with nickel-plated handle bar, brake set, saddle pillar, hubs, stay rods, cranks and pedals.

Price £18.

EXTRAS. Patent hollow rims, per wheel 10/-, ⅞in. tyres per wheel 5/-, Lining 7/6, chain guard 3/6, luggage carriers from 12/6.

Ivel Semi-Racer Safety, No. 7.

This machine is constructed for a similar purpose as our No. 3. In design it is a reproduction of No. 6 without brake set or mud guards, but with wheels and fittings precisely similar to those used for No. 3.

Price £18 18 0.

EXTRAS.—Brake set 10/-, mud guards 10/-, cork handles 3/6, chain guard 3/6, lining 7/6.

Biggleswade, Bedfordshire.

The Ivel Cycle Company, Limited,

Ivel Roadster Safety, No. 8.

This favorite design first manufactured by us late last season to meet the increasing demand for a thoroughly reliable diamond-framed safety, has proved itself worthy of the purpose. Perfected in detail we offer it as a thoroughly rigid and very fast machine.

SPECIFICATION.

Frame Work of the best weldless cold drawn steel tubes, and steel stampings; elliptical hollow steel forks; adjustable handle bar and saddle pin; specially designed crank axle bracket, and detachable roadster cranks, with adjustable throw from $5\frac{1}{2}$ to $6\frac{1}{2}$ inches; improved plunger brake; lamp bracket, rubber foot rests, and dirt guards.

Wheels.—Driving wheel, 30in. diam.; steerer, 32in.; best gun metal hubs of latest improved design; best high tension steel wire spokes; $\frac{3}{4}$in. solid U rims and best grey rubber tyres.

Bearings.—Æolus patent ball bearings throughout.

Fittings.—Abingdon Humber chain. Improved patent combination tension saddle and spring. Best Æolus ball rubber pedals. Ivel pattern black horn handles. Ivel pouch, adjustable wrench, oil can and spanners.

Gearing.—54in., 57in., or 60in.

Finish.—Finest stove black enamel, with nickel plated handle bar, brake set, saddle pillar, hubs, stay rods, cranks and pedals.

PRICE - - - £18

Extras.—Patent hollow rims, per wheel, 10/-; $\frac{7}{8}$in. tyres, per wheel, 5/-; lining, 7/6; chain guard, 3/6; luggage carriers from 12/6.

Ivel Racer Safety, No. 9.

This design (as No. 8) being "par excellence" characterised by its extreme rigidity, is eminently suitable for path racing. During a very short career last Autumn a marvellous proportion of victories fell to its riders. Like Racer No. 4, it is usually built to order, and follows that machine as regards size of wheels, and general fittings and finish.

PRICE - - - £20

Biggleswade, Bedfordshire.

The Ivel Cycle Company. Limited,

9

Ivel Lady's Safety, No. 10.

This carefully matured design is an adaptation of the principles of construction followed out in our No. 6 Safety. It is at once compact, comfortable, and strong. An additional loose stay rod, fitted between the neck and seat pillar, is supplied with each machine, affording an extra brace, rendering the frame thoroughly rigid, and suitable for the rougher riding of the stronger sex.

SPECIFICATION.

Frame Work of the best weldless cold drawn steel tubes and steel stampings; hollow elliptical steel forks; adjustable handle bar and saddle pin; improved crank axle bracket and detachable Roadster cranks, with throw of from 5 to 6 inches: also improved wire dress guard; improved plunger brake; lamp bracket; rubber foot rests; dirt guards.

Wheels.—Driving and steering wheels each 28in. diam.; best gun metal hubs of latest improved design; best high tension steel wire spokes; $\frac{5}{8}$in. solid U rims, and best grey rubber tyres.

Bearings.—Æolus patent ball bearings throughout.

Fittings.—Abingdon Humber chain; improved patent combination tension lady's saddle and spring; best Æolus ball rubber pedals; Ivel pattern black horn handles; Ivel pouch, adjustable wrench, oil can and spanners.

Gearing.—49in. and 52in.

Finish.—Finest stove black enamel, with nickel plated handle bar, brake set, saddle pillar, hubs, stay rods, cranks and pedals.

PRICE   -   -   £18 10 0

Extras.—Patent hollow rims, per wheel, 10/-.

Biggleswade, Bedfordshire.

The Ivel Cycle Company, Limited,

THE "IVEL"

Ivel Light Roadster Ordinary Bicycle.

SPECIFICATION.

FRAME WORK of the best weldless cold drawn steel tubes throughout, hollow elliptical steel forks, with Æolus patent ball bearings of latest improved pattern. Patent Abingdon ball bearing head; hollow handle bar and powerful spoon brake.

WHEELS.—Front wheel from 48 to 54 in. diameter to order; back wheel 20 in., $\frac{5}{8}$ or $\frac{3}{4}$ patent hollow rims, and best rubber tyres; best gun metal hubs, bell-shaped, to take bearings and narrow the tread of rider, high tension steel spokes, patent detachable cranks.

FITTINGS.—Improved patent combination tension saddle and spring, rubber or rat-trap Æolus patent ball pedals, Ivel pouch, adjustable wrench, oil can and spanners.

FINISH.—Finest black stoved enamel, best nickel-plated handle bar, brake set, hubs, cranks and pedals.

Price £18.

Ivel Racer Ordinary Bicycle.

This Machine is constructed on the same lines as the Light Roadster Ordinary, but built throughout as lightly as is consistent with strength. Made to order within about 14 days.

Price £18.

Biggleswade, Bedfordshire.

The Ivel Cycle Company, Limited,

II

THE "IVEL"

IVEL ROADSTER TRICYCLE, No. 1.

But slight deviation from our well-known pattern has been made by us. In placing before our patrons this well-constructed Machine, we specially draw attention to the lightness and simplicity of the crank axle bracket, so designed as to allow of rapid and effective adjustment of the driving chain, and rendered firm as a rock by the perfect bracing stays. The reputation of this Machine rests not only upon the many wonderful rides which have been accomplished on it, but also on the repeated testimony of its possessors.

SPECIFICATION.

Frame Work of the best weldless cold drawn steel tubes, and steel stampings, forged stay rod, our new improved driving bracket very strongly braced, detachable Roadster cranks, with adjustable throw of $5\frac{1}{2}$ to $6\frac{1}{2}$ in., elliptical hollow steel forks, adjustable hollow handle bar and saddle pin, four improved bearings to axle bridge, best steel axle, and balance gear. Improved powerful plunger brake, lamp bracket, rubber foot rests, mud guards.

Wheels.—Driving wheels 30 in., and steerer 32 in. diameter. Best gun metal hubs, high tension steel wire spokes $\frac{3}{4}$ solid **U** rims and best grey rubber tyres.

Bearings.—Æolus patent ball bearings throughout.

Fittings.—Abingdon Humber chain. Improved patent combination tension saddle and spring, best Æolus ball pedals, Ivel horn handles, Ivel pouch, adjustable wrench, oil can and spanners.

Gearing.—51, 54, 57, and 60 inches.

Finish.—Finest stove black enamel, with nickel plated handle bar, brake set saddle pin, hubs stay rods, axle and gear, cranks and pedals.

Price £23 10s.

Extras.—Hollow rims, per wheel, 10/-; $\frac{7}{8}$ tyres, per wheel, 5/-; luggage carriers, from 12/6; lining, 10/-

IVEL SEMI-RACER TRICYCLE, No. 2.

This Machine is constructed on precisely similar lines as No. 1, but is built specially to suit good roads and fast riding.

SPECIFICATION.

Of similar material as No. 1, but lighter throughout, $\frac{7}{8}$ hollow rims, and best rubber tyres, detachable racer cranks and chain, and rat trap ball pedals, without brake.

Price £25. Extras—Brake, 10/-

IVEL RACER TRICYCLE, No. 3.

Of same design as No. 1, but built throughout of the lightest possible material. The wheels used for this Machine are 28 in. drivers and 30 in. steerer, $\frac{3}{4}$ hollow rims, and rubber tyres. The handle bar and saddle pin are fixed to suit height of rider. WEIGHT, about 27lbs.

Price £25.

This Machine is usually built to order, and can be delivered in about 14 days from receipt of instructions. Straight forks are also fitted to the above Machines.

Biggleswade, Bedfordshire.

The Ivel Cycle Company, Limited,

12

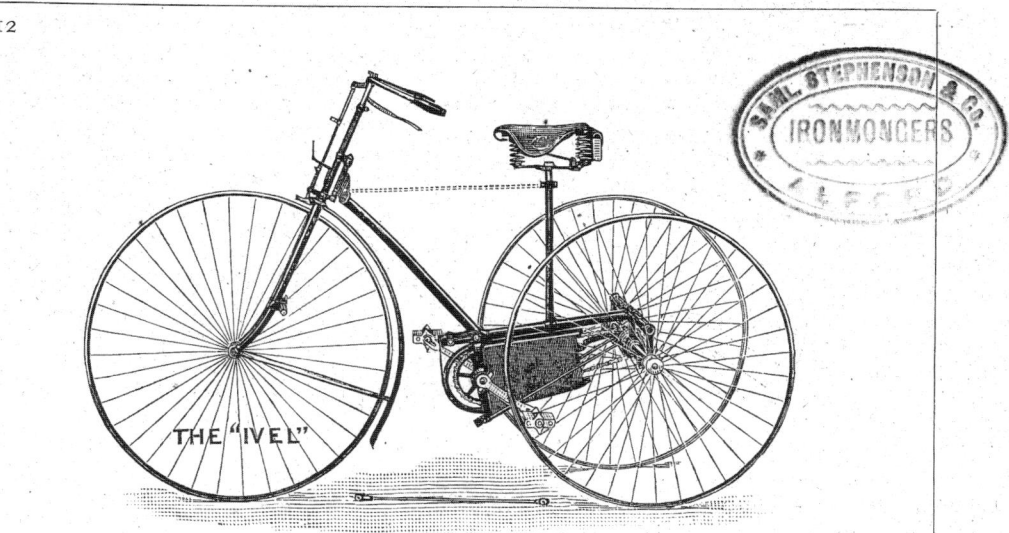

THE "IVEL"

Ivel Lady's Roadster Tricycle, No. 4.

This Machine combines all the high qualities of the No. 1 Tricycle, but is so constructed as to be suitable for Lady's riding. It is provided with a bracing stay to be fitted between saddle stem and neck when ridden by gentlemen.

SPECIFICATION.

Frame Work of best weldless cold drawn steel tubes and steel stampings, forged stay rod, our new improved driving bracket, very strongly braced detachable Roadster cranks, with adjustable throw $5\frac{1}{2}$ to $6\frac{1}{2}$ inches, hollow steel forks, adjustable hollow handle bar and saddle pin, four improved bearings to axle bridge, best steel axle and balance gear. Improved powerful plunger brake, lamp bracket, rubber foot rests, mud guard, leather dress guard.

Wheels.—Driving wheel 30 in., and steerer 32 in. diameter; best gun metal hubs, high tension steel wire spokes, $\frac{3}{4}$ solid U rims, and best grey rubber tyres.

Bearings.—Æolus patent ball bearings throughout.

Fittings.—Abingdon Humber chain. Improved patent combination tension saddle and spring, best Æolus ball pedals, Ivel horn handles, Ivel pouch, adjustable wrench, oil can, and spanners.

Gearing.—51, 54, 57, and 60 inches.

Finish.—Finest stoved black enamel, nickel-plated handle bar, brake set, saddle pin, hubs, stay rods, axle and gear, cranks and pedals.

PRICE £24.

Extras.—Hollow rims, per wheel, 10/-; $\frac{7}{8}$ tyres, per wheel, 5/-; luggage carriers, from 12/6; lining 10/-.

Biggleswade, Bedfordshire.

The Ivel Cycle Company, Limited,

13

Ivel Tandem Tricycle,

NO. 1.

Upon this Machine has been accomplished the greatest distance yet ridden in 24 hours by any type of Tandem, viz.: 298½ miles, certified by the N. C. U. It is admirably adapted for Touring purposes, and can be ridden by a Lady.

SPECIFICATION.

FRAME WORK of best weldless cold-drawn steel tubes and steel stampings, forged stay-rod, our new improved driving-bracket, very strongly braced; detachable Roadster-cranks, with adjustable throw of 5½ to 6½ inches, hollow steel forks, adjustable hollow handle-bar and saddle-pin, 4 improved bearings to axle-bridge, best steel axle and balance-gear. Improved powerful plunger-brake to front wheel, and band brake to axle. Lamp-bracket, rubber foot-rests. Leather guard to back chain. Mud guard.

WHEELS. Driving-wheel, 30-in., and steerer 32-in. diam.; best Gun Meta hubs, high tension steel wire spokes, ¾ solid U rims, and best grey rubber tyres.

BEARINGS. Æolus patent ball-bearings throughout.

FITTINGS. Abingdon Humber-chain. Improved patent combination tension-saddle and spring. Best Æolus ball-pedals. Ivel horn handles. Ivel pouch, adjustable wrench, oil-can and spanners.

GEARING. 57, 60, 63-in.

FINISH. Finest stoved black enamel, nickel-plated handle-bar, brake-set, saddle-pin hubs, stay-rods, axle and gear. Cranks and pedals.

PRICE £33.

EXTRAS. Hollow rims, per Wheel, 10/-. Lining, 9/-.

Biggleswade, Bedfordshire.

The Ivel Cycle Company, Limited,

14

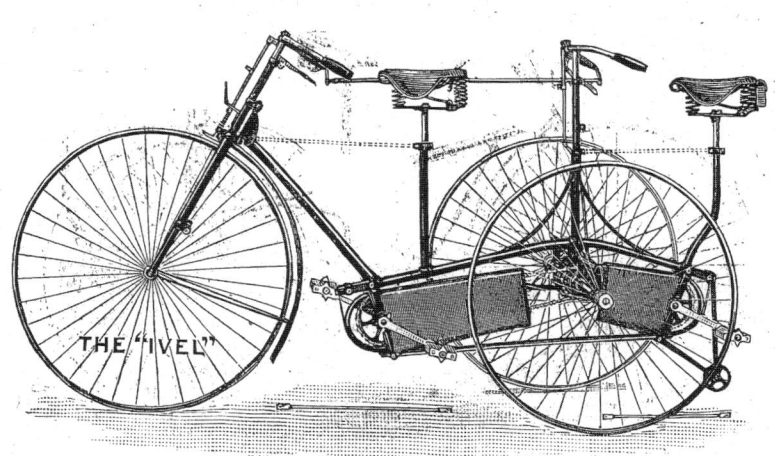

THE "IVEL"

Ivel Tandem Tricycle,

NO. 2.

This Machine is adapted to be ridden by Two Ladies, or by Lady on front seat. It is built of the same quality material, and generally fitted and finished as No. 1, but the steering is connected to the rear handle-bar, thus giving control to both riders.

FRAME WORK of the best weldless, cold-drawn steel tubes and steel stampings, forged stay-rod, our new improved driving-bracket, very strongly braced, detachable Roadster-cranks, with adjustable throw, $5\frac{1}{2}$ to $6\frac{1}{2}$ inches. Hollow steel forks, adjustable hollow handle-bar and saddle-pin ; 4 improved bearings to axle-bridge, best steel axle and balance-gear. Improved powerful plunger-brake to front wheel, and band brake to axle. Lamp-bracket. Rubber foot-rests, mud guard.

WHEELS. Driving-wheel, 30-in., and steerer, 32-in. diam. Best Gun Metal hubs, high tension steel wire spokes, $\frac{3}{4}$ solid U rims, and best grey rubber tyres.

BEARINGS. Æolus patent ball-bearings throughout.

FITTINGS. Abingdon Humber-chain. Improved patent combination tension saddle and spring. Best Æolus ball pedals. Ivel horn handles. Ivel pouch, adjustable wrench, oil-can, and spanners.

GEARING. 51, 54, 57 and 60-in.

FINISH. Finest stoved black enamel, with nickel-plated handle-bar, brake-set, saddle-pin, hubs, stay-rods, axle and gear, cranks and pedals.

PRICE £34 10.

EXTRAS. Hollow rims, per Wheel, 10/- ; $\frac{7}{8}$ tyres per Wheel, 5/- ; Luggage Carriers, from 12/6 ; Lining, 10/-.

Biggleswade, Bedfordshire.

The Ivel Cycle Company, Limited,

15

ACCESSORIES.

LAMPS.

THE "BELL-ROCK" LAMPS.

NEW PATTERNS FOR 1890.   No. 21.

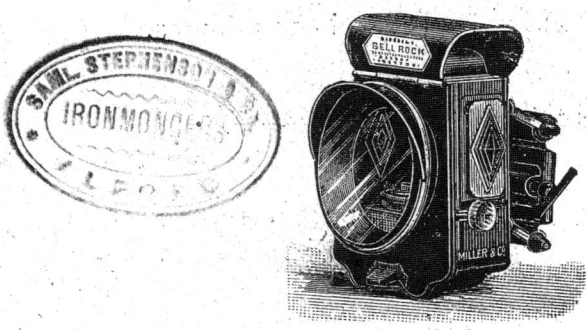

PATENTED AND REGISTERED.

No. 21.   Japanned 17/-

A little cheaper quality, but a First-class Lamp.

No. 36.   Japanned 13/6
No. 37.   Japanned 11/-

All the above are of the same design as No. 21, and have Instantaneous Detachable Reflectors, Adjustable Bracket Clips, and other improvements.

BELLS.

Harrison's Double Alarm No. 48, with Patent Band Clip,

Each 6/6

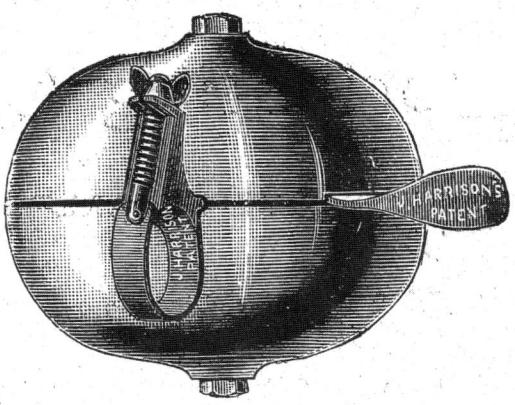

Biggleswade, Bedfordshire.

The Ivel Cycle Company, Limited,

17

Testimonials.

57, CANONBURY ROAD,
LONDON, N.,

4th December, 1889.

Dear Sir,

After a season's riding of an Ivel Safety, I feel so gratified at the way in which it has behaved, that I feel justified in giving my testimony as to its sterling virtues. Though a very light machine for the roads in and around London, it has stood them marvellously well, and although at first I was very careful with it—considering the weight being only 28lbs.—I found later on that I could ride it with impunity at top speed over the roughest macadam on the Barnet Road, on the lumpiest cobbles in North London.

Last week end, December 1st, I made up my mind to give it a thorough good testing, and rode to Hertford and back over the most vile and rutty road (hard frozen) I have ever ventured on, mounted on a machine. I did not spare it in the least, but being in good practice I drove it full pelt over the hard ruts to satisfy myself as to the soundness of the wheels, &c. Though the spokes are 16 gauge not one went; and it can be imagined the wheels had some terrific wrenches in the ruts, which were more like a succession of tram lines running parallel to each other than an ordinary road. The rims too—half inch only, with $\frac{5}{8}$ tyres—must be sound material to stand such a trying ordeal.

In conclusion I must say I am surprised the machine has stood my very hard usage, and I shall with confidence recommend the "IVEL" *for being the best machine obtainable, both for pace, ease and comfort in riding, and durability.* I shall not want a new machine next year, as my present mount is equal to new, though I have ridden it some few thousand miles. This I think is the best testimony I can give to its lasting qualities.

Wishing the "Ivel" a continued success,

I am,

Yours very truly,

Signed   W. HUTCHINGS.

Mr. DAN ALBONE,
    Ivel Cycle Company, Limited.

Biggleswade, Bedfordshire.

The Ivel Cycle Company, Limited,

18

44, DEANSGATE,
MANCHESTER,
28th May, 1889.

Dear Sirs,

Ivel Safety Tandem is a splendid machine, runs better than anything ever I was on.

Yours truly,

Signed JENNINGS & COMPANY.

THE IVEL CYCLE MANUFACTURING COMPANY.
Biggleswade.

1, MAY TERRACE,
ALPHA ROAD,
MILLWALL, LONDON, E.,
30th April, 1889.

Mr. Michael Moyle writes:

Dear Albone,

For lightness, rigidity, and ease of running, I think your machines are superior to any I have previously tried, and I have had some experience, having begun my riding in 1878.

On Friday April 19th, I succeeded upon an Ivel Tricycle in winning the " Beaumont " (People's Palace) 100 miles time medal.

On Monday April 22nd, at Bury St. Edmunds, I was second in the 5 miles open race, in which *I rode my Ivel Safety roadster against Racing Machines.*

On Saturday the 27th inst., in our Club Handicap of five miles, I started from scratch and did quickest time on *Ivel Tricycle against Safeties* and ordinaries of other makes some receiving over 3 minutes start from me.

These performances, I think, speak marvels of the machines, and plainly indicate what can be done upon them.

Yours truly,

Signed MICHAEL MOYLE.

10, CASTLE ROAD,
CARDIFF,
13th July, 1889.

Messrs. Wheeler & Co. write:

Gentlemen,

We beg to hand you enclosed cheque for diamond-framed Safety. *It is a gem,* and we ought to do good business with this pattern.

Yours truly,

Signed WHEELER & Co.

Biggleswade, Bedfordshire.

The Ivel Cycle Company, Limited,

19

THE CROSS, GLOUCESTER,
8th October, 1889.

Mr. E. Wright writes :

Dear Sirs,

The machines you supplied have given every satisfaction, and I hope to place a number of orders early next season.

Yours truly,

Signed   E. WRIGHT.

"LYNDALL,"
HORNSEY PARK,
LONDON, N.

Mr. Robert Ede writes :

Dear Sirs,

I have now ridden the Ivel Racing Safety you supplied me with, 2 years, and have found it to have no equal for easy running and steering. It has carried me to victory several times during the past year, both on path and road, as you will see by enclosed list.

Wishing you every success in the future,

Yours truly,

Signed   ROBT. L. EDE,
Southgate C.C.

10, CASTLE ROAD,
CARDIFF,
16th May, 1889.

Mr. H. Meager writes :

Dear Sirs,

The Safety you supplied me with, I can only speak of in the very highest terms. It is a most comfortable and fast machine, and I am very well pleased indeed with it, and hope it will lead to further orders.

Yours truly,

Signed   H. MEAGER.

GREAT NORTHERN RAILWAY,
KING'S CROSS, LONDON,
22nd October, 1889.

Mr. W. E. Hammerston writes :

Gentlemen,

The Tandem Tricycle which I bought a few days ago, I cannot speak too highly of, although the roads and weather have been most unfavourable for riding. Both myself and sisters are very much pleased with its performance.

Yours truly,

Signed   W. E. HAMMERSTON.

Biggleswade, Bedfordshire.

The Ivel Cycle Company, Limited,

20

2, Mincing Lane,
London,
2ud July, 1889.

Mr. A. E. Jewesbury writes:

Dear Dan,

I took an Ivel Spring Frame Roadster with me on the long Continental tour. I have just finished, and I may tell you that though I took it over some of the worst roads (!) in Italy, France and Switzerland, and crossed the Alps no less than 6 times with it, it never gave me a moment's trouble.

A machine behaving like this when so far from home, carrying as it did myself and over 30lbs. of luggage, adds considerably to the pleasure of a tour, and I am very grateful.

Yours very truly,
Signed   ARTHUR E. JEWESBURY,
North Road Club.

Fern Lodge,
Leytonstone Road,
Stratford, Essex.

Mr. W. H. Gray writes:

Dear Sirs,

With the easiest pedalling my machine fairly flies along the road. I attribute this solely to the well stayed and rigid frame and general excellence of the machine, as I am anything but a strong rider.

I may mention that I won our 10 mile road handicap a week or two ago from scratch, doing fastest time.

Wishing you every success,

Yours faithfully,
Signed   W. H. GRAY,
Pilot C.C., Sub-Captain.

Stapenhill House,
Burton-on-Trent.

Mr. A. J. Clay writes:

Dear Sirs,

Perhaps you remember selling me your Tandem Convertible Bicycle—Tricycle, of the Stanley Show, I write to say that I like it immensely, and find the joints perfectly rigid.

I have been using it in single bicycle form, and find it quite easy to ride without hands.

Yours very truly,
Signed   A. J. CLAY.

Biggleswade, Bedfordshire.

The Ivel Cycle Company, Limited,

21

24, ASHTON STREET, BRIGHTON,
28th September, 1889.

Mr. J. W. Herrington writes:

Dear Sirs,

I have ridden one of your Safeties—Light Roadster—for nearly two years, and it has stood the test of the roads round about Brighton, which are never in the best condition, and I have never come to grief. I am giving an order for another, and I only hope it will prove as satisfactory as its predecessor.

I am confident that the "IVEL" *machines are the best for workmanship and speed.*

I have won my Club Championship twice on an Ivel Safety, besides other minor events on the path.

Wishing you success with the Ivel machines,

Yours sincerely,
Signed   J. W. HERRINGTON.

———

POLYTECHNIC INSTITUTE,
309, REGENT STREET, W.

Louis Shute and Wm. Chas. Jones write:

Dear Sirs,

The Ivel Tandem Safety you so kindly placed at our disposal, though by no means the lightest machine of the kind that you build, yet, for ease of running, strength, design, workmanship, &c., &c., we think it could not be surpassed.

It was a pleasant revelation to us the easy manner in which it danced over the rough roads and the way the machine moved generally. Why! the first time we got on it, the machine moved so well, that several racing men on racing machines had all their work cut out to keep anywhere near us.

We are,
Yours faithfully,
Signed   LOUIS SHUTE,
„   WILLIAM CHARLES JONES,
Polytechnic Cycling Club.

———

ROTTERDAM,
13th August, 1889.

Dear Sirs,

The Ivels have done good service at Scheveningen, 4th August 1st prize; Nymegen, 10th August 1st and 2nd prize were on Ivels.

Racer Safety, two firsts at Nymegen, including Beger Cup (Silver) —a Challenge Cup.

Yours truly,
Signed   BINGHAM & Co.

Biggleswade, Bedfordshire.

The Ivel Cycle Company, Limited,

22

HULL,

21st March, 1889.

Gentlemen,

I beg to say with regard to the Ivel No. 1 you sent me last season that it is giving great satisfaction in every way ; I find it a very easy riding and fast machine. I can now ride quite easy without the *Handle Bar*, a thing which I cannot do on any other machine. I shall recommend it to all my friends.

Signed   Yours truly,

JAMES E. THIRSK.

Messrs. THE IVEL COMPANY, LIMITED.

BRIGHTON,

31st December, 1889.

Gentlemen,

I have the pleasure of informing you that this year I have ridden 7,180 miles on my Ivel Tricycle, which is over 1,000 miles more than I have ever ridden before in one year.

I am very pleased with the " Ivel," and think there is no better machine.

I remain,

Yours truly,

Signed   W. H. SCOTT.

To THE IVEL CYCLE COMPANY, LIMITED,
    Biggleswade.

Biggleswade, Bedfordshire.

ILLUSTRATED PRICE LIST

OF

" IVEL "

BICYCLES AND TRICYCLES

MANUFACTURED BY THE

"Ivel" Cycle Company,

LIMITED.

FACTORY AND REGISTERED OFFICES :

BIGGLESWADE, BEDFORDSHIRE, ENGLAND.

(41 MILES FROM LONDON, ON THE GREAT NORTHERN RAILWAY.)

TELEGRAPHIC ADDRESS: "DANNERIES, BIGGLESWADE."

LONDON DEPÔT AND SHOW ROOMS :

77, Fore Street, and 14, Fore Street Avenue,

LONDON, E.C.

(ONE MINUTE FROM MOORGATE STREET STATION.)

THE IVEL CYCLE COMPANY, LIMITED, have pleasure in presenting their New Illustrated Price List for 1891, in which they believe will be found a sufficient variety of first-class machines, fitted with solid, cushion, and pneumatic tyres, to satisfy the varied tastes and requirements of all customers.

It will be seen that the various patterns include both Diamond and Cross Frames, also Frames for Ladies' use. All Machines can be supplied with ball-steering, if desired.

During the year 1890 some of the most brilliant performances ever achieved on Cycles have been done on IVEL Machines. On August 30th, 334 miles were ridden in twenty-four hours by Mr. T. A. Edge, on an Ivel Safety ; and on October 18th, 100 miles was ridden on the North Road in 5 hours 27½ minutes, of which performance " Wheeling " says :—" **The Ivel has been ridden 100 miles in faster time than any other cycle in the world, under any circumstances whatever.**" Particulars of other important performances on these machines are given at the end of this Price List, pages 26 to 28.

Cushion Tyres.—We have had a special rim manufactured for us, for cushion tyres, which entirely prevents the rim from cutting the tyre, and these are used on all cushion-tyred machines sent out by us.

Inflated Cushion Tyres.—We also direct attention to the **Inflated Cushion Tyre**, which is stated to combine the advantages of both Pneumatic and Cushion Tyres, whilst avoiding the objections which have been raised to the former. An accidental puncture can be repaired in half an hour by a simple process ; but, in the meantime, the machine can be ridden without repair, as on an ordinary cushion-tyred one.

The Company desire to draw the attention of customers in London to their Depôt at No. 77, FORE STREET, E.C. (one minute's walk from Moorgate Street Station), where an extensive stock of all patterns of machines may be inspected.

❧ *TERMS.* ❧

PAYMENT.—Customers having no Ledger Accounts with the Company will be furnished with an Invoice of the goods ordered, against which remittance is to be made before the goods leave the Works; or References should be sent with the order.

REPAIRS are charged at NET CASH prices in all cases. CARRIAGE on Machines or parts sent for repair must be prepaid, and the sender's NAME AND ADDRESS SECURELY ATTACHED, to prevent their refusal by the Company. PAYMENT for Repairs must be made before the goods leave the Works.

DELIVERY of all goods is made by the Company Free on Rail, and they are signed for by the railway company as received in good condition. Thence they are FORWARDED AT THE RISK OF THE PURCHASER, by whom all charges are payable. Purchasers should therefore protect themselves by notifying any damage to the Carriers, against whom a claim for same should immediately be made.

CRATES, when used, are charged at net cost, and are not returnable.

EASY PAYMENT SYSTEM.—The Company sell their machines, when desired, on the system of deferred payments, spread over not more than 12 months—for particulars, see last leaf of this Catalogue;—and Forms for this purpose can be had of all Agents, or from the Company's Offices. Machines sold on this system are PRECISELY the SAME in QUALITY and PRICE as those bought for ready money, and bear no mark in any way to indicate how they are paid for.

The Ivel Cycle Company, Limited.

Ivel No. 1 Roadster Safety.

The established popularity of this machine enables us to place it again before our patrons with every confidence.

SPECIFICATION.

FRAMEWORK of best weldless cold drawn steel tubes, and steel stampings, strongly braced by front and back stay rods ; hollow elliptical steel forks, adjustable handle bar, and Γ saddle pillar ; improved crank axle bracket, and detachable roadster cranks, with throw adjustable from $5\frac{1}{2}$ to $6\frac{1}{2}$ inches ; improved plunger brake, lamp bracket, rubber foot rests, and mud guards.

WHEELS.—Best gun metal hubs, of improved design, best high tension steel wire spokes, $\frac{3}{4}$ in. solid U rims, and best grey rubber tyres.

BEARINGS.—Æolus patent ball bearings throughout, with widened bases.

FITTINGS.—Abingdon Humber chain, Brooks' patent combined tension saddle and spring, best ball rubber pedals, black horn handles, Ivel pouch, adjustable wrench, oil can and spanners.

GEARING.—54 in., 57 in., 60 in., or 63 in.. as ordered.

FINISH.—Finest stoved black enamel ; with handle bar, brake, saddle pin, hubs, stay rods, cranks and pedals, all nickel plated.

Price £16.

EXTRAS.—Patent hollow rims, per wheel, 10s. ; $\frac{1}{8}$ in. tyres, per wheel, 5s. ; coloured lines, 7s. 6d. ; chain guard, 3s. 6d. ; luggage carriers, from 12s. 6d ; ba steering, 10s. extra.

Cushion Tyres, with our improved Rims and Best Rubber, £3 extra.

Inflated Cushion Tyres, with valve and inflator, £3 10s. extra.

Ivel Roadster Safety No. 2.

As above, but built extra strong, with specially stout frame and forks, and $\frac{1}{8}$ in. tyres. Suitable for bad roads and heavy riders.

Price £17.

EXTRAS AS No. 1.

Factory : Biggleswade, Bedfordshire.

The Ivel Cycle Company, Limited.

5

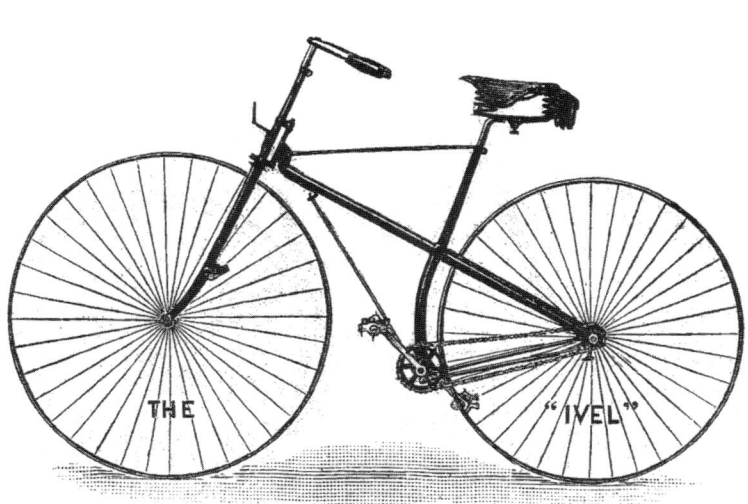

Ivel Semi-Racer Safety, No. 3.

This Machine is constructed to meet the requirements of those riders who desire a light yet strong machine for fast road riding and grass track racing. Upon it have been accomplished many of those performances which have rendered the reputation of Ivel Machines second to none.

SPECIFICATION.

FRAMEWORK of best weldless cold drawn steel tubes and steel stampings, strongly braced by front and back stay rods ; hollow elliptical steel forks, adjustable handle bar and saddle pin ; improved crank axle bracket, and detachable racer cranks, with throw adjustable from $5\frac{1}{2}$ to $6\frac{1}{2}$ in., improved plunge brake, lamp bracket, rubber foot rests, and mud guards.

WHEELS.—Best gun metal hubs of latest improved design, best high tension steel wire spokes, $\frac{5}{8}$ in. patent hollow rims, and best grey rubber tyres.

BEARINGS.—Æolus patent ball bearings throughout, with widened bases.

FITTINGS.—Abingdon Humber racer chain. Brooks' improved patent semi-racer combination tension saddle and spring, best rat trap ball pedals, Ivel pattern black horn handles, Ivel pouch, adjustable wrench, oil can, and spanners.

GEARING.—57 in., 60 in., and 63 in., as ordered.

FINISH.—Finest stoved black enamel, and nickel plated handle bar, saddle pin, hubs, stay rods, cranks and pedals.

Price £17 17s.

Or without mud guards 10/-, without brake 10/- less each.

EXTRAS.—Cushion Tyres, £3 ; Ball Steering, 10s. ; Inflated Cushion Tyres, with valve and inflator, £3 10 0.

Ivel Racer Safety, No. 4.

Similar to No. 3, but built lighter throughout.

WEIGHT.—About 20 lbs. **Price £18.**

London Depot : 77, Fore Street, E.C.

The Ivel Cycle Company, Limited.

Ivel Anti-Vibration Safety, No. 5.

The simplest and neatest spring frame made for attaining the desired effect, whilst avoiding any series of complicated springs and joints, noticeable in many machines designed for reducing vibration. Admirably suited to use on rough roads, whether in town or country.

For Woodcut of this Joint, see page 22.

SPECIFICATION.

In every respect similar to that of No. 1, but fitted with Laming's improved patent joint and spring.

Price £18.

EXTRAS as No. 1.

Also : Cushion Tyres, £3 ; Ball Steering, 10s.

Inflated Cushion Tyres, with Valve and Inflator, £3 10 0.

THE above patent is equally APPLICABLE to the design NO. 6, the PRICE of which, with Spring Frame, is £20.

Factory : Biggleswade, Bedfordshire.

The Ivel Cycle Company, Limited.

7

Ivel Roadster Safety, No. 6.

SPECIFICATION.

FRAMEWORK.—Best weldless cold drawn steel tubes and steel stampings, forged stay rods, elliptical hollow steel forks, adjustable handle bar and saddle pin, specially designed crank axle bracket, and detachable roadster cranks with adjustable throw from $5\frac{1}{2}$ to $6\frac{1}{2}$ inches, improved plunger brake, lamp bracket, rubber foot rests, and mud guards.

WHEELS.—Best gun metal hubs of latest improved design, best high-tension steel wire spokes, $\frac{3}{4}$ in. solid U rims, and best grey rubber tyres.

BEARINGS.—Æolus patent ball bearings throughout, with widened bases.

FITTINGS.—Abingdon Humber chain. Brooks' patent combination tension saddle and spring, best ball rubber pedals, black horn handles, Ivel pouch, adjustable wrench, oil can, and spanners.

GEARING.—54 in., 57 in., or 60 in., as ordered.

FINISH.—Finest stoved black enamel; with nickel plated handle bar, brake set, saddle pillar, hubs, stay rods, cranks and pedals.

Price £17.

EXTRAS.—Patent hollow rims, per wheel, 10/- ; $\frac{7}{8}$ in. tyres, per wheel, 5/-; lining, 7/6 ; chain guard, 3/6 ; luggage carriers, from 12/6.

Cushion Tyres, £3; Ball Steering, 10s.

Inflated Cushion Tyres, with Valve and Inflator, £3 10 0.

Ivel Semi-Racer Safety, No. 7.

This Machine is similar to No. 6, with brake and mud guards, but with wheels and fittings similar to those used for No. 3.

Price £18 18s.

Or without brake 10s., without mud guards 10s. less.

London Depot : 77, Fore Street, E.C.

The Ivel Cycle Company, Limited.

Ivel Roadster Safety, No. 8.

SPECIFICATION.

FRAMEWORK of best weldless cold drawn steel tubes, and steel stampings ; elliptical hollow steel forks ; adjustable handle bar and saddle pin ; specially designed crank axle bracket, and detachable roadster cranks, with adjustable throw from 5½ to 6½ inches ; improved plunger brake ; lamp bracket, rubber foot rests, and mud guards.

WHEELS.—Best gun metal hubs of latest improved design ; best high tension steel wire spokes ; ¾ in. solid U rims and best grey rubber tyres.

BEARINGS.—Æolus patent ball bearings throughout, with widened bases.

FITTINGS.—Abingdon Humber chain. Brooks' patent combination tension saddle and spring. Best Æolus ball rubber pedals. Black horn handles. Ivel pouch, adjustable wrench, oil can and spanners.

GEARING.—54 in., 57 in., or 60 in., as ordered.

FINISH.—Finest stoved black enamel, with nickel plated handle bar, brake set, saddle pillar, hubs, cranks and pedals.

Price £18.

EXTRAS.—Patent hollow rims, per wheel, 10/- ; ⅞ in. tyres, per wheel, 5/- ; lining, 7/6 ; chain guard, 3/6 ; luggage carriers from 12/6.

Ball Steering, 10s.

Ivel Semi-Racer Safety, No. 11.

This machine is constructed on similar lines to No. 8, but of lighter material than the Roadster machine. It is fitted with ⅝in. Warwicks's patent hollow felloes, special G.M. light hubs, best grey rubber tyres, rat-trap ball pedals, &c., and *includes detachable brake and mud guards.*

Price £19 10s.

EXTRAS, same as above. Can be supplied without brake and mud guards, if so ordered, at a reduction of 10/- for each.

Factory : Biggleswade, Bedfordshire.

The Ivel Cycle Company, Limited.

9

Ivel Roadster Safety, No. 12,

WITH CUSHION TYRES.

SPECIFICATION.

FRAMEWORK of the best weldless cold drawn steel tubes, and steel stampings; elliptical hollow steel forks; adjustable handle bar and saddle pin; specially designed crank axle bracket, and detachable roadster cranks, with adjustable throw from $5\frac{1}{2}$ to $6\frac{1}{2}$ inches; improved plunger brake; lamp bracket, rubber foot rests, and mud guards.

WHEELS.—Best gun metal hubs of latest improved design; best high tension steel wire spokes; our solid rims of special design to prevent cutting the tyres, the latter of best rubber.

BEARINGS.—Æolus patent ball bearings throughout, with widened bases.

FITTINGS.—Abingdon Humber chain. Brooks' improved patent combination tension saddle and spring. Best ball rubber pedals. Black horn handles. Ivel pouch, adjustable wrench, oil can and spanners.

GEARING.—54 in., 57 in., or 60 in., as ordered.

FINISH.—Finest stoved black enamel; with nickel plated handle bar, brake set, saddle pillar, hubs, cranks and pedals.

Price £21.

EXTRAS.—Ball Steering, 10s.; Inflated Cushion Tyres, with Valve and Inflator, 10s.

London Depot : 77, Fore Street, E.C.   B

Ivel Cycle Company, Limited.

Ivel Semi-Racer Safety, No. 12a,

WITH CUSHION TYRES.

SPECIFICATION.

FRAMEWORK of the best weldless cold drawn steel tubes, and steel stampings ; elliptical hollow steel forks ; adjustable handle bar and saddle pin ; specially designed crank axle bracket, and detachable racer cranks, with adjustable throw from $5\frac{1}{2}$ to $6\frac{1}{2}$ ins. ; lamp bracket, rubber foot rests, and mud guards.

WHEELS.—Best gun metal hubs of latest improved design ; best high tension steel wire spokes ; our solid rims of special design to prevent cutting the tyres, and best cushion tyres.

BEARINGS.—Æolus patent ball bearings throughout, with widened bases.

FITTINGS.—Abingdon Humber chain. Brooks' improved patent combination tension saddle and spring. Best ball rubber pedals. Black horn handles. Ivel pouch, adjustable wrench, oil can and spanners.

GEARING.—57 in., 60 in., or 63 in., as ordered.

FINISH.—Finest stoved black enamel, with nickel plated handle bar, brake set, saddle pillar, hubs, cranks, and pedals.

Price, with Ball Steering, Brake, and Mud Guards, £22 10s.

Inflated Cushion Tyres, with Valve and Inflator, 10s. extra.

If without Mud Guards, Brake, or Ball Steering, 10s. less for each of these.

Factory : Biggleswade, Bedfordshire.

The Ivel Cycle Company, Limited.

II

Ivel Semi-Racer Safety, No. 13,
WITH PNEUMATIC TYRES.

This is the Machine on which Mr. T. A. Edge rode 334 miles in 24 hours, and on which many other remarkable performances have been accomplished. (See page 28).

SPECIFICATION.

FRAMEWORK of the best weldless cold drawn steel tubes, and steel stampings; elliptical hollow steel forks; adjustable handle bar and saddle pin; specially designed crank axle bracket, and detachable racer cranks, with adjustable throw from 5½ to 6½ inches; lamp bracket, rubber foot rests.

WHEELS.—Best gun metal hubs of latest improved design; best high tension steel wire spokes; best solid rims, with 1¾in. (light-roadster) patent Pneumatic tyres.

BEARINGS.—Æolus patent ball bearings throughout, with widened bases.

FITTINGS.—Abingdon Humber chain. Brooks' patent tension saddle. Best ball rubber pedals. Black horn handles. Ivel pouch, adjustable wrench, oil can and spanners.

GEARING.—60in. or 63in.

FINISH.—Finest stoved black enamel, with nickel plated handle bar, brake set, saddle pillar, hubs, cranks and pedals.

Price, complete with Brake, and Mud Guards,

£25 0 0.

If without Mud Guards or Brake Set, 10s. less for each of these.

EXTRAS.—Coloured Lines, 7/6; Chain Guards, 3/6; Ball Steering, 10/-.

Ivel Racer Safety, No. 9.

Similar in Design of Frame to No. 13.

This Machine is made as light as possible throughout **FOR RACING ONLY.**

Fitted with ⅞in. Patent Hollow Rims.

Price, complete with Ball Steering, **£19 0 0.**

Extra if fitted with Pneumatic Racing Tyres, **£25 10 0.**

THIS MACHINE IS USUALLY BUILT TO ORDER.

London Depot: 77, Fore Street, E.C.

193

The Ivel Cycle Company, Limited.

12

Ivel Roadster Safety, No. 14,
WITH PNEUMATIC TYRES.

SPECIFICATION.

FRAMEWORK of the best weldless cold drawn steel tubes, and steel stampings; elliptical hollow steel forks; adjustable handle bar and saddle pin; specially designed crank axle bracket, and detachable roadster cranks, with adjustable throw from $5\frac{1}{2}$ to $6\frac{1}{2}$ inches; improved plunger brake; lamp bracket, rubber foot rests, and mud guards.

WHEELS.– Best gun metal hubs of latest improved design; best high tension steel wire spokes; best solid rims, with Pneumatic roadster tyres, $1\frac{3}{4}$ in. front and 2 in. back wheel.

BEARINGS.—Æolus patent ball bearings throughout, with widened bases.

FITTINGS.—Abingdon Humber chain. Brooks' patent combination tension saddle and spring. Best ball rubber pedals. Black horn handles. Ivel pouch, adjustable wrench, oil can and spanners.

GEARING.—57in., 60in., or 63in., as ordered.

FINISH.—Finest stoved black enamel; with nickel plated handle bar, brake set, saddle pillar, hubs, cranks and pedals.

Price, complete with Ball Steering Brake and Mud Guards,

£25 10 0.

Without Ball Steering, **10s. Less.**

Factory: Biggleswade, Bedfordshire.

The Ivel Cycle Company, Limited.

13

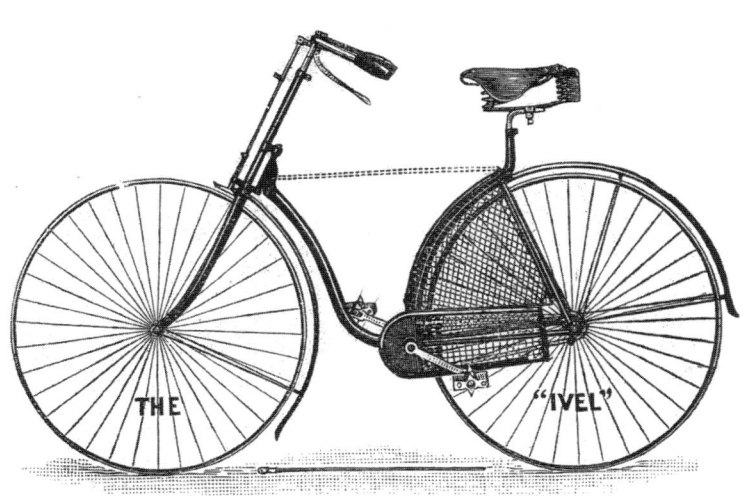

Ivel Lady's Safety, No. 10.

This carefully matured design is an adaptation of the principles of construction of our No. 6 Safety. It is at once compact, comfortable, and strong. An additional loose stay rod, fitted between the neck and seat pillar, is supplied with each machine, affording an extra brace, rendering the frame thoroughly suitable also for the riding of the stronger sex.

SPECIFICATION.

FRAMEWORK of the best weldless steel tubes and steel stampings; hollow elliptical steel forks; adjustable handle bar and Γ saddle pin; improved crank axle bracket and detachable roadster cranks, with throw from 5 to 6 inches : also improved dress guard; improved plunger brake; lamp bracket; rubber foot rests; and mud guards.

WHEELS.—Driving and steering wheels each 28 in. diameter; best gun metal hubs of latest improved design; best high tension steel wire spokes; $\frac{5}{8}$ in. solid U rims, and best grey rubber tyres.

BEARINGS. — Æolus patent ball bearings throughout, with widened bases.

FITTINGS.—Abingdon Humber chain; Brooks' patent combination tension lady's saddle and spring; best ball rubber pedals; black horn handles; Ivel pouch, adjustable wrench, oil can and spanners.

GEARING.—49 in. and 52 in., or as ordered.

FINISH.—Finest stoved black enamel, with nickel plated handle bar, brake set, saddle pillar, hubs, stay rod, cranks and pedals.

Price £18 10s.

EXTRAS. — Patent Hollow Rims, per wheel, 10/-. Ball Steering, 10s. Cushion Tyres, £3. Inflated Cushion Tyres, with Valve and Inflator, £3 10s.

London Depot : 77, Fore Street, E.C.

The Ivel Cycle Company, Limited.

14

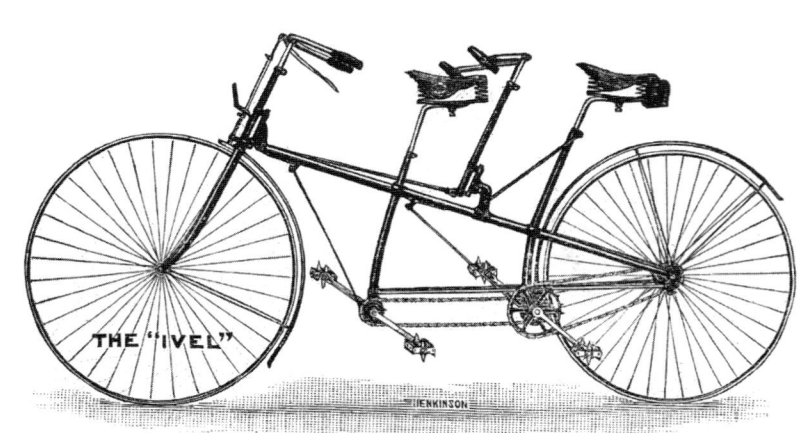

The Ivel Tandem Safety Bicycle.

SPECIFICATION.

FRAMEWORK of best weldless cold drawn steel tubes, and steel stampings, strongly braced by front and back stay rods; hollow elliptical steel forks, connected steering, adjustable handle bars and saddle pins, improved crank axle brackets and detachable roadster cranks, with throw adjustable from $5\frac{1}{2}$ to $6\frac{1}{2}$ inches, improved plunger brake, lamp bracket, rubber foot rests, mud guards.

WHEELS.—Best gun metal hubs, of latest improved design, best high tension steel wire spokes, $\frac{7}{8}$ in. solid U rims, and best grey rubber tyres.

BEARINGS.—Æolus patent ball bearings throughout, with widened bases.

FITTINGS.—Abingdon Humber chains, patent combination tension saddles and springs, best Æolus ball rubber pedals, black horn handles, Ivel pouch, adjustable wrench, oi can and spanners.

GEARING.—57 in., 60 in. or 63 in., as ordered.

FINISH.—Finest stoved black enamel, with nickel plated handle bars, brake sets, saddle pins, hubs, stay rods, cranks and pedals.

Price £28.

At the time of issuing our Price List of last year, our right to manufacture Tandem Safety Bicycles was *sub judice*. We have since succeeded in defending our rights from the attack made upon us, and continue to offer the IVEL TANDEM SAFETY BICYCLE as the best machine of the type on the market.

The Ivel Tandem Safety Bicycle,
WITH FRONT SEAT FOR LADY.

A similar machine to the last described, but with framework suitable for a lady to ride on the front seat, the steering controlled by the rear rider. Two brakes are fitted to this machine.

Price £30.

Factory : Biggleswade, Bedfordshire.

The Ivel Cycle Company, Limited.

15

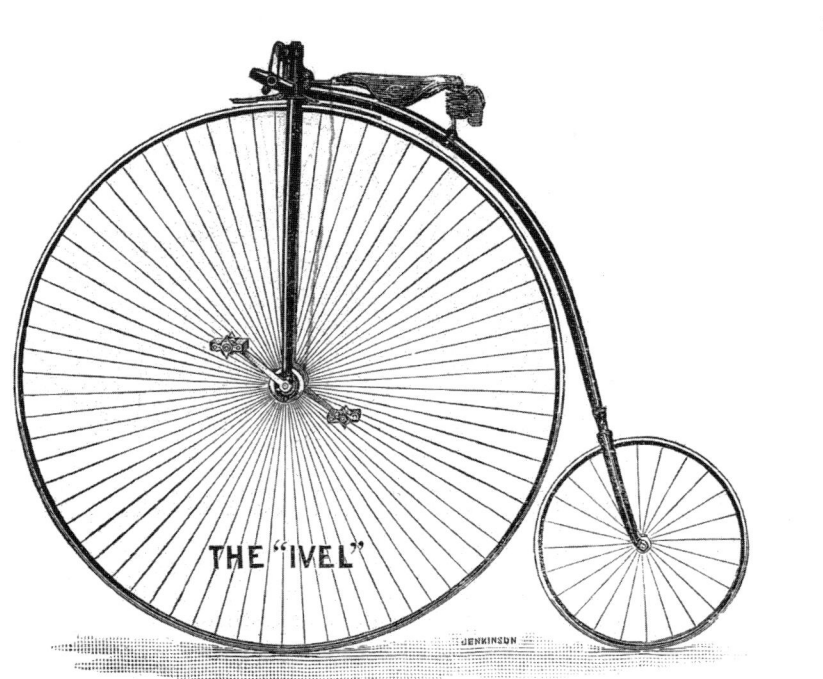

THE "IVEL"

Ivel Light Roadster Ordinary Bicycle.

SPECIFICATION.

FRAMEWORK of the best weldless cold drawn steel tubes throughout, hollow elliptical steel forks, with Æolus patent ball bearings of latest improved pattern. Patent ball bearing head; hollow handle bar and powerful spoon brake.

WHEELS.— Front wheel from 48 to 54 in. diameter, to order; back wheel 20 in., $\frac{5}{8}$ or $\frac{3}{4}$ patent hollow rims, and best rubber tyres; best gun metal hubs, bell-shaped, to take bearings and narrow the tread of rider, high tension steel spokes, patent detachable cranks.

FITTINGS.—Brooks' improved patent combination tension saddle and spring, Æolus patent ball pedals, rubber or rat trap, black horn handles, Ivel pouch, adjustable wrench, oil can and spanners.

FINISH.—Finest stoved black enamel; best nickel plated handle bar, brake set, hubs, cranks and pedals.

Price £18.

Extras: Cushion Tyre to Front Wheel, £4 0 0
" " Back " 1 7 6

Ivel Racer Ordinary Bicycle.

This Machine is constructed on the same lines as the Light Roadster Ordinary, but built throughout as lightly as is consistent with strength. Made to order.

Price £18.

London Depot: 77, Fore Street, E.C.

The Ivel Cycle Company, Limited.

IVEL ROADSTER TRICYCLE, No 1.

A light and very easy running machine, (see pp. 28 and 32), and fitted with an adjustable crank-axle bracket, allowing of easy adjustment of the driving chain. The reputation of this machine rests not only on the many wonderful rides done upon it, but also upon the unanimous testimony of its users.

SPECIFICATION.

FRAME of the best weldless steel tubes and steel stampings, forged stay rod, our improved driving bracket very strongly braced, detachable cranks, with adjustable throw of 5½ to 6½ in. ; elliptical hollow steel forks, adjustable hollow handle bar and saddle pin ; four improved bearings to axle bridge, best steel axle, and balance gear. Powerful plunger brake, lamp bracket, rubber foot rests, and mud guards.

WHEELS.—Best gun metal hubs, high tension steel wire spokes, ¾ in. solid U rims, and best grey rubber tyres.

BEARINGS.—Æolus patent ball bearings throughout.

FITTINGS.—Abingdon Humber chain, patent combination tension saddle and spring, best Æolus ball pedals, black horn handles, Ivel pouch, adjustable wrench, oil can and spanners.

GEARING.—51 in., 54 in., 57 in., and 60 in., as ordered.

FINISH.—Finest stoved black enamel, with nickel plated handle bar, brake set, saddle pin, hubs, stay rods, axle and gear, cranks and pedals.

Price £23 10s.

EXTRAS.—Hollow rims, per wheel, 10/- ; ⅞-in. tyres, per wheel, 5/- ; luggage carriers, from 12/6 ; lining, 9/- ; ball-steering, 10/-. **Cushion Tyres, £1 10s. per wheel.** Inflated cushion tyre, with valve and inflator, £1 15s. per wheel.

IVEL SEMI-RACER TRICYCLE, No. 2.

SPECIFICATION.

Of similar materials to No. 1, but lighter throughout, ⅝ hollow rims, and best rubber tyres, detachable racer cranks and chain, and rat trap ball pedals, without brake. **Price £25.**

Extras :—Brake, 10/- ; Ball steering, 10/- ; Cushion tyres, as No. 1.

IVEL RACER TRICYCLE, No. 3.

Of same design as No. 1, but built throughout of the lightest possible material. The wheels used for this Machine are 28 in. drivers, and 30 in. steerer, ⅝ hollow rims and rubber tyres. The handle bar and saddle pin are fixed to suit height of rider. WEIGHT, about 27 lbs.

Price £25.

This Machine is usually built to order.

Factory : Biggleswade, Bedfordshire.

The Ivel Cycle Company, Limited.

17

THE "IVEL"

Ivel Lady's Roadster Tricycle, No. 4.

This Machine combines all the high qualities of the No. 1 Tricycle, but is much lighter, and is so constructed as to be suitable for a lady's riding. It is provided with a bracing stay, to be fitted between saddle stem and neck when ridden by a gentleman.

SPECIFICATION.

FRAMEWORK of best weldless cold drawn steel tubes and steel stampings, forged stay rod, our new improved driving bracket, very strongly braced detachable light roadster cranks, with adjustable throw $5\frac{1}{2}$ to $6\frac{1}{2}$ inches, hollow steel forks, adjustable hollow handle bar and saddle pin, four improved bearings to axle bridge, best steel axle and balance gear. Improved powerful plunger brake, lamp bracket, rubber foot rests, mud guard, leather dress guard.

WHEELS.—Best gun metal hubs, high tension steel wire spokes, $\frac{3}{4}$ solid U rims, and best grey rubber tyres.

BEARINGS.—Æolus patent ball bearings throughout.

FITTINGS.—Abingdon Humber chain, Brooks' improved patent combination tension saddle and spring, best ball pedals, black horn handles, Ivel pouch, adjustable wrench, oil can and spanners.

GEARING.—51 in., 54 in., 57 in., and 60 in., as ordered.

FINISH.—Finest stoved black enamel, nickel plated handle bar, brake set, saddle pin, hubs, stay rods, axle and gear, cranks and pedals.

PRICE £24.

EXTRAS.—Hollow rims, per wheel, 10/-; $\frac{7}{8}$ tyres, per wheel, 5/-; luggage carriers, from 12/6; lining, 9/-; ball steering, 10s.

Cushion Tyres, £1 10s. per wheel.

Inflated Cushion Tyres, with Valve and Inflator, 35s. per wheel.

London Depot: 77, Fore Street, E.C.

The Ivel Cycle Company, Limited.

18

Ivel Roadster Tricycle, No. 5,

WITH PNEUMATIC TYRES.

Of this machine's excellence in quality and easy running, the best evidence is the fact that it **holds** the **"Record,"** for being ridden **100 miles** in **6 hours 10 minutes;** and **50 miles** in **2 hours 44 mins.** (see p. 28).

SPECIFICATION.

FRAMEWORK of the best weldless cold drawn steel tubes and steel stampings, forged stay rod, our new improved driving bracket very strongly braced, detachable roadster cranks, with adjustable throw of $5\frac{1}{2}$ to $6\frac{1}{2}$ in., elliptical hollow steel forks, adjustable hollow handle bar and saddle pin, four improved bearings to axle bridge, best steel axle and balance gear. Improved powerful plunger brake, lamp bracket, rubber foot rests, mud guards.

WHEELS.—Best gun metal hubs, high tension steel wire spokes, best solid rims, with $1\frac{3}{4}$ in. roadster pneumatic tyres.

BEARINGS.—Æolus patent ball bearings throughout.

FITTINGS.—Abingdon Humber chain, Brooks' improved patent combination tension saddle and spring, best Æolus ball pedals, black horn handles, Ivel pouch, adjustable wrench, oil can and spanners.

GEARING.—54 in., 57 in., 60 in., and 63 in., as ordered.

FINISH. Finest stoved black enamel; with nickel plated handle bar, brake set, saddle pin, hubs, stay rods, axle and gear, cranks and pedals.

Price, complete with Spoon Brake,

£34.

EXTRA.—Ball steering, 10s.

Factory : Biggleswade, Bedfordshire.

THE "IVEL"

Ivel Tandem Tricycle, No. 1.

Upon this Machine has been accomplished the greatest distance yet ridden in 24 hours by any type of Tandem, viz.: 298½ miles, certified by the N.C.U. It is admirably adapted for Touring purposes, and can be ridden by a Lady, by removing the adjustable stay from the back saddle pillar.

SPECIFICATION.

FRAMEWORK of best weldless cold drawn steel tubes and steel stampings, forged stay rod, our new improved driving bracket, very strongly braced; detachable roadster cranks, with adjustable throw of 5½ to 6½ inches, hollow steel forks, adjustable hollow handle bar, Γ saddle pillar, 4 bearings to axle bridge, best steel axle and balance-gear. Powerful plunger brake to front wheel, and band brake to axle. Lamp bracket, rubber foot rests. Leather guard to back chain. Mud guard. Curved or straight forks.

WHEELS. — Best gun metal hubs, high tension steel wire spokes, ¾ solid U rims, and best grey rubber tyres.

BEARINGS.—Æolus patent ball bearings throughout.

FITTINGS.—Abingdon Humber chain. Brooks' improved patent combination tension saddle and spring. Best ball pedals. Black horn handles. Ivel pouch, adjustable wrench, oil can and spanners.

GEARING.—57 in., 60 in., 63 in., as ordered.

FINISH.—Finest stoved black enamel, nickel plated handle bar, brake set, saddle pin, hubs, stay rods, axle and gear. Cranks and pedals.

Price £33.

EXTRAS.—Hollow rims, per wheel, 10/-. Lining, 10/-. Cushion tyres, per wheel, £1 15s.

London Depot : 77, Fore Street, E.C.

The Ivel Cycle Company, Limited.

20

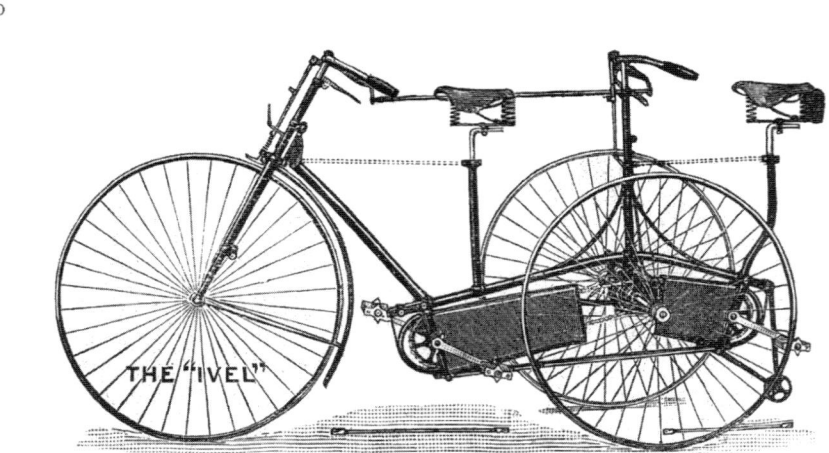

THE "IVEL"

Ivel Tandem Tricycle, No. 2.

This Machine is adapted to be ridden by Two Ladies, or by Lady on front seat. It is built of the same quality material, and generally fitted and finished as No. 1, but the steering is connected to the rear handle bar, thus giving control to both riders.

FRAMEWORK of the best weldless, cold drawn steel tubes and steel stampings, forged stay rod, our new improved driving bracket, very strongly braced, detachable roadster cranks, with adjustable throw, $5\frac{1}{2}$ to $6\frac{1}{2}$ inches. Hollow steel forks, adjustable hollow handle bar, ⌐ saddle pin ; 4 bearings to axle bridge, best steel axle and balance gear. Powerful plunger brake to front wheel, and band brake to axle. Lamp bracket. Rubber foot rests, mud guard.

WHEELS.—Best gun metal hubs, high tension steel wire spokes, $\frac{3}{4}$ solid ∪ rims, and best grey rubber tyres.

BEARINGS.—Æolus patent ball bearings throughout.

FITTINGS.—Abingdon Humber chain. Brooks' improved patent combination tension saddle and spring. Best ball pedals. Black horn handles. Ivel pouch, adjustable wrench, oil can, and spanners.

GEARING.—51 in., 54 in., 57 in., and 60 in., as ordered.

FINISH.—Finest stoved black enamel, with nickel plated handle bar, brake set, saddle pin, hubs, stay rods, axle and gear, cranks and pedals.

Price £34 10s.

EXTRAS.—Hollow rims, per wheel, 10/-; $\frac{7}{8}$ tyres, per wheel, 5/- ; Luggage Carriers, from 12/6 ; Lining, 10/- ; Cushion Tyres, £1 15s. per wheel.

Factory : Biggleswade, Bedfordshire.

The Ivel Cycle Company, Limited.

21

THE
Ivel Patent Ball Bearing
Carriage Wheels.

The attention of gentlemen owning horses is particularly requested to these wheels. The wheels are built on the unequalled direct suspension principle, and are fitted with rubber tyres of the very best quality, and revolve on patent adjustable ball bearings.

Carriages fitted with these wheels run smoothly and are perfectly noiseless, and the saving in horse labour is incalculable. The light and elegant appearance of carriages so fitted is at once noticeable, no others in any degree approaching them in this respect.

It might be imagined that the rubber tyres would soon be worn out. This, however, is not the case, the material being especially prepared for the purpose, and equal to a surprising amount of wear. Should new tyres be at any time required, they can be supplied at a moderate charge; the size of tyre recommended for an ordinary double-seated trap is $1\frac{1}{4}$-in., but larger or smaller tyres can be fitted to order.

Specially recommended for use in India,

and in other situations where it is desirable to reduce the labour of horses.

The spider wheels, rubber tyres, and patent ball bearings can be fitted to any vehicle now in use without any alteration, the axle being merely bolted or clamped to the old springs (see illustration). The price for these parts, viz., two 48-in. wheels, and patent ball bearings, complete, is 14 guineas, advancing half-a-guinea for each additional two inches in height of wheels.

London Depot: 77, Fore Street, London, E.C.

The Ivel Cycle Company, Limited.

22

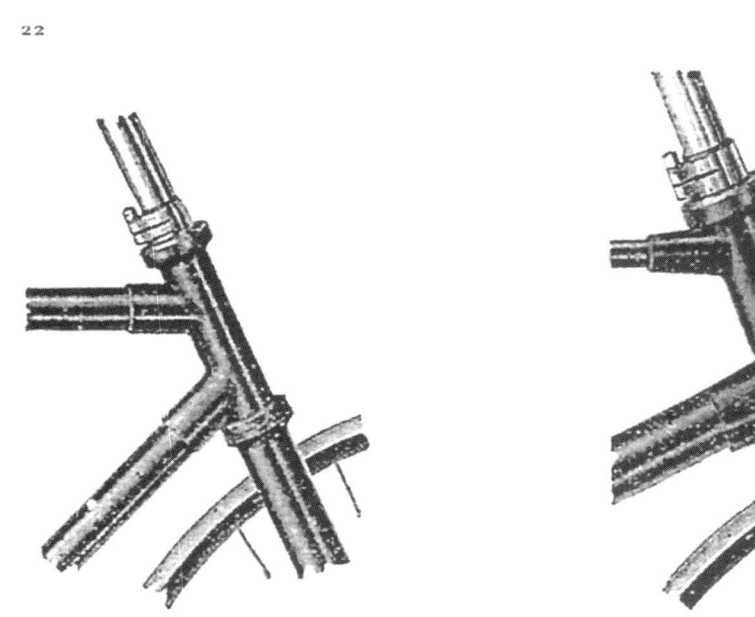

Ball Socket Steering.

As Fitted to Ivel Cycles.

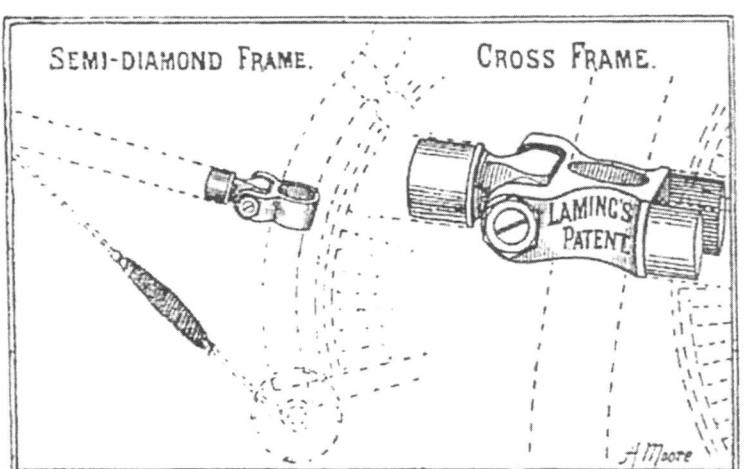

Laming's Patent Knuckle Joint.

Used with Spring in Anti-vibration
Ivel Frames.

Factory : Biggleswade, Bedfordshire.

The Ivel Cycle Company, Limited.

23

Sundries.

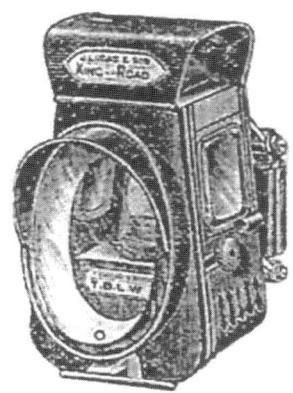 

"KING OF THE ROAD" SAFETY OR TRICYCLE LAMP,

From 14/6 to 16/6,

ACCORDING TO SIZE OF GLASS.

CLUB LAMP,
Price 9/6.

CYCLOE SPANNER,
Each 2/9.

WITH BAND CLIP,
3/-

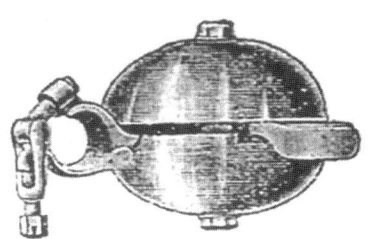

THE "CYCLARM,"
5 -

London Depot: 77, Fore Street, E.C.

Ivel Cycle Company, Limited.

24

Sundries.

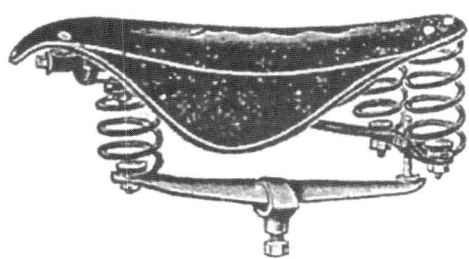

" INTERNATIONAL " COMBINED
SADDLE AND SPRING.
No. 80.
Price 18s. 6d.

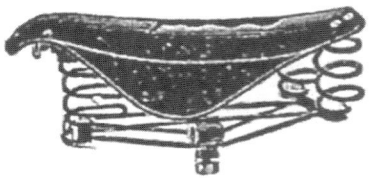

LIGHT ROADSTER
COMBINED
SADDLE AND SPRING.
No. 83.
Each 10s. 6d.

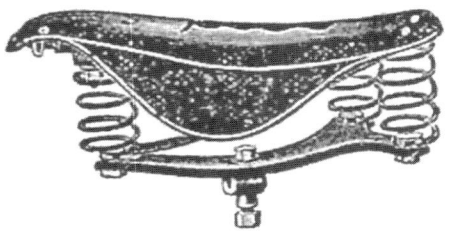

ROADSTER COMBINED SADDLE
AND SPRING.
No. 99.
Each 10s. 6d.

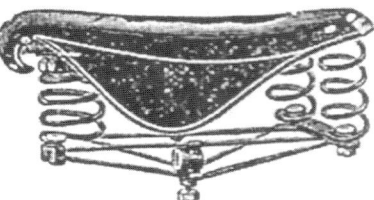

AS ABOVE, BUT FOR
LADY'S USE.
No. 85.
Each 12s. 6d.

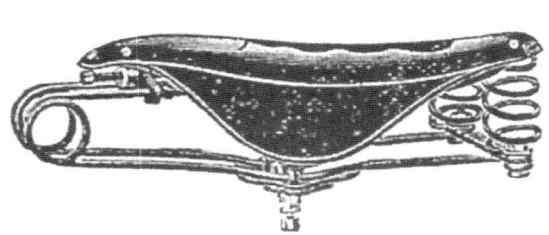

" EASY " COMBINED SPRING
AND SADDLE.
No. 90.
Each 15s.

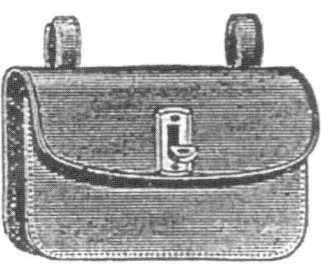

THE " IVEL " TOOL
POUCH.
Each 1s. 6d.

Factory : Biggleswade, Bedfordshire.

The Ivel Cycle Company, Limited.

25

Accessories.

———◆———

		s.	d.
Ball Rubber Pedals... ... ... per pair		17	6
Ball Rat-trap Pedals ... ... ,,		17	6
Tin Oilers ... ... each		0	3
Cork Handles, with Nickelled Ferrules ... per pair		3	6
Lamplugh's Pneumatic Handles... ... ,,		7	6
"Jet Vivement," a quick-drying Enamel per bottle		1	0
"Immobile," for securing rubber tyres by Poole's well-known process, obtainable only from us... ... ... per box		1	0
Lubricating Oil ... ... in bottles 6d. &		1	0
Cast Iron Cycle Stands ... ... from		4	0

London Depot : 77, Fore Street, E.C.

The Ivel Cycle Company, Limited.

26

334 Miles in 24 Hours,

RIDDEN BY MR. T. A. EDGE,

On AUGUST 30th, 1890,

In the North Road C.C.'s Competition.

AND

100 MILES

IN

Faster Time than any other 'Cycle' in the World.

We make bold to say that **never** in the whole history of cycling has there been a parallel to this tremendous performance; done, as it was, by a man who, on other machines, has never exceeded 225 miles in the same time. Mr. Edge was 32 miles ahead of the next fastest pneumatic-tyred safety, although many of his competitors had machines so fitted.

In the Bath Road 100 Miles Ride, 23rd August, 1890, the winner, E. DANGERFIELD, was nearly an hour ahead of the second pneumatic-tyred safety, and in this, as well as in the North Road 24 hours Ride, both riders attribute their success to the marvellously easy running of their mounts.

Also on the North Road, September 20, 1890, Mr. E. DANGERFIELD, on an **IVEL SAFETY,** "the best time made on a Safety in an open 100 miles competition."—*Cyclist.*

The PRESS is unanimous in its praises of

"THE IVEL,"

and the following are only a few of the many flattering notices published :—

CYCLIST, September 3rd, 1890, says:

" T. A. Edge, of Manchester, rode an 'Ivel' safety, fitted with pneumatic tyres, in the North Road 24 hours, on Saturday last. He covered **335 miles, beating the best previous record** by about **10 miles.** He rode the last 5 miles in 14 minutes ! "

Factory : Biggleswade, Bedfordshire.

The Ivel Cycle Company, Limited.

27

WHEELING, September 3rd, 1890, says:

" The 'Ivel' has once more taken its proper place among road machines, and evidently retains those qualities of speed and durability which made it '*nulli secundus*' a year or two ago."

SCOTTISH CYCLIST, August 27th, 1890, says:

" Again the 'Ivel' scores! In the **Bath Road 100 Miles Scratch Road Ride** last Saturday, Dangerfield, on a pneumatic-tyred 'Ivel' safety, was an easy first, covering the distance in **6h. 38m., or 29m. in front of any other competitor.** With the roads in a vile condition, and a heavy westerly wind up, this must rank as a splendid performance."

WHEELING, August 27th, 1890, says:

" We are truly pleased to see not only 'one of the best,' in Dangerfield, doing such a grand performance as that of last Saturday in the **Bath Road 100 Miles**—quite in the style of 'Eclipse first, rest nowhere'—but also our old friend the 'Ivel,' in its proper position, *i.e.*, right ahead. We congratulate the Ivel Cycle Co. on the fine way in which this light machine, weighing only 30 lb., stood the strain."

BRITISH SPORT, August 26th, 1890, says:

" No doubt, Dangerfield is a good man. But not a little is due to the excellent machine that he rode—an 'Ivel' pneumatic-tyred safety. The same machine was ridden by A. F. Ilsley last week, when he made the **fastest time in the North Road 50 Miles;** in fact I can safely say I have not seen a better safety on the road."

WHEELING, October 22nd, 1890, says:

" The 'Ivel' has been ridden **100 miles in faster time than any other Cycle in the world**, under any circumstances whatever."

CYCLIST, June 18th, 1890, says:

" During the past three weeks we have been subjecting an 'Ivel' light roadster safety (maker's and actual weight, all on, 31 lb.), to a thorough good bucketing over the north and south-western roads, and as we top the beam at 12 st. 7 lb., this riding may surely be regarded as a pretty severe test. The machine has stood grandly, the doubly-stayed crutched frame proving as stiff as a house. When we say that we have urged this machine over the summits of Petersham and Brockley more than twice, it would seem that Dan. Albone still retains the knack of constructing light, fast, and rigid machines, at all events. We have nothing but praise for the 'Ivel.'"

London Depot: 77, Fore Street, E.C.

The Ivel Cycle Company, Limited.

28

❧ "RECORDS" ❧

MADE IN 1890
ON IVEL CYCLES.

334 Miles in 24 hours.
> By T. A. EDGE on the North Road, in competition, on August 30th.

100 Miles in 5 hours 27 mins. 38 secs.
"THE FASTEST 100 MILES EVER ACCOMPLISHED ON A CYCLE IN THE WORLD."
> By T. A. EDGE, on the North Road, October 18th.

50 Miles in 2 hours 29 mins, 54 secs.
> By T. A. EDGE, on the North Road, on October 18th.

100 Miles Tricycle Record in 6 hours 10 mins.
> By T. A. EDGE, on September 22nd.

50 Miles Tricycle Record in 2 hours 44⅓ mins.
> By P. C. WILSON, on the North Road, September 15th.

50 Miles North Road Handicap.
> Won by F. CARLING, May 17th.

100 Miles North Road Competition in 6 h. 10¾ m.
> By EDMUND DANGERFIELD, September 20th.

"THE FASTEST 100 MILES EVER RIDDEN IN AN OPEN COMPETITION."

100 Miles Bath Road Competition.
> Won by EDMUND DANGERFIELD, August 23rd, in 6 hours 28 mins.

Factory : Biggleswade, Bedfordshire.

The Ivel Cycle Company, Limited.

29

TESTIMONIALS.

SAFETIES.

Fernbank, New Southgate, N., Dec. 6, 1890.

I have great pleasure in informing you that since April last I have ridden close upon 4,000 miles on the light Roadster Safety you built to my order. It has given me *great* satisfaction in every way, and I consider the **Ivel** to have no equal for easy running and sound workmanship.

Yours truly,

H. L. GIBBS, North Road Cycling Club.

West End Amateur Cycling Association, Sept. 17, 1890.

The Diamond-framed Ivel Safety supplied by you gives every satisfaction. I have ridden it some hundreds of miles this summer, and find it a very easy-running machine, combining lightness with strength. I shall not fail to recommend it to my friends.

Yours very truly,

M. W. SHEERMAN.

From the Boston (Linc.) Bicycle Club.

We, the undersigned, being members of the Boston Bicycle Club, and owners and riders of Ivel Safety Bicycles, wish to place on record our high approval of these machines. For speed, easy steering, general comfort in riding, and, above all, good workmanship, we are of opinion that they are equalled by few and excelled by none.

H. INGAMELLS, Captain.   J. C. PLATT, Sub-Captain.
J. H. TOOLEY, Bugler.   W. A. SYKES.
J. HASSNIP.   F. RICHARDSON.
A. W. HOVINTON.   T. M. ROBINSON.
JOSIAH D. CART.

April 2nd, 1890.

Galashiels, February 12, 1890.

Dear Sirs,—Two seasons ago I invested in an Ivel Safety. Since that time I have driven it over 6,400 miles of our Scotch roads, and to-day the machine is good enough for the same distance over again. The appearance of the machine after this ordeal is such as could only have resulted from superior workmanship.

I am, yours truly,

G. S. MICHIE, Galashiels C.C.

The Ivel Cycle Company, Limited.

4, Eton Terrace, Plymouth, June, 1890.

Dear Sir,—The Ivel which I purchased three years ago has given me the greatest satisfaction, during which time I have ridden about 6,000 miles over fairly rough country, and have never had a complaint to make. The machine is as firm and rigid as when new, and simply flies along with the greatest ease, and the steering is not to be bettered.

Yours very sincerely,

H. T. LAPTHORN.

The Ivel Cycle Company.

London Depot   77, Fore Street, E.C.

The Ivel Cycle Company, Limited.

30

Jesus College, Cambridge.

Dear Sir,—I may safely say that your " Safety Tandem " is vastly superior to any other in the market. Its principal advantage over other tandems is its great ease in steering.

I am, yours truly,

SYDNEY E. WILLIAMS, Camb. Univ. B.C.

———

King Street, Plymouth, Oct. 11th, 1890.

Gentlemen,—I have great pleasure in informing you that out of the number of machines—about 100 or so—of your make which I have sold *I have not had one complaint:* they have, one and all, given universal satisfaction.

Personally, with twenty years' practical experience, I consider your machines second to none in the market.

Trusting you will be still more successful next season,

I am, yours truly,

W. WHITTINGHAM.

To the Ivel Cycle Company, Limited, Biggleswade.

———

Edinburgh Evening News, Melrose,
18th April, 1890.

Gentlemen,—The Roadster Safety you built for me nearly two years ago has proved highly satisfactory in every respect, notwithstanding the hard usage to which it has been subjected at times.

I am always pleased to recommend your machine when I have an opportunity.

Yours faithfully,

JOHN WISHART.

———

32, Fitzroy Street, Northampton,
31 October, 1890.

Dear Sirs,—Your agent, Mr. A. Richardson, junr., having persuaded me to purchase one of your No. 1 Safeties at the beginning of 1889, I did so, and shall never regret it, for I have ridden it some thousands of miles, and it has borne the test splendidly. I may say that for workmanship and easy running these machines are not to be equalled.

Yours, &c.,

The Ivel Cycle Company.   JAMES LOE.

———

Cycle Depôt, Newland, Northampton,
Nov. 1st, 1890.

Gentlemen,—The " Ivels " are selling well in this district, and riders inform me that for easy running, durability, and workmanship they are not to be equalled. This speaks well for your mounts.   Yours faithfully,

A. RICHARDSON, Junr.

The Ivel Cycle Co., Biggleswade.

———

Rotterdam, 15 Sept., 1890.

Gentlemen,—Last week the Ivel Tandem Safety took the first and second at Brussels in a 3,000 metre race. Time for the first, 4 m. 59¾ secs.; second close up; or equal to 22⅜ Eng. miles per hour.

Yesterday in the 23 kilometre road race here an Ivel Roadster took the 2nd prize, and in the 50 km. road race an Ivel No. 3 took second and third prizes, all with solid tyres on a loose gravel road.

Truly yours,

The Ivel Cycle Company, Limited, Biggleswade.   BINGHAM & CO.

Factory : Biggleswade, Bedfordshire.

The Ivel Cycle Company, Limited.

31

10, Castle Road, Cardiff, May 9th, 1890.

To the Ivel Cycle Company, Limited, Biggleswade.

Dear Sirs —I beg to say I am very much pleased with the Diamond Frame Safety supplied to my order, and I think I never rode an easier going machine. The position of the rider is very good, and the ease of propulsion cannot be excelled.

Yours truly,
C. L. GEE.

———

Pool Valley, Brighton, 18/6/1890.

The Ivel Cycle Company, Limited.

Gentlemen,—We are pleased to inform you that the championship of the Newhaven Cyclists' Club was won this evening by A. E. Turner, Esq., on a No. 3 "Ivel" Safety Bicycle. This distance was about $7\frac{1}{2}$ miles on the road, and the winner's time was 27 mins. 18 secs. Among the other machines competing were "Premiers," "Raleighs," and Humbers.

Yours faithfully,
HALLIWELL & CO.

———

Milton Street, Fore Street, London,
August 12, 1890.

To the Ivel Cycle Company, Limited, Biggleswade.

Gentlemen,—The racing tricycle you built for me this season is second to none for easy running and speed.

Yours faithfully,
A. HERBERT TUBBS, Stanley C.C.

———

33, Castle Terrace, Edinburgh,
July 21st, 1890.

I have much pleasure in informing you that Mr. Muir, of the Edinburgh Southern C.C., won the 25 miles Championship and the "Gray" Challenge Shield on the Ivel Racing Safety; also, Mr. F. G. Townsend won the second prize in the Edinburgh Tricycle Club (10 miles race) on his "Ivel" Tricycle.

H. H. HALLY.

To the Ivel Cycle Company, Limited.

———

25 and 27, Jewin Crescent, Cripplegate, E.C.,
19th November, 1890.

Dear Sirs,—it is now three months since I purchased your Ivel Tricycle, and I think it only fair to you to bear testimony to the very satisfactory results I have obtained with the machine, and beg to state that I am very pleased with the Tricycle in every way.

Yours faithfully,
ALFRED DOUBLE, C.C.

The Ivel Cycle Company, Limited, Fore Street, E.C.

———

Cologne-on-the-Rhine, 29 November, 1890.

To the Ivel Cycle Company, Limited.

Gentlemen,—The machine is splendid, and we are highly pleased with it . . . . .

Yours faithfully,
BISCHOFF & CO.

London Depot: 77, Fore Street, London, E.C.

213

The Ivel Cycle Company, Limited.

3²

Paris, the 16 December, 1890.

The Ivel Cycle Company, Limited, Biggleswade.

Dear Sirs,—At the close of the cycling season we desire to express our entire satisfaction with all the " Ivel " machines you have supplied to us.

When we remember that at the beginning of the present year your make was almost unknown over here, as you had not, up till then, sought the French trade, we are surprised at the way in which it has won public favour. This is, no doubt, accounted for by *the excellence of the machines* you turn out. A proof of this is, that out of all the machines we have sold, *not one has come back for repairs*, though we give with each a twelve months' guarantee.

In the hope of a good 1891 season for the " Ivel,"

We remain, dear Sirs, yours very truly,

C. BREYER & FILS.

York, March 21, 1890.

To the Ivel Cycle Company, Limited.

Gentlemen,—I am much pleased with the principle of the " Ivel " **Patent Gig**. I have had mine some seven or eight months now, and have done some good work with it. My little cob can run it twenty miles without turning a hair, and it is the most comfortable trap I ever rode in.

Yours truly,

WILL. H. BRETT.

Coventry, December 19th, 1890.

Dear Mr. Albone,—I must tell you I am delighted with my " Ivel " Tricycle since it has been converted with pneumatic tyres, and I'm prepared to swear that it goes quite as easy as a *Safety* under all conditions except up steep hills; and there is no doubt that the " Ivel " Tricycle is the best built machine in the market for a gentleman to ride.

Yours faithfully,

GEORGE MOORE, Coventry District C.C.

79, Queen Victoria Street,

Jany., 1st, 1891.

Dear Sirs,—Our client writes us *re* your machines " I am delighted with my machine (No. 1 Ivel Safety) and so are several others here. I may secure you another order or two.

" I rode three miles in ten minutes this evening. The machine seems very *strong*, *light*, very easy running, and so very well adapted to the **Indian** roads.

Yours truly,

BYWATER, TANQUERY & CO.

Factory : Biggleswade, Bedfordshire.

The " IVEL " has been ridden 100 miles in faster time than any other Cycle in the World.

" WHEELING," Oct. 22nd, 1890.

334 Miles in 24 Hours.

August 30, 1890.

100 MILES IN 5 HOURS, 27½ MINS.

ALL PREVIOUS LISTS CANCELLED.

JANUARY, 1892.

THE

IVEL
CYCLES

MANUFACTURED BY

THE IVEL CYCLE COMPANY, LIMITED.

Managing Director - - H. G. WELCHMAN.

Works Manager - - DAN. ALBONE.

FACTORY AND REGISTERED OFFICES

BIGGLESWADE, BEDFORDSHIRE, ENGLAND.

41 miles from London, on the Great Northern Railway.

Tel aphic Address: "DANNERIES, BIGGLESWADE."

LONDON DEPOT AND SHOW ROOMS:

77, FORE STREET & 14, FORE STREET AVENUE,

LONDON, E.C.

One minute from Moorgate Street Station.

N607

A

2

Biggleswade, Bedfordshire,

January, 1892.

WE have much pleasure in presenting our NEW ILLUSTRATED PRICE LIST, which will be found to contain all those of our 1891 patterns which retain the approval of our customers, and into which we have introduced general improvements in details.

In addition to these well-tried patterns, we beg to draw attention to several important

NOVELTIES,

notably Nos. 15, 16 and 17, in Safety Bicycles, among which is a specially constructed PATH RACER, illustrated and described on page 8. It is a Diamond Frame machine, with extended wheel-base and lengthened ball socket steering head, having the crank-bracket well raised from the ground. The whole machine, with Dunlop's Patent Pneumatic Racing Tyres, weighs 25-lbs.

Also a NEWLY-DESIGNED TRICYCLE, which can easily be adapted for ladies' riding, by removing the top tube of the frame, which is made detachable, unless specified to the contrary by the purchaser.

Our patterns of Safety Bicycles include machines fitted with Cross Frames, Diamond Frames, and Anti-vibration Spring Frames; also patterns specially designed for the use of ladies.

Any of our machines, otherwise specified, can be fitted with Ball Socket Steering, if desired.

We continue to use our Special Rim for wheels to carry Cushion Tyres, it having proved most effective in preventing cutting of the tyre by the rim. The same section of rim is also used for 1-inch solid tyres, for which we anticipate a large demand.

The rivalry between the various descriptions of pneumatic tyres continues unabated. We imagine, that in the future, as in the past, Dunlop's Patent Pneumatic Tyre—which has been greatly improved for the coming season—will secure the largest share of public favour, while the Boothroyd and Clincher Tyres each possess special merits. We are prepared to fit either of these tyres according to the wishes of our customers. We still fit Cushion Tyres, which the experience of the past season has enabled manufacturers to perfect. Large Solid Tyres promise to be a feature of the season 1892. These we shall fit, as well as all smaller sizes, as hitherto.

We use none but the best materials and skilled workmanship in our manufactures; and neither trouble nor expense is spared to produce the most perfect machine that can be made. We make no second grade machine.

GUARANTEE.

We guarantee all our machines for twelve months from the date of purchase, and will make good any defects found within that time in material or workmanship. This guarantee does not apply, however, to Inflated Tyres of any description. Evidence as to place and date of purchase must accompany any claim under this guarantee.

THE IVEL CYCLE COMPANY, LIMITED.

3

TERMS.

PAYMENT. Customers having no Ledger Account with the Company will be furnished with an Invoice of the goods ordered, against which remittance is to be made before the goods leave the Works; or satisfactory references should be sent with the order.

REPAIRS are charged at Net Cash prices in all cases. CARRIAGE on Machines or parts sent for repair must be prepaid, and the sender's name and address securely attached, to prevent their refusal by the Company. PAYMENT FOR REPAIRS must be made before the goods leave the Works.

DELIVERY of all goods is made by the Company FREE ON RAIL, and they are signed for by the railway company as received in good condition. Thence they are forwarded at the risk of the purchaser, by whom all charges are payable. Purchasers should therefore protect themselves by notifying any damage to the Carriers, against whom a claim for compensation should be made immediately on delivery.

CRATES, when used, are charged at Net Cash, and are not returnable.

EASY PAYMENT SYSTEM. The Company sell their Machines, when desired, on the system of deferred payments, spread over not more than 12 months, without any addition whatever to the List Prices. The usual mode of procedure is to select a Machine, add the price of the Lamp, Bell, and other accessories, and divide the total by twelve to ascertain the amount of the monthly instalments. One payment is made at once, and the remainder monthly, until the whole amount is paid. Machines sold on this system are precisely the same in quality and price as those bought for ready money, and bear no mark in any way to indicate how they are paid for.

Forms for use under this system can be had of the Company at Biggleswade, or of any of their Agents.

All necessary enquiries of references given are conducted in a quiet and private manner—simply as to the trustworthiness of the purchaser—without disclosing the nature of the business.

THE IVEL CYCLE COMPANY, LIMITED.

GENERAL SPECIFICATION.

FRAMES. The frames of all our Machines are of the best weldless steel tubes and steel stampings, and are of remarkable strength and lightness. Forks are of hollow elliptical steel.

HANDLE-BARS and Saddle-pillars are adjustable.

CRANK-AXLE BRACKETS of improved design.

CRANKS detachable and adjustable from $5\frac{1}{2}$-ins. to $6\frac{1}{2}$-ins.

BRAKE, an improved pattern plunger.

LAMP-BRACKET, Foot-rests, and detachable Mud-guards.

WHEELS. Best gun metal hubs of improved design; best high-tension steel wire spokes; rims of improved designs to suit variety of tyres.

BEARINGS. Æolus patent ball bearings throughout, with widened bases.

FITTINGS. Abingdon Humber chain, or patent roller chain; Brooks' patent combination tension saddle and spring; best ball pedals, rat-trap or rubber; black horn handles; improved Ivel pouch, adjustable wrench, oil can, and spanners.

FINISH. Finest stoved black enamel. Nickel-plated handle-bar, brake-set, saddle-pillar, stay-rods, hubs, cranks, and pedals.

N.B.—We strongly recommend the use of Chain Guards in all cases where Mud Guards are dispensed with, to prevent the Chains running stiffly from the mud and wet thrown upon them by the wheel. This is especially important with large tyres.

HARRISON CARTER'S PATENT
Chain Lubricator, and Dirt, Dust, and Dress Guard.

We are Licensees of this Patent, which not only protects the chain from mud, dust, and rust, but also keeps every link constantly oiled.

This Gear Case can be fitted to our Safeties, Nos. 10, 12, 12a, 13, 14, 15, and 16; also to our Tricycles.

Price £2 0 0 extra.

BIGGLESWADE, BEDFORDSHIRE.

THE IVEL CYCLE COMPANY, LIMITED. 5

NO. 15.

IVEL ROADSTER SAFETY.

This represents the latest development in Safety Frame designs, comprising the extended wheel-base and lengthened ball socket head.

We have every confidence in recommending it to our numerous customers.

GEARING, 60-IN. OR 63-IN. AS ORDERED.

PRICES:

COMPLETE WITH BRAKE AND MUD GUARDS.

	£	s.	d.
Wheels fitted with best solid Rims and Dunlop's Patent Pneumatic Tyres	25	10	0
With turned edge Rims and 2-in. Boothroyd Tyres	24	10	0
With 1¾-in. front, and 2-in. back Clincher Tyres	24	0	0
With turned-edge Rims, and 1¼-in. best Cushion Tyres	21	10	0
With turned-edge Rims and 1-in. solid best Para Rubber Tyres	20	10	0
With crescent Rims and ⅞-in. best grey Rubber Tyres	18	10	0

EXTRAS.

Chain Guard, 3/6; Lining out in colours, 7/6; Carter's Patent Chain Lubricator and Gear Case, £2.

BIGGLESWADE, BEDFORDSHIRE.

B

6   THE IVEL CYCLE COMPANY, LIMITED.

NO. 16.

IVEL LIGHT ROADSTER SAFETY.

Similar to **No. 15**, but built lighter for fast road riding.

FITTED WITH RAT-TRAP PEDALS.

PRICES:

COMPLETE WITH BRAKE AND MUD-GUARDS.

	£	s.	d.
Wheels fitted with best solid Rims and Dunlop's Patent Pneumatic Tyres	25	10	0
With turned-edge Rims and 2-in. Boothroyd Tyres	24	10	0
With 1¾-in. front and 2-in. back Clincher Tyres	24	0	0
With turned-edge Rims and 1¼-in. best Cushion Tyres	21	10	0
With turned-edge Rims and 1-in. best solid Para Rubber Tyres	20	10	0
With crescent Rims and ¾-in. best grey Rubber Tyres	18	10	0

If without Brake or Mud-Guards, **10/-** less for each.

EXTRAS.

Chain-Guard, **3/6**; Lining out in Colours, **7/6**; Carter's Patent Chain Lubricator and Gear Case, **£2**.

BIGGLESWADE, BEDFORDSHIRE.

NO. 17.

IVEL RACER SAFETY.

This Machine has been constructed throughout with due regard to lightness and strength; the maximum weight being about 25-lbs.

It has Tangent Wheels, on steel hubs, with laced spokes, and the latest improved Dunlop's Patent Pneumatic Racing Tyres, fitted on Warwick's Patent Hollow Rims.

PRICE   ...   ...   £25 10 0.

77, FORE STREET, LONDON, E.C.

8   THE IVEL CYCLE COMPANY, LIMITED.

NO. 13.
IVEL SEMI-RACER SAFETY.

WITH DUNLOP'S PATENT PNEUMATIC TYRES.

This is the Machine on which Mr. T. A. EDGE rode 334 miles in 24 hours, on the road, and on which many other remarkable performances have been accomplished.

It is fitted with detachable racer cranks, and best rat-trap pedals.

GEARING: 60-IN. OR 63-IN., AS ORDERED.

PRICES:
COMPLETE WITH BRAKE AND MUD GUARDS.

	£	s.	d.
With Dunlop's Patent Pneumatic Tyres	25	10	0
With 1¾-in. front and 2-in. back Clincher Tyres	24	0	0
With turned-edge Rims and 2-in. Boothroyd Tyres	24	10	0

If without Brake or Mud-Guards, **10/-** less for each.

EXTRAS.

Chain-Guard, **3/6**; Lining out in Colours, **7/6**; Carter's Patent Chain Lubricator and Gear Case, **£2**.

BIGGLESWADE, BEDFORDSHIRE.

NO. 14.

IVEL ROADSTER SAFETY,

WITH DUNLOP'S PATENT PNEUMATIC TYRES.

Fitted with detachable roadster cranks and ball socket steering.

GEARING: 60-IN. OR 63-IN., AS ORDERED.

PRICES:

COMPLETE WITH BRAKE AND MUD GUARDS.

	£	s.	d.
With Dunlop's Patent Pneumatic Tyres	25	10	0
With 1¾-in. front and 2-in. back Clincher Tyres	24	0	0
With turned-edge Rims and 2-in. Boothroyd Tyres	24	10	0

EXTRAS.

Chain-Guard, **3/6**; Lining out in Colours, **7/6**; Carter's Patent Chain Lubricator and Gear Case, **£2.**

77, FORE STREET, LONDON, E.C.

NO. 1.

IVEL ROADSTER SAFETY.

The great popularity of this Machine is its best recommendation.

GEARING: 54-IN., 57-IN., 60-IN. OR 63-IN., AS ORDERED.

PRICES:

	£	s.	d.
With crescent Rims and ¾-in. best grey Rubber Tyres	16	0	0
With turned-edge Rims and 1-in. best Para Rubber Tyres	18	0	0
With turned edge Rims and 1¼-in. best Cushion Tyres	19	0	0

EXTRAS.

Chain Guard, **3/6**; Lining out in colours, **7/6**; Ball Socket Steering, **10/-**; Patent Hollow Rims for ¾-in. tyres, **10/-** per wheel.

NO. 2.

IVEL ROADSTER SAFETY.

Similar to **No. 1**, but built extra strong, with special stout frame and forks; suitable for bad roads and heavy riders.

PRICES AND EXTRAS AS No. 1.

EXTRA TO No. 2 ONLY: ⅞-in. best grey Rubber Tyres, **5/-** per wheel.

BIGGLESWADE, BEDFORDSHIRE.

THE IVEL CYCLE COMPANY, LIMITED. 11

NO. 3.

IVEL SEMI-RACER SAFETY.

This Machine is constructed to meet the requirements of those riders who desire a light, yet strong mount for fast road riding. Upon it have been achieved many of those performances which have contributed to raise the reputation of the Ivel Machines to the highest rank.

GEARING: 57-IN., 60-IN. OR 63-IN., AS ORDERED.

PRICES:

	£	.	d.
With turned-edge Rims and 1-in. solid best Para Rubber Tyres	19	0	0
With turned-edge Rims and 1½-in. best Cushion Tyres	20	0	0

If fitted with Centre Steering, in place of Ball Socket Steering, 10/- less.

EXTRAS.

Chain-Guard, **3/6**; Lining out in Colours, **7/6**.

77, FORE STREET, LONDON, E.C.

NO. 5.

IVEL ANTI-VIBRATION SAFETY.

Fitted with Laming's improved Patent Joint and Spring.

This Machine has a simple and effective spring frame, by which the vibration caused by rough roads is largely reduced, without the complicated series of joints and springs common to many Machines designed for the purpose.

A simple and effective spring can be fitted to the front fork, if desired, price on application.

GEARING: 54-IN., 57-IN., 60-IN. OR 63-IN., AS ORDERED.

PRICES:

	£	s.	d.
With crescent Rims and ⅞-in. best grey Rubber Tyres	18	0	0
With turned-edge Rims and 1-in. solid best Para Rubber Tyres	20	0	0
With turned-edge Rims and 1¼-in. best Cushion Tyres	21	0	0

Extras as No. 1.

BIGGLESWADE, BEDFORDSHIRE.

NO. 12.
IVEL ROADSTER SAFETY.

A Diamond Frame Machine of approved pattern, in great demand.

GEARING: 54-IN., 57-IN. OR 60-IN., AS ORDERED.

PRICES:

	£	s.	d.
With crescent Rims and ⅞-in. best grey Rubber Tyres	18	10	0
With turned-edge Rims and 1-in. solid best Para Rubber Tyres	20	10	0
With turned-edge Rims and 1¼-in. best Cushion Tyres	21	10	0

If fitted with Centre Steering, instead of Ball Socket Steering **10/-** less.

EXTRAS.

Carter's Patent Chain Lubricator and Gear Case, **£2**. Chain Guard, **3/6**; Lining out in colours, **7/6**.

NO. 12A.
IVEL SEMI-RACER SAFETY.

A Machine of similar design and price to **No. 12**, but of lighter pattern; suitable for fast road riding.

Gearing, 57 in., 60 in. or 63 in., as ordered.

PRICES AND EXTRAS AS FOR No. 12.

77, FORE STREET, LONDON, E.C.

NO. 10.

IVEL LADY'S SAFETY

Similar to last year's design; now fitted, however, with ball socket steering and improved dress and chain-guards. It has a detachable top stay, for use when ridden by a gentleman.

GEARING : 49-IN. OR 52-IN., AS ORDERED.

PRICES:

	£	s.	d.
With crescent Rims, and ¾-in. best grey rubber tyres	19	0	0
With turned-edge Rims, and 1-in. best Solid Para rubber tyres	21	0	0
With turned-edge Rims, and 1¼-in. best Cushion tyres	22	0	0
With 1⅜-in. front, and 2-in. back Clincher tyres	24	10	0
With turned-edge Rims, and 2-in. Boothroyd tyres	25	0	0
With best solid Rims, and Dunlop's Patent Pneumatic tyres	26	0	0

EXTRAS.

Lining out in Colours, **7/6**; Carter's Patent Chain Lubricator and Gear Case, **£2**.

BIGGLESWADE, BEDFORDSHIRE.

IVEL ROADSTER TRICYCLE.
NO. 1.

THE "IVEL"

This pattern remains unaltered; our past experience being that it has given entire satisfaction. It is fitted with our improved crank-bracket, which we believe to be the best in the Market.

GEARING: 51-IN., 54-IN., 57-IN. OR 60-IN., AS ORDERED.

PRICES:

	£	s.	d.
With crescent Rims and best ⅜-in. grey Rubber Tyres	23	10	0
With turned-edge Rims, and 1-in. best Para Rubber Tyres	26	10	0
With turned-edge Rims, and 1¼-in. best Cushion Tyres	28	0	0
With 1¾-in. front, and 2-in. back Clincher Tyres	31	15	0
With turned-edge Rims, and 2-in. Boothroyd Tyres	32	10	0
With best solid Rims, and Dunlop's Patent Pneumatic Tyres	34	0	0

EXTRAS.

Ball Socket Steering, **10/-**; Lining out in Colours, **9/-**; Carter's Patent Chain Lubricator and Gear Case, **£2**.

77, FORE STREET, LONDON, E.C.

THE IVEL CYCLE COMPANY, LIMITED.

IVEL TANDEM TRICYCLE

NO. 2.

This Machine can be ridden by two Ladies, or by a Lady on either seat. The handle-bars are connected together, thus giving both riders control over the steering. It is fitted with our improved crank-bracket, as named in Tricycle No. 1.

GEARING: 51-IN., 54-IN., 57-IN. OR 60-IN., AS ORDERED.

PRICES:

	£	s.	d.
With turned-edge Rims, and 1-in. solid best Para Rubber Tyres	37	10	0
With turned-edge Rims, and 1½-in. best Cushion Tyres	39	0	0
With 1¾-in. front, and 2-in. back Clincher Tyres	42	15	0
With turned-edge Rims, and 2-in Boothroyd Tyres	43	10	0
With best solid Rims and Dunlop's Patent Pneumatic Tyres	45	0	0

EXTRA.

Lining out in colours, 10/-

BIGGLESWADE, BEDFORDSHIRE.

THE IVEL CYCLE COMPANY, LIMITED. 17

IVEL ROADSTER TRICYCLE

NO. 6.

This Machine has been constructed with a view to its being used by either a Lady or Gentleman, the top tube of the frame being removable. It is fitted with our improved crank-bracket, as Tricycle No. 1.

GEARING, 64-IN., 67-IN., OR 60-IN., AS ORDERED.

PRICES:

	£	s.	d.
With crescent Rims, and ¾-in. best grey Rubber Tyres	24	10	0
With turned edge Rims, and 1-in solid best Para Rubber Tyres	27	10	0
With turned-edge Rims and 1¼-in. best Cushion Tyres	29	0	0
With 1¾-in. front, and 2-in back Clincher Tyres	32	15	0
With turned-edge Rims, and 2-in. Boothroyd Tyres	33	10	0
With best solid Rims, and Dunlop's Patent Pneumatic Tyres	35	0	0

EXTRAS.

Lining out in colours, 9/-; Carter's Patent Chain Lubricator and Gear Case, £2.

77, FORE STREET, LONDON, E.C.

18   THE IVEL CYCLE COMPANY, LIMITED.

IVEL RACER TRICYCLE

NO. 7.

In the construction of this Machine, lightness and strength have been very carefully studied and successfully combined.

It is fitted with Dunlop's Patent Pneumatic Racing Tyres, and all the very latest improvements, including our new Crank Bracket, as No. 1 Tricycle.

PRICE   ...   .   £35.

BIGGLESWADE, BEDFORDSHIRE.

20   THE IVEL CYCLE COMPANY, LIMITED.

SUNDRIES.

Brooks's
Improved
Combined

Tension Saddle
and
Spring.

No. B. 90.   Price, 15/-

Brooks's Light Roadster
Combined Saddle
and Spring,
No. 83.   Price, 10/6.

Brooks's Combination
Saddle and Spring.
B. 302.   Price, 9/6.

Brooks's Lady's Saddle
and Spring.
No. 85.   Price, 12/6.

Improved Ivel Tool Pouch.
2/-

The King of the Road.
No. 250 B.

Japanned, 15/- to 17/- ⎫ According to
Nickelled, 20/- to 22/- ⎬ size of
                        ⎭ front glass.

The Holophote
King of the Road.
No. 262.

Japanned, 22/- & 24/- ⎫ According
Nickelled, 28/- & 30/- ⎬ to size
                       ⎭ of lens.

The Captain.
No. 257.   Price, 6/6.

CONTINUOUS
ALARM

The "Warner."
No. 52   With band clip.   3/-

The Cycloe Spanner.
2/9.

The Cyclarm.
No. 53.   5/-

BIGGLESWADE, BEDFORDSHIRE.

238

THE IVEL CYCLE COMPANY, LIMITED.   21

ROAD PERFORMANCES.

The following are a few of the **Important Performances** made on IVEL Cycles, during the past six years.

All but the last, were achieved on the great North Road, and nearly all have been passed by the N.C.U., or the R.R.A.

We do not here include anything that has been done on the Racing Track.

All performances marked thus * are Records.

— 1886. —

*50 Miles in 3 hours 9 mins. 55½ secs.
by ALF. FLETCHER, August 21st, on an Ivel Safety. This was the first 50 miles record ever made on a Rear-Driving Safety Bicycle.

*50 Miles in 2 hours 47 mins. 35⅗ secs.
by G. P. MILLS, October 2nd, on an Ivel Safety. At that date this was the fastest 50 miles ever ridden on a cycle of any description.

*295 Miles in 24 hours.
by G. P. MILLS, October 5th, on an Ivel Safety. The longest distance that had ever been accomplished up to that time on a cycle in 24 hours.

— 1887. —

*50 Miles in 3 hours 7 mins. 24 secs.
by G. P. MILLS, June 10th, on an Ivel Tricycle. Beating the existing Record.

270¾ Miles in 24 hours.
by T. WATERHOUSE, September 3rd, on an Ivel Safety.

*264 Miles in 24 hours.
by G. P. MILLS, on an Ivel Tricycle. The last two were performed in the North Road 24 Hours' Competition, September 3rd. The Ivel Safety and Ivel Tricycle were respectively first and second in the race; G. P. Mills, with the Tricycle, beating the existing record by 17 miles.

*100 Miles in 7 hours 38 mins.
by G. P. MILLS, September 3rd, on an Ivel Tricycle.

*298½ Miles in 24 hours.
by G. P. MILLS and R. TINGEY, October 4th, on an Ivel Tandem Tricycle. The longest distance ever accomplished on any kind of cycle in 24 hours, up to that date, and the record still for this type of machine.

77, FORE STREET, LONDON, E.C.

THE IVEL CYCLE COMPANY, LIMITED.

--- 1888. ---

*50 Miles in 2 hours 59 mins. 39 secs.
By D. ALBONE and R. TINGEY, October 9th, on an Ivel Tandem Safety.   Record.

*50 Miles in 2 hours 52 mins. 3 secs.
By D. ALBONE and E. E. GLOVER, October 13th, on an Ivel Tandem Safety ; beating the previous record.

*50 Miles in 3 hours 2 mins. 44 secs.
By R. TINGEY, October 13th, on an Ivel Tricycle ; breaking the record.

--- 1889. ---

*50 Miles in 2 hours 51 mins. 51 secs.
By M. A. HOLBEIN and J. BLAIR, August 17th, on an Ivel Tandem Safety.

*164 Miles in 12 hours.
By M. A. HOLBEIN and P. C. WILSON, August 16th, on an Ivel Tandem Safety.   At the time this was the record for every class of cycle.

--- 1890. ---

50 Miles in 2 hours 48 mins.
By A. F. ILSLEY, August 16th, on an Ivel Safety.

100 Miles in 6 hours 28 mins.
By E. DANGERFIELD, August 23rd, winning in the Bath Road Competition on an Ivel Safety.

334 Miles in 24 hours.
By T. A. EDGE, August 30th, on an Ivel Safety, in the North Road Competition.

*50 Miles in 2 hours 44 mins. 20 secs.
By P. C. WILSON, September 5th, on an Ivel Tricycle ; beating the existing record.

100 Miles in 6 hours 10 mins. 45 secs.
By E. DANGERFIELD, September 20th, on an Ivel Safety, in the North Road Competition. The fastest 100 miles ever ridden in an open competition.

*100 Miles in 6 hours 10 mins.
By T. A. EDGE, September 22nd, on an Ivel Tricycle ; breaking existing record.

*50 Miles in 2 hours 29 mins. 54 secs.
By T. A. EDGE, October 18th, on an Ivel Safety.

*100 Miles in 5 hours 27 mins. 38 secs.
By T. A. EDGE October 18th, on an Ivel Safety, on the North Road.   "The fastest 100 miles ever ridden on a cycle in the world, under any circumstances whatever."

--- 1891. ---

175 Miles in 12 hours.
By H. H. SPENCER, September 9th, on an Ivel Safety.

178¼ Miles in 12 hours.
By H. H. SPENCER, October 9th, on an Ivel Safety.

*London to Brighton and Back.
By F. LOWE, September 4th, on an Ivel Tricycle ; breaking existing record.

BIGGLESWADE, BEDFORDSHIRE.

TESTIMONIALS.

Mr. W. D. STRADLING, Barry, Near Cardiff, writes, Dec. 19th, 1891.

Having been the owner of an Ivel machine for about three years, I am in a position to testify to the excellent workmanship, and easy running of this first-class machine.

I have ridden something like 7,500 miles on not very good roads, and not even a spoke has gone wrong.

Mr. F. W. DOWNING, Southampton, writes, June 25th, 1891.

My Ivel, which was bought in April, 1888, has been a splendid machine. It has been ridden hard, continuously, summer and winter, and has had very little attention given to it. The machine has required no repairs. I would not exchange it now for many of the improved machines which I see about.

Messrs. G. BISCHOF & Co., Cologne-on-the-Rhine, write, Oct. 9th, 1891.

At the close of the season we take great pleasure in informing you, that the machines you supplied, have given every satisfaction as in previous seasons. We prefer them to any other make. Our customers are full of praise for Ivels; expressing their high approval of these machines as regards speed, easy steering, great comfort in riding, and above all, sound workmanship combined with lightness and durability; and are of opinion that they are second to none.

Mr. T. A. EDGE, Manchester, writes, Feb. 7th, 1891.

The Safety itself is everything that could be desired, and it cannot fail to meet with the approbation and admiration of my friends.

Mr. HENRY J. BOYCE, Penge, S.E. (Catford and Mercury C.C's.), writes, Dec. 5th, 1891.

You will be pleased to hear that the machine you built for me in January, 1890, has given me the greatest satisfaction. I have ridden it since that time a distance of about 7,150 miles, without sparing it in the least, and I am glad to say that not the slightest mishap or breakage has occurred. It has not cost me a penny for repairs, and is now as sound as the day it left your works, nearly two years ago. This, considering the weight—about 30 lbs.—speaks well for the material and workmanship you put into your machines.

77 FORE STREET, LONDON, E.C.

Messrs. C. BREYER ET FILS, Paris, write, Nov. 25th, 1891.

In sending you our first stock order for 1892, we have but little to add to the testimonial we spontaneously gave you at the end of 1890.

Facts speak more loudly than words, and if we say that our sales in 1891 have tripled as compared with those of 1890, and that we are determined to follow the same rate of progression up to 1892, we think we have rendered all justice to the Ivel Cycles, which in all respects we more and more consider second to none.

Mr. G. HOODS, Liverpool, writes, March 11th, 1891.

I have ridden your No. 6, Roadster Safety over 2,000 miles in the North of England and it is as good as new.

Mr. L. VON LÜBBE, St. John's Wood, N.W., writes, Dec. 12th. 1891.

I am so thoroughly pleased with my machine, which I have now ridden about four years, that I would not change it for any other. All the time the repairs have been very little except new tires. My weight is 15 stone and I ride winter and summer.

Mr. R. E. SCALES, Earl's Court, writes, January 12th, 1891.

I have much pleasure in testifying to the excellence of the racing machine I had of you last April. From the day I had it I increased my speed considerably, and managed to secure the records in the fifty mile championship for 22 and 23 miles, which—for solid-tired machines—I still hold against the world.

The machine has been ridden over all kinds of courses ever since, and has done some real hard work on the roughest roads. It is just as good as on the day I had it, which, considering its weight—only 22 lbs.—speaks volumes for its splendid construction.

Mr. ARTHUR JEWESBURY, Stanley C.C., writes, January 8th, 1892.

With a Premier Grade Ivel, I crossed Europe from Pisa and Florence to Paris, viâ Genoa, Nice, and Grenoble without a single hitch. I have now ridden three consecutive tours, each year on an Ivel, of 1,700, 1,450, and 1,700 miles respectively, and have never had a moment's trouble. On each of the above tours the machine carried me—11 st. 3 lbs.—and over 30 lbs of luggage. I simply send this as a tribute which I candidly feel due to the sound and lasting workmanship which seems to form a chief feature in the Ivel. Messrs. C. Breyer, of Paris, furnished me with the machine.

Mr. E. W. DALLINGER, Bury St. Edmunds, writes, August, 1891.

The Light Roadster, with cushion tires, which you supplied me with in the early part of the season has won two first, two second, and one third prize in races; one among the number being a hotly contested Challenge Cup, which was finally won on the machine, the second man in, riding a Pneumatic. Altogether the machine has won golden opinions.

BIGGLESWADE, BEDFORDSHIRE.

THE DANGERFIELD PRINTING COMPANY, LONDON.

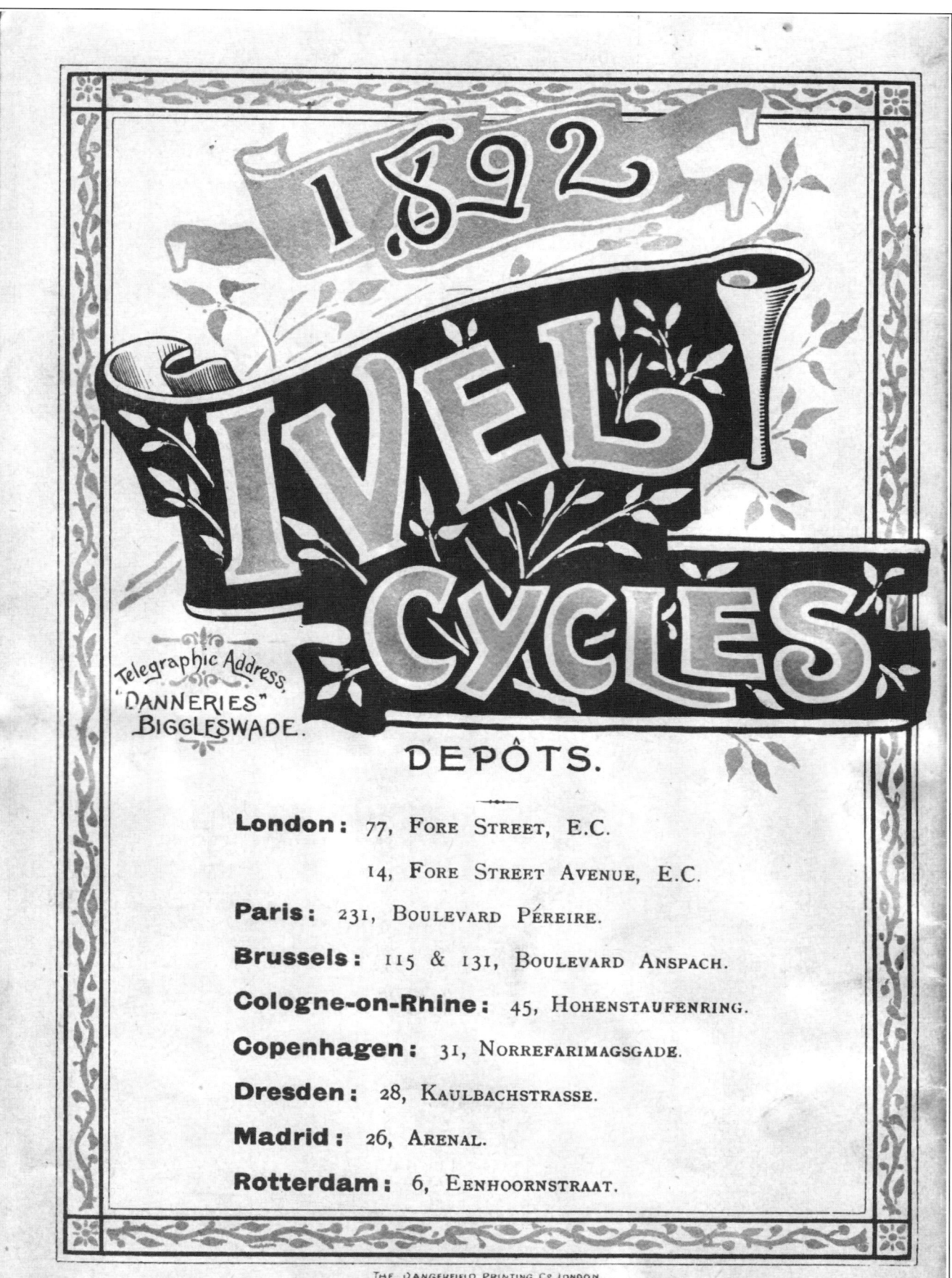

1892

IVEL CYCLES

Telegraphic Address,
"DANNERIES"
BIGGLESWADE.

DEPÔTS.

London: 77, FORE STREET, E.C.

14, FORE STREET AVENUE, E.C.

Paris: 231, BOULEVARD PÉREIRE.

Brussels: 115 & 131, BOULEVARD ANSPACH.

Cologne-on-Rhine: 45, HOHENSTAUFENRING.

Copenhagen: 31, NORREFARIMAGSGADE.

Dresden: 28, KAULBACHSTRASSE.

Madrid: 26, ARENAL.

Rotterdam: 6, EENHOORNSTRAAT.

THE DANGERFIELD PRINTING CO. LONDON

ALL PREVIOUS LISTS
CANCELLED.

January, 1893.

The IVEL

CYCLES

MANUFACTURED BY

THE IVEL CYCLE COMPANY, LIMITED.

Managing Director   -   -   H. G. WELCHMAN.

Works Manager   -   -   DAN. ALBONE.

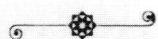

FACTORY AND REGISTERED OFFICES:

BIGGLESWADE, BEDFORDSHIRE, ENGLAND.

Telegraphic Address: "DANNERIES, BIGGLESWADE."

London Telegraphic Address: "IVEL, LONDON."

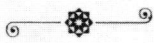

LONDON DEPOT AND SHOW ROOMS

22, FINSBURY PAVEMENT, LONDON, E.C.

OPPOSITE MOORGATE STREET STATION.

CARLING & CO., PRINTERS, HITCHIN

2   THE IVEL CYCLE COMPANY, LIMITED.

OUR 1893 MODEL SAFETY BICYCLES, which are illustrated and described in the following pages, are of improved design, and embody the following

SPECIAL FEATURES:

Frame of full length, having the crank bracket well raised from the ground.

Dust-proof Crank Bracket, of greatly improved design.

New Top Bracket, combined with simple and effective saddle tube grip.

Carefully designed Socket Head, with hard steel ball bearings, combined adjusting cone and handlebar grip, and Singer's patent steering lock.

The narrowest tread that can be obtained in machines fitted with pneumatic tyres and detachable pedals.

New Hubs and Axles, remarkably light and elegant in appearance, with ball races of full width.

Improved Spoon Brake, designed to obviate any danger of injury to the tyre by its use.

BIGGLESWADE, BEDFORDSHIRE.

GEAR CASES.

All our Machines for 1893 can be fitted with Harrison Carter's Gear Case, to order; special provision having been made for this, or other chain case, in designing the frames and hubs.

TYRES.

We are prepared to fit tyres and rims of any pattern that can be obtained in England, to order. But—while not committing ourselves to any expression of opinion as to the relative merits of any particular tyre, as against any other—those tyres which are quoted in this list are those which, from our observation and experience, we believe to be the most satisfactory forms for general use.

For list of prices of the principal tyres, see page 12, of this Catalogue.

WEIGHT.

The weights of machines according to specifications attached to the respective numbers, with Dunlop detachable tyres, are approximately as follow :—

No. 18	39lbs.
No. 19	30lbs.
No. 20	24lbs.
No. 21	36lbs.

WARRANTY.

Using only the best materials and skilled workmanship in our manufactures, and sparing neither trouble nor expense in our efforts to produce the most perfect article, we sell all our machines under guarantee, as expressed on page 5.

22, FINSBURY PAVEMENT, LONDON, E.C.

4   THE IVEL CYCLE COMPANY, LIMITED.

TERMS.

CORRESPONDENCE.

All communications should be addressed to the Company. Delay is often caused by the practice of addressing business letters to individuals.

ORDERS.

Orders for standard pattern machines are accepted for execution in rotation, and no responsibility is accepted by the Company for delay in delivery unless an explicit undertaking has been given by them to deliver at a stated time. Customers specifying any structural deviation from standard patterns must accompany their order by a remittance equal to a deposit of 25 % of the price of the machine.

PAYMENTS.

Customers having no Ledger Account with the Company will be furnished with an Invoice of the goods ordered, against which remittance is to be made before the goods leave the Works; or satisfactory references should accompany the order. All cheques and money orders to be made payable to THE IVEL CYCLE COY. LTD.

DELIVERY.

All goods are delivered by the Company Free on Rail; and they are signed for by the Railway Company as received in good condition. Thence they are forwarded at the risk of the purchaser, unless he gives special instructions to the contrary. All charges are payable by the consignee, by whom any claim for damage in transit should be made upon the carriers immediately on delivery.

CRATES

When used, are charged at Net Prices, and are *not returnable*.

REPAIRS AND SUNDRIES.

All machines and parts sent for repair must be *carriage paid*, and the sender's name and address must also be attached; otherwise they will not be received by the Company.

Repairs are charged at Net Prices in all cases, and *payment must be made* before the articles leave the Works.

BIGGLESWADE, BEDFORDSHIRE.

THE IVEL CYCLE COMPANY, LIMITED.   5

TO OUR CUSTOMERS.

GUARANTEE FOR TWELVE MONTHS.

WE GUARANTEE all our machines to be faultless in material and workmanship, and will make good any defect which may be disclosed within Twelve Months from the date of purchase and delivery to purchaser, and which does not arise from neglect, accident, or rough usage.

The alleged defective part or parts, together with evidence as to place and date of purchase, must be forwarded, carriage paid, to our Works at Biggleswade for inspection before any claim can be entertained.

The above guarantee applies to Solid and Cushion Tyres.

As regards PNEUMATIC TYRES of any description we can only undertake a responsibility equal to that admitted by their respective makers, from whom, however, we will always do our utmost to obtain for our customers the best possible terms in settlement of any complaint.

22, FINSBURY PAVEMENT, LONDON, E.C.

6   THE IVEL CYCLE COMPANY, LIMITED.

No. 18.
IVEL ROADSTER SAFETY.

SPECIFICATION.

FRAMEWORK.—Best weldless steel tube throughout. Saddle pillar and handle bar adjustable. Detachable mud guards. Steering lock. Detachable round cranks. Best ball rubber pedals. Roller chain. Detachable step, lamp-bracket, and foot-rests.

BEARINGS.—Balls to all parts, including steering.

WHEELS.—28-in. back and front, direct spokes.

GEARING.—60-in. or to order.

BRAKE.—Plated spoon brake to front wheel.

FINISH.—Finest stoved black enamel. Nickel-plated handlebar, fork crown, front fork ends, brake set, saddle pillar, chain wheel, cranks, and all bolts and nuts.
Brooks's B 24 saddle, with Ivel pouch and tools. Horn handles.

PRICES :

	£	s.	d.
With Dunlop Tyres	25	10	0
With Clincher Tyres	25	10	0
With Seddon Tyres	25	10	0

EXTRAS :
Hollow Rims, £1.   Lining-out in Colours, 7/6.   Harrison Carter's Gear Case, £2.
See page 12 for Prices of other Tyres.

BIGGLESWADE, BEDFORDSHIRE.

No. 19.
IVEL LIGHT ROADSTER SAFETY.

A light Machine of exceptional merit.

It has been thoroughly tested and proved to be remarkably fast; and, although so light, perfectly rigid and reliable.

SPECIFICATION.

FRAMEWORK.—Best weldless steel tube throughout. Saddle pillar and handlebar adjustable. Steering lock. Detachable round cranks. Roller chain. Best rat-trap ball pedals. Detachable step, lamp-bracket, and foot-rests.

BEARINGS.—Balls to all parts, including steering.

WHEELS.—28-in. back and front, 1¾-in. tyres, direct spokes.

GEARING.—63-in. or to order.

FINISH.—Finest stoved black enamel. Nickel-plated handle-bar, fork crown and front fork ends, saddle-pillar, chain-wheel, cranks, and all bolts and nuts.

Brooks's B 28 saddles, Ivel pouch and tools. Cork handles.

PRICES :

	£	s.	d.
With Dunlop Pneumatic Tyres	25	0	0
With Clincher Pneumatic Tyres	25	0	0
With Seddon Pneumatic Tyres...	25	0	0

EXTRAS :

Detachable brake, 10/- Detachable mud guards, 10/- Hollow rims, £1. Lining-out in colours, 7/6. Harrison Carter's gear case, £2.

See page 12 for Prices of other Tyres.

22, FINSBURY PAVEMENT, LONDON, E.C.

8   THE IVEL CYCLE COMPANY, LIMITED.

No. 20.

IVEL RACER SAFETY.

SPECIFICATION.

FRAMEWORK.—Best weldless steel tube throughout. Saddle-pillar and handle-bar
   adjustable. Detachable round cranks. Racing Humber chain. Best rat-
   trap ball pedals.

BEARINGS.—Balls to all parts, including steering.

WHEELS.—28-in. back and front, hollow rims, tangent spokes, Dunlop pneumatic
   tyres.

   N.B.—26-in. back wheel fitted to order.

GEARING.—66-in. or to order.

FINISH.—Finest stoved black enamel. Nickel-plated handle-bar, fork crown and
   front fork ends, saddle-pillar, chain-wheel, hubs, cranks, and all bolts and
   nuts.

   Brooks's B 19 saddle, with plated frame. Cork handles. Weight 24lbs.

PRICE £26 0 0

BIGGLESWADE, BEDFORDSHIRE.

THE IVEL CYCLE COMPANY, LIMITED. 9

No. 21.
IVEL LADY'S SAFETY.

To meet the growing demand for a light safety bicycle really adapted for use by a lady we have introduced this machine, which, as shown above, has the convenient drop frame, constructed with double tubes, so fashioned as to allow abundant room for the rider's dress, and for easy and safe mounting and dismounting. The rider sits well between the wheels, in the most comfortable position, and both the driving wheel and chain are so completely guarded that it is impossible for the dress to become entangled or injured in any way while riding.

It is a very light and easy-running machine.

SPECIFICATION.

FRAMEWORK.—Best weldless steel tube throughout. Saddle-pillar and handle-bar adjustable. Steering lock. Dust-proof crank bracket. Detachable round cranks. Roller chain. Best ball rubber pedals. Lamp-bracket and detachable foot-rests.

BEARINGS.—Balls to all parts, including steering.

WHEELS.—28-in. back and front, direct spokes, 1¾-in. tyres.

GEARING.—56-in. or to order.

BRAKE.—Plated convex spoon brake to front wheel.

FINISH.—Finest stoved black enamel. Nickel-plated handle-bar, fork crown and ends, brake-set, saddle-pillar, chain-wheel, hubs, cranks, and all bolts and nuts.

Brooks's B 28 lady's saddle, with Ivel pouch and tools. Cork handles.

PRICES :

	£	s.	d.
With Dunlop Pneumatic Tyres	26	0	0
With Clincher Pneumatic Tyres	26	0	0
With Seddon Pneumatic Tyres	26	0	0

EXTRAS :

Hollow rims, £1.   Lining-out in colours, 7/6.   Harrison Carter's gear case, £2.

See page 12 for Prices of other Tyres.

22, FINSBURY PAVEMENT, LONDON, E.C.

10   THE IVEL CYCLE COMPANY, LIMITED.

No. 6.

IVEL ROADSTER TRICYCLE.

This machine has been constructed with a view to its being used by either a lady or gentleman, the top tube of the frame being removable. It is fitted with our improved crank bracket, the excellence of which is generally admitted.

SPECIFICATION.

FRAMEWORK.—Best weldless steel tube throughout. Saddle-pillar and handle-bar adjustable. Axle-bridge trussed and stayed. Detachable round cranks. Humber pattern, or Roller chain to order. Best ball rubber pedals. Lamp-bracket and detachable foot-rests. Leather chain guard.

BEARINGS.—Balls to all parts, including steering.

WHEELS.—28-in. back and front, direct spokes, $1\frac{3}{4}$-in. tyres.

GEARING.—56-in. or to order.

BRAKE.—Convex spoon brake to front wheel.

FINISH.—Finest stove black enamel. Nickel-plated handle-bar, fork crown and ends, brake set, saddle-pillar, chain-wheel, cranks, crank bracket stays, back axle, hubs, and all bolts and nuts.

Brooks's B 28 saddle, with Ivel pouch and tools. Horn handles.

PRICES :

	£	s.	d.
With Dunlop Pneumatic Tyres	35	0	0
With Clincher Pneumatic Tyres	35	0	0
With Seddon Pneumatic Tyres	35	0	0

EXTRAS:

Lining-out in colours, 12/6. Carter's Patent Chain Lubricator and Gear Case, £2.

See page 12 for Prices of other Tyres.

BIGGLESWADE, BEDFORDSHIRE.

IVEL FRONT DRIVING SAFETY.

SPECIFICATION.

FRAMEWORK.—Best weldless steel tube throughout, strongly stayed.   Saddle-pillar and handle-bar adjustable.   Detachable mud-guards.   Lamp bracket.
BEARINGS.—Balls to all parts, including steering.
WHEELS.—30-in. front, 24-in. back, solid rims, direct spokes.
GEARING.—Perry's, geared to 60-in., or to order.   Round detachable cranks.   Best rat-trap ball pedals.
FINISH.—Finest stoved black enamel.   Nickel-plated handle-bar, front fork crown and ends, hubs and gearing case, cranks and all bolts and nuts.   Brooks's B 28 saddle, Ivel pouch and tools.   Horn handles.

PRICE (with Dunlop or Seddon Tyres) ... £25 10 0.
Prices of Tyres of other descriptions on application.

EXTRAS:
Hollow rims, 20/-.   Lining-out in colours, 7/6.   Brake, 12/6.

IVEL GEARED ORDINARY.

With Crypto gearing, wheels 36-in. to 40-in. front, 22-in. back, hollow rims, Dunlop or Seddon tyres.

PRICE ... ... £26 0 0.

EXTRAS:
Brake, 12/6.   Lining-out in colours, 7/6.

22, FINSBURY PAVEMENT, LONDON, E.C.

Additions to and Reductions from
Standard List Prices

For the undermentioned Tyres for 28 inch Wheels.

ADDITIONS.

	£	s.	d.
Dunlop ... ... per tyre	0	0	0
Clincher, 1¾ inches ... . ,, ,,	0	0	0
Do. 2 ,, ... ,, ,,	0	0	0
Seddon ... ... ,, ,,	0	0	0
Preston Davies ... ... ,, ,,	0	15	0
Michelin ... ... ,, ,,	1	10	0

REDUCTIONS.

	£	s.	d.
Silvertown Closure, 1¾ inches... ... ... per tyre	0	10	0
Do. do. 2 ,, ... ,, ,,	0	0	0
Boothroyd 1¾ ,, ... ,, ,,	1	5	0
Do. 2 ,, ... ,, ,,	0	15	0
Cushion, 1¼ inch ... ... Reduction per pair	4	10	0
Solid, 1 ,, ... ,, ,, ,,	5	10	0

Special Quotations for any Tyre not included in the above List.

THE IVEL CYCLE COMPANY, LIMITED.   13

SPECIAL NOTICE.

WE HAVE still a small surplus stock of machines of various patterns, of last and previous seasons' models, which we do not include in this list, having discontinued their manufacture.

These we can offer at

VERY ATTRACTIVE PRICES

and they will be found very satisfactory value for money.

Prices, specifications and illustrations on application.

TANDEM TRICYCLES.

The demand for these machines is so limited that we have ceased to stock them.

WE ARE PREPARED TO MAKE TO ORDER, having all necessary patterns and parts on hand; and will submit DESIGNS, SPECIFICATIONS and PRICES ON APPLICATION.

22, FINSBURY PAVEMENT, LONDON, E.C.

14   THE IVEL CYCLE COMPANY, LIMITED.

SUNDRIES.
BROOKS'S SADDLERY.

No. B. 90.   Price 14/6.

No. B. 28.   Price 10/-   Ivel Tool Pouch.   Price 2/-   No. B. 29.   Price 11/6.

No. B. 17. Price 7/-   No. B. 24.   Price 10/6.   No. B. 19. Price 8/6.

LUCAS'S CYCLEALITIES.
Telescopic Inflator.

Open.   Price 5/6.   Closed.

No. 2. Long Inflator.   Price 5/-   Cycloe Spanner.   Price 2/6.

TOE CLIPS.
For Rubber Pedals, No. 1, per pair 2/-   For Rat Trap Pedals, No. 2, per pair 2/6.
    ,,   ,,   No. 9,   ,,   2/-   ,,   ,,   ,,   No. 8,   ,,   2/6.

BIGGLESWADE,   BEDFORDSHIRE.

SUNDRIES—CONTINUED.

The " Pioneer," No. 266.

Size 0, Lens 2¾ ins. Japanned 11/6.
,, 1, ,, 3⅛ ins., ,, 12/6.

The " Alumophote," No. 272.

Height 4½ ins., Weight 10¾ ozs
Lens 2¼ ins., Japanned, 19/-

The "Warner," No. 273

Glass 3½ ins., Japanned 4/6.

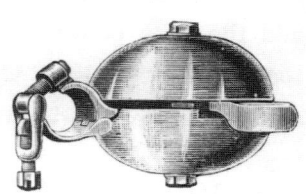

The "Warner," No. 52.

With Band Clip, 3/-

The "Captain," No. 274.

Glass 3½ ins. by 2⅞ ins., Japanned 7/-

The "Cyclarm," No. 53.

Price 5/-

OILERS

From 3d. to 2/6 each.

———

LAMP OILS,

LUBRICATING OILS

BY

VARIOUS MAKERS.

Repairing Outfits

FOR

PNEUMATIC TYRES

ON SALE AT

22, FINSBURY PAVEMENT,

LONDON, E.C.

The " Holophote," No. 262 B.

KING OF THE ROAD.

Size 00, Lens 2¼ ins., ... Japanned 18/6, Nickelled 24/6.
,, 0, ,, 2¾ ins., ... ,, 21/-, ,, 27/-
,, 1, ,, 3⅛ ins., ... ,, 22/-, ,, 28/-

22, FINSBURY PAVEMENT, LONDON, E.C.

EASY PAYMENT SYSTEM.

THE IVEL CYCLES can be purchased, when necessary, on the system of deferred payments, by which payment is spread over a period not exceeding Twelve Months, without any addition whatever to the List Prices.

To ascertain the amount of the monthly instalments, select a machine, add the price of the lamp, bell, and other accessories if desired, and divide the total by twelve. One payment is made at once, and the remainder monthly until the whole is paid.

Machines purchased on this system are precisely the same in quality and price as those bought for ready money; are delivered in the usual rotation of orders; and bear no mark in any way to indicate the terms of their purchase.

Forms for use under this system can be had of the Company at Biggleswade, or London, or of any of their Agents.

All necessary enquiries of references given, are conducted in the most private manner, and with the utmost discretion; the object being simply to ascertain the trustworthiness of the proposed purchaser, without disclosing the nature of the business.

BIGGLESWADE, BEDFORDSHIRE.

The Ivel Cycle Works,

BIGGLESWADE,

NOVEMBER, 1894.

SIR,

In June last I sent out a Circular informing you I had taken over the Business originally started by myself, but of recent years carried on by the IVEL CYCLE COMPANY, LIMITED. Since that time I have pleasure in announcing the Works have been, and are now, in full and thorough working order, and that I am prepared to supply from Standard Pattern or build to Customer's Order, a first class Cycle second to none on the Market.

The Ivel of to-day is indeed a Machine worthy of the Name,

and it is with the greatest possible confidence I ask for a continuance of your kind patronage.

Since taking over the Business among my numerous distinguished patrons have been:

COUNTESS COWPER.	LORD ALWYN COMPTON.	S. WHITBREAD, ESQ., M.P.
LORD AMPTHILL.	THE REV. LORD WM. CECIL.	MAJOR SHUTTLEWORTH.
	LENNOX PEEL, ESQ.	

The Ivel Company during the years of its existence built up for itself a good London connection, and it is my aim to do all I can to continue to hold this. Though I have decided not to open a London Depot, I have retained the services of MR. GEORGE COURSE, the late London Manager for the Company, who will be pleased to call on or meet at Biggleswade all old customers.

My decision to deal with my London Patrons direct from Biggleswade must be taken by them as one from which they gain very considerable benefit, inasmuch as not being taxed with the payment of excessive rents and the many other expenses necessarily attached to such a branch of the Business, I am enabled to offer at a Lower Figure, viz.—£15 15s. nett—a Machine better and more prettily designed, more skilfully built and more superbly finished in every detail than the one—good as it was—turned out by the Company last year.

To impress upon the mind if such be necessary, the extraordinary value embodied in my Machine I would mention it as a fact that none but the very best material procurable is used in their construction. Long ago it was proved the IVEL was a Safety to be depended upon. I am determined to keep this reputation and to do so I have spared no expense to place before the Public for 1895 an up to date Machine, I boldly assert, is excelled by none.

Full Particulars and Drawings of the IVEL Cycles will be found in my Illustrated Price List for 1895.

Earnestly soliciting a continuance of your favours and assuring you of my personal supervision and prompt attention to any order you may give me.

I am, Yours faithfully,

DAN ALBONE.

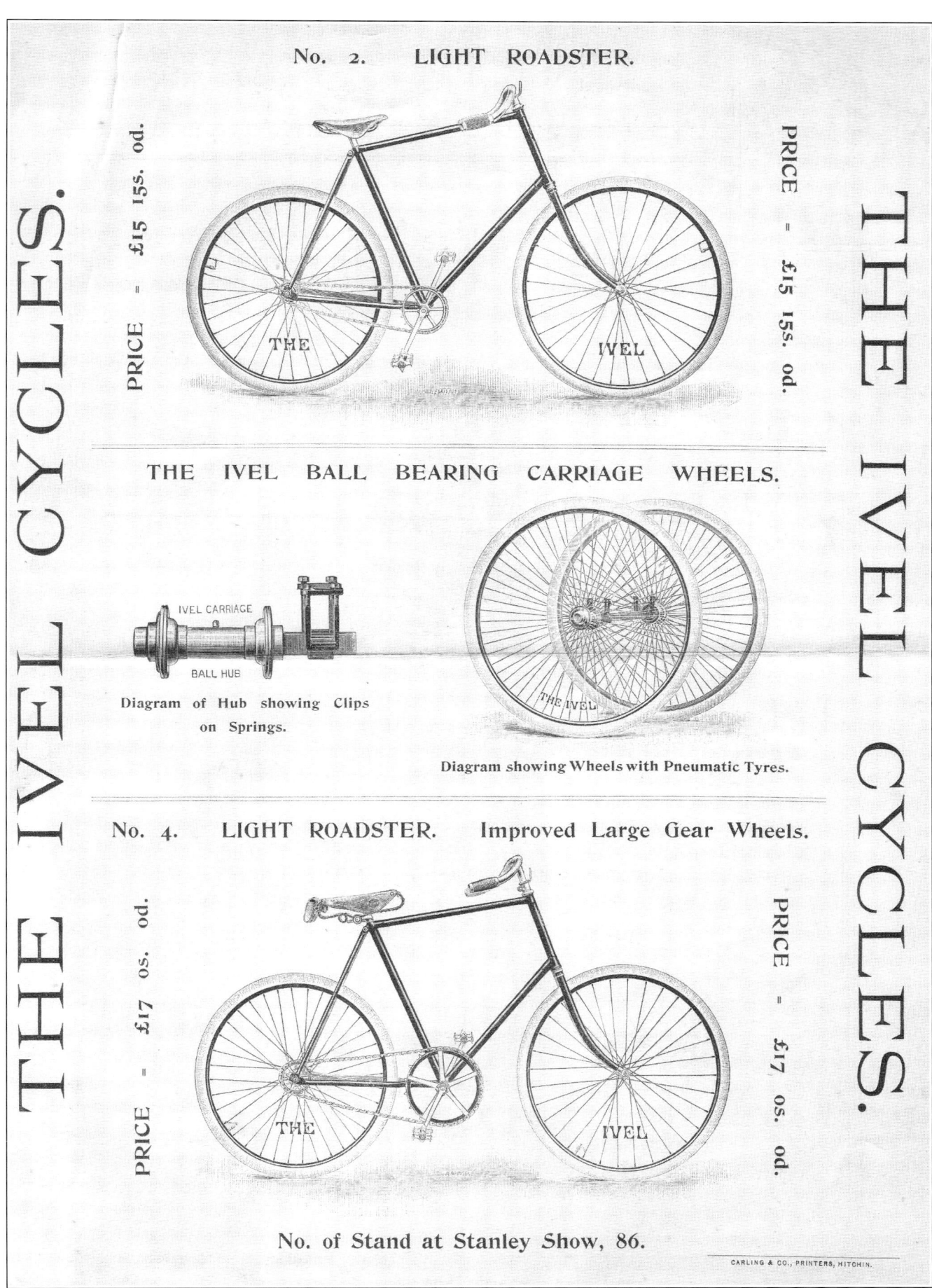

No. 2.   LIGHT ROADSTER.

THE IVEL BALL BEARING CARRIAGE WHEELS.

IVEL CARRIAGE

BALL HUB

Diagram of Hub showing Clips
on Springs.

Diagram showing Wheels with Pneumatic Tyres.

No. 4.   LIGHT ROADSTER.   Improved Large Gear Wheels.

No. of Stand at Stanley Show, 86.

CARLING & CO., PRINTERS, HITCHIN.

1896.

ILLUSTRATED PRICE LIST

OF THE

IVEL

 # CYCLES

AND BALL-BEARING

Carriage Axles and Boxes.

MANUFACTURED BY - - -

DAN ALBONE,

Ivel Cycle Works,

BIGGLESWADE, Beds.

W. CARLING & CO., PRINTERS, EXCHANGE YARD, HITCHIN.

TERMS OF BUSINESS.

CASH against Invoice to Customers having no Ledger Account.

CARRIAGE in all cases to be paid by PURCHASER.

REPAIRS will not be received unless sent CARRIAGE PAID with full Name and Address of Sender.

CRATES are charged Cost Price, and are NOT RETURNABLE.

NOTICES TO PURCHASERS - -

Most of my Machines are made specially to order, thus giving more satisfaction to the Purchaser and myself. All I require is the inside measurement of leg and the weight of the rider.

A Large Stock of all kinds of Accessories such as LAMPS, BELLS, TYRE INFLATORS, &c., &c., always kept in Stock. Old Machines are always taken as Part Payment, and a large number of second-hand Machines are always on sale at very low prices.

REPAIRS - - - -

All kinds of Repairs are done on the premises. As I have a complete plant for this branch, Customers may rely upon Prompt and Efficient attention. Any Enquiry respecting any of my Machines receives immediate attention, and inspection of my Stock of Machines and Accessories is respectfully invited at the Show Rooms at the Works.

SPECIAL - - - -

ALL KINDS OF NICKEL PLATING DONE ON THE PREMISES. I ALSO HAVE A SPECIAL PLANT FOR SILVERING SUCH ARTICLES AS FORKS, SPOONS, CRUETS, TRAYS, &c. See detailed List to be had on application.

Guarantee for Twelve Months.

I Guarantee all my Machines to be faultless in Material and Workmanship and will make good within twelve months of the date of purchase any defect which may be disclosed, not caused by accident, rough usage or neglect. Alleged defective parts must be forwarded to the Works (carriage paid) for examination before any claim can be allowed. This Guarantee does not hold good with regard to Tyres, I can only undertake a responsibility equal to that admitted by their respective Makers, from whom I will always do my utmost to obtain for Customers the best terms and settlement in the event of any complaint.

3

Introduction.

IT is now sixteen years since I had the pleasure of issuing my first Illustrated Catalogue of the celebrated IVEL Cycles, and it is with more than usual confidence and pleasure I send out my Illustrated Price List for 1896. So great and continual has been the run during the past season on the IVEL Machines, that next season—as in the one just passed—the IVEL Cycles will be

Up=to=Date in Every Way,

and for stability, ease of running, and finish, unsurpassed.

The increase of my business during 1895 has been phenomenal. During the whole year my Factory has been working at great pressure to keep pace with the ever increasing number of orders given to me. This, and the fact that every Machine sent out has had nothing but praise bestowed upon it, justifies me in making the arrangements I have made for the output of the IVEL Cycles in even greater numbers than last season.

The list of Patrons on the next page speaks for itself, and it only remains for me to say I shall continue to turn out a Machine I know is as well constructed and lower in price than any other first-grade Machine in the Market. To the making of the Ladies' Safety I am giving special attention. I was the first to introduce this pattern 10 years ago, and my experience in the building of this class of Machine puts me in a position to say the

Ivel Ladies' Safety Bicycle

possesses advantages in construction which contribute to the ease of propulsion and the comfort of the rider, found in few of the similarly built Machines.

Although I have no London Depôt for the convenience of my customers in town. I may make mention of the capital service of trains existing between London and Biggleswade—which allows a Machine put in at King's Cross (G.N.R.) to be at my works in

4

little more than an hour. This is a boon few Makers can offer to their London patrons, for it is certainly a great advantage to have any accident to a Bicycle attended to and repaired at the works of the Maker of the Machine. My trade in London has so much increased that I or my Representative, Mr. GEORGE COURSE, will visit town once or twice each week, and will be glad to call upon intending purchasers or any one wishing for fuller details or particulars of my Cycles.

As was the case last year I have priced my Cycles at the amount for which they can be bought. What is known as the " discount " has already been subtracted, **and no Agent** can sell less than the figure shown. The testimony I have received (some of which is printed on pages 13, 14, 15 in this list) both from my more distinguished patrons as well as from many other Ladies and Gentlemen, and the knowledge that my Machines are conscientiously well-made and to be depended upon, enables me to state with truth that the purchase of an IVEL Cycle will not, be regretted.

I would here draw attention to the fact that I am making a speciality of

Ball Bearing Carriage Wheel Hubs

which were introduced by me in 1885, also Pneumatic and solid rubber Tyred Wheels for Vehicles of all kinds. There is no doubt that before long such will be in general use, and I ask those, in or out of the coach building trade, interested in the construction of all descriptions of Carriages, to refer carefully to the pages (Nos. 12 and 16) devoted to this branch of business in this List.

I thank all for their past support and kindness in recommending my Machines and Patent Ball Bearing Carriage Axles, and assure them that it will be my constant endeavour to give individual and personal attention and satisfaction to every buyer of an IVEL Cycle and Carriage Axle. In conclusion, I would remind my readers I am a practical and experienced Maker, and having been a racing man, both on road and path, winning over 180 prizes, I know the requirements of every purchaser.

DAN ALBONE.

5

List of Patrons.

Countess Cowper,
Countess Grey,
Countess Listowell,
Lady Colthurst,
Lady Oxenbridge,
Honourable Mrs. Forbes,
Mrs. Shuttleworth,
Mrs. Captain Barnett,
Mrs. Colonel Josselyn,
Mrs. George Barnett,
Mrs. Heysham,
Mrs. Kerr,
Mrs. S. Bruce,
Mrs. Cooke,
Mrs. G. Taddy,
Miss Astell,
Miss M. Dimsdale,
Miss F. Cochrane,
Miss Osborne,
Mrs. Algernon Talbot,
Mrs. J. Trotter,
Mrs. A. Tyrrell,
His Grace the Duke of Bedford,
Viscount Peel,
Earl Grey,
Earl Jersey,
Earl of Mount Edgcumbe,
Lord Alwyne Compton, M.P.,
Lord Ampthill,
Rev. Lord William Cecil,
Sir Algernon Osborne,
Honourable C. A. Pelham,
Honourable Mark McDonnell,
Colonel Astell,
Colonel Gregson,
Major-General T. B. Bevan,
Major Shuttleworth,
Major Mellor,
Sydney Mills, Esq.,
Captain C. H. Fenwick,
Captain Duberley,
Captain Chas. J. Briggs, R.N.,
Guy Pym, Esq., M.P.,
Howard S. Whitbread, Esq.,

Howard Gilliat, Esq.,
Algernon Gilliat, Esq.,
Reginald B. Loder, Esq.,
J. Harvey, Esq.,
J. H. St. Q. Astell, Esq.,
Lennox Peel, Esq.,
G. Peel, Esq.,
F. Archdale, Esq.,
Henry J. B. Kendall, Esq.,
W. H. Attenborough, Esq.,
E. O. Fordham, Esq.,
H. A. Vernet, Esq.,
F. W. Greenfield, Esq.,
F. B. Greenfield, Esq.,
Robert Dimsdale, Esq.,
J. H. Mossop, Esq.,
Jos. F. Green, Esq.,
Francis R. Pryor, Esq.,
Marlborough Pryor, Esq.,
C. S. Lindsell, Esq.,
Robert Lindsell, Esq.,
Gerald Smith, Esq.,
Julian Godfrey, Esq.,
Cyril B. Tubbs, Esq.,
John Corrie Carter, Esq.,
S. Whitbread, Esq.,
A. Harter, Esq.,
C. F. St. Quinton, Esq.,
C. F. M. Hodgkins, Esq.,
Hubert S. Payne, Esq.,
Henry J. B. Kendall, Esq.,
E. Morse, Esq.,
William Tyrer, Esq.,
Martin Pirie, Esq.,
Philip Bright, Esq.,
J. Dryon Moore, Esq.,
J. N. Stewart, Esq.,
A. Tyrrell, Esq.,
T. A. Gibb, Esq.,
W. T. Nash, Esq.,
R. E. V. Lang, Esq.,
J. S. W. Beachett, Esq.,
Bedfordshire Constabulary.

6

No. 1 ROADSTER
SAFETY.

THIS Machine is built for Touring and General Purposes, and will carry anything up to fifteen stone. For heavier weights Machines are made specially.

SPECIFICATION:

Best weldless steel tubes; 28″ driving and 30″ steering wheels; tangent or direct spokes; best ball bearings throughout; improved dust proof bottom bracket; gear 60 or to order; powerful detachable spoon brake; detachable light metal mud-guards; adjustable foot-rests; rubber pedals; weight as illustrated, 39lbs.

PRICE - - £16 10/-

With Dunlop, Clincher or other well-known Pneumatic Tyres.

EXTRAS.—Carter Detachable Gear Case, £1 15s.; IVEL Gear Case, £1; Lining, 7/6; if enamelled any other colour than Black, 5s.

7

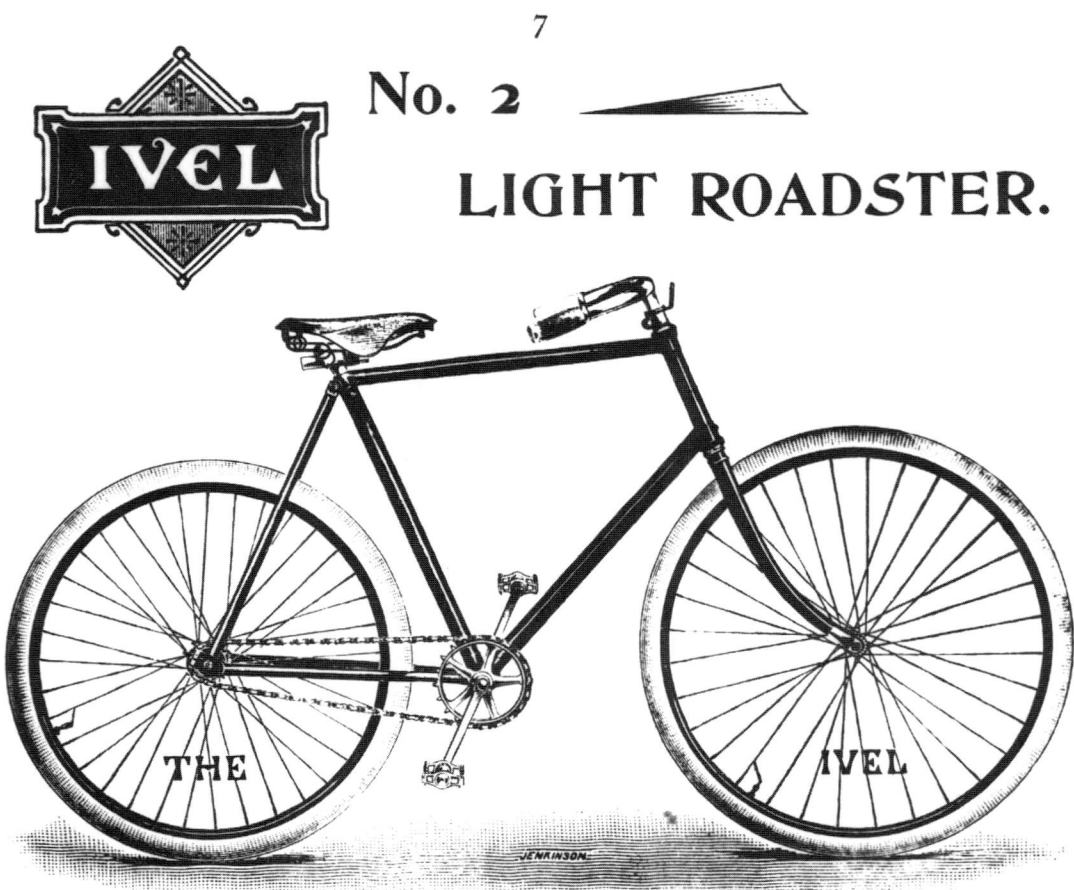

No. 2
LIGHT ROADSTER.

THIS Machine has demanded a large Sale, and is equal to any on the Market. Several improvements have been made, reducing weight and increasing strength.

SPECIFICATION :—Best weldless tubes ; 28″ driving and 30″ steering wheels, improved dust proof bottom bracket, narrow tread, gear 63″ or to order, rat-trap or rubber pedals, latest pattern flat cranks, 6½″ throw, tangent or direct spokes. Weight 29lbs.

PRICE - - £15 15/-

With Dunlop, Clincher, or other well-known Pneumatic Tyres.

EXTRAS.—Carter detachable Gear Case, £1 15s. ; IVEL Gear Case, £1 ; Brake and Guards, 15s. ; Lining, 7/6 ; If enamelled any other colour than Black, 5s.

IVEL NO. 3 ROAD RACER.—A splendid reproduction of the IVEL No. 2 Light Roadster cut down in lightness consistent with strength. Hollow rims, tangent spokes. Gear 66 or to order. Weight, 25lbs.

PRICE - - £16 16/-

EXTRAS.—Same as No. 2.

IVEL NO. 4 PATH RACER.—Made of special light parts with pure racing rims, tyres and chain. Weight, 20½lbs. Although this Machine has been used on the road without mishap, we do not guarantee to make good any breakage should it occur when being used off the path.

PRICE - - £17 17/-

EXTRAS.—Same as No. 2.

8

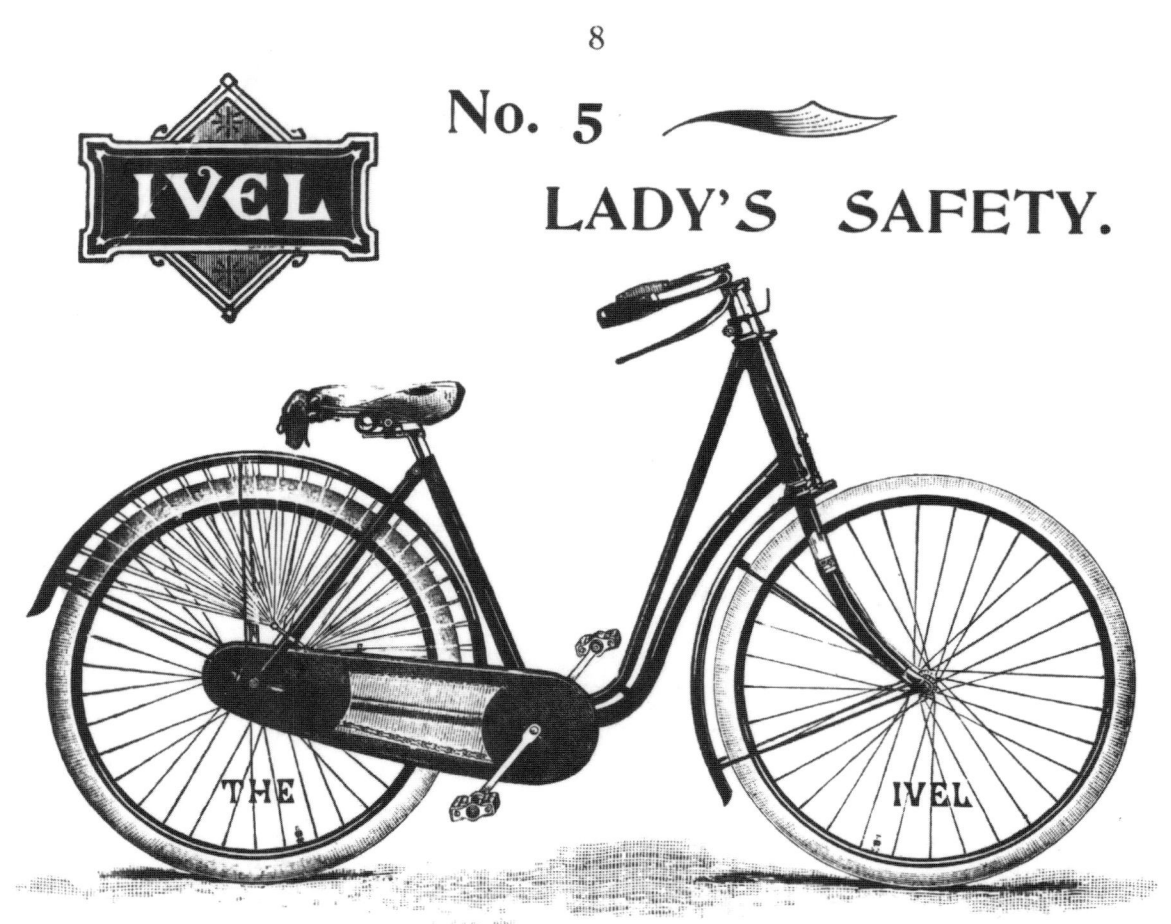

No. 5

LADY'S SAFETY.

THE experience I have had in the construction of this Machine has been very great. The Lady's Safety was first introduced by me in 1886, and since that time I have turned out a very large number each season. So much satisfaction has my last year's machine given that I have made little change in the pattern.

SPECIFICATION :

Strong dropped frame with double tubes, 28″ wheels complete with IVEL Gear Case, Brake and Mud Guards.

PRICE - - £17.

With Dunlop, Clincher, or other well-known Tyres.

EXTRAS.—If fitted with Carter Case instead of IVEL., 15s. ; Hollow Rims, 12. 6d. ; Lining, 7s. 6d. If enamelled any other colour than Black, 5s.

Reprint      as introduced and

of Lady's Safety   sold by me in 1886.

9

No. 6 = = TRICYCLE.

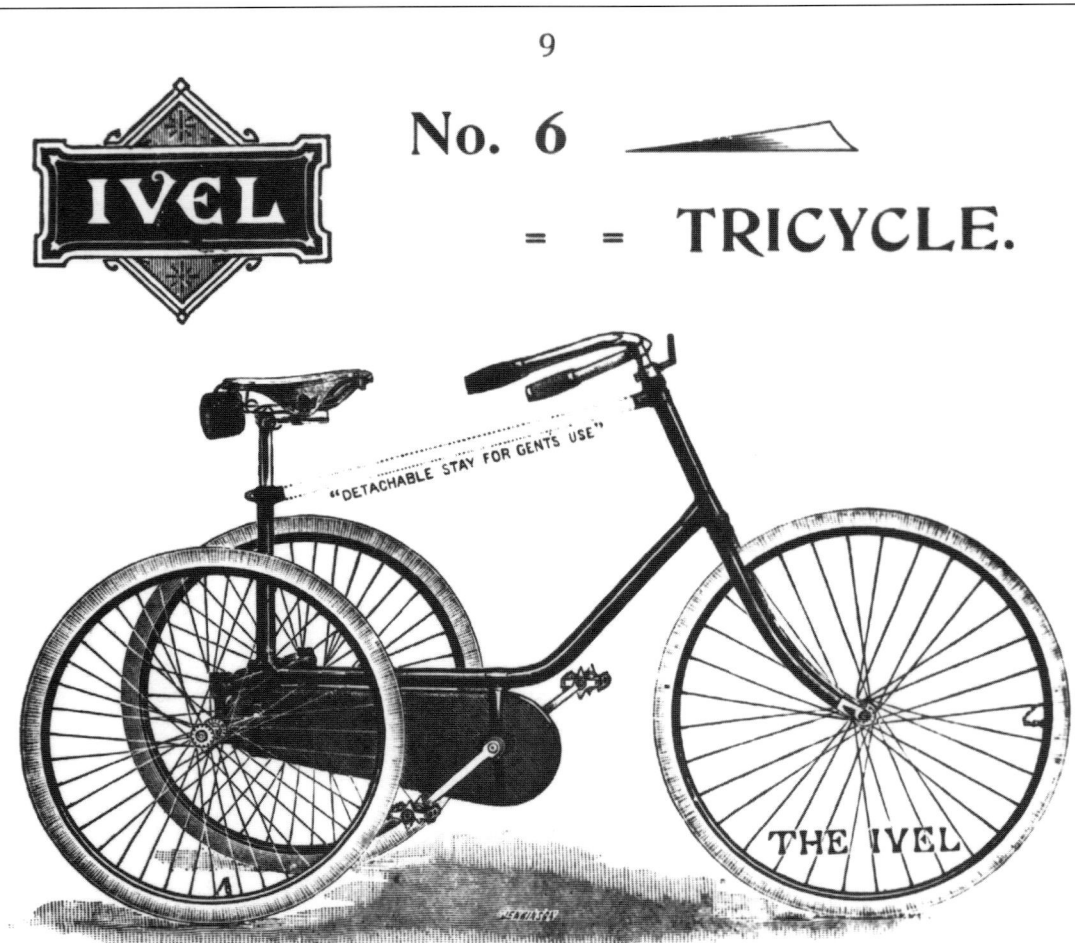

"DETACHABLE STAY FOR GENTS USE"

THE IVEL

THE Ivel Tricycle has been constructed with a view to its being used by either a lady or gentleman, the top tube of the frame being removable. I have always done a large business with Tricycles and each year the demand is increasing. It is made with fixed top tube if required for the use of gentlemen only or for fast road riding purposes.

PRICE - - £26.

With Dunlop, Clincher, or other well-known Pneumatic Tyres,and Improved Dress Guard.

If fitted with best 1¼" Cushion Tyres £21.

Lining, 10s. If enamelled any other colour than Black, 7s. 6.

TANDEM SAFETIES.

THOUGH not illustrating this Machine I am prepared to make to order a Tandem Safety of the latest pattern.

Designs, Specifications, and Prices on Application.

10

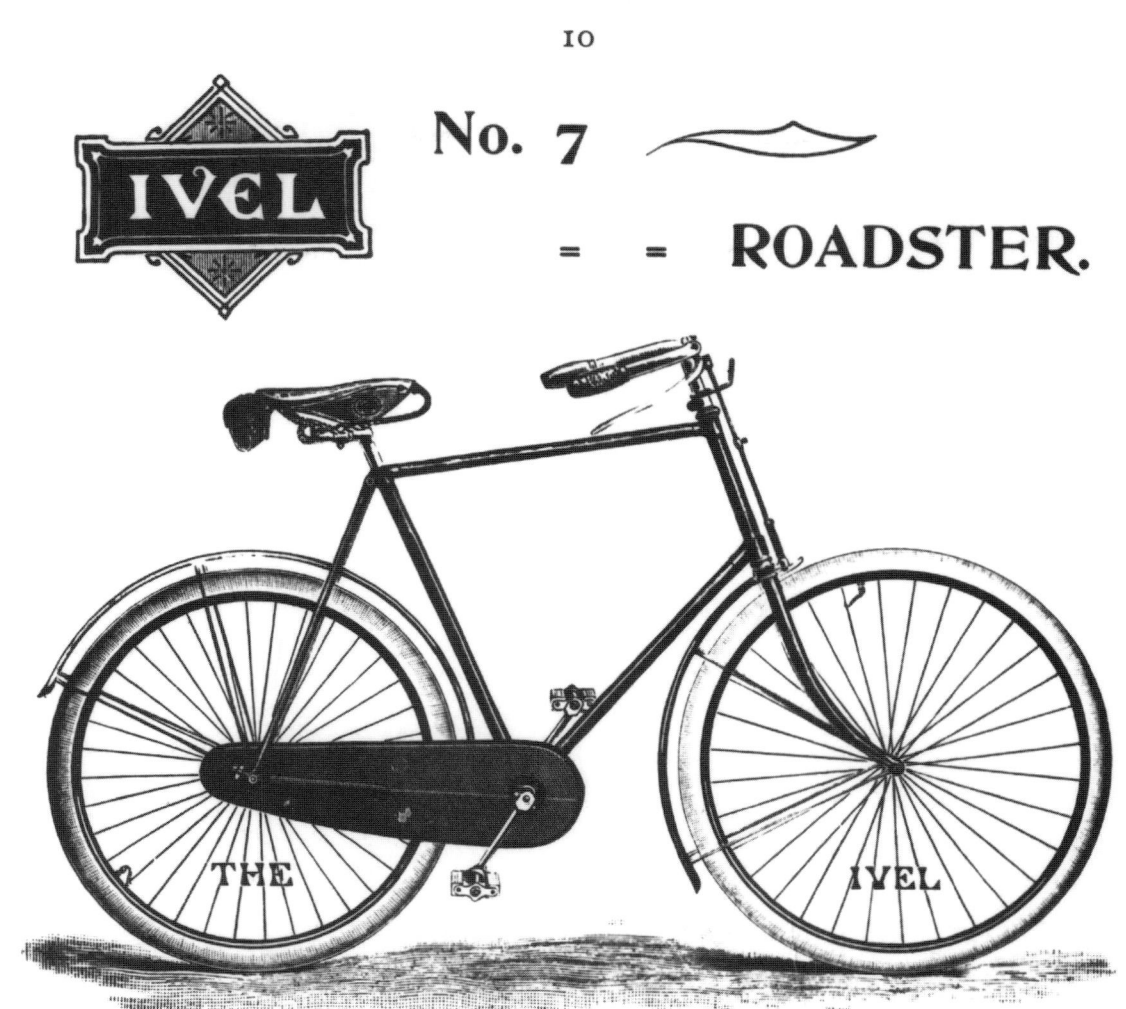

No. 7 = = ROADSTER.

THESE Machines are made of the very best material, including ball bearings throughout. They are my last year's best safety, therefore not *quite* up-to-date in minor details. The reason I am enabled to supply these at a less price than my other Machines is on account of having in stock a large quantity of machined parts which I have decided to make up througout this season.

SPECIFICATION:

Best weldless steel tubes; 28″ driving and 30″ steering wheels; direct spokes; best ball bearings throughout; improved dust proof bottom bracket; gear 60 or to order; brake; mud guards; ball pedals.

PRICE - - £14.

With Pneumatic Tyres.

————

EXTRAS.—Carter Detachable Case, £1 15s.; IVEL Gear Case, £1.

I I

DAN ALBONE'S
CHILD CARRIER
AND PARCEL CARRIER.

The CHILD CARRIER is a very neat and light Wicker Basket made on steel wire framework, the weight of which is carried by means of tubing direct on to the axle of front wheel, with Leg Troughs, as sketch. Plated Clips to fasten to the Handle Bar, and Back Irons

to bolt on back of Basket. Two holes are made in the back of Basket, so that a strap can be put through to fasten the child safely in.

When ordering, the only Particulars necessary are the Diameters of Front Wheel and Handle Bar.

EASILY FIXED TO ANY SAFETY BICYCLE OR TRICYCLE.

PARCEL CARRIER.

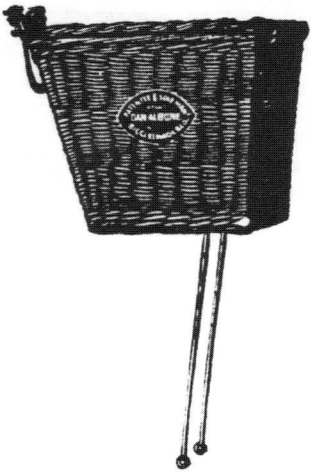

The Basket is easily put on and taken off in a minute, by taking the bottom screw out of the clips and leaving the clips on Handle Bar.

CHILD CARRIER.

Complete £1 1s. 0d

With Cushions Complete £1 7s. 6d.

Full Instructions for fitting sent with Carrier, which must be strictly adhered to when fixing same to Cycle.

Further Particulars, see Abridged List which contains Testimonials, &c., to be had on application.

274

12

Ball Bearing

Carriage Wheels.

WHICH CAUSE A SAVING OF ONE-THIRD IN DRAUGHT.

IVEL, BALL BOX

SECTION OF ALL BEARINGS.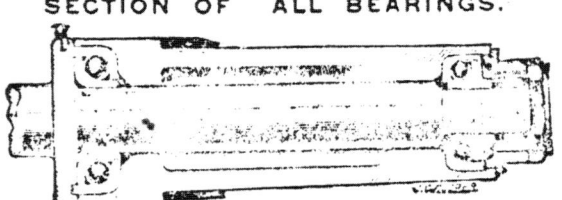

FOR WOOD WHEELS.
(PATENTED BY ME.)

BALL BEARINGS FOR WOOD WHEELS

Are now coming into general use, having undergone for a long time a thorough test even when fitted to ordinary iron-tyred wheels (see testimonial from H. EDWARDS, Esq., page No. 16), let alone rubber shod ones, and gentlemen whom I have supplied have testified to their stability, great ease of running and reduction in draught. Having had repeat orders proves conclusively their superiority over other kinds of bearings. Amongst my patrons for the PATENT IVEL BALL BEARING BOX have been :—

His Grace the Duke of Bedford
Reginald B. Loder, Esq.
London Improved Cab Co.
North British Rubber Co.
A. J. Clay, Esq.
H. Sturke, Esq.
W. H. Brett, Esq.
H. Edwards, Esq.
Pneumatic Tyre Co.

Gooding & Priestley.
M. D. Rucker, Esq.
Hayes & Sons
W. H. Sewell, Esq.
Universal Electric
      Carriage Syndicate, Ltd.
Edward Kuhlstein, Esq.
Messrs. G. & A. Chariot.

CYCLE SPOKED WHEELS.

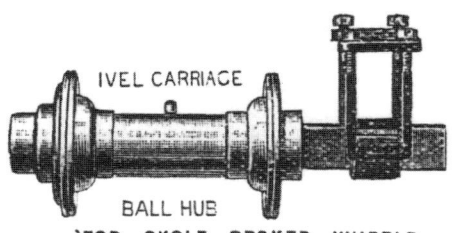

IVEL CARRIAGE

BALL HUB

'FOR CYCLE SPOKED WHEELS.

Diagram of Hub shewing Clips for Springs.

I am still making numbers of Cycle Spoked Vehicle Wheels with ball bearings and have supplied them to customers ever since 1884, when I first introduced them. These still continue to create a demand and give entire satisfaction. Having had twelve years' experience in manufacturing ball bearings for Carriage Wheels I have a thorough knowledge of adapting them for all kinds of Vehicles. (See Testimonial dated June 18th, 1886, from HERBERT WILSON, Esq., page No. 16.)

13

Testimonials.

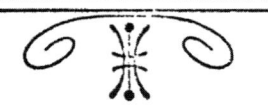

COUNTESS COWPER, Panshanger, Hertford, January 29th, 1895.
"The Machine runs lightly and well."

COUNTESS LISTOWELL, Convamore Mallow, Co. Cork, October 26th, 1895.
"I am much pleased with the Bicycle, as it suits me well."

HONOURABLE MRS. FORBES, Goodwood, Chichester, September 10th, 1895.
"I am very pleased with my Bicycle."

MRS. G. HARTER, The Grotto, Basildon, Reading, January 2nd, 1896.
"I like my Bicycle very much indeed, and find it very easy to ride. There is a great difference between it and the one I have been learning on."

EARL JERSEY, 43, Grosvenor Place, London, July 7th, 1895.
"Please make a new machine for my son. The one [you made for me is excellent."

LORD AMPTHILL, Ampthill Park, Beds., October 2nd, 1894.
"I am delighted with Bicycle, which is the finest I have ever seen up to my weight and size. It is also beautifully light, and a real pleasure to ride upon."

LORD ALWYNE COMPTON, M.P., Castle Ashby, December 2nd, 1894.
"I should like to write a line and tell you how pleased I am with the Light Roadster Bicycle you made for me in the summer. I have travelled some distance on it now, and am delighted with the way in which it carries me—so smoothly and strongly. I have the more pleasure in writing this because you have not asked me for a testimonial.

SIR ALGERNON OSBORNE, Chicksands Priory, Shefford, Beds., Jan. 18th, 1896.
"I am greatly pleased with the Bicycle, and shall recommend your Machines to my friends who intend buying Bicycles."

HON. MARK McDONNELL, Mount Pleasant, Old Warden, Oct. 28th, 1895.
"I have ridden the IVEL Bicycle you made for me six months over all kinds of roads and have never had a screw loose, not even a puncture ; and am satisfied a better Machine cannot be made."

HON. CHAS. A. PELHAM, Gartsherrie House, Coatbridge, N.B., Oct. 5th, 1895.
"I cannot tell you how pleased I am with the Bicycle you sent me. It is a little marvel, and every one who sees it says the same. The more I ride it the more I like it. It is the most easy running machine I have ever ridden."

HOWARD S. WHITBREAD, ESQ., Southill, Biggleswade, August 10th, 1895.
"I have had a fair opportunity of trying the Bicycle and am happy to say I am very much pleased with it. It appears to answer my requirements in every way."

14

TESTIMONIALS—continued.

JOSEPH F. GREEN, Esq., West Lodge, Blackheath, May 19th, 1895.
"The Bicycle arrived and is first-rate."

J. CORRIE CARTER, Esq., 43, Sussex Gardens, Hyde Park, London, Jan. 19th, 1896.
"I am glad to say that I find the Machine you made for me an excellent one, and have every reason to speak well of it."

J. HARVEY, Esq., Trinity Hall, Cambridge, February 12th, 1895.
"I am most satisfied with your Machine, which is so comfortable and pleasant to ride."

ARTHUR HARTER, Esq., 28, Eaton Terrace, London, December 23rd, 1895.
"I like the Bicycle very much indeed."

MAJOR MELLOR, The King's Regiment, October 5th, 1895.
"The Machine is an excellent one, and has been most satisfactory in every way."

J. N. STEWART, Esq., Roxborough Park, Harrow, June 18th, 1895.
"I am glad to say I am thoroughly satisfied with my Bicycle. It carries me well, and is much admired by my friends."

CYRIL B. TUBBS, Esq., Denholme, Datchett, December 18th, 1895.
"I like Bicycle very much—it looks very smart."

FRANCIS R. PRYOR, Esq., Woodfield, Hatfield, July 11th, 1895.
"The Bicycle has given me much satisfaction."

R. C. V. LANG, Esq., Pottingdean, Sussex, October 9th, 1895.
"I like the Bicycle immensely, and it goes well. I rode it out from Brighton in pouring rain and it went as easily as possible. It is also a very handsome Machine."

AUGUSTUS HILL, Esq., High Street, Bedford, May 28th, 1895.
Having now ridden over a thousand miles on the Machine you built for me. I should like to say what a constant pleasure it is to use it. I have tried many, but never one that goes as easily and pleasantly as the 'IVEL,' and many owners of others have, after a spin on mine, said : 'That's what I call a perfect machine,' with which sentiment I quite agree. With many thanks for your careful attention to all my requests.

MR. G. C. FLANDERS, Cycle Agent, Hitchin, Jan. 11th, 1895.
"Machine received and I am very pleased with it, never having seen a better one."

ERNEST O. FORDHAM, Esq., Odsey House, Ashwell, Oct. 26th, 1895.
"I am very pleased with the Machine and have had a number of good rides on it."

PHILIP BRIGHT, Esq., Pall Mall, London, Jan. 13th, 1896.
"I am very pleased with the Bicycle, which is a very strong, easy running Machine."

F. N. BUTLER, Esq., Cross Hall Lodge, St. Neots, Oct. 12th, 1895.
"I am entirely satisfied with the Machine, and have not had any mishaps whatever."

15

PRESS NOTICES Re STANLEY SHOW EXHIBIT, 1895.

"THE EVENING NEWS AND POST," November 26th, 1895.

"At Stand 73 cyclists will find the ever smiling and obliging DAN ALBONE, the designer of the IVEL Cycles. DAN was the first maker to turn out a Lady's Bicycle as far back as 1886, and next season he will probably reap the harvest of his foresight. He also shews on his stand the IVEL Ball Bearing, which is adapted for vehicles such as carriages, dog carts, &c. MR. ALBONE has made many of these, notably for the Duke of Bedford, and as an adjunct to a light running carriage they are a great success."

"THE LADY," December 12th, 1895.

"Up-to-date, reliable, and splendid Machines were shown by the IVEL at their stall. The frames were light, strong, and of the newest pattern, well finished and perfect in detail. DAN ALBONE, of Biggleswade, made the first ladies' Bicycle, in 1886, and those who possess IVELS will not require a better or sounder mount."

"IRISH CYCLIST," November 29th, 1895.

"Dan Albone has an interesting exhibit. Of two things he is particularly proud. With some degree of pleasure he recalls the fact that ten years ago he made the first lady's safety, and indeed reprints in his current list a block, which illustrated it in his catalogue of 1886. The Ivel Lady's Safety of '96 is not so far in advance as it was then, but it is, nevertheless, quite up-to-date. The double-tube curved frame is used with the tubes coming from the top and bottom of the head, tied in the centre and giving ample dress accommodation. Dan Albone (no one would think of saying Mr. Albone) has supplied a number of aristocrats in his own neighbourhood with Ivels and some flattering testimonials from them are shown. The Gent's Safeties are also up-to-date machines, with top tubes which are almost parallel and moderately long heads. Humber-type brackets, and neat head-locks are among their features. The second thing which Dan is at present priding himself on is his carriage ball-bearing which is now in its 13th year. It is an excellent thing of its kind, and the day may not be far distant when it will be universal. It was first applied to bicycle wheels only, but is now made so that it can be adapted to wooden wheels with or without pneumatic tyres."

"SCOTTISH CYCLIST," November 27th, 1895.

73, Dan Albone, Biggleswade.

"Ten machines of this well-known make from the banks of the Ivel in charge of the pleasant and ever-courteous Dan himself, who, by the way, points with pride to the fact that he was making ladies' machines, almost identical in pattern with those of the present day, as far back as 1887 and, indeed, produces a list of that year showing an illustration to prove his words. The Ladies' Machine is, therefore, kept well to the front to-day, and the three exhibited are equal to anything in the show. In the Ivel machines generally simplicity of design is apparent, and all are kept well up to the times without exaggeration of fashion. Few alterations have been made in detail since last season, for the simple reason that little room for improvement could be found.

Copy of Illuminated Testimonial presented to me by a large number of Cyclists who frequented the North Road :—

November 29th, 1885.

DEAR DAN,

The Cyclists visiting Biggleswade having for many years past received at your hands at all times and at all hours numerous acts of kindness and self-denying attention, desire to express to you their hearty thanks for the considerate treatment you have invariably shown them, and the assistance you have rendered by pace-making for them when racing or during long distance rides, and in numerous other ways doing all in your power to administer to their comfort and convenience. They also wish to make some slight acknowledgement of your exertions on their behalf and combining to express to you their high opinion of your sterling good qualities, request your acceptance of a tangible token of their regard in the shape of a **GOLD CHAIN** which they hope you will accept and wear with the consciousness of its being a tribute of the esteem in which you are held by the subscribers."

16

TESTIMONIALS ᴀᴺᴰ PRESS NOTICES
Re Ball Bearing Carriage Axles.

HERBERT WILSON, Esq., Emmanuel College, Cambridge, June 18th, 1886.
    " I have now given the pony trap I purchased of you a good trial ; and I am more than satisfied with it. It is without exception the most comfortable vehicle of any kind I have ever used, and runs delightfully, freely and noiselessly. It is a great saving of labour to the horse, **and answers my expectations and your own recommendations** in every respect. The Tyres wear surprisingly well, and altogether I can conscientiously recommend your vehicle without the slightest reserve in any particular.

W. H. BRETT, Esq., York, March 21st, 1890.
    " I am much pleased with the principle of the **Ivel Patent Gig.** I have had mine some seven or eight months now, and have done some good work with it. My little cob can run it twenty miles without turning a hair, and it is the most comfortable trap I ever road in."

H. EDWARDS, Esq., C.C., Tinwell, Stamford, January 31st, 1896.
    " Some **five months ago** ago I had your Ivel Ball Bearing Axles fitted to the ordinary Wooden Wheels with **Iron Tyres** of my Norfolk Cart, since then I have driven a distance **exceeding 1200 miles** over every description of road including Cobbles, indeed I have put it to the severest test I could think of, being somewhat sceptical as to its performance over rough country roads, but I am glad to say that your invention has proved an unqualified success, indeed I cannot speak too highly of it, not the least of its advantages is the fact that my groom can (single-handed) readily remove the bearings for cleaning and subsequently replace the same without the slightest difficulty.
    It is, I apprehend, but seldom that inventors understate the advantages of their appliances, but I consider you have done so in saying that there is a saving of one-third in draught, I am convinced that this is considerably exceeded by the adoption of your system.
    I shall be very glad to answer any enquiries, and you have my permission to refer intending purchasers to me direct."

A. J. CLAY, Esq., Burton-on-Trent, November 5th, 1895.
    " I am pleased to be able to report most favourably of your suspension wheels and ball bearings which you built for my dog cart."

"THE SPORTSMAN," November 20th, 1894.
    " Novelties were not particularly easy to find at the Show last year. Then it was much like many of the Shows which have gone before. This year, however, there are several exhibits which have the charm of novelty. In addition thereto are sundry innovations of comparatively recent years which have been submitted to the process of latest improvements. Amongst the latter may be mentioned Dan Albone's **Ball Bearing Hubs** for Carriage Wheels. It is not quite the novelty which some folks suppose, having been originally brought out by the inventor about ten years ago. Since then the idea has been greatly developed and improved and some of the improvements are quite equal to new ideas as generally understood.

"THE TIMES," August 21st, 1895.
Institute of British Carriage Manufacturers held at Tunbridge Wells.
    " The eighth Autumnal Meeting of the Institute of British Carriage Manufacturers began at Tunbridge Wells yesterday, when the Members were welcomed by the Mayor, Sir David Salamons, at the Town Hall. The President, Mr. John Philipson, of Newcastle-on-Tyne, afterwards delivered an address, in which he said, ' The great aim in life was to reduce friction to a minimum, and the pneumatic tire afforded great assistance in that direction. But it seemed to him that in the efforts to reduce friction they had not devoted **to ball bearing axles** the attention they deserved.' "

"THE MORNING," November 26th, 1895.
    " The Ivel Ball Bearing Carriage Wheels have everything to recommend them, and that they deserve the success they have achieved is undeniable."

"THE IRISH CYCLIST," November 27th, 1895."
    " Re Carriage Ball Bearing ' It is an excellent thing of its kind and the day may not be far distant when it will be univ. d.' "

ILLUSTRATED PRICE LIST

OF

The IVEL ❋

❖ Cycles,

1897,

AND BALL BEARING

Carriage Axles & Boxes.

MANUFACTURED BY - -

DAN ALBONE,

Ivel Cycle Works

BIGGLESWADE, Beds.

W. CARLING & CO., PRINTERS, EXCHANGE YARD, HITCHIN.

2

TERMS OF BUSINESS.

CASH against Invoice to Customers having no Ledger Account.

CARRIAGE in all cases to be paid by PURCHASER.

REPAIRS will not be received unless sent **Carriage Paid** with full Name and Address of Sender.

CRATES are charged Cost Price, and are NOT RETURNABLE.

NOTICES TO PURCHASERS - -

Most of my Machines are made specially to order, thus giving more satisfaction to the Purchaser and myself. All I require is the inside measurement of leg and the weight of the rider.

A Large Stock of all kinds of Accessories such as LAMPS, BELLS, TIRE INFLATORS, &c., &c., always kept in Stock. Old Machines are always taken as Part Payment, and a large number of second-hand Machines are always on sale at very low prices.

REPAIRS - - - -

All kinds of Repairs are done on the premises. Having a complete plant for this branch, Customers may rely upon Prompt and Efficient attention. Enquiries respecting any of my Machines receive immediate attention, and inspection of my Stock of Machines and Accessories is respectfully invited at the Show Rooms at the Works.

SPECIAL - - - -

ALL KINDS OF COPPER AND NICKEL PLATING DONE ON THE PREMISES. I ALSO HAVE A SPECIAL PLANT FOR SILVERING SUCH ARTICLES AS FORKS, SPOONS, CRUETS, TRAYS, &c. See detailed list to be had on application.

FORM OF GUARANTEE.

I Guarantee, subject to the conditions mentioned below, that all precautions which are usual and reasonable have been taken by me to secure excellence of materials and workmanship in all my Machines, and I undertake to make good, at any time within twelve months of this date, any defects which result from inherent flaws or defective workmanship, and are not caused by wear and tear, misuse or neglect.

CONDITIONS.—If a defective part should be found in any of my machines, it must be sent to me **Carriage Paid** and accompanied by an intimation from the Sender that he desires to have it repaired free of charge under this guarantee. The number of the machine must be quoted.

Failing compliance with this rule no notice will be taken of anything that may arrive, but such articles will lie here at the risk of the Sender.

This Guarantee does not apply to the specialities of other Firms, such as Tires, Gear Cases, Lamps, Bells, &c., but the makers of these, whose names usually appear thereon, are in nearly every case willing to replace defective parts, and I will at all times furnish the maker's name as a proof of the quality.

3

INTRODUCTION.

WITH more than usual pleasure and confidence I place before the public my seventeenth annual Illustrated Price List for 1897. My endeavours to place a

High Class Machine

in the Market at a *reasonable* price have been most satisfactory both to purchasers and myself. That this has been the case is proved to the full extent by the repeat orders I have had from customers, by the recommendations purchasers have made to their friends as to the sterling merits the "Ivel" Machines possess; the large and very distinguished list of patrons, some of whom are herein mentioned, and the numerous

Unsolicited Testimonials

I have received.

As in the past two years, <u>instead of the old method of listing my machines at a high figure and allowing a large discount—a system useful to many for taking the advantage of the inexperienced in the buying of cycles</u>—I have listed them at a fair price, which does not admit of a large discount being deducted by an agent. At the same time I would point out that <u>my machines are made throughout of the very best material</u> procurable, and by skilled workmen, and the apparent disparity which seems to exist between a bicycle priced at £28 and mine is that one is fictitious and the other is not.

Frequent visits to London are made **by me** or m.... ....presentative, **Mr. GEORGE COURSE,** and appointments arranged by wire or letter. I need hardly say that personal interviews have proved most successful in the past both to purchasers and myself. Appointments to other places are also made.

4

By the capital service of trains existing between London and Biggleswade intending purchasers can visit the Works and inspect the various processes of Cycle manufacturing. A Machine (put on at King's Cross G.N.R.) can be at the Works in little more than an hour, thus considerably obviating the loss of time incurred when any repairs are rendered necessary by accidents, &c., to the machine, and moreover can have the attention of the workmen who built it, and the personal supervision of me or my representatives. This is a boon few Makers can offer to London Patrons.

Ivel Patent Ball Bearings

for **Carts** and **Carriages** are now in general use, and by the number of Vehicles which are now fitted with them, and the general satisfaction they have given, their success is assured. Any carriage can now be fitted with IVEL Ball Bearing Boxes. They not only save

One=Third in Draught,

but cause the wheels to run smoothly, and are free from rattle and jarring. Everyone owning horses and carriages ought to have these bearings fitted to their wheels, for the saving in horse labour is incalculable. I would specially draw attention to the **unsolicited testimonials** and press notices I have received, which date back as far as 1886. (See pages 12, 13, 19, 20.)

In conclusion, I again take the opportunity to thank all my patrons for their support and kind recommendations, to offer them my apologies for what inconvenience may have been caused them by my inability to cope with the phenominal demand for my machines during the past year ; and to say that arrangements have been made to prevent a recurrence of disappointment. I assure them that no effort on my part shall be wanting to merit not only a continuance of their patronage, but an extension of the same.

DAN ALBONE,
SOLE PROPRIETOR.

5

List of Patrons.

Countess Cowper	Mrs. E. Osborn	Miss Agnes Keyser
Countess Grey	Mrs. Lawson	Miss L. Bernard
Countess Listowell	Mrs. S. Scott	Miss Madeline S. Beaden
Countess de Grey	Mrs. Gibson Carmichael	Miss Batchellor
Countess Guildford	Mrs. Algernon Talbot	Miss E. Wilshere
Countess Tweeddale	Mrs. J. Trotter	Miss M. F. Prickard
Lady Colthurst	Mrs. D. H. F. Peploe	Miss B. Greenfield
Lady Oxenbridge	Mrs. A. Tyrrell	Miss Sinclair
Lady Payne	Mrs. D. Stuart	Miss E. Gregory
Lady Bertie	Mrs. Sutton Sams	Miss K. M. F. Brooks
Lady Constance Harris	Mrs. R. Ord	Miss K. L. Lawrence
Lady Barbara Smith	Mrs. M. P. Foster	His Grace the Duke of
Lady Brabourne	Mrs. J. Richardson	Bedford
Lady Lawson	Mrs. Jervoise Huddleston	Marquis of Tweeddale
Lady Napier of Magdala	Miss Bulkeley Hughes	Marquis of Granby
Hon. Mrs. C. Bagot	Miss F. Keyser	Marquis of Cholmondeley
Hon. Mrs. Forbes	Miss C. Astell	Viscount Peel
Hon. Mrs. Astell	Miss M. Dimsdale	Earl Grey
Hon. Mrs. Charles Brand	Miss F. Cochrane	Earl Jersey
Hon. Constance Russell	Miss O. Marshall	Earl Compton
Mrs. Shuttleworth	Miss N. Hulbert	Earl of Mount Edgcumbe
Mrs. G. Barnett	Miss E. Lindsell	Lord Napier of Magdala
Mrs. F. J. Josselyn	Miss L. Hawksley	Lord Massey
Mrs. C. Barnett	Miss E. F. Humphries	Lord St. John
Mrs. Heysham	Miss Archdale	Lord Ampthill
Mrs. Kerr	Miss St. Quinton	Lord Alwyne Compton, M.P.
Mrs. S. Bruce	Miss L. Osborn	Sir Algernon Osborn, Bart.
Mrs. Cooke	Miss E. Williams	Rev. Lord Wm. Cecil
Mrs. E. G. Taddy	Miss Hawkinson	Monsieur ███████,
Mrs. W. Earle	Miss K. Ladds	███ ███ *an Embassy*
Mrs. Madeline McCarthy	Miss Helen Douglas	Sir T. O'Brien, Bart.
Mrs. Blackwood	Miss May Irwin	Sir Robert Turin
Mrs. E Lennox Peel	Miss G. Archdale	Sir Edward Jenkinson
Mrs. Capt. C. F. Lindsell	Miss D. Pearson	Hon. C. A. Pelham

6

LIST OF PATRONS—continued,

Hon. Mark McDonald	F. Archdale, Esq.	F. Penn, Esq.
Col. The Hon. C. Crichton	H. J. B. Kendall, Esq.	W. Penn, Esq.
Colonel Astell	W. A. Attenborough, Esq.	F. G. Payne. Esq.
Colonel Gregson	E. O. Fordham, Esq.	W. H. B. Drayson, Esq.
Colonel Blane	H. A. Vernet, Esq.	A. Lewis Jones, Esq.
Colonel Oldham	M. J. Godby, Esq.	J. H. Williams, Esq.
Lieut.-Col. Lindsell	F. B. Greenfield, Esq.	S. F. Cotton, Esq.
Colonel Ellison	Robert Dimsdale, Esq.	J. G. O'Brien, Esq.
Colonel Josselyn	J. H. Mossop, Esq.	Edward O'Brien, Esq.
Capt. Com. The Hon. Sey-	J. F. Green, Esq.	Willoughby Josselyn, Esq.
mour Fortescue	Francis R. Pryor, Esq,	Arthur G. Murrell, Esq.
Com. G. R. Bethell, M.P.	C. S. Lindsell, Esq.	J. Clunes, Esq.
J. G. Talbot, Esq., M.P.	R. J. Lindsell, Esq.	W. G. Quihampton, Esq.
Com. P. H. Wright, R.N.	A. K. Lindsell, Esq.	G. A. Newton, Esq.
Major Gen. T. B. Bevan	Gerald Smith, Esq.	C. C. Jury, Esq.
Major F. Shuttleworth	Julian Godfrey, Esq.	A. Rawlinson, Esq.
Major A. Duberly	Cyril B. Tubbs, Esq.	J. Leveson-Gower, Esq.
Major F. A. B. Talbot	John Corrie Carter, Esq.	E. Talbot, Esq.
Major Mellor	A. Harter, Esq.	J. Phillips, Esq.
Captain C. H. Fenwick	C. F. St. Quinton, Esq.	J. S. Wood, Esq.
Captain Duberley	C. M. Hodgins, Esq.	A. F. Robertson, Esq.
Captain C. J. Briggs, R.N.	J. J. Dunne, Esq.	W. Jameson, Esq.
Captain Dugald Stuart	Hubert S. Payne, Esq.	Arthur Lane, Esq.
Captain Stapylton Marshall	E. Morse, Esq.	Beds. Constabulary
Captain H. M. Stanley	William Tyrer, Esq.	F. Preedy, Esq., F.S.I.
Captain C. J. Blunt, R.A.	Martin Pirie, Esq.	W. Armstrong, Esq.
The Rev. Canon Stone-Wigg	Philip Bright, Esq.	J. A. Pomeroy, Esq.
Guy Pym Esq. M.P.	J. Dyson Moore, Esq.	A. W. W. Dale, Esq.
W. F. Archdale, Esq.	J. N. Stewart, Esq.	T. M. Bear, Esq.
H. S. Whitbread, Esq.	A. Tyrrell, Esq.	W. A. St. Quinton, Esq.
S. Whitbread, Esq.	T. A. Gibb, Esq.	H. A. Block, Esq.
Algernon Gilliat, Esq.	W. T. Nash, Esq.	G. P. Talbot, Esq.
Howard Gilliat, Esq.	R. E. V. Lang, Esq.	R. J. Vyner, Esq.
Reginald B. Loder, Esq.	J. S. W. Blackett, Esq.	W. C. Palcolologues, Esq.
J. Harvey, Esq.	E. Snow Fordham, Esq.	H. Sylston Hodgson, Esq.
J. H. St. Q. Astell, Esq.	A. Duberly, Esq.	G. V. Fiddes, Esq.
P. C. Gaul, Esq.	J. E. Talbot, Esq.	W. Francis Higgins, Esq.
Lennox Peel, Esq.	Sydney Mills, Esq.	G. P. Evans, Esq.
G. Peel, Esq.	J. W. Walter, Esq.	George Hunt, Esq.

7

No. 1 ROADSTER SAFETY.

The established popularity of this Machine enables me to place it again before my patrons with every confidence. It has been designed for general use, and its strength is equal to any weight rider.

SPECIFICATION :

Best Weldless Steel Tubes ; 28″ driving and 30″ steering wheels ; tangent or direct spokes ; best ball bearings throughout ; improved dust proof bottom bracket ; gear 60 or to order ; powerful detachable rubber brake ; detachable light metal mudguards ; adjustable foot-rests ; rubber pedals ; weight as illustrated, 36lbs.

PRICE - - £17 10/-

With Dunlop, Clincher, or other well-known Pneumatic Tires.

EXTRAS.—Carter Detachable Gear Case, £1 17s. 6d. ; IVEL Detachable Gear Case, £1 ; Lining, 7/6 ; if enamelled any other colour than Black, 7/6.

8

NO. 2

LIGHT ROADSTER.

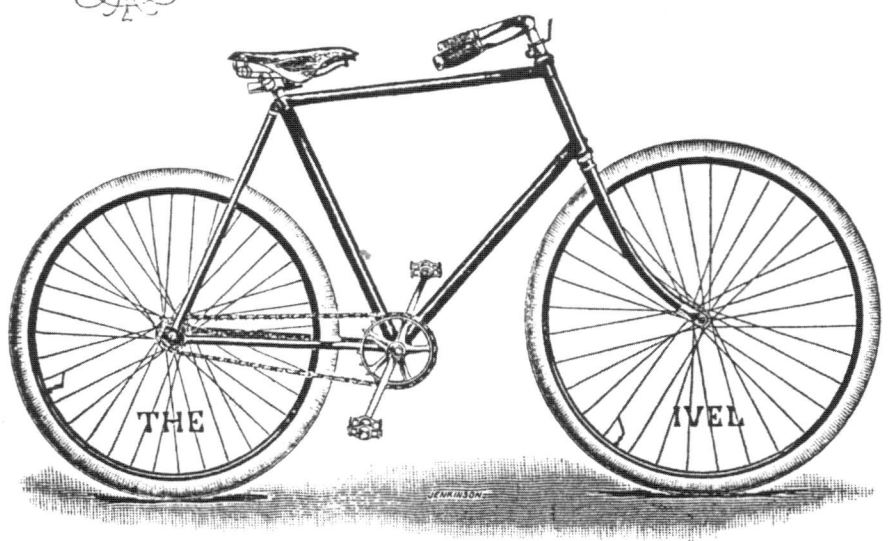

A Light Machine of exceptional merit. It has been thoroughly tested and proved to be remarkably fast. It is entirely suitable for touring purposes, being perfectly rigid and reliable.

SPECIFICATION :—Best weldless tubes ; 28″ driving and 30″ steering wheels ; improved dust proof bottom bracket ; narrow tread ; gear 63″ or to order ; rat-trap or rubber pedals ; latest pattern flat cranks ; 6½″ throw ; tangent spokes. Weight 28lbs.

PRICE - - £16 16/-

With Dunlop, Clincher, or other well-known Pneumatic Tires.
EXTRAS.—Carter Detachable Gear Case, £1 17s. 6d. ; IVEL Gear Case, £1 ; Brake and Guards, 15/- ; Lining, 7/6. If enamelled any other colour than Black, 7/6.

———————

IVEL NO. 3 ROAD RACER.—This machine is identical with the Light Roadster, but built lighter where possible. It has been a great success during 1896, and has in every case given satisfaction. It is the very best value in the Cycle Trade. Hollow rims, tangent spokes, gear 66″ or to order. Weight 25lbs.

PRICE - - £17 17/-

EXTRAS.—Same as No. 2.

———————

IVEL NO. 4 PATH RACER.—This Machine has been constructed throughout with due regard to lightness and strength, the maximum weight being about 21lbs.

PRICE - - £18 18/-

9

No. 5

LADY'S SAFETY.

This machine has given such entire satisfaction during the past season that I have decided to alter the pattern very little. The experience I have had in making Ladies' Cycles has been very great. The Lady's Safety was first introduced by me in 1886, and since that time I have turned out a very large number each year.

SPECIFICATION :

Strong dropped frame with double tubes ; 28″ wheels ; with IVEL gear case, brake and mudguards.

PRICE - - £18 10/-

With Dunlop, Clincher, or other well-known Pneumatic Tires.

EXTRAS.—If fitted with Carter Case instead of IVEL., **17s. 6d.** ; Hollow Rims, **12s. 6d.** Lining, **7/6.**   If Enamelled any other colour than Black, **7/6.**

Reprint of      as introduced and sold

Lady's Safety   by me in 1886.

10

No. 6

= = TRICYCLE.

THE IVEL

Ever since 1886 this machine has been to the front. The simple construction of the first Tricycle I made, adopting the line of the safety bicycle with equal size wheels, was copied by nearly every other maker. Since that time Tricycles have had my most careful attention, and this year's machine, which has a very light truss frame, is perfectly rigid, and suitable for either a lady or gentleman. The 1897 IVEL Tricycle will, I feel sure, be a most popular machine, and will have a good sale.

Size of wheels, 26″ back and 28″ front.

PRICE - - £28.

With Dunlop, Clincher, or other well-known Pneumatic Tires, and Improved Dress Guard. Detachable rubber brake.

Lining, 10/-. If enamelled any other colour than Black, 10/-.

TANDEM SAFETIES.

I am prepared to make these machines to order, although I do not illustrate them.

II

No. 7

= = ROADSTER.

This Machine is a good bargain, as it is made of the very best material procurable, including ball bearings throughout. Owing to the change which takes place each year in the manufacture of cycles there is always a number of the last year's machined parts in stock. These are worked up, and as they are not so thoroughly up-to-date, the price is less than that of the very latest machines.

SPECIFICATION :

Best weldless steel tubes ; 28″ driving and 30″ steering wheels ; direct spokes ; best ball bearings throughout ; improved dust proof bottom bracket ; brake ; mud guards ; ball pedals.

PRICE - - £14 14/-

With Pneumatic Tires.

———

EXTRAS.—IVEL Gear Case, £1.

12

Ball Bearing Carriage
& Motor Car Wheels.

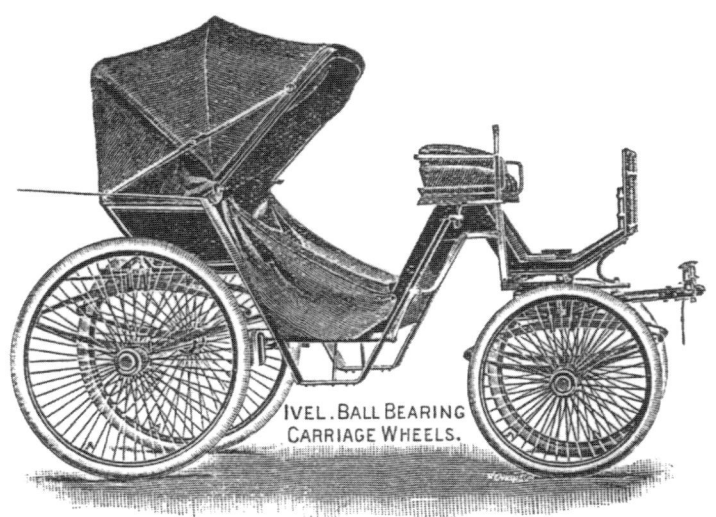

IVEL. BALL BEARING
CARRIAGE WHEELS.

As fitted by me for His Grace the Duke of Bedford.

IVEL. BALL BOX

FOR WOOD WHEELS.
(PATENTED BY ME.)

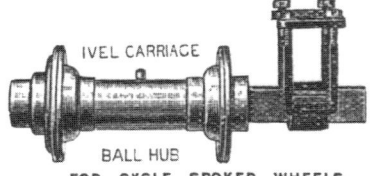

IVEL CARRIAGE

BALL HUB
FOR CYCLE SPOKED WHEELS.
Diagram of Hub shewing Clibs for Springs.

CYCLE SPOKED WHEELS.

I am still making these wheels for ordinary carts and carriages, and they continue to give entire satisfaction. During the past year I have also made a number of Motor Car Wheels on the same principle, sometimes leaving each hind hub longer to allow for the fixing of a sprocket wheel for driving purposes. Having had 13 years' experience in making these wheels and bearings I have acquired a thorough knowledge of adapting them to all kinds of vehicles.

13

Patent Ball Bearing Axles
AND BOXES
FOR ORDINARY
Wood Carriage Wheels.

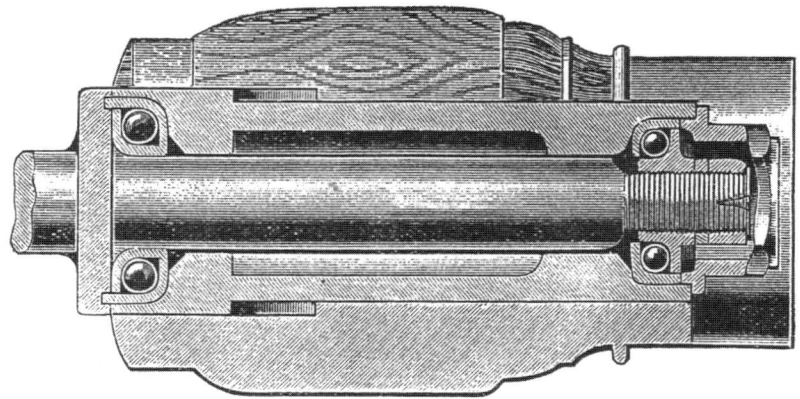

SECTION SHOWING BALL BOX FITTED IN NAVE OR WOOD STOCK.   (PATENTED BY ME.)

I have supplied and fitted these Ball Bearing Boxes for coach builders and private customers in both new and old wheels when fitted with ordinary **Iron Tires**.   I would ask those who are interested to read the unsolicited testimonials of Miss Barnett, H. Edwards, Esq., A. Palmer, Esq., printed on pages 19 and 20.

Having proved they are a great success when in wheels with **Iron Tires** (see pages 19 and 20), it is obvious that they run extremely nicely and wear exceptionally well when they are fitted to wheels with rubber tires.   The repeat orders I have received confirms this.

IMPORTANT.—

When present old wheels are to be fitted with my patent ball bearing axle and boxes, measurements are taken, and after axles are made and finished I only require the old wheels about a day or so to fit ball boxes and axles in them—thus depriving customers of the use of their vehicle for a few days only.

The following is a list of patrons whom I have supplied with Ball Bearing Carriage axles :—

His Grace the Duke of Bedford
Lord Alwyne Compton, M.P.
Miss H. Barnett
London & North Western Railway Co.
Headlands Electric Battery Co.
Reginald B. Loder, Esq.
London Improved Cab Co.
North British Rubber Co.
R. C. de Grey Vyner, Esq.
A. J. Clay, Esq.
H. Starke, Esq.
W. H. Brett, Esq.
H. Edwards, Esq.
Dunlop Pneumatic Tyre Co.
E. E. Dymond, Esq.

Gooding & Priestly.
M. D. Rucker, Esq.
Hayes & Sons
Universal Electric Carriage Syndicate, Ltd.
Edward Kuhlstein, Esq.
H. H. Mulliner, Esq.
Alfred Palmer, Esq.
F. L. Merritt, Esq.
Cyril B. Tubbs, Esq.
Harry T. Shaw, Esq.
W. C. Bersey, Esq., A.I.C.E.
Messrs. Thorn
James Saunders, Esq.
Messrs. A. Ferris & Co.

14

DAN ALBONE'S
CHILD CARRIER
AND PARCEL CARRIER.

The CHILD CARRIER is a very neat and light Wicker Basket made on steel wire framework, the weight of which is carried by means of tubing direct on to the axle of front wheel, with Leg Troughs, as sketch, Plated Clips to fasten to the Handle Bar and Back Irons

to bolt on back of Basket. Two holes are made in the back of Basket, so that a strap can be put through to fasten the child safely in.

When ordering, the only Particulars necessary are the Diameters of Front Wheel and Handle Bar.

EASILY FIXED TO ANY SAFETY BICYCLE OR TRICYCLE.

PARCEL CARRIER.

CHILD CARRIER.

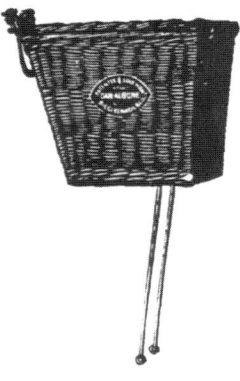

The Basket is easily put on and taken off in a minute, by taking the bottom screw out of the clips and leaving the clips on Handle Bar.

Complete £1 1s. 0d.

With Cushions Complete £1 7s. 6d.

Full Instructions for fitting sent with Carrier, which must be strictly adhered to when fixing same to cycle.

Further Particulars see Abridged List, which contains Testimonials, &c., to be had on application.

15

EXTRACTS FROM TESTIMONIALS.
CYCLES.

Countess Guildford, Thorpe End, Chertsey, Surrey, October 23rd, 1896.
" I am delighted with the Bicycle."

Lady Evelyn Bertie, Uffington House, Stamford, June 16th, 1896.
" The Bicycle has arrived safely.   I am very much pleased with it."

The Hon. Mrs. Charles Bagot, Hinchingbrooke, Huntingdon, Jan. 15th, 1897.
" I am very pleased indeed with the Bicycle."

The Hon. Mrs. Forbes, Goodwood, Chichester, July 21st, 1896.
" I have found my Bicycle excellent and have been many long rides on it."

The Hon. Mrs. Charles Brand, Littledene, Lewis, October 19th, 1896.
" I like the Bicycle very much indeed."

Miss E. Gregory, The Deanery, St. Paul's, September 17th, 1896.
" I cannot speak too highly of your machine, or the comfort and pleasure of riding it. I shall always recommend your make."

Miss L. Hawksley, 60, Porchester Terrace, London, July 26th, 1896.
" Everyone admires the make and finish and think the Bicycle very smart."

Miss May Irwin, Napton, Rugby, September 14th, 1896.
" Everything is as I like it and the Machine has been much admired.   I will always recommend your Bicycles."

Mrs. W. Earle, 18, Wilton Crescent, London, S.W., Feb. 1st, 1897.
" I am perfectly delighted with the Bicycle and it is most satisfactory."

Miss R. H. Sumner, New Haw Farm, Addlestone, May 13th, 1896.
" I find the Machine you have made for me most comfortable and in every way to my liking."

Miss Julia Turing, Chilgrove, Chichester, May 31st, 1896.
" I am very pleased with my Bicycle, it runs so easily and the more I ride it the more I like it."

Mrs. Lawson, Brayton, Carlisle, Oct. 29th, 1896.
" I wish to say ' How pleased I am with my Bicycle.'   I rode it **22** miles yesterday, on very hilly roads, and it ran with wonderful great ease."

Miss L. M. Scott, Allan House, Stourbridge, June 15th, 1896.
" I like the Bicycle immensely, it gives such great satisfaction and is admired by everyone."

Mrs. F. J. Josselyn, Banstead, Bedford, April 23rd, 1896.
" My Bicycle gives me more satisfaction every day."

16

EXTRACTS FROM TESTIMONIALS (CYCLES)—continued.

Miss Mortlock, Caxton Hall, Cambridge, July 30th, 1896.

" My Machine is very satisfactory. I have gone many long journeys on it and am more pleased with it each time I ride it."

Miss Eleanor Appleton, 16, Albion Street, London, W., June 4th, 1896.

" I am most exceedingly pleased with the bicycle."

Miss Olive E. Marshall, Castlerigg Manor, Keswick, July 28th, 1896.

" My Bicycle is very satisfactory and goes beautifully, it also goes well both up and down hill, which in this hilly country is a great recommendation."

Miss Beadon, Beechfield, Basset, Southampton, Jan. 4th, 1897.

" I am very pleased indeed with my Bicycle, which suits me admirably. Everything about it seems perfect and it is an easy Bicycle to go up hill."

Mrs. A. Gibson Carmichael, Oak Hill, Mount Hermon, Woking, July 27th, 1896.

" I like the Bicycle immensely. I have recommended you to a lady friend."

Miss M. F. Prickard, Ddwer, Rhayader, Oct. 28th, 1896.

" The Bicycle is most satisfactory. I don't think I have ever ridden one I liked better."

Miss R. Douglas, St. George's Lodge, Winchester, Oct. 19th, 1896.

" I am exceedingly well satisfied with my Bicycle."

Miss Duberly, Fenlake, Bedford, May 8th, 1896.

" I am extremely pleased with the Bicycle. It goes remarkably smoothly."

Miss Ewen, Skerryvone, St. Andrew's Road, Bedford, June 15th, 1896.

" I like my Bicycle very much indeed. It is most comfortable and satisfactory in every way."

Miss Margaret Thompson, 25, Leazes Terrace, Newcastle-on-Tyne, July 2nd, 1896.

" I take the opportunity of telling you how exceedingly pleased I am with the " Ivel " machine altogether ; it is one of the prettiest looking and most graceful ladies' Bicycles I have ever seen. It is a very easy and pleasant machine to ride."

Mrs. Maples, Kingsbury, Stevenage, Herts, Aug. 18th, 1896.

" I am very pleased indeed with the Bicycle you made for me. It is the most comfortable and easy going one I have ever ridden."

Marquis of Tweeddale, Yester, Gifford, Haddington, October 23rd, 1896.

" The Machine has given entire satisfaction."

Lord St. John, Melchbourne Park, Bedford, Dec. 7th, 1896.

" The Bicycles give most ample satisfaction and my daughters are delighted with them."

Lord Alwyne Compton, M.P., 7, Balfour Place, London, Jan. 7th, 1897.

" I am more than satisfied with the new Road-Racer you have made me. I can ride up almost any hill with it geared as it is to 66 inches, and being as light as it is, *i.e.*, 26 lbs., on a good road it as near perfection as possible. I hear your machines praised on all sides."

17

EXTRACTS FROM TESTIMONIALS (CYCLES)—continued.

Admiral-Commander G. R. BETHELL, M.P., Aug. 13th, 1896.

" I find your machine goes excellently."

———

The Hon. Colonel Crichton, Oct. 1st, 1896.

" I like my Bicycle very much, and so does my daughter hers."

———

Captain Stapylton Marshall, Newnton, Tetbury, Gloucester, July 19th, 1896.

" I am delighted with the machine you built me. The finish and workmanship are perfect. I do not think I have ever seen a neater looking or better turned out machine."

———

Cyril B. Tubbs, Esq., Denholme, Datchett.

" Everyone here admires and likes the machine you last built me. It runs well."

———

Algernon Gilliat, Esq., Duffield, Stoke Green, Slough, May 10th, 1896.

" The Bicycle I had from you has given perfect satisfaction."

———

A. W. W. DALE, Esq., Trinity Hall, Cambridge, Oct. 31st, 1896.

" Kindly make and forward a Bicycle for Mrs. DALE. My own **" IVEL "** is excellent in every way and suits me admirably."

———

JAS. CLUNES, Esq., Palace Court, London, W. April 22nd, 1896.

" Both Machines have been much admired, and they have given pleasure and satisfaction in every way."

———

A. F. Robertson, Esq., Clynderwen House, Clynderwen, South Wales, Sept. 30th, 1896.

" The Bicycle goes splendidly. The ease with which it runs is wonderful."

———

G. E. D. Brown, Esq., The Elms, Houghton, Huntingdon, Aug. 11th, 1896.

" I have been thoroughly satisfied with my Bicycle."

———

John W. Walter, Esq., Hastoe House, Tring, Herts, Aug. 19th, 1896.

" I am very pleased with the Machine, which has stood the rough wear of bad country roads exceedingly well."

———

Richard Ord, Esq., Laxton Park, Stamford, July 28th, 1896.

" The Machine gives every satisfaction. I have ridden it about 800 miles and shall have pleasure in recommending your machines to my friends."

———

Julian Godfrey, Esq.. Berrycote, Ennerdale Road, Kew, Jan. 22nd, 1897.

" I have to thank you for the trouble you have taken in building the Bicycle for me, it is excellent in all respects."

———

H. A. Block, Esq., Llanover, Churt, Farnham, Dec. 18th, 1896.

" The Bicycle you supplied to Miss Bernard certainly looks extremely smart and well turned out. She is very pleased with her Machine."

———

J. G. Wall, Esq., The Hollies, Old Warden, Oct. 15th, 1896.

" The Road Racer you built for me in March has given every satisfaction. I have been a rider of cycles for 17 years, during which I have purchased many of the best make machines, but never have I had one which runs more freely than the **IVEL ROAD RACER.**

18

PRESS NOTICES (CYCLES.)

"THE QUEEN," The Lady's Newspaper, January 23rd, 1897.

A second-hand good make of machine will be found much more satisfactory than one of the cheap glittering affairs sold first hand at £13 or so. These will often spend a large portion of their time in the local repairer's, and in the end be found more costly than a good one to begin with. Premiers are very good, so too are the **IVELS**, made by **ALBONE** of **BIGGLESWADE**. In fact, reliance can always be placed on any machine coming from Singer, J. K. Starley, or **ALBONE**, of **BIGGLESWADE**.

"THE GENTLEWOMAN," November 14th, 1896.

THE IVEL LADIES' SAFETY BICYCLE.—Among the many names of well-known manufacturers of ladies' safety bicycles, perhaps none has had more praise bestowed on it by the public than that of Mr. Dan Albone, the maker of the "Ivel" machines. Some sixteen years ago he first issued his illustrated catalogue of this famous make of machines, and in 1886 patented the first ladies' safety ever made, which has undergone many alterations and improvements since that time ; until to-day the Ivel ladies' safety bicycle is one which possesses every advantage in construction and all modern appliances which can add to the comfort of the rider. Mr. Albone himself having had life-long experience as a practised rider on roads, and on the best known bicycle tracks in the world, is eminently fitted to gauge and test the newest and most important inventions for bicyclists ; whilst his own ready inventive power stands him in good stead as maker and manufacturer.

At his bicycle works in Biggleswade, Bedfordshire, many hundreds of machines are turned out, all fitted with his particular speciality to suit the requirements of each individual rider.

In short, the knowledge that everything which comes from the Ivel Cycle Works is conscientiously well made, and thoroughly to be relied upon, makes one recommend very heartily this firm to the attention of anyone about to buy a bicycle.

"BICYCLING NEWS," NOVEMBER 26th, 1896.

RE STANLEY SHOW.

Mr. Dan Albone has been doing an excellent business among well known people and almost all the machines he exhibits are marked and sold to ladies and gentlemen of title. It will be in the recollection of many that Dan Albone exhibited a **lady's safety bicycle ten years ago** at the Royal Aquarium and got considerably chaffed for his trouble. He shows several machines all of excellent finish and such has been the success of his ladies' safety that he has made very little alteration in its structure. His light roadster is a well built bicycle, particular attention having been given to details. The fact that he does such a big recommendation business is a sufficient guarantee of the reliability of the wares of this maker.

"THE IRISH CYCLIST," November 25th, 1896.

The ever-smiling Dan was as usual the first man in the hall to have his exhibit ready, and very neatly, indeed, was it staged. He has confined himself to making two patterns of machines, and shows eight ladies' machines, with double-curved frames, and eight gents' machines ot. the generally accepted lines, varying only in methods of tyring and in colour of enamel. Dan still proudly points to the fact that he was one of the first makers to build safeties for ladies, and just as the Ivel is the first it is still amongst the best.

Copy of Illuminated Testimonial presented to me by a large number of Cyclists who frequented the North Road:—

DEAR DAN,   November 29th, 1885.

The Cyclists visiting Biggleswade having for many years past received at your hands at all times and at all hours numerous acts of kindness and self-denying attention, desire to express to you their hearty thanks for the considerate treatment you have invariably shown them, and the assistance you have rendered by pace-making for them when racing or during long distance rides, and in numerous other ways doing all in your power to administer to their comfort and convenience. They also wish to make some slight acknowledgement of your exertions on their behalf and combining to express to you their high opinion of your sterling good qualities, request your acceptance of a tangible token of their regard in the shape of a **GOLD CHAIN** which they hope you will accept and wear with the consciousness of its being a tribute of the esteem in which you are held by the subscribers.

19

TESTIMONIALS
Re BALL BEARING CARRIAGE AXLES.

EAST THORPE, READING,
November, 1896.

MR. DAN ALBONE,
DEAR SIR,

I am desired by Mr. ALFRED PALMER to say he finds the introduction of the Ball Bearings has done away with the drumming in the brougham. They run very nicely, and have made it much easier for the horses.

I am, yours truly, H. H. JONES, *Secretary.*

MR. PALMER, in giving his opinion of the Ivel Ball Bearing Axles and Boxes privately, says :—" I did not have new wheels put to my brougham, but Albone had the old wheels and supplied axle trees with his own patent Ball Bearings. They have only been on about three weeks, so that I cannot say anything as to whether they wear well, although I see no reason why they should not, but as regards the easy running I am perfectly satisfied. The horses trot up hills which they used to walk up, and the drumming in the brougham of which we used to complain has been completely silenced. One of the horses which we never used singly, because he was not strong enough, now draws the brougham about the town nicely."

TINWELL, STAMFORD, *Nov. 7th,* 1896.

DEAR SIR,

Some 14 months ago, I had your Ivel Ball Bearing Axles fitted to the ordinary wooden wheels with **iron tyres** of my Norfolk Cart. Since then I have driven a distance exceeding **2,000** miles over every description of road, **including cobbles ;** indeed I have put it to the severest test I could think of, being somewhat sceptical as to its performance over rough country roads, but I am glad to say that your invention has proved an unqualified success. Indeed I cannot speak too highly of it. Not the least of its advantages is the fact that my groom can (single handed) readily remove the bearings for clearing, and subsequently replace the same without the slightest difficulty.

It is, I apprehend, but seldom that inventors understate the advantages of their appliances, but I consider you have done so in saying that there is a saving of one third in draught. I am convinced that this is considerably exceeded by the adoption of your system.

I shall be very glad to answer any inquiries, and you have my permission to refer intending purchasers to me direct.

Yours faithfully, H. EDWARDS, C.C.

MR. DAN ALBONE, Biggleswade, Beds.

MARKET SQUARE, BIGGLESWADE,
Feb. 2nd, 1897.

DEAR SIR,

I have great pleasure in informing you that after supplying and fitting some of your Patent Ball Bearing Axles and Boxes to all kinds of carriage wheels (both old and new) I have come to the conclusion that they are quite a success. My customers have expressed entire satisfaction with them and have remarked that their carriages run much more easily for the horses and with more comfort for the occupants. While writing this I may add that your Ball Bearing Axles and Boxes are just as easily fitted to ordinary wood wheels as the Collings Axle.

Yours faithfully, JAMES SAUNDERS,
(*Coach Builder.*)

COTTESBROOKE PARK, NORTHAMPTON, *Nov. 3rd,* 1896.

DEAR SIR,

In reply to your letter, I have great pleasure in saying that the Patent **Ball Bearing** Axles you put into Lady Margaret's pony cart last autumn have given complete satisfaction, and I see no reason why they should not continue to do so.

Yours truly, REGINALD B. LODER.

20

TESTIMONIALS and PRESS NOTICES
Re Ball Bearing Carriage Axles.

THE GRANGE, BEESTON, SANDY,
Dec. 19th, 1896.

MR. DAN ALBONE,
DEAR SIR,

Miss Barnett is so much pleased with the Ball Bearings she has had put in the ordinary **iron tired** wood wheels of her Victoria that she wishes to have them for her Brougham. They make it considerably lighter for her horse and much more comfortable for the occupants of the carriage.

EMMANUEL COLLEGE, CAMBRIDGE,
June 18th, **1886.**

" I have now given the pony trap I purchased of you a good trial ; and I am more than satisfied with it. It is without exception the most comfortable vehicle of any kind I have ever used, and runs delightfully, freely and noiselessly. It is a great saving of labour to the horse, **and answers my expectations and your own recommendations** in every respect. The Tyres wear surprisingly well, and altogether I can conscientiously recommend your vehicle without the slightest reserve in any particular.

HERBERT WILSON.

PRESS NOTICES.

"THE COACH BUILDERS', HARNESS MAKERS' and SADDLERS' ART JOURNAL."

Ball Bearing axles not only largely reduce friction to a minimum, but they also considerably relieve much of the strain put upon the horse in drawing a vehicle, and effectually render locomotion quicker and easier, while at the same time diminishing the unpleasant rumbling noise.

"THE TIMES," August 21st, 1895.

Institute of British Carriage Manufacturers held at Tunbridge Wells.

" The eighth Autumnal Meeting of the Institute of British Carriage Manufacturers began at Tunbridge Wells yesterday, when the Members were welcomed by the Mayor, Sir David Salamons, at the Town Hall. The President, Mr. John Phillipson, of Newcastle-on-Tyne, afterwards delivered an address, in which he said, ' The great aim in life was to reduce friction to a minimum, and the pneumatic tire afforded great assistance in that direction. But it seemed to him that in the efforts to reduce friction they had not devoted **to ball bearing axles** the attention they deserved.' "

"EVENING NEWS and POST," November 24th, 1896.

Mr. Albone's stand is well worth visiting by those interested in ball bearings for vehicles. He claims a ball bearing which can be fitted to any carriage or dog-cart in a short time without breaking up the wheel in any way. This bearing is also useful for Motor Cars and Mr. Albone is certain to find a ready sale for it.'

"THE SPORTSMAN," November 20th, 1894.

" Novelties were not particularly easy to find at the Show last year. Then it was much like many of the Shows which have gone before. This year, however, there are several exhibits which have the charm of novelty. In addition thereto are sundry innovations of comparatively recent years which have been submitted to the process of latest improvements. Amongst the latter may be mentioned Dan Albone's **Ball Bearing Hubs** for Carriage Wheels. It is not quite the novelty which some folks suppose, having been originally brought out by the inventor about ten years ago. Since then the idea has been greatly developed and improved and some of the improvements are quite equal to new ideas as generally understood."

"IRISH CYCLIST," November 25th, 1896.

" He also shows his well known ball bearing axles for vehicles, which have proved such a thorough success."

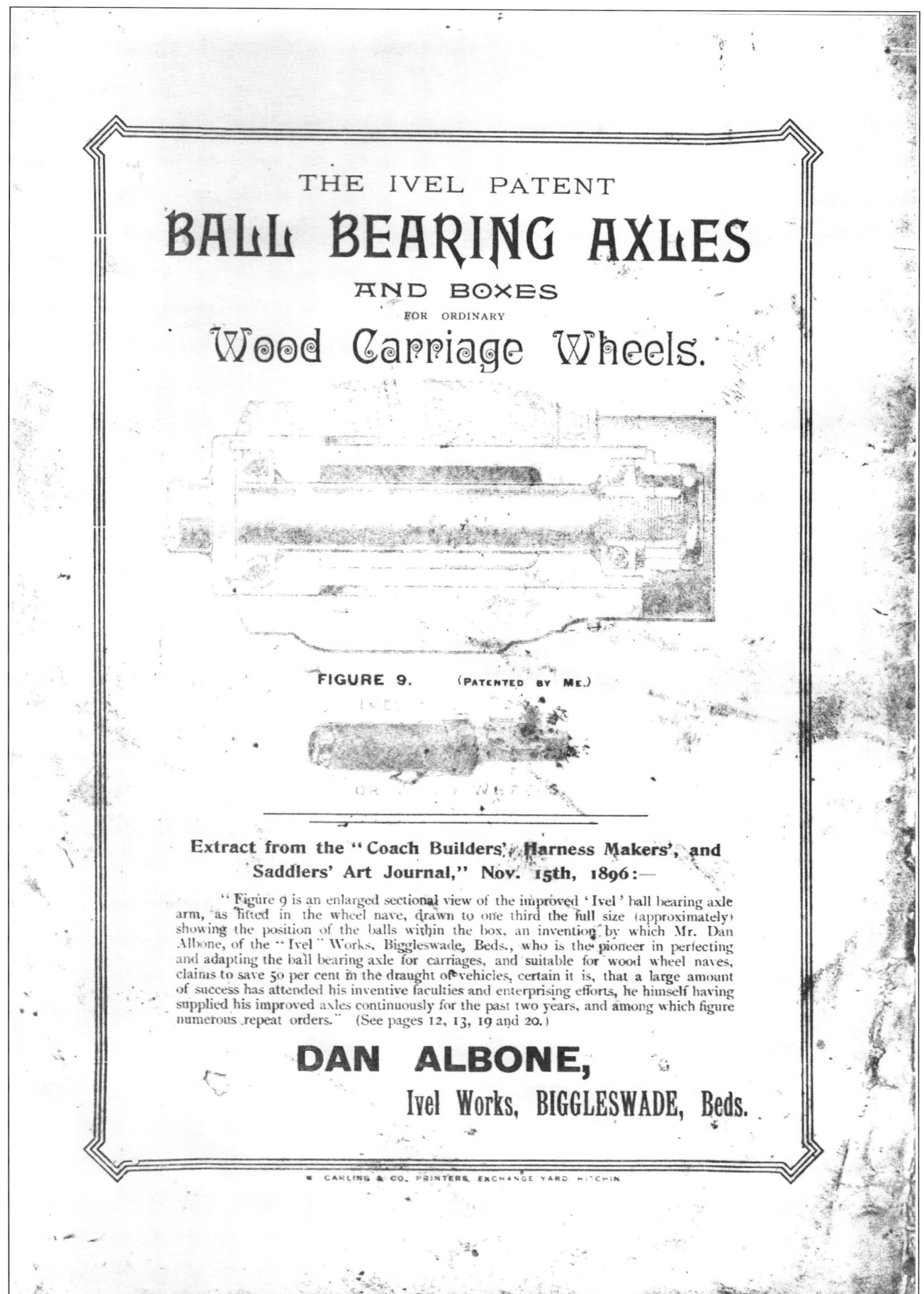

THE IVEL PATENT
BALL BEARING AXLES
AND BOXES
FOR ORDINARY
Wood Carriage Wheels.

FIGURE 9.   (PATENTED BY ME.)

Extract from the "Coach Builders', Harness Makers', and Saddlers' Art Journal," Nov. 15th, 1896:—

"Figure 9 is an enlarged sectional view of the improved 'Ivel' ball bearing axle arm, as fitted in the wheel nave, drawn to one third the full size (approximately) showing the position of the balls within the box, an invention by which Mr. Dan Albone, of the "Ivel" Works, Biggleswade, Beds., who is the pioneer in perfecting and adapting the ball bearing axle for carriages, and suitable for wood wheel naves, claims to save 50 per cent in the draught of vehicles, certain it is, that a large amount of success has attended his inventive faculties and enterprising efforts, he himself having supplied his improved axles continuously for the past two years, and among which figure numerous repeat orders." (See pages 12, 13, 19 and 20.)

DAN ALBONE,
Ivel Works, BIGGLESWADE, Beds.

W. CARLING & CO., PRINTERS, EXCHANGE YARD, HITCHIN.

View of the River Ivel which runs through Biggleswade

BLACKSMITHS' SHOP AT THE
IVEL WORKS.

Blacksmiths

ESTABLISHED 20
YEARS.

ILLUSTRATED PRICE LIST

OF THE

IVEL ─

CYCLES,

1900.-1.

ALSO

Ball Bearing Carriage Axles and
Boxes and Motor Cars.

MANUFACTURED BY

DAN

ALBONE,

BIGGLESWADE,
Beds.

TELEGRAPHIC ADDRESS.
DAN ALBONE, BIGGLESWADE.

CARLING & CO., PRINTERS, HITCHIN.

Terms of Business.

CASH against Invoice to Customers having no Ledger Account.

CARRIAGE in all cases to be paid by **Purchaser.**

REPAIRS will not be received unless sent **Carriage Paid** with full Name and Address of Sender.

CRATES are charged Cost Price, and are NOT RETURNABLE.

NOTICES TO PURCHASERS

Most of my Machines are made specially to order, thus giving more satisfaction to the Purchaser and myself. All I require is the inside measurement of leg, from fork to ball of foot, and the weight of the rider. Easy payments are arranged when required by customers.

A Large Stock of all kinds of Accessories such as LAMPS, OIL and ACETYLENE, BELLS, TIRE INFLATORS, &c., &c., always kept in Stock. A large number of Second-hand Machines are always on sale at very low prices.

REPAIRS

All kinds of Repairs are done on the premises. Having a complete plant for this branch customers may rely upon Prompt and Efficient attention. Enquiries respecting Machines receive immediate attention, and inspection of my Stock of Machines and Accessories is respectfully invited at the Show Rooms of the Works.

SPECIAL

ALL KINDS OF COPPER AND NICKEL PLATING DONE ON THE PREMISES. I ALSO HAVE A SPECIAL PLANT FOR SILVERING SUCH ARTICLES AS FORKS, SPOONS, CRUETS, TRAYS, &c. See detailed List, to be had on application.

FORM OF GUARANTEE.

I Guarantee, subject to the conditions mentioned below, that all precautions which are usual and reasonable have been taken by me to secure excellence of materials and workmanship in all my Machines, and I undertake to make good, at any time within twelve months of this date, any defects which result from inherent flaws or defective workmanship, and are not caused by wear and tear, misuse or neglect.

CONDITIONS.—If a defective part should be found in any of my Machines, it must be sent to me **Carriage Paid** and accompanied by an intimation from the Sender that he desires to have it repaired free of charge under the guarantee. The number of the Machine must be quoted.

Failing compliance with this rule no notice will be taken of anything that may arrive, but such articles will lie here at the risk of the Sender.

This Guarantee does not apply to the specialities of other Firms, such as Tires, Gear Cases, Saddles, Tool Bags, Lamps, Bells, &c., but the makers of these, whose names usually appear thereon, are in nearly every case willing to replace defective parts, and I will at all times furnish the maker's name as a proof of the quality.

2

Introduction.

IT is now twenty years since I had the pleasure of submitting my first Catalogue of the celebrated IVEL Cycles, and it is with more than usual confidence and pleasure I now issue my illustrated Price List for 1900, and in so doing I will ask my numerous friends and patrons to accept my best thanks for their kind support and recommendations which have in no small measure assisted me to keep the IVEL Cycles in the very front rank of the world's best machines.

The distinguished list of patrons on the following pages and the innumerable

UNSOLICITED TESTIMONIALS

I have received (see pages 20, 21 and 22) prove that IVEL Cycles not only possess sterling merits, but that they are second to none.

I shall continue to turn out machines of the

VERY HIGHEST CLASS

at a reasonable price which cannot fail to be to the purchasers' satisfaction.

The immense popularity of IVEL Cycles, gained by their always giving entire satisfaction, was greatly enhanced **six years ago** when I determined to do away with the old method of listing machines at a high figure and allowing a large discount (see pages 9, 11, 12 and 14). There was nothing to be gained by running the price of a machine up in order to bring it down again, except that it gave an unscrupulous dealer an opportunity to take advantage of the inexperienced in the purchase of a cycle.

IVEL machines will be made throughout of the very best material procurable and by skilled workmen. The requirements of each individual customer will be carefully studied and the twenty years' experience I have had in general engineering, and being a practical rider (having won over 180 prizes on the path and road) is a guarantee that customers' wants are thoroughly known and understood.

The same arrangements as regards London business will be continued as during the past few years, and either myself or my chief representative, **Mr. GEORGE COURSE,** will make appointments by wire or letter at the works or at customers' residences. Appointments to other places are also made.

One great advantage my patrons in London have is that Biggleswade is on the Great Northern Railway main line, about an hour's run from King's Cross, and a machine put on at the terminus or at any of their Depôts

4

reaches me very soon after its despatch, lessening the time incurred when any repairs are necessary to the machine. The repairs are executed by the workmen who built it; an important consideration. Intending customers themselves can visit the Works and inspect the various branches of the industry, seeing the raw material itself and the machine in all its stages while under construction.

IVEL PATENT BALL BEARINGS

for **CARTS, CARRIAGES, MOTOR CARS and 'BUSES** are now well-known and those supplied during the past few years have given entire satisfaction. The repeat orders I have received from customers who have given them a **long trial** proves this, and they have testified to the enormous **saving in draught.** For reference to some of the Testimonials and Press Notices which I have received from as far back as 1886 (pages 23 and 24) will confirm this statement.

MOTOR CARS.

Having now had some three or four years experience in the Motor Car industry, I am pleased to state that I am now in a position to make and supply complete IVEL Motor Cars. Neither time nor expense have been spared in order to produce a really successful IVEL Motor Car, one which I can confidently put on the market, knowing that it will make for itself a reputation equal to that which the IVEL Cycle has possessed for a great number of years.

The IVEL Motor Car has been severely and thoroughly tested over all sorts of roads, and the results of these tests have been so gratifying that I venture to think that it will find a great many admirers and purchasers. There are novelties and improvements in its construction which are not to be seen on any other make and which cannot fail to attract considerable attention. It is built on sound lines and is made of the very best material obtainable, and it is with great confidence that I anticipate that no Car has a better future before it than **THE IVEL.**

Besides making and supplying IVEL Cars, I am sole agent in my own immediate district for several other best known Cars, Tricycles, &c., and I can supply them as cheaply as anyone else in this country. I would respectfully point out that every purchaser of a Car supplied by me will have the advantage of dealing with a man who thoroughly understands Motor Cars, and I shall be pleased at all times to give them my best attention, and I shall be pleased to give any intending purchaser a trial trip on a Car and any information as regards the management of these vehicles.

In conclusion I would once more assure customers that their enquiries and orders will at all times have prompt attention, and I trust that the support they have hitherto accorded me will be continued; no effort on my part shall be wanting to merit it.

DAN ALBONE,
SOLE PROPRIETOR.

5

LIST OF PATRONS.

Her Grace the Duchess of
   Bedford
Marchioness of Tweeddale
Marchioness of Granby
Countess Cowper
Countess Grey
Countess of Listowel
Countess de Grey
Countess of Guildford
Countess Rosslyn
Lady Dora Yeoman
Lady Colthurst
Lady Oxenbridge
Lady Payne
Lady Bertie
Lady Constance Harris
Lady Barbara Smith
Lady Brabourne
Lady Lawson
Lady Napier of Magdala
Lady Ampthill
Lady Griffin
Lady St. John
Lady Primrose
The Honble. Mrs. Bagot
The Honble. Mrs. Forbes
The Honble. Mrs. Astell
The Honble. Mrs. Charles
   Brand
The Honble. Constance
   Russell
The Honble. Mrs.
   Hastings
Mrs. M. S. Reeves
Mrs. John Sinclair
Mrs. G. Barnett
Mrs. F. J. Josselyn
Mrs. Barnett
Mrs. Heysham
Mrs. C. Kerr
Mrs. S. Bruce
Mrs. Cooke
Mrs. E. G. Taddy
Mrs. W. Earle
Mrs. Madeline McCarthy
Mrs. Blackwood
Mrs. E. Lennox Peel
Mrs. W. Appleton
Mrs. C. F. Lindsell
Mrs. E. Osborn
Mrs. Lawson
Mrs. S. Scott
Mrs. Gibson Carmichael
Mrs. Algernon Talbot

Mrs. J. Trotter
Mrs. D. H. F. Peploe
Mrs. A. Tyrell
Mrs. D. Stuart
Mrs. R. Ord
Mrs. M. P. Foster
Mrs. J. Richardson
Mrs. Jervoise Huddleston
Mrs. Griffith Jones
Mrs. Elmhirst
Mrs. Gribble
Mrs. Pechy Phipson, M.D.
Mrs. Middleton
Mrs. Callander
Mrs. Frank Penn
Mrs. Charlotte Villiers
Mrs. H. G. Thornton
Mrs. L. Mounteney
   Jephson
Mrs. Oscar Berry
Mrs. E. Hill
Mrs. Henniker
Mrs. Mitchell Gill
Mrs. Sam Hopkins
Mrs. B. Baxter
Mrs. Clifford Smith
Mrs. Ben Haworth Booth
Mrs. Sumner
Mrs. Reckett
Mrs. J. Atkinson
Mrs. Coldham
Mrs. Wilfred Kempe
Mrs. Alexandra Landale
Mrs. Harold Brocklebank
Mrs. Madeline S. Beaden
Miss Sutton Sams
Miss Bulkeley Hughes
Miss F. Keyser
Miss C. Astell
Miss M. Dimsdale
Miss F. Cockrane
Miss O. Marshall
Miss N. Hulbert
Miss E. Lindsell
Miss L. Hawksley
Miss E. F. Humphries
Miss Archdale
Miss St. Quintin
Miss Beatrice Stuart
   Wortley
Miss L. Osborn
Miss E. Williams
Miss Hawkinson
Miss K. Ladds

Miss Helen Douglas
Miss May Irwin
Miss G. Archdale
Miss D. Pearson
Miss Agnes Keyser
Miss L. Bernard
Miss Batchelor
Miss E. Wilshere
Miss M. F. Prichard
Miss B. Greenfield
Miss Sinclair
Miss E. Gregory
Miss K. M. F. Brooks
Miss K. L. Laurance
Miss C. Hulbert
Miss E. Gibbs
Miss Holt
Miss Geraldine Magniac
Miss F. J. Dewar
Miss Constance Cochrane
Miss Chamberlayne
Miss M. Tryon
Miss Tait
Miss Briscoe
Miss Ethel Hartley
Miss H. Coltman
Miss C. T. Wood
Miss E. Phipps
Miss Marion Cureton
Miss Aimée Curll
Miss H. Chapman
Miss A. E. Gregory
Miss Constance Pym
Miss Adelaide Pym
Miss M. Thompson
Miss Caroline Astell
Miss A. P. Haines
Miss M. Humphries
Miss M. Grierson
Miss Beatrice Dunbar
   Kilburn
Miss K. Rintoul
Miss D. Higgins
Miss L. M. Richardson
Miss W. Barker
Miss A. K. Higgins
Miss Aikenhead
Miss Mary Pearson
Miss S. Hesketh
Miss Augusta Mary Wing
Miss J. C. Palmer
Miss Dunbar Kilburn
Miss M. Tower
Miss F. A. Cooper

6

LIST OF PATRONS—Continued.

Miss C. A. J. Dimsdale
Miss E. Hewetson
Miss Mortlock
Miss Olive Hill
Miss D. Hill
His Grace the Duke of Bedford
Marquis of Tweeddale
Marquis of Granby
Marquis of Northampton
Viscount Peel
Earl Grey
Earl Jersey
Earl of Mount Edgcumbe
Lord Napier of Magdala
Lord Massey
Lord St. John
Lord Ampthill
Lord Alwyne Compton, M.P.
Sir Algernon Osborn, Bart.
Lord Arthur Hay
Rev. Lord Wm. Cecil
Count Deym
Austrian Embassy
Viscount Duncannon
Monsieur Bolatzell
Russian Embassy
Capt. The Hon. H. S. Davey
Sir T. O'Brien, Bart.
Sir Robert Turin
Sir Robert Edgcumbe
Sir Edward Jenkinson
Sir Hugh R. Beevor, Bart., M.D.
Sir Arthur de Copell Brooke
The Honble. C. A. Pelham
The Honble. Mark McDonnell
The Honble. G. Peel
The Honble. M. B. Peel
The Honble. Henry B. O. St. John
The Honble. Roland St. John
Col. The Honble. C. Crichton
The Honble. Mowbray A. T. St. John
The Hon. Alfred Lyttelton, Q.C., M.P.
The Honble. Spencer Lyttelton
Colonel Law

Colonel Astell
Colonel Gregson
Colonel Blane
Colonel Oldham
Colonel Ellison
Colonel Josselyn
Colonel Jackson
Colonel M. Bowers
Colonel J. Burn
Colonel Hunt
Colonel Johnston
Colonel V. Dawson
Colonel Cumberlege
Lieut.-Col. A. W. Bentley
Lieut.-Col. Everard
Lieut.-Col. Broughton
Surgeon Lieut.-Colonel Crombie
Major Elmhirst
Major M. Block
Major Braithwaite
Major J. M. Richardson
Captain G. G. Lang
Capt. Com. The Honble. Seymour Fortescue
Capt. G. R. Bethell, M.P.
J. G. Talbot, Esq., M.P.
Com. P. H. Wright, R.N.
Major-Gen. T. B. Bevan
Major F. Shuttleworth
Major A. Duberley
Major F. A. B. Talbot
Major Mellor
Major S. Haines
Major A. H. Block, R.A.
Captain Street, R.N.
Lt. Chas. Bissett, R.N.
Captain C. H. Fenwick
Captain Duberly
Captain C. J. Briggs, R.N.
Captain Leetham
Captain Dugald Stuart
Captain Stapylton Marshall
Captain H. M. Stanley
Captain H. A. Street
Captain J. C. Blunt, R.A.
Captain F. Hulton
Capt. Chas. Windham, R.N.
Captain N. G. Frazer
Captain J. P. Coote
Captain R. C. Broome
Guy Pym, Esq., M.P.
B. C. Molloy, Esq., M.P.

Ellis J. Griffiths, Esq., M.P.
Reginald McKenna, Esq., M.P.
T. R. Buchanan, Esq., M.P.
Dr. Dent
Dr. H. Bond
Dr. T. W. Smyth
Dr. Welsh
Dr. R. R. Hatherell
Dr. Davies
Dr. Shaw
Dr. Symes
Dr. James
Dr. Emmerson
Dr. Argo
Dr. C. A. Lees
Dr. M. Cameron Blair
Dr. Mivart
The Right Rev. Lord Bishop of New Guinea
Rev. Ruston
Rev. C. M. Greenstreet
Rev. J. R. H. Duke
Rev. F. Jickling
Rev. T. S. Toolis
Rev. F. C. Hartley
Rev. F. Kinglake
Rev. W. P. Henderson
Rev. A. Kirke Smith
Rev. C. B. Bevan
Rev. R. Hugh Gundry
Rev. F. Sullivan
Rev. Richardson
Rev. Gwynne
Rev. R. S. Bagshaw
Rev. E. P. Gatty
Rev. Watkins
Rev. C. B. Bevan
Rev. C. D. Ash
Rev. R. C. Whitworth
Rev. W. S. Edgell
Rev. C. H. Brocklebank
Rev. H. S. Payne
Rev. J. A. Hervey
Rev. J. Halliburton Young
Rev. G. M. Osborne
Rev. E. L. Colebrooke
Rev. R. Lang
Rev. L. Clutterbuck
W. F. Archdale, Esq.
H. S. Whitbread, Esq.
S. Whitbread, Esq.
Algernon Gilliat, Esq.
Howard Gilliat, Esq.
Reginald B. Loder, Esq.
J. Harvey, Esq.

7

LIST OF PATRONS Continued.

J. H. St. Q. Astell, Esq.
Bateman Brown, Esq.
Percival Bosanquet, Esq.
Lennox Peel, Esq.
F. Archdale, Esq.
H. J. B. Kendall, Esq.
W.A.Attenborough, Esq.
E. O. Fordham, Esq.
H. A. Vernet, Esq.
M. J. Godby, Esq.
F. F. Greenfield, Esq.
Robert Dimsdale, Esq.
J. H. Mossop, Esq.
J. T. Green, Esq.
Francis R. Pryor, Esq.
C. S. Lindsell, Esq.
R. J. Lindsell, Esq.
A. K. Lindsell, Esq.
Gerald Smith, Esq.
Julian Godfrey, Esq.
Cyril B. Tubbs, Esq.
John Corrie Carter, Esq.
A. Harter, Esq.
C. F. St. Quintin, Esq.
C. M. Hodgkins, Esq.
A. Lewis Jones, Esq.
E. Morse, Esq.
William Tyrer, Esq.
Martin Pirie, Esq.
Philip Bright, Esq.
J. Dyson Moore, Esq.
J. N. Stuart, Esq.
A. Tyrell, Esq.
T. A. Gibb, Esq.
W. T. Nash, Esq
R. C. V. Lang, Esq.
J. S. W. Blackett, Esq.
E. Snow Fordham, Esq.
A. Duberley, Esq.
J. E. Talbot, Esq.
J. W. Walter, Esq.
F. Penn, Esq.
W. Penn, Esq.
F. G. Payne, Esq.
W. H. B. Drayson, Esq.
J. H. Williams, Esq.
Redfern Williams, Esq.
S. F. Cotton, Esq.
J. G. O'Brien, Esq.
Edward O'Brien, Esq.
Willoughby Josselyn, Esq.
Arthur G. Murrell, Esq.
J. Clunes, Esq.
W. G. Quihampton, Esq.
G. A. Newton, Esq.
C. C. Jury, Esq.

A. Rawlinson, Esq.
J. Leveson-Gower, Esq.
E. Talbot, Esq.
J. Phillips, Esq.
J. S. Wood, Esq.
A. F. Robertson, Esq.
W. Jameson, Esq.
Arthur Lane, Esq.
Beds. Constabulary
F. Preedy, Esq., F.S.I.
W. Armstrong, Esq.
J. A. Pomeroy, Esq.
A. W. W. Dale, Esq.
T. M. Bear, Esq.
W. A. St. Quintin, Esq.
J. G. W. James, Esq.
H. A. Block, Esq.
G. P. Talbot, Esq.
W. C. Palceologues, Esq.
H. Tylston Hodgson, Esq.
G. V. Fiddes, Esq.
G. P. Evans, Esq.
George Hunt, Esq.
A. J. Beckett, Esq.
George Farquharson, Esq.
F. G. Le Marchant, Esq.
Tobias Williams, Esq.
T. D. Lawrance, Esq.
Arthur G. Kendall, Esq.
E. Evelyn Barron, Esq.
C. Alington, Esq.
H. P. J. Cowell, Esq.
E. Lumley, Esq.
J. G. Gribble, Esq.
Rimmington Wilson, Esq.
F. J. Thynne, Esq.
A Crossman, Esq.
G. K. Paley, Esq.
John Browning, Esq.
J. Barker, Esq.
F. Lowrey, Esq.
A. C. Mitchell, Esq.
W. Andrew, Esq.
J. Taylor, Esq.
T. G. D. Hendley, Esq.
A. D. Carlisle, Esq.
J. W. Orde, Esq.
Montague Loftus, Esq.
N. S. Talbot, Esq.
W. H. Haughton, Esq.
John Russell Villiers, Esq.
C. T. Newton, Esq.
A. D. Tait, Esq.
E. G. Cubitt, Esq.
D. Henry T. Peploe, Esq.
Henry J.L.Graham, Esq.

Arthur J. Ashton, Esq.
Oswald Norman, Esq.
C. K. Bayley, Esq.
Sydney Stephenson, Esq.
W. Appleton, Esq.
Francis J.Blackwood,Esq.
R. I. Dale, Esq.
Ben Haworth Booth, Esq.
Joseph Smith, Esq.
F. N. Butler, Esq.
F. Giles, Esq.
H. H. Green, Esq.
George Wilkinson, Esq.
W. H. Hulbert, Esq.
R. C. H. Millar, Esq.
E. M. Kendall, Esq.
Jan Robertson, Esq.
G. J. Bruce, Esq.
C. S. Newton, Esq.
C. S. Newton, Esq.
J. A. Kemp, Esq.
R. W. Wileman, Esq.
Gordon Hooper, Esq.
K. D. Hutchinson, Esq.
Marlborough R.Pryor,Esq.
E. Wahab, Esq.
C. C. James, Esq.
R. C. Vyner, Esq,
C. A. Turner, Esq.
Leslie, Keith, Esq.
A. Clifford Smith, Esq.
L. Dawson Campbell, Esq.
Clarence Bird, Esq.
J. H. Dalton, Esq.
R. H. Dun, Esq.
Theodore Thompson, Esq.
Walter Adams, Esq.
H. B. Green, Esq.
W. A. W. Dawn, Esq.
Alex Landale, Esq.
Cecil F. Parr, Esq.
E. S. A. Littlewood, Esq.
J. Annan Bryce, Esq.
R. Taunton Raikes, Esq.
Esme Howard, Esq.
H. Temple Prior, Esq.
C. R. Wade Gery, Esq.
H. Chaundler, Esq.
Thomas Hartley, Esq.
J. A. Bright, Esq.
C. W. Patchell, Esq.
J. McNab, Esq.
P. M. Buchanan, Esq.
Alfred J. Boult, Esq.
Arthur C. Beck, Esq.
William Tennant, Esq.

8

THE MAYPOLE ON ICKWELL GREEN.

One of the prettiest
and most old fashioned
Village Greens in Eng-
land.

Close to Biggleswade.

Ivel No. 1
Roadster Safety.

Specification.

Best steel weldless tubes, 28″ driving and 30″ steering wheels; tangent spokes; best ball bearings throughout; improved dust proof bottom bracket; barrel hubs, oil containing; bright parts heavily coppered and nickelled; steering lock; geared 60″ or to order; powerful detachable rubber brake; detachable light metal mudguards; adjustable foot rests; rubber or rat trap pedals; best quality saddle; tool bag; spanners; oil can; pump, &c. Weight as illustrated, 36lbs.

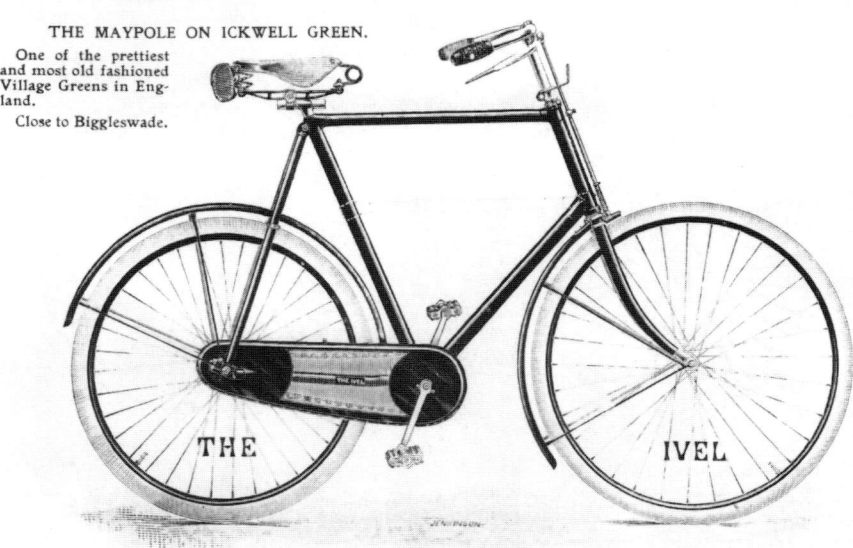

THE   IVEL

This Machine is a splendid full roadster, and is capable of carrying any weight rider. For touring and general use it cannot be beaten. When made for exceptionally tall and heavy riders an extra tube in frame is used.

PRICE - - - £16.

As illustrated, with Dunlops, "A" Clinchers, or other well-known pneumatic tires with hollow rims, brake, mudguards and IVEL gear case.

EXTRAS. Carter detachable gear case, **17/6**; lining gold, **10/6**; any other colour, **7/6**; if enamelled any other colour than black, **7/6**; if fitted with extra tube in frame as shown by dotted line, **15/=**; free wheel and Bowden back rim brake, **£1 15/=**.

Extract from *Cycling*, Nov. 26th, 1898. — "It is worth while to note cheery Dan Albone has, for the last few years, marked nett prices in his catalogue." (*See introduction, page 4.*)

9

SUTTON, an old and picturesque Village near Biggleswade.
Showing Bridge and Ford.

Ivel No. 2

LIGHT = ROADSTER.

Specificaton.

Best weldless steel tubes ; 28 in. driving and 30 in. steering wheels ; improved dust proof bottom bracket ; narrow tread ; barrel hubs, oil containing ; bright parts heavily coppered and nickelled ; steering lock ; tangent spokes ; gear 63 in. or to order ; best quality saddle ; tool bag ; spanners ; oil can ; pump, &c. Weight 28lbs.

THE   IVEL

It was the IVEL Light Roadster which made such a reputation in the early days of the present type of safety bicycle by so many world's road records being made on it. This machine, though light in weight, is built with strength, safety and durability, for any weight rider up to 12 stone.

PRICE - - - £16.

Complete with Dunlop, "A" Clincher, or other well-known pneumatic tires, with hollow rims, brake, mudguards and IVEL gear case.

EXTRAS.—Carter detachable gear case, 17/6 ; lining gold, 10/6 ; any other colour, 7/6 ; if enamelled any other colour than black, 7/6 ; free wheel and Bowden back rim brake, £1 15 0.

IVEL No. 3 ROAD RACER.— This Machine is identical with the Light Roadster, but built lighter where possible. It has been a great success, and has in every case given satisfaction. It is the very best value in the cycle trade. Hollow rims, tangent spokes, gear, 70 in. or to order. Weight 25lbs. **PRICE,** without brake, mudguards or gear case, **£15 10/-**

EXTRAS.—Same as No. 2.

IVEL No. 4 PATH RACER.—This Machine has been constructed throughout with due regard to lightness and strength, the Maximum weight being about 21lbs.

PRICE - - - £16.

10

A VIEW OF SUTTON.
From the Bridge showing Village and Church
in the distance.

Ivel No. 5
LADY'S
SAFETY.

Specification.

Strong dropped frame with double tubes; 28″ wheels with barrel hubs, oil containing; bright parts heavily coppered and nickelled; steering lock; IVEL gear case, brake and mudguards; best quality saddle; tool bag; spanners; oil can; pump, &c.

The established popularity of this machine enables me to place it again before my Patrons with every confidence. It is a fact that no Lady's Bicycle has been more popular than the "IVEL No. 5." Fourteen years ago I made this type of machine and during the whole of this long period it has never been surpassed either in design, material, or workmanship.

PRICE - - £16.

As illustrated with Dunlops, "A" Clinchers, or other well-known Pneumatic Tyres with hollow rims.

EXTRAS.—If fitted with Carter gear case instead of IVEL, 17/6; Lining gold, 10/6; any other colour, 7/6; if enamelled any other colour than black, 7/6; Free Wheel and Bowden Back Rim Brake, £1 15s. 0d.

For particulars of a cheaper safety machine, but of this pattern, see page 13.

Extract from *Athletic News*, Sept. 26th, 1898:—" Dan Albone was undoubtedly the first man to drop the discount system."
(See Introduction, page 4.)

Reprint of Lady's Safety which I advertised and sold 14 years ago.

11

313

NORTHILL CHURCH.
Near Biggleswade.

Ivel No. 6

Lady's Safety.

Specification.

Strong frame with curved top tube and straight lower one; 28" wheels; barrel hubs, oil containing; bright parts heavily coppered and nickelled; steering lock; IVEL gear case, brake and mudguards; best quality saddle; tool bag; spanner; oil can; pump, &c.

This pattern of IVEL Ladies' Safety is especially made to meet the special requirements of some of my customers who prefer the kind of frame as illustrated, to that of the No. 5. It is a splendid machine, and is equal to the No. 5 in every respect as regards material and workmanship, and the price is the same. Every care and attention will be given to this machine so as to make it create a big demand.

PRICE - - - £16.

As illustrated, with Dunlops, Clincher, or other well-known pneumatic tyres, with hollow rims.

EXTRAS.—If fitted with Carter Gear Case instead of IVEL, 17/6; any other colour Enamel but Black, 7/6; lining gold, 10/6; any other colour, 7/6. Free wheel and Bowden Back Rim Brake, £1 15s. 0d.

Extract from *Cyclist*, Nov. 23rd, 1898.—**Now that nett prices** are coming into vogue, we must not forget to add that Dan Albone was one of **the first** to adopt the system **of nett prices**; in fact he may be considered quite a pioneer in the matter. (*See Introduction, page 4.*)

12

OLD WARDEN.
A model Village near Biggleswade.

Ivel No. 7.
Roadster Safety.

Specification.

Best weldless steel tubes; 28in. and 30in. wheels; direct or laced spokes; best ball bearings throughout; improved dust proof bottom bracket; brake; mudguards; ball pedals.

PRICE - - - £12.

Complete with " B " Clincher tyres, brake and mudguards.

Ivel No. 5c
- Lady's Safety.

Specification.

Strong dropped frame with double tubes; 28in. wheels; IVEL gear case; brake and mudguards; best ball bearings; improved dust proof bottom bracket; ball pedals.

PRICE - - - £12 12/-.

Complete with " B " Clincher tyres, brake, mudguards and IVEL gear case.

Owing to the demand for Machines at a somewhat less price than that of the highest grade Cycles, I have resolved to supply both a Gents' and a Lady's Machine at a popular price, and I have every confidence in doing a big trade with both No. 7 Gents' and No. 5c Lady's.

These Machines are in every way first-class ones with the exception of their being thoroughly up-to-date in detail. They are practically last season's patterns fitted with " B " Clincher tyres, and a little cheaper saddle, gear case, &c., than usually fitted. I can confidently recommend both machines and am sure of their giving great satisfaction.

13

Ivel No. 8

Tricycle.

Another view of Ickwell Green.

Size of Wheels:

26-in. back and 28-in. front.

THE IVEL

Eighteen years ago I made the first IVEL Tricycle, and it was the **very first** to gain a world-wide reputation. This machine is built with a truss frame, which is very rigid, though light. It is made suitable for either a lady or gentleman, and for a first-class machine at a moderate price, it has no equal.

PRICE - - - £25.

With Dunlop's "A" Clinchers, or any other well-known pneumatic tyres with hollow rims ; bright parts heavily coppered and nickelled ; leather gear case ; detachable rubber brake and mudguards ; best quality saddle ; tool bag ; spanners ; oil can ; pump, &c.

Lining gold, 15/- ; any other colour, 10/- : if enamelled any other colour than black, 10/-

---

TANDEM SAFETIES.

Though not illustrating these Machines, I am prepared to make them to order. *Prices on application.*

Extract from *Financial News*, Nov. 12th, 1898. — "Dan Albone has, by placing a **high-class machine** on the market at a **reasonable price**, secured a good many distinguished patrons. (*See Introduction, page 4.*)

14

DAN ALBONE'S
Child Carrier and
Parcel Carrier.

The CHILD CARRIER is a very neat and light Wicker Basket made on steel wire framework, the weight of which is carried by means of tubing direct on to the axle of front wheel, with Leg Troughs, as sketch, Plated Clips to fasten to the Handle Bar and Back Irons to bolt on back of Basket. Two holes are made in the

back of Basket, so that a strap can be put through to fasten the child safely in.

When ordering the only Particulars necessary are the Diameters of Front Wheel and Handle Bar.

Easily fixed to any Safety Bicycle or Tricycle.

PARCEL CARRIER.

CHILD CARRIER.

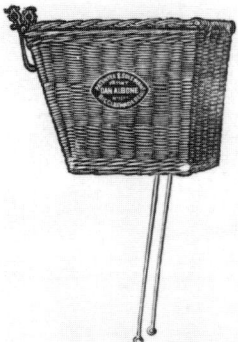

The Basket is easily put on and taken off in a minute, by taking the bottom screw out of the clips and leaving the clips on Handle Bar.

Complete £1.

With Cushions complete, £1 7s. 6d.

Full Instructions for fitting sent with Carrier, which must be strictly adhered to when fixing same to Cycle.

Further particulars see Abridged List, which contains Testimonials, &c., to be had on application.

TESTIMONIAL.

"SELBOURNE," DURHAM ROAD, WIMBLEDON, SURREY,
November 3rd, 1899.

DEAR SIR,

I am pleased to inform you that the child carrier is much appreciated. My little daughter has travelled just 1000 miles in it with great delight and she evidently thinks it as safe as I do, as it fits well without impeding the movement of the machine in the slightest, allowing of course for the slight extra weight to carry. The carrier has been continuously left on the machine for over four months and has proved thoroughly safe and reliable.

As my wife always travels with me you have the complete satisfaction of my small family.

Yours very truly,
(signed) C. TILLINGHAST.

15

Ball Bearing Carriage
and Motor Car Wheels.

IVEL. BALL BEARING
CARRIAGE WHEELS.

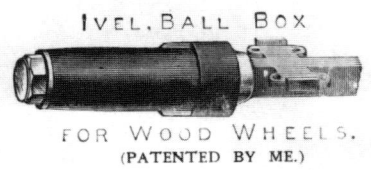

IVEL. BALL BOX

FOR WOOD WHEELS.
(PATENTED BY ME.)

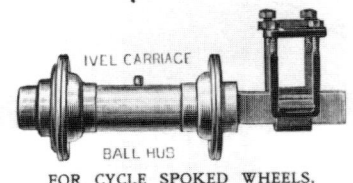

IVEL CARRIAGE

BALL HUB
FOR CYCLE SPOKED WHEELS.
Diagram of Hub shewing Clips for Springs.

CYCLE SPOKED WHEELS.

The demand for Cycle Spoked Wheels for ordinary carts, carriages, and motor cars, is still on the increase, and those I have supplied for the **past 15 years** have given such great satisfaction that I have had the pleasure of receiving many repeat orders. When fitted to motor cars, sometimes the head hubs are left a little longer so that there is room for the fixing on of a sprocket wheel for driving purposes.

Acetylene Gas, Carriage and Motor Car Lamps supplied to order.

16

Patent Ball Bearing Axles
AND BOXES
For WOOD CARRIAGE and = =
= = = MOTOR CAR WHEELS.

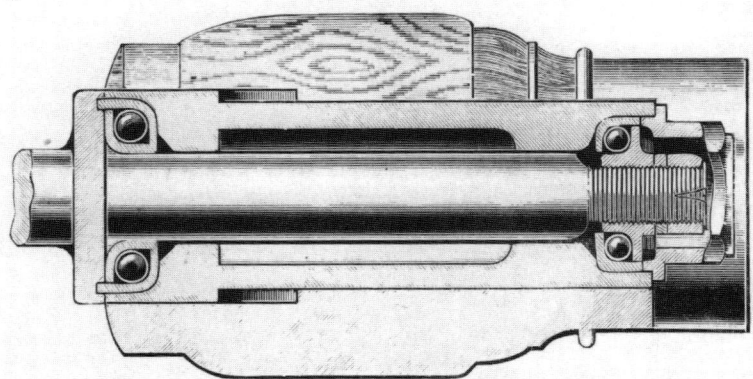

Section showing Ball Box fitted in nave or wood stock.   (Patented by me.)

The big business I have done with Ball Bearing Boxes, both with coach builders and private customers, during the past 12 months has come quite up to my expectation. The number sold being far greater than that of any previous year, and the orders I have now in hand proves conclusively that I shall supply a far greater number during the coming season. I would kindly ask those who take an interest in Ball Bearings for vehicles to read the unsolicited testimonials of Mrs. Ben Haworth-Booth, Miss Barnet, Mrs. Osborn, Lord Alwyne Compton, M.P., A Tyrell, Esq., A. Palmer, Esq., Captain Bethell M.P., A. J. Clay, Esq., A. K. Stothert, Esq., and Mr. D. Campbell, on pages 23 and 24.

Having proved they are a great success when in wheels with **Iron Tyres** it is obvious that they run extremely nicely and wear exceptionally well when they are fitted to wheels with rubber tires. The repeat orders received confirm this.

IMPORTANT.

When present old wheels are to be fitted with my patent ball bearing axles and boxes, measurements are taken, and after axles are made and finished I only require the old wheels about a day or so to fit ball boxes and axles in them—thus depriving customers of the use of their vehicle for a few days only.

The following is a list of patrons supplied with IVEL Ball Bearing Carriage Axles :

His Grace the Duke of Bedford	Mrs. Ben Haworth-Booth
Lord Alwyne Compton, M.P.	Goodling & Priestly
Miss H. Barnett	M. D. Rucker, Esq.
London & North Western Railway Co.	Hayes & Sons
Great Northern Railway Co.	Universal Electric Carriage
Headlands Electric Battery Co.	Syndicate, Ltd.
Reginald B. Loder, Esq.	H. H. Mulliner, Esq.
London Improved Cab Co.	Alfred Palmer, Esq.
North British Rubber Co.	F. L. Merritt, Esq.
R. C. de Grey Vyner, Esq.	Cyril B. Tubbs, Esq.
A. J. Clay, Esq.	Harry T. Shaw, Esq.
H. Starke, Esq.	W. C. Bersey, Esq., A.I.C.E.
W. H. Brett, Esq.	Messrs. Thorn
Howard Whitbread, Esq.	Mr. James Saunders
A. Tyrell, Esq.	Messrs. A. Ferris & Co.
H. Edwards, Esq.	E. Ventham & Co.
Dunlop Pneumatic Tyre Co.	Maythorn & Son.
Higgins, Bessemer, Nicholson & Co.	Barker & Co.
Captain G. R. Bethel, M.P.	Thrupp & Maberly
Mrs. L. Chadwick	Messrs. Carpenter & Co.
Major Frank Shuttleworth	Mr. J. A. Croucher
Mrs. Osborn	Mr. D. Campbell
Sir Algernon Osborn	Messrs. Rock, Hawkins & Thorpe
A. K. Stothert, Esq.	F. E. Metcalfe, Esq.

A fact worthy of the attention of all interested in such vehicles as vans, 'buses, &c., for London as well as country traffic is that I am receiving repeat orders from the London and North Western and Great Northern Railways, who have had IVEL Patent Ball Bearing Axles and Boxes fitted to such vehicles, some of which have been in constant use in London for some years past.

IVEL MOTOR CAR.

THE Ivel Motor Car is a vehicle which departs very much from the usual type now before the public. The frame is constructed of steel tubing, after the manner of the bicycle, and the arrangement of the tubes is such that all the various strains to which the frame is exposed, both from road vibration and that caused by the motor itself, are scientifically taken up, a double cantilever system being adopted. The frame is mounted upon the axles on four spiral springs, those of the rear axle being enclosed in steel cylinders which are inclined towards the rear of the car, in order that the springs may act in the same plane as the lines of vibration from the wheels. These cylinders further prevent any movement of one spring without a duplicate motion on the part of the other. The importance of this arrangement is very great, for it does what has not yet been previously accomplished upon cars having two chains, namely, keeps the chain wheels in proper alignment, thus, not only saving a great deal of friction, but also greatly prolonging the wearing powers of the chains. The front axle springs are vertical, and are designed to allow the wheels to rise or fall to accommodate themselves to the inequalities of the road. Upon this frame, the petrol motor, which is of five horse power (and of English manufacture, the ignition being electric), is carried, while the body of the car, designed to seat four persons, is supported upon four "Cee" springs, being thus entirely separate from the frame and working parts. By this means the occupants of the car are completely insulated from the vibration of the motor, as well as from that caused by road inequalities, and, in addition to this, a different body can at any time be attached to the frame in a few minutes, so that the purchaser may have practically two or three cars to one frame and motor. To tradesmen and others this is a great advantage. The main brakes act upon steel drums within the chain wheels. A pair of tyre brakes are also provided, while the lever which applies these is so arranged that when pushed forward it automatically opens a switch, thus breaking the current of the electric ignition and so stopping the motor. These tyre brakes are really only used in cases of emergency. A great feature of the Ivel car is that all the levers are within easy reach of the driver while the steering is remarkably steady, being controlled by a chain, and therefore free from the shake inevitable where a number of jointed rods are employed. It should also be noted that the motor is started from the driver's seat without the employment of a detachable crank, which is always objectionable on account of its liability to fly off should the motor back fire. The petrol tank is situated under the front seat and is a long way from the motor, so that the car is proof against fire. The tank holds close upon nine gallons, which is sufficient to run the vehicle a couple of hundred miles. The water tank is also of large capacity and a hundred miles can be covered before a fresh supply is required. Four cooling tubes pass through the tank and take the place of the condenser commonly employed, while placing the water tank well above the motor does away with the necessity of automatic pumps and their attendant complications. Two or three speed gearing is provided and also a reversing gear which allows the car to be backed if necessary. The motor and chains are enclosed, so that the cleaning and wear are greatly reduced. A convenient box is fitted behind the back seat to convey tools, the necessary accumulator and induction coil. The motor is so arranged that the flywheel runs in the same direction as the car, and a certain amount of power is thus saved which would otherwise be wasted, and is wasted with many other motor cars now manufactured. Moreover, as the driving belts are not crossed but run straightly between the pulleys, there is a considerable saving in friction. With these advantages, in addition to the fact that they are fitted with Ivel patent ball bearings, which are larger and wider apart than usual, it has been found that the motor does work equal to that performed by cars fitted with six-horse power engines and naturally at a very much less cost. The convenience of the driver has been most carefully studied and it should be noted that every part of the machinery can be easily reached, so that all adjustments can be made with the greatest nicety without the trouble usually involved. As stated in the Introduction (page 5) this car has been most successful in all kinds of tests and may be thoroughly relied upon.

18

IDEAL CAR (Benz System).

These Cars are propelled by patent spirit gas motors. They are 3 h.p. and have 3 speeds, and are fitted with patent wired-on solid rubber tyres and powerful brakes.

They are very efficient cars and will seat 3 persons.

THE VICTORIA—Combination.

These Cars have been made to meet a growing demand for a rather small carriage to seat 2 persons side by side. They are fitted with a De Dion-Bouton 2¼ h.p. motor with electric ignition. They have 2 speeds, and are fitted with most powerful brakes.

Particulars, prices, &c., of Motor Tricycles and other kinds of Cars, can be had on application.

19

Extracts from Testimonials.

CYCLES.

The Hon. Mrs. HASTINGS, Myton, Warwick, November 1st, 1899.

" I am delighted with the IVEL bicycle, it has given me every satifaction."

The Hon. Mrs. ASTELL, Hazlewood, Kings Langley, Jan. 4th, 1899.

" The bicycles are very satisfactory."

Miss A. P. HAINES, Westmill House, Ware.

" I have now had the machine about a year and am pleased to say it has always given me every satisfaction. I shall be pleased to strongly recommend your machines to my friends."

Miss S. HESKETH, 6, Castle Road, Bedford, June 13th, 1899.

" I like the machine very much and it runs very easily and looks very nice."

Mrs. BLACKWOOD, Norton Court, Sittingbourne, Kent, March 8th, 1898.

" I cannot speak too highly of the machine. It is quite perfect and so very easy and comfortable, I shall always recommend IVELS."

Mrs. L. RECKETT, c/o Major Reckett, R.A.M.C., North Camp, Aldershot, August 25th, 1899.

" I like the machine very much and it exactly fits me."

Miss RINTOUL, Butler House, High Wycombe, July 3rd, 1899.

" I am much pleased with the bicycle."

Miss GREGORY, Deanery, St. Pauls, E.C., Nov. 8th, 1898.

" Miss Alice Gregory is delighted with the bicycle."

Miss M. THOMPSON, Ashdale, Stamford, January 25th, 1899.

" I am very pleased indeed with the IVEL bicycle you have made for me."

Miss JESSIE G. YOUNG, Westbook, House, Faringdon, Berks., August 2nd, 1898.

" I like the appearance of the machine immensely and find it very comfortable to ride, it runs so smoothly that I find it easier to guide than any machine I have hitherto ridden."

Mrs. CLIFFORD SMITH, The Old House, Totteridge, May, 16th, 1898.

" I am delighted with my bicycle ; it is most comfortable and suits me perfectly."

Miss ADELAIDE PYM, The Firs, Ampthill, October 3rd, 1898.

" I am much pleased with the tricycle as it runs so lightly."

Miss F. A. COOPER, 8, Ashley Place, S.W.

" I am very pleased with the tricycle you made for me."

20

EXTRACTS FROM TESTIMONIALS (CYCLES)—continued.

Miss ROSIE JOHNSTONE, Rothsay, Cowes, Isle of Wight, Nov. 7th, 1899.
   " I received the bicycle in perfect condition this morning and I am very pleased with it."

Mrs. JOSSELYN, Banstead, Bedford, May 24, 1899.
   " Miss Bulkley Hughes is very pleased with her machine and I think it is a very nice one."

Mrs. SINCLAIR, Arundel House, Fulham, S.W., March 21st, 1898.
   " I am much pleased with my IVEL bicycle."

Miss N. ASHFIELD, Fen Ditton Rectory, Cambridge, April 15th, 1898.
   " I am exceedingly pleased with my bicycle and consider it the nicest I have ever ridden."

Miss WYNTER, 1, Rockingham Place, Eastbourne, May 27th, 1898.
   " I am much pleased with the appearance of the machine and particularly with the lightness and ease of motion.   I will certainly recommend IVELS."

Miss M. M. NORTON, 13, Hilgrove Road, South Hampstead, Jan. 20th, 1899.
   " I have now had the bicycle for more than two years and am still extremely satisfied with it."

Miss AUGUSTA MARY WING, Market Overton, Oakham, May 6th, 1899.
   " The machine runs beautifully and it is a great pleasure to ride it."

A. W. W. DALE, Esq., Trinity Hall, Cambridge, Oct. 9th, 1899.
   " The machine is all one can wish; it is better even than the old one, and that is saying much."

Sir HUGH BEEVOR, Bart., M.D., 17, Wimpole Street, London, W., May 7th, 1898.
   " I am very satisfied with the machine."

GEORGE TURNER, Esq., 40, St. John's, Bedford, June 25th, 1898.
   " I am exceedingly pleased in every way with the machine.   It runs so smoothly and easily.   The general appearance of the bicycle and its smartness have been remarked upon by a number of my friends."

MONTAGUE LOFTUS, Esq., H.B.M. Consulate, Ajaccio, Feb. 1st, 1898.
   " Both Mrs. Loftus and myself are exceedingly pleased with the machines and they get a great deal of admiration.

Sir EDWARD JENKINSON, 2, High Beach, Felixstowe, Suffolk.
   " All the machines which you have supplied to my order have given great satisfaction."

T. MONAGHAN, Esq., Stroud, June 6th, 1898.
   " I think there is no machine like the IVEL.   I have not had to touch the bearings or any nuts yet."

The Hon. Lieut.-Col. CHRICTON, 38, Walton Street, London, S.W., June 23rd, 1898.
   " I like the bicycle very much indeed, and am always glad to recommend your bicycles."

PERCIVAL BOSANQUET, Esq., Ponfield, Near Hertford, January 6th, 1900.
   " The tricycle runs uncommonly well."

C. W. PATCHELL, Esq., Trinity College, Glenalmond, Perth, Feb. 13th, 1899.
   " I am delighted with the running of the machine and with the comfort of its fit.   All my friends here admire the general lines on which the machine is built and its external finish."

The Hon. MARK McDONNELL, Mount Pleasant, Old Warden, Beds., Nov. 15th, 1898.
   " I have ridden the bicycle you made for me 4500 miles, and it is as good as on the day I bought it."

21

EXTRACTS FROM TESTIMONIALS (CYCLES)—continued.

Lieut.-Col. EVERARD, Roydon, King's Lynn, Aug. 26th 1898.

" The machine gives every satisfaction and runs beautifully."

Dr. W. BELGARIE, The Dutch House, Winchfield, June 9th, 1899.

" I thought it would interest you to know how the bicycle which you supplied me with three years ago has gone on. I have ridden it 13000 miles or more and it now goes almost as well as when I first had it. I am accustomed to ride the bicycle through every weather and over any ground and so I consider it speaks very highly for its construction."

EDWARD WAHAB, Esq., 14, St. Mary Axe, E.C.

" I like the new machine very much."

The Hon. MOWBRAY ST. JOHN, Weybridge, May 9th, 1899.

" I received my bicycle all right and find it is most satisfactory. I have ridden it a good deal lately and it goes splendidly."

WILLIAM TENNANT, Esq., Paulsgrove, Cosham, Hants.

" The bicycle gives me every satisfaction."

FRANK J. POTTER, Esq., 1, Verulam Buildings, Gray's Inn, W.C., Jan. 30, 1899.

" I have now ridden the machine about 1300 miles and have not turned a nut or a screw, nor opened the gear case except to put oil in through the lubricator."

Lord AMPTHILL, 109, Park Street, London, W., Feb. 15th, 1898.

" I am much pleased with the new bicycles."

G. W. MANNING, Esq., Surveyor's Office, London Road, Ashford, Staines, January 4th, 1899.

" My machine has carried me splendidly all through this winter, in fact I have been riding it almost continuously instead of driving."

The Hon. HENRY B. O. St. JOHN, Magdalene College, Cambridge, May 31st, 1898.

" I am exceedingly pleased with the bicycle."

R. H. DUN, Esq., Walsingham, Chislehurst, August 16th, 1899.

" The more I use the bicycle the better I am pleased with it."

GORDAN HOOPER, Esq., 44, Devonshire Street, Harley Street, W., August 5th, 1898.

" I have tried the bicycle and find it goes beautifully."

Lord NAPIER OF MAGDALA, 9, Loundes Square, London, Jan. 9th, 1899.

" I have bought two bicycles from you—one has been running **3 years** at home and abroad, the other **2 years,** without any need of repairs, and to ride they have been as good as the best."

BRIDGE HOUSE, HUNTINGDON,
June 18th, 1898.

DEAR SIR,

You will be pleased to hear the Car ran home last Saturday alright after we parted with you. We were out on Monday, Tuesday, Wednesday and Friday and the Car performed FIRST RATE. The other night we ran to Norman Cross and back *via* Stukleys, and the Car took all hills both going and coming back. I shall be pleased to show the Car to any intending purchaser and you can make any use of this letter as you please,

Yours truly, BATEMAN BROWN.

N.B.—I am now making a new IVEL Motor Car for Mr. Brown.

22

TESTIMONIALS
Re Ball Bearing Carriage & Motor Car Axles.

MRS. OSBORN.   CHICKSANDS PRIORY, SHEFFORD,
                                                                October 5th, 1898.
          "I am delighted with the Phæton which has your Ball Bearing Axles and Boxes
fitted."

MRS. B. HAWORTH-BOOTH.   ROLSTON HALL, HORNSEA, HULL,
                                                                August 18th, 1898.
          The Ball Bearings you fitted to my Pony Cart are certainly a very great advantage,
as it now runs so easily.

CAPT. G. R. BETHELL, M.P.   SIGGLESTHORNE, HULL,
                                                                August 3rd, 1897.
          "I like the Ball Bearing wheels.   The trap runs very easily."

LORD ALWYNE COMPTON, M.P.   7, BALFOUR PLACE, PARK LANE, W.
                                                                January 15th, 1899.
          I have much pleasure in testifying to the success of the Ball Bearing Axles which
you fitted to my brougham.   After a practical trial of over a year, I have no hesitation in
saying that the advantages gained in the case of a carriage of heavy draught (such as a
brougham is) can not be exaggerated.   It reduces the draught so much that quite a light horse
can manage it, and the carriage runs smoothly and well as far as the occupant is concerned.   I
consider these Ball Bearings are an advantage in any carriage whether for London or for the
country.

A. TYRELL, ESQ.   BERKIN MANOR, HORTON, SLOUGH,
          SIR,   *May 28th, 1897.*
          The Ball Bearings which I had fitted to the Carriage and Dog Cart are capital ;
we like them very much.

MR. DAN ALBONE,   EAST THORPE, READING,
          DEAR SIR,   *November, 1896.*
          I am desired by Mr. ALFRED PALMER to say he finds the introduction of the Ball
Bearings has done away with the drumming in the brougham.   They run very nicely, and
have made it much easier for the horses.
                              I am, yours truly, H. H. JONES, *Secretary.*
          MR. PALMER, in giving his opinion of the Ivel Ball Bearing Axles and Boxes privately,
says :—" I did not have new wheels put to my brougham, but Albone had the old wheels
and supplied axle trees with his own patent Ball Bearings.   They have only been on about
three weeks, so that I cannot say anything as to whether they wear well, although I see no
reason why they should not, but as regards the easy running I am perfectly satisfied.   The
horses trot up hills which they used to walk up, and the drumming in the brougham of which
we used to complain has been completely silenced.   One of the horses which we never used
singly, because he was not strong enough, now draws the brougham about the town nicely."

ARTHUR J. CLAY, ESQ.   HOLLY BUSH, BURTON-ON-TRENT,
                                                                August 4th, 1897.
          "I am very much pleased at the way in which the Ball Bearing wheels have
stood."
          N.B.—These wheels have now been running nearly 3½ years.

A. K. STOTHERT, ESQ.   53, VICTORIA STREET, WESTMINSTER,
                                                                February 28th, 1900.
          I have now run my brougham for two years with your Ball Bearings, during which time
I have only had to adjust them once.   They have more than answered my expectations.

MR. D. CAMPBELL.   CAMBRIDGE ROAD, HASTINGS,
                                                                January 3rd 1900.
          I am very pleased to tell you that the axles which you supplied in July 1898, have
given unqualified satisfaction to me and my customers.

23

PRESS NOTICES.

"The Irish Cyclist," November 30th, 1898.

The Stanley Show would lack an interesting feature if the time honoured " Dan " were not there with his faithful IVELS. Though working on rather unconventional lines and preferring to teach the public rather than feed its every whim, DAN ALBONE has built up a steady business and caters for a school in enthusiastic clients who include some of England's best riders. The IVELS are the outcome of long experience, and are made with a care and precision which the hasty methods of many modern makes do not allow of. An individuality is given to each machine. It is not an incongruous assemblage of parts, but a compact instrument of "life" and speed. Twelve machines in all were shown by him, and these included two dainty road racers and a racer built on grand speed lines. He showed some ladies' machines of a new pattern, which are at once graceful and strong, and have every indication of possessing the good running qualities of all the IVELS.

"The Ladies' Field," December 3rd, 1898.

" The New Ladies' IVEL is, both in theory and practice, an admirable cycle."

"Cyclists' Touring Club Gazette," July, 1897.

SIR,—Having read your correspondent's letter, headed " A Plaint from Gibralter," and as a cyclist who for a good many years has suffered from agents and makers, I should like to mention my this year's experience, which stands in pleasing contrast with a past list of annoyances and disappointments. Being in the neighbourhood of Biggleswade, I heard much of the excellence of the Ivel bicycle, manufactured there by Dan Albone, and ordered a machine for myself. I allowed a month, but it was invoiced to me as completed within a fortnight. Being much pleased with the result, I then ordered a lady's machine. It was promised within a fortnight, but completed within ten days. The lady only objected to the narrowness of the saddle (a Brooks), and this was immediately changed for a broader and costlier one (another Brookes'), without extra charge. In fact, the particular attentive, obliging and generous dealing of the maker with me throughout, down to the smallest details, has been quite a novel experience. I also consider that very exceptional value is given with these machines for the prices. In heartily commending it to your readers, I hope that it is superfluous for me to add that my testimony is entirely honest and disinterested.

A HAMPSHIRE CLERGYMAN (32,953).

Copy of Illuminated Testimonial presented to me by a large number of Cyclists who frequented the North Road :—

November 29th, 1885.

DEAR DAN,

The cyclists visiting Biggleswade having for many years past received at your hands at all times and at all hours numerous acts of kindness and self-denying attention, desire to express to you their hearty thanks for the considerate treatment you have invariably shown them, and the assistance you have rendered by pace-making for them when racing or during long-distance rides, and in numerous other ways, doing all in your power to adminster to their comfort and convenience. They also wish to make some slight acknowledgment of your exertions on their behalf and combining to express to you their high opinion of your sterling good qualities, request your acceptance of a tangible token of their regard in the shape of a **Gold Chain**, which they hope you will accept and wear with the consciousness of its being a tribute of the esteem in which you are held by the subscribers.

THE AUTO CAR.

December 3rd, 1898.

Earl and Countess Cowper recently entertained a large party of distinguished guests at their beautiful seat at Wrest Park, near Silsoe. Mr. Dan Albone, the well-known cycle manufacturer of Biggleswade, drove out in his motor car, and had the honour of taking the following notable personages in the car : Earl and Countess Cowper, Right Hon. A. J. Balfour, M.P., Lord Cranbourne, M.P., Hon. A. Lyttleton, M.P., and Mrs. Lyttleton, Lord Warkworth, M.P., Lord and Lady York, Lord and Lady Hythe, Countess Gleichen Féodor, Mr. and Lady Margaret Graham, Major and Mrs. Drummond, Hon. and Mrs. R. Spencer, W. H. Grenfell and Family, Lady Edward Cecil, Mr. Bagot, Mr. Charteris, Lord Alwyne Compton, M.P., Mr. M. Baring, Major Putteney, all of whom were highly pleased with the behaviour of the vehicle. This is not the first occasion on which Mr. Albone has had distinguished persons as passengers on his car, for not long since, the Duke and Duchess of Bedford, Marquis of Tavistock, Marquis of Granby, the Rev. Lord William and Lady Cecil, Lord St. John, Lord and Lady Ampthill, Lady Barbara Smith, Hon. George Peel, Hon. Agnes Peel, Guy Pym, Esq., M.P., Sir Edward and Lady Mallett, Sir Algernon Osborn, Bart., Major F. Shuttleworth, Miss Agnes Keyser, Lord Basil Blackwood Sir John Burgoyne, the Dowager Lady Ampthill, The Hon. Constance Russell, C. A. Park, Esq., the Countess of Dysart, the Hon. F. Stanley, Captain G. Dundas, Mrs. F. J. Josselyn, John Harvey, Esq., Cecil F. Parr, Esq., C. S. Lindsell, Esq., J.P., Sir Lepel Henry Griffin, Lady Griffin, F. L. Cook, Esq., M.P., G. J. Gribble, Esq., J.P., G. Kemp, Esq., M.P., G. P. Evans, Esq., the Hon. Mowbray A. T. St. John and many others have had a ride upon it.

24

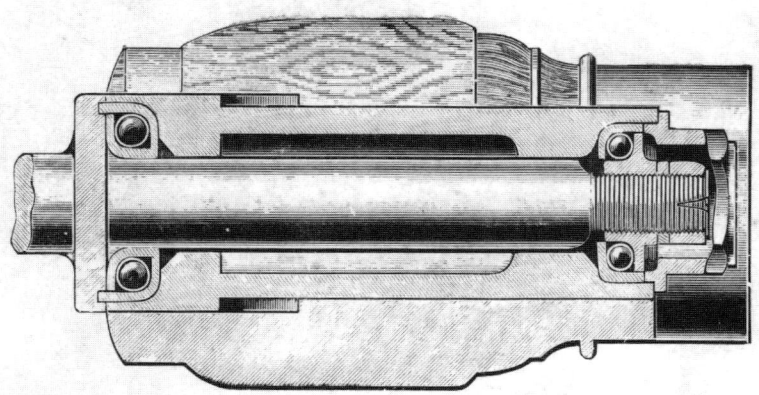

ILLUSTRATED PRICE LIST

TELEGRAPHIC ADDRESS:
DAN ALBONE, BIGGLESWADE.

IVEL·CYCLES 1902

AND Ball-Bearing Carriage Axles and Boxes.

DAN ALBONE

Manufactured by

DAN ALBONE,
Biggleswade,
Beds.

View of the River Ivel which runs through Biggleswade.

BLACKSMITHS' SHOP AT THE
IVEL WORKS.

Blacksmiths

ILLUSTRATED
PRICE LIST
OF THE

IVEL CYCLES,

MOTOR CYCLES,

ALSO

Ball Bearing Carriage Axles and Boxes and
Motor Cars,

ESTABLISHED 22 YEARS.

Manufactured by

DAN ALBONE,

BIGGLESWADE,

Beds.

FOR 1902.

TELEGRAPHIC ADDRESS:
DAN ALBONE, BIGGLESWADE

CARLING & CO., PRINTERS, HITCHIN.

Terms of Business.

CASH against Invoice to Customers having no Ledger Account.

CARRIAGE in all cases to be paid by **Purchaser.**

REPAIRS. Machines or parts will not be received unless sent **Carriage Paid** with full Name and Address of Sender at back of label. Invoices are sent out when the work is complete. In no case can repairs be booked, my terms being Nett Cash on receipt of invoice. I am compelled to insist on this owing to the difficulty experienced in collecting small accounts and the cost of booking and postage when numerous applications for payment have to be made, this often taking the whole profit off repairs. Enquiries respecting machines receive immediate attention.

CRATES are charged Cost Price, and are NOT RETURNABLE.

NOTICES TO PURCHASERS.

Most of my Machines are made specially to order, thus giving more satisfaction to the Purchaser and myself. All I require is the inside measurement of leg, from fork to ball of foot, and the weight of rider. Easy payments are arranged when required by customers, and, if desired, old machines are taken in exchange as part payment.

A Large Stock of all kinds of Accessories such as LAMPS, OIL and ACETYLENE, BELLS, TYRE INFLATORS, &c., &c., always kept in Stock. A large number of **Second=hand Machines** are always on sale at very low prices.

SPECIAL.

ALL KINDS OF COPPER AND NICKEL PLATING DONE ON THE PREMISES. I ALSO HAVE A SPECIAL PLANT FOR SILVERING SUCH ARTICLES AS FORKS, SPOONS, CRUETS, TRAYS, &c. See detailed List, to be had on application.

FORM OF GUARANTEE.

I Guarantee, subject to the conditions mentioned below, that all precautions which are usual and reasonable have been taken by me to secure excellence of materials and workmanship in all my Machines, and I undertake to make good, at any time within twelve months of this date, any defects which result from inherent flaws or defective workmanship, and are not caused by wear and tear, misuse or neglect.

CONDITIONS.—If a defective part should be found in any of my Machines, it must be sent to me **Carriage Paid** and accompanied by an intimation from the Sender that he desires to have it repaired free of charge under the guarantee. The number of the Machine must be quoted.

Failing compliance with this rule no notice will be taken of anything that may arrive, but such articles will lie here at the risk of the Sender.

This Guarantee does not apply to the specialities of other Firms, such as Tyres, Gear Cases, Saddles, Tool Bags, Lamps, Bells, &c., but the makers of these, whose names usually appear thereon, are in nearly every case willing to replace defective parts, and I will at all times furnish the maker's name as a proof of the quality.

N.B.—This guarantee does not apply to Motor Bicycles or Motor Cars. These are guaranteed to be in perfect order when leaving the works. No other guarantee is given or implied,

2

Introduction.

❦❦❦❦❦❦

THIS being the 21st issue of the Catalogue of **Ivel Cycles**, marks its "coming of age," and this important epoch of its career must not pass without my once more tendering to my friends and the public generally, my hearty thanks for their continued patronage and business recommendations.

The list of some of the

UNSOLICITED TESTIMONIALS

which I again include on pages 21, 22 and 23, give ample evidence of the maintenance of that quality in

IVEL CYCLES

which has ever made them second to none, and that quality is the

ABSOLUTELY BEST

combined with fair prices for the **best goods**.

The system I introduced 8 years ago of listing machines at their nett cash prices (see pages 10, 12, 13 and 15), still proves acceptable to buyers, and my constant efforts during the coming season will be to enhance the reputation of **IVELS** by embodying in them the highest grade of material and workmanship, combined with my own long and varied experience in their manufacture.

I am always prepared to wait upon customers by appointment, either personally or by MR. GEORGE COURSE, my chief representative, and either at my works or elsewhere. I think it well to remind customers of the great advantage of easy communication by G.N.R. between London (King's Cross Terminus or any of their Depots) and Biggleswade station, enabling repairs to machines to be effected and returned in a very short time, and allowing of expedition in delivery of machines generally. To have the necessary repairs executed by the workmen who built the machines is an important consideration.

4

I shall be pleased at any time to receive a personal visit at the works from any prospective buyers, and shall be glad to show them over the works where they may examine the **IVELS** in the various stages of manufacture.

IVEL PATENT BALL BEARINGS

for Vehicles, such as Dog Carts, Vans, Buses, &c., also Motor Cars still form a staple item in my productions, and have only to be used to be appreciated. Here again I have the experience of many years to guide me in producing the best article, and one which I may claim to be a **Speciality.** At the end of the Catalogue will be found some of the testimonials as to these Ball Bearings.

IVEL MOTOR CYCLES.

The season of 1901 saw the introduction of a practicable form of **Motor Bicycle** and a steady demand at once set in for this form of vehicle. Realising its practicability, I was among the very earliest to adapt the Motor to IVEL CYCLES, and there is no other Motor Cycle **more renowned.** The numerous samples I have already supplied to customers have given unqualified satisfaction. One of the great points of superiority in a Motor Bicycle is the small space necessary for its storage, another is the small amount it costs for fuel, for 100 miles can be ridden for the small sum of about one shilling. These I venture to think will prove its best **Selling Points.** The manipulation of the machine is a simple matter; and every facility will be given to buyers to master any little technicality that is not at first clear.

Although anticipating a big demand in 1902 for the **Ivel Motor Bicycle,** I shall still be prepared to supply **Motor Cars,** and am agent for almost every type of well-known Car as heretofore; and will place my wide experience in this department at the disposal of intending purchasers.

I shall be always glad to give my best and prompt attention to enquiries; and any orders that are entrusted to me will receive my personal attention, and be executed in such a manner as to maintain the high reputation that **IVELS** have acquired in the past.

DAN ALBONE,

SOLE PROPRIETOR.

5

LIST OF PATRONS.

Her Grace the Duchess of
 Bedford
Marchioness of Tweeddale
Marchioness of Granby
Countess Cowper
Countess Grey
Countess of Listowel
Countess de Grey
Countess of Guildford
Countess Rosslyn
Lady Dora Yeoman
Lady Colthurst
Lady Oxenbridge
Lady Bertie
Lady Constance Harris
Lady Barbara Smith
Lady Brabourne
Lady Lawson
Lady Napier of Magdala
Lady Margaret Cameron of
 Lochiel
Lady Ampthill
Lady Griffin
Lady St. John
Lady Primrose
The Honble. Mrs. Bagot
The Honble. Mrs. Forbes
The Honble. Mrs. Astell
The Hon. Mrs. Charles Brand
The Honble. Constance Russell
The Honble. Mrs. Hastings
Mrs. M. S. Reeves
Mrs. John Sinclair
Mrs. G. Barnett
Mrs. F. J. Josselyn
Mrs. Barnett
Mrs. Heysham
Mrs. C. Kerr
Mrs. S. Bruce
Mrs. Cooke
Mrs. E. G. Taddy
Mrs. C. Payne

Mrs. W. Earle
Mrs. Madeline McCarty
Mrs. Blackwood
Mrs. E. Lennox Peel
Mrs. W. Appleton
Mrs. C. F. Lindsell
Mrs. E. Osborn
Mrs. Lawson
Mrs. S. Scott
Mrs. Gibson Carmichael
Mrs. Algernon Talbot
Mrs. Duberly
Mrs. J. Trotter
Mrs. D. H. F. Peploe
Mrs. A. Tyrell
Mrs. D. Stuart
Mrs. R. Orde
Mrs. M. P. Foster
Mrs. J. Richardson
Mrs. Jervoise Huddleston
Mrs. Griffith Jones
Mrs. Elmhurst
Mrs. Gribble
Mrs. Pechy Phipson, M.D.
Mrs. Middleton
Mrs. Callander
Mrs. Frank Penn
Mrs. Charlotte Villiers
Mrs. H. G. Thornton
Mrs. L. Mounteney Jephson
Mrs. Oscar Berry
Mrs. E. Hill
Mrs. Henniker
Mrs. Mitchell Gill
Mrs. Sam Hopkins
Mrs. R. A. Baxter
Mrs. Clifford Smith
Mrs. Ben Haworth-Booth
Mrs. Sumner
Mrs. Reckett
Mrs. J. Atkinson
Mrs. Coldham

Mrs. St. Quintin
Mrs. Evan Hanbury
Mrs. Wilfred Kempe
Mrs. Alexandra Landale
Mrs. Harold Brocklebank
Mrs. Madeline S. Beaden
Miss Sutton Sams
Miss Bulkeley Hughes
Miss F. Keyser
Miss C. Astell
Miss M. Dimsdale
Miss F. Cochrane
Miss O. Marshall
Miss N. Hulbert
Miss E. Lindsell
Miss L. Hawksley
Miss E. F. Humphries
Miss Archdale
Miss St. Quintin
Miss Beatrice Stuart-Wortley
Miss E. Williams
Miss Hawkinson
Miss K. Ladds
Miss A. H. Prior
Miss Helen Douglas
Miss May Irwin
Miss G. Archdale
Miss D. Pierson
Miss Agnes Keyser
Miss L. Bernard
Miss Batchelor
Miss E. Wilshere
Miss M. F. Pritchard
Miss B. Greenfield
Miss Sinclair
Miss E. Gregory
Miss K. M. F. Brooks
Miss K. L. Laurance
Miss C. Hulbert
Miss E. Gibbs
Miss Holt
Miss Geraldine Magniac

6

LIST OF PATRONS—continued.

Miss F. J. Dewar
Miss Constance Cochrane
Miss Chamberlayne
Miss M. Tryon
Miss Tait
Miss Briscoe
Miss Ethel Hartley
Miss H. Coltman
Miss C. J. Wood
Miss E. Phipps
Miss Marion Cureton
Miss Aimée Curll
Miss H. Chapman
Miss A. E. Gregory
Miss Constance Pym
Miss Adelaide Pym
Miss M. Thompson
Miss Caroline Astell
Miss A. P. Haines
Miss M. Humphries
Miss M. Grierson
Miss Beatrice Dunbar Kilburn
Miss K. Rintoul
Miss D. Higgins
Miss L. M. Richardson
Miss W. Barker
Miss A. K. Higgins
Miss Ada St. Quinton
Miss Winckworth
Miss Margaret Talbot
Miss Alice Williams
Miss Harnet
Miss O. Hulbert
Miss Aikenhead
Miss Mary Pearson
Miss S. Hesketh
Miss Augusta Mary Wing
Miss J. C. Palmer
Miss Dunbar Kilburn
Miss M. Tower
Miss F. A. Cooper
Miss J. Craven
Miss Johnson
Miss E. Shaw-Lefevre
Miss C. A. J. Dimsdale
Miss E. Hewetson

Miss Mortlock
Miss Olive Hill
Miss D. Hill
His Grace the Duke of Bedford
Marquis of Tweeddale
Marquis of Granby
Marquis of Northampton
Viscount Peel
Earl Grey
Earl Jersey
Earl of Mount Edgcumbe
Earl Scarborough
Lord Edward Hay
Lord Napier of Magdala
Lord Massey
Lord St. John
Lord Ampthill
Lord Alwyne Compton, M.P.
Sir Algernon Osborn, Bart.
Lord Arthur Hay
Rev. Lord Wm. Cecil
Count Deym

Austrian Embassy

Viscount Duncannon
Monsieur Bolatzell

Russian Embassy

Capt. the Hon. H. S. Davey
Sir T. O'Brien, Bart.
Sir Robert Turin
Sir Robert Edgcumbe
Sir Edward Jenkinson
Sir Hugh R. Beevor, Bart. M.D.
Sir Arthur de Copell Brooke
Sir John Burgoyne, Bart.
The Rt. Hon. A. Graham Murray, M.P. (Lord Advocate).
The Honble. C. A. Pelham
The Honble. Mark McDonnell
The Honble. G. Peel
The Honble. M. B. Peel
The Hon. Henry B. O. St. John
The Honble. Roland St. John
The Honble. Col. Crichton
The Honble. Mowbray A. T. St. John

The Hon. Alfred Lyttelton, K.C., M.P.
The Honble. Spencer Lyttelton
Colonel Law
Colonel Astell
Colonel Gregson
Colonel Blane
Colonel Oldham
Colonel Ellison
Colonel Josselyn
Colonel Jackson
Colonel M. Bowers
Colonel J. Burne
Colonel Hunt
Colonel Johnson
Colonel V. Dawson
Colonel Cumberlege
Colonel Young
Colonel R. K. Ridgway, V.C.
Colonel F. Shuttleworth
Lieut.-Col. A. W. Bentley
Lieut.-Col. Everard
Lieut.-Col. Broughton
Surgeon Lieut.-Col. Crombie
Major R. C. Broome
Major Elmhirst
Major M. Block
Major Braithwaite
Major J. M. Richardson
Captain G. G. Lang
Capt. Com. The Hon. Seymour Fortescue
Captain G. R. Bethell
The Rt. Honble. J. G. Talbot, M.P.
Com. P. H. Wright, R.N.
Major H. Hoare
Major James
Major-Gen. T. B. Bevan
Major A. Duberly
Major F. A. B. Talbot
Major Mellor
Major G. Haines
Major A. H. Block, R.A.
Captain Street, R.N.
Lieut. Chas. Bissett, R.N.

7

LIST OF PATRONS—continued.

Captain C. H. Fenwick
Captain Duberly
Captain C. J. Briggs, R.N.
Captain Leetham
Captain Dugald Stuart
Captain Stapylton Marshall
Captain Perkins
Captain H. M. Stanley
Captain H. A. Street
Captain J. C. Blunt, R.A.
Captain F. Hulton
Captain Chas. Windham, R.N.
Captain N. G. Frazer
Captain J. P. Coote
Captain G. Francis Higgins
Captain A. J. Hills
Col. George Kemp, M.P.
Guy Pym, Esq., M.P.
B. C. Molloy, Esq.,
Ellis J. Griffiths, Esq., M.P.
Reginald McKenna, Esq. M.P.
T. R. Buchanan, Esq.,
Dr. Dent
Dr. H. Bond
Dr. T. W. Smyth
Dr. Welsh
Dr. R. R. Hatherell
Dr. Davies
Dr. Shaw
Dr. Syme
Dr. James
Dr. Emmerson
Dr. C. A. Lees
Dr. M. Cameron Blair
Dr. Mivart
Dr. T. P. Greenwood
The Right Rev. Lord Bishop of
    New Guinea
Rev. Ruston
Rev. C. M. Greenstreet
Rev. J. R. H. Duke
Rev. F. Jickling
Rev. T. S. Toolis
Rev. F. C. Hartley
Rev. F. Kinglake
Rev. W. P. Henderson

Rev. A. Kirke Smith
Rev. R. Hugh Gundry
Rev. F. Sullivan
Rev. Richardson
Rev. Gwynne
Rev. R. S. Bagshaw
Rev. A. A. Honey
Rev. E. P. Gatty
Rev. Watkins
Rev. C. B. Bevan
Rev. C. D. Ash
Rev. R. C. Whitworth
Rev. W. S. Edgell
Rev. C. H. Brocklebank
Rev. H. S. Payne
Rev. J. A. Hervey
Rev. J. Halliburton Young
Rev. G. M. Osborne
Rev. E. L. Colebrooke
Rev. R. Lang
Rev. L. Clutterbuck
Rev. N. Royds
Rev. Henry Moore
W. F. Archdale, Esq.
H. S. Whitbread, Esq.
S. Whitbread, Esq.
Algernon Gilliat, Esq.
Howard Gilliat, Esq.
Reginald B. Loder, Esq.
J. Harvey, Esq.
J. H. St. Q. Astell, Esq.
Bateman Brown, Esq.
Percival Bosanquet, Esq.
Lennox Peel, Esq.
F. Archdale, Esq.
H. J. B. Kendall, Esq.
W. A. Attenborough, Esq.
E. O. Fordham, Esq.
H. A. Vernet, Esq.
M. J. Godby, Esq.
F. F. Greenfield, Esq.
Robert Dimsdale, Esq.
J. H. Mossop, Esq.
J. T. Green, Esq.
Francis R. Pryor, Esq.
C. S. Lindsell, Esq.

R. J. Lindsell, Esq.
A. K. Lindsell, Esq.
H. M. Lindsell, Esq.
Gerald Smith, Esq.
Julian Godfrey, Esq.
Cyril B. Tubbs, Esq.
John Corrie Carter, Esq.
A. Harter, Esq.
C. F. St. Quintin, Esq.
C. M. Hodgkins, Esq.
A. Lewis Jones, Esq.
E. Morse, Esq.
William Tyrer, Esq.
Martin Pirie, Esq.
Philip Bright, Esq.
J. Dyson Moore, Esq.
J. N. Stuart, Esq.
A. Tyrell, Esq.
T. A. Gibb, Esq.
W. T. Nash, Esq.
R. C. V. Lang, Esq.
J. S. W. Blackett, Esq.
E. Snow Fordham, Esq.
A. Duberley, Esq.
J. E. Talbot, Esq.
J. W. Walter, Esq.
F. Penn, Esq.
W. Penn, Esq.
F. G. Payne, Esq.
W. H. B. Drayson, Esq.
J. H. Williams, Esq.
Redfern Williams, Esq.
S. F. Cotton, Esq.
J. G. O'Brien, Esq.
Edward O'Brien, Esq.
Willoughby Josselyn, Esq.
Arthur G. Murrell, Esq.
J. Clunes, Esq.
W. G. Quihampton, Esq.
G. A. Newton, Esq.
C. C. Jury, Esq.
F. A. V. Morse, Esq.
Sidney Morse, Esq.
H. Wakley, Esq.
S. R. Pryor, Esq.

8

LIST OF PATRONS—continued.

G. Hereford, Esq.	A. D. Carlisle Esq.	J. C. Monteith, Esq.
A. Rawlinson, Esq.	J. W. Orde, Esq.	J. F. St. Q. Archdale, Esq.
J. Leveson-Gower, Esq.	Montague Loftus, Esq.	R. H. Dun, Esq.
E. Talbot, Esq.	N. S. Talbot, Esq.	Theodore Thomson, Esq.
J. Phillips, Esq.	W. H. Haughton, Esq.	S. G. Wallis-Adams, Esq.
J. S. Wood, Esq.	John Russell Villiers, Esq.	H. B. Green, Esq.
A. F. Robertson, Esq.	C. T. Newton, Esq.	W. A. W. Dawn, Esq.
W. Jameson, Esq.	A. D. Tait, Esq.	Alex Landale, Esq.
Arthur Lane, Esq.	E. G. Cubitt, Esq.	Cecil F. Parr, Esq.
Beds. Constabulary	D. Henry T. Peploe, Esq.	E. S. A. Littlewood, Esq.
E. Preedy, Esq., F.S.I.	Henry J. L. Graham, Esq.	J. Annan Bryce, Esq.
W. Armstrong, Esq.	J. R. Clifton, Esq.	R. Taunton Raikes, Esq.
J. A. Pomeroy, Esq.	A. R. Berry, Esq.	Esme Howard Esq.
A. W. W. Dale, Esq.	D. Butler, Esq.	H. Temple Prior, Esq.
T. M. Bear, Esq.	Arthur J. Ashton, Esq.	C. R. Wade Gery, Esq.
W. A. St. Quintin, Esq.	Oswald Norman, Esq.	H. Chaundler, Esq.
J. G. W. James, Esq.	C. K. Baley, Esq.	Thomas Hartley, Esq.
H. A. Block, Esq.	Sydney Stephenson, Esq.	J. A. Bright, Esq.
G. P. Talbot, Esq.	W. Appleton, Esq.	C. W. Patchell, Esq.
W. C. Palceologues, Esq.	R. I. Dale, Esq.	J. McNab, Esq.
H. Tylston Hodgson, Esq.	Ben Haworth-Booth, Esq.	P. M. Buchanan, Esq.
G. V. Fiddes, Esq.	Joseph Smith, Esq.	Alfred J. Boult, Esq.
G. P. Evans, Esq.	F. N. Butler, Esq.	Arthur C. Beck, Esq.
George Hunt, Esq.	F. Giles, Esq.	Lockett Agnew, Esq.
A. J. Beckett, Esq.	H. H. Green, Esq.	Frank Gordon, Esq.
George Farquharson, Esq.	George Wilkinson, Esq.	E. E. St. Quinton, Esq.
F. G. Le Marchant, Esq.	W. H. Hulbert, Esq.	T. Hammond Clark, Esq.
Tobias Williams, Esq.	R. C. H. Millar, Esq.	H. A. Arkwright, Esq.
T. D. Lawrance, Esq.	E. M. Rendall, Esq.	H. E. A. Craven, Esq.
Arthur G. Kendall, Esq.	Jan Robertson, Esq.	H. B. Chinnery, Esq.
E. Evelyn Barron, Esq.	G. J. Bruce, Esq.	G. A. C. Thynne, Esq.
C. Alington, Esq.	C. S. Newton, Esq.	Kenneth Walker, Esq.
H. P. J. Cowell, Esq.	J. A. Kemp, Esq.	E. T. St. Quintin, Esq.
E. Lumley, Esq.	R. W. Wileman, Esq.	H. W. St. Quintin, Esq.
J. G. Gribble, Esq., J.P.	Gordon Hooper, Esq.	W. J. Thody, Esq.
Rimmington Wilson, Esq.	K. D. Hutchinson, Esq.	W. J. F. Giffard, Esq.
F. J. Thynne, Esq.	Marlborough R. Pryor, Esq.	A. R. Burton, Esq.
A. Crossman, Esq.	E. Wahab, Esq.	S. Stagoll Higham, Esq.
G. K. Paley, Esq.	C. C. James, Esq.	H. V. L. Kelham, Esq.
John Browning, Esq.	C. A. Turner, Esq.	R. W. Shaw, Esq.
J. Barker, Esq.	Leslie Keith, Esq.	C. T. Newbery, Esq.
F. Lowrey, Esq.	A. Clifford Smith, Esq.	N. A. Block, Esq.
A. C. Mitchell, Esq.	L. Dawson Campbell, Esq.	F. J. Jenkins, Esq.
W. Andrew, Esq.	Clarence Bird, Esq.	T. E. Hurst-Hodgson, Esq.
J. Taylor, Esq.	J. H. Dalton, Esq.	J. M. Fraser, Esq.
T. G. D. Hendley, Esq.	J. Page, Esq.	J. K. Lewis, Esq.

9

SUTTON, an old picturesque Village near Biggleswade.
Showing Bridge and Ford.

Ivel No. I

ROADSTER - SAFETY.

Specification.

Best steel weldless tubes, 28in. driving and 30in. steering wheels; tangent spokes; best ball bearings throughout; improved dust proof bottom bracket; barrel hubs, oil containing; bright parts heavily coppered and nickelled; steering lock; geared 63in. or to order; free or fixed wheel; two powerful rim brakes; detachable light metal mudguards; rubber or rat trap pedals; best quality saddle; tool bag; spanners; oil can; pump, &c. Weight as illustrated, 36lbs.

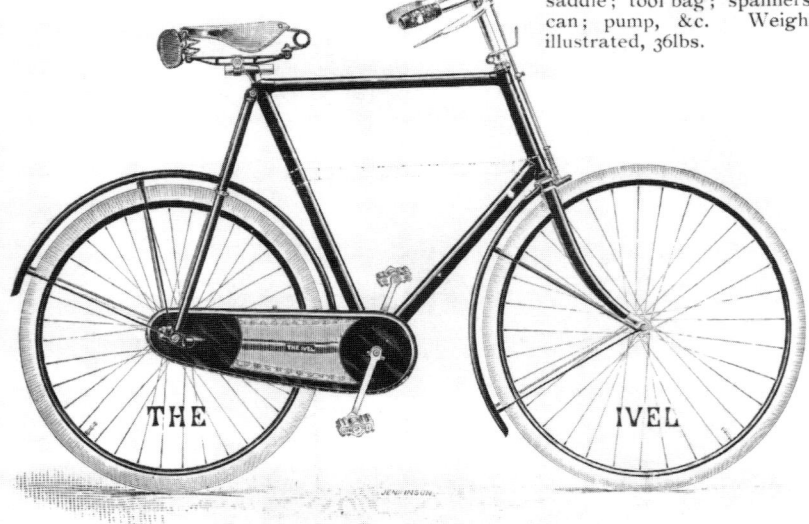

THE IVEL

This machine has a world-wide reputation as a splendid full roadster. It is easy running, and is capable of carrying any weight rider. For touring and general use it cannot be beaten. When made for exceptionally tall and heavy riders an extra tube in frame is used.

PRICE - £16.

Complete with Dunlop, "A" Clinchers, or other well-known pneumatic tyres, with hollow rims, and IVEL gear case.

EXTRAS.—Carter detachable gear case, 15/-; lining gold, 10/6; any other colour. 7/6; if enamelled any other colour than black, 7/6; if fitted with extra tube in frame as shown by dotted line, 15/-; plated rims, 10/-

Extract from *Cycling*, Nov. 26th, 1898.—"It is worth while to note cheery Dan Albone has, for the last few years, marked nett prices in his catalogue." (*See introduction, page 4.*)

10

A VIEW OF SUTTON
From the Bridge, showing Village and Church
in the distance.

Ivel No. 2

LIGHT - ROADSTER.

Specification.

Best weldless steel tubes; 28 in. driving and 30 in. steering wheels: improved dust proof bottom bracket: barrel hubs, oil containing; free or fixed wheel; two rim brakes; bright parts heavily coppered and nickelled; steering lock; tangent spokes; gear 68 in. or to order; best quality saddle; tool bag; spanners; oil can; pump, &c. Weight 28 lbs.

As a Light Roadster Bicycle this machine is unsurpassed. It was on this machine so many world's records were made in the early days of the present type of safety bicycle. It is made of the very best material procurable and is supplied with either fixed or free wheel.

PRICE - £16.

Complete with Dunlop, "A" Clincher, or other well-known pneumatic tires, with hollow rims, and IVEL gear case.

EXTRAS.—Carter detachable gear case, 15/-; lining gold, 10/6; any other colour, 7/6; if enamelled any other colour than black, 7/6; plated rims, 10/-

IVEL No. 3 ROAD RACER.—This machine is a light and speedy mount built specially suitable for fast riding. It is the best value in the cycle trade, and for ease of running is incomparable. Hollow rims; tangent spokes; fixed wheel; gear, 75 in. or to order; weight 25 lbs. **PRICE, £13 10/-** without brake, mudguards or gear case. If fitted with free wheel, two rim brakes, mudguards and gear case, **PRICE, £16 15/-**

EXTRAS.—Same as No. 2.

IVEL No. 4 PATH RACER.—This machine has been constructed throughout with due regard to lightness and strength, the maximum weight being about 21 lbs.

PRICE - £14.

11

THE MAYPOLE ON ICKWELL GREEN.

One of the prettiest and most old fashioned Village Greens in England.

Close to Biggleswade.

Ivel No. 5

LADY'S SAFETY.

Specification.

Strong dropped frame with double tubes; 28 in. wheels with barrel hubs, oil containing; free or fixed wheel; two rim brakes; bright parts heavily coppered and nickelled; steering lock; IVEL gear case, mudguards; best quality saddle; tool bag; spanners; oil can; pump, &c.

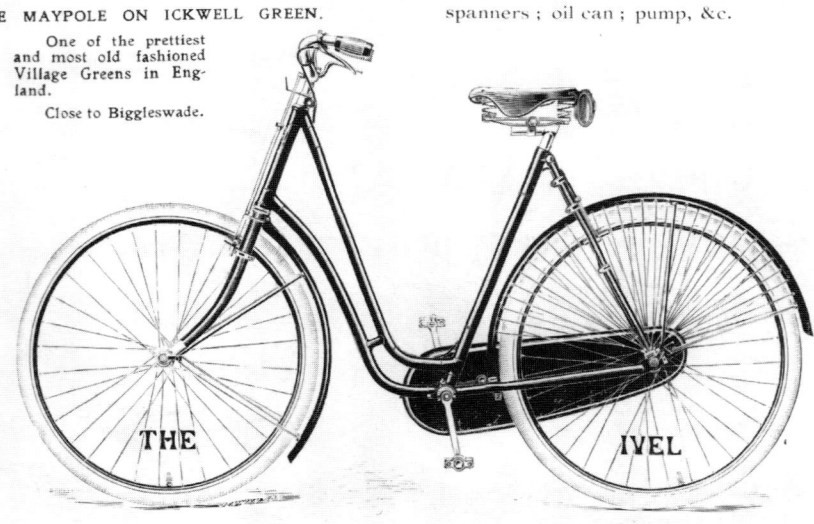

For sixteen years I have made this type of machine. The material, workmanship and finish, are of the highest quality and equal to many machines sold at higher prices. The popularity of this machine has never diminished since it was first put on the market.

PRICE - £16.

As illustrated with Dunlops, "A" Clinchers, or other well-known Pneumatic Tyres with hollow rims.

EXTRAS.—If fitted with Carter gear case instead of IVEL, 15/-; lining gold, 10/6; any other colour, 7/6; if enamelled any other colour than black, 7/6; plated rims, 10/-

For particulars of a cheaper machine, but of this pattern, see page 14.

Extract from *Athletic News*, Sept, 26th, 1898.—"Dan Albone was undoubtedly the first man to drop the discount system."

(*See Introduction, page 4.*)

Reprint of Lady's Safety which I advertised and sold 16 years ago.

12

NORTHILL CHURCH.
Near Biggleswade.

Ivel No. 6 ☙

LADY'S SAFETY.

Specification.

Strong frame with curved top tube and straight lower one; 28 in. wheels; barrel hubs, oil containing; free or fixed wheel; two rim brakes; bright parts heavily coppered and nickelled; steering lock; IVEL gear case, mudguards; best quality saddle; tool bag; spanner; oil can; pump, &c.

This type of IVEL Ladies' Safety is built to meet the special requirements of some of my customers who prefer the kind of frame as illustrated, to that of the No. 5. It is a smart cycle of the highest class, and is equal to the No. 5 in every respect as regards material and workmanship, and the price is the same. It has been a great success, having in each case given every satisfaction.

PRICE - £16.

As illustrated, with Dunlops, Clinchers, or other well-known pneumatic tyres, with hollow rims.

EXTRAS.—If fitted with Carter Gear Case instead of IVEL, 15/-; any other colour enamel but black, 7/6; lining gold, 10/6; any other colour, 7/6; plated rims, 10/-

---

Extract from *Cyclist*, Nov. 23rd, 1898.—**Now that nett prices** are coming into vogue, we must not forget to add that Dan Albone was one of **the first** to adopt the system **of nett prices;** in fact he may be considered quite a pioneer in the matter. (*See Introduction, page 4.*)

13

Ivel No. 7

ROADSTER SAFETY.

OLD WARDEN.
A Model Village near Biggleswade.

Specification.

Best weldless steel tubes; 28in. and 30in. wheels; tangent spokes; best ball bearings throughout; improved dust proof bottom bracket; plunger brake; mudguards; rubber or rat trap pedals.

PRICE - £11 10s.

Complete with "B" Clincher tyres, plunger brake and mudguards.

Ivel No. 5c

LADY'S SAFETY.

Specification.

Strong dropped frame with double tubes; 28in. wheels; IVEL gear case; plunger brake and mudguards; best ball bearings; improved dust proof bottom bracket.

PRICE - £11 17s. 6d.

Complete with "B" Clincher tyres, plunger brake, mudguards and IVEL gear case.

If desired, Free Wheel and Bowden Back Rim Brake can be fitted to either of the above Machines at an extra cost.

Owing to the demand for Machines at a somewhat less price than that of the highest grade Cycles, I have resolved to supply both a Gents.' and a Lady's Machine at a popular price, and I have every confidence in doing a big trade with both No. 7 Gents.' and No. 5c Lady's.

These Machines are in every way first-class ones with the exception of their being thoroughly up-to-date in detail. They are practically last season's patterns fitted with "B" Clincher tyres, and a little cheaper saddle, gear case, &c., than usually fitted. I can confidently recommend both machines and am sure of their giving great satisfaction.

14

Another view of Ickwell Green.

Ivel No. 8

TRICYCLE.

Size of Wheels:

26-in. back and 28-in. front.

THE IVEL

This machine is very popular, especially with those riders who are not so active as they have been, and who might find it difficult to learn to ride a bicycle. Twenty years ago I made the first IVEL Tricycle, and it was the **very first** to gain a world-wide reputation.   This machine is built with a truss frame, which is very rigid, though light.   It is made suitable for either a lady or gentleman, and for a first-class machine at a moderate price, it has no equal.

PRICE   -   £25.

With Dunlops, "A" Clinchers, or any other well-known pneumatic tyres with hollow rims; bright parts heavily coppered and nickelled; leather gear case; rim brake and mud-guards; best quality saddle; tool bag; spanners; oil can; pump, &c.

EXTRAS.—Lining gold, 15/-; any other colour, 10/-; if enamelled any other colour than black, 10/-; if fitted with free wheel, 25/-

Extract from *Financial News*, Nov. 12th, 1898.—"Dan Albone has, by placing a **high-class machine** on the market at a **reasonable price,** secured a good many distinguished patrons. (*See Introduction, page 4.*)

15

IVEL GENT'S MOTOR BICYCLE.

EASY TO
STEER AND
REGULATE
AND IS
PERFECTLY
SAFE
AND UNDER
CONTROL.

NO
STOPPINC
AS BICYCLE
CAN BE
RIDDEN AS
AN
ORDINARY
MACHINE.

NO
DISACREEABLE
SMELL.

NO NOISE
OR VIBRATION.

£45 - - COMPLETE

With Free Wheel, Two Powerful Rim Brakes, Rims nickelled, Gear Case and Valve Lifter.

MOTOR driven vehicles are becoming more popular every day and the most easy to manipulate and which will be within the easy reach of many who cannot afford the luxury of a Motor Car will undoubtedly be the Motor Bicycle. The Ivel Motor Bicycle is not only one of the **first** but it is one of the **best** that has yet been placed on the market.

The Motor Bicycle has one very great advantage over the Motor Car or Tricycle, and that is, it requires no specially large space when stored away. It takes up no more room than an ordinary bicycle.

Its construction is very simple, the frame being an ordinary standard pattern, but made specially stronger to take the extra weight of the engine. Therefore it is unlike many motor cycles which are clumsy, unevenly balanced and unsightly. It is very neat in appearance, and what is most important, the weight is equally distributed between the two wheels, the engine being fixed to the frame tube leading from the bottom of the head to the bottom bracket.

The engine is full 1½ H.P. (Minerva patents), and is driven by twisted raw hide belting, which is easily tightened or taken off altogether if necessary. It has electric ignition, and can be driven from a walking pace up to 35 miles an hour.

The ease and facility in working and controlling the engine is most simple, and any person of ordinary intelligence who is able to ride a safety bicycle can learn to ride the Ivel Motor Bicycle after two or three lessons of 1 hour each.

The whole weight of the machine is only about 70 lbs., and it is fitted with a free wheel and two powerful rim brakes, gear case and valve lifter, and Brook's B 90 saddle.

The Motor is so simple that it will never go wrong if worked properly and the directions for using it are carefully carried out ; but if not used properly, and through neglect the motor refuses to work, and it would take too long to re-adjust at the roadside, the belt is taken off and the machine ridden home almost as easily as an ordinary bicycle.

Should the rider desire to pedal for exercise, as if on an ordinary bicycle, he can easily do so by partly closing the throttle valve, thus reducing the power of engine.

Purchasers of Ivel Motor Bicycles will be given lessons free of charge by a competent instructor on machines kept in stock for the purpose, and no effort will be spared to give customers every satisfaction with both lessons and the new machines they order. Printed instructions will be given to purchasers.

Every Ivel Motor Bicycle supplied during the past season has given entire satisfaction—**see some of the testimonials** I have received (on page 23) proves the machine to have been a success in every way. The **numerous** and **great improvements** in the 1902 Motor will undoubtedly make the machine a bigger success than ever, and the demand for Ivel Motor Bicycles is sure to be very great during the coming season. The following is a list of some of the improvements in 1902 pattern.

Greater Power. Although only called 1½ H.P., the new pattern gives on the break double the power of the 1901 1½ H.P. pattern. **Inlet Valve** and **Exhaust Valve** are both enlarged. **Compression tap** done away with and replaced by a new patent Compression Valve. **New Sparking Plug** which is practically indestructible. **Trembler** is a great improvement on the old one and will last much longer.

An Automatic Oiling apparatus has been fitted so as to enable lubricating the engine from the saddle for over 200 miles. **A Tap for waste oil** is fitted instead of hexagon nut.

A new pattern Induction Coil which will last an indefinite period.

16

A Multiple Tool is supplied with each machine. This contains everything necessary for handling a motor and its accessories.

Other Improvements have also been made to ensure every motor being perfect before it is sent out from the works.

A Back Attachment furnishing a seat for another rider (in tandem fashion) is also supplied with Motor Bicycles when ordered. This will be found a most simple and useful article when the owner of Motor Bicycle wishes to take a gentleman friend for a trip. It is fastened to the hub back wheel pin and the seat lug of either Lady's or Gent's Motor Safety. **Price £3 3 0**

IVEL LADY'S MOTOR BICYCLE.

Reprint of Lady's Safety which I advertised and sold 16 years ago.

PRICE £47 - - COMPLETE

With Free Wheel, Two Powerful Rim Brakes, Rims nickelled, Gear Case, and Valve Lifter.

BEING the first to introduce the ordinary Lady's Safety Bicycle, now some 16 years ago, and with that great success which is generally known (notwithstanding adverse criticisms made upon it for the first few years of its inception) I have resolved to place the IVEL LADY'S MOTOR BICYCLE on the market, believing it will in a very short period become almost as popular a mount as the IVEL GENT'S MOTOR BICYCLE.

Every care and attention has been bestowed on this machine, the frame being specially constructed throughout and the material, workmanship and finish are of the highest excellence.

The Ivel Trailer.

THIS Trailer is a safe and comfortable carriage for either a lady or a gentleman, and can be attached to either a lady's or gentleman's Motor Bicycle.

Price £9 9 0

Specification.

Wheels, 26 in. × 1½ in. ; Clincher tyres and plated springs. Sent out complete with cushion, mat and mudguards.

17

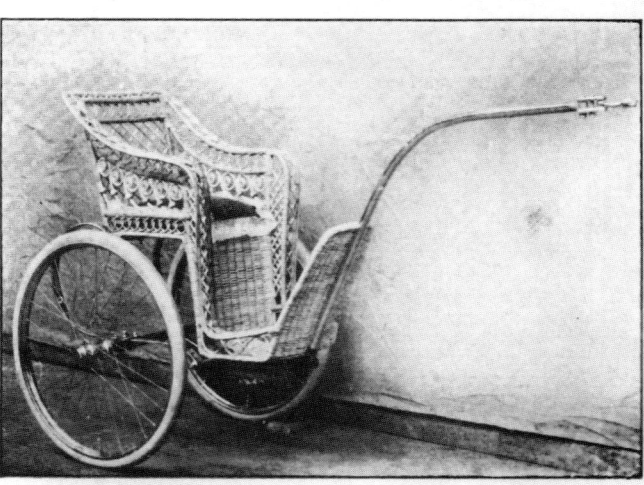

Patent Ball Bearing
Axles & Boxes for Wood Carriage and Motor Car Wheels.

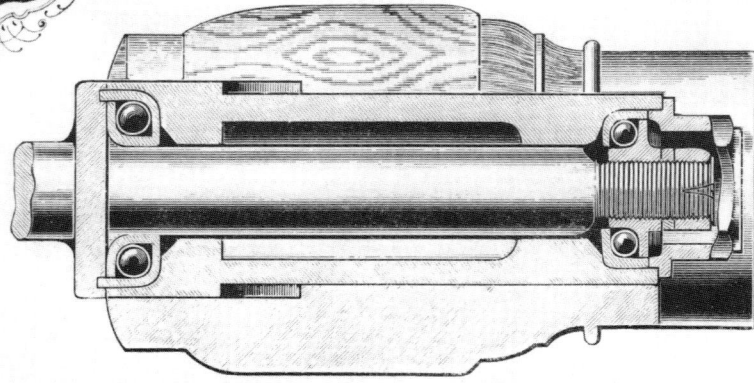

SECTION SHEWING BALL BOX FITTED IN NAVE OR WOOD STOCK.   (PATENTED BY ME)

IVEL Patent Ball Bearings for **Carts, Carriages, Motor Cars** and **Busses,** are now well known and are in general use. The past few years have been the best I have ever had in this branch of my business, and I feel sure that this year there will be a much bigger demand for them. The **saving in draught** is enormous, consequently there is much less work for the horse to do- the life of the horse is prolonged, and the expenses are much less for all owners of horses who have my Ball Bearing Axles and Boxes fitted to their vehicles.

The number of public companies who are now having Ivel Patent Ball Bearings fitted to their carts, vans, &c., with ordinary iron tyred wheels, is ample proof that these bearings have all the merits which are claimed for them, and they can be fitted by any ordinary coach builder.

Having proved they are a great success when in wheels with **Iron Tyres** it is obvious that they run extremely nicely and wear exceptionally well when they are fitted to wheels with rubber Tyres. The repeat orders received confirm this.

IMPORTANT. —When present old wheels are to be fitted with my patent ball bearing axle and boxes, measurements (see list opposite) are taken, and after axles are made and finished I only require the old wheels about a day or so to fit ball boxes and axles in them —thus depriving customers of the use of their vehicle for a few days only.

I would kindly ask those who take an interest in Ball Bearings, to read the unsolicited testimonials on page 24.

A fact worthy of the attention of all interested in such vehicles as vans busses, &c., for London as well as country traffic is that I am receiving repeat orders from the London and North Western and Great Northern Railways, who have had IVEL Patent Ball Bearing Axles and Boxes fitted to such vehicles, some of which have been in constant use in London for some years past.

The following is a List of Patrons supplied with IVEL Patent Ball Bearing Carriage Axles:

His Grace the Duke of Bedford
Lord Alwyne Compton, M.P.
London & North Western Railway Co.
Great Northern Railway Co.
Headlands Electric Battery Co.
Reginald B. Loder, Esq.
London Improved Cab Co.
North British Rubber Co.
A. J. Clay, Esq.
H. Starke, Esq.
W. H. Brett, Esq.
Howard Whitbread, Esq.
A. Tyrell, Esq.
H. Edwards, Esq.
Dunlop Pneumatic Tyre Co.
Higgins, Bessemer, Nicholson & Co.
Captain G. R. Bethel
Mrs. L. Chadwick
Colonel Frank Shuttleworth
Mrs. Osborn

Sir Algernon Osborn
A. K. Stothert, Esq.
Mrs. Ben Haworth-Booth
Goodling and Priestly
M. D. Rucker, Esq.
Hayes and Sons
Universal Electric Carriage Syndicate Ltd.,
H. H. Mulliner, Esq.
Alfred Palmer, Esq.
F. L. Merritt, Esq.
Cyril B. Tubbs, Esq.
Harry T. Shaw, Esq.
W. T. Bersey, Esq., A.I.C.E.
Messrs. Thorn,
Mr. James Saunders
Messrs. A. Ferris & Co.
E. Ventham & Co.
Maythorn & Son
Barker & Co.
Thrupp and Maberly
Messrs. Carpenter & Co.

J. W. & T. Connolly
F. E. Metcalfe, Esq.
Messrs. Rock, Hawkins & Thorpe
Mr. D. Campbell
Mr. J. A. Croucher
T. Mackrill, Esq.
C. Purrott, Esq.
Francis Pym, Esq., J.P.
Steuart & Co. (Calcutta).
A Barnes & Sons
Morgan & Co.
Mrs. Berney Ficklin
Laurie and Marner, Ltd.
W. Parkyn & Sons
J. Strangward & Son, Ltd.
Matthew T. Shaw & Co., Ltd.
Mr. G. Heath
E. E. Pullman, Esq.
H. A. Hamshaw, Esq.
W. & F. Thorn
Earl Jersey

18

Ball Bearing Carriage, Motor Car and Rickshaw Wheels.

IVEL. BALL BEARING
CARRIAGE WHEELS.

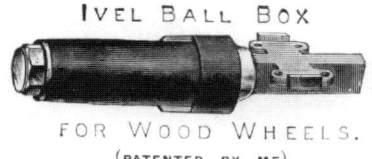

IVEL BALL BOX

FOR WOOD WHEELS.
(PATENTED BY ME).

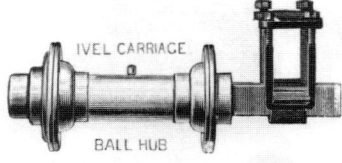

IVEL CARRIAGE

BALL HUB

FOR CYCLE SPOKED WHEELS.
Diagram of Hub showing Clips for Springs.

CYCLE SPOKED WHEELS.

I am still making these wheels for ordinary **Carts, Carriages** and **Rickshaws,** and they continue to give entire satisfaction. During the past 4 years I have also made a number of Motor Car Wheels on the same principle, sometimes leaving each hind hub longer to allow for fixing of a sprocket wheel for driving purposes. Having had 16 years' experience in making these wheels and bearings I have acquired a thorough knowledge of adapting them to all kinds of vehicles.

When ordering Axles and Boxes for WOOD Wheels, please state:—

	Front.	Back.
Size and kind of Axle		
Kind of flaps		
Width of springs		
Length of axle between springs		
Length of axle between springs and collars		
Length of stock or wood hub not measuring outside ring		
Diameter of stock each end		
Colour of caps (brassed or nickelled)		

19

347

DAN ALBONE'S
Child Carrier and
Parcel Carrier.

The CHILD CARRIER is a very neat and light Wicker Basket made on steel wire framework, the weight of which is carried by means of tubing direct on to the axle of front wheel, with Leg Troughs, as sketch, Plated Clips to fasten to the Handle Bar and Back Irons to bolt on back of Basket. Two holes are made in the back of Basket, so that a strap can be put through to fasten the child safely in.

When ordering, the only Particulars necessary are the Diameters of Front Wheel and Handle Bar.

Easily fixed to any Safety Bicycle or Tricycle.

PARCEL CARRIER.

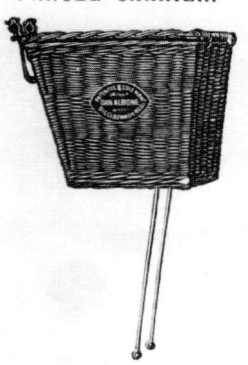

CHILD CARRIER.

The Basket is easily put on and taken off in a minute, by taking the bottom screw out of the clips and leaving the clips on Handle Bar.

Complete £1.

With Cushions complete, £1 7s. 6d.

Full Instructions for fitting sent with Carrier, which must be strictly adhered to when fixing same to Cycle.

Further particulars see Abridged List, which contains Testimonials. &c., to be had on application.

TESTIMONIAL.

"Selbourne," Durham Road, Wimbledon, Surrey,

November 3rd, 1899.

DEAR SIR,

I am pleased to inform you that the child carrier is much appreciated. My little daughter has travelled just 1,000 miles in it with great delight and she evidently thinks it as safe as I do, as it fits well without impeding the movement of the machine in the slightest, allowing of course for the slight extra weight to carry. The carrier has been continuously left on the machine for over four months and has proved thoroughly safe and reliable.

As my wife always travels with me you have the complete satisfaction of my small family.

Yours very truly,

(signed) C. TILLINGHAST.

20

Extracts from Testimonials.

CYCLES.

The Hon. Mrs. HASTINGS, Myton, Warwick, November 1st, 1899.
" I am delighted with the IVEL bicycle, it has given me every satisfaction."

The Hon. Mrs. ASTELL, Hazelwood, Kings Langley, Jan. 4th, 1899
" The bicycles are very satisfactory."

Miss A. P. HAINES, Westmill House, Ware.
" I have now had the machine about a year and am pleased to say it has always given me every satisfaction. I shall be pleased to strongly recommend your machines to my friends."

Miss S. HESKETH, 6, Castle Road, Bedford, June 13th, 1899.
" I like the machine very much and it runs very easily and looks very nice."

Miss ROSIE JOHNSTONE, Rothsay, Cowes, Isle of Wight, Nov. 7th, 1899.
" I received the bicycle in perfect condition this morning and I am very pleased with it."

Mrs. JOSSELYN, Banstead, Bedford, May 24, 1899.
" Miss Bulkeley Hughes is very pleased with her machine and I think it is a very nice one."

Mrs. SINCLAIR, Arundel House, Fulham, S.W., March 21st, 1898.
" I am very much pleased with my IVEL bicycle."

Mrs. L. RECKETT, c/o Major Reckett, R.A.M.C., North Camp, Aldershot, August 25th, 1899.
" I like the machine very much and it exactly fits me."

Miss RINTOUL, Butler House, High Wycombe, July 3rd, 1899.
" I am much pleased with the bicycle."

Miss GREGORY, Deanery, St. Paul's, E.C., Nov. 8th, 1898.
" Miss Alice Gregory is delighted with the bicycle."

Miss M. THOMPSON, Ashdale, Stamford, January 25th, 1899.
" I am very pleased indeed with the IVEL bicycle you have made for me."

Miss ADELAIDE PYM, The Firs, Ampthill, October 3rd, 1898.
" I am much pleased with the tricycle as it runs so lightly."

Miss M. M. NORTON, 13, Hilgrove Road, South Hampstead, Jan. 20th, 1899.
" I have now had the bicycle for more than two years and am still extremely satisfied with it."

Miss AUGUSTA MARY WING, Market Overton, Oakham, May 6th, 1899.
" The machine runs beautifully and it is a great pleasure to ride it."

Miss MURIEL WINCKWORTH, Shefford.
" I am delighted with my bicycle and have never ridden one which has been so easy to ride. I shall recommend all my friends to get an IVEL now."

Miss WOOD, The Nurses Hostel, Francis Street, London, W.C., Jan. 28th, 1901.
" I have received my tricycle and think the small repair required after the amount of running it has done speaks volumes for the good workmanship put into the machine."

Miss ANNIS M. THORNLEY, Brookdale, Upper Tooting, S.W., April 4th, 1901.
" A year ago last May you supplied me with an IVEL Ladies Bicycle which has given me the greatest satisfaction, and I shall always have great pleasure in recommending it to my friends."

Miss MAUD BLAKE, 38, High Street, Bedford.
" I am more than pleased with the bicycle and like it better each time I ride it."

Miss FANNY KEYSER, King Edward's Hospital, Windsor, Sept. 1st, 1901.
" Miss Agnes and I are very pleased with our machines ; they are most comfortable and run beautifully."

Miss O. HULBERT, Stakes Hill Lodge, Cosham, April 9th, 1901.
" The bicycle is most satisfactory."

21

EXTRACTS FROM TESTIMONIALS (CYCLES)—continued.

MRS. R. BAXTER, Mozufferpore, Bengal, June 6th, 1900.
  " My husband likes his IVEL very much.   I only hope it will last as well as mine has."

F. J. THYNNE, Esq., Conan House, Rossshire, N.B., Sept. 23rd, 1901.
  " I am pleased to say that my son is very much satisfied with the bicycle I ordered from you."

Major H. HOARE, Mayes, Near East Grinstead, Sussex, June 25th, 1901.
  " The two machines are a great success in every way."

S. G. WALLIS ADAMS, Esq., Abbots Court, Hoo, Rochester, Aug. 24th, 1900.
  " My machine has given me every satisfaction and is as good as ever."

E. LUMLEY, Esq., County Club, Nottingham, Sept. 15th, 1900.
  " I have tried my new cycle, and like it very much."

H. V. KELHAM, Esq., Felbrig, Park Hill, Carshalton.
  " You will be pleased to hear that the machine suits me in every way, and that I am thoroughly satisfied with it."

G. FRANCIS HIGGINS, Esq., Government House, Madras, India, Jan. 1st, 1901.
  " Thanks to careful packing, the bicycle arrived here without a scratch.   I am pleased to tell you that I am more than satisfied with it in every respect."

Lieut. CHARLES BISSETT, R.N., H.M.S. Pembroke, Chatham, May 2nd, 1900.
  " I want you to make a machine for my wife. The machine you made for me a year ago has given every satisfaction."

Lieut.-Col. EVERARD, Roydon, King's Lynn, Aug. 26th, 1898.
  " The machine gives every satisfaction and runs beautifully."

Dr. W. BELGARIE, The Dutch House, Winchfield, June 9th, 1899.
  " I thought it would interest you to know how the bicycle which you supplied me with three years ago has gone on. I have ridden it 13000 miles or more and it now goes almost as well as when I first had it.   I am accustomed to ride the bicycle through every weather and over any ground and so I consider it speaks very highly for its construction."

Sir EDWARD JENKINSON, 2, High Beach, Felixstowe, Suffolk.
  " All the machines which you have supplied to my order have given great satisfaction."

The Hon. Lieut.-Col. CRICHTON, 38, Walton Street, London, S.W., June 23rd, 1898.
  " I like the bicycle very much indeed, and am always glad to recommend your bicycles."

PERCIVAL BOSANQUET, Esq., Ponfield, Near Hertford, January 6th, 1900.
  " The tricycle runs uncommonly well."

C. W. PATCHELL, Esq., Trinity College, Glenalmond, Perth, Feb. 13th, 1899.
  " I am delighted with the running of the machine and with the comfort of its fit.   All my friends here admire the general lines on which the machine is built and its external finish."

The Hon. MOWBRAY ST. JOHN, Weybridge, May 9th, 1899.
  " I received my bicycle all right and find it is most satisfactory.   I have ridden it a good deal lately and it goes splendidly."

FRANK J. POTTER, Esq., 1, Verulam Buildings, Gray's Inn, W.C., Jan. 30th, 1899.
  " I have now ridden the machine about 1300 miles and have not turned a nut or a screw, nor opened the gear case except to put oil in through the lubricator,"

A. W. W. DALE, Esq., Trinity Hall, Cambridge, Oct. 9th, 1899.
  " The machine is all one can wish ; it is better even than the old one, and that is saying much."

SIR HUGH BEEVOR, Bart., M.D., 17, Wimpole Street, London, W., May 7th, 1898.
  " I am very satisfied with the machine."

Lord NAPIER OF MAGDALA, 9, Loundes Square, London, Jan. 9th, 1899.
  " I have bought two bicycles from you—one has been running **3 years** at home and abroad, the other **2 years,** without any need of repairs, and to ride they have been as good as the best."

R. H. DUN, Esq., Walsingham, Chislehurst, August 16th, 1899.
  " The more I use the bicycle the better I am pleased with it."

T. E. HURST HODGSON, Esq., St. Mary's Abbey, Bedford, February 4th, 1902.
  " The machine I had from you last year is as good as the day I received it.   I have had a large number of cycles during the past 15 years and yours is the easiest running one of the lot."

22

350

EXTRACTS FROM TESTIMONIALS (CYCLES)—continued.

HAROLD M. LANG, Esq., Trumpington Street, Cambridge, Oct. 1900.
" I am much pleased with my new bicycle."

Mr. J. ROULSTONE, Wortley Hall, Sheffield, Nov. 15th, 1900.
" I am glad to say the bicycles have given every satisfaction."

G. HEREFORD, Esq., Paymaster General's Office, Whitehall, June 8th, 1900.
" The bicycle you built for me is excellent."

W. H. ARCHBUTT, Esq., Bramhall Lane, Stockport, Aug. 29th, 1900.
" The bicycle you made for me some few weeks ago now runs exceedingly well and I am much pleased with it. My wife is equally well pleased with her machine.

Copy of Illuminated Testimonial presented to me by a large number of Cyclists who frequented the North Road :—

November 29th, 1885.

DEAR DAN,

The cyclists visiting Biggleswade having for many years past received at your hands at all times and at all hours numerous acts of kindness and self-denying attention, desire to express to you their hearty thanks for the considerate treatment you have invariably shown them, and the assistance you have rendered by pace-making for them when racing or during long-distance rides, and in numerous other ways, doing all in your power to administer to their comfort and convenience. They also wish to make some slight acknowledgment of your exertions on their behalf and combining to express to you their high opinion of your sterling good qualities, request your acceptance of a tangible token of their regard in the shape of a **Gold Chain,** which they hope you will accept and wear with the consciousness of its being a tribute of the esteem in which you are held by the subscribers.

MOTOR BICYCLE TESTIMONIALS.

The Rt. Hon. A. GRAHAM MURRAY, K.C., M.P., Stenton, Dunkeld,
(Lord Advocate)
October 3rd, 1901.
" I am very pleased with the Motor Bicycle which continues to give every satisfaction."

H. B. CHINNERY, Esq., Hatchford Cobham, September 30th, 1901.
" I am delighted with the Motor Bicycle, and have recommended it to many friends."

W. H. GREENWOOD, Esq., Metheringham, Lincoln, August 27th, 1901.
" The more I ride the Ivel Motor Bicycle the more I like it. I did 96 miles on one supply of petrol. The machine runs well when the belt is off, and I tried it up a stiff hill just to know how it ran when motor was not in use."

The Rev. A. A. HONEY, Cowper's House, Huntingdon, January 16th, 1902.
DEAR SIR,
" I think it is only due to you and your firm that I should let you know how satisfactorily the Motor Bicycle is going.

I have no trouble with it—thanks to the great pains you took at the first to explain everything connected with the machine.

I may say that I have not been obliged to pedal the machine home on any journey—and this is a matter of importance to me, particularly on Sundays when I have several services to take, and long distances to travel, and of course punctuality is a necessity.

I have ridden the Ivel Motor now 1200 miles in all kinds of weather, on roads in all kinds of condition, and it has certainly come up to all my expectations.

I have to thank you for building such an excellent machine and also for such instruction that has enabled me not only to master my own Motor but also to help others whom I have found in difficulties on the road.

After seeing and trying other Motor bicycles of the same pattern, I certainly prefer your make, and therefore I have strongly recommended intending purchasers to go to you, for I am firmly convinced you will give them every satisfaction."

H. J. BEDFORD, Esq., Silsoe, Beds., January 23rd, 1902.
DEAR SIR,
" Having now had my new Ivel Motor Bicycle just a month I thought you would like to hear how I am getting on with it. Well, I am pleased to say " I am more than delighted with it." I have ridden it practically every day over all sorts of roads and up some very stiff hills and it has not yet failed to give me every satisfaction. I rode it 72 miles the second day I had it, and I have ridden it 600 miles altogether. And as this is the first Motor of any kind I have ridden, I think I have done fairly well. I attribute a great deal of my success to the attention given me in the first lessons at your works."

23

TESTIMONIALS
Re Ball Bearing Carriage & Motor Car Axles

Chicksands Priory, Shefford,
October 5th, 1898.

MRS. OSBORN.
"I am delighted with the Phæton which has your Ball Bearing Axles and Boxes fitted."

Rolston Hall, Hornsea, Hull,
August 18th, 1898.

MRS. B. HAWORTH-BOOTH.
"The Ball Bearings you fitted to my Pony Cart are certainly a very great advantage, as it now runs so easily."

Sigglesthorne, Hull,
August 3rd, 1897.

CAPT. G. R. BETHELL.
"I like the Ball Bearing wheels. The trap runs very easily."

7, Balfour Place, Park Lane, W.,
January 15th, 1899.

LORD ALWYNE COMPTON, M.P.
"I have much pleasure in testifying to the success of the Ball Bearing Axles which you fitted to my brougham. After a practical trial of over a year, I have no hesitation in saying that the advantages gained in the case of a carriage of heavy draught (such as a brougham is) cannot be exaggerated. It reduces the draught so much that quite a light horse can manage it, and the carriage runs smoothly and well as far as the occupant is concerned. I consider these Ball Bearings are an advantage in any carriage whether for London or for the country."

Berkin Manor, Horton, Slough,
May 28th, 1897.

A. TYRELL, ESQ.,
SIR,
"The Ball Bearings which I had fitted to the Carriage and Dog Cart are capital; we like them very much."

East Thorpe, Reading,
November, 1896.

MR. DAN ALBONE.
DEAR SIR,
"I am desired by MR. ALFRED PALMER to say he finds the introduction of the Ball Bearings has done away with the drumming in the brougham. They run very nicely, and have made it much easier for the horses."

I am, yours truly, H. H. JONES, *Secretary.*

MR. PALMER in giving his opinion of the Ivel Ball Bearing Axles and Boxes privately, says:—"I did not have new wheels put to my brougham, but Albone had the old wheels and supplied axle trees with his own patent Ball Bearings. They have only been on about three weeks, so that I cannot say anything as to whether they wear well, although I see no reason why they should not, but as regards the easy running I am perfectly satisfied. The horses trot up hills which they used to walk up, and the drumming in the brougham of which we used to complain has been completely silenced. One of the horses which we never used singly, because he was not strong enough, now draws the brougham about the town nicely."

Holly Bush, Burton-on-Trent,
August 4th, 1897.

ARTHUR J. CLAY, ESQ.
"I am very much pleased at the way in which the Ball Bearing wheels have stood."

October 12th, 1901.

"The Dog Cart with the Ball Bearings and Cycle spoked wheels which I have had so long (5½ years) is still in excellent order."

53, Victoria Street, Westminster,
February 28th, 1900.

A. K. STOTHERT, ESQ.
"I have now run my brougham for two years with your Ball Bearings, during which time I have only had to adjust them once. They have more than answered my expectations."

Cambridge Road, Hastings,
January 3rd, 1900.

MR. D. CAMPBELL.
"I am very pleased to tell you that the axles which you supplied in July, 1898, have given unqualified satisfaction to me and my customers."

The Hazells, Sandy, Beds.
December 2nd, 1900.

FRANCIS PYM, ESQ., J.P.
"I am much pleased with the Ivel Ball Bearings you have fitted to my cart."
N.B.—I have since made a set for a new brougham to Mr. Pym's order.

24

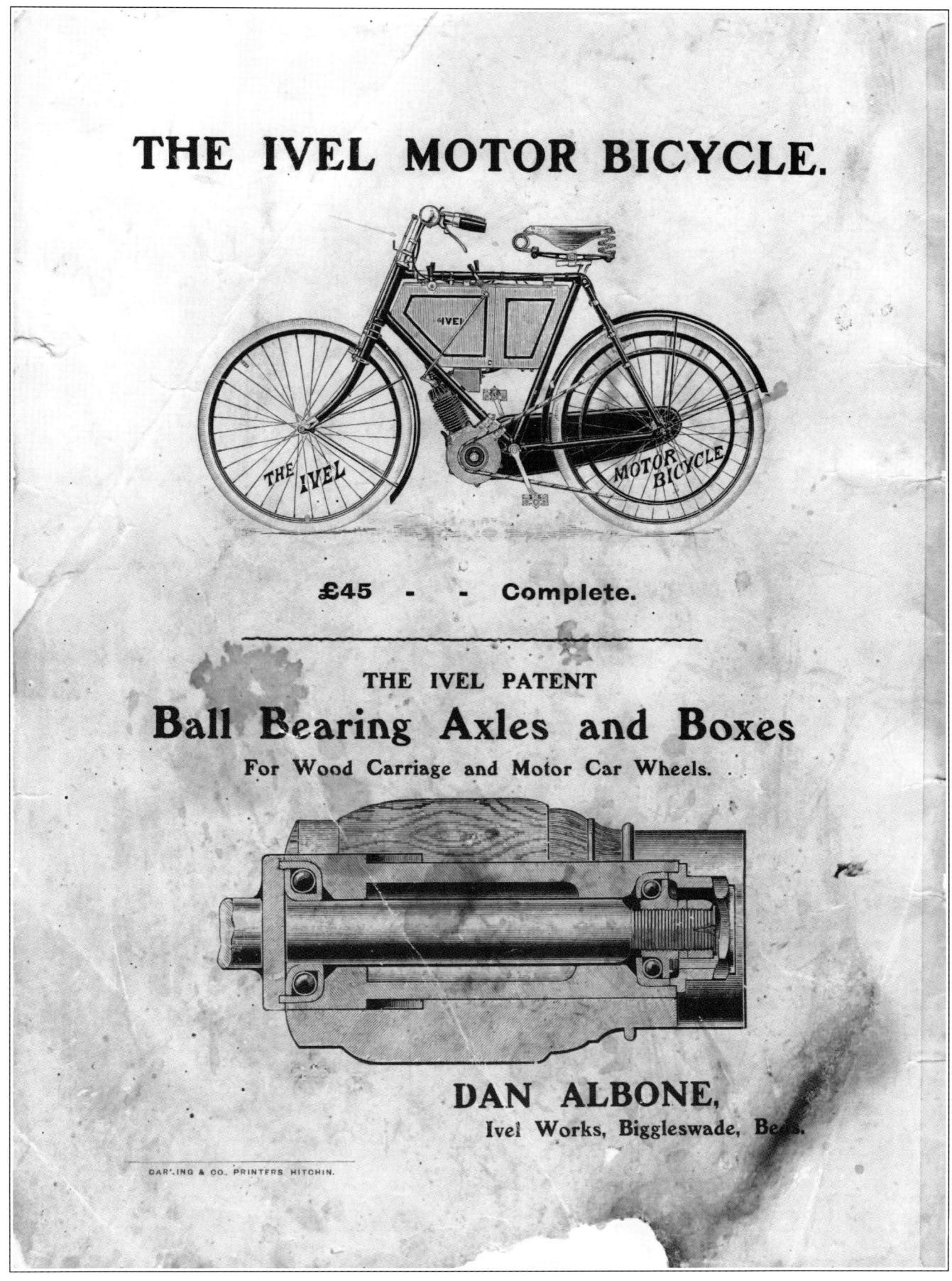

THE IVEL MOTOR BICYCLE.

£45 - - Complete.

THE IVEL PATENT

Ball Bearing Axles and Boxes

For Wood Carriage and Motor Car Wheels.

DAN ALBONE,

Ivel Works, Biggleswade, Beds.

DARLING & CO. PRINTERS HITCHIN.

Introduction.

IT is just a quarter of a century since I introduced the IVEL Cycle, and during the whole of this period the IVEL has stood in the front rank among the leading makes. Notwithstanding the introduction of the so-called cheap cycle, the IVEL has always commanded its fair share of patronage, due undoubtedly to its sterling merits, lasting qualities, and to the kind recommendation of one customer to another.

I have received hundreds of

UNSOLICITED TESTIMONIALS

from all parts of the world, and a few of these are printed on pages 11 and 12. It is with pride that I can point to the fact that I still retain the patronage of many customers who dealt with me when I first started business, and it is my pleasing duty to once more thank my numerous friends and patrons for their past support and kind recommendations.

The IVEL will still be my leading line in cycles, and it will be made of the best material procurable and of the highest excellence, but in order to meet the increased demand for cheap but good reliable machines, I am this year introducing the RUNWELL, which I can confidently recommend to those of my customers who desire a reliable but lower priced machine than the IVEL.

My machines are priced at the **actual amount** for which they can be purchased. I introduced this method eleven years ago, doing away with the discount system (see Press Notices on pages 4, 5, 6, 7, 8 and 9).

In order to meet with the increased trade in cycles in the immediate district I have opened a branch depôt situated in **Hitchin Street**, where there will always be a good display of cycles and accessories of every kind, and I cordially invite all intending purchasers to pay a visit either to my works or the show-room in Hitchin Street, and they will find that my stock will not only be much larger than anyone elses in the district, but that my prices will in many cases be lower, for having an extensive knowledge of everything belonging to the cycle industry, and being a large buyer, I am enabled to compete with anyone in the market.

A competent workman has been engaged for the Hitchin Street Depôt, and customers can always rely upon having best and prompt attention to enquiries, both at the Works and at the Depôt. They can see or communicate with either myself or my manager, Mr. GEORGE COURSE, for I have arranged that one of us will always be in attendance at the works during business hours as hitherto.

MOTOR CARS.

Having been one of the first to take up the manufacture of **Motor Cars**, and being the inventor and maker of the **Ivel Agricultural Motor**, my experience in all matters pertaining to Motor Cars has been considerable, and although I am not at present manufacturing this particular class of machine, I have sold a good number during the last few years to customers who have commissioned me to purchase for them. I am agent for nearly every well-known car on the market, and my experience and services will be at the disposal of any of my customers.

In conclusion I can assure my customers that I shall endeavour to retain their patronage by continuing to supply them with articles that will give them entire satisfaction.

DAN ALBONE,
SOLE PROPRIETOR.

2

Terms of Business.

CASH against Invoice to Customers having no Ledger Account.

CARRIAGE in all cases to be paid by **Purchaser.**

REPAIRS. Machines or parts will not be received unless sent **Carriage Paid** with full name and Address of Sender at back of label. Invoices are sent out when the work is complete. In no case can repairs be booked, my terms being Nett Cash on receipt of invoice. I am compelled to insist on this owing to the difficulty experienced in collecting small accounts and the cost of booking and postage when numerous applications for payment have to be made, this often taking the whole profit off repairs. Enquiries respecting machines receive immediate attention.

CRATES are charged Cost Price, and are NOT RETURNABLE.

. . . .

NOTICES TO PURCHASERS.

Most of my Machines are made specially to order, thus giving more satisfaction to the Purchaser and myself. All I require is the inside measurement of leg, from fork to ball of foot, and the weight of rider. Easy payments are arranged when required by customers, and, if desired, old machines are taken in exchange as part payment.

A Large Stock of all kinds of Accessories such as LAMPS, OIL and ACETYLENE, BELLS, TYRE INFLATORS, &c., &c., always kept in Stock. A large number of **Second=hand Machines** are always on sale at very low prices.

SPECIAL.

ALL KINDS OF NICKEL PLATING DONE ON THE PREMISES. I ALSO HAVE A SPECIAL PLANT FOR SILVERING SUCH ARTICLES AS FORKS, SPOONS, CRUETS, TRAYS, &c. See detailed List, to be had on application.

. . . .

FORM OF GUARANTEE.

I Guarantee, subject to the conditions mentioned below, that all precautions which are usual and reasonable have been taken by me to secure excellence of materials and workmanship in all my IVEL Machines, and I undertake to make good, at any time within twelve months of this date, any defects which result from inherent flaws or defective workmanship, and are not caused by wear and tear, misuse or neglect.

CONDITIONS.—If a defective part should be found in any of my Machines, it must be sent to me **Carriage Paid** and accompanied by an intimation from the Sender that he desires to have it repaired free of charge under the guarantee. The number of the Machine must be quoted.

Failing compliance with this rule no notice will be taken of anything that may arrive, but such articles will lie here at the risk of the Sender.

This Guarantee does not apply to the specialities of other Firms, such as Tyres, Gear Cases, Saddles, Tool Bags, Lamps, Bells, &c., but the makers of these, whose names usually appear thereon, are in nearly every case willing to replace defective parts, and I will at all times furnish the maker's name as a proof of the quality.

N.B.—This guarantee does not apply to Motor Bicycles or Motor Cars. These are guaranteed to be in perfect order when leaving the works. No other guarantee is given or implied.

3

A VIEW OF SUTION
From the Bridge, showing Village and Church in the distance.

Ivel No. 1
ROADSTER.

Specification.

Best weldless steel tubes; 28in. wheels; free wheel; two latest pattern Bowden rim brakes; plated rims; bright parts heavily nickelled; steering lock; mudguards; gear case; gear 68in. or to order; best quality saddle; tool bag; spanners; oil can; pump, etc. Weight 32 lbs.

Complete with Dunlop, "A Won" Clincher, or other well-known pneumatic tires.

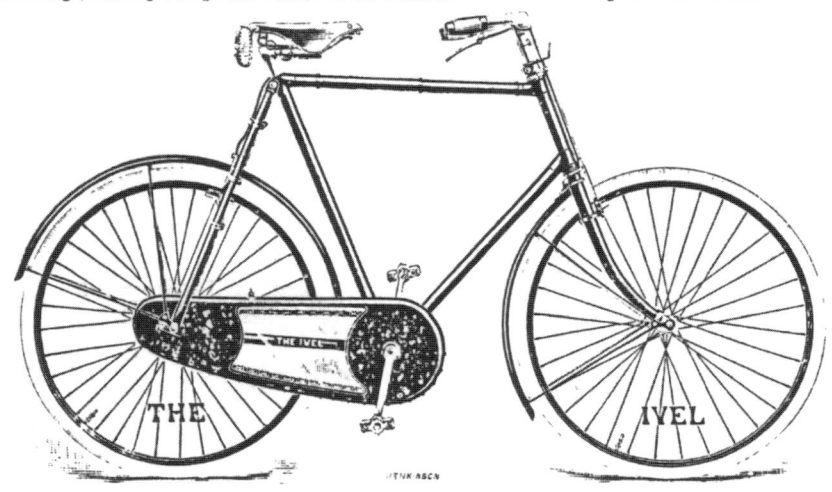

PRICE - - £11.

With Hub Two-Speed Gear, **Price £12 12'-**   With Three-Speed Gear, **Price £13 13'-**

EXTRAS.—Lining gold, 10/6; any other colour, 7/6; if enamelled any other colour than black, 7/6.

IVEL No. 2 LIGHT ROADSTER.—Complete as No. 1; weight 25lbs.
PRICE - - - £11 10/-
EXTRAS.—Same as No. 1.

IVEL No. 3 PATH RACER.—This Machine has been constructed throughout with due regard to lightness and strength. PRICE - - £10.

IVEL JUVENILE CYCLES for BOYS from **£5 5/-**

The IVEL Safety Bicycle was one of the very first put on the market, and it held nearly every worlds road record during the early years of the Safety Bicycle.

Extract from *Cycling Times*, Sept. 1st, 1886.—" Alfred Fletcher, of the Anfield Club, on Tuesday last covered 265½ miles in 24 hours on the road. He rode a geared-up safety bicycle made by Dan Albone, which carried him grandly. This ride establishes a record for safety machines."

4

SUTTON, an old picturesque Village near Biggleswade.
Showing Bridge and Ford.

Ivel No. 4

Lady's Safety.

+ +

Specification.

Strong dropped frame with double tubes ; 28in. wheels ; free wheel ; two latest pattern Bowden rim brakes ; plated rims ; bright parts heavily nickelled ; steering lock ; IVEL gear case ; mud guards ; best quality saddle ; tool bag ; spanners ; oil can ; pump, etc.

Complete with Dunlop, " A Won " Clincher, or other well-known pneumatic tires.

PRICE - - £11.

With Hub Two-Speed Gear, **Price £12 12/-**   With Three-Speed Gear, **Price £13 13/-**

EXTRAS.—Lining gold, 10/6 ; any other colour, 7/6 ; if enamelled any other colour than black, 7/6.

IVEL JUVENILE CYCLES for GIRLS from **£5 5/-**

Reprint of Lady's Safety which I advertised and sold 20 years ago, although many critics doubted whether ladies would ever take to the cycle.

Extract from *Bicycling News*, Feb. 5th, 1887.—" I do not believe the fair sex will ever take seriously to the narrow-guager (Lady's Bicycle), but for those who do intend doing so, this is the first really practicable Lady's Bicycle brought out."

5

MAYPOLE ON ICKWELL GREEN.
One of the prettiest and most old
fashioned Village Greens in England.
Close to Biggleswade.

Ivel No. 5

Lady's Tricycle.

✠ ✠ ✠ ✠

Specification.

26in Back and 28in. front wheels; fixed
wheel; powerful rim brake; gear 58; leather
gear case; front mudguard; side shields; best
quality saddle; tool bag; spanners; and oil can.

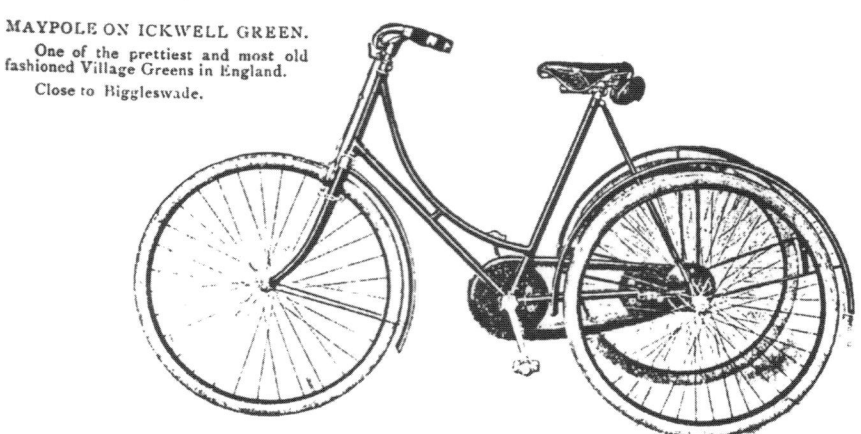

PRICE - - £20.

If fitted with free wheel and patent back pedalling brake, **PRICE £23.**

Ivel Gent's Tricycle.

Specification.—This Machine is built on the same lines as No. 5, with the exception of
the bottom curve tube, this being replaced with the straight top tube as in Gent's Bicycles.

PRICE - - £20.

If fitted with free wheel and patent back pedalling brake, **PRICE £23.**

Extract from *Cyclist*, Nov. 23rd, 1898.—"**Now that nett prices** are coming into vogue,
we must not forget to add that Dan Albone was one of **the first** to adopt the system **of nett
prices**; in fact he may be considered quite a pioneer in the matter."

6

NORTHILL CHURCH.
Near Biggleswade.

The

Rnwell No. 6

Roadster Safety.

✠ ✠ ✠ ✠

Specification.

28in. Wheels ; free wheel ; two rim brakes ; plated rims ; mudguards ; gear 75.

I have introduced this cheap cycle in order to meet the increasing demand for a low priced machine. It is a well made and useful machine, and although priced at a low figure, it is thoroughly reliable and well worth the figure it is priced at.

PRICE - - £7.

Extract from *Athletic News*, Sept. 26th, 1898.—" Dan Albone was undoubtedly the first man to drop the discount system."

7

Another view of Ickwell Green.

The

Runwell No. 7

= Lady's Safety.

⁺ ⁺ ⁺ ⁺

Specification.

28in. Wheels ; free wheel ; two rim brakes ; plated rims ;
mudguards ; dress guard ; gear case ; gear 62.

This Machine is built on the same lines as the No. 6 RUNWELL, but with
curved bottom tube instead of straight top tube, and although a low priced
machine, great care has been bestowed upon it and there is no better value
for money on the market.

PRICE - - £7 10/-.

Extract from *Cycling*, Nov. 26th, 1898.—"It is worth while to note cheery Dan Albone
has, for the last few years, marked nett prices in his catalogue."

8

The Ivel - =

Motor Bicycle.

Specification.

Engine either 2 h.p. or 2¾ h.p.; mechanically operated valves; special strong frame; girder front forks; two powerful rim brakes; electric ignition; latest spray carburettor; tank contains compartments for oil, petrol, twin accumulators, and coil; best quality V belt; pump lubricator fixed to oil reservoir; Clincher, Dunlop, or any other well-known tyres.

PRICES:

£29 - with **2 h.p. engine.**

£32 - „ **2¾** „ „

Purchasers of Ivel Motor Bicycles will be given lessons free of charge by a competent instructor.

Extract from *Financial News*, Nov. 12th, 1898.—" Dan Albone has, by placing a **high-class machine** on the market at a **reasonable price**, secured a good many distinguished patrons."

9

Dan Albone's - =

- - Child Carrier.

The CHILD CARRIER is a very neat and light Wicker Basket made on steel wire framework, the weight of which is carried by means of tubing direct on to the axle of front wheel, with Leg Troughs, as sketch, Plated Clips to fasten to the Handle Bar and Back Irons to bolt on the back of Basket. Two holes are made in the back of Basket, so that a strap can be put through to fasten the child safely in.

When ordering, the only Particulars necessary are the Diameters of Front Wheel and Handle Bar.

Easily fixed to any Safety Bicycle or Tricycle.

The Basket is easily put on and taken off in a minute, by taking the bottom screw out of the clips and leaving the clips on Handle Bar.

✢ ✢ ✢ ✢ ✢

Full Instructions for fitting sent with Carrier, which must be strictly adhered to when fixing same to Cycle.

✢ ✢ ✢ ✢ ✢

Further particulars see Abridged List, which contains Testimonals, &c., to be had on application.

With Cushions complete, £1 7s. 6d.

TESTIMONIALS.

"SELBOURNE," DURHAM ROAD, WIMBLEDON, SURREY.

DEAR SIR,   November 3rd, 1899.

I am pleased to inform you that the Child Carrier is much appreciated. My little daughter has travelled just 1,000 miles in it with great delight and she evidently thinks it as safe as I do, as it fits well without impeding the movement of the machine in the slightest, allowing of course for the slight extra weight to carry. The Carrier has been continuously left on the machine for over four months and has proved thoroughly safe and reliable.

As my wife always travels with me you have the complete satisfaction of my small family.—Yours very truly, (signed) C. TILLINGHAST.

THE VICARAGE, TOTTERIDGE,

DEAR SIR,   May 9th, 1897.

I have lately given the Child Carrier and the Bicycle you made me a thorough good test. Starting from Totteridge, near Barnet, on Monday, April 26th, I rode, with my little daughter of 4½, weight about 2½ stone, 60 miles in the day, to Newbury, with perfect ease. On the 27th we travelled 42 miles on to Calne and Devizes, and finished up on Wednesday with 20 miles to Frome by 12. We travelled 112 miles in 2½ days. The return journey was even better. On May 5th we returned by a different road—Warminster, Stonehenge, Andover, Basingstoke, Staines, and Harrow, to Totteridge. On the 5th we road 67 miles to Hartley Row, and got back on the 6th, about 46 miles. In two days we came 113 miles. We had a most enjoyable journey both ways. Besides the child I took luggage sufficient for my daughter and myself to manage comfortably for 3 days. This is sufficient to show how strong and safe the Carrier must be, and is a strong recommendation. **I hope the Bicycle you are making for Mrs. Edgell will soon be ready, and that it will turn out as successful as mine.**—Yours faithfully, W. S. EDGELL.

10

Extracts from Testimonials.

❖ CYCLES. ❖

Mr. H. P. PURSER, Holmeside, Biggleswade, Beds., April 6th, 1906.

"The Bicycle you built for me 4 years ago is a splendid machine. Well made in every part, and the running powers are as good to-day as when I first had it."

Mr. ARTHUR DEBNEY, Market Gardener and Seed Grower, Biggleswade, April 6th, 1906.

"I have pleasure in informing you that the 3 'Ivel' Bicycles which I have had from you have given me entire satisfaction. As you are aware I have used them all the year round in my business, and I am delighted with the way they have carried me. I always recommend your machines to my friends."

RICHARD WHITE, Esq., 40, Chelsea Gardens, London, S.W., March, 1906.

"Instead of having a new Ivel Bicycle this year as I intended, I am sending you my old one to be done up, for it is running as well as ever. As I use my machine all the year round, and it having been in use for 4 years without having anything done to it, and considering I ride 16 stone, I think it speaks for itself as to its stability and workmanship. My previous Ivel, which I rode for 4 years, and then sold to a tradesman for shop work, is still in use."

GEORGE TURNER, Esq., 40, St. John's, Bedford, March 10th, 1906.

"Just a line to say how pleased I am with my last new Cycle. It goes splendidly and seems strong enough for any amount of rough work.

You know I cycle a lot and this is the third machine I have had built by you, and each of the others I disposed of readily for £5, after 3 years hard work in each case. I think it speaks well for the stability of your Cycles to be able to make that price after 3 years wear."

H. V. L. KELHAM, Esq., Tangley Court, Burgh Heath Road, Epsom, April 3rd, 1905.

"I am well satisfied with the machine you have built for me which is quite as good as those you have previously built, and my wife is also very pleased with the way in which her machine goes."

Miss C. J. WOOD, The Nurses' Hostel, Francis Street, W.C., March 22nd, 1905.

"I have pleasure in enclosing cheque for the Tricycle received yesterday. If it has as honourable a career as its predecessor which has carried me to perfect satisfaction for eight years, I shall be quite content ; I think it only visited your Works for an overhaul once during that time."

E. H. OLIPHANT, Esq., Crow Holt Lodge, Woburn, R.S.O. Beds., Jan. 24th, 1904.

"The Bicycle has been very satisfactory. I have used it in all weathers, and it continues to run as well as when new."

THEODORE HAUGHTON, Esq., School House, Rugby, May 14th, 1903.

"The machine is very satisfactory, and runs beautifully."

LADY DORA YEOMAN, 5, Royal Crescent, Whitby, April 30th, 1903.

"Lady Dora Yeoman has been most thoroughly satisfied with her Bicycle which Mr. Albone built for her 3 years ago."

R. A. BAXTER, Esq., Beckington, Bath, May 24th, 1903.

"The Bicycle came yesterday and I rode it at once, and could not wish for a better looking or running machine."

F. E. WALLIS ADAMS, Esq., The Elms, Hoo, Rochester, Feb. 25th, 1902.

"I cannot say too much in favour of the Bicycle you made for me just 3 years ago. It has been an excellent machine."

C. V. DUNGEY, Esq., Middletons, Granbrook, October 21st, 1902.

"My Ivel Bicycle goes very well indeed, and I am quite satisfied with it. Many have admired the machine."

11

W. H. GREENWOOD, Esq., Metherington, November 10th, 1902.

" I have not expended one penny on the ' Ivel ' Bicycle nor had occasion to make only the slightest adjustment in any way, and it is as good as when I had it. I am perfectly satisfied with it in every way, for, having been in constant use for 15 months it speaks for itself."

Mrs. E. J. GRIFFITHS, Ty-Coch, Brynsiencyn, Anglesey, May 29th, 1902.

" I am delighted with my new Bicycle. It is really a beautifully made machine in every way."

G. FRANCIS HIGGINS, Esq., Government House, Madras, February 6th, 1902.

" The machine you made me about a year ago, has given every satisfaction."

Mrs. MARY E. KENNARD, The Barn, Market Harboro,' October 31st, 1902.

" I have enjoyed riding my ' Ivel ' very much, and only regret that the Winter will put a stop to long outings."

B. E. DUNBAR KILBURN, Esq., 6, Stanhope Street, Hyde Park, W. Sept. 4th, 1902.

" The machine runs excellently and has been much commented on and admired."

C. W. KINGSTON, Esq., Langley Lodge, Lemsford Road, St. Albans, May 20th, 1902.

" I returned home to-day after a week's tour on my ' Ivel ' and as my Cycle now records 383 miles, I consider I have thoroughly tested the machine. I have ridden it over all sorts of roads and in all kinds of weather, chiefly bad, and I am more than satisfied with my mount. It is in every way a magnificent machine, and I can find no fault with it. The Bicycle has been greatly admired and I shall lose no opportunity of recommending my friends to come to you when they want a machine."

JOSHUA PAGE, Esq., Westbury House, Ashwell, Herts., April 11th, 1902.

" I wish to thank you for having built for me such a splendid machine. It is in every way quite satisfactory."

MOTOR CYCLES.

PERCY H. JORDAN, Esq., Manor Street, Braintree, January 5th, 1906.

" You may be pleased to hear that the Ivel Motor Cycle I had from you 3 years ago is still in good running order, although it has been driven over 33,000 miles on all roads and in all weathers. Its consistency in running has been wonderful and only on one occasion, through a short circuit in the coil, was I unable to reach my destination on it, and I am afraid it will yet be some time before you receive an order for a new machine from me."

ALFRED R. BURTON, Esq., 2, George Street, Richmond, Surrey, Sept. 24th, 1903.

" I have great pleasure in testifying to the good workmanship and general excellency of the Ivel Motor Bicycle I purchased of you in July last. It has been much admired by all my friends and pronounced a first-class machine. I may say I have had four Bicycles of you all good and most satisfactory, but the Motor Bicycle more than retains your reputation."

CHAS. E. DONALDSON, Esq., Matang, Perak, Straits Settlements, Oct. 1st, 1903.

" I have now given the Ivel Motor Bicycle a month's trial and it has given me perfect satisfaction. I can confidently recommend my friends to go to you, if they require a serviceable Motor Cycle at a reasonable cost."

Copy of Illuminated Testimonial presented to me by a large number of Cyclists who frequented the North Road :—

DEAR DAN,   November 29th, 1885.

The Cyclists visiting Biggleswade having for many years past received at your hands at all times and at all hours numerous acts of kindness and self-denying attention, desire to express to you their hearty thanks for the considerable treatment you have invariably shown them, and the assistance you have rendered by pace-making for them when racing or during long distance rides, and in numerous other ways doing all in your power to administer to their comfort and convenience. They also wish to make some slight acknowledgement of your exertions on their behalf and combining to express to you their high opinion of your sterling good qualities, request your acceptance of a tangible token of their regard in the shape of a **Gold Chain** which they hope you will accept and wear with the consciousness of its being a tribute of the esteem in which you are held by the subscribers.

12

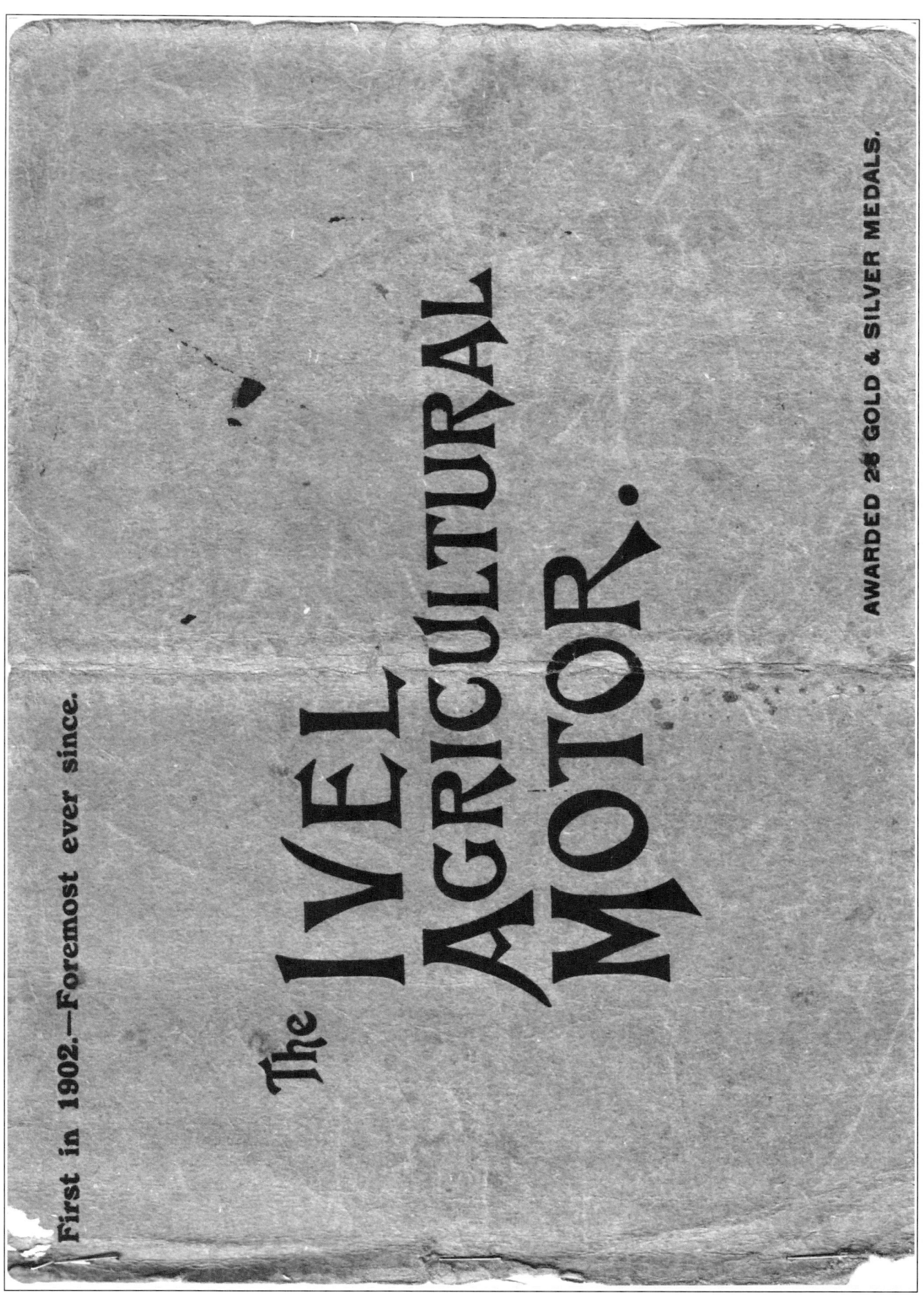

First in 1902.—Foremost ever since.

The IVEL AGRICULTURAL MOTOR.

AWARDED 26 GOLD & SILVER MEDALS.

All Previous Lists Cancelled.

The Ivel Agricultural Motor.

The Ivel Agricultural Motors, Ltd.,

Head Office: 45, GREAT MARLBOROUGH STREET,

London, W.

Telegrams: "IVEL, LONDON."
A.B.C. code, 5th Edition used.
Telephone No. 9295 CENTRAL.

The Ivel Agricultural Motor.

IN bringing before your notice the Ivel Agricultural Motor, it is unnecessary for us to set out the innumerable advantages which must accrue particularly to the agriculturist and farmer in being able to dispense with cattle. The expense of upkeep, sickness, and the necessity for having reserve animals, and the slow manner in which the work is accomplished where cattle are employed, all tend to make their use an expensive and burdensome item in the cultivation of land and for general use in agriculture.

In the Ivel Agricultural Motor we have a machine which will do agricultural work. The machine is reliable, easy to control, simple in construction, and applicable to nearly every form of implement at present drawn by cattle, and every type of machine such as chaff cutters, threshers, pumps, mills, dynamos, etc., where engine power has now to be employed. We would like to emphasise the fact that the Ivel is in no way an experiment; it was placed on the market more than four years ago, was the first practical Agricultural Motor, and is a machine that should be owned by every farmer.

The Ivel Agricultural Motor has competed at a large number or ploughing matches and other competitions and has carried out all the work that it has been put to with absolute success. Altogether 26 gold and silver medals have been won by the Ivel Motor, including the Silver Medal of the Royal Agricultural Society of England, and the Gold Medal of the Highland and Agricultural Society of Scotland, and the two premier societies of the British Isles ; in fact, the Ivel Agricultural Motor has proved to be the best Agricultural Motor on the market. Copies of testimonials received from users of Ivel Motors will be sent on application.

Since the Ivel Agricultural Motor was placed on the market a number of the machines have been sold in the United Kingdom ;

**The late Dan Albone,
Inventor of the Ivel Agricultural Motor.**

2

many have also been exported and are working satisfactorily in the following countries :—

Portugal, Egypt, Transvaal, East Griqualand, Orange River Colony, Natal, Tasmania, Germany, France, Belgium, Hungary, India, Cuba, Turkey, Sweden, Austria, Victoria, New South Wales, Cape Colony, New Zealand, South Australia, West Australia, Philippine Islands, Sandwich Islands, Nigeria, United States of America, Peru, Canada, British East Africa, Straits Settlements, Brazil, Argentine.

The Ivel Agricultural Motor is capable of hauling a 2, 3 or 4-furrow plough, the number of furrows to be ploughed at a time depending of course on the field whether undulating or flat, and the nature of the soil. It can also haul a cultivator, two reapers and binders, two mowing machines, or in fact any agricultural implement used for the cultivation of the land. Any existing agricultural machine can be attached to the Ivel Agricultural Motor; for mowers and binders the connection is made by taking out the poles usually used, when cattle are used, and a small spring coupling (which is supplied with the motor) substituted.

Apart from working in the field, the capabilities of the Ivel Agricultural Motor are invaluable on the farm. Among other things it can be used for driving a full-size threshing machine, chaff-cutter, grinding machine, mill, pump, dynamo, and any other work at present accomplished by the ordinary oil or steam engine generally used for three purposes.

With the Ivel Agricultural Motor it is possible to turn in quite as small a space when ploughing as one can with horses or oxen. It is therefore unnecessary to leave wider headlands than when cattle are used for doing similar work.

The motive power of the Ivel Agricultural Tractor is supplied by a double cylinder, governed engine which develops 18/20 h.p. when using petrol as fuel. The engine is extremely simple in construction, and is made so that petrol, paraffin, kerosene or alcohol can be used. The carburettor fitted is suitable for running the engine on petrol, but we can fit our patent Ivel Vapouriser at an extra cost so that the heavier fuels, such as paraffin, kerosene and alcohol, can be utilised.

The power of the engine is transmitted through a friction clutch and thence by chains to the back axle to which are attached the driving road wheels. One speed forward and a reverse are fitted to the Ivel Agricultural Motor. Band brakes are fitted to the road wheels which have extra wide rims with grips.

For stationary work, such as driving a threshing machine, grinding mill, chaff-cutter, dynamo, etc., a pulley is fitted, which is coupled direct to the engine.

The machine complete weighs 32 cwts., and as this weight is distributed over the three wide wheels the machine hardly makes any impression on the land, in fact, comparing it with cattle, it is very much less.

The Ivel Agricultural Motor is made of the most suitable material and best workmanship throughout, and every care is taken in its manufacture to secure the best results. Should however, any part of the machine prove defective, through bad material or workmanship, and this part is returned to the Works carriage paid within six months from its delivery to the purchaser, we undertake to repair, or if necessary supply a new part free of charge. Every motor or part is sold by us upon the condition that the purchaser shall accept this undertaking in lieu of all warranties implied by Law, and shall have no further claim against us on account of any delay, damage or loss arising from such defect.

PRICES.

The Ivel Agricultural Motor	£300
Vapouriser for paraffin, kerosene or alcohol, extra	£12 10
Magneto Ignition, extra	£30
Mowing and Reaping Attachment for either two Binders or Mowers	£6 10
Sunshade (see illustration, page 15), suitable for tropical climates, extra	£10
Three-furrow Plough	£16 10

All the above prices are delivered at our works. Packing extra, which we charge at cost.

3

PLOUGHING.

Ploughing is without doubt the most expensive work that has to be done on the farm when it is done by horses or oxen. This work is performed in exactly the same way by the Ivel Agricultural Motor as when ploughing with cattle, that is, the plough is hauled in the rear. Any kind of 2, 3 or 4-furrow plough is suitable for use with the motor and the number of furrows that can be worked at a time, of course, depends entirely on the nature of the field, whether the soil is undulating or flat, and the depth required to be ploughed.

The weight of the Ivel Motor being only 32 cwts. it hardly makes any impression on the land, in fact, when compared with cattle ploughing, the weight on the land is very much less. It is not necessary to leave wider headlands when ploughing with the Ivel Motor, as it is able to turn on the same headlands as when cattle are employed for doing similar work. Another important point that agriculturists have to take into consideration when using mechanical traction is that with this motor they can plough by night (with the aid of acetylene lamps) as well as by day.

The cost of ploughing with the Ivel Agricultural Motor varies somewhat on account of the different conditions prevailing, such as nature of soil, depth required to be ploughed, size and condition of field, &c. By actual trials made in the vicinity of our works near Biggleswade, we have found that the Ivel Motor hauling a 3-furrow plough on medium soil to a depth of 7-in. is able to plough about 6 acres in 9 hours, the cost of doing this work being as follows :—

	£	s.	d.
20 gallons of kerosene or paraffin at 7d.	0	11	8
1 gallon of lubricating oil	0	3	0
Driver's wages	0	4	6
Ploughman's wages	0	3	0
Depreciation, wear and tear, and renewals	0	5	0
	£1	7	2

4

PLOUGHING.

FIRST IN 1902, FOREMOST EVER SINCE.

The Ivel Agricultural Motor hauling a three-furrow plough.

5

PLOUGHING.

The Ivel Agricultural Motor hauling a 3-furrow plough, with a Potato Planter.

CULTIVATING.

FIRST IN 1902,
FOREMOST
EVER SINCE.

The Ivel Agricultural Motor hauling a Cultivator.

The Ivel Agricultural Motor is specially adapted for cultivating, the motor, on account of its light weight, being able to travel over land that has already been ploughed. The cultivator, or scuffle, is attached to the rear of the motor, in the same way as when cattle are employed. Any kind of cultivator can be used, but it is as well to have one which is at least as wide as the motor.

The Ivel Agricultural Motor can also be used for cultivating land that has not already been ploughed. The cost of cultivating land with an Ivel Motor depends a good deal on the conditions prevailing. However, one may take it that the cost is always somewhat less than when ploughing.

7

REAPING AND BINDING.

The Ivel Agricultural Motor hauling Two Binders at Night.

mechanical traction is a great advantage, for in addition to being able to accomplish the work during the day, the Ivel Motor can continue its work during the night. The cost of reaping and binding with the Ivel Motor differs somewhat on account of various conditions, but with one 6 ft. binder attached to the motor, 2½ acres could be cut in an hour, the consumption of fuel being 2¼ gallons of paraffin and 1 pint of lubricating oil. If the field is such so that two binders can be used, the work accomplished would be about 4 acres, the consumption of fuel being about the same. We might mention that when the Ivel Motor is doing this work it is done in a similar manner as when horses are used, with the exception that the corners of the field are cut round, this being the best and quickest way, a good deal of time being saved by this, as there never is any necessity to back the binder. The Ivel Patent Attachment, by which two binders can be hauled satisfactorily, is supplied at extra cost ; part of this attachment can also be used for hauling two mowers.

This work can also be done by the Ivel Agricultural Motor; it is lighter work than ploughing, and the motor is therefore able to travel faster. One or two binders can be hauled, according to the condition of the field and crop, the binders being fixed to the motor by the Ivel Patent Attachment. Reaping and binding, as all agriculturists know, has to be done very quickly, and here again

8

375

REAPING AND BINDING.

The Ivel Agricultural Motor hauling two Reapers and Binders.

9

MOWING.

The Ivel Agricultural Motor hauling two Mowing Machines.
(FITTED WITH THE IVEL PATENT ATTACHMENT.)

The Ivel Agricultural Motor can be used for hauling mowers, either one, two or three, the number of machines that can be hauled at a time depending on conditions, such as size of field, crop, etc. No special mowers are necessary, any ordinary standard machine being suitable.

The work is done in exactly the same way as when animals are employed, i.e., the mower or mowers are fitted to the back of the motor. When two mowers are being hauled by an Ivel Motor about four acres can be cut in an hour, the quantity of fuel consumed would come out to about $2\frac{1}{4}$ gallons.

The Ivel Patent Attachment, so that two mowers can be used satisfactorily, can be supplied at an extra cost; part of this attachment can also be used for hauling two binders.

10

377

THRESHING.

FIRST IN 1902, FOREMOST EVER SINCE.

The Ivel Agricultural Motor driving a Threshing Machine (54in. Double Blast), and Chaff-Cutter.

Farm machinery such as threshers, chaff-cutters, mills, pumps, etc., can be driven successfully with the Ivel Agricultural Motor. For doing this work a pulley is fitted on the main engine shaft of the motor, and the power is transmitted from this pulley by a belt to the machine that is required to be driven. The engine has governors fitted, so that if the load is suddenly made lighter the engine at once cuts out. The consumption of fuel depends on the work that is being done, but when the motor is working to its fullest capacity it uses about 2½ gallons per hour.

I hereby certify that the Ivel Agricultural Motor was at work at Elm Farm, Caldecote, near Biggleswade, and drove one of the largest threshing machines and elevator (5ft. double blast), and threshed some very long rough sheaves of oats. It was fed for testing purposes, and came through the trial without any stoppage and with very great success. The motor was driven at its full speed.

(Signed) THOS. COCKRILL. A.M.I.C.E.

11

The Ivel Agricultural Motor

Obtained the HIGHEST AWARD,
The SILVER MEDAL of the

Royal Agricultural Society of England,

At the 1904 SHOW.

"There can be no doubt that Motors are of much interest at the present time and may become a great factor in the agriculture of the future. It was somewhat surprising, therefore, to find so poor an exhibit in view of the capabilities that have been shown by motor cars, and still more surprising to find how little those who do exhibit in this class (and in that of motor-driven agricultural implements) have profited by the experience of makers of pleasure vehicles. **Only one can be said to be worthy of favourable mention in this Report, viz., the Ivel Agricultural Motor.**

"Article 2353.—*The Ivel Agricultural Motors, Ltd.,* 45, Great Marlborough Street, London, W. The Ivel. Price £300.—This tractor has come within the range of what may be considered a practical agricultural machine. It is driven by a two-cylinder horizontal petrol engine which is stated to give 14 B.H.P. The crank-shaft is parallel to the axle of the driving wheels. The revolutions are approximately 800 per minute. The first reduction from the clutch shaft to the intermediate shaft for going ahead is by a Renold silent chain gear, and for going astern by pinion and spur wheels, both gears being always in mesh. The drive from the intermediate shaft to the differential gear on the main driving wheel axle is by sprocket wheels and roller chain. The driving wheels are 41½ in. in diameter with 9 in. treads. The normal speed is about four miles an hour, which can be varied by changing the sprocket pinion on the intermediate shaft, for which provision is made. The tractor is fitted with one speed ahead and one astern, each driven by a separate cone clutch, and both operated by one and

the same lever. The ahead clutch is held into gear by springs (there being no end thrust when in gear) and out of gear by the lever; the astern clutch has no springs, but is forced into gear by the lever; thus the change is as simple and positive as possible. There are no cogged wheels to be brought into or out of mesh, and there is no possibility of both gears being in action at the same moment. The engine shaft is continued through the casing and carries a pulley for use in driving stationary machinery by belt.

"We saw a tractor ploughing with a three-furrow plough, plough-man riding upon the plough. The land at Biggleswade is light, and so the test was not such a good one as we should have wished; but owing to three days of almost constant rain the ground was very soft, requiring the wheels of the tractor to be fitted with paddles. It made light of its task, however, at a speed of about three and a half miles an hour, the depth of the furrows being about 6 in. and their average width about 8¾ in. The turning at the headlands did not present any difficulty, the motor being adapted for turning in a very small circle. It was evident that the tractor was of ample power.

"We did not see the tractor pull a reaper and binder, but we were satisfied that it was well adapted for the purpose; in fact its capabilities would probably show to the greatest advantage in such work. It is also capable of driving a threshing machine, chaff-cutter, and other stationary farm machinery."—*Extract from Judges' report.*

12

FIRST IN 1902, FOREMOST EVER SINCE.

Hauling a Cultivator.

Driving a Chaff Cutter.

Hauling a Reaper and Binder.

Driving an Ice Making Machine.

The Ivel Agricultural Motor

Obtained the
HIGHEST AWARD of the

Suffolk Agricultural Association.

TRIALS HELD AT IPSWICH, JUNE 7th and 8th, 1906.

A prize of £10 and a diploma for the best combination of machinery for ploughing by power (other than horse power), which, in the opinion of the judges, would be most suitable for landowners and farmers.

The Ploughing Trials commenced at 10.30 a.m. on the first day of the show.

Just over an acre of land was allotted to each competitor, but the soil was very light and exceedingly dry, in fact, many of the spectators considered that a heavier soil would have afforded a far more satisfactory test. Although the friable character of the ground made ploughing easy work, it was a disadvantage so far as the tractors were concerned, for at the headlands the wheels of the engine sometimes sank into the soft soil and made turning a difficult matter. The ploughing was, according to the judges' directions, to be 8 in. deep, and the competitors were to get through their work as quickly as they could with the least possible expenditure of fuel.

Some very good and uniform work was accomplished by all the competitors, but it was soon evident that the Ivel motor would finish first. The Ivel motor finished its plot at 12.45, having covered the acre in 2¼ hours; and in looking admiringly at the completed work an eminent authority characterised it as a "very creditable performance."

Six gallons of petrol was consumed by the engine, the paraffin served out not having been touched. The —— tractor was stopped by the judges soon after the Ivel had finished; whilst the —— tractor, which had evidently been worked too fast, had just previously been rendered *hors de combat* by burning out its fusible plug.

The Ivel Motor not only demonstrated its suitability for ploughing, but on the second day of the Show was likewise to be seen working a 7-tine Martin cultivator, and also drawing two of Harrison, McGregor & Co.'s 6 ft. "Albion" mowers. Asked as to the motor's behaviour when worked by paraffin instead of alcohol, the inventor answered our question by immediately running on that fuel; and its graceful evolutions on that occasion, followed by the two mowers, were indeed eloquent of the ease with which the engine can be controlled, and the facility with which it can be made to travel in the most tortuous track.

The Judges in the Implement classes were Mr. T. Stirton, of Ipswich, and Mr. F. W. Stearn, of Old Newton, whose awards were as follows:— Diploma of merit and £15 to the Ivel Agricultural Motors, Ltd., for the Ivel Agricultural Motor working Ransomes' plough.— Extract from *Implement and Machinery Review*.

The Ivel Agricultural Motor

Obtained the HIGHEST AWARD,
The GOLD MEDAL of the

Highland and Agricultural Society of Scotland.

TRIALS HELD AT PERTH, SEPTEMBER 15th, 1904.

The first part of the trial consisted in the cutting of a portion of a field of oats. The crop was of medium height, the greater part standing up regularly, thus enabling the cutting to be done continuously round two plots which had been measured and set apart for the trials.

The Ivel Motor, to which was attached 5-feet-cut, reaper and binder, was set to cut a plot measuring 2·73 acres. This task it accomplished in 1 hour 54 minutes, using 2·02 gallons of petrol, or at the rate of one acre in 41¾ minutes, with an expenditure of 0·74 gallons of petrol per acre, practically costing 9½ pence, not including the wages of the men and the interest on the cost of Motor and depreciation.

The Ivel Motor worked satisfactorily and the engines did not stop once during the trial; the motor was required to stop on several occasions for a few seconds on account of objects interfering with the working of the binder.

The Ivel motor was also tried on a portion of the field in which the crop was slightly heavier than the rest, while some bits were laid, thus necessitating the machine to cut one way and return empty.

The Ivel drew a three-furrow plough made specially for the motor. This plough can be altered if required into a two-furrow implement without using a spanner. The Ivel seemed to experience no difficulty in executing the task allotted to it, the depth of the furrows varying from 6 inches to 8 inches.

The adaptability of the motor to so many operations pertaining to farming renders it a most useful and valuable source of power. The quickness with which the work is done is especially noticeable. Beyond the interest on outlay, and depreciation, the agricultural motor does not cost anything until it is put into motion.— *Extract from Judges' report.*

14

THE IVEL AGRICULTURAL MOTOR.

FIRST IN 1902, FOREMOST EVER SINCE.

The Ivel Agricultural Motor, fitted with Sunshade for Colonial use.
Beside the Motor is the crate in which machines are packed for abroad.

The Ivel Agricultural Motor

Obtained the HIGHEST AWARDS,
TWO GOLD MEDALS of the

Essex Agricultural Association.

At the TRIALS HELD AT BRENTWOOD, JUNE 14th and 15th, 1906.

Class B. Best Motors to plough not less than half-an-acre of land, time and draught to be taken into consideration, the depth of ploughing to be not less than 6 inches.

There were two entries in this class, but only one put in an appearance. This was the Ivel, which was attached to a 3-furrow Ransome's plough, and put to the test of ploughing half-an-acre. This it accomplished without a stoppage in 1 hour 16 minutes, keeping to rather more than 6 inches deep, and laying the land perfectly level with a straight furrow. The length of the land being only 16 rods of course accounted for a longer time than it would be otherwise. The weight of the motor is 1½ tons, and as one wheel which takes half the weight runs in the bottom of the furrow, very little compression of the land need be feared, in fact, the track made by the wheel running on the unploughed land made no more impression than a Cambridge roll would do. We unhesitatingly awarded it the Gold Medal.

Class C. Best Motors suitable for Agricultural purposes, to be tested for any work required.

The Ivel was again the only entry in this class. Taking ploughing as one of the "purposes," and that a most important one, we thought it most satisfactory, and difficult to beat. It was next tried upon a 5-ft. threshing machine—unthreshed corn not being available, wheat straw was put through the drum. It then hauled the machine, showing plenty of power it this direction. It was then used to draw two 6-ft. mowers, but one machine being unfit, owing to its cutting bar being out of order, one only was used, which it worked at a good pace, turning very short corners with marvellous ease.

It was a matter of regret to us that there were no other competitors, but as this motor did all we asked of it, and went through all the tests provided for it in a satisfactory manner, we awarded it the Gold Medal.—*Extract from Judges' report.*

R. W. CHRISTY, *Referee.*

W. DANNATT. }
JAMES F. BENSON. } *Judges.*

The Ivel Agricultural Motor

Obtained the HIGHEST AWARD,
The GOLD MEDAL of the

Essex Agricultural Association.

At the TRIALS HELD AT SOUTHEND, JUNE 14th and 15th, 1905.

Class 138 (Best Motors to plough not less than half-an-acre of land). Four very busy Motors of varied design and of steam and petrol power, in this class, formed one of the greatest attractions of the Show during the time of working.

The little Ivel was a marvel of energy and efficiency reminding one of its inventor, for it was here, there, and everywhere hauling plough, mowers, cultivators, driving a threshing machine, and never out of place, always coming up smiling, apparently as happy and cheerful in its various duties as the inventor himself. It was really extraordinary how an implement of only 1½ tons weight could get sufficient grip of the land to haul a 3-furrow plough 6-in. deep in stiff soil that has been seven years down to lucerne. This, however, it managed with marvellous ease, and not only performed the 4-bout non-stop run which the Judges arranged to test for overheating, &c., but immediately this was over it operated the 3-furrow plough, 8-in. deep, with very little difficulty, so that your Judges had no hesitation in awarding this the GOLD MEDAL. The 4-bout non-stop run works out about ·621 of an acre per hour.—*Extract from Judges' report.*

Signed { J. W. MOSS.
W. DANNATT.
REUBEN HUNT.

16

SOME PRESS OPINIONS.

From 1902-1906.

"The Times," *August 30th, 1902.*

HARVESTING BY MOTOR.—Harvesting in Lincolnshire has been conducted with the aid of a petrol motor specially invented for farm use. The motor, attached to a reaper and binder, cut a field of barley at Tinwell. The motor has also been tried with a double furrow plough, and cut some deep and even furrows through stubble.

SEPT. 4, 1902.—The motor employed was the Ivel agricultural motor, of which Mr. D. Albone is the inventor and maker.

"The Field," *November 22nd, 1902.*

In response to requests from readers abroad concerning the efficiency and adaptability of the Ivel Agricultural Motor, we were privileged to witness the contrivance at work last week. The motor had been successfully employed, first in drawing the mowing machine and then the reaper and binder, while it has also been found to answer as a substitute for horses in drawing scuffles and ploughs. On the occasion of our visit it was doing duty in the plough,

an ordinary double furrow implement, which is usually drawn by three horses. In this capacity it certainly answered very satisfactorily indeed, working quite smoothly, and generally, in such a way as to satisfy the most fastidious. The land was soft enough after the recent rains to afford a fair indication of its action in compressing the soil, a rich loam, and yet no objectionable results were attained, either in the upturned furrow or in packing the subsoil. In all probability it will be less harmful, even to soft land, than the three or four horses it displaces, at least as regards the subsoil. The furrows last week were 10in. × 7in., but any reasonable width and depth is well within its capacity, and travelling at the unvarying rate of four miles an hour, and being easily turned and readily tractable, it covers in a day at least as large an area as two similar ploughs drawn by horses.

The application of the Ivel Agricultural Motor on farms and estates is practically limitless. It is portable, and attachable to any description of implement: with equal ease it can be used for the driving of machinery in the barn, threshing, pumping water, &c.

An Ivel Agricultural Motor cultivating in the Straits Settlements.

An Ivel Agricultural Motor ploughing in Cuba.

SOME PRESS OPINIONS.

From 1902-1906.

"The Daily Telegraph," *July 26th,* 1902.

The motor has been regarded with unfriendly eye by the farmer, but it may be that it will come to be received by him as an ally. Some interesting trials were carried out by Mr. Albone, at Biggleswade, of a motor designed for agricultural purposes. It is of eight-horse power, and runs on three wheels; and it was shown drawing a mowing machine, performing the work satisfactorily and expeditiously. Reaping and other machines may be attached to it; or it can be employed as a stationary engine to drive chaff-cutting, pulping and other machines. Now that agricultural labour is scarce, it may be that the motor will prove a boon to the farmer, even though it displaces his beloved horses. At this early stage it is impossible, of course, to compare the relative cost of working, which is the crux of the question. But it is something in favour of the motor that it only eats when it works, and that it can continue its labours as long as its driver wishes; while the speed at which it can travel is greatly in excess of that of the horse.

"The Standard," *June 25th,* 1903.

This machine has been so thoroughly tested in many parts of the kingdom for drawing a plough, a cultivator, mower, reaper and binder, and for the work of a stationary engine, that there is no doubt as to its efficiency.

"The Times," *November 4th,* 1903.

Ploughing by motor formed a novel feature at the annual competitions in connection with The North Kent Agricultural Association. The tractor used was an Ivel Agricultural Motor of 12-horse power. A three-furrow Canadian plough did not prove to be suited to the wet and heavy condition of the land, but when subsequently the motor was attached to a double-furrow balance plough, an implement well known to be adapted to the soil of the district, some excellent work was done. The motor, it should be explained, can be used with any kind of plough, and travelled when at work yesterday at the rate of about three and a half miles per hour.

"The Scotsman," *September 16th,* 1904.

AGRICULTURE.—Yesterday the practical trial of agricultural motors in the cutting of corn and ploughing of land took place at Picton's Hill, near Perth, in presence of a large attendance of farmers from all parts of Scotland. The motors entered were the Ivel and the ——, the former being by the Ivel Agricultural Company, and the latter by ——. The Ivel is an 18 h.p. with double cylinder petrol motor. A friction clutch is employed for transmitting the power of the engine. One speed and a reverse are fitted, and the speed is regulated by a single little lever. Two band brakes are fitted to the road wheels. The motor is also useful for stationary work, such as driving a thresher, dynamo, pump, mill, etc., a belt pulley being driven directly off the engine. The machine complete weighs about 30 cwt., and as this weight is distributed over three wide wheels, it makes hardly any impression on the ground. The motors were first of all tried in the cutting of a field of oats. The crop was of medium height, the greater portion standing up regularly, which enabled the cutting to be done round the plots. The work was therefore a comparatively easy task. Attached to the Ivel was a Harrison MacGregor, Albion reaper and binder. The —— motor headed a Hornsby reaper and binder. Both machines did admirable work, and general satisfaction was expressed with what they had done. Unfortunately the —— motor broke down for a time, and was unable to finish the cutting, although later in the day it took part in the ploughing. The Ivel was by far the quicker of the two machines, and cut the three acres allotted to it in one hour and forty minutes. Doubts were expressed, however, as to the expedience of such rapid cutting, the view being that in a very short time the binder would be useless. The cutting by both machines was very clean, and even the most sceptical admitted that in the near future the agricultural motor would take the place of horses. After lunch a portion of the field heavier than the rest was tried, while some bits were laid with the view of testing the machines. Owing to the break-down, the —— motor was unable to take part in this, but the Ivel gave a satisfactory display.

The motors were thereafter tried with the plough, and both made a highly creditable appearance, the Ivel again, however, covering the ground at a more rapid pace than the ——. What struck the spectators, perhaps, as much as anything was the handiness of the machines. While the cutting was very favourably commented on the criticisms on the ploughing were not less favourable. The furrows were evenly turned and about 7 inches deep. Taking the exhibition as a whole it excited great interest, and was in every way a success, so much so that the judges awarded each motor one of the Highland and Agricultural Society's gold medals, not in the light that the machines were perfect, but in the recognition of the substantial progress which the makers exhibited in the bringing out of a thoroughly useful agricultural motor. The Committee are also to prepare a detailed report, which will be published in due course.

"The Daily Telegraph," *September 4th,* 1905.

NOVEL HARVESTING.—For the purpose of showing the usefulness of the agricultural motor, an interesting demonstration has been given on Mrs. K. Kendall's farm, near Biggleswade. The field was illuminated by acetylene gas, and drawing two 6ft. mowers, the motor cut fifteen acres in three hours and thirty-five minutes, the start having taken place at 9 p.m. The demonstration was given to show that the motor can be used day and night, so enabling a field to be mowed or ploughed in the shortest possible time.

18

SOME PRESS OPINIONS.

From 1902-1906.

"Motor Traction," *June 29th, 1905.*

The Ivel Agricultural Motors, Ltd., 45, Gt. Marlborough Street, W., are well known from the successes of their motor, which is capable of doing practically any work that may be desired about a farm. The machines have from time to time been illustrated in *Motor Traction*, and these representations and their recent performances in the colonies and abroad well illustrate their capabilities. This firm may be said to be the pioneer firm in agricultural motoring.

"The Times," *August 7th, 1906.*

A very interesting experiment was tried by the Ivel Agricultural Motors (Limited) last Thursday afternoon and night on a farm near Biggleswade, occupied by Mr. George Pope. With one of their motors hauling two binders they started cutting and binding in a field of corn during the afternoon, and when darkness fell, the work was continued with success by the light of acetylene lamps fitted to the binders. Unfortunately the storm which visited many parts of England that night did not omit Biggleswade, and operations were necessarily discontinued when the wheat became too wet to be fit for cutting. Up to that point the experiment was entirely successful, and there can be no question as to its value. Economy apart—and we have no exact materials for forming a judgment on that point—any person at all familiar with the exigencies of farming, particularly in the more humid districts of our islands, will perceive at once that occasions on which it is desirable, if it be possible, to carry on the work of harvesting by night as well as by day, are numerous; and, even if the expense be considerably greater than that of harvest work by day, it is obvious that the gain by contrast with the possible and probable loss from delay, would often be far in excess of any additional expense upon which it would be reasonable to reckon. Even in this case the chances are that the experiment paid its expenses handsomely.

"The Standard," *October 26th, 1906.*

Motor Plough Competition.—The annual ploughing match of the Boston and District Agricultural Society was held yesterday, in splendid weather, on Mr. W. Dennis's farm at Wyberton. A large number of horse teams competed, and the class open to all England for the silver cup, presented by Mr. G. H. Faber, M.P., went to Mr. Walter Leggatt, of Lincoln. As is now usual at ploughing matches, there was a class open to the world, for motor ploughs, and the first prize (a gold medal) was won by the Ivel Agricultural Motor, which was shown hauling a three-furrow plough, 9 inches deep, as well as cultivating. The president of the society, Mr. W. Gar^nt, late M.P. for Boston, was present at the proceedings.

"The Review of the River Plate," Buenos Aires, *January, 1907.*

Much discussion has taken place in agricultural papers at home and in America, as to the possibilities of motors for agricultural work. The general opinion appears to be that there is an enormous scope for the motor, especially in countries where cereal areas and grazing tracks are so very extensive. The most successful agricultural motor yet placed on the market is the "Ivel," made in England, and which has literally swept the board of gold and silver medals for its class at shows since 1902.

THE LATEST IVEL AGRI-CULTURAL MOTOR.

THE FIRST PRACTICAL AGRI-CULTURAL MOTOR. THE IVEL, 1902.

19

The Ivel Agricultural Motor

HAS BEEN AWARDED

26 Gold and Silver Medals,

HIGHEST AWARDS.

Silver Medal, 1904, Royal Agricultural Society of England.

Gold Medal   ,,   The Highland and Agricultural Society of Scotland.

Gold Medal   ,,   The Agricultural Society of Egypt.

Gold Medal   ,,   The Upton-by-Chester Ploughing Association.

Gold Medal   ,,   The Stow-on-the-Wold and Chipping Norton Agricultural Association.

Silver Medal   ,,   The Royal Lancashire Agricultural Association.

Silver Medal   ,,   The Peterborough Agricultural Association.

Gold Medal   ,,   The North Kent Agricultural Association.

Silver Medal   ,,   The Royal Freebridge Association.

First Class Certificate of Merit, 1904, Pietermaritzburg, Natal.

Gold Medal, 1905, The Upton-by-Chester Ploughing Association.

Gold Medal   ,,   The Sheepy and District Ploughing Association.

Gold Medal   ,,   The Essex Agricultural Association.

Gold Medal   ,,   The Royal Lancashire Agricultural Association.

Gold Medal and Silver Cup, 1905, The Devon County Agricultural Association.

Silver Medal, 1905, The Cambs. and Isle of Ely Agricultural Society.

Gold Medal   ,,   The North Kent Agricultural Association.

Gold Medal   ,,   The Boston and District Agricultural Association.

Diploma of Merit, 1905, Suffolk Agricultural Association.

Gold Medal, 1906, The Rhuddlan and District Ploughing Association.

Gold Medal   ,,   The Upton-by-Chester Ploughing Association.

Gold Medal   ,,   The Alsager and District Ploughing Association.

Gold Medal   ,,   The Sheepy and District Ploughing Association.

Gold Medal   ,,   The Essex Agricultural Association.

Gold Medal   ,,   The Essex Agricultural Association.

First Prize   ,,   The Suffolk Agricultural Association.

Silver Medal   ,,   The Royal Freebridge Association.

Gold Medal   ,,   The Boston and District Ploughing Association.

Gold Medal   ,,   The Sheepy and District Ploughing Association.

Barclay & Fry—5,000—6.07.

20

387

Date of Application, 30th Apr., 1886
Complete Left, 31st Jan., 1887.
Complete Accepted, 1st Mar., 1887

~~~~~~

A.D. 1886, 30th APRIL. N° 5909.

~~~~~~

PROVISIONAL SPECIFICATION.

An Improved Construction of Road Vehicle.

I, DANIEL ALBONE, of the Ivel Cycle Works, Biggleswade in the County of Bedfordshire, Bicycle and Tricycle Maker, do hereby declare the nature of this invention to be as follows :—

My invention relates to an improved construction of road vehicle, and is applicable
5 more especially to that class of vehicles known as trotting traps and the like, which require to be built both light and strong.

In carrying this invention into effect I make the shafts of a length of metal tube, steel by preference, taking it round the body of the trap. The body is framed in metal (steel tubing by preference) and may be left open or panelled in.
10 The springs are attached to the body in any convenient way.

The bearings are of the double ball type, and their connection to the axle is by means of a detachable lower cap.

A suitable knuckle joint, the axis of which is at right angles to that of the ball bearing, is inserted in each of the brackets by which the bearings are bolted to the
15 springs, to allow of lateral oscillation of the body.

PHILLIPS & LEIGH,
Agents for the Applicant.

COMPLETE SPECIFICATION.

_____

An Improved Construction of Road Vehicle.

I, DANIEL ALBONE, of the "Ivel" Cycle Works, Biggleswade, in the County of Bedfordshire, Bicycle & Tricycle Maker, do hereby declare the nature of this invention and in what manner the same is to be performed, to be particularly described and ascertained in and by the following statement :—

My invention relates to an improved construction of road vehicle, and is applicable 5 more especially to that class of vehicles known as trotting traps and the like, which require to be built both light and strong.

In carrying this invention into effect I make the shafts of a length of metal tube, steel by preference, taking it round the body of the trap. The body is framed in metal (steel tubing by preference) and may be left open or panelled in.   10

The springs are attached to the body in any convenient way.

The bearings are of the double ball type, and their connection to the axle is by means of a detachable lower cap.

A suitable knuckle joint, the axis of which is at right angles to that of the ball bearing is inserted in each of the brackets by which the bearings are bolted to the 15 springs, to allow of lateral oscillation of the body.

In order that my invention and the means by which it can be carried into practical effect may be thoroughly understood, I will now describe it in detail referring in so doing to the accompanying figures which are to be taken as part of this specification and read therewith.   20

Fig. 1 is a side elevation, with the near wheel removed for the sake of clearness.

Fig. 2 is a detail elevation on a larger scale illustrating the connection of the spring to the ball bearing by means of a knuckle joint.

The shafts A are shewn as continuous and tubular, although I wish it to be distinctly understood that my invention does not limit me to this method of making 25 them, inasmuch as both the materials and the construction may be varied.

The body of the trap is shewn as constructed of metal tubing B and filled in with removeable panels C.

The axle D revolves in double ball bearings E, the boxes of which are fixed to the springs by means of clamps as illustrated in Fig. 1 or by bolts and nuts as illustrated 30 in Fig. 2.

Between the box of the bearing and the extensions by which it is attached to the spring I interpose a knuckle joint F the axis of which is at right angles with that of the axle D.

The wheels are of the kind known as double suspension spider wheels.   35

Complete
Specification.
A.D. 1886.—N° 5909.   3

Albone's Improved Construction of Road Vehicle.

The practical advantages of the embodiment of the above described structural novelties are

1. Great strength with diminished weight.
2. Abolition of rattle.
5   3. Easy running as far as the occupants of the vehicle are concerned.
4. Frictionless and light running as far as the horse or pony is concerned.
5. The facility with which the vehicle can be changed from one type to another by removing or putting in the panels, e.g., from an ordinary trap to a trotting-machine.

Having now particularly described and ascertained the nature of my said invention
10 and in what manner the same is to be performed, I declare that what I claim is :—

1. In a road vehicle the combination of metallic tubular framing, spider wheels and double ball bearings substantially for the purpose described with reference to the accompanying figures.
2. In a road vehicle the combination with the springs thereof of a knuckle joint
15 interposed between the body of the vehicle and the springs, the axis of said knuckle joint being at right angles with the axis of the axle of the vehicle substantially as described with reference to the accompanying figures.

PHILLIPS & LEIGH,
Patent Agents,
22, Southampton Buildings, Chancery Lane, W.C.,
Agents for the Applicant.

20

LONDON : Printed by DARLING AND SON.
For Her Majesty's Stationery Office.

1887.

[*This Drawing is a reproduction of the Original on a reduced scale*]

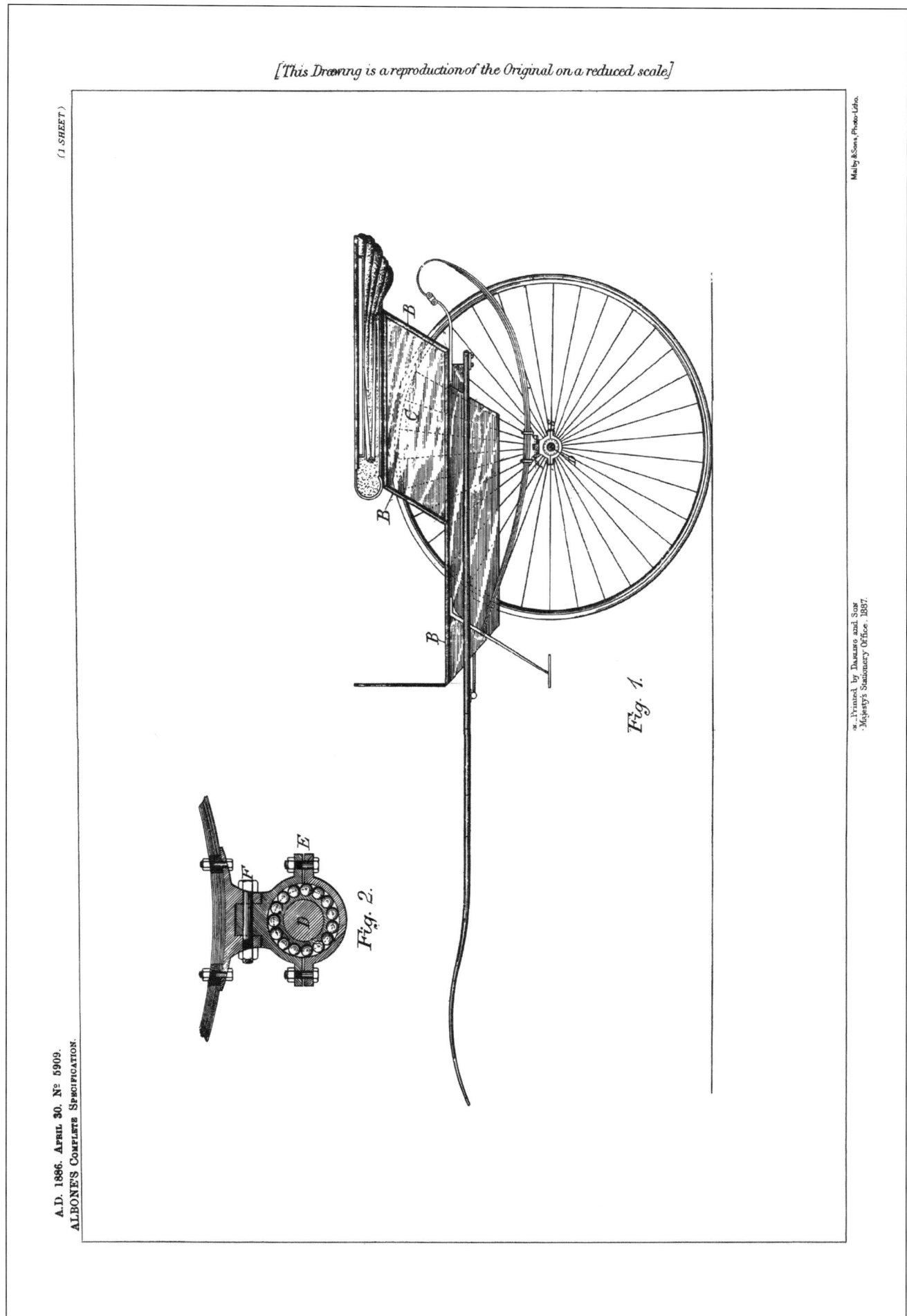

Fig. 1.

Fig. 2.

(1 SHEET)

A.D. 1886. APRIL 30. № 5909.
ALBONE'S COMPLETE SPECIFICATION.

Malby & Sons, Photo-Litho.

...Printed by DARLING and SON
Majesty's Stationery Office. 1887.

Date of Application, 24th Jan., 1888.
Complete Specification Left, 24th Oct., 1888
Complete Specification Accepted, 7th Dec., 1888

A.D. 1888. *24th January.* N° 1098.

PROVISIONAL SPECIFICATION.

An Improved Velocipede.

I, DAN ALBONE, of the "Ivel" Cycle Works, Biggleswade, in the County of Bedford, Manufacturer, do hereby declare the nature of this invention to be as follows :—

My invention relates to improvements in the manufacture of convertible velocipedes,
5   according to which the machine may be a tandem safety bicycle ; a safety bicycle ; a front steering tricycle, or a rear driving tandem tricycle, as may be desired ; and when the machine is set as a " safety " to carry two riders, they will both be between the front and the driving wheels, and both drive on to the same wheel.

In carrying my invention into effect, I make the frame longer than usual, by
10   inserting a removable piece therein, making the connections by means of knuckle-joints, or their equivalents. This removable piece carries a second saddle-tube, saddle, handle-bar, and the necessary additional chain-wheel, chain, and cranks.

To make the machine a tandem safety bicycle, the frame is lengthened by the insertion of the removable piece above mentioned. The chain wheel on the stalk thereof
15   drives on to the wheel on the back stalk, and the latter on to the rear wheel as usual.

To convert a tandem safety bicycle constructed according to my invention into a single safety bicycle, the removable piece is taken out with its attachments and the frame closed by means of the joint above described.

20   To convert a tandem safety bicycle constructed according to my invention into a single tricycle, the removable piece with its adjuncts is taken out the frame shut up and the rear wheel replaced by an axle and pair of wheels. The axle is strengthened by the addition of a bridge, and is furnished with a pair of lugs adapted to be connected to the fork ends of the frame.

25   To convert a tandem safety bicycle constructed according to my invention into a rear driving tandem tricycle, I replace the rear wheel of the bicycle in the manner explained in the last paragraph.

Dated this 24th day of January 1888.

PHILLIPS & LEIGH,
Agents for the Applicant.

30

Albone's Improved Velocipede.

COMPLETE SPECIFICATION.

An Improved Velocipede.

I, DAN ALBONE, of the " Ivel " Cycle Works, Biggleswade, in the County of Bedford, Manufacturer, do hereby declare the nature of this invention, and in what manner the same is to be performed, to be particularly described and ascertained in and by the following statement :—

My invention relates to improvements in the manufacture of convertible velocipedes, 5 according to which the machine may be a tandem safety bicycle ; a safety bicycle ; a front steering tricycle ; or a rear driving tandem tricycle, as may be desired.

When a machine constructed according to my invention is set as a " safety " to carry two riders, they will both be between the front and the driving wheels, and will both drive onto the same wheel. 10

In order that my invention, and the means by which the same is to be carried into practical effect, may be thoroughly understood, I will now describe them in detail, referring in so doing to the accompanying drawings, which are to be taken as part of this specification and read therewith.

Figure 1 is a side elevation of a machine fitted with my invention, and put together 15 as a tandem safety bicycle.

Figure 2 is a side elevation of the same machine converted into a tandem tricycle.

Figure 3 is a rear elevation of the driving wheels, axle, bridge, and connections of the machine illustrated in Figure 2.

Figure 4 is a plan, to a larger scale, of a knuckle-joint such as is adapted for the 20 purpose of my invention for use in the machine-backbone.

Referring to Figure 1,

The ordinary backbone is divided into two portions a, a^1, and has its adjacent ends finished as parts of knuckle-joints, and thereby adapted to receive a lengthening tube B, the ends of which are finished to correspond with the respective ends of the 25 divided backbone.

The lengthening tube is furnished with a stalk C, saddle c, and handle bar d. It carries at its lower extremity a chain-wheel E, the chain e of which drives onto a wheel f fast on the axis of the back chain-wheel g.

A tandem safety bicycle constructed as illustrated in Figure 1 and described there- 30 with is converted into a safety bicycle by freeing both knuckle-joints h and i, taking out the lengthening tube and its attachments, removing the chain e from the wheel f, bringing the two portions a, a^1 of the back-bone together, and bolting them up.

A safety or a tandem bicycle is converted, according to my invention, into a front 35 steering single or tandem tricycle in the following manner.

The back chain j is taken off the chain-wheel k on the axle of the driving wheel ; and the latter, with its chain-wheel, is taken out of the back-fork, and replaced by the pair of driving wheels illustrated in Figure 3. The axle l is strengthened by a bridge piece m and two braces n, n. From the latter project two studs o, o, adapted 40

Albone's Improved Velocipede.

in respect of position and size to receive the slotted ends of the back-fork, and to hold it by their nuts o^1, o^1.   The chain j is then fixed round the chain-wheel p upon the axle l.

5   I am aware that it is not new to convert safety into tandem bicycles by the use of an auxiliary frame carrying an additional seat, pedal, crank, axis and handle bar, and I make no general claim, therefore, for the use of such arrangements.

Having now particularly described and ascertained the nature of my said invention, and in what manner the same is to be performed, I declare that what I claim is :—

10   1. The combination of divided backbone and lengthening tube, as set forth.

2. The combination of divided backbone, lengthening tube, and knuckle-joint or equivalent connection, by which the said tube may be inserted in the said backbone and made a rigid part thereof, as set forth.

3. The combination of divided backbone, lengthening tube, additional stalk, saddle,
15 handle bar, chain-wheel, and chain, as and for the purpose set forth.

4. The method of making safety and tandem bicycles mutually convertible, as the same is hereinbefore set forth.

5. The method of making single rider and tandem tricycles mutually convertible, as the same is hereinbefore set forth.

20   Dated this 22nd day of October 1888.

PHILLIPS & LEIGH,
22, Southampton Buildings, Chancery Lane, W.C.,
Agents for the Applicant.

London : Printed for Her Majesty's Stationery Office, by Darling & Son, Ltd.—1889.

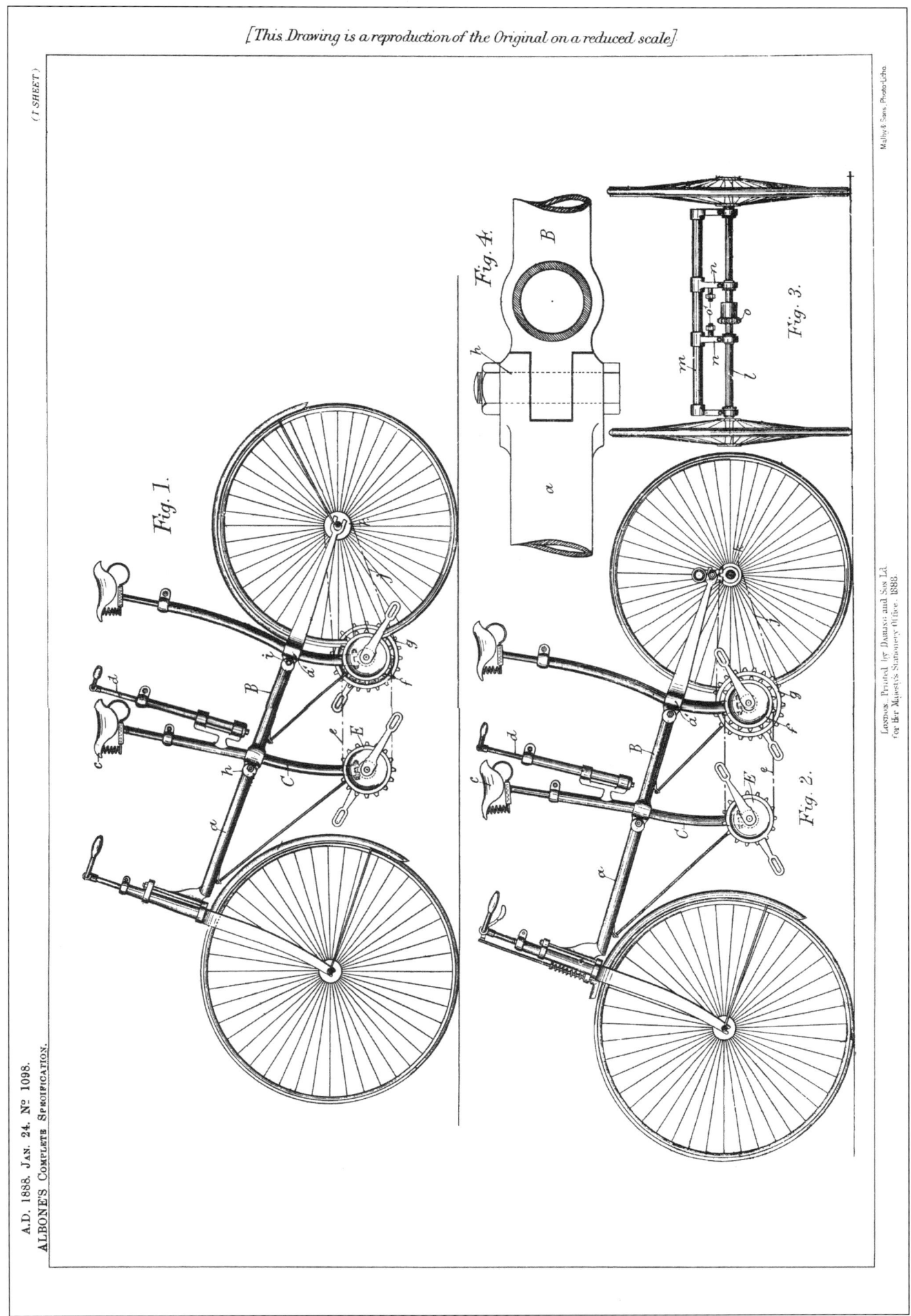

[This Drawing is a reproduction of the Original on a reduced scale]

(1 SHEET)

Malby & Sons, Photo-Litho.

A.D. 1888. Jan. 24. Nº 1098.
ALBONE'S COMPLETE SPECIFICATION.

Fig. 1.

Fig. 2.

Fig. 3.

Fig. 4.

London: Printed by Darling and Son Ld.
for Her Majesty's Stationery Office. 1888.

N° 7300  A.D. 1891

Date of Application, 28th Apr., 1891
Complete Specification Left, 26th Jan., 1892—Accepted, 27th Feb., 1892

PROVISIONAL SPECIFICATION.

Improvements in and relating to Velocipedes.

I DANIEL ALBONE, of the Ivel Hotel Biggleswade in the County of Bedford-shire, Hotel Proprietor do hereby declare the nature of this invention to be as follows :—

5   My invention relates to an improved seat for carrying a child as a passenger on a front-steering cycle, and it consists of a seat preferably made of basket or wicker-work mounted on an iron frame adapted to be attached to the front of the handle bar of the cycle, by any form of simple clip adapted to embrace the said bar. The iron frame is extended below the seat to carry a platform for the feet. This plat-form is cut away in the centre to allow of the seat being brought as near down to

10   the periphery of the steering wheel as possible, in order that the centre of gravity may be kept as low as possible. The "cut away" portion of the platform is closed by a suitable cover preferably forming part of the said platform, and the said cover together with the sides of the platform form suitable recesses for the feet of the child.

15   The seat, or the frame carrying it, is carried on a fork attached to the axle of the steering wheel outside the prongs of the main fork, a spring of rubber or metal being interposed between the crown of the fork and the seat or frame. The fork is attached to the seat, or to the frame carrying it, in such a position that it is vertical with the horizontal plane and thus directly supports the weight carried on the seat,

20   the connections to the handle bar being merely to support the back of the seat and steady it.

In order that this seat may be adapted to all machines having a single front-steering wheel, the fork carrying it is made adjustable in length in any convenient manner, and the width of the fork and also of the clearance in the platform is such

25   that the seat may be used with any type of tyre. The attachments to the handle bar are also made adjustable both in diameter and height so that this seat may be fitted to machines with any sized handle bar, or with any length of steering pillar.

Dated this 28th day of April 1891.

30   ROBT. ED. PHILLIPS, M.I.M.E., ETC.,
                              Consulting Engineer and Patent Agent,
                    70—72, Chancery Lane, London, W.C., Agent for Applicant.

COMPLETE SPECIFICATION.

Improvements in and relating to Velocipedes.

35   I DANIEL ALBONE of the Ivel Hotel, Biggleswade, in the County of Bedford-shire, Hotel Proprietor, do hereby declare the nature of this invention and in what manner the same is to be performed to be particularly described and ascertained in and by the following statement :—

My invention relates to an improved seat for carrying a child as a passenger on

40   a front-steering cycle, and it consists of a seat preferably made of basket or wicker work mounted on an iron frame adapted to be attached to the front of the handle bar of the cycle by any form of simple clip adapted to embrace the said bar. The iron frame is extended below the seat to carry a platform for the feet. This plat-form is cut away in the centre to allow of the seat being brought close down to

45   the periphery of the steering wheel in order that the centre of gravity may be

Albone's Improvements in and relating to Velocipedes.

kept as low as possible. The " cut away " portion of the platform is closed by a suitable cover preferably forming part of the said platform, and the said cover together with the sides of the platform form suitable recesses for the feet of the child.

The seat, or the frame carrying it, is carried on a fork attached to the axle of 5 the steering wheel outside the prongs of the main fork, a spring of rubber or metal being interposed between the crown of the fork and the seat or frame. The fork is attached to the seat, or to the frame carrying it, in such a position that it is vertical with the horizontal plane and thus directly supports the weight carried on the seat, the connections to the handle bar being merely to support the back of the 10 seat and steady it.

In order that this seat may be adapted to all machines having a single front-steering wheel, the fork carrying it is made adjustable in length in any convenient manner and the width of the fork and also of the clearance in the platform is such that the seat may be used with any type of tyre. The attachments to the handle 15 bar are also made adjustable both in diameter and height so that this seat may be fitted to machines with any sized handle bar or with any length of steering pillar.

In order that my invention may be fully understood I append a drawing hereto showing how it is carried into practical effect. 20

In the drawing

Figure 1 is a view in perspective showing the application of my carrier to a rear driving safety bicycle.

Figure 2 is a view in perspective of the carrier alone.

Figures 3, 4, and 5 are views in side & back elevation and plan respectively of 25 the carrier, and

Figure 6 is a view showing the construction of the metal framework when the carrier is made of wicker or basketwork.

Throughout these views similar parts are marked with like letters of reference.

Referring to the drawings. A designates the seat. B designates the platform the 30 centre of which is cut away and covered in, forming a recess b to fit over the steering wheel of the cycle. The covered in portion of the platform forms with the sides thereof two recesses b^1 b^1 for the feet of the child. The seat A is carried by a vertical fork C adapted to be fixed to the axle of the steering wheel. The prongs of this fork may if desired be made adjustable in length so as to fit a 35 machine with any sized steering wheel. This fork is bolted to the underside of the seat as illustrated, and if the cycle to which it is to be fitted has not pneumatic tyres a block of rubber is inserted between the crown of the said fork and the underside of the seat. To the back of the seat A are fixed two arms D, D, carrying adjustable clips d, d, adapted to embrace the handle bar of the machine 40 and so steady and support the carrier. These arms are fixed to the back of the seat by bolts passing through the back of the seat at the desired positions. As a modification the arms may be made adjustable in length.

It will be seen that with this carrier the centre of gravity of the machine and rider is not materially raised, and therefore the stability of the machine is not 45 impaired.

I do not limit myself to the use of any particular material for the construction of the carrier neither do I bind myself to attach or support it in the specific manner hereinbefore described and illustrated by the accompanying drawing, but I hold myself at liberty to make such modifications as fairly fall within the spirit and 50 scope of my invention.

Having now particularly described and ascertained the nature of my said invention and in what manner the same is to be performed I declare that what I claim is :—

1. The improved child carrier as hereinbefore described and illustrated by the 55 accompanying drawing.

N° 7300.—A.D. 1891.

Albone's Improvements in and relating to Velocipedes.

2. In a child carrier adapted to be fixed over the steering wheel of a cycle, the combination with the seat, of a platform recessed to receive the steering wheel and form pockets or recesses for the feet of the child, as set forth.

Dated this 27th day of January 1892.

5

ROBT. ED. PHILLIPS, M.I.M.E.,
Consulting Engineer and Patent Agent,
70, Chancery Lane, London, W.C., Agent for the Applicant.

London : Printed for Her Majesty's Stationery Office, by Darling & Son. Ltd.—1892

A.D. 1891. April 28. N.º. 7300.
ALBONE'S Complete Specification.

(1 SHEET)

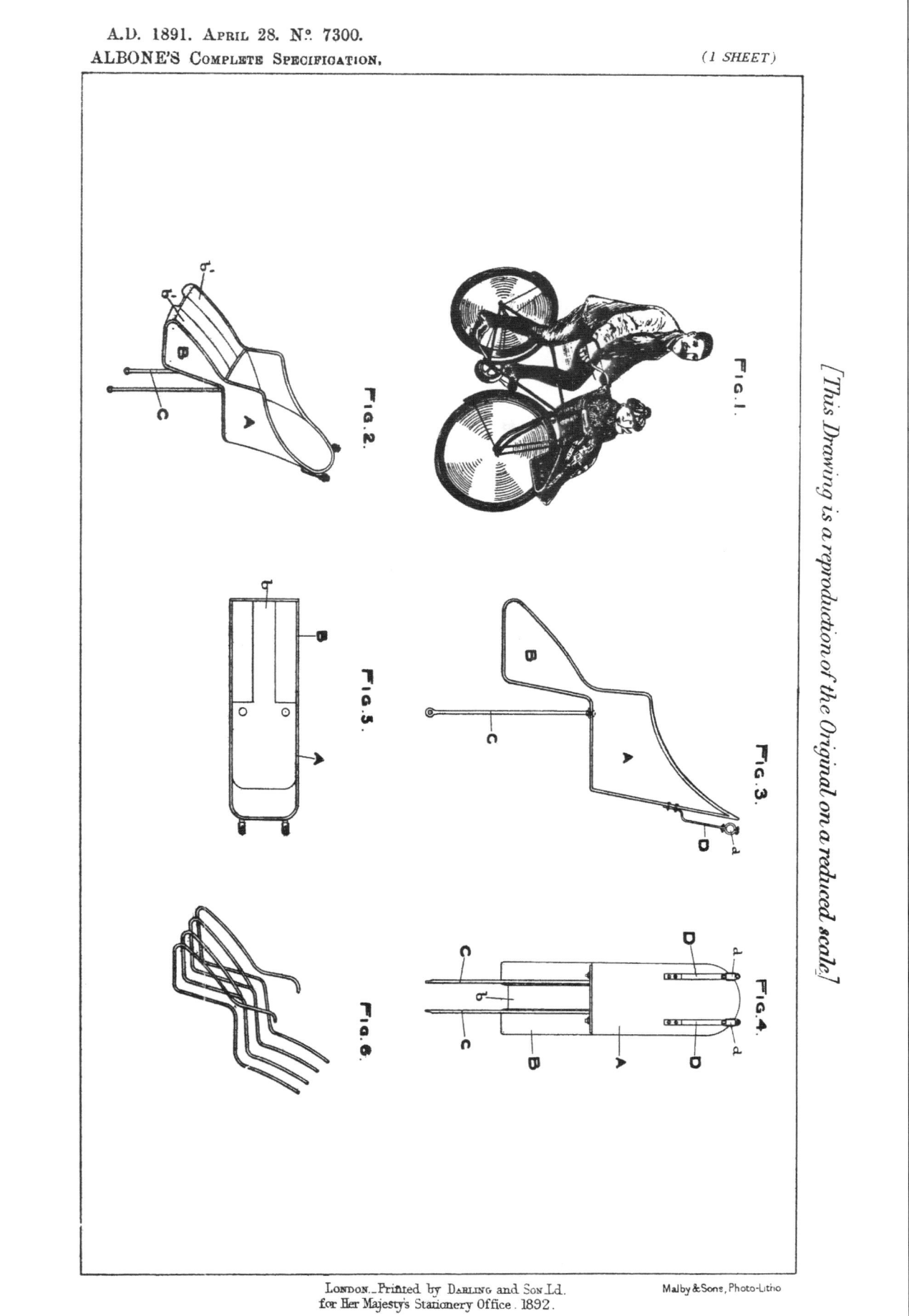

[This Drawing is a reproduction of the Original on a reduced scale.]

London._Printed by Darling and Son.Ld.
for Her Majesty's Stationery Office. 1892.

Malby&Sons, Photo-Litho

399

N° 14,705 A.D. 1891

Date of Application, 31st Aug., 1891
Complete Specification Left, 31st May, 1892—Accepted, 31st Aug., 1892

PROVISIONAL SPECIFICATION.

Improvements in and relating to Velocipedes.

We DAN ALBONE of the Ivel Hotel, Biggleswade, in the County of Bedfordshire, Licensed Victualler, and RICHARD TINGEY, of Ivel House, Caldecote, near Biggleswade, in the County aforesaid, Foreman of Works, do hereby declare the nature of this invention to be as follows :—

5   Our invention relates to a device for carrying an inflation pump—such as is used for inflating pneumatic tyres—on the frame of a cycle, and it consists essentially of two clips or their equivalents, the one adapted to embrace the barrel of the pump, and the other the piston thereof, so that both parts of the pump are gripped. The clips may take the form of **U**-shaped spring clips or of sockets, each clip or socket
10   being adjustably attached to the frame of the cycle—at any convenient part—by any suitable form of clip or claw bracket. A convenient form of bracket consists of a length of band steel attached at or about its centre to the clip or socket adapted to carry one part of the inflation pump. The free ends of this band are provided with holes through which—when the ends are overlapped—a set screw
15   is passed and threaded into a nut lying on the underside of the overlapping ends of the band. The set screw on being screwed into the nut bears on the tube of the frame passing through the loop or clip made by the band—or on a plate bedding thereon—and so forces the ends of them away from the tube, and thus binds the clip or socket carried by it firmly to the said tube. By mounting the clips or
20   sockets adjustably on the tube of the frame their positions with respect to one another may be varied to suit pumps of different lengths.

Dated this 31st day of August 1891.

ROBT. ED. PHILLIPS, M.I.M.E.,
Consulting Engineer and Patent Agent,
25   70, Chancery Lane, London, W.C., Agent for the Applicants.

COMPLETE SPECIFICATION.

Improvements in and relating to Velocipedes.

We DAN ALBONE of the Ivel Hotel Biggleswade in the County of Bedfordshire Licensed Victualler and RICHARD TINGEY of Ivel House Caldecote near
30   Biggleswade in the County aforesaid Engineer do hereby declare the nature of this invention and in what manner the same is to be performed, to be particularly described and ascertained in and by the following statement :—

Our invention relates to a device for carrying an inflation pump,—such as is used for inflating pneumatic tyres,—on the frame of a cycle.
35   It consists essentially of and is attained by the use of two spring clips or sockets the one adapted to embrace the barrel of the pump and the other the piston thereof so that both parts of the pump are gripped. The clips take the form of **U** shaped spring clips or sockets each clip or socket being fixed at or about its centre to any suitable form of clip or claw bracket such clip or claw bracket being made adjustable
40   to fit any portion of the frame of the cycle as may be required.

A convenient form of bracket consists of a length of band steel attached at or about its centre to the spring clip or socket adapted to carry one part of the inflator pump. The free ends of this band are provided with holes through which —when the ends are overlapped—a set screw is passed and threaded into a nut
45   lying on the underside of the overlapping ends of the band.

The set screw on being screwed into the nut bears on the tube of the frame

2   Nº 14,705.—A.D. 1891.

Albone & Tingey's Improvements in and relating to Velocipedes.

passing through the loop or clip made by the band—or on a plate bedding on such tube or frame—and so forces the ends of them away from the tube and thus binds the spring clip or socket carried by it firmly to the said tube or frame. By mounting the spring clips or sockets adjustably on the tube of the frame their positions with respect to one another may be varied to suit pumps of different 5 lengths.

The accompanying drawings shew more clearly the nature of our invention.

Fig. 1 is a front view in section shewing the band passing round the tube of frame and overlapping the nut and also the spring clip or socket adapted for passing round the barrel of the pump. 10

Figs. 2 and 3 shew the pump held in position by the spring clips or sockets.

The same letters apply to the same part in each figure.

(*a*) is the band clip. (*b*) the nut. (*c*) the screw. (*d*) the spring clip or bracket embracing the barrel of the pump and (*e*) in Fig. 3 the spring clip or socket embracing the piston of the pump. 15

The pump is placed in the spring clips or sockets and is held firmly on the tube by means of the band clip as will readily be seen from the drawings. The spring clips or sockets are readily adjusted to suit pumps of different lengths.

Having now particularly described and ascertained the nature of our said invention and in what manner the same is performed we declare that what we 20 claim is.

1. The spring clips or sockets for holding an inflation pump as above described.
2. The adjustable bracket or steel band for attaching such clips to the frame of the cycle as above described.

Dated this 27th day of May 1892. 25

DAN ALBONE.
RICHARD TINGEY.

London : Printed for Her Majesty's Stationery Office by Darling & Son, Ltd.—1892.

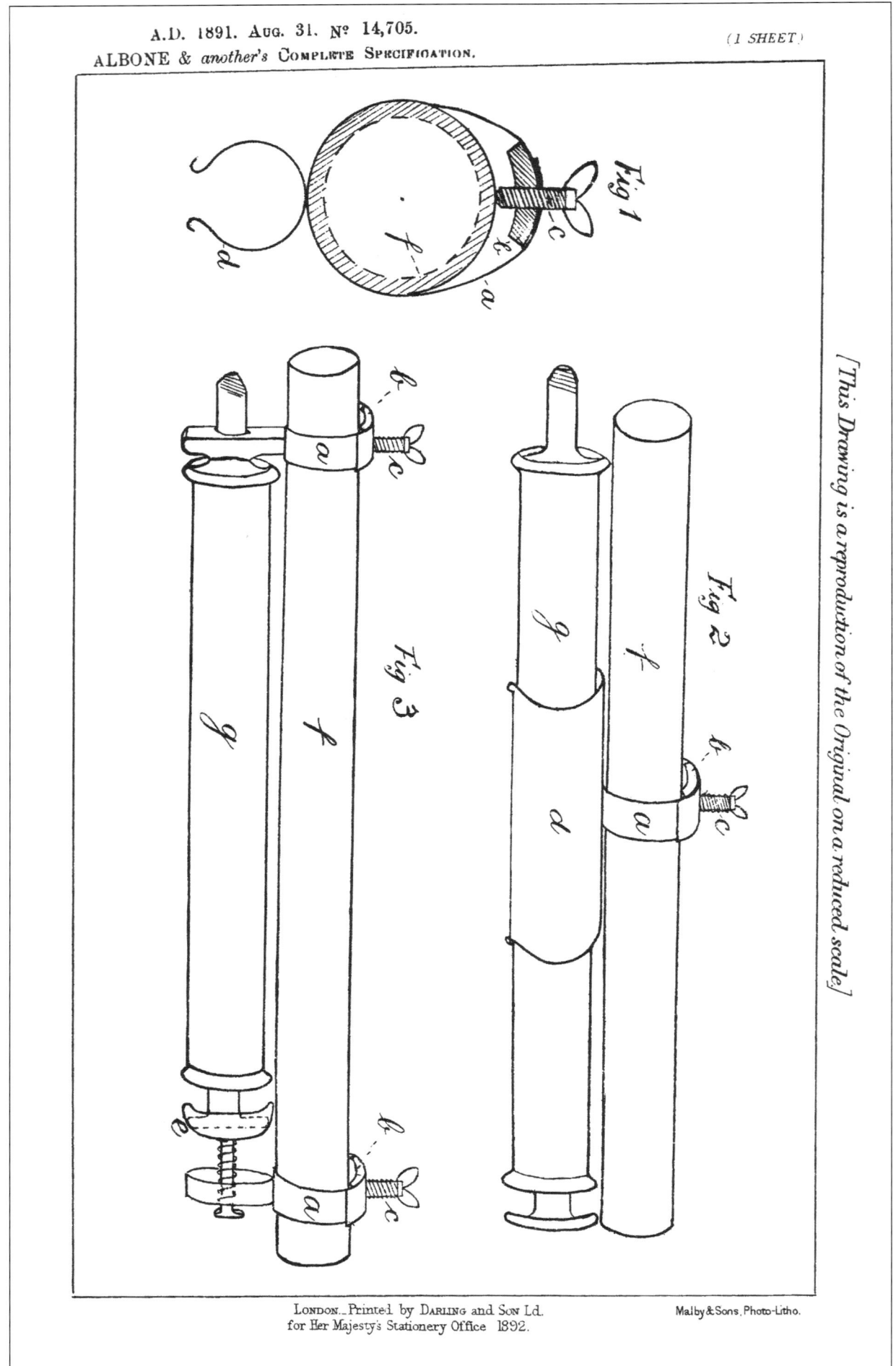

N° 4427  A.D. 1895

Date of Application, 1st Mar., 1895
Complete Specification Left, 30th Nov., 1895--Accepted, 4th Jan., 1896

PROVISIONAL SPECIFICATION.

Improvements in Axle Boxes for Vehicle Wheels.

I, DANIEL ALBONE, of the Ivel Cycle Works, Biggleswade, in the County of Bedfordshire, Cycle Manufacturer, do hereby declare the nature of this invention to be as follows :—

5 My invention relates to an improved construction of axle box for an anti-friction ball bearing for vehicle wheels having wooden naves and spokes.

The axle box consists essentially of a hollow metal cylinder preferably slightly tapered on the outside to adapt it to be driven and wedged into the wooden nave, and having one or more feathers adapted to fit in slots or recesses in the said nave to prevent the metallic axle box rotating with respect thereto.

10 In each end of the metallic axle box is fitted a steel cup forming parts of the race for the balls, the other part of each of the said races being formed by a cup or cone mounted on the axle, the one cup or cone being fixed thereto and the other being capable of adjustment thereon by means of the well-known methods, and fitted with any suitable form of locking nut or equivalent device. The outer end

15 of the metallic axle box is threaded internally to receive a suitable cap closing in the end of the axle.

Dated this 1st day of March 1895.

ROBERT E. PHILLIPS, M.I. Mech. E.,
Consulting Engineer and Patent Agent,
20 70, Chancery Lane, London, W.C., Agent for the Applicant.

COMPLETE SPECIFICATION.

Improvements in Axle Boxes for Vehicle Wheels.

I, DANIEL ALBONE, of the Ivel Cycle Works, Biggleswade, in the County of Bedfordshire, Cycle Manufacturer, do hereby declare the nature of this invention
25 and in what manner the same is to be performed to be particularly described and ascertained in and by the following statement :—

This invention relates to an improved construction of axle box for the application of ball bearings to vehicle wheels having wooden naves.

In the accompanying drawing which illustrates this invention ;
30 Figure 1 is a view in section,
Figure 2 is a view in transverse section on line *x, x,* Figure 1, and
Figure 3 is a view in transverse section on line *y, y,* Figure 1.
Throughout the views similar parts are marked with like letters of reference.

The axle box consists essentially of a metal cylinder A preferably slightly
35 tapered on the outside to adapt it to be driven and wedged into the wooden nave or the wheel, and having one or more feathers *a* or their equivalents adapted to wedge in slots or recesses in the said nave to prevent the axle box rotating with respect thereto.

The ends a^1 and a^2 of the axle box A are recessed to receive steel cups B, B
40 forming parts of the races for the balls C, the other part of each of the said races

Albone's Improvements in Axle Boxes for Vehicle Wheels.

being formed by cups or cones D, D¹ mounted on the axle E.   The cup or cone D¹ is fixed on the axle up against a shoulder *e* thereon and the other cup or cone D is threaded on the axle to provide for adjustment.   The adjustable cup or cone D is locked by means of a lock nut *d*¹ acting against an interposed washer *d* having a D-shaped hole to fit over the axle which has a flat cut on it.   The outer end *a*² of 5 the axle box A is threaded internally to receive a suitable cap F adapted to close the said box and cover in the end of the axle.

Instead of forming the cup B independent of the axle box A, they may be made all in one piece either out of a steel stamping or by being pressed or formed up out of a piece of steel tube in which case the feathers *a* would be either pressed up 10 out of the thickness of the metal or they would take the form of dowel pins or the like.

By this construction of axle box, ball bearings can readily be applied to wheels having wooden naves and also to wheels having metal naves bushed or lined with wood.   15

Having now particularly described and ascertained the nature of my said invention and in what manner the same is to be performed I declare that what I claim is :—

(1) The improvements in axle boxes whereby ball bearings can be applied to vehicle wheels having naves made wholly or partially of wood, as set forth.   20

(2) An axle box, for vehicle wheels the naves of which are either made of wood or are bushed or lined with wood, having feathers or their equivalents such as *a* on its exterior surface and recesses at its ends adapted to receive or form cups such as B, as and for the purpose set forth.

Dated this 30th day of November 1895.   25

ROBERT E. PHILLIPS, Assoc. M. Inst. C.E., M.I. Mech. E.,
Consulting Engineer and Patent Agent,
70, Chancery Lane, London, W.C., Agent for the Applicant.

London : Printed for Her Majesty's Stationery Office, by Darling & Son, Ltd.—1896

A.D. 1895. March 1. N.° 4427.
ALBONE'S Complete Specification.

(1 SHEET)

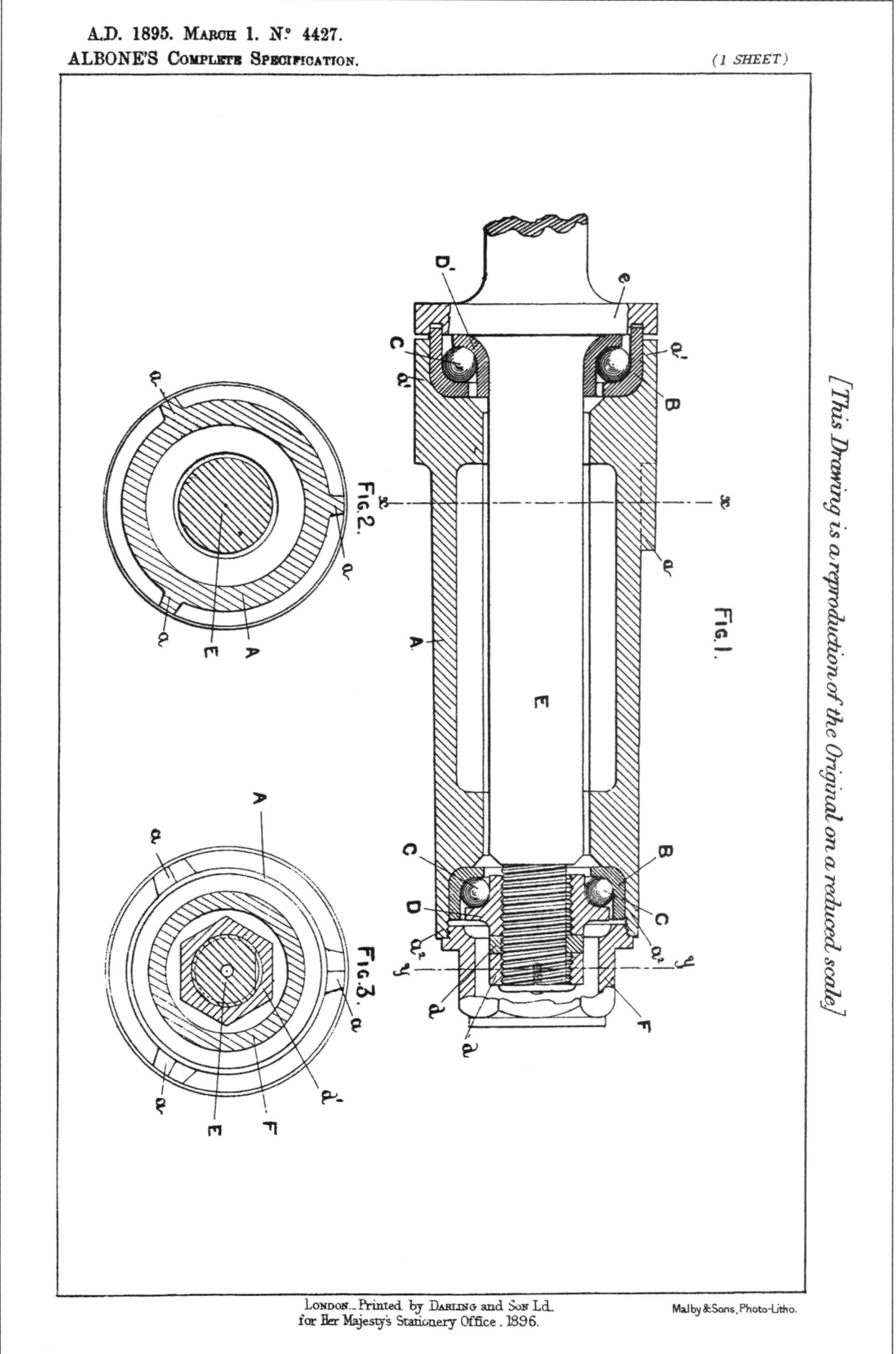

Fig. 2.

Fig. 1.

Fig. 3.

[This Drawing is a reproduction of the Original on a reduced scale]

London. Printed by Darling and Son Ld.
for Her Majesty's Stationery Office. 1896.

Malby & Sons, Photo-Litho.

N° 24,388   A.D. 1896

Date of Application, 2nd Nov., 1896
Complete Specification Left, 2nd Sept., 1897—Accepted, 2nd Nov., 1897

PROVISIONAL SPECIFICATION.

Improvements in Chucks.

We WILLIAM CRAWLEY Brampton Huntingdonshire Engineer and DANIEL ALBONE of the Ivel Cycle Works, Biggleswade in the County of Bedford Cycle Manufacturer do hereby declare the nature of this invention to be as follows:—

5   A Round Faceplate A to fit Lathe having Slots B & C in Face as shown in drawing or other suitable arrangement to which is attached by Bolts or Studs D D sliding in slots B & C a plate E with Brackets to form Bearings or Journals F fitted with caps G G & bored to fit Pivots or Trunions H H of Plate I. Said Caps G. G. to be bolted or screwed to Brackets to allow of free movement of Pivot or Trunions H H but capable of being screwed tight to lock Plate I at any desired
10   angle.

Plate I is bored through centre and is also recessed to take round Plate J with boss to fit centre bore and fitted with nut K to be moved with Hook or other suitable spanner. Plate J revolves freely in Plate I, but may be fixed at any angle by Nut K or other suitable device and is indexed on top Face to degrees of
15   circle.

One Bracket of Plate E is also fitted with segment of circle M and divided to degrees & Index or Indicator fitted to Pivot or Trunion H to show angle of Plate I.

Plate E to be adjusted or moved across main Faceplate by screw L, Rack &
20   Pinion or other suitable device.

Main Faceplate A may also be fitted with an extra Plate to allow of a second cross movement at right angles thus giving 4 movements *viz*. 2 cross movements at right angles & 2 Circular or Revolving motions in Plains at right angles.

Work or Castings may be fixed to Plate J by means of centre Stud, Bolt or
25   any other suitable arrangement.

October 30th 1896.

WILLIAM CRAWLEY.

COMPLETE SPECIFICATION.

Improvements in Chucks.

30   We WILLIAM CRAWLEY of Brampton in the County of Huntingdon, Engineer, and DANIEL ALBONE of the Ivel Cycle Works, Biggleswade in the County of Bedford, Cycle Manufacturer do hereby declare the nature of this invention and in what manner the same is to be performed to be particularly described and ascertained in and by the following statement:—

35   This invention relates to chucks more particularly for use in connection with cycle manufacture.

[*Price 8d.*]

Crawley and Albone's Improvements in Chucks.

We will particularly describe our invention making reference to the accompanying drawings in which:—

Figure 1 is a view in front elevation of a chuck constructed according to our invention.

Figure 2 is a side view in section thereof.   5

Figure 3 is a view in back elevation of a modified form thereof, and

Figure 4 is a view in side elevation thereof.

Throughout the views similar parts are marked with like letters of reference.

A face plate A adapted to fit the lathe is provided with a bracket B free to slide and be adjusted thereon by means of bolts or studs b sliding in slots a on 10 the plate A or in any other convenient manner. In Figures 1 and 2 the bracket B is only capable of sliding and being adjusted in a vertical direction whereas in Figures 3 and 4 movement of the bracket is possible in a vertical and horizontal direction, this may be accomplished in any suitable manner as for example by means of T-headed bolts. The heads b^1 of the bolts being capable of sliding in 15 horizontal slots formed in the bracket whilst the shanks are capable of sliding in a vertical direction in the slots a of the plate.

A circular plate C is fitted to revolve in and be locked to the plate C^1 by means of a nut c.

This plate C^1 is furnished with trunnions or pivots c^1 adapted to pivot in 20 bearings b^2 formed on the bracket B and to be moved (preferably by means of a worm and pinion) and locked to any desired angle with respect to the face plate. A hand or pointer c^2 is attached to one of the said trunnions or pivots so as to indicate the angle on a scale b^3 formed on the side of the bracket.

The plate C^1 is divided on its edge into degrees or divisions so as to indicate by 25 means of a finger on the plate C, the angle through which the said plate C is turned.

The work to be operated on is secured to the plate C in any suitable manner; a convenient method is to form in one with or to fix to the plate C a screw threaded spindle E on which the work is held by means of a washer and nut e as shown 30 on the drawings in which a seat pillar lug is shown being turned in Figures 1 and 2 and a bottom bracket in Figure 4.

Having now particularly described and ascertained the nature of our said invention and in what manner the same is to be performed, we declare that what we claim is:—   35

(1) A new or improved chuck constructed arranged and adapted to be operated substantially as hereinbefore described and shown.

(2) A chuck consisting essentially of a face plate, a bracket adapted to slide and be adjusted thereon and furnished with bearings for the trunnions or pivots of a plate on which is mounted a second plate capable of revolving and being 40 locked thereto and which is adapted to hold the work to be turned.

Dated this 2nd day of September 1897.

ROBERT E. PHILLIPS, Assoc. M. Inst. C.E., M. I. Mech. E.
Consulting Engineer and Patent Agent,
70 Chancery Lane, London, W.C., Agent for the Applicant.   45

Redhill : Printed for Her Majesty's Stationery Office, by Malcomson & Co., Ltd.—1897.

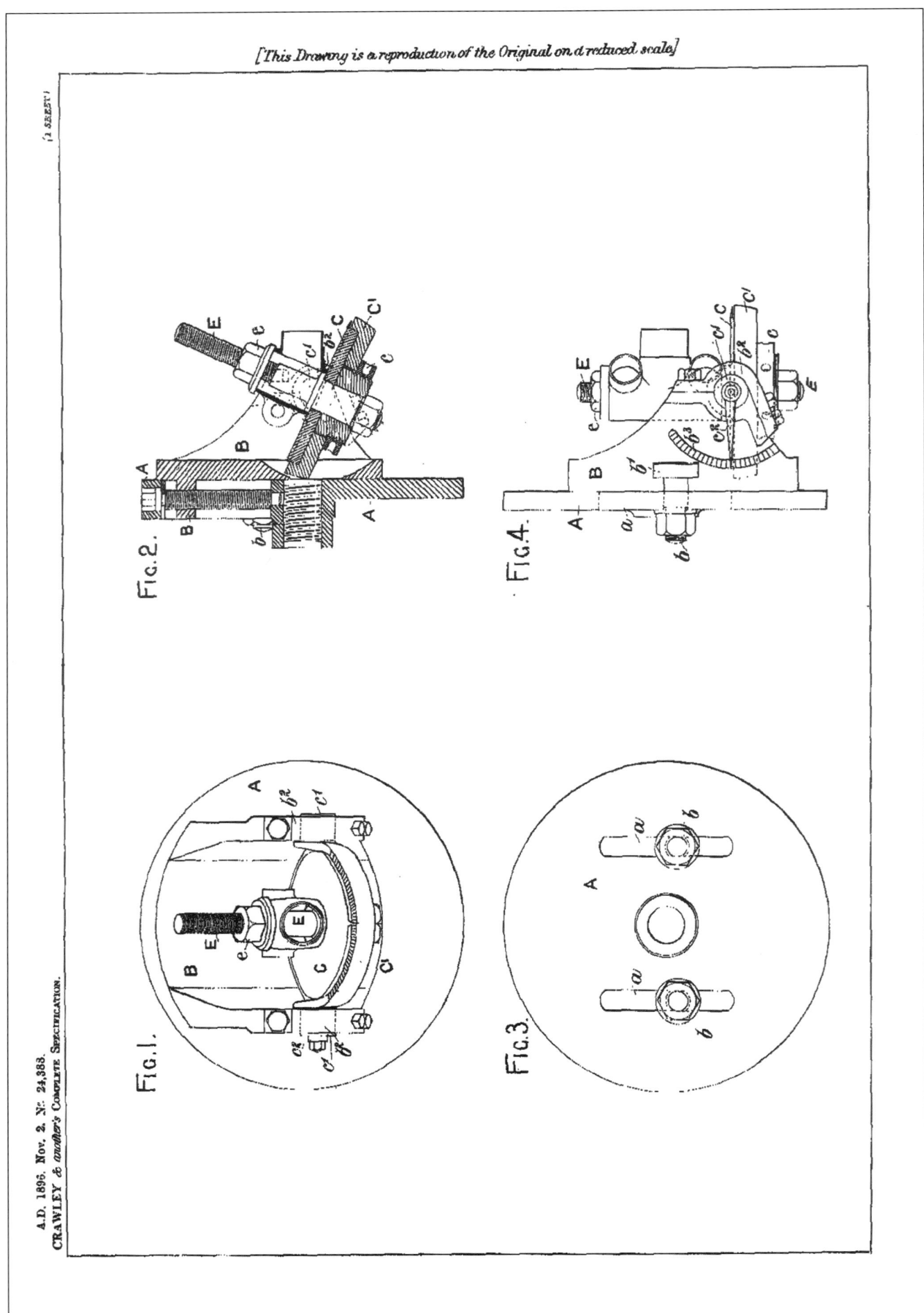

N° 3920      A.D. 1902

Date of Application, 15th Feb., 1902
Complete Specification Left, 14th Nov., 1902—Accepted, 8th Jan., 1903

PROVISIONAL SPECIFICATION.

" **Motor Tractor for Agricultural Purposes also Applicable as a Portable Motor**"

I, DAN ALBONE of the "Ivel" Cycle Works, Biggleswade, in the County of Bedford, Engineer, do hereby declare the nature of this invention to be as follows :—

This invention relates to a mechanical tractor for use in conjunction with
5 agricultural implements.

This tractor consists essentially of a pair of driving wheels mounted on a balance-geared axle supported in a suitable frame which extends forward and carries one or more steering wheels. On the frame in close proximity to the back axle is mounted an internal combustion engine of any suitable type which drives
10 the balance-geared axle carrying the driving wheels either direct by means of spur or chain gearing, or through a countershaft and gearing, the gear being so arranged as to impart a uniform speed of about 5 miles per hour with the motor running at its normal speed.

The wheels are preferably of the type usually employed in agricultural imple-
15 ments, viz, metallic construction with grip tyres.

The frame carries a suitably arranged seat for the driver and the necessary storage tanks for the liquid hydrocarbon employed and for water if such is used for cooling purposes.

The frame is also adapted to support and carry the various agricultural imple-
20 ments with which it is intended to be employed such as mowing machines, reaping machines, grain drills, ploughs, carts and wagons etc. Where the implement is entirely carried by the tractor the motion is transmitted to the mechanism of the implement either directly from the motor shaft or indirectly from the driving axle, but where as in the case of grain drills the implement is self-supporting, the
25 necessary motion may be imparted to its mechanism by means of any suitable flexible drive and in the case—as with ploughs—where the implement has no mechanism that require motion imparted to it the tractor is merely used as such, viz, for traction or propelling purposes only.

Provision is also made whereby the motor may be disconnected from the
30 driving axle and used as a stationary motor for driving any desired machinery such as chaff cutters, pulpers, pumps, and the like.

Dated this 15th day of February 1902

PHILLIPSS
Chartered Patent Agents
70, Chancery Lane, London, W.C.
Agents for the Applicant.

35

Motor Tractor for Agricultural Purposes also Applicable as a Portable Motor.

COMPLETE SPECIFICATION.

"Motor Tractor for Agricultural Purposes also Applicable as a Portable Motor".

I DAN ALBONE of the "Ivel" Cycle Works, Biggleswade, in the County of Bedford, Engineer, do hereby declare the nature of this invention and in what manner the same is to be performed to be particularly described and ascertained in and by the following statement:—

This invention relates to a mechanical tractor for use in conjunction with agricultural implements.   5

In the accompanying drawing which illustrates this invention:—

Figure 1 is a view in side elevation, and

Figure 2 is a view in plan.

In both views similar parts are marked with like letters of reference.   10

The tractor consists essentially of a pair of driving wheels B mounted on a balance-geared axle b carried in suitable bearings supported by a frame A which extends forward and carries a steering wheel C. On the stem c of the wheel C is mounted a fixed sprocket wheel c^1 geared by means of a chain c^2 to a second sprocket wheel d fixed on to a steering pillar D mounted in bearings at the rear   15 end of the frame, and carrying a steering wheel D^1. Behind the steering pillar D is mounted a seat pillar e supporting a seat E for the driver.

At or about the centre of the frame and on one side thereof is mounted an internal combustion engine F of any suitable type, the crank shaft f of which is arranged transversely to the frame. The crank shaft of the motor is connected   20 with a counter-shaft K by any suitable form of gearing but preferably by that shown in the drawing which will provide for the transmission of the driving motion in such a manner as to propel the tractor in either direction. On the shaft f is a sprocket wheel f^1 and a spur wheel g either of which can be fixed to the shaft by means of a clutch H—preferably of the friction type—operated by a   25 lever I, located near the seat E through suitable connecting mechanism. The sprocket wheel f^1 gears by means of a chain f^2 with a sprocket wheel k on a transversely arranged countershaft K which is mounted in suitable bearings carried by the frame. The spur wheel g gears with another spur wheel k^1 on the countershaft K. It will thus be seen that if the clutch H is so operated as to cause   30 the sprocket wheel f^1 to be connected with the motor shaft f the countershaft K will rotate in one direction—preferably for the forward movement of the tractor—whereas if the spur wheel g is connected with the shaft f the countershaft K will rotate in the reverse direction, thus providing for the backward movement of the tractor, it being understood that the engine F will run free when the clutch is in   35 such a position that neither of the wheels f^1 or g are connected to the crank shaft f.

The countershaft K is geared with the driving axle b by means of a sprocket wheel k^2 on the shaft K chain k^3 and sprocket wheel b^1 carried by the box or casing of the balance gear b^2 of the driving axle. The whole of the gearing is   40 so arranged as to impart a uniform speed of about five miles per hour to the tractor when the motor is running at its normal speed.

To enable the motor to be used independent of the tractor the shaft b is disconnected from the countershaft K. This may be effected either by removing the chain k^3 or by connecting the sprocket wheel k^2 to the axle K by means of a   45 clutch. Driving pulleys are provided either on the crank shaft f of the motor or on the countershaft K. In the former case a fast and loose pulley is provided and in the latter case a single pulley k^4 as shown.

N° 3920.—A.D. 1902.   3

Motor Tractor for Agricultural Purposes also Applicable as a Portable Motor.

The frame A also carries a storage tank L for the liquid hydrocarbon, a carburettor M of any suitable type and a water storage tank N for the water employed for cooling purposes.

5 The tractor is connected to the agricultural implement to be used by means of a spring draw bar O of any suitable construction, the attachment of the bar to the frame of the tractor being such as will permit of its point of attachment being varied to suit the type of implement to be drawn.

In the case of mowing and reaping machines and also with ploughs the tractor must be on one side, sometimes on the right and sometimes on the left. In 10 others such as seed drills, scuffles, wagons *etc* it may pull quite centrally it is therefore necessary either to provide two or more brackets P as shown, or a single bracket may be used, capable of being adjusted transversely on the said member *a* of the frame.

15 Having now particularly described and ascertained the nature of my said invention and in what manner the same is to be performed, I declare that what I claim is:—

(1) A mechanical tractor for agricultural purposes consisting of a frame, of a balance-geared driving axle carried thereby, of a pair of driving wheels carried by said axle, of a wheel carried by said frame and adapted to have angular 20 movement imparted to it for steering purposes, of an internal combustion engine carried on said frame, of gearing for transmitting the motion of the motor to the driving wheels, and of means for attaching the frame of the tractor to the implement to be drawn, as set forth.

(2) A mechanical tractor for agricultural purposes consisting of a frame, of 25 a balanced-geared driving axle carrying a pair of driving wheels, of a wheel carried by said frame in advance of the driving wheels and adapted to have angular movement imparted to it for steering purposes, of means for imparting steering motion to the said wheel, of an internal combustion engine mounted on said frame, of a transversely arranged countershaft mounted in bearings on said 30 frame, of gearing for transmitting motion from the motor to the countershaft in either direction, of gearing for transmitting motion from the countershaft to the balance-gear of the driving axle, of a carburettor mounted on said frame, of a water storage tank mounted on said frame, of a hydrocarbon storage tank mounted on said frame, of one or more driving pulleys mounted either on the 35 crank shaft of the motor or on the countershaft, of a draw bar for connecting the tractor to the implement to be drawn, as set forth.

(3) The improved motor tractor for agricultural purposes substantially as described and illustrated in the accompanying drawing

Dated this 15th day of November 1902.
40

PHILLIPSS
Chartered Patent Agents
70, Chancery Lane, London, W.C.
Agents for the Applicant.

Redhill: Printed for His Majesty's Stationery Office, by Love & Malcomson, Ltd.—1903.

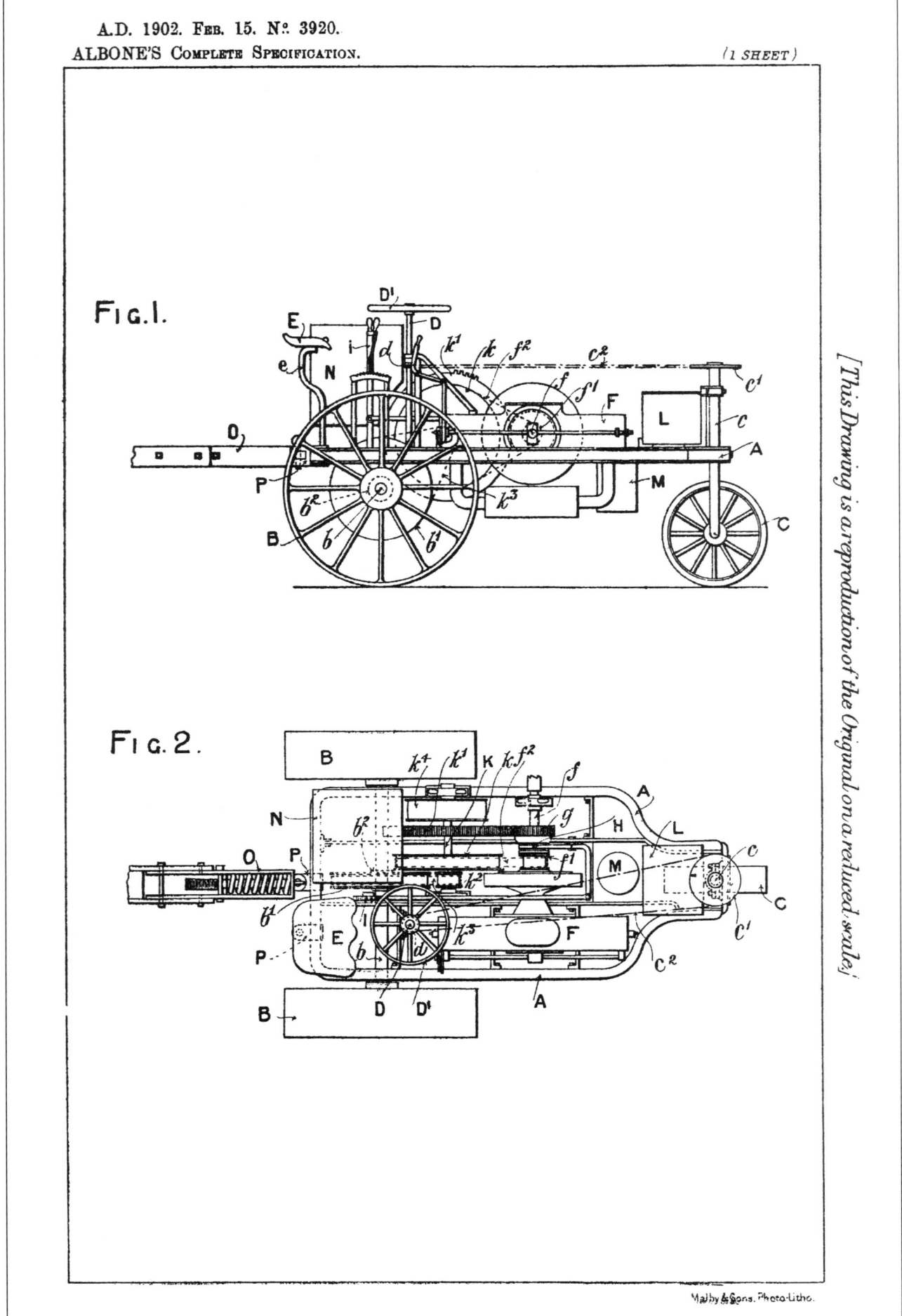

N° 10,064
A.D. 1904

Date of Application, 2nd May, 1904

Complete Specification Left, 2nd Feb., 1905 – Accepted, 2nd Mar., 1905

PROVISIONAL SPECIFICATION.

"Improvements in Automatic-feed Oil Lubricators".

We, THE IVEL AGRICULTURAL MOTORS, LIMITED, of 45, Great Marlborough Street, Regent Street, in the County of London, Manufacturers, and DAN ALBONE, of Biggleswade, in the County of Bedford, Engineer, do hereby declare the nature of this invention to be as follows:—

5   This invention relates to automatic-feed oil lubricators, the object being to provide a device for obtaining an automatic and adequate supply of lubricant in a closed chamber under pressure, such for example, as the crank case of an explosion engine.

According to the invention the improved device comprises a pump cylinder in 10 connection with an oil supply tank, and with a discharge pipe through which the oil is forced from the cylinder into the delivery pipe within the closed chamber. The plunger is reciprocated in the cylinder through the medium of a rod and crank or crank-disc, the said crank or crank-disc being actuated in any suitable way, say by means of a ratchet wheel adapted to be rotated by a pawl upon a 15 pawl arm which is oscillated by any suitable means; for example, in the case of the crank case of a motor, the said pawl arm can be oscillated by a rod which passes through a gland in the crank-case and is actuated by an eccentric upon one of the motor shafts.

Valves, say ball valves, are provided in the inlet and outlet pipes to and from 20 the pump cylinder and to enable the delivery of the pump to be tested, the delivery pipe is provided outside the closed chamber with a cock, above which is provided a chamber containing a valve normally held upon its seat by a spring.

The apparatus operates as follows, that is to say, the pawl arm being oscillated 25 intermittently rotates the ratchet wheel and thus reciprocates the pump plunger which draws the oil from the supply tank and forces it into the delivery pipe which is provided with a number of orifices so that the oil is sprayed into the crank case or other closed chamber, where it is delivered in the form of spray as above described. The throw of the pump plunger can be adjusted by varying the 30 throw of the ratchet crank-disc.

When it is desired to test the delivery of the pump, the cock is opened, the spring valve above the same then closing the passage through the delivery pipe to the crank case or other closed chamber.

Dated the 2nd day of May 1904

35

G. F. REDFERN & Co.,
4, South Street, Finsbury, London.
Agents for the Applicants.

COMPLETE SPECIFICATION.

"Improvements in Automatic-feed Oil Lubricators."

40   We, THE IVEL AGRICULTURAL MOTORS, LIMITED, of 45, Great Marlborough Street, Regent Street, in the County of London, Manufacturers, and DAN ALBONE,

Improvements in Automatic-feed Oil Lubricators.

of Biggleswade, in the County of Bedford, Engineer, do hereby declare the nature of this invention and in what manner the same is to be performed, to be particularly described and ascertained in and by the following statement:—

This invention relates to automatic-feed oil lubricators, the object being to provide a device for obtaining an automatic and adequate supply of lubricant 5 in a closed chamber under pressure, such, for example, as the crank-case of an explosion engine.

According to the invention the improved device comprises a pump cylinder in connection with an oil supply tank, and with a discharge pipe through which the oil is forced from the cylinder into the delivery pipe within the closed chamber. 10 The plunger is reciprocated in the cylinder through the medium of a rod and crank or crank-disc, the said crank or crank-disc so being actuated in any suitable way, say, by means of a ratchet wheel adapted to be rotated by a pawl upon a pawl arm which is oscillated by any suitable means; for example, in the case of the crank case of a motor, the said pawl arm can be oscillated by a rod 15 actuated by an eccentric upon one of the motor shafts.

Valves, say ball-valves, are provided in the inlet and outlet pipes to and from the pump cylinder and to enable the delivery of the pump to be tested, the delivery pipe is provided outside the closed chamber with a cock, above which is provided a chamber containing a valve normally held upon its seat by a 20 spring.

In the accompanying drawing:—

Figure 1 is a sectional elevation of an automatic-feed oil lubricator shown fitted to the crank-case of an explosion engine.

Figure 2 is a horizontal section thereof, and   25

Figure 3 is a view similar to Figure 2 of a slightly modified construction.

Referring first to the arrangement illustrated in Figures 1 and 2 *a* represents the closed chamber, in this case the crank-case of an explosion engine. *b* is the pump cylinder which, as above described, is in communication with an oil supply tank (not shown) by the pipe *c* opening into the pipe *d* at the lower end 30 of the cylinder *b*. *e* is the plunger which works in the cylinder *b*, the said plunger being reciprocated by the connecting rod *f* and crank disc *g*. This disc *g* is mounted upon the fixed pivot *h* and its periphery is toothed and has engaging with it the pawl *i* held upon the end of the arm *j* loosely supported on the aforesaid pivot *h* and adapted to be reciprocated by the eccentric rod *k*; the 35 latter is driven from the eccentric *l* keyed upon the half-speed shaft *m* outside the casing *a*.

n is the outlet pipe for the oil discharged by the pump *b*, the said discharge pipe being fitted to a valve chamber *o* at the upper end of a pipe *p* extending from the pipe *d*. The other end of the outlet pipe *n* passes into the crank-case *a*, 40 as shown, and is provided within the said chamber with orifices through which the lubricant is discharged.

The apparatus operates as follows, that is to say, the pawl arm *j* being oscillated by the eccentric rod *k* rotates the ratchet wheel *g* and thus reciprocates the pump plunger *e* which draws the oil from the supply tank and forces it into the 45 delivery pipe *n* so that the oil is sprayed through the orifices with which the pipe is provided within crank case, and is delivered in the form of spray on to the rotating crank-shaft. The throw of the pump plunger can be adjusted by altering the throw of the ratchet crank-disc *g*.

In the modification illustrated in Figure 3, two pumps are provided, each of 50 which has its own separate outlet pipe *n*. Furthermore, these two pipes, instead of spraying the oil on to the crank-shaft discharge the same into the eccentric casings *q*, *q*, which are provided around the two ends of the crank-shaft and from the outer ends of which passages *r* extend within the crank; these passages open on the surfaces of the crank pins. With this construction it will be clear that 55 the lubricant is forced by the pumps into the eccentric casings *q*, *q*, whence,

Improvements in Automatic-feed Oil Lubricators.

under the action of the centrifugal force, it flows to that end of each of the casings which is farthest from the centre of the crank-shaft, and thus escapes through the aforesaid passages r to the bearings designed to be lubricated.

5 s is the ball-valve in the inlet pipe to the pump, and t is the ball-valve in the outlet pipe thereof, u being a ball-valve in the chamber o which is normally held upon its seat by the spring u^1; v is the cock which is fitted to the valve chamber o below the ball-valve u. This cock is intended to enable the delivery of the pump to be tested, the spring u^1 preventing the suction action in the crank-case from lifting the valve u whilst this is being effected.

10 Having now particularly described and ascertained the nature of our said invention and in what manner the same is to be performed, we declare that what we claim is:—

Automatic-feed oil lubricators consisting of the parts, constructed, arranged and operating substantially as hereinbefore described and illustrated respectively 15 in Figures 1 and 2 and Figure 3 of the accompanying drawing.

Dated the 2nd day of February, 1905.

G. F. REDFERN & Co.,
4, South Street, Finsbury, London.
Agents for the Applicants.

Redhill: Printed for His Majesty's Stationery Office, by Love & Malcomson, Ltd.—1905.

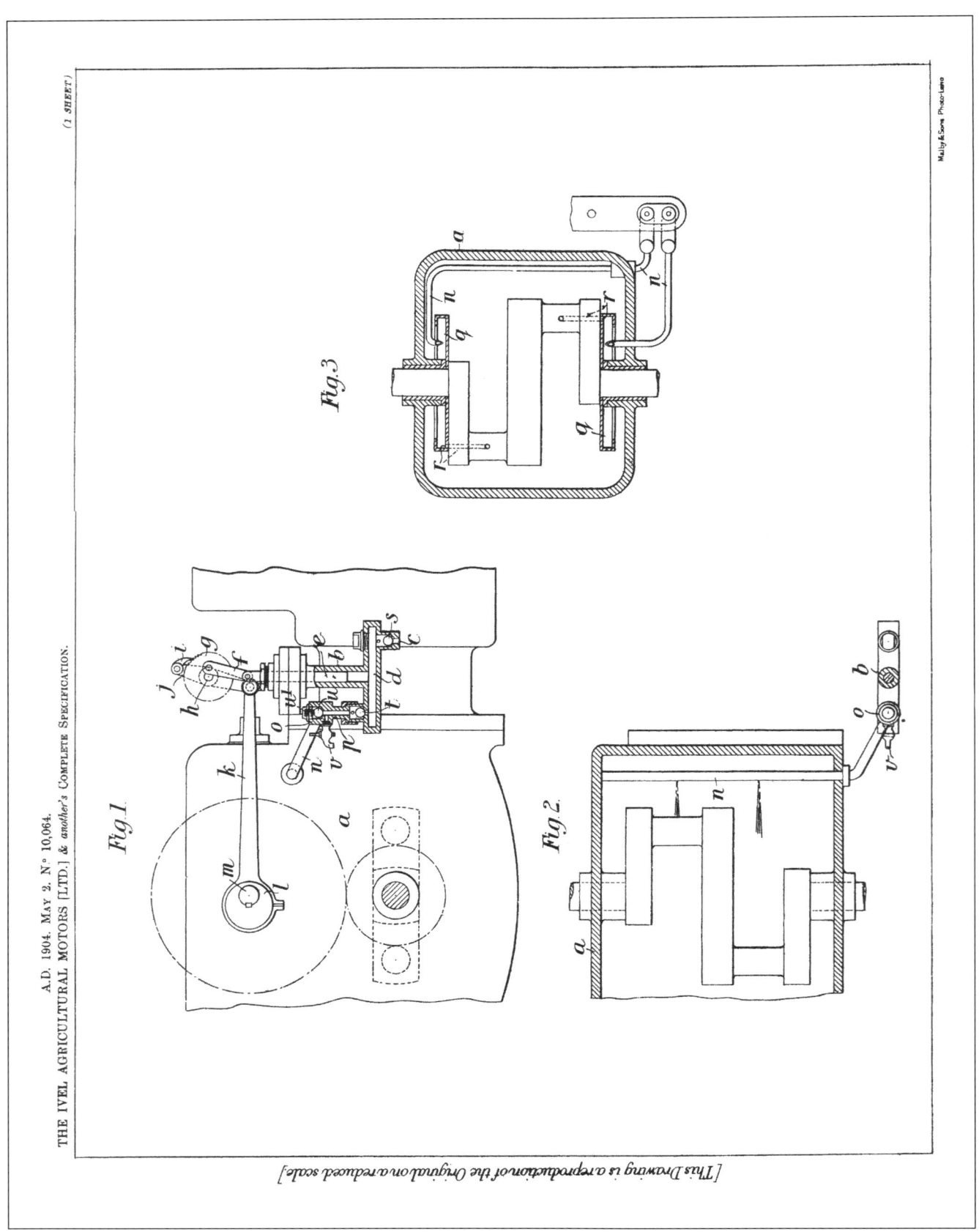

Nº 13,663  A.D. 1904

Date of Application, 16th June, 1904
Complete Specification Left, 16th Mar., 1905—Accepted, 27th Apr., 1905

PROVISIONAL SPECIFICATION.

"Improvements in or connected with the Attachment of Mowers, Reapers, Binders and like Implements or Machines to Motor-tractors ".

I, DAN ALBONE, of The Ivel Agricultural Motors, Limited, of 45, Great Marlborough Street, in the County of London, Engineer, do hereby declare the nature of this invention to be as follows :—

5   My invention relates to the attachment of mowers, reapers, binders and like implements or machines to motor-tractors.

The power of a motor-tractor is usually considerably in excess of that necessary for hauling a single mower, reaper, binder or the like, and there are practical difficulties in constructing such a machine of a cutting capacity proportionate to the power of the tractor.

10   According to my invention I provide for connecting two or more mowers or the like to a single tractor, and I advantageously accomplish this in the following manner, that is to say, one mowing or other machine is attached to the tractor in the usual manner, preferably by a spring connection, and this mower or the like has attached to the pole or other suitable part, a laterally projecting

15   arm or bracket to the extremity of which the second mower or the like is attached in a similar manner to that in which the leading mower is attached to the tractor. This arm or bracket may project to such an extent that the second mower will trail in a proper position for cutting its full width behind the first mower, but in practice, I prefer to provide at the end of the said arm or bracket

20   a head having in it a series of holes which will permit of the pole of the second mower being arranged nearer to or farther from the adjacent travelling wheel of the leading mower according to requirements.

The pole of the second machine is advantageously carried on a caster wheel so that the bracket will be relieved of the weight of the said pole.

25   With the arrangement hereinbefore described the two machines will trail in a correct manner and can be manœuvred around sharp curves with facility without missing any of the crop.

When more than two machines are connected to a single tractor they are successively attached in the same manner as the second machine, which in this

30   case would be provided with an arm or bracket like the leading machine.

Dated the 16th day of June, 1904.

G. F. REDFERN & Co.,
4, South Street, Finsbury, London,
Agents for the Applicant.

Improvements in the Attachment of Mowers, Reapers, &c., to Motor-tractors.

COMPLETE SPECIFICATION.

"Improvements in or connected with the Attachment of Mowers, Reapers Binders and like Implements or Machines to Motor-tractors".

I, DAN ALBONE, of The Ivel Agricultural Motors, Limited, of 45, Great Marlborough Street, in the County of London, Engineer, do hereby declare the nature of this invention and in what manner the same is to be performed, to be particularly described and ascertained in and by the following statement :—

My invention relates to the attachment of mowers, reapers, binders and like 5 implements or machines to motor-tractors.

The power of a motor-tractor is usually considerably in excess of that necessary for hauling a single mower, reaper, binder or the like, and there are practical difficulties in constructing such a machine of a cutting capacity proportionate to the power of the tractor. 10

According to my invention I provide for connecting two or more mowers or the like to a single tractor, and I advantageously accomplish this in the following manner, that is to say, one mowing or other machine is attached to the tractor in the usual manner, preferably by a spring connection, and this mower or the like has attached to the pole or other suitable part, a laterally projecting 15 arm or bracket to the extremity of which the second mower or the like is attached in a similar manner to that in which the leading mower is attached to the tractor. This arm or bracket may project to such an extent that the second mower will trail in a proper position for cutting its full width behind the first mower, but in practice, I prefer to provide at the end of the said arm or bracket 20 a head having in it a series of holes which will permit of the pole of the second mower being arranged nearer to or farther from the adjacent travelling wheel of the leading mower according to requirements.

The pole of the second machine is advantageously carried on a caster wheel so that the bracket will be relieved of the weight of the said pole. 25

With the arrangement hereinbefore described the two machines will trail in a correct manner and can be manœuvred around sharp curves with facility without missing of the crop.

To enable the invention to be fully understood, I will describe it by reference to the accompanying drawings, in which :— 30

Figure 1 is a plan view illustrating a pair of mowing machines attached to a motor-tractor.

Figure 2 is an elevation of a detail hereinafter described.

Figure 3 is a plan illustrating the invention in connection with a binder.

Referring to Figures 1 and 2 a represents the motor-tractor and b, c the two 35 mowers. The pole d of the first machine b is attached to the motor-tractor a by means of the spring connection e and has secured to it the arm or bracket f. This arm or bracket is attached to the pole d by means of a single bolt g and a stay h pivoted at one end to a bracket i upon the arm f, and at the other end upon a similar bracket j upon the pole. By connecting the arm in this manner to the 40 pole d the said arm can have slight vertical play, sufficient to compensate for inequalities of the ground over which the two mowers b and c are drawn by the tractor a. The rear end of the arm f is provided with a bracket k having a number of holes k^1, k^1, and the pole l of the machine c is connected to this bracket k by means of a spring connection m similar to the spring connection e 45 on the pole d of the machine b. The pin n (Figure 2) can be passed through any one of the series of holes k^1 so that the pole l of the mower c can have its distance from the pole of the mower b adjusted within certain limits.

Improvements in the Attachment of Mowers, Reapers, &c., to Motor-tractors.

o (Figure 2) is the caster wheel upon which the pole l of the mower c is carried in order to relieve the bracket k of the weight of the said pole.

In Figure 3, which illustrates the invention in connection with a binder, the arm or bracket f is attached at one end to the footboard p, the stay h for the said
5 bracket being advantageously connected to the seat pillar q. In this arrangement the bracket k hereinbefore described can be dispensed with, the holes k^1 for the attachment of another binder being formed on the stay h.

When more than two machines are connected to a single tractor they are successively attached in the same manner as the second machine, which in this
10 case would be provided with an arm or bracket like the leading machine.

Although in the foregoing description I have particularly described and illustrated my invention as applied to mowers and binders, it will be clear that it is also applicable to reapers, and other agricultural implements or machines.

Having now particularly described and ascertained the nature of my said
15 invention and in what manner the same is to be performed, I declare that what I claim is;—

1. The method of coupling two or more mowers, reapers, binders or other agricultural implements for attachment to a motor-tractor, wherein a lateral arm or bracket is secured to the leading machine, and has connected to it the
20 pole of the following machine, substantially in the manner hereinbefore described.

2. A coupling attachment for motor drawn agricultural implements constructed substantially as hereinbefore described and illustrated in Figures 1 and 2 and Figure 3 of the accompanying drawings.

Dated the 16th day of March, 1905.

25

G. F. REDFERN & Co.,
4, South Street, Finsbury, London.
Agents for the Applicant.

Redhill: Printed for His Majesty's Stationery Office, by Love & Malcomson, Ltd.—1905.

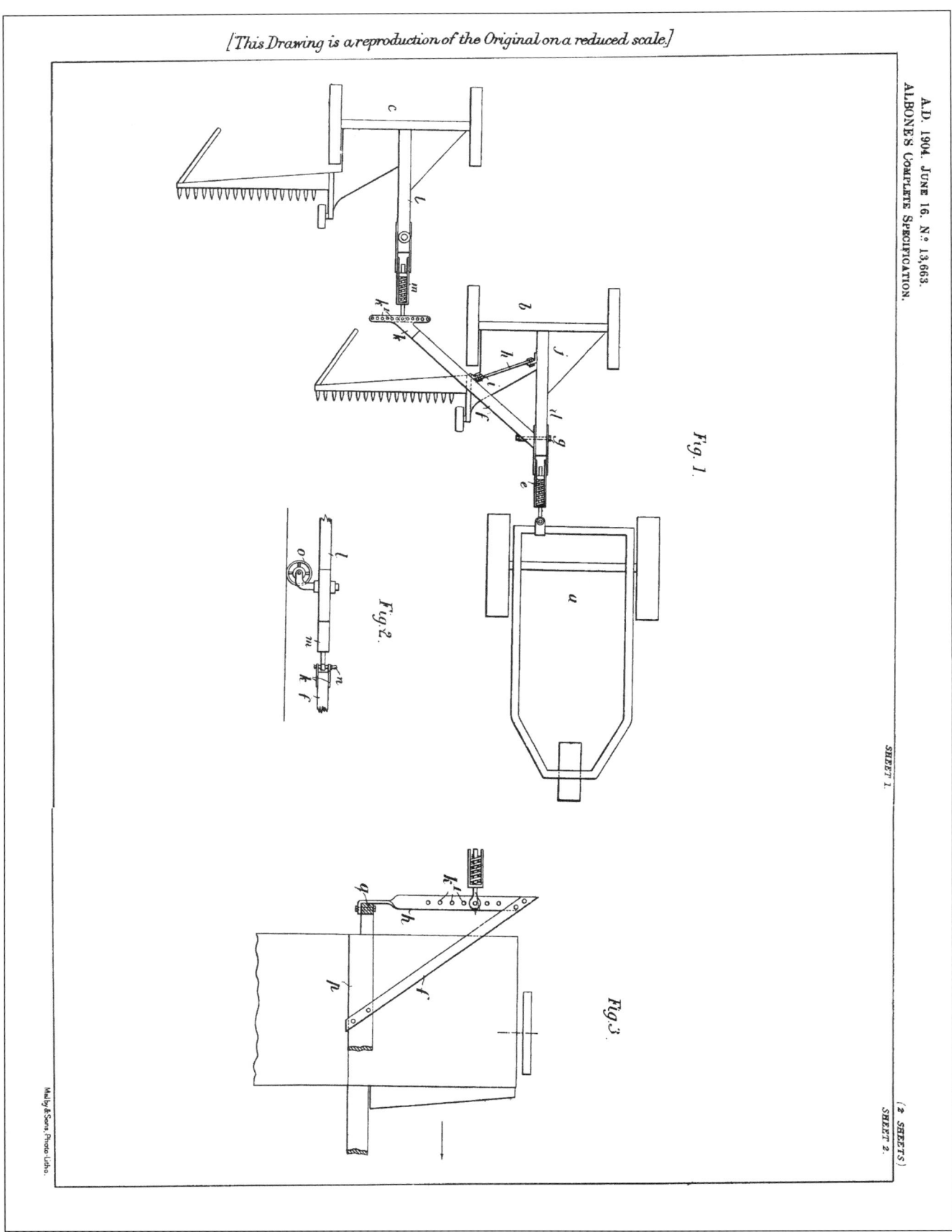

Nº 24,489

A.D. 1904

Date of Application, 11th Nov., 1904
Complete Specification Left, 5th Aug., 1905—Accepted, 7th Sept., 1905

PROVISIONAL SPECIFICATION.

" Improvements in Means for Vaporising Heavy Hydrocarbons for use in Internal Combustion Engines ".

We, DAN ALBONE, of the "Ivel" Cycle Works, Biggleswade, in the County of Bedford, and FREDERICK BOSWELL, of 1, Claremont Cottages, Biggleswade, aforesaid, Engineers, do hereby declare the nature of this invention to be as follows :—

5   This invention relates to improved means for vaporising a heavy hydrocarbon, such as paraffin, as it is drawn from the carburetter to the combustion chamber of an internal combustion engine.

According to the invention the mixture of air and paraffin from the carburetter is conveyed through a pipe traversed by a number of tubes, preferably 10 of copper, through which the products of combustion from the motor are led. The diameter and number of the tubes are so chosen as to provide as large a heating surface for the paraffin mixture as possible, and to this end also the said tubes, instead of traversing the mixture induction or mixture pipe at right angles thereto, are arranged at a considerable inclination so that as much 15 as possible of their length is contained within the mixture pipe.

In a suitable arrangement for carrying out the invention the copper tubes are mounted within a metal casing fitted at an angle of about 45° to the induction or mixture pipe, the tubes being fixed in copper plates provided at each end of the casing and held therein by means of suitable screws or unions.

20   It will be understood that the device operates as follows, that is to say, the engine or motor in conjunction with which the device is employed, is started in the usual way by means of petrol, and the exhaust gases, or a portion thereof, are conducted through the aforesaid copper tubes so as to heat the same. After the motor has been running for a short time the supply 25 of paraffin can be turned on and the petrol cut off, the said paraffin being vaporised by the heat conveyed to it from the copper tubes.

Or, as will be obvious, the device can be initially heated by means of a spirit or other lamp, thus obviating the necessity for employing petrol.

Dated the 11th day of November 1904.

30   G. F. REDFERN & Co.
                           4, South Street, Finsbury, London,
                             Agents for the Applicants.

COMPLETE SPECIFICATION.

" Improvements in Means for Vaporising Heavy Hydrocarbons for use in Internal Combustion Engines ".

35

We, DAN ALBONE, of the "Ivel" Cycle Works, Biggleswade, in the County of Bedford, and FREDERICK BOSWELL, of 1, Claremont Cottages, Biggleswade,

2   Nº 24,489.—A.D. 1904.

Means for Vaporising Heavy Hydrocarbons for use in Internal Combustion Engines.

aforesaid, Engineers, do hereby declare the nature of this invention and in what manner the same is to be performed to be particularly described and ascertained in and by the following statement:—

This invention relates to improved means for vaporising a heavy hydrocarbon, such as paraffin, as it is drawn from the carburetter to the combustion 5 chamber of an internal combustion engine.

According to the invention the mixture of air and paraffin from the carburetter is conveyed through a pipe traversed by a number of tubes, preferably of copper, through which the products of combustion from the motor are led. The diameter and number of the tubes are so chosen as to provide as large a 10 heating surface for the paraffin mixture as possible, and to this end also the said tubes, instead of traversing the induction or mixture pipe at right angles thereto, are arranged at a considerable inclination so that as much as possible of their length is contained within the mixture pipe.

In a suitable arrangement for carrying out the invention the copper tubes 15 are mounted within a metal casing fitted at an angle to the induction or mixture pipe, the tubes being fixed in copper plates provided at each end of the casing and held therein by means of suitable screws or unions.

It will be understood that the device operates as follows, that is to say, the engine or motor in conjunction with which the device is employed, is 20 started in the usual way by means of petrol, and the exhaust gases, or a portion thereof, are conducted through the aforesaid copper tubes so as to heat the same. After the motor has been running for a short time the supply of paraffin can be turned on and the petrol cut off, the said paraffin being vaporised by the heat conveyed to it from the copper tubes. 25

Or, as will be obvious, the device can be initially heated by means of a spirit or other lamp, thus obviating the necessity for employing petrol.

To enable the invention to be fully understood, we will describe it by reference to the accompanying drawing, in which:—

Figure 1 is a sectional elevation of a device for vaporising heavy hydro- 30 carbons constructed according to the invention.

Figure 2 is a section on the line 2—2, Figure 1, and

Figure 3 is a side view of a detail hereinafter described.

a is the mixture pipe which is secured by means of the union *b* to the carburetter and *c* is the metal casing which is fitted to the said mixture pipe *a* 35 at an angle of about 60° therewith. *d, d* are the tubes which, as above described, are preferably of copper and which are located within the casing *c*, the said tubes being fixed to end plates *e, e¹*. The end plate *e¹* bears against a shoulder *f* formed upon the nozzle *g* which connects the interior of the casing *c* with the exhaust silencer and the upper tube plate *e* bears against a similar 40 shoulder *h* upon the fitting *i* which is elastically connected to the end of the casing *c* through the medium of studs *j* projecting from the casing *c* and passing through holes in the flange *i¹* of the fitting *i*, each of the said bolts *j* having coiled around it a spring *k* and being screw-threaded at its outer end to receive a nut *l*. The fitting *i*, which is connected with the exhaust from 45 the motor, is provided with the tap or cock *m* for controlling the discharge of the exhaust gases through the tubes *d*.

n is a branch pipe provided at the lower part of the device, that is to say, near the lower end of the tubes *d, d*, the said branch being normally closed by the pivoted cover *o* secured in place by the wing-nut *p*, the object of this 50 branch pipe is to enable the vaporiser to be initially heated by means of a blow lamp as hereinafter described.

Our improved vaporising device is employed as follows: The engine or motor may be started in the ordinary way by means of petrol, (the cock *m* being turned off), the exhaust gases or a portion thereof from the motor being 55 conveyed through the fitting *i* and the tubes *c* which latter quickly become highly heated. When the motor has been running for a short time the petrol

Means for Vaporising Heavy Hydrocarbons for use in Internal Combustion Engines.

is cut off and the mixture of paraffin and air from the carburetter is allowed to enter the mixing tube *a* where it bathes the relatively large surface of the tubes *d* and thus becomes efficiently vaporised by the heat conveyed to it by the said tubes. The vaporisation which is effected in this manner is of such a
5 nature that there is practically no deposit upon the valves and other parts of the motor.

Or, instead of employing petrol to start the motor and initially heat the tubes *d* for vaporising the paraffin, we may dispense with the use of petrol, in which case the tubes *d* are heated before starting by means of a spirit or
10 other lamp, the flame of which is introduced through the aforesaid branch pipe *n* so as to be applied to the lower ends of the tubes *c* and thus raise the same to the necessary temperature.

It will be clear that an engine fitted with our device can be driven by a petrol mixture without the necessity of making alterations of any kind to the
15 carburetter or other parts of the engine.

Having now particularly described and ascertained the nature of our said invention and in what manner the same is to be performed, we declare that what we claim is:—

1. A device for vaporising heavy hydrocarbons for internal combustion
20 engines, comprising a chamber or pipe for the mixture of heavy hydrocarbon and air and a number of tubes traversing the said pipe or chamber, preferably at an angle thereto, and through which the products of combustion from the motor are passed, substantially as hereinbefore described.

2. A device for vaporising heavy hydrocarbons, constructed substantially as
25 hereinbefore described and illustrated in the accompanying drawing.

Dated the 5th day of August, 1905.

G. F. REDFERN & Co.
4, South Street, Finsbury, E.C. and
21, Southampton Buildings, W.C.
30 Agents for the Applicants.

Redhill: Printed for His Majesty's Stationery Office, by Love & Malcomson, Ltd.—1905.

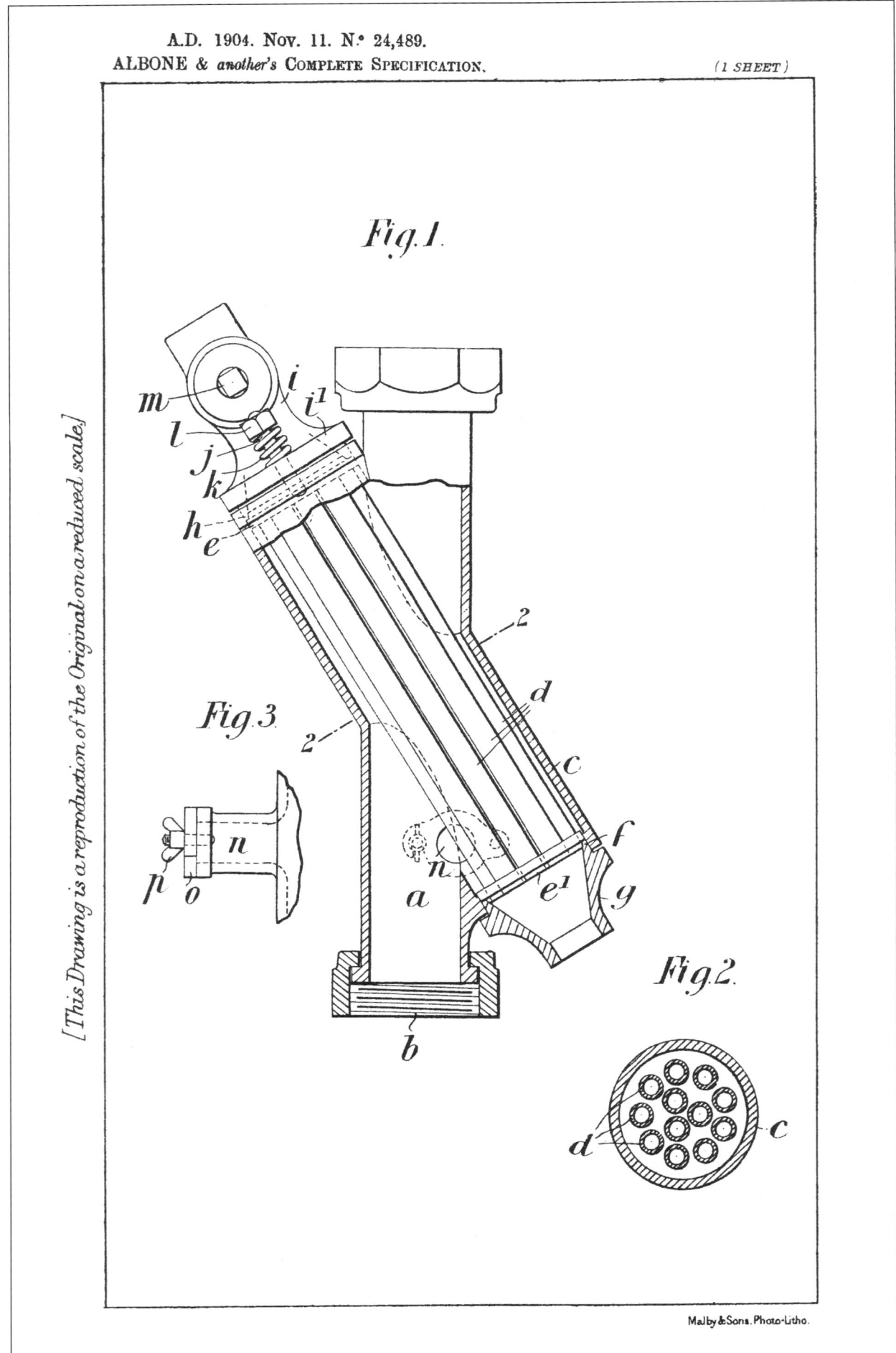